Data-Centric Systems and Applications

Intelligent data management is the backbone of all information processing and has hence been one of the core topics in computer science from its very start. This series is intended to offer an international platform for the timely publication of all topics relevant to the development of data-centric systems and applications. All books show a strong practical or application relevance as well as a thorough scientific basis. They are therefore of particular interest to both researchers and professionals wishing to acquire detailed knowledge about concepts of which they need to make intelligent use when designing advanced solutions for their own problems.

Special emphasis is laid upon:

- Scientifically solid and detailed explanations of practically relevant concepts and techniques
  (what does it do)
- Detailed explanations of the practical relevance and importance of concepts and techniques
  (why do we need it)
- Detailed explanation of gaps between theory and practice
  (why it does not work)

According to this focus of the series, submissions of advanced textbooks or books for advanced professional use are encouraged; these should preferably be authored books or monographs, but coherently edited, multi-author books are also envisaged (e.g. for emerging topics). On the other hand, overly technical topics (like physical data access, data compression etc.), latest research results that still need validation through the research community, or mostly product-related information for practitioners ("how to use Oracle 9i efficiently") are not encouraged.

Alejandro Vaisman • Esteban Zimányi

Data Warehouse Systems

Design and Implementation

Second Edition

 Springer

Alejandro Vaisman 🆔
Instituto Tecnológico de Buenos Aires
Buenos Aires, Argentina

Esteban Zimányi 🆔
Université Libre de Bruxelles
Brussels, Belgium

ISSN 2197-9723   ISSN 2197-974X   (electronic)
Data-Centric Systems and Applications
ISBN 978-3-662-65169-8   ISBN 978-3-662-65167-4   (eBook)
https://doi.org/10.1007/978-3-662-65167-4

This Springer imprint is published by the registered company Springer-Verlag GmbH, DE part of Springer Nature.
The registered company address is: Heidelberger Platz 3, 14197 Berlin, Germany

To Andrés and Manuel,
who bring me joy and
happiness day after day
A.V.

To Elena,
the star that shed light upon my path,
with all my love
E.Z.

Foreword to the Second Edition

Dear reader,

Assuming you are looking for a textbook on data warehousing and the analytical processing of data, I can assure you that you are certainly in the right spot. In fact, I could easily argue how panoramic and lucid the view from this spot is, and in the next few paragraphs, this is exactly what I am going to do.

Assembling a good book from the bits and pieces of writings, slides, and article commentaries that an author has in his folders, is no easy task. Even more, if the book is intended to serve as a textbook, it requires an extra dose of love and care for the students who are going to use it (and their instructors, too, in fact). The book you have at hand is the product of hard work and deep caring by our two esteemed colleagues, Alejandro Vaisman and Esteban Zimányi, who have invested a large amount of effort to produce a book that is (a) comprehensive, (b) up-to-date, (c) easy to follow, and, (d) useful and to-the-point. While the book is also addressing the researcher who, coming from a different background, wants to enter the area of data warehousing, as well as the newcomer to data processing, who might prefer to start the journey of working with data from the neat setup of data cubes, the book is perfectly suited as a textbook for advanced undergraduate and graduate courses in the area of data warehousing.

The book comprehensively covers all the fundamental modeling issues, and addresses also the practical aspects on querying and populating the warehouse. The usage of concrete examples, consistently revisited throughout the book, guide the student to understand the practical considerations, and a set of exercises help the instructor with the hands-on design of a course. For what it's worth, I have already used the first edition of the book for my graduate data warehouse course and will certainly switch to the new version in the years to come.

If you, dear reader, have already read the first edition of the book, you already know that the first part, covering the modeling fundamentals, and the second part, covering the practical usage of data warehousing are both comprehensive and detailed. To the extent that the fundamentals have not changed (and are not really expected to change in the future), apart from a set of extensions spread throughout the first part of the book, the main improvements concern readability on the one hand, and the technological advances on the other. Specifically, the dedicated chapter 7 on practical data analysis with lots of examples over a specific example, as well as the new topics covering partitioning and parallel data processing in the physical management of the data warehouse provide an even more easy path to the novice reader into the areas of querying and managing the warehouse.

I would like, however, to take the opportunity and direct your attention to the really new features of this second edition, which are found in the last unit of the book, concerning advanced areas of data warehousing. This part goes beyond the traditional data warehousing modeling and implementation and is practically completely refreshed compared to the first edition of the book. The chapter on temporal and multiversion warehousing covers the problem of time encoding for evolving facts and the management of versions. The part on spatial warehouses has been significantly updated. There is a brand-new chapter on graph data processing, and its application to graph warehousing and graph OLAP. Last but extremely significant, the crown jewel of the book, a brand-new chapter on the management of Big Data and the usage of Hadoop, Spark and Kylin, as well as the coverage of distributed, in-memory, columnar, and Not-Only-SQL DBMS's in the context of analytical data processing. Recent advents like data processing in the cloud, polystores and data lakes are also covered in the chapter.

Based on all that, dear reader, I can only invite you to dive into the contents of the book, feeling certain that, once you have completed its reading (or maybe, targeted parts of it), you will join me in expressing our gratitude to Alejandro and Esteban, for providing such a comprehensive textbook for the field of data warehousing in the first place, and for keeping it up to date with the recent developments, in this, current, second edition.

Ioannina, Greece   Panos Vassiliadis

Foreword to the First Edition

Having worked with data warehouses for almost 20 years, I was both honored and excited when two veteran authors in the field asked me to write a foreword for their new book and sent me a PDF file with the current draft. Already the size of the PDF file gave me a first impression of a very comprehensive book, an impression that was heavily reinforced by reading the Table of Contents. After reading the entire book, I think it is quite simply the most comprehensive textbook about data warehousing on the market.

The book is very well suited for one or more data warehouse courses, ranging from the most basic to the most advanced. It has all the features that are necessary to make a good textbook. First, a running case study, based on the Northwind database known from Microsoft's tools, is used to illustrate all aspects using many detailed figures and examples. Second, key terms and concepts are highlighted in the text for better reading and understanding. Third, review questions are provided at the end of each chapter so students can quickly check their understanding. Fourth, the many detailed exercises for each chapter put the presented knowledge into action, yielding deep learning and taking students through all the steps needed to develop a data warehouse. Finally, the book shows how to implement data warehouses using leading industrial and open-source tools, concretely Microsoft's suite of data warehouse tools, giving students the essential hands-on experience that enables them to put the knowledge into practice.

For the complete database novice, there is even an introductory chapter on standard database concepts and design, making the book self-contained even for this group. It is quite impressive to cover all this material, usually the topic of an entire textbook, without making it a dense read. Next, the book provides a good introduction to basic multidimensional concepts, later moving on to advanced concepts such as summarizability. A complete overview of the data warehouse and online analytical processing (OLAP) "architecture stack" is given. For the conceptual modeling of the data warehouse, a concise and intuitive graphical notation is used, a full specification of which is given in

an appendix, along with a methodology for the modeling and the translation
to (logical-level) relational schemas.

Later, the book provides a lot of useful knowledge about designing and
querying data warehouses, including a detailed, yet easy to read, description
of the de facto standard OLAP query language: MultiDimensional eXpressions (MDX). I certainly learned a thing or two about MDX in a short time.
The chapter on extract-transform-load (ETL) takes a refreshingly different
approach by using a graphical notation based on the Business Process Modeling Notation (BPMN), thus treating the ETL flow at a higher and more
understandable level. Unlike most other data warehouse books, this book also
provides comprehensive coverage on analytics, including data mining and reporting, and on how to implement these using industrial tools. The book even
has a chapter on methodology issues such as requirements capture and the
data warehouse development process, again something not covered by most
data warehouse textbooks.

However, the one thing that really sets this book apart from its peers is
the coverage of advanced data warehouse topics, such as spatial databases
and data warehouses, spatiotemporal or mobility databases and data warehouses, and semantic web data warehouses. The book also provides a useful
overview of novel "big data" technologies like Hadoop and novel database
and data warehouse architectures like in-memory database systems, column
store systems, and right-time data warehouses. These advanced topics are a
distinguishing feature not found in other textbooks.

Finally, the book concludes by pointing to a number of exciting directions
for future research in data warehousing, making it an interesting read even
for seasoned data warehouse researchers.

A famous quote by IBM veteran Bruce Lindsay states that "relational
databases are the foundation of Western civilization." Similarly, I would say
that "data warehouses are the foundation of twenty-first-century enterprises."
And this book is in turn an excellent foundation for building those data warehouses, from the simplest to the most complex.

Happy reading!

Aalborg, Denmark   Torben Bach Pedersen

Preface

Since the late 1970s, relational database technology has been adopted by most organizations to store their essential data. However, nowadays, the needs of these organizations are not the same as they used to be. On the one hand, increasing market dynamics and competitiveness led to the need to have the right information at the right time. Managers need to be properly informed in order to take appropriate decisions to keep up with business successfully. On the other hand, data held by organizations are usually scattered among different systems, each one devised for a particular kind of business activity. Further, these systems may also be distributed geographically in different branches of the organization.

Traditional database systems are not well suited for these new requirements, since they were devised to support day-to-day operations rather than for data analysis and decision making. As a consequence, new database technologies for these specific tasks emerged in the 1990s, namely, data warehousing and online analytical processing (OLAP), which involve architectures, algorithms, tools, and techniques for bringing together data from heterogeneous information sources into a single repository suited for analysis. In this repository, called a data warehouse, data are accumulated over a period of time for the purpose of analyzing their evolution and discovering strategic information such as trends, correlations, and the like. Data warehousing is a well-established and mature technology used by organizations to improve their operations and better achieve their objectives.

Objective of the Book

This book is aimed at consolidating and transferring to the community the experience of many years of teaching and research in the field of databases and data warehouses conducted by the authors, individually as well as jointly. However, this is not a compilation of the authors' past publications. On the contrary, the book aims at being a main textbook for undergraduate and graduate computer science courses on data warehousing and OLAP. As such, it is written in a pedagogical rather than research style to make the work of the instructor easier and to help the student understand the concepts being delivered. Researchers and practitioners who are interested in an introduction to the area of data warehousing will also find in the book a useful reference. In summary, we aim at providing in-depth coverage of the main topics in the field, yet keeping a simple and understandable style.

Throughout the book, we cover all the phases of the data warehousing process, from requirements specification to implementation. Regarding data warehouse design, we make a clear distinction between the three abstraction levels of the American National Standards Institute (ANSI) database architecture, that is, conceptual, logical, and physical, unlike the usual approaches, which do not distinguish clearly between the conceptual and logical levels. A strong emphasis is placed on querying using the de facto standard language MDX (MultiDimensional eXpressions) as well as the popular language DAX (Data Analysis eXpressions). Though there are many practical books covering these languages, academic books have largely ignored them. We also provide in-depth coverage of the extraction, transformation, and loading (ETL) processes. In addition, we study how key performance indicators (KPIs) and dashboards are built on top of data warehouses. An important topic that we also cover in this book is temporal and multiversion data warehouses, in which the evolution over time of the data and the schema of a data warehouse are taken into account. Although there are many textbooks on spatial databases, this is not the case with spatial data warehouses, which we study in this book, together with mobility data warehouses, which allow the analysis of data produced by objects that change their position in space and time, like cars or pedestrians. Data warehousing and OLAP on graph databases and on the semantic web are also studied. Finally, big data technologies led to the concept of big data warehouses, which are also covered in this book.

A key characteristic that distinguishes this book from other textbooks is that we illustrate how the concepts introduced can be implemented using existing tools. Specifically, throughout the book we develop a case study based on the well-known Northwind database using representative tools of different kinds. In particular, the chapter on logical design includes a complete description of how to define an OLAP cube in Microsoft SQL Analysis Services using both the multidimensional and the tabular models. Similarly, the chapter on physical design illustrates how to optimize SQL Server and Analysis Services applications. Further, in the chapter on ETL we give a complete example of a process that loads the Northwind data warehouse, implemented using Integration Services. We also use Analysis Services for defining KPIs, and use Reporting Services to show how dashboards can be implemented. To illustrate spatial and spatiotemporal concepts we use the open-source database PostgreSQL, its spatial extension PostGIS, and its mobility extension MobilityDB. In this way, the reader can replicate most of the examples and queries presented in the book. Finally, in the chapter on graph data warehouses we use Neo4j.

We also include review questions and exercises for all the chapters in order to help the reader verify that the concepts have been well understood. Support material for the book is available online at http://cs.ulb.ac.be/DWSDIbook2e/. This includes electronic versions of the figures, slides for each chapter, solutions to the exercises, and other pedagogic material that can be used by instructors using this book as a course text.

This second edition of the book updates several chapters with new results and technologies that have appeared since the publication of the first edition. In Chaps. 5, 6, and 7, the tabular model and DAX have been included. Chapter 15 covers big data warehouse technologies, which have considerably evolved since the first edition. Further, we have added new chapters covering temporal, multiversion, and graph data warehouses. Also, all application examples that make use of software tools have been updated to the latest versions of them. In addition to this new material, all chapters of the first edition have been revised and updated with the feedback obtained through seven years of teaching at undergraduate and graduate levels, and to professional teams in different industries.

Organization of the Book and Teaching Paths

Part I of the book starts with Chap. 1, giving a historical overview of data warehousing and OLAP. Chapter 2 introduces the main concepts of relational databases needed in the remainder of the book. We also introduce the case study that we will use throughout the book, based on the well-known Northwind database. Data warehouses and the multidimensional model are introduced in Chap. 3, as well as the suite of tools provided by SQL Server. Chapter 4 deals with conceptual data warehouse design, while Chap. 5 is devoted to logical data warehouse design. Part I closes with Chaps. 6 and 7, which study SQL/OLAP, the extension of SQL with OLAP features, as well as MDX and DAX.

Part II covers data warehouse implementation issues. This part starts with Chap. 8, which tackles classical physical data warehouse design, focusing on indexing, view materialization, and database partitioning. Chapter 9 studies conceptual modeling and implementation of ETL processes. Finally, Chap. 10 provides a comprehensive method for data warehouse design.

Part III covers advanced data warehouse topics. This part starts with Chap. 11, which studies temporal and multiversion data warehouses, for both *data* and *schema* evolution of the data warehouse. Then, in Chap. 12, we study spatial data warehouses and their exploitation, denoted spatial OLAP (SOLAP), illustrating the problem with a spatial extension of the Northwind data warehouse denoted GeoNorthwind. We query this data warehouse using PostGIS, PostgreSQL's spatial extension. The chapter also covers mobility data warehousing, using MobilityDB, a spatiotemporal extension of PostgreSQL. Chapters 13 and 14 address OLAP analysis over graph data represented, respectively, natively using property graphs in Neo4j and using RDF triples as advocated by the semantic web. Chapter 15 studies how novel techniques and technologies for distributed data storage and processing can be applied to the field of data warehousing. Appendix A summarizes the notations used in this book.

The figure below illustrates the overall structure of the book and the interdependencies between the chapters described above. Readers may refer to this figure to tailor their use of this book to their own particular interests. The dependency graph in the figure suggests many of the possible combinations that can be devised to offer advanced graduate courses on data warehousing.

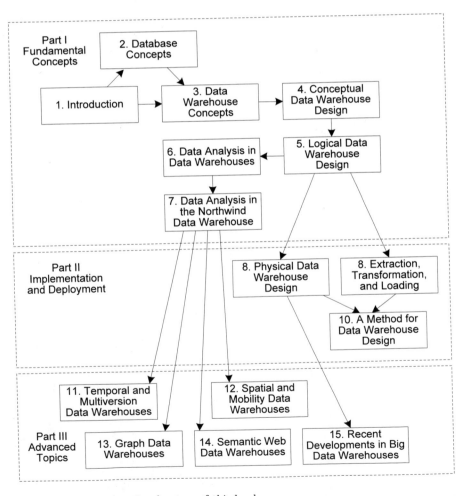

Relationships between the chapters of this book

Acknowledgments

We would like to thank Innoviris, the Brussels Institute for Research and Innovation, which funded Alejandro Vaisman's work through the OSCB project; without its financial support, the first edition of this book would never have been possible. As mentioned above, some content of this book finds its roots in a previous book written by one of the authors in collaboration with Elzbieta Malinowski. We would like to thank her for all the work we did together in making the previous book a reality. This gave us the impetus to start this new book.

Parts of the material included in this book have been previously presented in conferences or published in journals. At these conferences, we had the opportunity to discuss with research colleagues from all around the world, and we exchanged viewpoints about the subject with them. The anonymous reviewers of these conferences and journals provided us with insightful comments and suggestions that contributed significantly to improve the work presented in this book. We would like to thank Zineb El Akkaoui, with whom we have explored the use of BPMN for ETL processes, and Judith Awiti, who continued this work. A very special thanks to Waqas Ahmed, a doctoral student of our laboratory, with whom we explored the issue of temporal and multiversion data warehouses. Waqas also suggested to include tabular modeling and DAX in the second edition of the book, and without his invaluable help, all the material related to the tabular model and DAX would have not been possible. A special thanks to Mahmoud Sakr, Arthur Lesuisse, Mohammed Bakli, and Maxime Schoemans, who worked with one of the authors in the development of MobilityDB, a spatiotemporal extension of PostgreSQL and PostGIS that was used for mobility data warehouses. This work follows that of Benoit Foé, Julien Lusiela, and Xianling Li, who explored this topic in the context of their master's thesis. Arthur Lesuisse also provided invaluable help in setting up all the computer infrastructure we needed, especially for spatializing the Northwind database. He also contributed in enhancing some of the figures of this book. Thanks also to Leticia Gómez from the Buenos Aires Technological Institute for her help on the implementation of graph data warehouses and for her advice on the topic of big data technologies. Bart Kuijpers, from Hasselt University, also worked with us during our research on graph data warehousing and OLAP. We also want to thank Lorena Etcheverry, who contributed with comments, exercises, and solutions in Chap. 14.

Special thanks go to Panos Vassiliadis, professor at the University of Ioannina in Greece, who kindly agreed to write the foreword for this second edition. Finally, we would like to warmly thank Ralf Gerstner of Springer for his continued interest in this book. The enthusiastic welcome given to our book proposal for the first edition and the continuous encouragements to write the second edition gave us enormous impetus to pursue our project to its end.

Alejandro Vaisman   Esteban Zimányi
Buenos Aires, Argentina,   Brussels, Belgium
February 2022

About the Authors

Alejandro Vaisman is a professor at the Instituto Tecnológico de Buenos Aires, where he also chairs the graduate program in data science. He has been a professor and chair of the master's program in data mining at the University of Buenos Aires (UBA) and professor at Universidad de la República in Uruguay. He received a BE degree in civil engineering, and a BCS degree and a doctorate in computer science from the UBA, under the supervision of Prof. Alberto Mendelzon, from the University of Toronto (UoT). He has been a postdoctoral fellow at UoT, and visiting researcher at UoT, Universidad Politécnica de Madrid, Universidad de Chile, University of Hasselt, and Université Libre de Bruxelles (ULB). His research interests are in the field of databases, business intelligence, and geographic information systems. He has authored and coauthored many scientific papers published at major conferences and in major journals.

Esteban Zimányi is a professor and a director of the Department of Computer and Decision Engineering (CoDE) of Université Libre de Bruxelles (ULB). He started his studies at the Universidad Autónoma de Centro América, Costa Rica, and received a BCS degree and a doctorate in computer science from ULB. His current research interests include spatiotemporal and mobility databases, data warehouses and business intelligence, geographic information systems, as well as semantic web. He has coauthored and coedited eight books and published many papers on these topics. He was editor-in-chief of the *Journal on Data Semantics* (JoDS) published by Springer from 2012 to 2020. He coordinated the Erasmus Mundus master's and doctorate programmes "Information Technologies for Business Intelligence" (IT4BI) and "Big Data Management and Analytics" (BDMA) as well as the Marie Skłodowska-Curie doctorate programme "Data Engineering for Data Science" (DEDS).

Contents

Part II Implementation and Deployment

Part I
Fundamental Concepts

Chapter 1
Introduction

Organizations face increasingly complex challenges in terms of management and problem solving in order to achieve their operational goals. This situation compels people in those organizations to use analysis tools that can better support their decisions. **Business intelligence** comprises a collection of methodologies, processes, architectures, and technologies that transform raw data into meaningful and useful information for decision making. Business intelligence and **decision-support systems** provide assistance to managers at various organizational levels for analyzing strategic information. These systems collect vast amounts of data and reduce them to a form that can be used to analyze organizational behavior. This data transformation involves a set of tasks that take the data from the sources and, through extraction, transformation, integration, and cleansing processes, store the data in a common repository called a **data warehouse**. Data warehouses have been developed and deployed as an integral part of decision-support systems to provide an infrastructure that enables users to obtain efficient and accurate responses to complex queries.

A wide variety of systems and tools can be used for accessing and exploiting the data contained in data warehouses. From the early days of data warehousing, the typical mechanism for those tasks has been **online analytical processing (OLAP)**. OLAP systems allow users to interactively query and automatically aggregate the data contained in a data warehouse. In this way, decision makers can easily access the required information and analyze it at various levels of detail. **Data mining** tools have also been used since the 1990s to infer and extract interesting knowledge hidden in data warehouses. The business intelligence market is shifting to provide sophisticated analysis tools that go beyond the data navigation techniques that popularized the OLAP paradigm. This new paradigm is generically called **data analytics**. Many business intelligence techniques are used to exploit a data warehouse. These techniques can be broadly summarized as follows (this list by no means attempts to be comprehensive):

© Springer-Verlag GmbH Germany, part of Springer Nature 2022
A. Vaisman, E. Zimányi, *Data Warehouse Systems*, Data-Centric Systems and Applications, https://doi.org/10.1007/978-3-662-65167-4_1

- Reporting, such as dashboards and alerts.
- Performance management, such as metrics, key performance indicators (KPIs), and scorecards.
- Analytics, such as OLAP, data mining, time series analysis, text mining, web analytics, and advanced data visualization.

Although in this book the main emphasis will be put on OLAP as a tool to exploit a data warehouse, many of these techniques will also be discussed.

In this chapter, we present an overview of the data warehousing field, covering both established topics and new developments, and indicate the chapters in the book where these subjects are covered. In Section 1.1 we provide a brief overview of data warehousing, referring to the chapters in the book that cover their different topics. Section 1.2 discusses relevant emerging fields such as spatial and mobility data warehousing, which are being increasingly used in many application domains. We also discuss new domains and challenges that are being explored in order to meet the requirements of today's analytical applications, as well as new big data technologies that are making the implementation of those new applications possible.

1.1 An Overview of Data Warehousing

In the early 1990s, as a consequence of an increasingly competitive and rapidly changing world, organizations realized that they needed to perform sophisticated data analysis to support their decision-making processes. Traditional **operational** or **transactional databases** did not satisfy the requirements for data analysis, since they were designed and optimized to support daily business operations, and their primary concern was ensuring concurrent access by multiple users, and, at the same time, providing recovery techniques to guarantee data consistency. Typical operational databases contain detailed data, do not include historical data, and perform poorly when executing complex queries that involve many tables or aggregate large volumes of data. Furthermore, data from several different operational systems must be integrated, a difficult task to accomplish because of the differences in data definition and content. Therefore, **data warehouses** were proposed as a solution to the growing demands of decision-making users.

The classic data warehouse definition, given by Inmon, characterizes a data warehouse as a collection of subject-oriented, integrated, nonvolatile, and time-varying data to support management decisions. This definition emphasizes some salient features of a data warehouse. **Subject oriented** means that a data warehouse targets one or several subjects of analysis according to the analytical requirements of managers at various levels of the decision-making process. For example, a data warehouse in a retail company may contain data for analysis of the inventory and sales of products. The term

integrated means that the contents of a data warehouse result from the integration of data from various operational and external systems. **Nonvolatile** indicates that a data warehouse accumulates data from operational systems for a long period of time. Thus, data modification and removal are not allowed in data warehouses, and the only operation allowed is the purging of obsolete data that is no longer needed. Finally, **time varying** emphasizes that a data warehouse keeps track of how its data have evolved over time, for instance, to know the evolution of sales over the last months or years.

The basic concepts of databases are studied in Chap. 2. The design of operational databases is typically performed in four phases: **requirements specification**, **conceptual design**, **logical design**, and **physical design**. During the requirements specification process, the needs of users at various levels of the organization are collected. The specification obtained serves as a basis for creating a database schema capable of responding to user queries. Databases are designed using a **conceptual model**, such as the entity-relationship (ER) model, which describes an application without taking into account implementation considerations. The resulting design is then translated into a **logical model**, which is an implementation paradigm for database applications. Nowadays, the most-used logical model for databases is the relational model. Finally, physical design particularizes the logical model for a specific implementation platform in order to produce a **physical model**.

Relational databases must be highly normalized in order to guarantee consistency under frequent updates and a minimum level of redundancy. This is usually achieved at the expense of a higher cost of querying, because normalization implies partitioning the database into multiple tables. Several authors have pointed out that this design paradigm is not appropriate for data warehouse applications. Data warehouses must aim at ensuring a deep understanding of the underlying data and deliver good performance for complex analytical queries. This sometimes requires a lesser degree of normalization or even no normalization at all. To account for these requirements, a different model was needed. Thus, multidimensional modeling was adopted for data warehouse design. **Multidimensional modeling**, studied in Chap. 3, represents data as a collection of facts linked to several dimensions. A **fact** represents the focus of analysis (e.g., analysis of sales in stores) and typically includes attributes called **measures**, usually numeric values, that allow a quantitative evaluation of various aspects of an organization. **Dimensions** are used to study the measures from several perspectives. For example, a *store* dimension might help to analyze sales activities across various stores, a *time* dimension can be used to analyze changes in sales over various periods of time, and a *location* dimension can be used to analyze sales according to the geographical distribution of stores. Dimensions typically include attributes that form **hierarchies**, which allow users to explore measures at various levels of detail. Examples of hierarchies are month–quarter–year in the time dimension and city–state–country in the location dimension.

From a methodological point of view, data warehouses must be designed analogously to operational databases, that is, following the four-step process consisting of requirements specification and conceptual, logical, and physical design. However, there is still no widely accepted conceptual model for data warehouse applications. Thus, data warehouse design is usually performed at the logical level, leading to schemas that are difficult for a typical user to understand. We believe that a conceptual model on top of the logical level is required for data warehouse design. In this book, we use the **MultiDim model**, which is powerful enough to represent the complex characteristics of data warehouses at an abstraction level higher than the logical model. We study conceptual modeling for data warehouses in Chap. 4.

At the **logical level**, the multidimensional model is usually represented by relational tables organized in specialized structures called star schemas and snowflake schemas. These relational schemas relate a fact table to several dimension tables. **Star schemas** use a unique table for each dimension, even in the presence of hierarchies, which yields denormalized dimension tables. On the other hand, **snowflake schemas** use normalized tables for dimensions and their hierarchies. Then, over this relational representation of a data warehouse, an OLAP server builds a data cube, which provides a multidimensional view of the data warehouse. Logical modeling is studied in Chap. 5.

Once a data warehouse has been implemented, analytical queries may be addressed to it. MDX (MultiDimensional eXpressions) is the de facto standard language for querying a multidimensional database. More recently, the Data Analysis Expressions (DAX) language was proposed by Microsoft as an alternative. The MDX and the DAX languages are studied (and compared to SQL) in Chaps. 6 and 7.

The **physical level** is concerned with implementation issues. Physical design is crucial to ensure adequate response time to the complex ad hoc queries that must be supported. Three techniques are normally used for improving system performance: materialized views, indexing, and data partitioning. In particular, bitmap indexes are used in the data warehousing context, as opposed to operational databases, where B-tree indexes are typically used. A huge amount of research in these topics has been performed, particularly during the second half of the 1990s. The results of this research have been implemented in traditional OLAP engines, as well as in modern OLAP engines for big data. In Chap. 8, we review and study these efforts.

A key difference between operational databases and data warehouses is the fact that, in the latter, data are extracted from several source systems. Thus, data must be transformed to fit the data warehouse model, and loaded into the data warehouse. This process is called **extraction, transformation, and loading** (ETL), and it has been proven crucial for the success of a data warehousing project. However, in spite of the work carried out on this topic, again, there is still no consensus on a methodology for ETL design, and most problems are solved in an ad hoc manner. There exist several proposals regarding ETL conceptual design. We study the design and implementation of ETL processes in Chap. 9.

Data analysis is the process of exploiting the contents of a data warehouse in order to provide essential information to the decision-making process. Three main tools can be used for this. **Querying** consists in using the OLAP paradigm for extracting relevant data from the warehouse in order to discover useful knowledge that is not easy to obtain from the detailed original data. **Key performance indicators** (KPIs) are measurable organizational objectives that are used for characterizing how an organization is performing. Finally, **dashboards** are interactive reports that present the data in a warehouse, including the KPIs, in a visual way, providing an overview of the performance of an organization for decision-support purposes. We study data analysis in Chaps. 6 and 7.

Designing a data warehouse is a complex endeavor that needs to be carefully carried out. As for operational databases, several phases are needed to design a data warehouse, where each phase addresses specific considerations that must be taken into account. As mentioned above, these phases are requirements specification, conceptual design, logical design, and physical design. There are three different approaches to requirements specification, which differ on how requirements are collected: from users, by analyzing source systems, or by combining both. The choice of the particular approach followed determines how the subsequent phase of conceptual design is undertaken. In Chap. 10 we present a methodology for data warehouse design.

1.2 Emerging Data Warehousing Technologies

By the beginning of this century, the foundational concepts of data warehouse systems were mature and consolidated. Nevertheless, the field has been steadily growing in many different ways. On the one hand, new kinds of data and data models have been introduced. Some of them have been successfully implemented into commercial and open-source systems. This is the case for spatial data. On the other hand, new architectures are being explored for coping with the massive amount of data that must be processed in modern decision-support systems. We comment on these issues in this section.

A simplifying hypothesis used in most data warehouses is that dimensions do not change, and thus facts and their measures are the only data that are associated with a time frame. However, this does not correspond to reality, since dimensions also evolve in time; for instance, a product may change its price or its category. The most popular approach for solving this problem, in the context of relational databases, is the so-called slowly changing dimensions. An alternative approach to this problem is based on the notion of **Temporal databases**, which provide structures and mechanisms for representing and managing time-varying information. The combination of temporal databases and data warehouses leads to **temporal data warehouses**.

Current database and data warehouse systems give limited support for manipulating time-varying data. Querying time-varying data with SQL involves writing extremely complex and probably inefficient queries. Further, MDX currently does not provide temporal support. What is needed is to extend the traditional OLAP operators for exploring time-varying data, which is referred to as **temporal OLAP** (TOLAP). Temporal data warehouses are studied in Chap. 11.

In addition to the above, in real-world scenarios, the schema of a data warehouse evolves across time in order to accommodate new application requirements. The common approach to address this situation consists of modifying the data in the warehouse to comply with the new version of the schema: this implies removing data that are no longer needed and adding new data that were not previously collected. When this is not possible or desirable, the versions of the schema and their data should be maintained, leading to **multiversion data warehouses**. In such data warehouses, new data are added according to the current schema, while data associated with previous schemas are kept for analysis purposes. Thus, users and applications can continue working with the previous schema versions, while new users and applications can target the current version of the schema. Multiversion data warehouses are studied in Chap. 11.

Over the years, **spatial data** has been increasingly used in various areas, such as public administration, transportation networks, environmental systems, and public health, among others. Spatial data can represent either *objects* located on the Earth's surface, such as streets and cities, or geographic *phenomena*, such as temperature and altitude. The amount of spatial data available is growing considerably due to technological advances in areas such as remote sensing and global navigation satellite systems (GNSS), namely the Global Positioning System (GPS) and the Galileo system.

Spatial databases offer sophisticated capabilities for storing and manipulating spatial data. However, such databases are typically targeted toward daily operations and therefore are not well suited to support the decision-making process. As a consequence, **spatial data warehouses** emerged as a combination of the spatial database and data warehouse technologies. Spatial data warehouses provide improved data analysis, visualization, and manipulation. This kind of analysis is called **spatial OLAP** (SOLAP), which enables the exploration of spatial data in the same way as in OLAP with tables and charts. We study spatial data warehouses in Chap. 12.

Many applications require the analysis of data about **moving objects**, that is, objects that change their position in space and time. The possibilities and interest of mobility data analysis have expanded dramatically with the availability of positioning devices. Traffic data, for example, can be captured as a collection of sequences of positioning signals transmitted by the cars' GPS along their itineraries. This kind of analysis is called **mobility**

data analysis. In addition, since the sequences generated by moving objects' positions can be very long, they are often processed by being divided into segments of movement called **trajectories**, which are the unit of interest in the analysis of movement data. Extending data warehouses to cope with mobility data leads to **mobility data warehouses**. These are studied in Chap. 12.

A common characteristic of the web, transportation networks, communication networks, biological data, and economic data, among others, is that they are highly connected. Since connectedness is naturally modeled by graphs, the interest in **graph databases** and **graph analytics** lead to the notion of graph **data warehousing** and **graph OLAP**. Two main approaches have been proposed in this respect. On the one hand, the property graph data model is used for *native* graph databases and graph analytics, where graph data structures composed of nodes and vertices are the basis for storing the data. This approach is very effective for computing path traversals. Chapter 13 is devoted to property graph databases and graph analytics, mainly based on Neo4j, one of the most popular graph databases in the marketplace.

The web is an important source of multidimensional information, although this is usually too volatile to be permanently stored. The **semantic web** aims at representing web content in a machine-processable way. The basic layer of the data representation for the semantic web recommended by the World Wide Web Consortium (W3C) is the Resource Description Framework (RDF), on top of which the Web Ontology Language (OWL) is based. In a semantic web scenario, domain ontologies (defined in RDF or some variant of OWL) define a common terminology for the concepts involved in a particular domain. Semantic annotations are especially useful for describing unstructured, semistructured, and textual data. Many applications attach metadata and semantic annotations to the information they produce (e.g., in medical applications, medical imaging, and laboratory tests). Thus, large repositories of semantically annotated data are currently available, opening new opportunities for enhancing current decision-support systems. The data warehousing technology must be prepared to handle semantic web data. In Chap. 14 we study semantic web data warehouses.

In the current **big data** scenario, which will be predominant in the coming years, massive-scale data sources are becoming common, posing new challenges to the data warehouse community. New database architectures are gaining momentum. As an answer to these challenges, distributed storage and processing, NoSQL database systems, column-store database systems, and in-memory database systems are part of new emerging data warehouse architectures. In addition, traditional ETL processes and data warehouse solutions are unable to cope with the massive amounts and variety of data. The need to combine structured, unstructured, and real-time analytics demands for solutions that can integrate data analysis in a single system. The NewSQL and HTAP paradigms, Data lakes, Delta Lake, Polyglot architectures, and cloud data warehouses are responses to this demand from academia and industry. Chapter 15 presents and discusses these recent developments in the field.

1.3 Review Questions

1.1 Why are traditional databases called operational or transactional? Why are these databases inappropriate for data analysis?

1.2 Discuss four main characteristics of data warehouses.

1.3 Describe the different components of a multidimensional model, that is, facts, measures, dimensions, and hierarchies.

1.4 What is the purpose of online analytical processing (OLAP) systems and how are they related to data warehouses?

1.5 Specify the different steps used for designing a database. What are the specific concerns addressed in each of these phases?

1.6 Explain the advantages of using a conceptual model when designing a data warehouse.

1.7 What is the difference between the star and the snowflake schemas?

1.8 Specify several techniques that can be used for improving performance in data warehouse systems.

1.9 What is the extraction, transformation, and loading (ETL) process?

1.10 What languages can be used for querying data warehouses?

1.11 Describe what is meant by the term data analytics. Give examples of techniques that are used for exploiting the content of data warehouses.

1.12 Why do we need a method for data warehouse design?

1.13 What is spatial data? What is mobility data? Give examples of applications for which such kinds of data are important.

1.14 Explain the differences between spatial databases and spatial data warehouses.

1.15 What is big data and how is it related to data warehousing? Give examples of technologies that are used in this context.

1.16 Give examples of applications where graph data models can be used.

1.17 Describe why it is necessary to take into account web data in the context of data warehousing. Motivate your answer by elaborating an example application scenario.

Chapter 2
Database Concepts

This chapter introduces the basic database concepts, covering modeling, design, and implementation aspects. Section 2.1 begins by describing the concepts underlying database systems and the typical four-step process used for designing them, starting with requirements specification, followed by conceptual, logical, and physical design. These steps allow a separation of concerns, where requirements specification gathers the requirements about the application and its environment, conceptual design targets the modeling of these requirements from the perspective of the users, logical design develops an implementation of the application according to a particular database technology, and physical design optimizes the application with respect to a particular implementation platform. Section 2.2 presents the Northwind case study that we will use throughout the book. In Sect. 2.3, we review the entity-relationship model, a popular conceptual model for designing databases. Section 2.4 is devoted to the most used logical model of databases, the relational model. Finally, physical design considerations for databases are covered in Sect. 2.5.

The aim of this chapter is to provide the necessary knowledge to understand the remaining chapters in this book, making it self-contained. However, we do not intend to be comprehensive and refer the interested reader to the many textbooks on the subject.

2.1 Database Design

Databases are the core component of today's information systems. A **database** is a shared collection of logically related data, and a description of that data, designed to meet the information needs and support the activities of an organization. A database is deployed on a **database management system** (DBMS), which is a software system used to define, create, manipulate, and administer a database.

© Springer-Verlag GmbH Germany, part of Springer Nature 2022
A. Vaisman, E. Zimányi, *Data Warehouse Systems*, Data-Centric Systems and Applications, https://doi.org/10.1007/978-3-662-65167-4_2

Designing a database system is a complex undertaking typically divided into four phases, described next.

- **Requirements specification** collects information about the users' needs with respect to the database system. A large number of approaches for requirements specification have been developed by both academia and practitioners. These techniques help to elicit necessary and desirable system properties from prospective users, to homogenize requirements, and to assign priorities to them.
- **Conceptual design** aims at building a user-oriented representation of the database that does not contain any implementation considerations. This is done by using a **conceptual model** in order to identify the relevant concepts of the application at hand. The entity-relationship model is one of the most frequently used conceptual models for designing database applications. Alternatively, object-oriented modeling techniques can also be applied, based on the UML (Unified Modeling Notation) notation.
- **Logical design** aims at translating the conceptual representation of the database obtained in the previous phase into a **logical model** common to several DBMSs. Currently, the most common logical model is the relational model. Other logical models include the object-relational model, the object-oriented model, and the semistructured model. In this book, we focus on the relational model.
- **Physical design** aims at customizing the logical representation of the database obtained in the previous phase to a **physical model** targeted to a particular DBMS platform. Common DBMSs include SQL Server, Oracle, DB2, MySQL, and PostgreSQL, among others.

A major objective of this four-level process is to provide **data independence**, that is, to ensure as much as possible that schemas in upper levels are unaffected by changes to schemas in lower levels. Two kinds of data independence are typically defined. **Logical data independence** refers to immunity of the conceptual schema to changes in the logical one. For example, changing the structure of relational tables should not affect the conceptual schema, provided that the requirements of the application remain the same. **Physical data independence** refers to immunity of the logical schema to changes in the physical one. For example, physically sorting the records of a file on a disk does not affect the conceptual or logical schema, although this modification may be perceived by the user through a change in response time.

In the following sections, we briefly describe the entity-relationship model and the relational models, to cover the most widely used conceptual and logical models, respectively. We then address physical design considerations. Before doing this, we introduce the use case we will use throughout the book, which is based on the popular Northwind relational database. In this chapter, we explain the database design concepts using this example. In the next chapter, we will use a data warehouse derived from this database, over which we will explain the data warehousing and OLAP concepts.

2.2 The Northwind Case Study

The Northwind company exports a number of goods. In order to manage and store the company data, a relational database must be designed. The main characteristics of the data to be stored are the following:

- Customer data, which must include an identifier, the customer's name, contact person's name and title, full address, phone, and fax.
- Employee data, including the identifier, name, title, title of courtesy, birth date, hire date, address, home phone, phone extension, and a photo. Photos must be stored in the file system, together with a path them. Further, employees report to other employees of higher level in the organization.
- Geographic data, namely, the territories where the company operates. These territories are organized into regions. For the moment, only the territory and region description must be kept. An employee can be assigned to several territories, but these territories are not exclusive to an employee: Each employee can be linked to multiple territories, and each territory can be linked to multiple employees.
- Shipper data, that is, information about the companies that Northwind hires to provide delivery services. For each one of them, the company name and phone number must be kept.
- Supplier data, including the company name, contact name and title, full address, phone, fax, and home page.
- Data about the products that Northwind trades, such as identifier, name, quantity per unit, unit price, and an indication if the product has been discontinued. In addition, an inventory is maintained, which requires to know the number of units in stock, the units ordered (i.e., in stock but not yet delivered), and the reorder level (i.e., the number of units in stock such that, when it is reached, the company must produce or acquire). Products are further classified into categories, each of which has a name, a description, and a picture. Each product has a unique supplier.
- Data about the sale orders. This includes the identifier, the date at which the order was submitted, the required delivery date, the actual delivery date, the employee involved in the sale, the customer, the shipper in charge of its delivery, the freight cost, and the full destination address. An order can contain many products, and for each of them the unit price, the quantity, and the discount that may be given must be kept.

2.3 Conceptual Database Design

The entity-relationship (ER) model is one of the most often used conceptual models for designing database applications. Although there is general agreement about the meaning of the various concepts of the ER model, a number of different visual notations have been proposed for representing these concepts. Appendix A shows the notations we use in this book.

Figure 2.1 shows the ER model for the Northwind database. We next introduce the main ER concepts using this figure.

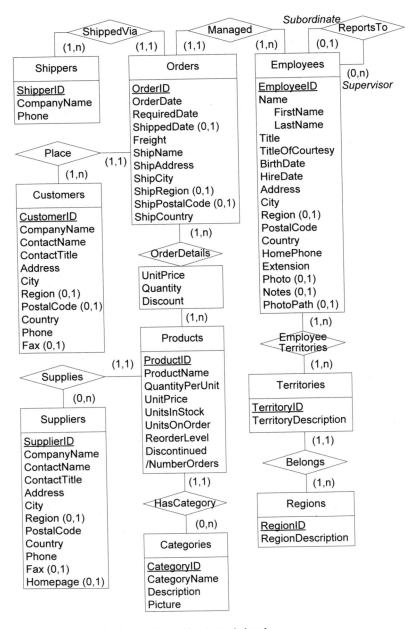

Fig. 2.1 Conceptual schema of the Northwind database

Entity types are used to represent a set of real-world objects of interest to an application. In Fig. 2.1, Employees, Orders, and Customers are examples of entity types. An object belonging to an entity type is called an **entity** or an **instance**. The set of instances of an entity type is called its **population**. From the application point of view, all entities of an entity type have the same characteristics.

Real world objects do not live in isolation; they are related to other objects. **Relationship types** are used to represent these associations between objects. In our example, Supplies, ReportsTo, and HasCategory are examples of relationship types. An association between objects of a relationship type is called a **relationship** or an **instance**. The set of associations of a relationship type is called its **population**.

The participation of an entity type in a relationship type is called a **role** and is represented by a line linking the two types. Each role of a relationship type has associated with it a pair of **cardinalities** describing the minimum and maximum number of times that an entity may participate in that relationship type. For example, the role between Products and Supplies has cardinalities (1,1), meaning that each product participates exactly once in the relationship type. The role between Supplies and Suppliers has cardinality (0,n), meaning that a supplier can participate between 0 and n times (i.e., an undetermined number of times) in the relationship. On the other hand, the cardinality (1,n) between Orders and OrderDetails means that each order can participate between 1 and n times in the relationship type. A role is said to be **optional** or **mandatory** depending on whether its minimum cardinality is 0 or 1, respectively. Further, a role is said to be **monovalued** or **multivalued** depending on whether its maximum cardinality is 1 or n, respectively.

A relationship type may relate two or more object types: It is called **binary** if it relates two object types, and **n-ary** if it relates more than two object types. In Fig. 2.1, all relationship types are binary. Depending on the maximum cardinality of each role, binary relationship types can be categorized into **one-to-one**, **one-to-many**, and **many-to-many** relationship types. In Fig. 2.1, the relationship type Supplies is a one-to-many relationship, since one product is supplied by at most one supplier, whereas a supplier may supply several products. On the other hand, the relationship type OrderDetails is many-to-many, since an order is related to one or more products, while a product can be included in many orders.

It may be the case that the same entity type occurs more than once in a relationship type, as is the case of the ReportsTo relationship type. In this case, the relationship type is called **recursive**, and **role names** are necessary to distinguish between the different roles of the entity type. In Fig. 2.1, Subordinate and Supervisor are role names.

Both objects and the relationships between them have a series of structural characteristics that describe them. **Attributes** are used for recording these characteristics of entity or relationship types. For example, in Fig. 2.1

Address and Homepage are attributes of Suppliers, while UnitPrice, Quantity, and Discount are attributes of OrderDetails.

Like roles, attributes have associated **cardinalities**, defining the number of values that an attribute may take in each instance. Since most of the time the cardinality of an attribute is (1,1), we do not show this cardinality in our diagrams. Thus, each supplier will have exactly one Address and at most one Homepage. Therefore, its cardinality is (0,1). and we say that the attribute is **optional**. When the cardinality is (1,1) we say that the attribute is **mandatory**. Similarly, attributes are called **monovalued** or **multivalued** depending on whether they may take at most one or several values, respectively. In our example, all attributes are monovalued. However, if a customer has one or more phones, then the attribute Phone will be labeled (1,n).

Further, attributes may be composed of other attributes. For example, the attribute Name in entity type Employees, is composed of FirstName and Last-Name. Such attributes are called **complex attributes**, while those that do not have components are called **simple attributes**. Finally, some attributes may be **derived**, as shown for the attribute NumberOrders of Products. This means that the number of orders in which a product participates may be derived using a formula that involves other elements of the schema, and stored as an attribute. In our case, the derived attribute records the number of times that a particular product participates in the relationship OrderDetails.

A common situation in real-world applications is that one or several attributes uniquely identify a particular object; such attributes are called **identifiers**. In Fig. 2.1, identifiers are underlined; for example, EmployeeID is the identifier of the entity type Employees, meaning that every employee has a unique value for this attribute. In the figure, all entity type identifiers are simple, that is, they are composed of only one attribute, although it is common to have identifiers composed of two or more attributes.

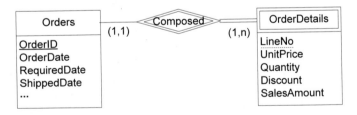

Fig. 2.2 Relationship type OrderDetails modeled as a weak entity type

Entity types that do not have an identifier of their own are called **weak entity types**, and are represented with a double line on its name box. In contrast, regular entity types that do have an identifier are called **strong entity types**. In Fig. 2.1, there are no weak entity types. However, note that the relationship OrderDetails between Orders and Products can be modeled as shown in Fig. 2.2.

A weak entity type is dependent on the existence of another entity type, called the **identifying** or **owner entity type**. The relationship type that relates a weak entity type to its owner is called the **identifying relationship type** of the weak entity type. A relationship type that is not an identifying relationship type is called a **regular relationship type**. Thus, in Fig. 2.2, Orders is the owner entity type for the weak entity type OrderDetails, and Composed is its identifying relationship type. As shown in the figure, the identifying relationship type and the role that connects it to the weak entity type are distinguished by their double lines. Note that identifying relationship types have cardinality (1,1) in the role of the weak entity type and may have (0,n) or (1,n) cardinality in the role of the owner.

A weak entity type typically has a **partial identifier**, which is a set of attributes that uniquely identifies weak entities related to the same owner entity. For example, attribute LineNo of OrderDetails stores the line number of each product in an order. Thus, the same number can appear several times in different orders, although it is unique within each order. As shown in the figure, partial identifier attributes are underlined with a dashed line.

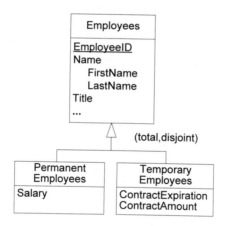

Fig. 2.3 Entity type Employees and two subtypes

Finally, it is usual that people refer to the same concept using several different perspectives with different abstraction levels. The **generalization** (or **is-a**) **relationship** captures such a mental process. It relates two entity types, called the **supertype** and the **subtype**, meaning that both types represent the same concept at different levels of detail. The Northwind database does not include a generalization. To give an example, consider Fig. 2.3, in which we have a supertype Employees, and two subtypes, PermanentEmployees and TemporaryEmployees. The former has an additional attribute Salary, and the latter has attributes ContractExpiration and ContractAmount.

Generalization has three essential characteristics. The first one is **population inclusion**, meaning that every instance of the subtype is also an instance of the supertype. In our example, this means that every temporary employee is also an employee of the Northwind company. The second characteristic is **inheritance**, meaning that all characteristics of the supertype (e.g., attributes and roles) are inherited by the subtype. Thus, in our example, temporary employees also have, for instance, a name and a title. Finally, the third characteristic is **substitutability**, meaning that each time an instance of the supertype is required (e.g., in an operation or in a query), an instance of the subtype can be used instead.

A generalization can be either **total** or **partial**, depending on whether every instance of the supertype is also an instance of one of the subtypes. In Fig. 2.3, the generalization is total, since employees are either permanent or temporary. On the other hand, a generalization can be either **disjoint** or **overlapping**, depending on whether an instance may belong to one or several subtypes. In our example, the generalization is disjoint, since a temporary employee cannot be a permanent one.

2.4 Logical Database Design

In this section, we describe the most used logical data model for databases, that is, the relational model. We also study two well-known query languages for the relational model: the relational algebra and SQL.

2.4.1 The Relational Model

Relational databases have been successfully used for several decades for storing information in many application domains. In spite of alternative database technologies that have appeared in the last decades, the relational model is still the most often used approach for storing the information that is crucial for the day-to-day operation of an organization.

Much of the success of the relational model, introduced by Codd in 1970, is due to its simplicity, intuitiveness, and its foundation on a solid formal theory: The relational model builds on the concept of a mathematical relation, which can be seen as a table of values and is based on set theory and first-order predicate logic. This mathematical foundation allowed the design of declarative query languages, and a rich spectrum of optimization techniques that led to efficient implementations. Note that in spite of this, only in the early 1980s the first commercial relational DBMS (RDBMS) appeared.

The relational model has a simple data structure, a **relation** (or **table**) composed of one or several **attributes** (or **columns**). Thus, a **relational schema** describes the structure of a set of relations. Figure 2.4 shows a relational schema that corresponds to the conceptual schema of Fig. 2.1. As

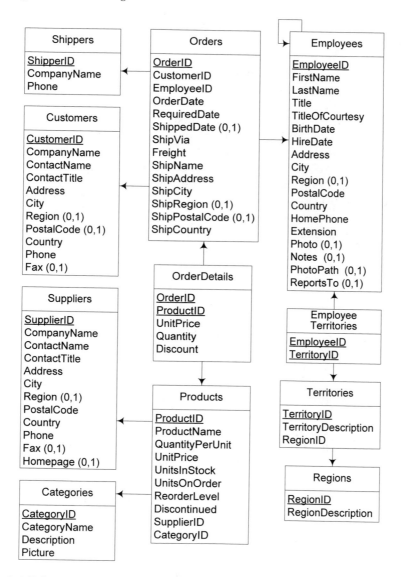

Fig. 2.4 Relational schema of the Northwind database that corresponds to the conceptual schema in Fig. 2.1

we will see later in this section, this relational schema is obtained by applying a set of translation rules to the corresponding ER schema. The relational schema of the Northwind database is composed of a set of relations, such as Employees, Customers, and Products. Each of these relations is composed of several attributes. For example, EmployeeID, FirstName, and LastName are some attributes of the relation Employees. In what follows, we use the notation $R.A$ to indicate the attribute A of relation R.

In the relational model, each attribute is defined over a **domain**, or **data type**, that is, a set of values with an associated set of operations, the most typical ones being integer, float, date, and string. One important restriction to the model is that attributes must be atomic and monovalued. Thus, complex attributes like Name of the entity type Employees in Fig. 2.1 must be split into atomic values, like FirstName and LastName in the table of the same name in Fig. 2.4. Therefore, a relation R is defined by a schema $R(A_1 : D_1, A_2 : D_2, \ldots, A_n : D_n)$, where R is the name of the relation, and each attribute A_i is defined over the domain D_i. The relation R is associated to a set of **tuples** (or **rows** if we see the relation as a table) $(t_1, t_2, \ldots, t_n)$. This set of tuples is a subset of the Cartesian product $D_1 \times D_2 \times \cdots \times D_n$, and it is sometimes called the **instance** or **extension** of R. The **degree** (or **arity**) of a relation is the number of attributes n of its relation schema.

The relational model allows several types of **integrity constraints** to be defined declaratively.

- An attribute may be defined as being **non-null**, meaning that **null values** (or blanks) are not allowed in that attribute. In Fig. 2.4, only the attributes marked with a cardinality (0,1) allow null values.
- One or several attributes may be defined as a **key**, that is, it is not allowed that two different tuples of the relation have identical values in such columns. In Fig. 2.4, keys are underlined. A key composed of several attributes is called a **composite key**, otherwise it is a **simple key**. In Fig. 2.4, the table Employees has a simple key, EmployeeID, while the table EmployeeTerritories has a composite key, composed of EmployeeID and TerritoryID. In the relational model, each relation must have a **primary key** and may have other **alternate keys**. Further, the attributes composing the primary key do not accept null values.
- **Referential integrity** specifies a link between two tables (or twice the same table), where a set of attributes in one table, called the **foreign key**, references the primary key of the other table. This means that the values in the foreign key must also exist in the primary key. In Fig. 2.4, referential integrity constraints are represented by arrows from the referencing table to the table that is referenced. For example, the attribute EmployeeID in table Orders references the primary key of the table Employees. This ensures that every employee appearing in an order also appears in the table Employees. Note that referential integrity may involve foreign keys and primary keys composed of several attributes.
- Finally, a **check constraint** defines a predicate that must be valid when adding or updating a tuple in a relation. For example, a check constraint can be used to verify that in table Orders the values of attributes OrderDate and RequiredDate for a given order are such that OrderDate $\leq$ RequiredDate. Note that many DBMSs restrict check constraints to a single tuple: references to data stored in other tables or

in other tuples of the same table are not allowed. Therefore, check constraints can be used only to verify simple constraints.

The above declarative integrity constraints do not suffice to express the many constraints that exist in any application domain. Such constraints must then be implemented using triggers. A **trigger** is a named event-condition-action rule that is automatically activated when a relation is modified. Triggers can also be used to compute derived attributes, such as attribute NumberOrders in table Products in Fig. 2.4. A trigger will update the value of the attribute each time there is an insert, update, or delete in table OrderDetails.

The translation of a conceptual schema (written in the ER or any other conceptual model) to an equivalent relational schema is called a *mapping*. This is a well-known process, implemented in most database design tools, where conceptual schemas are automatically translated to logical ones, mainly into the relational model. This process includes the definition of the tables in various RDBMSs.

We now outline seven rules that are used to map an ER schema into a relational one.

Rule 1: A strong entity type E is mapped to a table T containing the simple monovalued attributes and the simple components of the monovalued complex attributes of E. The identifier of E defines the primary key of T. T also defines non-null constraints for the mandatory attributes. Note that additional attributes will be added to this table by subsequent rules. For example, the strong entity type Products in Fig. 2.1 is mapped to the table Products in Fig. 2.4, with key ProductID.

Rule 2: Let us consider a weak entity type W, with owner (strong) entity type O. Assume W_{id} is the partial identifier of W, and O_{id} is the identifier of O. W is mapped in the same way as a strong entity type, that is, to a table T. In this case, T must also include O_{id} as an attribute, with a referential integrity constraint to attribute $O.O_{id}$. Moreover, the identifier of T is the union of W_{id} and O_{id}.

As an example, the weak entity type OrderDetails in Fig. 2.2 is mapped to the table of the same name in Fig. 2.5. The key of the latter is composed of the attributes OrderID and LineNo, where the former is a foreign key referencing table Orders.

Rule 3: A regular binary one-to-one relationship type R between two entity types E_1 and E_2, which are mapped, respectively, to tables T_1 and T_2 is mapped embedding the identifier of T_1 in T_2 as a foreign key. In addition, the simple monovalued attributes and the simple components of the monovalued complex attributes of R are also included in T_2. This table also defines non-null constraints for the mandatory attributes.

Note that, in general, we can embed the key of T_1 in T_2, or conversely, the key of T_2 in T_1. The choice depends on the cardinality of the roles of R. In Fig. 2.1, assume the relationship Supplies has cardinalities (1,1)

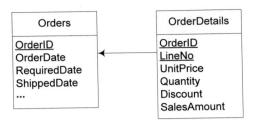

Fig. 2.5 Relationship translation of the schema in Fig. 2.2

with Products and (0,1) with Suppliers. Embedding ProductID in table Suppliers may result in several tuples of the Suppliers relation containing null values in the ProductID column, since there can be suppliers that do not supply any product. Thus, to avoid null values, it would be preferable to embed SupplierID in table Products.

Rule 4: Consider a regular binary one-to-many relationship type R relating entity types E_1 and E_2, where T_1 and T_2 are the tables resulting from the mapping of these entities. R is mapped embedding the key of T_2 in table T_1 as a foreign key. In addition, the simple monovalued attributes and the simple components of the monovalued complex attributes of R are included in T_1, defining the corresponding non-null constraints for the mandatory attributes.

As an example, in Fig. 2.1, the one-to-many relationship type Supplies between Products and Suppliers is mapped by including the attribute SupplierID in table Products, as a foreign key, as shown in Fig. 2.4.

Rule 5: Consider a regular binary many-to-many relationship type R between entity types E_1 and E_2, such that T_1 and T_2 are the tables resulting from the mapping of the former entities. R is mapped to a table T containing the keys of T_1 and T_2, as foreign keys. The key of T is the union of these keys. Alternatively, the relationship identifier, if any, may define the key of the table. T also contains the simple monovalued attributes and the simple components of the monovalued complex attributes of R, and also defines non-null constraints for the mandatory attributes.

In Fig. 2.1, the many-to-many relationship type EmployeeTerritories between Employees and Territories is mapped to a table with the same name containing the identifiers of the two tables involved, as shown in Fig. 2.4.

Rule 6: A multivalued attribute of an entity or relationship type E is mapped to a table T, which also includes the identifier of the entity or relationship type. A referential integrity constraint relates this identifier to the table associated with E. The primary key of T is composed of all of its attributes.

Suppose that in Fig. 2.1, the attribute Phone of Customers is multivalued. In this case, the attribute is mapped to a table CustomerPhone with attributes CustomerID and Phone both composing the primary key.

Rule 7: A generalization relationship between a supertype E_1 and subtype E_2 can be dealt with in three different ways:

Rule 7a: Both E_1 and E_2 are mapped, respectively, to tables T_1 and T_2, in which case the identifier of E_1 is propagated to T_2. A referential integrity constraint relates this identifier to T_1.

Rule 7b: Only E_1 is associated with a table T_1, which contains all attributes of E_2. All these attributes become optional in T_1.

Rule 7c: Only E_2 is associated with a table T_2, in which case all attributes E_1 are inherited in T_2.

As an example, the possible translations of the generalization given in Fig. 2.3 are shown in Fig. 2.6.

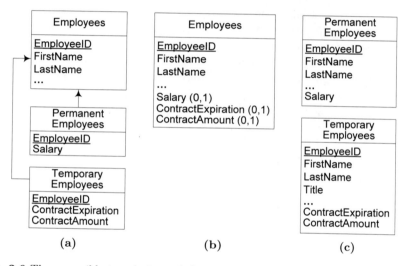

Fig. 2.6 Three possible translations of the schema in Fig. 2.3 (**a**) Using Rule 7a; (**b**) Using Rule 7b; (**c**) Using Rule 7c

Note that the generalization type (total vs. partial and disjoint vs. overlapping) may preclude one of the above three approaches. For example, the third possibility is not applicable for partial generalizations. Also, note that the semantics of the partial, total, disjoint, and overlapping characteristics are not fully captured by this translation mechanism. The conditions must be implemented when populating the relational tables. For example, assume a table T, and two tables T_1 and T_2 resulting from the mapping of a total and overlapping generalization. Referential integrity does not fully capture the semantics. It must be ensured, among other conditions, that when deleting an element from T, this element is also deleted from T_1 and T_2 (since it can exist in both tables). Such constraints are typically implemented with triggers.

Applying these mapping rules to the ER schema given in Fig. 2.1 yields the relational schema shown in Fig. 2.4. Note that the above rules apply in the general case; however, other mappings are possible. For example, binary one-to-one and one-to-many relationships may be represented by a table of its own, using Rule 5. The choice between alternative representation depends on the characteristics of the particular application at hand.

It must be noted that there is a significant difference in expressive power between the ER model and the relational model. This difference may be explained by the fact that the ER model is a *conceptual* model aimed at expressing concepts as closely as possible to the users' perspective, whereas the relational model is a *logical* model targeted toward particular implementation platforms. Several ER concepts do not have a correspondence in the relational model, and thus they must be expressed using only the available concepts in the model, that is, relations, attributes, and the related constraints. This translation implies a semantic loss in the sense that data invalid in an ER schema are allowed in the corresponding relational schema, unless the latter is supplemented by additional constraints. Many of such constraints must be manually coded by the user using mechanisms such as triggers or stored procedures. Furthermore, from a user's perspective, the relational schema is much less readable than the corresponding ER schema. This is crucial when one is considering schemas with hundreds of entity or relationship types and thousands of attributes. This is not a surprise, since this was the reason for devising conceptual models back in the 1970s, that is, the aim was to better understand the semantics of large relational schemas.

2.4.2 Normalization

When considering a relational schema, we must determine whether or not the relations in the schema have potential redundancies, and thus may induce anomalies in the presence of insertions, updates, and deletions.

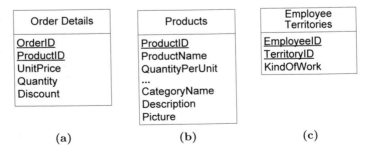

Fig. 2.7 Examples of relations that are not normalized

For example, assume that in relation OrderDetails in Fig. 2.7a, each product, no matter the order, is associated with a discount percentage. Here, the discount information for a product p will be repeated for all orders in which p appears. Thus, this information will be redundant. To solve this problem, the attribute Discount must be removed from the table OrderDetails and must be added to the table Products in order to store only once the information about the product discounts.

Consider now the relation Products in Fig. 2.7b, which is a variation of the relation with the same name in Fig. 2.4. In this case, we have included the category information (name, description, and picture) in the Products relation. It is easy to see that such information about a category is repeated for each product with the same category. Therefore, when, for example, the description of a category needs to be updated, we must ensure that all tuples in the relation Products, corresponding to the same category, are also updated, otherwise there will be inconsistencies. To solve this problem, the attributes describing a category must be removed from the table and a table Category like the one in Fig. 2.4 must be used to store the data about categories.

Finally, let us analyze the relation EmployeeTerritories in Fig. 2.7c, where an additional attribute KindOfWork has been added with respect to the relation with the same name in Fig. 2.4. Assume that an employee can do many kinds of work, independently of the territories in which she carries out her work. Thus, the information about the kind of work of an employee will be repeated as many times as the number of territories she is assigned to. To solve this problem, the attribute KindOfWork must be removed from the table, and a table EmpWork relating employees to the kinds of work they perform must be added.

Dependencies and normal forms are used to describe the redundancies above. A **functional dependency** is a constraint between two sets of attributes in a relation. Given a relation R and two sets of attributes X and Y in R, a functional dependency $X \rightarrow Y$ holds if and only if, in all the tuples of the relation, each value of X is associated with at most one value of Y. In this case it is said that X *determines* Y. Note that a key is a particular case of a functional dependency, where the set of attributes composing the key functionally determines all of the attributes in the relation.

The redundancies in Fig. 2.7a,b can be expressed by means of functional dependencies. For example, in the relation OrderDetails in Fig. 2.7a, there is the functional dependency ProductID $\rightarrow$ Discount. Also, in the relation Products in Fig. 2.7b, we have the functional dependencies ProductID $\rightarrow$ CategoryName and CategoryName $\rightarrow$ Description.

The redundancy in the relation EmployeeTerritories in Fig. 2.7c is captured by another kind of dependency. Given two sets of attributes X and Y in a relation R, a **multivalued dependency** $X \rightarrow\rightarrow Y$ holds if the value of X determines a set of values for Y, which is independent of $R \backslash XY$, where '$\backslash$' indicates the set difference. In this case we say that X *multidetermines* Y. In the relation in Fig. 2.7c, the multivalued dependency EmployeeID $\rightarrow\rightarrow$ KindOfWork holds, and consequently TerritoryID $\rightarrow\rightarrow$ KindOfWork. Functional dependencies are special cases of multivalued dependencies, that is, every functional dependency is also a multivalued dependency.

A **normal form** is an integrity constraint aimed at guaranteeing that a relational schema satisfies particular properties. Since the beginning of the relational model in the 1970s, many types of normal forms have been defined. In addition, normal forms have also been defined for other models, such as the entity-relationship model. We refer the reader to database textbooks for the definition of the various normal forms.

2.4.3 Relational Query Languages

Data stored in a relational database can be queried using different formalisms. Two kinds of query languages are typically defined. In a *procedural* language, a query is specified indicating the operations needed to retrieve the desired result. In a *declarative* language, the user only indicates *what* she wants to retrieve, leaving to the DBMS the task of determining the equivalent procedural query that is to be executed.

In this section, we introduce the relational algebra and SQL, which we will be using in many parts of this book. While the relational algebra is a procedural query language, SQL is a declarative one.

Relational Algebra

The relational algebra is a collection of operations for manipulating relations. These operations can be of two kinds: **unary**, which receive as argument a relation and return another relation, or **binary**, which receive as argument two relations and return a relation. As the operations always return relations, the algebra is *closed*, and operations can be combined in order to compute the answer to a query. Another classification of the operations is as follows. **Basic** operations cannot be derived from any combination of other operations, while **derived** operations are a shorthand for a sequence of basic operations, defined for making queries easier to express. In what follows, we describe the relational algebra operations. We start first with the unary operations.

The **projection** operation, denoted by $\pi_{C_1,...,C_n}(R)$, returns the columns $C_1, \ldots, C_n$ from the relation R. Thus, it can be seen as a vertical partition of R into two relations: one containing the columns mentioned in the expression, and the other containing the remaining columns.

For the database given in Fig. 2.4, an example of a projection is:

$\pi_{\mathsf{FirstName,LastName,HireDate}}(\mathsf{Employees})$.

This operation returns the three specified attributes from the Employees table.

The **selection** operation, denoted by $\sigma_\varphi(R)$, returns the tuples from the relation R that satisfy the Boolean condition φ. In other words, it partitions a table horizontally into two sets of tuples: the ones that do satisfy the condition and the ones that do not. Therefore, the structure of R is kept in the result.

A selection operation over the database given in Fig. 2.4 is:

$$\sigma_{\text{HireDate}\geq\text{'}01/01/2012\text{'}\wedge\text{HireDate}\leq\text{'}31/12/2014\text{'}}(\text{Employees}).$$

This operation returns the employees hired between 2012 and 2014.

Since the result of a relational algebra operation is a relation, it can be used as input for another operation. To make queries easier to read, sometimes it is useful to use temporary relations to store intermediate results. We will use the notation $T \leftarrow Q$ to indicate that relation T stores the result of query Q. Thus, combining the two previous examples, we can ask for the first name, last name, and hire date of all employees hired between 2012 and 2014. The query reads:

$\text{Temp1} \leftarrow \sigma_{\text{HireDate}\geq\text{'}01/01/2012\text{'}\wedge\text{HireDate}\leq\text{'}31/12/2014\text{'}}(\text{Employees})$
$\text{Result} \leftarrow \pi_{\text{FirstName,LastName,HireDate}}(\text{Temp1}).$

The **rename** operation, denoted by $\rho_{A_1\rightarrow B_1,\ldots,A_k\rightarrow B_k}(R)$, returns a relation where the attributes $A_1,\ldots,A_k$ in R are renamed to $B_1,\ldots,B_k$, respectively. Therefore, the resulting relation has the same tuples as the relation R, although the schema of both relations is different.

We present next the binary operations, which are based on classic operations of the set theory. Some of these operations require that the relations be **union compatible**. Two relations $R_1(A_1,\ldots,A_n)$ and $R_2(B_1,\ldots,B_n)$ are said to be union compatible if they have the same degree n and for all $i = 1,\ldots,n$, the domains of A_i and B_i are equal.

The three operations union, intersection, and difference on two union-compatible relations R_1 and R_2 are defined as follows:

- The **union** operation, denoted by $R_1 \cup R_2$, returns the tuples that are in R_1, in R_2, or in both, removing duplicates.
- The **intersection** operation, denoted by $R_1 \cap R_2$, returns the tuples that are in both R_1 and in R_2.
- The **difference** operation, denoted by $R_1 \setminus R_2$, returns the tuples that are in R_1 but not in R_2.

If the relations are union compatible, but the attribute names differ, by convention the attributes names of the first relation are kept in the result.

The union can be used to express queries like "Identifier of employees from the UK or who are reported by an employee from the UK," which reads:

$\text{UKEmps} \leftarrow \sigma_{\text{Country}=\text{'}\text{UK}\text{'}}(\text{Employees})$
$\text{Result1} \leftarrow \pi_{\text{EmployeeID}}(\text{UKEmp})$
$\text{Result2} \leftarrow \rho_{\text{ReportsTo}\rightarrow\text{EmployeeID}}(\pi_{\text{ReportsTo}}(\text{UKEmps}))$
$\text{Result} \leftarrow \text{Result1} \cup \text{Result2}.$

Relation UKEmps contains the employees from the UK. Result1 contains the projection of the former over EmployeeID, and Result2 contains the EmployeeID of the employees reported by an employee from the UK. The union of Result1 and Result2 yields the desired result.

The intersection can be used to express queries like "Identifier of employees from the UK who are reported by an employee from the UK," which is obtained by the replacing the last expression above by the following one:

Result ← Result1 ∩ Result2.

Finally, the difference can be used to express queries like "Identifier of employees from the UK who are not reported by an employee from the UK," which is obtained by the replacing the expression above by the following one:

Result ← Result1 \ Result2.

The **Cartesian product**, denoted by $R_1 \times R_2$, takes two relations and returns a new one, whose schema is composed of all the attributes in R_1 and R_2 (renamed if necessary), and whose instance is obtained concatenating each pair of tuples from R_1 and R_2. Thus, the number of tuples in the result is the product of the cardinalities of both relations.

Although by itself the Cartesian product is usually meaningless, it is very useful when combined with a selection. For example, suppose we want to retrieve the name of the products supplied by suppliers from Brazil. To answer this query, we use the Cartesian product to combine data from the tables Products and Suppliers. For the sake of clarity, we only keep the attributes we need: ProductID, ProductName, and SupplierID from table Products, and SupplierID and Country from table Suppliers. Attribute SupplierID in one of the relations must be renamed, since a relation cannot have two attributes with the same name.

Temp1 ← $\pi_{ProductID,ProductName,SupplierID}$ (Products)
Temp2 ← $\rho_{SupplierID \rightarrow SupID}$ ($\pi_{SupplierID,Country}$ (Suppliers))
Temp3 ← Temp1 × Temp2.

The Cartesian product combines each product with all the suppliers. We are only interested in the rows that relate a product to its supplier. For this, we filter the meaningless tuples, select the ones corresponding to suppliers from Brazil, and project the column we want, that is, ProductName:

Temp4 ← $\sigma_{SupplierID=SupID}$ (Temp3)
Result ← $\pi_{ProductName}$ ($\sigma_{Country='Brazil'}$ (Temp4)).

The **join** operation, denoted by $R_1 \bowtie_\varphi R_2$, where φ is a condition over the attributes in R_1 and R_2, takes two relations and returns a new one, whose schema consists in all attributes of R_1 and R_2 (renamed if necessary), and whose instance is obtained concatenating each pair of tuples from R_1 and R_2 that satisfy condition φ. The operation is basically a combination of a Cartesian product and a selection.

Using the join operation, the query "Name of the products supplied by suppliers from Brazil" will read:

Temp1 ← $\rho_{\text{SupplierID}\rightarrow\text{SupID}}$(Suppliers)
Result ← $\pi_{\text{ProductName}}(\sigma_{\text{Country}=\text{'Brazil'}}(\text{Product} \bowtie_{\text{SupplierID}=\text{SupID}} \text{Temp1}))$.

Note that the join combines the Cartesian product in Temp3 and the selection in Temp4 in a single operation, making the expression much more concise.

There are a number of variants of the join operation. An **equijoin** is a join $R_1 \bowtie_\varphi R_2$ such that condition φ states only equality comparisons. A **natural join**, denoted by $R_1 * R_2$, is a type of equijoin that states the equality between *all* the attributes with the same name in R_1 and R_2. The resulting table is defined over the schema $R_1 \cup R_2$ (i.e., all the attributes in R_1 and R_2, without duplicates). In the case that there are no attributes with the same names, a cross join is performed.

For example, the query "List all product names and category names" reads:

Temp ← Products * Categories
Result ← $\pi_{\text{ProductName},\text{CategoryName}}$(Temp).

The first query performs the natural join between relations Products and Categories. The attributes in Temp are all the attributes in Product, plus all the attributes in Categories, except for CategoryID, which is in both relations, so only one of them is kept. The second query performs the final projection.

The joins introduced above are known as **inner joins**, since tuples that do no match the join condition are eliminated. In many practical cases we need to keep in the result all the tuples of one or both relations, independently of whether or not they verify the join condition. For these cases, a set of operations, called **outer joins**, were defined. There are three kinds of outer joins: left outer join, right outer join, and full outer join.

The **left outer join**, denoted by $R_1 \bowtie_\varphi R_2$, performs the join as defined above, but instead of keeping only the matching tuples, it keeps every tuple in R_1 (the relation of the left of the operation). If a tuple in R_1 does not satisfy the join condition, the tuple is kept, and the attributes of R_2 in the result are filled with null values.

As an example, the query "Last name of employees, together with the last name of their supervisor, or null if the employee has no supervisor," reads in relational algebra:

Supervisors ← $\rho_{\text{EmployeeID}\rightarrow\text{SupID},\text{LastName}\rightarrow\text{SupLastName}}$(Employees)
Result ← $\pi_{\text{EmployeeID},\text{LastName},\text{SupID},\text{SupLastName}}($
Employees $\bowtie_{\text{ReportsTo}=\text{SupID}}$ Supervisors$)$.

The resulting table has tuples such as (2, Fuller, NULL, NULL), which correspond to employees who do not report to any other employee.

The **right outer join**, denoted by $R_1 \bowtie_\varphi R_2$, is analogous to the left outer join, except that the tuples that are kept are the ones in R_2. The **full outer join**, denoted by $R_1 \bowtie_\varphi R_2$, keeps all the tuples in both R_1 and R_2.

Suppose that in the previous example we also require the information of the employees who do not supervise anyone. Then, we would have:

$\pi_{EmployeeID,LastName,SupID,SupLastName}$(Employees $⟖_{ReportsTo=SupID}$ Supervisors)

With respect to the left outer join shown above, the resulting table has in addition tuples such as (NULL, NULL, 1, Davolio), which correspond to employees who do not supervise any other employee.

The **division**, denoted by $R_1 \div R_2$, is used to express queries involving *universal quantification*, that is, those that are typically state using the word *all*. It returns tuples from R_1 that have combinations with all tuples from R_2. More precisely, given two tables $R_1(A_1, \ldots, A_m, B_1, \ldots, B_n)$ and $R_2(B_1, \ldots, B_n)$, $R_1 \div R_2$ returns the tuples $(a_1, \ldots, a_m)$ such that R_1 contains a tuple $(a_1, \ldots, a_m, b_1, \ldots, b_n)$ for every tuple $(b_1, \ldots, b_n)$ in R_2.

For example, the query "Suppliers that have products in *all* categories" is written as follows.

SuppCat $\leftarrow \pi_{CompanyName, CategoryID}$(Suppliers $*$ Products $*$ Categories)
Result $\leftarrow$ SuppCat $\div \pi_{CategoryID}$(Categories)

Table SuppCat finds the couples of supplier and category such that the supplier has at least one product from the category. The result is obtained by dividing this table by a table containing the identifiers of the categories.

SQL

SQL (structured query language) is the most common language for creating, manipulating, and retrieving data from relational DBMSs. SQL is composed of several sublanguages. The **data definition language** (DDL) is used to define the schema of a database. The **data manipulation language** (DML) is used to query a database and to modify its content (i.e., to add, update, and delete data in a database). In what follows, we present a summary of the main features of SQL that we will use in this book. For a detailed description, we refer the reader to the references provided at the end of this chapter.

Below we show the SQL DDL command for defining table Orders in the schema of Fig. 2.4 (only some of attributes are shown). The basic DDL statement is CREATE TABLE, which creates a relation and defines the data types of the attributes, the primary and foreign keys, and the constraints.

```
CREATE TABLE Orders (
        OrderID INTEGER PRIMARY KEY,
        CustomerID INTEGER NOT NULL,
        EmployeeID INTEGER NOT NULL,
        OrderDate DATE NOT NULL,

        ...
        FOREIGN KEY (CustomerID) REFERENCES Customers(CustomerID),
        FOREIGN KEY (ShippedVia) REFERENCES Shippers(ShipperID),
        FOREIGN KEY (EmployeeID) REFERENCES Employees(EmployeeID),
        CHECK (OrderDate <= RequiredDate) )
```

SQL provides a DROP TABLE statement for deleting a table, and an ALTER TABLE statement for modifying the structure of a table.

The **DML** part of SQL is used to insert, update, and delete tuples from the database tables. For example, the following INSERT statement

```
INSERT INTO Shippers(CompanyName, Phone)
VALUES ('Federal Express', '02 752 75 75')
```

adds a new shipper in the Northwind database. This tuple is modified by the following UPDATE statement:

```
UPDATE Shippers
SET      CompanyName = 'Fedex'
WHERE  CompanyName = 'Federal Express'
```

Finally, the new shipper is removed in the following DELETE statement.

```
DELETE FROM Shippers
WHERE CompanyName = 'Fedex'
```

SQL also provides statements for retrieving data from the database. The basic structure of an SQL expression is:

```
SELECT ⟨ list of attributes ⟩
FROM    ⟨ list of tables ⟩
WHERE ⟨ condition ⟩
```

where ⟨ list of attributes ⟩ indicates the attribute names whose values are to be retrieved by the query, ⟨ list of tables ⟩ is a list of the relation names that will be included in the query, and ⟨ condition ⟩ is a Boolean expression that must be satisfied by the tuples in the result. The semantics of an SQL expression

```
SELECT R.A, S.B
FROM    R, S
WHERE R.B = S.A
```

is given by the relational algebra expression

$$\pi_{R.A,S.B}(\sigma_{R.B=S.A}(R \times S)),$$

that is, the SELECT clause is analogous to a projection π, the WHERE clause is a selection σ, and the FROM clause indicates the Cartesian product $\times$ between all the tables included in the clause.

It is worth noting that an SQL query, opposite to a relational algebra one, returns a set *with duplicates* (or a bag). Therefore, the keyword DISTINCT must be used to remove duplicates in the result. For example, the query "Countries of customers" must be written:

```
SELECT DISTINCT Country
FROM    Customers
```

This query returns the set of countries of the Northwind customers, without duplicates. If the DISTINCT keyword is removed from the above query, then it would return as many results as the number of customers in the database.

As another example, the query "Identifier, first name, and last name of the employees hired between 2012 and 2014," which we presented when discussing the projection and selection operations, reads in SQL:

```
SELECT EmployeeID, FirstName, LastName
FROM    Employees
WHERE HireDate >= '2012-01-01' and HireDate <= '2014-12-31'
```

The binary operations of the relational algebra are supported in SQL: union, intersection, difference, and the different kinds of joins. Recall the query "Identifiers of employees from the UK, or who are reported by an employee from the UK." In SQL it would read:

```
SELECT EmployeeID
FROM    Employees
WHERE Country='UK'
     UNION
SELECT ReportsTo
FROM    Employees
WHERE Country='UK'
```

The UNION in the above query removes duplicates in the result, whereas the UNION ALL keeps them, that is, if an employee from the UK is reported by at least one employee from the UK, it will appear twice in the result.

The join operation can be implemented as a projection of a selection over the Cartesian product of the relations involved. However, in general, it is easier and more efficient to use the join operation. For example, the query "Name of the products supplied by suppliers from Brazil" can be written as:

```
SELECT ProductName
FROM    Products P, Suppliers S
WHERE P.SupplierID = S.SupplierID AND Country = 'Brazil'
```

An alternative formulation of this query is as follows:

```
SELECT ProductName
FROM    Products P JOIN Suppliers S ON P.SupplierID = S.SupplierID
WHERE Country = 'Brazil'
```

The outer join operation must be explicitly stated in the FROM clause. For example, the query "First name and last name of employees, together with the first name and last name of their supervisor, or null if the employee has no supervisor" can be implemented using the LEFT OUTER JOIN operation.

```
SELECT E.FirstName, E.LastName, S.FirstName, S.LastName
FROM    Employees E LEFT OUTER JOIN Employees S
        ON E.ReportsTo = S.EmployeeID
```

Analogously, we can use the FULL OUTER JOIN operation to also include in the answer the employees who do not supervise anybody.

```
SELECT E.FirstName, E.LastName, S.FirstName, S.LastName
FROM   Employees E FULL OUTER JOIN Employees S ON E.ReportsTo = S.EmployeeID
```

As shown in the examples above, SQL is a declarative language, that is, we tell the system *what* we want, whereas in relational algebra, being a procedural language, we must specify *how* we will obtain the result. In fact, SQL query processors usually translate an SQL query into some form of relational algebra in order to optimize it.

Aggregation is used to summarize information from multiple tuples into a single one. For this, tuples are grouped and then an aggregate function is applied to every group. In data warehouses, particularly in OLAP, aggregation plays a crucial role, as we will study in subsequent chapters of this book.

Typically, DBMSs provide five basic aggregate functions, namely, COUNT, SUM, MAX, MIN, and AVG. The COUNT function returns the number of tuples in each group. Analogously, the functions SUM, MAX, MIN, and AVG are applied over numeric attributes and return, respectively, the sum, maximum value, minimum value, and average of the values in those attributes, for each group. Note that all of these functions can be applied to the whole table considered as a group. Further, the functions MAX and MIN can also be used with attributes that have nonnumeric domains if a total order is defined over the values in the domain, as is the case for strings.

The general form of an SQL query with aggregate functions is as follows:

```
SELECT    ⟨ list of grouping attributes ⟩ ⟨ list of aggr_funct(attribute) ⟩
FROM      ⟨ list of tables ⟩
WHERE     ⟨ condition ⟩
GROUP BY  ⟨ list of grouping attributes ⟩
HAVING    ⟨ condition over groups ⟩
ORDER BY  ⟨ list of attributes ⟩
```

When there is a GROUP BY clause, the SELECT clause must contain *only* aggregates or grouping attributes. The HAVING clause is analogous to the WHERE clause, except that the condition is applied over each group rather than over each tuple. Finally, the result can be sorted with the ORDER BY clause, where every attribute in the list can be ordered either in ascending or descending order by specifying ASC or DESC, respectively.

We next present some examples of aggregate SQL queries. We start with the query "Total number of orders handled by each employee, in descending order of number of orders. Only list employees with more than 100 orders."

```
SELECT    EmployeeID, COUNT(*) AS OrdersByEmployee
FROM      Orders
GROUP BY  EmployeeID
HAVING    COUNT(*) > 100
ORDER BY  COUNT(*) DESC
```

Consider now the query "For customers from Germany, list the total quantity of each product ordered. Order the result by customer ID, in ascending order, and by quantity of product ordered, in descending order."

```
SELECT     C.CustomerID, D.ProductID, SUM(Quantity) AS TotalQty
FROM       Orders O JOIN Customers C ON O.CustomerID = C.CustomerID
           JOIN OrderDetails D ON O.OrderID = D.OrderID
WHERE      C.Country = 'Germany'
GROUP BY C.CustomerID, D.ProductID
ORDER BY C.CustomerID ASC, SUM(Quantity) DESC
```

This query starts by joining three tables: Orders, Customers (where we have the country information), and OrderDetails (where we have the quantity ordered for each product in each order). Then, the query selects the customers from Germany. We then group by pairs (CustomerID, ProductID), and for each group, we take the sum in the attribute Quantity.

A **subquery** (or **nested query**) in SQL is used within a SELECT, FROM, or WHERE clause. The external query is called the **outer query**. In the WHERE clause, this is typically used to look for a certain value that is then used in a comparison condition through two special predicates: IN and EXISTS (and their negated versions, NOT IN and NOT EXISTS).

As an example of the IN predicate, the query "Identifier and name of products ordered by customers from Germany", is written as follows:

```
SELECT ProductID, ProductName
FROM   Products P
WHERE P.ProductID IN (
       SELECT D.ProductID
       FROM   Orders O JOIN Customers C ON O.CustomerID = C.CustomerID
              JOIN OrderDetails D ON O.OrderID = D.OrderID
       WHERE C.Country = 'Germany' )
```

The inner query computes the products ordered by customers from Germany. This returns a bag of product identifiers. The outer query scans the Products table, and for each tuple, it compares the product identifier with the set of identifiers returned by the inner query. If the product is in the set, the product identifier and the product name are listed.

The query above can be formulated using the EXISTS predicate, yielding what are referred to as **correlated nested queries**, as follows:

```
SELECT ProductID, ProductName
FROM   Products P
WHERE EXISTS (
       SELECT *
       FROM   Orders O JOIN Customers C ON
              O.CustomerID = C.CustomerID JOIN
              OrderDetails D ON O.OrderID = D.OrderID
       WHERE C.Country = 'Germany' AND D.ProductID = P.ProductID )
```

In the outer query we define an alias (or variable) P. For each tuple in Products, the variable P in the inner query is instantiated with the values in such tuple; if the result set of the inner query instantiated in this way is not empty, the EXISTS predicate evaluates to true, and the values of ProductID and ProductName are listed. The process is repeated for all tuples in Products.

To illustrate the **NOT EXISTS** predicate, consider the query "Names of customers who have not purchased any product," which is written as follows:

```
SELECT C.CompanyName
FROM   Customers C
WHERE  NOT EXISTS (
       SELECT *
       FROM   Orders O
       WHERE  C.CustomerID = O.CustomerID )
```

Here, the **NOT EXISTS** predicate will evaluate to true if, when P is instantiated in the inner query, the query returns the empty set.

The division operator we introduced in the previous section is not explictly implemented in SQL. It must be expressed by nesting two **NOT EXISTS** predicates. For example, the query "Names of suppliers who have products in *all* categories" can be written as follows:

```
SELECT S.CompanyName
FROM   Suppliers S
WHERE  NOT EXISTS (
       SELECT *
       FROM   Categories C
       WHERE  NOT EXISTS (
              SELECT *
              FROM   Products P
              WHERE  P.CategoryID = C.CategoryID AND
                     S.SupplierID = P.SupplierID ) )
```

This query uses double negatives to express the query condition. Indeed, it can be read as follows: "Suppliers for which there is no category such that no product of the category is supplied by the supplier."

In SQL, a **view** is just a query that is stored in the database with an associated name. Thus, views are like virtual tables. A view can be created from one or many tables or other views.

Views can be used for various purposes. They are used to structure data in a way that users find it natural or intuitive. They can also be used to restrict access to data such that users can have access only to the data they need. Finally, views can also be used to summarize data from various tables, which can be used, for example, to generate reports.

Views are created with the **CREATE VIEW** statement. To create a view, a user must have appropriate system privileges to modify the database schema. Once a view is created, it can then be used in a query as any other table.

For example, the following statement creates a view **CustomerOrders** that computes for each customer and order the total amount of the order.

```
CREATE VIEW CustomerOrders AS
        SELECT    O.CustomerID, O.OrderID,
                  SUM(D.Quantity * D.UnitPrice) AS Amount
        FROM      Orders O, OrderDetails D
        WHERE     O.OrderID = D.OrderID
        GROUP BY O.CustomerID, O.OrderID
```

This view is used in the next query to compute for each customer the maximum amount among all her orders.

```
SELECT    CustomerID, MAX(Amount) AS MaxAmount
FROM      CustomerOrders
GROUP BY CustomerID
```

As we will see in Chap. 8, views can be materialized, that is, they can be physically stored in a database.

A **common table expression** (CTE) is a temporary table defined within an SQL statement. Such temporary tables can be seen as views within the scope of the statement. A CTE is typically used when a user does not have the necessary privileges for creating a view.

For example, the following query combines in a single statement the view definition and the subsequent query given in the previous section.

```
WITH CustomerOrders AS (
          SELECT    O.CustomerID, O.OrderID,
                    SUM(D.Quantity * D.UnitPrice) AS Amount
          FROM      Orders O, OrderDetails D
          WHERE     O.OrderID = D.OrderID
          GROUP BY O.CustomerID, O.OrderID )
SELECT    CustomerID, MAX(Amount) AS MaxAmount
FROM      CustomerOrders
GROUP BY CustomerID
```

Note that several temporary tables can be defined in the WITH clause.

2.5 Physical Database Design

The objective of **physical database design** is to specify how database records are stored, accessed, and related in order to ensure adequate performance of a database application. Physical database design is related to query processing, physical data organization, indexing, transaction processing, and concurrency management, among other characteristics. In this section, we provide a very brief overview of some of those issues that will be addressed in detail for data warehouses in Chap. 8.

Physical database design requires knowing the specificities of the given application, in particular the properties of the data and the usage patterns of the database. The latter involves analyzing the transactions or queries that are run frequently and will have a significant impact on performance, the transactions that are critical to the operations of the organization, and the periods of time during which there will be a high demand on the database (called the **peak load**). This information is used to identify the parts of the database that may cause performance problems.

Various factors can be used to measure the performance of database applications. **Transaction throughput** is the number of transactions that can be processed in a given time interval. In some systems, such as electronic payment systems, a high transaction throughput is critical. **Response time** is the elapsed time for the completion of a single transaction. Minimizing response time is essential from the user's point of view. Finally, **disk storage** is the amount of disk space required to store the database files. Normally, a trade-off among these factors must be made, for example:

1. **Space-time trade-off:** It is often possible to reduce the time taken to perform an operation by using more space, and vice versa. For instance, a compression algorithm can be used to reduce the space occupied by a large file, but this implies extra time for the decompression process.
2. **Query-update trade-off:** Access to data can be made more efficient by imposing some structure upon it. However, the more elaborate the structure, the more time it takes to build it and to maintain it when its contents change. For example, sorting the records of a file according to a key field allows them to be located more easily but there is a greater overhead upon insertions to keep the file sorted.

Once an initial physical design has been implemented, it is necessary to monitor the system and to tune it as a result of the observed performance and any changes in requirements. Many DBMSs provide utilities to monitor and tune the system operations.

As the functionality provided by current DBMSs varies widely, physical design requires one to know the various techniques for storing and finding data that are implemented in the particular DBMS that will be used.

A database is organized on **secondary storage** into one or more **files**, where each file consists of one or several **records** and each record consists of one or several **fields**. Typically, each tuple in a relation corresponds to a record in a file. When a user requests a particular tuple, the DBMS maps this logical record into a physical disk address and retrieves the record into main memory using the file access routines of the operating system.

Data are stored on a computer disk in **disk blocks** (or **pages**) that are set by the operating system during disk formatting. Transfer of data between the main memory and the disk and vice versa takes place in units of disk blocks. DBMSs store data on **database blocks** (or **pages**). One important aspect of physical database design is the need to provide a good match between disk blocks and database blocks, on which logical units such as tables and records are stored. Most DBMSs provide the ability to specify a database block size. The selection of a database block size depends on several issues. For example, most DBMSs manage concurrent access to the records using some kind of locking mechanism. If a record is locked by one transaction that aims at modifying it, then no other transaction will be able to modify this record (however, normally several transactions are able to read a record if they do not try to write it). In some DBMSs, the finest locking granularity is at the page level, not at the record level. Therefore, the larger the page size, the larger the chance that two transactions will request access to entries on the same page. On the other hand, for optimal disk efficiency, the database block size must be equal to or be a multiple of the disk block size.

DBMSs reserve a storage area in the main memory that holds several database pages, which can be accessed for answering a query without reading those pages from the disk. This area is called a **buffer**. When a request is issued to the database, the query processor checks if the required data records are included in the pages already loaded in the buffer. If so, data are read from the buffer and/or modified. In the latter case, the modified pages are marked as such and eventually written back to the disk. If the pages needed to answer the query are not in the buffer, they are read from the disk, probably replacing existing ones in the buffer (if it is full, which is normally the case) using well-known algorithms, for example, replacing the least recently used pages with the new ones. In this way, the buffer acts as a **cache** that the DBMS can access to avoid going to disk, enhancing query performance.

File organization is the physical arrangement of data in a file into records and blocks on secondary storage. There are three main types of file organization. In a **heap** (or **unordered**) file organization, records are placed in the file in the order in which they are inserted. This makes insertion very efficient. However, retrieval is relatively slow, since the various pages of the file must be read in sequence until the required record is found. **Sequential** (or **ordered**) **files** have their records sorted on the values of one or more fields, called **ordering fields**. Ordered files allow fast retrieving of records, provided that the search condition is based on the sorting attribute. However, inserting and deleting records in a sequential file are problematic, since the order must be maintained. Finally, **hash files** use a **hash function** that calculates the address of the block (or **bucket**) in which a record is to be stored, based on the value of one or more attributes. Within a bucket, records are placed in order of arrival. A **collision** occurs when a bucket is filled to its capacity and a new record must be inserted into that bucket. Hashing provides the fastest possible access for retrieving an arbitrary record given the value of its hash field. However, collision management degrades the overall performance.

Independently of the particular file organization, additional access structures called **indexes** are used to speed up the retrieval of records in response to search conditions. Indexes provide efficient ways to access the records based on the **indexing fields** that are used to construct the index. Any field(s) of the file can be used to create an index, and multiple indexes on different fields can be constructed in the same file.

There are many different types of indexes. We describe below some categories of indexes according to various criteria.

- One categorization of indexes distinguishes between **clustered** and **nonclustered indexes**, also called **primary** and **secondary indexes**. In a clustered index, the records in the data file are physically ordered according to the field(s) on which the index is defined. This is not the case for a nonclustered index. A file can have at most one clustered index and in addition can have several nonclustered indexes.

- Indexes can be **single-column** or **multiple-column**, depending on the number of indexing fields on which they are based. When a multiple-column index is created, the order of columns in the index has an impact on data retrieval. Generally, the most restrictive value should be placed first for optimum performance.
- Indexes can be **unique** or **nonunique**: the former do not allow duplicate values, while nonunique indexes do.
- Indexes can be **sparse** or **dense**: in a dense index there is one entry in the index for every data record. This requires data files to be ordered on the indexing key. A sparse index contains less index entries than data records. Thus, a nonclustered index is always dense, since it is not ordered on the indexing key, while clustered indexes are sparse.
- Finally, indexes can be **single-level** or **multilevel**. When an index file becomes large and extends over many blocks, the search time required for the index increases. A multilevel index attempts to overcome this problem by splitting the index into a number of smaller indexes and maintaining an index to the indexes. Although a multilevel index reduces the number of blocks accessed when one is searching for a record, it also has problems in dealing with insertions and deletions in the index because all index levels are physically ordered files. A **dynamic multilevel index** solves this problem by leaving some space in each of its blocks for inserting new entries. This type of index is often implemented by using data structures called **B-trees** and **B$^+$-trees**, which are supported by most DBMSs.

Most DBMSs give the designer the option to set up indexes on any fields, thus achieving faster access at the expense of extra storage space for indexes, and overheads when updating. Because the indexed values are held in a sorted order, they can be efficiently exploited to handle partial matching and range searches, and in a relational system they can speed up join operations on indexed fields.

We will see in Chap. 8 that data warehouses require physical design solutions that are different from the ones required by DBMSs in order to support heavy transaction loads.

2.6 Summary

This chapter introduced the background database concepts that will be used throughout the book. We started by describing database systems and the usual steps followed for designing them, that is, requirements specification, conceptual design, logical design, and physical design. Then, we presented the Northwind case study, which was used to illustrate the different concepts introduced throughout the chapter. We presented the entity-relationship model, a well-known conceptual model. With respect to logical models, we studied the relational model and also gave the mapping rules that are used to translate an entity-relationship schema into a relational schema. In addition, we briefly discussed normalization, which aims at preventing redundancies and inconsistency in a relational database. Then, we presented two different languages for manipulating relational databases, namely, the relational algebra and SQL. We finished this introduction to database systems by describing several issues related to physical database design.

2.7 Bibliographic Notes

For a general overview of all the concepts covered in this chapter, we refer the reader to the textbooks [70, 79]. An overall view of requirements engineering is given in [59]. Conceptual database design is covered in [171] although it is based on UML [37] instead of the entity-relationship model. Logical database design is covered in [230]. A thorough overview of the components of the SQL:1999 standard is given in [151, 153], and later versions of the standard are described in [133, 152, 157, 272]. Physical database design is detailed in [140].

2.8 Review Questions

2.1 What is a database? What is a database management system?

2.2 Describe the four phases used in database design.

2.3 Define the following terms: entity type, entity, relationship type, relationship, role, cardinality, and population.

2.4 Illustrate with an example each of the following kinds of relationship types: binary, n-ary, one-to-one, one-to-many, many-to-many, and recursive.

2.5 Discuss different kinds of attributes according to their cardinality and their composition. What are derived attributes?

2.6 What is an identifier? What is the difference between a strong and a weak entity type? Does a weak entity type always have an identifying relationship? What is an owner entity type?

2.7 Discuss the different characteristics of the generalization relationship.

2.8 Define the following terms: relation (or table), attribute (or column), tuple (or line), and domain.

2.9 Explain the various integrity constraints that can be described in the relational model.

2.10 Discuss the basic rules for translating an ER schema into a relational schema. Give an example of a concept of the ER model that can be translated into the relational model in different ways.

2.11 Illustrate with examples the different types of redundancy that may occur in a relation. How can redundancy in a relation induce problems in the presence of insertions, updates, and deletions?

2.12 What is the purpose of functional and multivalued dependencies? What is the difference between them?

2.13 Describe the different operations of the relational algebra. Elaborate on the difference between the several types of joins. How can a join be expressed in terms of other operations of the relational algebra?

2.14 What is SQL? What are the sublanguages of SQL?

2.15 What is the general structure of SQL queries? How can the semantics of an SQL query be expressed with the relational algebra?

2.16 Discuss the differences between the relational algebra and SQL. Why is relational algebra an operational language, whereas SQL is a declarative language?

2.17 Explain what duplicates are in SQL and how they are handled.

2.18 Describe the general structure of SQL queries with aggregation and sorting. State the basic aggregation operations provided by SQL.

2.19 What are subqueries in SQL? Give an example of a correlated subquery.

2.20 What are common table expressions in SQL? What are they needed for?

2.21 What is the objective of physical database design? Explain some factors that can be used to measure the performance of database applications and the trade-offs that have to be resolved.

2.22 Explain different types of file organization. Discuss their respective advantages and disadvantages.

2.23 What is an index? Why are indexes needed? Explain the various types of indexes.

2.24 What is clustering? What is it used for?

2.9 Exercises

Exercise 2.1. A French horse race fan wants to set up a database to analyze the performance of the horses as well as the betting payoffs.

A racetrack is described by a name (e.g., Hippodrome de Chantilly), a location (e.g., Chantilly, Oise, France), an owner, a manager, a date opened, and a description. A racetrack hosts a series of horse races.

A horse race has a name (e.g., Prix Jean Prat), a category (i.e., Group 1, 2, or 3), a race type (e.g., thoroughbred flat racing), a distance (in meters), a track type (e.g., turf right-handed), qualification conditions (e.g., 3-year-old excluding geldings), and the first year it took place.

A meeting is held on a certain date and a racetrack and is composed of one or several races. For a meeting, the following information is kept: weather (e.g., sunny, stormy), temperature, wind speed (in km per hour), and wind direction (N, S, E, W, NE, etc.).

Each race of a meeting is given a number and a departure time and has a number of horses participating in it. The application must keep track of the purse distribution, that is, how the amount of prize money is distributed among the top places (e.g., first place: €228,000, second place: €88,000, etc.), and the time of the fastest horse.

Each race at a date offers several bet types (e.g., tiercé, quarté+) each type offering zero or more bet options (e.g., in order, in any order, and bonus for the quarté+). The payoffs are given for a bet type and a base amount (e.g., quarté+ for €2) and specify for each option the win amount and the number of winners.

A horse has a name, a breed (e.g., thoroughbred), a sex, a foaling date (i.e., birth date), a gelding date (i.e., castration date for male horses, if any), a death date (if any), a sire (i.e., father), a dam (i.e., mother), a coat color (e.g., bay, chestnut), an owner, a breeder, and a trainer.

A horse that participates in a race with a jockey is assigned a number and carries a weight according to the conditions attached to the race or to equalize the difference in ability between the runners. Finally, the arrival place and the margin of victory of the horses are kept by the application.

a. Design an ER schema for this application. If you need additional information, you may look at the various existing French horse racing web sites.
b. Translate the ER schema above into the relational model. Indicate the keys of each relation, the referential integrity constraints, and the non-null constraints.

Exercise 2.2. A Formula One fan club wants to set up a database to keep track of the results of all the seasons since the first Formula One World championship in 1950.

A season is held on a year, between a starting and an ending date, has a number of races, and is described by a summary and a set of regulations. A race has a number (stating its order in a season), an official name (e.g., 2013 Formula One Shell Belgian Grand Prix), a race date, a race time (expressed in both local and UTC time), a description of the weather when the race took place, the pole position (consisting of driver name and time realized), and the fastest lap (consisting of driver name, time, and lap number).

Each race of a season belongs to a Grand Prix (e.g., Belgian Grand Prix), for which the following information is kept: active years (e.g., 1950–1956, 1958, etc. for the Belgian Grand Prix), total number of races (58 races as of 2013 for the Belgian Grand Prix), and a short historical description. The race of a season is held on a circuit, described by its name (e.g., Circuit de Spa-Francorchamps), location (e.g., Spa, Belgium), type (such as race, road, street), number of laps, circuit length, race distance (the latter two expressed in kilometers), and lap record (consisting of time, driver, and year).

Notice that the course of the circuits may be modified over the years. For example, the Spa-Francorchamps circuit was shortened from 14 to 7 km in 1979. Further, a Grand Prix may use several circuits over the years, as we the case for the Belgian Grand Prix.

A team has a name (e.g., Scuderia Ferrari), one or two bases (e.g., Maranello, Italy), and one or two current principals (e.g., Stefano Domenicali). In addition, a team keeps track of its debut (the first Grand Prix entered), the number of races competed, the number of world championships won by constructor and by driver, the highest race finish (consisting of place and number of times), the number of race victories, the number of pole positions, and the number of fastest laps. A team competing in a season has a full name, which typically includes its current sponsor (e.g., Scuderia Ferrari Marlboro from 1997 to 2011), a chassis (e.g., F138), an engine (e.g., Ferrari 056), and a tyre brand (e.g., Bridgestone).

For each driver, the following information is kept: name, nationality, birth date and birth place, number of races entered, number championships won, number of wins, number of podiums, total points in the career, number of pole positions, number of fastest laps, highest race finish (consisting of place and number of times), and highest grid position (consisting of place and number of times). Drivers are hired by teams competing in a season as either main drivers or test drivers. Each team has two main drivers and usually two test drivers, but the number of test drivers may vary from none to six. In addition, although a main driver is usually associated to a team for the whole season, it may only participate in some of the races of the season. A team participating in a season is assigned two consecutive numbers for its main drivers, where the number 1 is assigned to the team that won the constructor's world title the previous season. Further, the number 13 is usually not given to a car, it only appeared once in the Mexican Grand Prix in 1963.

A driver participating in a Grand Prix must participate in a qualifying session, which determines the starting order for the race. The results kept for a driver participating in the qualifying session are the position and the time realized for the three parts (called Q1, Q2, and Q3). Finally, the results kept for a driver participating in a race are the following: position (may be optional), number of laps, time, the reason why the driver retired or was disqualified (both may be optional) and the number of points (scored only for the top eight finishers).

a. Design an ER schema for this application. Note any unspecified requirements and integrity constraints, and make appropriate assumptions to make the specification complete. If you need additional information, you may look at the various existing Formula One web sites.

b. Translate the ER schema above into the relational model. Indicate the keys of the relations, and the referential integrity constraints, and the non-null constraints.

Exercise 2.3. Consider the following queries for the Northwind database. Write in relational algebra queries (a)–(g) and in SQL all the queries.

a. Name, address, city, and region of employees.
b. Name of employees and name of customers located in Brussels related through orders that are sent by Speedy Express.
c. Title and name of employees who have sold at least one of the products "Gravad Lax" or "Mishi Kobe Niku."
d. Name and title of employees as well as the name and title of the employee to whom they report.
e. Name of products that were sold by employees or purchased by customers located in London.
f. Name of employees and name of the city where they live for employees who have sold to customers located in the same city.
g. Names of products that have not been ordered.
h. Names of customers who bought all products.
i. Name of categories and the average price of products in each category.
j. Identifier and name of the companies that provide more than three products.
k. Identifier, name, and total sales of employees ordered by employee identifier.
l. Name of employees who sell the products of more than seven suppliers.

Chapter 3
Data Warehouse Concepts

This chapter introduces the basic concepts of data warehouses. A data warehouse is a particular database targeted toward decision support. It takes data from various operational databases and other data sources and transforms it into new structures that fit better for the task of performing business analysis. Data warehouses are based on a multidimensional model, where data are represented as hypercubes, with dimensions corresponding to the various business perspectives and cube cells containing the measures to be analyzed. In Sect. 3.1, we study the multidimensional model and present its main characteristics and components. Section 3.2 gives a detailed description of the most common operations for manipulating data cubes. In Sect. 3.3, we present the main characteristics of data warehouse systems and compare them against operational databases. The architecture of data warehouse systems is described in detail in Sect. 3.4. As we shall see, in addition to the data warehouse itself, data warehouse systems are composed of back-end tools, which extract data from the various sources to populate the warehouse, and front-end tools, which are used to extract the information from the warehouse and present it to users. We finish in Sect. 3.5, describing SQL Server, a representative business intelligence suite of tools.

3.1 Multidimensional Model

The importance of data analysis has been steadily increasing from the early 1990s, as organizations in all sectors are being required to improve their decision-making processes in order to maintain their competitive advantage. Traditional database systems like the ones studied in Chap. 2 do not satisfy the requirements of data analysis. They are designed and tuned to support the daily operations of an organization, and their primary concern is to ensure fast, concurrent access to data. This requires transaction processing and concurrency control capabilities, as well as recovery techniques that guaran-

© Springer-Verlag GmbH Germany, part of Springer Nature 2022
A. Vaisman, E. Zimányi, *Data Warehouse Systems*, Data-Centric Systems and Applications, https://doi.org/10.1007/978-3-662-65167-4_3

tee data consistency. These systems are known as **operational databases** or **online transaction processing (OLTP)** systems. The OLTP paradigm is focused on transactions. In the Northwind database example, a simple transaction could involve entering a new order, reserving the products ordered, and, if the reorder point has been reached, issuing a purchase order for the required products. Eventually, a user may want to know the status of a given order. If a database is indexed following one of the techniques described in the previous chapter, a typical OLTP query like the above would require accessing only a few records of the database (and normally will return a few tuples). Since OLTP systems must support heavy transaction loads, their design should prevent update anomalies, and thus, OLTP databases are highly normalized using the techniques studied in Chap. 2. Thus, they perform poorly when executing complex queries that need to join many tables together or to aggregate large volumes of data. Besides, typical operational databases contain detailed data and do not include historical data.

The above needs called for a new paradigm specifically oriented to analyze the data to support decision making. This paradigm, called **online analytical processing (OLAP)**, is focused on analytical queries. OLAP-oriented databases should support a heavy query load. Typical OLAP queries over the Northwind database would ask, for example, for the total sales amount by product and by customer, or for the most ordered products by customer. These kinds of queries involve aggregation, and thus, processing them will require, most of the time, accessing all the records in a database table. Indexing techniques aimed at OLTP are not efficient in this case: new indexing and query optimization techniques are required for OLAP. Further, normalization is not good for these queries, since it partitions the database into many tables. Reconstructing the data would require a high number of joins.

Therefore, the need for a different database model to support OLAP was clear and led to the notion of **data warehouses**, which are (usually) large repositories that consolidate data from different sources (internal and external to the organization). Being dedicated analysis databases, data warehouses can be designed and optimized to efficiently support OLAP queries. In addition, data warehouses are also used to support other kinds of analysis tasks, like reporting, data mining, and statistical analysis.

Data warehouses and OLAP systems are based on the **multidimensional model**, which views data in an n-dimensional space, usually called a **data cube** or a **hypercube**. A data cube is defined by dimensions and facts. **Dimensions** are perspectives used to analyze the data. For example, consider the data cube in Fig. 3.1, based on a portion of the Northwind database. We can use this cube to analyze sales figures. The cube has three dimensions: Product, Time, and Customer. A **level** represents the **granularity**, or level of detail, at which measures are represented for each dimension of the cube. In the example, sales figures are aggregated to the levels Category, Quarter, and City, respectively. Instances of a dimension are called **members**. For example, Seafood and Beverages are members of the Product dimension at

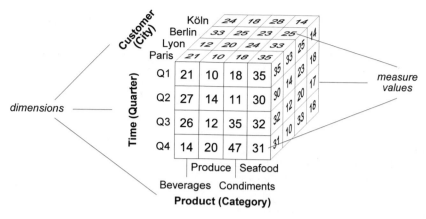

Fig. 3.1 A three-dimensional cube for sales data with dimensions Product, Time, and Customer, and a measure Quantity

the Category level. Dimensions also have associated **attributes** describing them. For example, the Product dimension could contain attributes such as ProductNumber and UnitPrice, which are not shown in the figure.

On the other hand, the **cells** of a data cube, or **facts**, have associated numeric values (we will see later that this is not always the case), called **measures**. These measures are used to evaluate quantitatively various aspects of the analysis at hand. For example, each number shown in a cell of the data cube in Fig. 3.1 represents a measure Quantity, indicating the number of units sold (in thousands) by category, quarter, and customer's city. A data cube typically contains several measures. For example, another measure, not shown in the figure, could be Amount, indicating the total sales amount.

A data cube may be **sparse** or **dense** depending on whether it has measures associated with each combination of dimension values. In the case of Fig. 3.1, this depends on whether all products are bought by all customers during the period of time considered. For example, not all customers may have ordered products of all categories during all quarters of the year. Actually, in real-world applications, cubes are typically sparse.

3.1.1 Hierarchies

The **granularity** of a data cube is determined by the combination of the levels corresponding to each axis of the cube. In Fig. 3.1, the dimension levels are indicated between parentheses: Category for the Product dimension, Quarter for the Time dimension, and City for the Customer dimension.

In order to extract strategic knowledge from a cube, it is necessary to view its data at several levels of detail. In our example, an analyst may want to see the sales figures at a finer granularity, such as at the month level, or at a coarser granularity, such as at the customer's country level. **Hierarchies** allow this possibility by defining a sequence of mappings relating lower-level, detailed concepts to higher-level, more general concepts. Given two related levels in a hierarchy, the lower level is called the **child** and the higher level is called the **parent**. The hierarchical structure of a dimension is called the dimension **schema**, while a dimension **instance** comprises the members at all levels in a dimension. Figure 3.2 shows the simplified hierarchies for our cube example. In the next chapter, we give full details of how dimension hierarchies are modeled. In the Product dimension, products are grouped in categories. For the Time dimension, the lowest granularity is Day, which aggregates into Month, which in turn aggregates into Quarter, Semester, and Year. Similarly, for the Customer dimension, the lowest granularity is Customer, which aggregates into City, State, Country, and Continent. It is usual to represent the top of the hierarchy with a distinguished level called All.

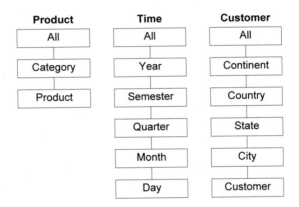

Fig. 3.2 Hierarchies of the Product, Time, and Customer dimensions

At the instance level, Fig. 3.3 shows an example of the Product dimension.[1] Each product at the lowest level of the hierarchy can be mapped to a corresponding category. All categories are grouped under a member called all, which is the only member of the distinguished level All. This member is used for obtaining the aggregation of measures for the whole hierarchy, that is, for obtaining the total sales for all products.

In real-world applications, there exist many kinds of hierarchies. For example, the hierarchy depicted in Fig. 3.3 is **balanced**, since there is the same number of levels from each individual product to the root of the hierarchy. In Chaps. 4 and 5, we shall study these and other kinds of hierarchies in detail, covering both their conceptual representation and their implementation in current data warehouse and OLAP systems.

---

[1] Note that, as indicated by the ellipses, not all nodes of the hierarchy are shown.

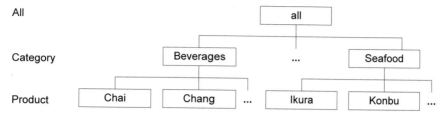

Fig. 3.3 Members of a hierarchy Product → Category

3.1.2 Measures

Each measure in a cube is associated with an aggregation function that combines several measure values into a single one. Aggregation of measures takes place when one changes the level of detail at which data in a cube are visualized. This is performed by traversing the hierarchies of the dimensions. For example, if we use the Customer hierarchy in Fig. 3.2 for changing the granularity of the data cube in Fig. 3.1 from City to Country, then the sales for all customers in the same country will be aggregated using, for example, the SUM operation. Similarly, total sales figures will result in a cube containing one cell with the total sum of the quantities of all products, that is, the cube visualized at the All level of all dimension hierarchies.

Summarizability refers to the correct aggregation of cube measures along dimension hierarchies, to obtain consistent aggregation results. To ensure summarizability, a set of conditions may hold. Some of them are listed below.

- **Disjointness of instances**: The grouping of instances in a level with respect to their parent in the next level must result in disjoint subsets. For example, in the hierarchy of Fig. 3.3, a product cannot belong to two categories. If this were the case, each product sales would be counted twice, one for each category.
- **Completeness**: All instances must be included in the hierarchy and each instance must be related to one parent in the next level. For example, the instances of the Time hierarchy in Fig. 3.2 must contain all days in the period of interest, and each day must be assigned to a month. If this condition were not satisfied, the aggregation of the results would be incorrect, since there would be dates for which sales will not be counted.
- **Correctness**: It refers to the correct use of the aggregation functions. As explained next, measures can be of various types, and this determines the kind of aggregation function that can be applied to them.

According to the way in which they can be aggregated, measures can be classified as follows.

- **Additive measures** can be meaningfully summarized along all the dimensions, using addition. These are the most common type of measures.

For example, the measure Quantity in the cube of Fig. 3.1 is additive: it can be summarized when the hierarchies in the Product, Time, and Customer dimensions are traversed.

- **Semiadditive measures** can be meaningfully summarized using addition along *some*, but not all, dimensions. As a typical example, inventory quantities cannot be meaningfully aggregated along the Time dimension, for instance, adding the inventory quantities for two different quarters.
- **Nonadditive measures** cannot be meaningfully summarized using addition across any dimension. Typical examples are item price, cost per unit, and exchange rate.

The aggregation functions to be used in the various dimensions must be defined for each measure. This is particularly important in the case of semiadditive and nonadditive measures. For example, a semiadditive measure representing inventory quantities can be aggregated computing the average along the Time dimension and the sum along other dimensions. Averaging can also be used for aggregating nonadditive measures such as item price or exchange rate. However, depending on the semantics of the application, other functions such as the minimum, maximum, or count could be used instead.

Allowing users to interactively explore the data cube at different granularities, optimization techniques based on aggregate precomputation are used. Incremental aggregation mechanisms avoid computing the whole aggregation from scratch each time the data warehouse is queried. However, this is not always possible, since this depends on the aggregate function used. This leads to another classification of measures, which we explain next.

- **Distributive measures** are defined by an aggregation function that can be computed in a distributed way. Suppose that the data are partitioned into n sets, and that the aggregate function is applied to each set, giving n aggregated values. The function is distributive if the result of applying it to the whole data set is the same as the result of applying a function (not necessarily the same) to the n aggregated values. The usual aggregation functions such as the count, sum, minimum, and maximum are distributive. However, the distinct count function is not. For instance, if we partition the set of measure values $\{3, 3, 4, 5, 8, 4, 7, 3, 8\}$ into the subsets $\{3, 3, 4\}$, $\{5, 8, 4\}$, and $\{7, 3, 8\}$, summing up the result of the distinct count function applied to each subset gives us a result of 8, while the answer over the original set is 5.
- **Algebraic measures** are defined by an aggregation function that can be expressed as a scalar function of distributive ones. A typical example of an algebraic aggregation function is the average, which can be computed by dividing the sum by the count, the latter two functions being distributive.
- **Holistic measures** are measures that cannot be computed from other subaggregates. Typical examples include the median, the mode, and the rank. Holistic measures are expensive to compute, especially when data are modified, since they must be computed from scratch.

3.2 OLAP Operations

A fundamental characteristic of the multidimensional model is that it allows viewing data from multiple perspectives and at several levels of detail. The OLAP operations allow these perspectives and levels of detail to be materialized and provide an interactive data analysis environment. These OLAP operations can be defined in a way analogous to the relational algebra operations introduced in Chap. 2.

Figure 3.4 shows the OLAP operations that can be used in order to analyze a data cube in different ways. The analysis starts from Fig. 3.4a, a cube containing quarterly sales quantities (in thousands) by product categories and customer cities for the year 2012.

Roll-up

The **roll-up** operation aggregates measures along a dimension hierarchy to obtain measures at a coarser **granularity**. The syntax for this operation is:

ROLLUP(CubeName, (Dimension → Level)*, AggFunction(Measure)*)

where Dimension → Level is the level in a dimension to which the roll-up is performed and AggFunction is the aggregation function applied to summarize the measure. An aggregation function must be specified for each measure to be kept in the resulting cube. The measures for which an aggregation is not specified are removed from the cube. Notice that specifying Dimension → All amounts to removing one dimension of the cube.

In our example, the following roll-up operation computes the sales quantities by country

ROLLUP(Sales, Customer → Country, SUM(Quantity))

The result is shown in Fig. 3.4b. While the original cube contained four values in the Customer dimension, one for each city, the new cube contains two values, one for each country. The remaining dimensions are not affected. Thus, the values in cells pertaining to Paris and Lyon in a given quarter and category contribute to the aggregation of the corresponding values for France. The computation of the cells pertaining to Germany proceeds analogously.

When querying a cube, a usual operation is to roll-up a few dimensions to particular levels and to remove the other dimensions through a roll-up to the All level. In a cube with n dimensions, this can be obtained by applying n successive roll-up operations. The ROLLUP* operation provides a shorthand notation for this sequence of operations. The syntax is as follows:

ROLLUP*(CubeName, [(Dimension → Level)*], AggFunction(Measure)*)

For example, the total quantity by quarter can be obtained as follows:

ROLLUP*(Sales, Time → Quarter, SUM(Quantity))

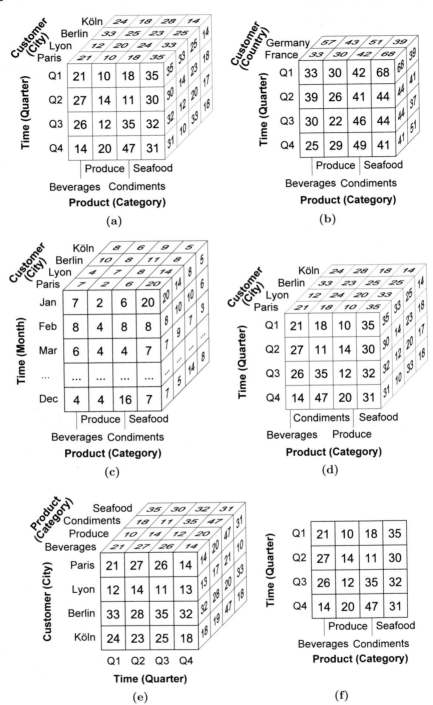

Fig. 3.4 OLAP operations. (**a**) Original cube; (**b**) Roll-up to the Country level; (**c**) Drill-down to the Month level; (**d**) Sort product by name; (**e**) Pivot; (**f**) Slice on City='Paris'

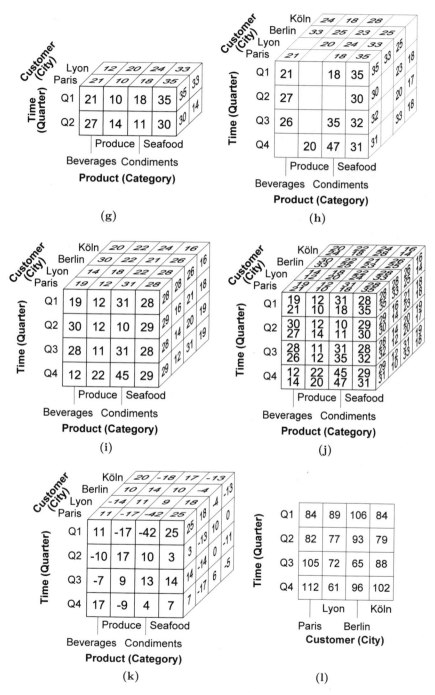

Fig. 3.4 OLAP operations (continued). (**g**) Dice on City='Paris' or 'Lyon' and Quarter='Q1' or 'Q2'; (**h**) Dice on Quantity > 15; (**i**) Cube for 2011; (**j**) Drill-across; (**k**) Percentage change; (**l**) Total sales by quarter and city

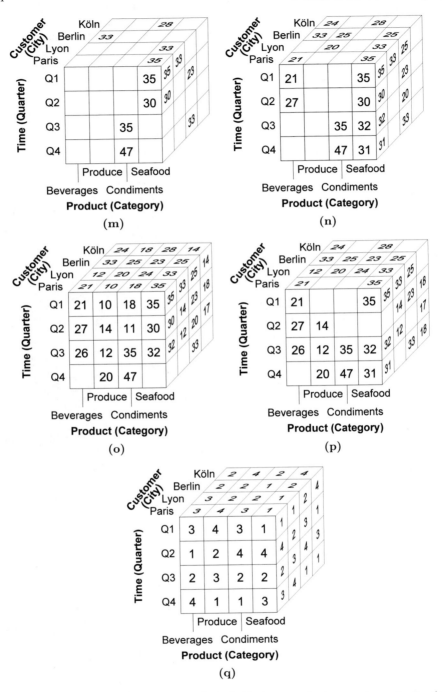

Fig. 3.4 OLAP operations (continued). (**m**) Maximum sales by quarter and city; (**n**) Top two sales by quarter and city; (**o**) Top 70% sales by city and category ordered by ascending quarter; (**p**) Top 70% sales by city and category ordered by descending quantity; (**q**) Rank quarter by category and city ordered by descending quantity

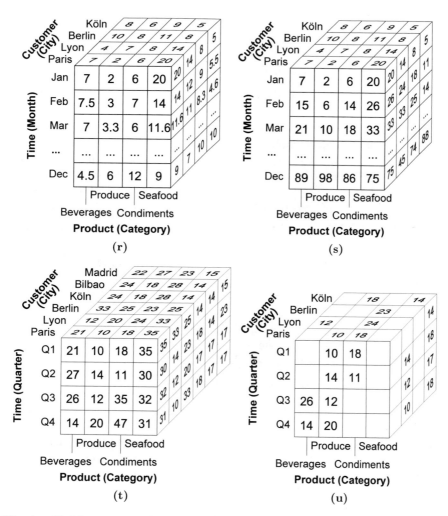

Fig. 3.4 OLAP operations (continued). (**r**) Three-month moving average; (**s**) Year-to-date sum; (**t**) Union of the original cube and another cube with data from Spain; (**u**) Difference of the original cube and the cube in Fig. 3.4n

which performs a roll-up along the Time dimension to the Quarter level and the other dimensions (in this case Customer and Product) to the All level. On the other hand, if the dimensions are not specified as in

ROLLUP*(Sales, SUM(Quantity))

all the dimensions of the cube will be rolled-up to the All level, yielding a single cell containing the overall sum of the Quantity measure.

A usual need when applying a roll-up operation is to count the number of members in one of the dimensions removed from the cube. For example, the following query obtains the number of distinct products sold by quarter:

ROLLUP*(Sales, Time → Quarter, COUNT(Product) AS ProdCount)

In this case, a new measure ProdCount will be added to the cube. We will see below other ways to add measures to a cube.

In many real-world situations hierarchies are **recursive**, that is, they contain a level that rolls-up to itself. A typical example is a supervision hierarchy over employees. Such hierarchies are discussed in detail in Chap. 4. The particularity of such hierarchies is that the number of levels of the hierarchy is not fixed at the schema level, but it depends on its members. The RECROLLUP operation is used to aggregate measures over recursive hierarchies by iteratively performing roll-ups over the hierarchy until the top level is reached. The syntax of this operation is as follows:

RECROLLUP(CubeName, Dimension → Level, Hierarchy, AggFunction(Measure)*)

Drill down

The **drill-down** operation performs the inverse of the roll-up operation, that is, it goes from a more general level to a more detailed level in a hierarchy. The syntax of this operation is as follows:

DRILLDOWN(CubeName, (Dimension → Level)*)

where Dimension → Level is the level in a dimension to which the drill down is performed.

For example, in the cube shown in Fig. 3.4b, the sales of category Seafood in France are significantly higher in the first quarter compared to the other ones. Thus, we can take the original cube and apply a drill-down along the Time dimension to the Month level to find out whether this high value occurred during a particular month, as follows

DRILLDOWN(Sales, Time → Month)

As shown in Fig. 3.4c, we discover that, for some reason yet unknown, sales in January soared both in Paris and in Lyon.

Sort

The **sort** operation returns a cube where the members of a dimension have been sorted. The syntax of the operation is as follows:

SORT(CubeName, Dimension, (Expression [{ASC | DESC | BASC | BDESC}])*)

where the members of Dimension are sorted according to the value of Expression either in ascending or descending order. In the case of ASC or DESC, members are sorted within their parent (i.e., respecting the hierarchies), whereas, in the case of **BASC** or **BDESC** the sorting is performed across all members (i.e., irrespective of the hierarchies). The **ASC** is the default option.

For example, the following expression

SORT(Sales, Product, ProductName)

sorts the members of the Product dimension on ascending order of their name, as shown in Fig. 3.4d. Here, ProductName is an attribute of products. When the cube contains only one dimension, the members can be sorted based on its measures. For example, if SalesByQuarter is obtained from the original cube by aggregating sales by quarter for all cities and all categories, the expression

SORT(SalesByQuarter, Time, Quantity DESC)

sorts the members of Time on descending order of the Quantity measure.

Pivot

The **pivot** (or **rotate**) operation rotates the axes of a cube to provide an alternative presentation of the data. The syntax of the operation is as follows:

PIVOT(CubeName, (Dimension → Axis)*)

where the axes are specified as $\{X, Y, Z, X1, Y1, Z1, \ldots\}$.

In our example, to see the cube with the Time dimension on the x axis, we can rotate the axes of the original cube as follows

PIVOT(Sales, Time → X, Customer → Y, Product → Z)

The result is shown in Fig. 3.4e.

Slice

The **slice** operation removes a dimension in a cube (i.e., a cube of $n - 1$ dimensions is obtained from a cube of n dimensions) by selecting one instance in a dimension level. The syntax of this operation is:

SLICE(CubeName, Dimension, Level = Value)

where the Dimension will be dropped by fixing a single Value in the Level. The other dimensions remain unchanged.

In our example, to visualize the data only for Paris, we apply a slice operation as follows:

SLICE(Sales, Customer, City = 'Paris')

The result is the subcube of Fig. 3.4f, a two-dimensional matrix where each column represents the evolution of the sales quantity by category and quarter, that is, a collection of time series. The slice operation assumes that the granularity of the cube is at the specified level of the dimension (in the example above, at the city level). Thus, a granularity change by means of a roll-up or drill-down operation is often needed prior to the slice operation.

Dice

The **dice** operation keeps the cells in a cube that satisfy a Boolean condition φ. The syntax for this operation is

DICE(CubeName, Condition)

where Condition is a Boolean condition over dimension levels, attributes, and measures. The resulting cube has the same dimensionality as the original cube. The dice operation is analogous to a selection in the relational algebra.

In our example, we can obtain a subcube of the original cube, containing only the sales figures for the first two quarters for Lyon and Paris as follows:

DICE(Sales, (Customer.City = 'Paris' OR Customer.City = 'Lyon') AND
            (Time.Quarter = 'Q1' OR Time.Quarter = 'Q2'))

and the result is shown in Fig. 3.4g. As another example, we can select the cells of the original cube that have a measure greater than 15 as

DICE(Sales, Quantity > 15)

and the result is shown in Fig. 3.4h.

Rename

The **rename** operation returns a cube where some schema elements or members have been renamed. The syntax is:

RENAME(CubeName, ({SchemaElement | Member} → NewName)*)

It is worth mentioning that a rename operation is usually necessary prior to combining two cubes with the drill-across operation (see next).

For example, the following expression

RENAME(Sales, Sales → Sales2012, Quantity → Quantity2012)

renames the cube in Fig. 3.4a and its measure. As another example

RENAME(Sales, Customer.all → AllCustomers)

renames the all member of the customer dimension.

Drill across

The **drill-across** operation combines cells from two data cubes that have the same schema and instances, using a join condition. The syntax of the operation is:

DRILLACROSS(CubeName1, CubeName2, [Condition]).

where Condition is a Boolean condition over dimension levels, attributes, and measures. This operation is analogous to a full outer join in the relational algebra. If the condition is not stated, it corresponds to an outer equijoin.

In our example, to compare the sales quantities in 2012 with those in 2011, we need the cube in Fig. 3.4i, which has the same structure as the one for 2012 given in Fig. 3.4a. To have the measures in the two cubes consolidated in a single one we can use the drill-across operation as follows

Sales2011-2012 ← DRILLACROSS(Sales2011, Sales2012)

This is shown in Fig. 3.4j.

On the other hand, given the Sales cube in Fig. 3.4c, to compare the sales of a month with those of the previous month can be obtained in two steps as follows:

Sales1 ← RENAME(Sales, Quantity → PrevMonthQuantity)
Result ← DRILLACROSS(Sales1, Sales, Sales1.Time.Month+1 = Sales.Time.Month)

In the first step, we create a temporary cube Sales1 by renaming the measure. In the second step, we perform the drill across of the two cubes by combining a cell in Sales1 with the cell in Sales corresponding to the subsequent month. As already stated, the join condition above corresponds to an outer join. Notice that the Sales cube in Fig. 3.4a contains measures for a single year. Thus, in the result above the cells corresponding to January and December will contain a null value in one of the two measures. As we will see in Sect. 4.4, when the cube contains measures for several years, the join condition must take into account that measures of January must be joined with those of December of the preceding year. Notice also that the cube has three dimensions and the join condition in the query above pertains to only one dimension. For the other dimensions it is supposed that an outer equijoin is performed.

Add measure

The **add measure** operation adds new measures to the cube computed from other measures or dimensions. The syntax for this operation is as follows:

ADDMEASURE(CubeName, (NewMeasure = Expression, [AggFunction])*)

where Expression is a formula over measures and dimension members, and AggFunction is the function for the measure, SUM being the default.

In our example, to compute the percentage change of sales between the two years, we take the cube resulting from the drill-across operation above and apply to it the add measure operation as follows

ADDMEASURE(Sales2011-2012, PercentageChange =
          (Quantity2011-Quantity2012)/Quantity2011)

The new measure is shown in Fig. 3.4k.

Drop measure

The **drop measure** operation removes one or several measures from a cube. The syntax is as follows:

DROPMEASURE(CubeName, Measure*)

For example, given the result of the add measure above, the cube illustrated in Fig. 3.4k is expressed by:

DROPMEASURE(Sales2011-2012, Quantity2011, Quantity2012)

Aggregation

We have seen that the roll-up operation aggregates measures when displaying the cube at coarser level. On the other hand, we also need to aggregate measures of a cube at the current granularity, that is, without performing a roll-up operation. The syntax for this operation is as follows:

AggFunction(CubeName, Measure) [BY Dimension*]

Usual aggregation functions are SUM, AVG, COUNT, MIN, and MAX. In addition to these, we use extended versions of MIN and MAX, which have an additional argument that is used to obtain the n minimum or maximum values. Further, TOPPERCENT and BOTTOMPERCENT select the members of a dimension that cumulatively account for x percent of a measure. Also, RANK and DENSERANK are used to rank the members of a dimension according to a measure. We show next examples of these functions.

In our example, given the original cube in Fig. 3.4a, the total sales by quarter and city can be computed as follows

SUM(Sales, Quantity) BY Time, Customer

This will yield the two-dimensional cube in Fig. 3.4l. On the other hand, to obtain the total sales by quarter we can write

SUM(Sales, Quantity) BY Time

which returns a one-dimensional cube with values for each quarter. In the query above, a roll-up along the Customer dimension up to level All is performed before the aggregation. Finally, to obtain the overall sales we write

SUM(Sales, Quantity)

which will result in a single cell.

OLAP aggregation functions can be classified in two types. **Cumulative aggregation functions** compute the measure value of a cell from several other cells. Examples of cumulative functions are SUM, COUNT, and AVG. On the other hand, **filtering aggregation functions** filter the members of a dimension that appear in the result. Examples are are MIN and MAX. The distinction between these two types of aggregation functions is important in

OLAP since filtering aggregation functions must not only compute the aggregated value but also determine the associated dimension members. As an example, to obtain the best-selling employee, we must compute the maximum sales amount and identify who is the employee that performed best.

When applying an aggregation operation, the dimension members in the resulting cube will depend on the aggregation function used. For example, given the cube in Fig. 3.4a, the total overall quantity is obtained as

SUM(Sales, Quantity)

This yields a single cell whose coordinates for the three dimensions will be all equal to all. Also, when computing the overall maximum quantity as:

MAX(Sales, Quantity)

we obtain the cell with value 47 and coordinates Q4, Condiments, and Paris (we suppose that cells that are hidden in Fig. 3.4a contain a smaller value for this measure). Similarly, the following expression

SUM(Sales, Quantity) BY Time, Customer

returns the total sales by quarter and customer, resulting in the cube given in Fig. 3.4l. This cube has three dimensions, where the Product dimension only contains the member all. On the other hand,

MAX(Sales, Quantity) BY Time, Customer

will yield the cube in Fig. 3.4m, where only the cells containing the maximum by time and customer will have values, while the other ones will be filled with null values. Similarly, the two maximum quantities by product and customer as shown in Fig. 3.4n can be obtained as follows:

MAX(Sales, Quantity, 2) BY Time, Customer

Notice that in the example above, we requested the two maximum quantities by time and customer. If in the cube there are two or more cells that tie for the last place in the limited result set, then the number of cells in the result could be greater than two. For example, this is the case in Fig. 3.4n for Berlin and Q1, where there are three values in the result, that is, 33, 25, and 25.

To compute top or bottom percentages, the order of the cells must be specified. For example, to compute the top 70% of the measure quantity by city and category ordered by quarter, as shown in Fig. 3.4o, we can write

TOPPERCENT(Sales, Quantity, 70) BY City, Category ORDER BY Quarter ASC

The operation computes the running sum of the sales by city and category starting with the first quarter and continues until the target percentage is reached. In this example, the sales in the first three quarters cover the required 70%. Similarly, the top 70% of the measure quantity by city and category ordered by quantity, shown in Fig. 3.4p, can be obtained by

TOPPERCENT(Sales, Quantity, 70) BY City, Category ORDER BY Quantity DESC

The rank operation also requires the specification of the order of the cells. As an example, to rank quarters by category and city order by descending quantity, as shown in Fig. 3.4q, we can write

RANK(Sales, Time) BY Category, City ORDER BY Quantity DESC

The rank and the dense rank operations differ in the case of ties. The former assigns the same rank to ties. For example, in Fig. 3.4q there is a tie in the quarters for Seafood and Köln, where Q2 and Q4 are in the first rank and Q3 and Q1 are in the third and fourth ranks, respectively. Using dense rank, Q3 and Q1 would be in the second and third ranks, respectively.

We often need to compute measures where the value of a cell is obtained by aggregating the measures of several nearby cells. Examples of these include moving average and year-to-date computations. For this, we need to define a subcube that is associated with each cell, and perform the aggregation over this subcube. These functions correspond to the window functions in SQL that will be described in Chap. 5. For example, given the cube in Fig. 3.4c, the 3-month moving average in Fig. 3.4r can be obtained by

ADDMEASURE(Sales, MovAvg3M = AVG(Quantity) OVER Time 2 CELLS PRECEDING)

Here, the moving average for January is equal to the measure in January, since there are no previous cells. Analogously, the measure for February is the average of the values of January and February. Finally, the average for the remaining months is computed from the measure value of the current month and the two preceding ones. In the window functions it is supposed that the members of the dimension over which the window is constructed are already sorted. For this, a sort operation can be applied prior to the application of the window aggregate function.

Similarly, to compute the year-to-date sum in Fig. 3.4s we can write

ADDMEASURE(Sales, YTDQuantity = SUM(Quantity) OVER Time
      ALL CELLS PRECEDING)

Here, the aggregation function is applied to a window that contains the current cell and all the previous ones, as indicated by ALL CELLS PRECEDING.

Union

The **union** operation merges two cubes that have the same schema but disjoint instances. The syntax of the operation is:

UNION(CubeName1, CubeName2).

If CubeSpain has the same schema as our original cube but containing only the sales to Spanish customers, the cube in Fig. 3.4t is obtained by

UNION(Sales, SalesSpain)

The union operation is also used to display different granularities on the same dimension. For example, if SalesCountry is the cube in Fig. 3.4b, then the following operation

UNION(Sales, SalesCountry)

results in a cube with sales measures summarized by city and by country.

Difference

Given two cubes with the same schema, the **difference** operation removes the cells in a cube that exist in another one. The syntax of the operation is:

DIFFERENCE(CubeName1, CubeName2).

In our example, we can remove from the original cube in Fig. 3.4a the cells of the top-two sales by quarter and city shown in Fig. 3.4n, which is called TopTwoSales, as follows

DIFFERENCE(Sales, TopTwoSales)

This will result in the cube in Fig. 3.4u.

Drill Through

Finally, the **drill-through** operation allows one to move from data at the bottom level in a cube to data in the operational systems from which the cube was derived. This could be used, for example, if one were trying to determine the reason for outlier values in a data cube. Formally, the drill through is not an OLAP operator since its result is not a multidimensional cube.

Table 3.1 summarizes the OLAP operations we have presented in this section. In addition to these basic operations, OLAP tools provide a great variety of mathematical, statistical, and financial operations for computing ratios, variances, interest, depreciation, currency conversions, etc.

3.3 Data Warehouses

A **data warehouse** is a repository of integrated data obtained from several sources for the specific purpose of multidimensional data analysis. More technically, a data warehouse is defined as a collection of subject-oriented, integrated, nonvolatile, and time-varying data to support management decisions. We explain next these characteristics.

- **Subject-oriented** means that data warehouses focus on the analytical needs of different areas of an organization. These areas vary depending

Operation	Purpose
Add measure	Adds new measures to a cube computed from other measures or dimensions.
Aggregation operations	Aggregate the cells of a cube, possibly after performing a grouping of cells.
Dice	Keeps the cells of a cube that satisfy a Boolean condition over dimension levels, attributes, and measures.
Difference	Removes the cells of a cube that are in another cube. Both cubes must have the same schema.
Drill-across	Merges two cubes that have the same schema and instances using a join condition.
Drill-down	Disaggregates measures along a hierarchy to obtain data at a finer granularity. It is the opposite of the roll-up operation.
Drop measure	Removes measures from a cube.
Pivot	Rotates the axes of a cube to provide an alternative presentation of its data.
Recursive roll-up	Performs an iteration of roll-ups over a recursive hierarchy until the top level is reached.
Rename	Renames one or several schema elements of a cube.
Roll-up	Aggregates measures along a hierarchy to obtain data at a coarser granularity. It is the opposite of the drill-down operation.
Roll-up*	Shorthand notation for a sequence of roll-up operations.
Slice	Removes a dimension from a cube by selecting one instance in a dimension level.
Sort	Orders the members of a dimension according to an expression.
Union	Combines the cells of two cubes that have the same schema but disjoint members.

Table 3.1 Summary of the OLAP operations

on the kind of activities performed by the organization. For example, in a retail company, the analysis may focus on product sales or inventory management. In operational databases, on the contrary, the focus is on specific functions that applications must perform, for example, registering sales of products or inventory replenishment.

- **Integrated** means that data obtained from operational and external systems must be joined together, which implies solving problems due to differences in data definition and content, such as differences in data format and data codification, synonyms (fields with different names but the same data), homonyms (fields with the same name but different meanings), multiplicity of occurrences of data, and many others. In operational databases these problems are typically solved in the design phase.
- **Nonvolatile** means that durability of data is ensured by disallowing data modification and removal, thus expanding the scope of the data to a longer period of time than operational systems usually offer. A data

warehouse gathers data encompassing several years, typically 5–10 years or beyond, while data in operational databases is often kept for only a short period of time, for example, 2–6 months, as required for daily operations, and it may be overwritten when necessary.

- **Time-varying** indicates the possibility of retaining different values for the same information, as well as the time when changes to these values occurred. For example, a data warehouse in a bank might store information about the average monthly balance of clients' accounts for a period covering several years. In contrast, an operational database may not have explicit temporal support, since sometimes it is not necessary for day-to-day operations, and also it is difficult to implement.

A data warehouse is aimed at analyzing the data of an entire organization. It is often the case that particular departments or divisions of an organization only require a portion of the organizational data warehouse specialized for their needs. For example, a sales department may only need sales data, while a human resources department may need demographic data and data about the employees. These departmental data warehouses are called **data marts**. However, these data marts are not necessarily private to a department, they may be shared with other interested parts of the organization.

A data warehouse can be seen as a collection of data marts. This view represents a **bottom-up** approach in which a data warehouse is built by first building the smaller data marts and then merging these to obtain the data warehouse. This can be a good approach for organizations not willing to take the risk of building a large data warehouse, which may take a long time to complete, or organizations that need fast results. On the other hand, in the classic data warehouse view, data marts are obtained from the data warehouse in a **top-down** fashion. In this approach, a data mart is sometimes just a logical view of a data warehouse.

Table 3.2 shows several aspects that differentiate operational database (or OLTP) systems from data warehouse (or OLAP) systems. We analyze next in detail some of these differences.

Typically, the users of OLTP systems are operations and employees who perform predefined operations through transactional applications, like payroll systems or ticket reservation systems. Data warehouse users, on the other hand, are usually located higher in the organizational hierarchy and use interactive OLAP tools to perform data analysis (lines 1–2). Therefore, data for OLTP systems should be current and detailed, while data analytics require historical, summarized data (line 3). The difference on data organization (line 4) follows from the type of use of OLTP and OLAP systems.

Data structures for OLTP are optimized for rather small and simple transactions, carried out frequently and repeatedly. Data access for OLTP requires reading and writing data files. For example, in the Northwind database application, a user may frequently insert new orders, modify old ones, and delete orders if customers cancel them. Thus, the number of records accessed by an OLTP transaction is usually small (e.g., the records involved in a particular

Table 3.2 Comparison between operational databases and data warehouses

	Aspect	Operational databases	Data warehouses
1	User type	Operators, office employees	Managers, account executives
2	Usage	Predictable, repetitive	Ad hoc, nonstructured
3	Data content	Current, detailed data	Historical, summarized data
4	Data organization	According to operational needs	According to analysis needs
5	Data structures	Optimized for small transactions	Optimized for complex queries
6	Access frequency	High	From medium to low
7	Access type	Read, insert, update, delete	Read, append only
8	# records/access	Few	Many
9	Response time	Short	Can be long
10	Concurrency level	High	Low
11	Lock utilization	Needed	Not needed
12	Update frequency	High	None
13	Data redundancy	Low (normalized tables)	High (denormalized tables)
14	Data modeling	UML, ER model	Multidimensional model

sales order). On the other hand, data structures for OLAP must support complex aggregation queries, thus requiring access to all the records in one or more tables, resulting in long, complex SQL queries. Further, OLAP systems are less frequently accessed than OLTP systems (e.g., a system handling purchase orders is frequently accessed, while a performing analysis of orders may not be that frequent). Also, data warehouse records are usually accessed in read mode (lines 5–8). OLTP systems usually have a short query response time, provided the appropriate indexing structures are defined, while complex OLAP queries can take longer time to complete (line 9).

OLTP systems have normally a high number of concurrent accesses and require locking or other concurrency management mechanisms to ensure safe transaction processing (lines 10–11). On the other hand, OLAP systems are read only, and thus queries can be submitted and computed concurrently. Also, the number of concurrent users in an OLAP system is usually low.

Finally, OLTP systems are modeled using UML or some variation of the ER model studied in Chap. 2, since such models lead to a highly normalized schema, adequate for databases that support frequent transactions, to guarantee consistency and reduce redundancy. OLAP designers use the multidimensional model, which, at the logical level (as we will see in Chap. 5), leads in general to a denormalized database schema, with a high level of redundancy, which favors query processing (lines 12–14).

3.4 Data Warehouse Architecture

We now show the general data warehouse architecture that will be used throughout the book. This architecture is composed of several tiers, depicted in Fig. 3.5 and described next.

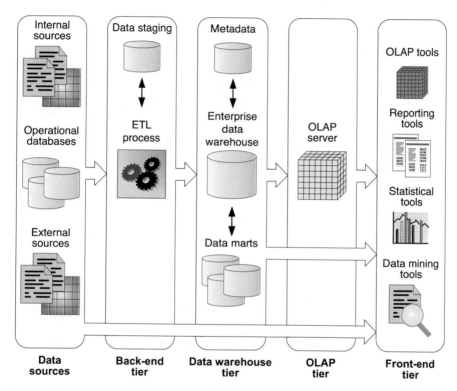

Fig. 3.5 Typical data warehouse architecture

3.4.1 Back-End Tier

The **back-end tier** is composed of **extraction, transformation, and loading (ETL) tools**, used to feed data into the data warehouse from operational databases and other **data sources**, which can be **internal** or **external** to the organization. There is also a **data staging area**, a database in which the data extracted from the sources undergoes successive modifications to eventually be ready to be loaded into the data warehouse. Such a database is usually called **operational data store**.

The **extraction, transformation, and loading** process, as the name indicates, is a three-step process as follows:

- **Extraction** gathers data from multiple, heterogeneous data sources. These sources may be operational databases but may also be files in various formats; they may be **internal** to the organization or **external** to it. In order to solve interoperability problems, data are extracted whenever possible using application programming interfaces (APIs) such as ODBC (Open Database Connectivity) and JDBC (Java Database Connectivity).
- **Transformation** modifies the data from the format of the data sources to the warehouse format. This includes several aspects: *cleaning*, which removes errors and inconsistencies in the data and converts it into a standardized format; *integration*, which reconciles data from different data sources, both at the schema and at the data level; and *aggregation*, which summarizes the data obtained from data sources according to the level of detail, or granularity, of the data warehouse.
- **Loading** feeds the data warehouse with the transformed data. This also includes **refreshing** the data warehouse, that is, propagating updates from the data sources to the data warehouse at a specified frequency in order to provide up-to-date data for the decision-making process. Depending on organizational policies, the refresh frequency may vary from monthly to several times a day, or even near to real time.

3.4.2 Data Warehouse Tier

The **data warehouse tier** in Fig. 3.5 is composed of an **enterprise data warehouse** and/or several **data marts**, and a **metadata repository** storing information about the data warehouse and its contents.

An **enterprise data warehouse** is centralized and encompasses an entire organization, while a **data mart** is a specialized data warehouse targeted toward a particular functional or departmental area in an organization. A data mart can be seen as a small, local data warehouse. Data in a data mart can be either derived from an enterprise data warehouse or collected directly from data sources.

Another component of the data warehouse tier is the metadata repository. **Metadata** can be defined as "data about data", and has been traditionally classified into technical and business metadata. **Business metadata** describes the meaning (or semantics) of the data, and organizational rules, policies, and constraints related to the data. **Technical metadata** describes how data are structured and stored in a computer system, and the applications and processes that manipulate such data.

In a data warehouse context, technical metadata can be of various natures, describing the data warehouse system, the source systems, and the ETL process. The metadata repository may contain information such as:

- Metadata describing the structure of the data warehouse and the data marts at the conceptual, logical and/or physical levels. These metadata contain security information (user authorization and access control) and monitoring information (e.g., statistics, error reports, and audit trails).
- Metadata describing the data sources and their schemas (at the conceptual, logical, and/or physical levels), and descriptive information such as ownership, update frequencies, legal limitations, and access methods.
- Metadata describing the ETL process, including data lineage (i.e., tracing warehouse data back to the source data from which it was derived), data extraction, cleaning, transformation rules and defaults, data refresh and purging rules, algorithms for summarization, etc.

3.4.3 OLAP Tier

The **OLAP tier** in the architecture of Fig. 3.5 is composed of an **OLAP server**, which presents business users with multidimensional data, regardless of the actual way in which data are stored in the underlying system.

Most database products provide OLAP extensions and related tools allowing the construction and querying of cubes, as well as navigation, analysis, and reporting. However, there is not yet a standardized language for defining and manipulating data cubes, and the underlying technology differs between the available systems. In this respect, several languages are worth mentioning. XMLA (XML for Analysis) aims at providing a common language for exchanging multidimensional data between client applications and OLAP servers. Further, MDX (MultiDimensional eXpressions) and DAX (Data Analysis eXpressions) are query languages for OLAP databases. As MDX is supported by a number of OLAP vendors, it became a de facto standard for querying OLAP systems. On the other hand, DAX has been proposed by Microsoft as an alternative to MDX as it is supposed to be easier to learn by business end users. The SQL standard has also been extended for providing analytical capabilities; this extension is referred to as SQL/OLAP. In Chaps. 6 and 7, we study in detail MDX, DAX, and SQL/OLAP.

3.4.4 Front-End Tier

The **front-end tier** in Fig. 3.5 is used for data analysis and visualization. It contains **client tools** that allow users to exploit the contents of the data warehouse. Typical client tools include the following:

- **OLAP tools** allow interactive exploration and manipulation of the warehouse data. They facilitate the formulation of complex queries that may involve large amounts of data. These queries are called **ad hoc queries**, since the system has no prior knowledge about them.
- **Reporting tools** enable the production, delivery, and management of reports, which can be paper-based, interactive, or web-based. Reports use **predefined queries**, that is, queries asking for specific information in a specific format that are performed on a regular basis. Modern reporting techniques include key performance indicators and dashboards.
- **Statistical tools** are used to analyze and visualize the cube data using statistical methods.
- **Data mining tools** allow users to analyze data in order to discover valuable knowledge such as patterns and trends; they also allow predictions to be made on the basis of current data.

In Chap. 7, we show some of the tools used to exploit the data warehouse, like data analysis tools, key performance indicators, and dashboards.

3.4.5 Variations of the Architecture

Some of the components illustrated in Fig. 3.5 can be missing in a real environment. In some situations there is only an enterprise data warehouse without data marts or, alternatively, an enterprise data warehouse does not exist. Building an enterprise data warehouse is a complex task that is very costly in time and resources. In contrast, a data mart is typically easier to build than an enterprise warehouse. However, when several data marts are created independently, they need to be integrated into a data warehouse for the entire enterprise, which is usually complicated.

In other situations, an OLAP server does not exist and/or the client tools directly access the data warehouse. This is indicated by the arrow connecting the data warehouse tier to the front-end tier. This situation is illustrated in Chap. 7, where the same queries for the Northwind case study are expressed both in MDX and DAX (targeting the OLAP server) and in SQL. In an extreme situation, there is neither a data warehouse nor an OLAP server. This is called a **virtual data warehouse**, which defines a set of views over operational databases that are materialized for efficient access. The arrow connecting the data sources to the front-end tier depicts this situation. A virtual data warehouse, although easy to build, does not contain historical data, does not contain centralized metadata, and does not have the ability to clean and transform the data. Furthermore, a virtual data warehouse can severely impact the performance of operational databases.

Finally, a data staging area may not be needed when the data in the source systems conforms very closely to the data in the warehouse. This situation arises when there are few data sources having high-quality data, which is rarely the case in real-world situations.

3.5 Overview of Microsoft SQL Server BI Tools

Nowadays, there is a wide offer in business intelligence tools. The major database providers, such as Microsoft, Oracle, IBM, and Teradata, have their own suite of such tools. Other popular tools include SAP, MicroStrategy, Qlik, and Tableau. In addition to the above commercial tools, there are also open-source tools, of which Pentaho is the most popular one. In this book, we have chosen a representative suite of tools for illustrating the topics presented: Microsoft's SQL Server tools. We briefly describe next these tools, and provide references to other well-known business intelligence tools in the bibliographic notes.

Microsoft SQL Server provides an integrated platform for building analytical applications. It is composed of three main components, described below.

- **Analysis Services** is used to define, query, update, and manage analytical databases. It comes in two modes: multidimensional and tabular. The difference between them stems from their underlying paradigm (multidimensional or relational). Each mode has an associated query language, MDX and DAX, respectively. In this book, we cover both modes and its associated languages MDX and DAX in Chaps. 5, 6, and 7 when we define and query the analytical database for the Northwind case study.
- **Integration Services** supports ETL processes previously introduced. It is used to extract data from a variety of data sources, to combine, clean, and summarize this data, and, finally, to populate a data warehouse with the resulting data. We cover Integration Services when we describe the ETL process for the Northwind case study in Chap. 9.
- **Reporting Services** is used to define, generate, store, and manage reports. Reports can be built from various types of data sources, including data warehouses and OLAP cubes, and can be personalized and delivered in a variety of formats. Users can view reports with a variety of clients, such as web browsers or mobile applications. Clients access reports via Reporting Services' server component. We will explain Reporting Services when we build dashboards for the Northwind case study in Chap. 7.

Several tools can be used for developing and managing these components. **Visual Studio** is a development platform that supports Analysis Services,

Reporting Services, and Integration Services projects. **SQL Server Management Studio** (SSMS) provides integrated management of all SQL Server components. In addition, **Power BI** is a business intelligence tool that aims at enabling business end users to analyze data and create their own data visualizations in the form of reports and dashboards without involving IT specialists, which is referred to as **self-service BI**. Finally, **Power Pivot** is an add-in for Excel that enables to create and analyze data models.

3.6 Summary

In this chapter, we introduced the multidimensional model, which is the basis for data warehouse systems. We defined the notion of online analytical processing (OLAP) systems as opposite to online transaction processing (OLTP) systems. We then studied the data cube concept and its components: dimensions, hierarchies, and measures. In particular, we presented several classifications of measures and defined the notions of measure aggregation and summarizability. Then, we defined a set of OLAP operations, like roll-up and drill-down, that are used to interactively manipulate a data cube. We then described data warehouse systems and highlighted their differences with respect to traditional database systems. We discussed the basic architecture of data warehouse systems and several variants of it that may be considered. Finally, we provided an overview of Microsoft SQL Server BI tools.

3.7 Bibliographic Notes

Basic data warehouse concepts can be found in the classic books by Kimball [129] and by Inmon [117]. In particular, the definition of data warehouses we gave in Sect. 3.3 is from Inmon. The notion of hypercube underlying the multidimensional model was studied in [94], where the roll-up and cube operations were defined for SQL. Hierarchies in OLAP are studied in [144]. The notion of summarizability of measures was defined in [138] and has been studied, for example, in [109, 110, 166]. Other classification of measures are given in [94, 129]. More details on these concepts are given in Chap. 5, where we also give further references.

There is not yet a standard definition of the OLAP operations, in a similar way as the relational algebra operations are defined for the relational algebra. Many different algebras for OLAP have been proposed in the literature, each one defining different sets of operations. A comparison of these OLAP algebras is given in [202], where the authors advocate the need for a reference algebra for OLAP. The definition of the operations we presented in this chapter was inspired from [50].

For SQL Server, the books devoted to Analysis Services [108], Integration Services [52], and Reporting Services [135] cover extensively these components. The tabular model in Microsoft Analysis Services is studied in [204], while DAX is covered in [205].

3.8 Review Questions

3.1 What is the meaning of the acronyms OLAP and OLTP?

3.2 Using an example of an application domain that you are familiar with, describe the various components of the multidimensional model, that is, facts, measures, dimensions, and hierarchies.

3.3 Why are hierarchies important in data warehouses? Give examples of various hierarchies.

3.4 Discuss the role of measure aggregation in a data warehouse. How can measures be characterized?

3.5 Give an example of a problem that may occur when summarizability is not verified in a data warehouse.

3.6 Describe the various OLAP operations using the example you defined in Question 3.2.

3.7 What is an operational database system? What is a data warehouse system? Explain several aspects that differentiate these systems.

3.8 Give some essential characteristics of a data warehouse. How do a data warehouse and a data mart differ? Describe two approaches for building a data warehouse and its associated data marts.

3.9 Describe the various components of a typical data warehouse architecture. Identify variants of this architecture and specify in what situations they are used.

3.10 Briefly describe the components of Microsoft SQL Server.

3.9 Exercises

Exercise 3.1. A data warehouse of a telephone provider consists of five dimensions, namely, caller customer, callee customer, date, call type, and call program, and three measures, namely, number of calls, duration, and amount.

Define the OLAP operations to be performed in order to answer the following queries. Propose dimension hierarchies when needed.

a. Total amount collected by each call program in 2012.
b. Total duration of calls made by customers from Brussels in 2012.
c. Total number of weekend calls made by customers from Brussels to customers in Antwerp in 2012.

  d. Total duration of international calls started by customers in Belgium in
     2012.
  e. Total amount collected from customers in Brussels who are enrolled in
     the corporate program in 2012.

Exercise 3.2. A data warehouse of a train company contains information
about train segments. It consists of six dimensions, namely, departure station, arrival station, trip, train, arrival time, and departure time, and three
measures, namely, number of passengers, duration, and number of kilometers.

  Define the OLAP operations to be performed in order to answer the following queries. Propose dimension hierarchies when needed.

  a. Total number of kilometers made by Alstom trains during 2012 departing
     from French or Belgian stations.
  b. Total duration of international trips during 2012, that is, trips departing
     from a station located in a country and arriving at a station located in
     another country.
  c. Total number of trips that departed from or arrived at Paris during July
     2012.
  d. Average duration of train segments in Belgium in 2012.
  e. For each trip, average number of passengers per segment, that is, take all
     the segments of each trip, and average the number of passengers.

Exercise 3.3. Consider the data warehouse of a university that contains
information about teaching and research activities. On the one hand, the
information about teaching activities is related to dimensions department,
professor, course, and time, the latter at a granularity of academic semester.
Measures for teaching activities are number of hours and number of credits.
On the other hand, the information about research activities is related to
dimensions professor, funding agency, project, and time, the latter twice for
the start date and the end date, both at a granularity of day. In this case,
professors are related to the department to which they are affiliated. Measures
for research activities are the number of person months and amount.

  Define the OLAP operations to be performed in order to answer the following queries. For this, propose the necessary dimension hierarchies.

  a. By department, total number of teaching hours during the academic year
     2012–2013.
  b. By department, total amount of research projects during the calendar
     year 2012.
  c. By department, total number of professors involved in research projects
     during the calendar year 2012.
  d. By professor, total number of courses delivered during the academic year
     2012–2013.
  e. By department and funding agency, total number of projects started in
     2012.

Chapter 4
Conceptual Data Warehouse Design

The advantages of using conceptual models for designing databases are well known. Conceptual models facilitate communication between users and designers since they do not require knowledge about the underlying implementation platform. Further, schemas developed using conceptual models can be mapped to various logical models, such as relational, object-oriented, or even graph models, thus simplifying responses to changes in the technology used. Conceptual models also facilitate database maintenance and evolution, since they focus on users' requirements; as a consequence, they provide better support for subsequent changes in the logical and physical schemas.

In this chapter, we study conceptual modeling for data warehouses. In particular, we base our presentation in the MultiDim model, which can be used to represent the data requirements of data warehouse and OLAP applications. The definition of the model is given in Sect. 4.1. Since hierarchies are essential for exploiting data warehouse and OLAP systems to their full capabilities, in Sect. 4.2 we consider various kinds of hierarchies that exist in real-world situations. We classify these hierarchies, giving a graphical representation of them and emphasizing the differences between them. We also present advanced aspects of conceptual modeling in Sect. 4.3. Finally, in Sect. 4.4, we revisit the OLAP operations that we presented in Chap. 2 by addressing a set of queries to the Northwind data warehouse.

4.1 Conceptual Modeling of Data Warehouses

As studied in Chap. 2, the conventional database design process includes the creation of database schemas at the conceptual, logical, and physical levels. A **conceptual schema** is a concise description of the users' data requirements without taking into account implementation details. Conventional databases are generally designed at the conceptual level using the entity-relationship

© Springer-Verlag GmbH Germany, part of Springer Nature 2022
A. Vaisman, E. Zimányi, *Data Warehouse Systems*, Data-Centric Systems
and Applications, https://doi.org/10.1007/978-3-662-65167-4_4

(ER) model or the Unified Modeling Language (UML). Conceptual schemas are translated to the relational model by applying a set of mapping rules.

There is no well-established conceptual model for multidimensional data. Due to this, data warehouse design is usually directly performed at the logical level, based on star and/or snowflake schemas (which we will study in Chap. 5), leading to schemas that are difficult to understand by a typical user. Therefore, conceptual data warehousing modeling requires a model that clearly stands on top of the logical level.

In this chapter, we use the MultiDim model to represent at the conceptual level the elements required in data warehouse and OLAP applications. The graphical notation of the model is given in Appendix A. To give a general overview of the model, we shall use the example in Fig. 4.1, which illustrates the conceptual schema of the Northwind data warehouse. We will refer to this schema as the Northwind data cube.

A **schema** in the MultiDim model is composed of a set of dimensions and a set of facts.

A **dimension** is composed of either one level, or one or more hierarchies. A hierarchy is in turn composed of a set of levels. There is no graphical element to represent a dimension, it is depicted by means of its constituent elements.

A **level** is analogous to an entity type in the ER model. It describes a set of real-world concepts that, from the application perspective, have similar characteristics. Instances of a level are called **members**. For example, Product and Category are some of the levels in Fig. 4.1. A level has a set of **attributes** that describe the characteristics of their members. In addition, a level has one or several **identifiers** that uniquely identify its members. Each identifier is composed of one or several attributes. For example, in Fig. 4.1, CategoryID is an identifier of the Category level. Each attribute of a level has a type, that is, a domain for its values. Typical value domains are integer, real, and string. We do not include type information for attributes in the graphical representation of our conceptual schemas.

A **fact** relates several levels. For example, the Sales fact in Fig. 4.1 relates the Employee, Customer, Supplier, Shipper, Order, Product, and Date levels. The same level can participate several times in a fact, playing different **roles**. Each role is identified by a name and is represented by a separate link between the level and the fact. For example, in Fig. 4.1 the Date level participates in the Sales fact with the roles OrderDate, DueDate, and ShippedDate. Instances of a fact are called **fact members**. The **cardinality** of the relationship between facts and levels indicates the minimum and maximum number of fact members that can be related to level members. For example, in Fig. 4.1 the Sales fact is related to the Product level with a one-to-many cardinality, meaning that one sale is related to only one product and that each product can have many sales. The Sales fact is also related to the Order level with a one-to-one cardinality, which means that a sale is related to only one order line and that an order line has only one sale.

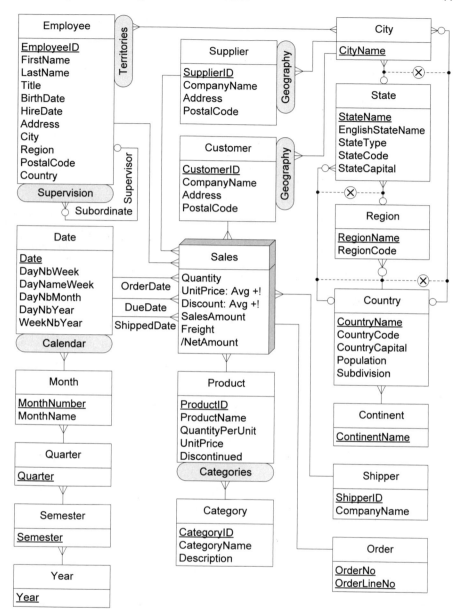

Fig. 4.1 Conceptual schema of the Northwind data warehouse

A fact may contain attributes commonly called **measures**. These contain data (usually numerical) that are analyzed using the various perspectives represented by the dimensions. For example, Quantity, UnitPrice, and Discount are some of the measures of the Sales fact in Fig. 4.1. The identifier attributes of the levels involved in a fact indicate the **granularity** of the measures, that is, the level of detail at which measures are represented.

Measures are aggregated along dimensions when performing roll-up operations. As shown in Fig. 4.1, the aggregation function associated with a measure can be specified next to the measure name, where the SUM aggregation function is assumed by default. In Chap. 3 we classified measures as **additive, semiadditive**, or **nonadditive**. We assume by default that measures are additive. For semiadditive and nonadditive measures, we include the symbols '+!' and '≠', respectively. For example, in Fig. 4.1 the measures Quantity and UnitPrice are, respectively, additive and semiadditive. Further, measures and level attributes may be **derived**, if they are calculated on the basis of other measures or attributes in the schema. We use the symbol '/' for indicating them. For example, in Fig. 4.1 the measure NetAmount is derived.

A **hierarchy** comprises several related levels. Given two related levels of a hierarchy, the lower level is called the **child** and the higher level is called the **parent**. Thus, the relationships composing hierarchies are called **parent-child relationships**. The **cardinalities** in parent-child relationships indicate the minimum and the maximum number of members in one level that can be related to a member in another level. For example, in Fig. 4.1 the child level Product is related to the parent level Category with a one-to-many cardinality, which means that a product belongs to only one category and that a category can have many products.

A dimension may contain several hierarchies, each one expressing a particular criterion used for analysis purposes; thus, we include the **hierarchy name** to differentiate them. For example, in Fig. 4.1, the Employee dimensions has two hierarchies, namely, Territories and Supervision. When the user is not interested in employing a hierarchy for aggregation purposes, she will represent all the attributes in a single level. This is the case of the attributes City, Region, and Country in the Employee dimension in Fig. 4.1, .

Levels in a hierarchy are used to analyze data at various **granularities**, or levels of detail. For example, the Product level contains information about products, while the Category level may be used to see these products from the more general perspective of the categories to which they belong. The level in a hierarchy that contains the most detailed data is called the **leaf level**. The name of the leaf level defines the dimension name, except for the case where the same level participates several times in a fact, in which case the role name defines the dimension name. These are called **role-playing dimensions**. The level in a hierarchy representing the most general data is called the **root level**. It is usual (but not mandatory) to represent the root of a hierarchy using a distinguished level called All, which contains a single member, denoted by all. The decision of including this level in multidimensional schemas is left to the designer. In the remainder, we do not show the All level in the hierarchies (except when we consider it necessary for clarity of presentation), since we consider that it is meaningless in conceptual schemas.

The identifier attributes of a parent level define how child members are grouped. For example, in Fig. 4.1, CategoryID in the Category level is an identifier attribute, used for grouping different product members during the roll-up operation from the Product to the Category levels. However, in the case of many-to-many parent-child relationships, we need to determine how to distribute the measures from a child to its parent members. For this, we can use a **distributing attribute**. For example, in Fig. 4.1, the relationship between Employee and City is many-to-many (i.e., an employee can be assigned to several cities). A distributing attribute can be used to store the percentage of time that an employee devotes to each city.

Finally, it is sometimes the case that two or more parent-child relationships are **exclusive**. This is represented using the symbol '⊗'. An example is given in Fig. 4.1, where states can be aggregated either into regions or into countries. Thus, according to their type, states participate in only one of the relationships departing from the State level.

4.2 Hierarchies

Hierarchies are key elements in analytical applications, since they provide the means to represent the data under analysis at different abstraction levels. In real-world situations, users must deal with complex hierarchies of various kinds. Even though we can model complex hierarchies at a conceptual level, logical models of data warehouse and OLAP systems only provide a limited set of kinds of hierarchies. Therefore, users are often unable to capture the essential semantics of multidimensional applications and must limit their analysis to only the predefined kinds of hierarchies provided by the tools in use. Nevertheless, a data warehouse designer should be aware of the problems that the various kinds of hierarchies introduce and be able to deal with them. In this section, we discuss several kinds of hierarchies that can be represented using the MultiDim model, although the classification of hierarchies that we will provide is independent of the conceptual model used to represent them.

4.2.1 Balanced Hierarchies

A **balanced hierarchy** has only one path at the schema level, where all levels are mandatory. An example is given by hierarchy Product → Category in Fig. 4.1. At the instance level, the members form a tree where all the branches have the same length, as shown in Fig. 3.3. All parent members have at least one child member, and a child member belongs exactly to one parent member. For example, in Fig. 3.3 each category is assigned at least one product, and a product belongs to only one category.

4.2.2 Unbalanced Hierarchies

An **unbalanced hierarchy** has only one path at the schema level, where at least one level is not mandatory. Therefore, at the instance level there can be parent members without associated child members. Figure 4.2a shows a hierarchy schema where a bank is composed of several branches, a branch may have agencies, and an agency may have ATMs. As a consequence, at the instance level the members represent an unbalanced tree, that is, the branches of the tree have different lengths, since some parent members do not have associated child members. For example, Fig. 4.2b shows a branch with no agency, and several agencies with no ATM. As for balanced hierarchies, the cardinalities imply that every child member belongs to at most one parent member. For example, in Fig. 4.2 every agency belongs to one branch. These hierarchies are useful either when facts may come at different granularities (a case we study later), or the same hierarchy is used by different facts at different levels of granularity. For example, one fact may be associated with ATMs and another one with agencies.

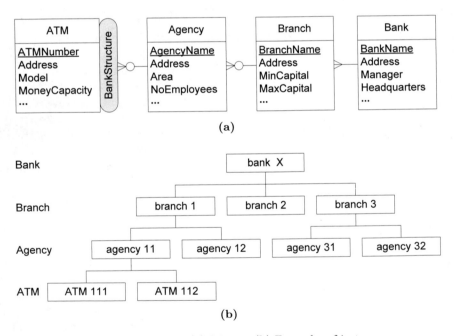

Fig. 4.2 An unbalanced hierarchy. (**a**) Schema; (**b**) Examples of instances

Unbalanced hierarchies include a special case that we call **recursive hierarchies**, or **parent-child hierarchies**. In this kind of hierarchy, the same level is linked by the two roles of a parent-child relationship (note the difference between the notions of parent-child hierarchies and relationships).

An example is given by dimension **Employee** in Fig. 4.1, which represents an organizational chart in terms of the employee-supervisor relationship. The **Subordinate** and **Supervisor** roles of the parent-child relationship are linked to the **Employee** level. As seen in Fig. 4.3, this hierarchy is unbalanced since employees with no subordinate will not have descendants in the instance tree.

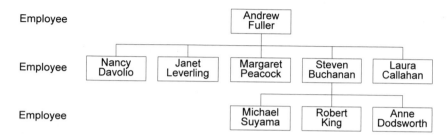

Fig. 4.3 Instances of the parent-child hierarchy in the Northwind data warehouse

4.2.3 Generalized Hierarchies

Generalized hierarchies represent the situation when the members of a level are of different types. A typical example arises with customers, which can be either companies or persons. This is usually captured in an ER model using the generalization relationship studied in Chap. 2. Further, suppose that measures pertaining to customers must be aggregated differently according to the customer type, where for companies the aggregation path is **Customer** → **Sector** → **Branch**, while for persons it is **Customer** → **Profession** → **Branch**. The MultiDim model represents such kinds of hierarchies as shown in Fig. 4.4a, where the common and specific hierarchy levels and also the parent-child relationships between them are clearly represented.

At the schema level, a generalized hierarchy contains multiple exclusive paths sharing at least the leaf level; they may also share some other levels, as depicted in Fig. 4.4a. This figure shows the two aggregation paths described above, one for each type of customer, where both belong to the same hierarchy. At the instance level, each member of the hierarchy belongs to only one path, shown in Fig. 4.4b. The symbol '⊗' indicates that the paths are exclusive for every member. The levels at which the alternative paths split and join are called, respectively, the **splitting** and **joining levels**.

The distinction between splitting and joining levels is important to ensure correct measure aggregation during roll-up operations, a property called summarizability, which we discussed in Chap. 3. Generalized hierarchies are, in general, not summarizable. For example, not all customers are mapped

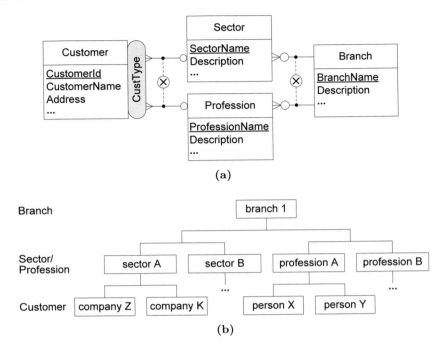

Fig. 4.4 A generalized hierarchy. (**a**) Schema; (**b**) Examples of instances

to the Profession level. Thus, the aggregation mechanism should be modified when a splitting level is reached in a roll-up operation.

In generalized hierarchies, it is not necessary that splitting levels are joined. An example is the hierarchy in Fig. 4.5, which is used for analyzing international publications. Three kinds of publications are considered: journals, books, and conference proceedings. The latter can be aggregated to the conference level. However, there is not a common joining level for all paths.

Generalized hierarchies include a special case commonly referred to as **ragged** hierarchies. An example is the Geography hierarchy given in Fig. 4.1. As can be seen in Fig. 4.6, some countries, such as Belgium, are divided into regions, whereas others, such as Germany, are not. Furthermore, small countries like the Vatican have neither regions nor states. A ragged hierarchy is a generalized hierarchy where alternative paths are obtained by skipping one or several intermediate levels. At the instance level, every child member has only one parent member, although the path length from the leaves to the same parent level can be different for different members.

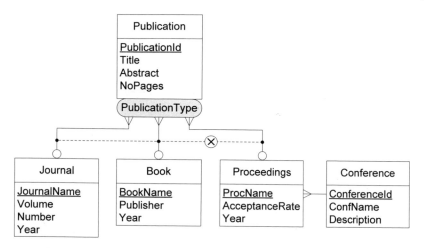

Fig. 4.5 A generalized hierarchy without a joining level

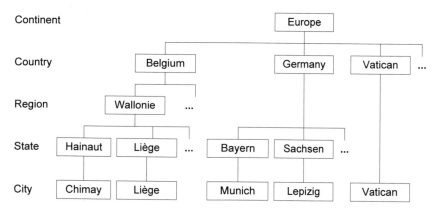

Fig. 4.6 Examples of instances of the ragged hierarchy in Fig. 4.1

4.2.4 Alternative Hierarchies

Alternative hierarchies represent the situation where at the schema level several nonexclusive hierarchies share at least the leaf level. An example is given in Fig. 4.7a, where the Date dimension includes two hierarchies corresponding to different groupings of months into calendar years and fiscal years. Figure 4.7b shows an instance of the dimension (we do not show members of the Date level), where it is supposed that fiscal years begin in February. It can be seen that the hierarchies form a graph, since a child member is associated with more than one parent member, and these parent members belong to different levels. Alternative hierarchies are used to analyze measures from a unique perspective (e.g., time) using alternative aggregations.

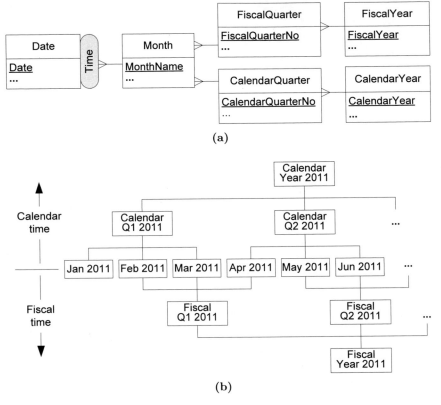

Fig. 4.7 An alternative hierarchy. (**a**) Schema; (**b**) Examples of instances

Although generalized and alternative hierarchies share some levels (see Figs. 4.4 and 4.7), they represent different situations. In a generalized hierarchy, a child member is related to *only one* of the paths, whereas in an alternative hierarchy a child member is related to *all paths*, and the user must choose one of them for analysis.

4.2.5 Parallel Hierarchies

When a dimension has several hierarchies associated with it (even of different kinds), accounting for different analysis criteria, we are in the presence of **Parallel hierarchies**.

Parallel hierarchies can be **dependent** or **independent** based on whether or not the component hierarchies share levels. Figure 4.8 shows an example of a dimension that has two parallel independent hierarchies. The hierarchy ProductGroups is used for grouping products according to categories or de-

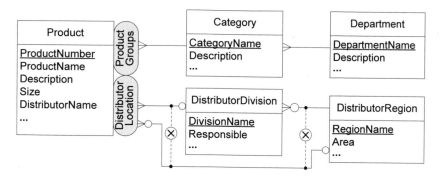

Fig. 4.8 An example of parallel independent hierarchies

partments, while the hierarchy DistributorLocation groups them according to distributors' divisions or regions. On the other hand, the parallel dependent hierarchies given in Fig. 4.9 represent a company that requires sales analysis for stores located in several countries. The hierarchy StoreLocation represents the geographic division of the store address, while the hierarchy SalesOrganization represents the organizational division of the company. Since the two hierarchies share the State level, this level plays different roles according to the hierarchy chosen for the analysis. Sharing levels in a conceptual schema reduces the number of its elements without losing its semantics, thus improving readability. In order to unambiguously define the levels composing the various hierarchies, the hierarchy name must be included in the sharing level for hierarchies that *continue beyond* that level. This is the case of StoreLocation and SalesOrganization indicated on level State.

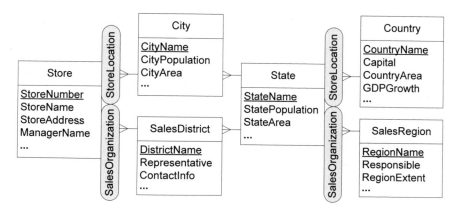

Fig. 4.9 An example of parallel dependent hierarchies

Alternative and parallel hierarchies represent different situations and should be clearly distinguishable at the conceptual level. This is done by including one (for alternative hierarchies) or several (for parallel hierarchies) hierarchy names, which account for various analysis criteria. In this way, the user knows that, for alternative hierarchies, it is not meaningful to combine levels from different component hierarchies, but this can be done for parallel hierarchies. For example, for the schema in Fig. 4.9 the user can safely issue a query "Sales figures for stores in city A that belong to sales district B."

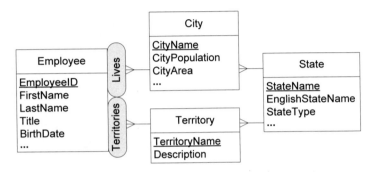

Fig. 4.10 Parallel dependent hierarchies leading to different parent members of the shared level

Further, in parallel dependent hierarchies a leaf member may be related to various different members in a shared level, which is not the case for alternative hierarchies that share levels. For instance, consider the schema in Fig. 4.10, which refers to the living place and the territory assignment of sales employees. It should be obvious that traversing the hierarchies Lives and Territory from the Employee to the State level will lead to different states for employees who live in one state and are assigned to another. As a consequence of this, aggregated measure values can be reused for shared levels in alternative hierarchies, whereas this is not the case for parallel dependent hierarchies. For example, suppose that the amount of sales generated by employees E1, E2, and E3 are $50, $100, and $150, respectively. If all employees live in state A, but only E1 and E2 work in this state, aggregating the sales of all employees to the State level following the Lives hierarchy gives a total amount of $300, whereas the corresponding value will be equal to $150 when the Territories hierarchy is traversed. Note that both results are correct, since the two hierarchies represent different analysis criteria.

4.2.6 Nonstrict Hierarchies

In the hierarchies studied so far, we have assumed that each parent-child relationship has a one-to-many cardinality, that is, a child member is related to at most one parent member and a parent member may be related to several child members. However, many-to-many relationships between parent and child levels are very common in real-life applications. For example, a diagnosis may belong to several diagnosis groups, 1 week may span 2 months, a product may be classified into various categories, etc.

A hierarchy that has *at least* one many-to-many relationship is called **nonstrict**, otherwise it is called **strict**. The fact that a hierarchy is strict or not is orthogonal to its kind. Thus, the hierarchies previously presented can be either strict or nonstrict. We next analyze some issues that arise when dealing with nonstrict hierarchies.

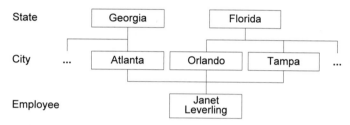

Fig. 4.11 Examples of instances of the nonstrict hierarchy in Fig. 4.1

Figure 4.1 shows a nonstrict hierarchy where an employee may be assigned to several cities. Some instances of this hierarchy are shown in Fig. 4.11, where the employee Janet Leverling is assigned to three cities that belong to two states. Since at the instance level a child member may have more than one parent member, the members of the hierarchy form an acyclic graph. Note the slight abuse of terminology. We use the term "nonstrict hierarchy" to denote an acyclic graph for several reasons. The term "hierarchy" conveys the notion that users need to analyze measures at different levels of detail; the term "acyclic classification graph" is less clear in this sense. Further, the term "hierarchy" is widely used by practitioners and data warehouse researchers.

Nonstrict hierarchies induce the problem of **double counting** of measures when a roll-up operation reaches a many-to-many relationship. Let us consider the example in Fig. 4.12, which illustrates sales by employees with aggregations along City and State levels (defined in Fig. 4.11), and employee Janet Leverling with total sales equal to 100. Figure 4.12a shows a situation where the employee has been assigned to Atlanta, in a strict hierarchy scenario. The sum of sales by territory and by state can be calculated straightforwardly, as the figure shows. Figure 4.12b shows a nonstrict hierarchy scenario, where the employee has been assigned the territories Atlanta, Orlando, and Tampa.

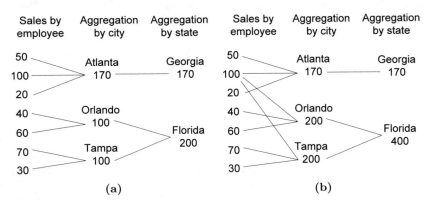

Fig. 4.12 Double-counting problem when aggregating a sales amount measure in Fig. 4.11. (**a**) Strict hierarchy; (**b**) Nonstrict hierarchy

This approach causes incorrect aggregated results, since the employee's sales are counted three times instead of only once.

One solution to the double-counting problem would be to transform a nonstrict hierarchy into a strict one by creating a new member for each set of parent members participating in a many-to-many relationship. In our example, a new member that represents the three cities Atlanta, Orlando, and Tampa will be created. However, a new member must also be created at the state level, since two cities belong to the state of Florida, and one to Georgia. Another solution would be to ignore the existence of several parent members and to choose one of them as the primary member. For example, we may choose the city of Atlanta. However, neither of these solutions correspond to the users' analysis requirements, since in the former, artificial categories are introduced, and in the latter, some pertinent analysis scenarios are ignored.

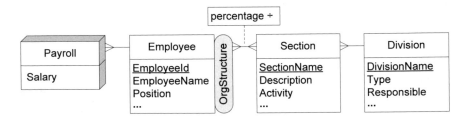

Fig. 4.13 A nonstrict hierarchy with a distributing attribute

An alternative approach to the double-counting problem would be to indicate how measures are distributed between several parent members for many-to-many relationships. For example, Fig. 4.13 shows a nonstrict hierarchy where employees may work in several sections. The schema includes a measure that represents an employee's overall salary, that is, the sum of the salaries paid in each section. Suppose that an attribute stores the percentage of time for which an employee works in each section. In this case, we annotate this attribute in the relationship with an additional symbol '÷' indicating that it is a **distributing attribute** determining how measures are divided between several parent members in a many-to-many relationship.

Choosing an appropriate distributing attribute is important in order to avoid approximate results when aggregating measures. For example, suppose that in Fig. 4.13 the distributing attribute represents the percentage of time that an employee works in a specific section. If the employee has a higher position in one section, although she works less time in that section she may earn a higher salary. Thus, applying the percentage of time as a distributing attribute for measures representing an employee's overall salary may not give an exact result. Note also that in cases where the distributing attribute is unknown, it can be approximated by considering the total number of parent members with which the child member is associated. In the example of Fig. 4.12, since Janet Leverling is associated with three cities, one third of the value of the measure will be accounted for each city.

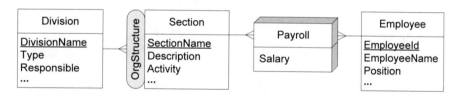

Fig. 4.14 Transforming a nonstrict hierarchy into a strict one with an additional dimension

Figure 4.14 shows another solution to the problem of Fig. 4.13 where we transformed a nonstrict hierarchy into independent dimensions. However, this solution corresponds to a different conceptual schema, where the focus of analysis has been changed from employees' salaries to employees' salaries by section. Note that this solution can only be applied when the exact distribution of the measures is known, for instance, when the amounts of salary paid for working in the different sections are known. It cannot be applied to nonstrict hierarchies without a distributing attribute, as in Fig. 4.11.

Although the solution in Fig. 4.14 aggregates correctly the Salary measure when applying the roll-up operation from the Section to the Division levels, the problem of double counting of the same employee is still present. Suppose that we want to use the schema in Fig. 4.14 to calculate the number of employees by section or by division; this value can be calculated by counting the instances of employees in the fact. The example in Fig. 4.15a considers five employees who are assigned to various sections. Counting the

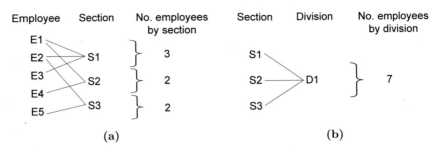

Fig. 4.15 Double-counting problem for a nonstrict hierarchy

number of employees who work in each section gives correct results. However, the aggregated values for each section cannot be reused for calculating the number of employees in every division, since some employees (E1 and E2 in Fig. 4.15a) will be counted twice and the total result will give a value equal to 7 (Fig. 4.15b) instead of 5.

In summary, nonstrict hierarchies can be handled in several ways:

- Transforming a nonstrict hierarchy into a strict one:
    - Creating a new parent member for each group of parent members linked to a single child member in a many-to-many relationship.
    - Choosing one parent member as the primary member and ignoring the existence of other parent members.
    - Replacing the nonstrict hierarchy by two independent dimensions.
- Including a distributing attribute.
- Calculating approximate values of a distributing attribute.

Since each solution has its advantages and disadvantages and requires special aggregation procedures, the designer must select the appropriate solution according to the situation at hand and users' requirements.

4.3 Advanced Modeling Aspects

In this section, we discuss particular modeling issues, namely, facts with multiple granularities, many-to-many dimensions, and links between facts, and show how they can be represented in the MultiDim model.

4.3.1 Facts with Multiple Granularities

Sometimes measures are captured at **multiple granularities**. An example is given in Fig. 4.16, where, for instance, sales for USA might be reported per state, while European sales might be reported per city. As another example, in a medical data warehouse there is a diagnosis dimension with levels diagnosis, diagnosis family, and diagnosis group. A patient may be related to a diagnosis at the lowest granularity, but may also have (more imprecise) diagnoses at the diagnosis family and diagnosis group levels.

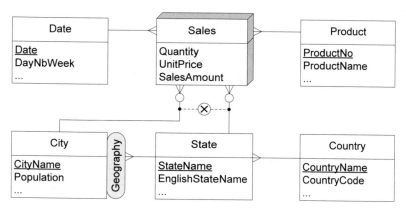

Fig. 4.16 Multiple granularities for a Sales fact

As shown in Fig. 4.16, this situation can be modeled using exclusive relationships between the various granularity levels. The issue is to get correct analysis results when fact data are registered at multiple granularities.

4.3.2 Many-to-Many Dimensions

In a **many-to-many dimension**, several members of the dimension participate in the same fact member. An example is shown in Fig. 4.17. Since an account can be jointly owned by several clients, aggregation of the balance according to the clients will count this balance as many times as the number of account holders. For example, as shown in Fig. 4.18, suppose that at date D1 the two accounts A1 and A2 have balances of, respectively, 100 and 500. Suppose further that both accounts are shared between several clients: account A1 is shared by C1, C2, and C3, and account A2 by C1 and C2. The total balance of the two accounts is equal to 600; however, aggregation (e.g., according to the Date or the Client dimension) gives a value equal to 1,300.

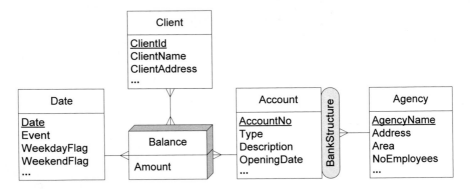

Fig. 4.17 Multidimensional schema for the analysis of bank accounts

The problem of **double counting** introduced above can be analyzed through the concept of **multidimensional normal forms** (MNFs). MNFs determine the conditions that ensure correct measure aggregation in the presence of the complex hierarchies studied in this chapter. The first multidimensional normal form (1MNF) requires each measure to be uniquely identified by the set of associated leaf levels. The 1MNF is the basis for correct schema design. To analyze the schema in Fig. 4.17 in terms of the 1MNF, we need to find out the functional dependencies that exist between the leaf levels and the measures. Since the balance depends on the specific account and the time when it is considered, the account and the time determine the balance. Therefore, the schema in Fig. 4.17 does not satisfy the 1MNF, since the measure is not determined by all leaf levels, and thus the fact must be decomposed.

Date	Account	Client	Balance
D1	A1	C1	100
D1	A1	C2	100
D1	A1	C3	100
D1	A2	C1	500
D1	A2	C2	500

Fig. 4.18 An example of double-counting problem in a many-to-many dimension

Let us recall the notion of multivalued dependency we have seen in Chap. 2. There are two possible ways in which the Balance fact in Fig. 4.17 can be decomposed. In the first one, the same joint account may have different clients assigned to it during different periods of time, and thus the time and the account multidetermine the clients. This situation leads to the solution shown in Fig. 4.19a, where the original fact is decomposed into two facts, that is, AccountHolders and Balance. If the joint account holders do not change over time, clients are multidetermined just by the accounts (but not the date).

In this case, the link relating the Date level and the AccountHolders fact can be eliminated. Alternatively, this situation can be modeled with a nonstrict hierarchy as shown in Fig. 4.19b.

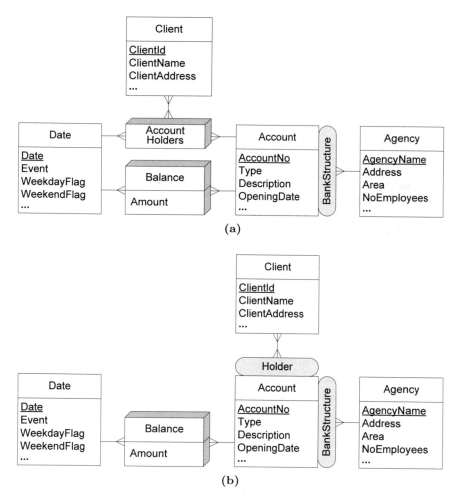

Fig. 4.19 Two possible decompositions of the fact in Fig. 4.17. (**a**) Creating two facts; (**b**) Including a nonstrict hierarchy

Even though the solutions proposed in Fig. 4.19 eliminate the double-counting problem, the two schemas require programming effort for queries that ask for information about individual clients. In Fig. 4.19a a drill-across operation (see Sect. 3.2) between the two facts is needed, while in Fig. 4.19b special procedures for aggregation in nonstrict hierarchies must be applied. In the case of Fig. 4.19a, since the two facts represent different granularities, queries with drill-across operations are complex, demanding a conversion either from a finer to a coarser granularity (e.g., grouping clients to know who holds a specific balance in an account) or vice versa (e.g., distributing a balance between different account holders). Note also that the two schemas in Fig. 4.19 could represent the information about the percentage of ownership of accounts by customers (if this is known). This could be represented by a measure in the AccountHolders fact in Fig. 4.19a and by a distributing attribute in the many-to-many relationship in Fig. 4.19b.

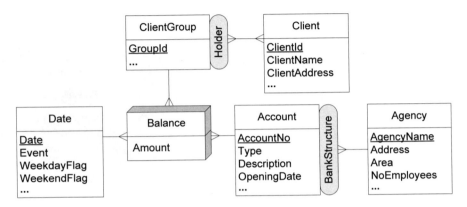

Fig. 4.20 Alternative decomposition of the fact in Fig. 4.17

Another solution to this problem is shown in Fig. 4.20. In this solution, an additional level is created, which represents the groups of clients participating in joint accounts. In the case of the example in Fig. 4.18, two groups should be created: one that includes clients C1, C2, and C3, and another with clients C1 and C2. Note, however, that the schema in Fig. 4.20 is not in the 1MNF, since the measure Balance is not determined by all leaf levels, that is, it is only determined by Date and Account. Therefore, the schema must be decomposed leading to schemas similar to those in Fig. 4.19, with the difference that in this case the Client level in the two schemas in Fig. 4.19 is replaced by a nonstrict hierarchy composed of the ClientGroup and the Client levels.

Finally, to avoid many-to-many dimensions we can choose one client as the primary account owner and ignore the other clients. In this way, only one client will be related to a specific balance, and the schema in Fig. 4.17 can be used without any problems related to double counting of measures. However, this solution may not represent the real-world situation and may exclude from the analysis the other clients of joint accounts.

In summary, many-to-many dimensions in multidimensional schemas can be avoided by using one of the solutions presented in Fig. 4.19. The choice between these alternatives depends on the functional and multivalued dependencies existing in the fact, the kinds of hierarchies in the schema, and the complexity of the implementation.

4.3.3 Links between Facts

Sometimes we need to define a link between two related facts even if they share dimensions. Fig. 4.21a shows an example where the facts Order and Delivery share dimensions Customer and Date, while each fact has specific dimensions, that is, Employee in Order and Shipper in Delivery. As indicated by the link between the two facts, suppose that several orders can be delivered by a single delivery and that a single order (e.g., containing many products) can be delivered by several deliveries. Possible instances of the above facts and their link are shown in Fig. 4.21b. In the figure, the links between the fact instances and the members of dimensions Customer and Date are not shown. Notice that, even if the facts share dimensions, an explicit link between the facts is needed to keep the information of how orders were delivered. Indeed, neither Customer nor Date can be used for this purpose.

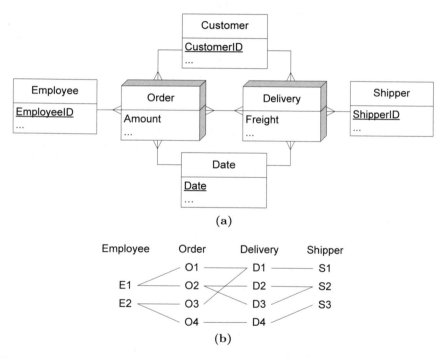

Fig. 4.21 An excerpt of a conceptual schema for analyzing orders and deliveries. (**a**) Schema; (**b**) Examples of instances

The cardinalities of the links between facts can be one-to-one, one-to-many, and many-to-many. In the example above, we consider the last case. If instead the cardinality of the link between Delivery and Order were one-to-many, in this case an order would be delivered by only one delivery, but one delivery may concern multiple orders.

4.4 Querying the Northwind Cube Using the OLAP Operations

We conclude the chapter showing how the OLAP operations studied in Chap. 3 can express queries over a conceptual schema, regardless the actual underlying implementation. We use for this the Northwind cube in Fig. 4.1.

Query 4.1. *Total sales amount per customer, year, and product category.*

ROLLUP*(Sales, Customer → Customer, OrderDate → Year,
              Product → Category, SUM(SalesAmount))

The ROLLUP* operation specifies the levels at which each of the dimensions Customer, OrderDate, and Product are rolled-up. For the other dimensions, a roll-up to All is performed. The SUM operation aggregates the measure SalesAmount. All other measures of the cube are removed from the result.

Query 4.2. *Yearly sales amount for each pair of customer and supplier countries.*

ROLLUP*(Sales, OrderDate → Year, Customer → Country,
              Supplier → Country, SUM(SalesAmount))

As in the previous query, a roll-up to the specified levels is performed, while performing a SUM operation to aggregate the measure SalesAmount.

Query 4.3. *Monthly sales by customer state compared to those of the previous year.*

Sales1 ← ROLLUP*(Sales, OrderDate → Month, Customer → State,
              SUM(SalesAmount))
Sales2 ← RENAME(Sales1, SalesAmount → PrevYearSalesAmount)
Result ← DRILLACROSS(Sales2, Sales1,
              Sales2.OrderDate.Month = Sales1.OrderDate.Month AND
              Sales2.OrderDate.Year+1 = Sales1.OrderDate.Year AND
              Sales2.Customer.State = Sales1.Customer.State)

Here, we first apply a ROLLUP operation to aggregate the measure SalesAmount. Then, a copy of the resulting cube, with the measure renamed as PrevYearSalesAmount, is kept in the cube Sales2. The two cubes are joined with the DRILLACROSS operation, where the join condition ensures that cells corresponding to the same month of two consecutive years and to the same client state are merged in a single cell. Although we include the join condition for the Customer dimension, since it is an equijoin, this is not mandatory, it is assumed by default for all the dimensions not mentioned in the join condition. In the following, we do not include the equijoins in the conditions in the DRILLACROSS operations.

Query 4.4. *Monthly sales growth per product, that is, total sales per product compared to those of the previous month.*

```
Sales1 ← ROLLUP*(Sales, OrderDate → Month, Product → Product,
          SUM(SalesAmount))
Sales2 ← RENAME(Sales1, SalesAmount → PrevMonthSalesAmount)
Sales3 ← DRILLACROSS(Sales2, Sales1,
           ( Sales1.OrderDate.Month > 1 AND
            Sales2.OrderDate.Month+1 = Sales1.OrderDate.Month AND
            Sales2.OrderDate.Year = Sales1.OrderDate.Year ) OR
           ( Sales1.OrderDate.Month = 1 AND Sales2.OrderDate.Month = 12 AND
            Sales2.OrderDate.Year+1 = Sales1.OrderDate.Year ) )
Result ← ADDMEASURE(Sales3, SalesGrowth =
          SalesAmount - PrevMonthSalesAmount )
```

Agin, we first apply a **ROLLUP** operation, make a copy of the resulting cube, and then join the two cubes with the **DRILLACROSS** operation. However, in the join condition two cases must be considered. In the first one, for the months starting from February (**Month** > 1) the cells to be merged must be consecutive and belong to the same year. In the second case, the cell corresponding to January must be merged with the one of December from the previous year. In the last step we compute a new measure **SalesGrowth** as the difference between the sales amount of the two corresponding months.

Query 4.5. *Three best-selling employees.*

```
Sales1 ← ROLLUP*(Sales, Employee → Employee, SUM(SalesAmount))
Result ← MAX(Sales1, SalesAmount, 3)
```

Here, we roll-up all the dimensions in the cube, except **Employee**, to the **All** level, while aggregating the measure **SalesAmount**. Then, the **MAX** operation is applied while specifying that cells with the top three values of the measure are kept in the result.

Query 4.6. *Best-selling employee per product and year.*

```
Sales1 ← ROLLUP*(Sales, Employee → Employee,
          Product → Product, OrderDate → Year, SUM(SalesAmount))
Result ← MAX(Sales1, SalesAmount) BY Product, OrderDate
```

In this query, we roll-up the dimensions of the cube as specified. Then, the **MAX** operation is applied after grouping by **Product** and **OrderDate**.

Query 4.7. *Countries that account for top 50% of the sales amount.*

```
Sales1 ← ROLLUP*(Sales, Customer → Country, SUM(SalesAmount))
Result ← TOPPERCENT(Sales1, Customer, 50) ORDER BY SalesAmount DESC
```

Here, we roll-up the **Customer** dimension to **Country** level and the other dimensions to the **All** level. Then, the **TOPPERCENT** operation selects the countries that cumulatively account for top 50% of the sales amount.

Query 4.8. *Total sales and average monthly sales by employee and year.*

Sales1 ← ROLLUP*(Sales, Employee → Employee, OrderDate → Month,
        SUM(SalesAmount))
Result ← ROLLUP*(Sales1, Employee → Employee, OrderDate → Year,
        SUM(SalesAmount), AVG(SalesAmount))

Here, we first roll-up the cube to the Employee and Month levels by summing the SalesAmount measure. Then, we perform a second roll-up to the Year level to obtain to overall sales and the average of monthly sales.

Query 4.9. *Total sales amount and discount amount per product and month.*

Sales1 ← ADDMEASURE(Sales, TotalDisc = Discount * Quantity * UnitPrice)
Result ← ROLLUP*(Sales1, Product → Product, OrderDate → Month,
        SUM(SalesAmount), SUM(TotalDisc))

Here, we first compute a new measure TotalDisc from three other measures. Then, we roll-up the cube to the Product and Month levels.

Query 4.10. *Monthly year-to-date sales for each product category.*

Sales1 ← ROLLUP*(Sales, Product → Category, OrderDate → Month,
        SUM(SalesAmount))
Result ← ADDMEASURE(Sales1, YTD = SUM(SalesAmount) OVER
        OrderDate BY Year ALL CELLS PRECEDING)

We start by performing a roll-up to the category and month levels. Then, a new measure is created applying the aggregate function SUM to a window composed of all preceding cells of the same year. Note that it is supposed that the members of the Date dimension are ordered by calendar time.

Query 4.11. *Moving average over the last 3 months of the sales amount by product category.*

Sales1 ← ROLLUP*(Sales, Product → Category, OrderDate → Month,
        SUM(SalesAmount))
Result ← ADDMEASURE(Sales1, MovAvg3M = AVG(SalesAmount) OVER
        OrderDate 2 CELLS PRECEDING)

In the first roll-up, we aggregate the SalesAmount measure by category and month. Then, we compute the moving average over a window containing the cells corresponding to the current month and the two preceding months.

Query 4.12. *Personal sales amount made by an employee compared with the total sales amount made by herself and her subordinates during 2017.*

Sales1 ← SLICE(Sales, OrderDate.Year = 2017)
Sales2 ← ROLLUP*(Sales1, Employee → Employee, SUM(SalesAmount))
Sales3 ← RENAME(Sales2, SalesAmount → PersonalSales)
Sales4 ← RECROLLUP(Sales2, Employee → Employee, Supervision,
        SUM(SalesAmount))
Result ← DRILLACROSS(Sales4, Sales3)

We first restrict the data in the cube to the year 2017. Then, we perform the aggregation of the sales amount measure by employee, obtaining the sales figures independently of the supervision hierarchy. In the third step the obtained measure is renamed, after which we apply the recursive roll-up that iterates over the supervision hierarchy, aggregating children to parent until the top level is reached. The last step obtains the cube with both measures.

Query 4.13. *Total sales amount, number of products, and sum of the quantities sold for each order.*

```
ROLLUP*(Sales, Order → Order, SUM(SalesAmount),
          COUNT(Product) AS ProductCount, SUM(Quantity))
```

Here, we roll-up all the dimensions, except Order, to the All level, while adding the SalesAmount and Quantity measures and counting the number of products.

Query 4.14. *For each month, total number of orders, total sales amount, and average sales amount by order.*

```
Sales1 ← ROLLUP*(Sales, OrderDate → Month, Order → Order,
          SUM(SalesAmount))
Result ← ROLLUP*(Sales1, OrderDate → Month, SUM(SalesAmount),
          AVG(SalesAmount) AS AvgSales, COUNT(Order) AS OrderCount)
```

Here we first roll-up to the Month and Order levels. Then, we roll-up to remove the Order dimension and obtain the requested measures.

Query 4.15. *For each employee, total sales amount, number of cities, and number of states to which she is assigned.*

```
ROLLUP*(Sales, Employee → State, SUM(SalesAmount), COUNT(DISTINCT City)
          AS NoCities, COUNT(DISTINCT State) AS NoStates)
```

Recall that Territories is a nonstrict hierarchy in the Employee dimension. In this query, we roll-up to the State level while adding the SalesAmount measure and counting the number of distinct cities and states. Notice that the ROLLUP* operation takes into account the fact that the hierarchy is nonstrict and avoids the double-counting problem studied in Sect. 4.2.6.

4.5 Summary

This chapter focused on conceptual modeling for data warehouses. As it the case for databases, conceptual modeling allows user requirements to be represented while hiding actual implementation details, that is, regardless of the actual underlying data representation. To explain conceptual multidimensional modeling we used the MultiDim model, which is based on the entity-relationship model and provides an intuitive graphical notation. It is well known that graphical representations facilitate the understanding of application requirements by users and designers.

We presented a comprehensive classification of hierarchies, taking into account their differences at the schema and at the instance level. We started by describing balanced, unbalanced, and generalized hierarchies, all of which account for a single analysis criterion. Recursive (or parent-child) and ragged hierarchies are special cases of unbalanced and generalized hierarchies, respectively. Then, we introduced alternative hierarchies, which are composed of several hierarchies defining various aggregation paths for the same analysis criterion. We continued with parallel hierarchies, which are composed of several hierarchies accounting for different analysis criteria. When parallel hierarchies share a level, they are called dependent, otherwise they are called independent. All the above hierarchies can be either strict or nonstrict, depending on whether they contain many-to-many relationships between parent and child levels. Nonstrict hierarchies define graphs at the instance level. We then presented advanced modeling aspects, namely, facts with multiple granularities and many-to-many dimensions. These often arise in practice but are frequently overlooked in the data warehouse literature. In Chap. 5, we will study how all these concepts can be implemented at the logical level. We concluded showing how the OLAP operations introduced in Chap. 3 can be applied over the conceptual model, using as example a set of queries over the Northwind data cube.

4.6 Bibliographic Notes

Conceptual data warehouse design was first introduced by Golfarelli et al. [84]. A detailed description of conceptual multidimensional models can be found in [236]. Many multidimensional models have been proposed in the literature. Some of them provide graphical representations based on the ER model (e.g., [210, 240]), as is the case of the MultiDim model, while others are based on UML (e.g., [2, 143, 239]). Other models propose new notations (e.g., [86, 114, 241]), while others do not refer to a graphical representation (e.g., [111, 186, 191]). There is great variation in the kinds of hierarchies supported by current multidimensional models. A detailed comparison of how the various multidimensional models cope with hierarchies is given in [145, 185]. The inclusion of explicit links between cubes in multidimensional models was proposed in [206]. Multidimensional normal forms were defined in [136, 137]. A survey in multidimensional design is given in [203].

The Object Management Group (OMG) has proposed the Common Warehouse Model (CWM)[1] as a standard for representing data warehouse and OLAP systems. This model provides a framework for representing metadata

---

[1] https://www.omg.org/spec/CWM/1.1/PDF

about data sources, data targets, transformations, and analysis, in addition to processes and operations for the creation and management of warehouse data. The CWM model is represented as a layered structure consisting of a number of submodels. One of these submodels, the resource layer, defines models that can be used for representing data in data warehouses and includes the relational model as one of them. Further, the analysis layer presents a metamodel for OLAP, which includes the concepts of a dimension and a hierarchy. In the CWM, it is possible to represent all of the kinds of hierarchies presented in this chapter.

4.7 Review Questions

4.1 Discuss the following concepts: dimension, level, attribute, identifier, fact, role, measure, hierarchy, parent-child relationship, cardinalities, root level, and leaf level.

4.2 Explain the difference, at the schema and at the instance level, between balanced and unbalanced hierarchies.

4.3 Give an example of a recursive hierarchy. Explain how to represent an unbalanced hierarchy with a recursive one.

4.4 Explain the usefulness of generalized hierarchies. To which concept of the entity-relationship model are these hierarchies related?

4.5 What is a splitting level? What is a joining level? Does a generalized hierarchy always have a joining level?

4.6 Explain why ragged hierarchies are a particular case of generalized hierarchies.

4.7 Explain in what situations alternative hierarchies are used.

4.8 Describe the difference between parallel dependent and parallel independent hierarchies.

4.9 Illustrate with examples the difference between generalized, alternative, and parallel hierarchies.

4.10 What is the difference between strict and nonstrict hierarchies?

4.11 Illustrate with an example the problem of double counting of measures for nonstrict hierarchies. Describe different solutions to this problem.

4.12 What is a distributing attribute? Explain the importance of choosing an appropriate distributing attribute.

4.13 What does it mean to have a fact with multiple granularities?

4.14 Relate the problem of double counting to the functional and multi-valued dependencies that hold in a fact.

4.15 Why must a fact be decomposed in the presence of dependencies? Show an example of a fact that can be decomposed differently according to the dependencies that hold on it.

4.16 Think of real-world examples where two fact tables must be related to each other.

4.8 Exercises

Exercise 4.1. Design a MultiDim schema for an application domain that you are familiar with. Make sure that the schema has a fact with associated levels and measures, at least two hierarchies, one of them with an exclusive relationship, and a parent-child relationship with a distributing attribute.

Exercise 4.2. Design a MultiDim schema for the telephone provider application in Ex. 3.1.

Exercise 4.3. Design a MultiDim schema for the train application in Ex. 3.2.

Exercise 4.4. Design a MultiDim schema for the university application given in Ex. 3.3 taking into account the different granularities of the time dimension.

Exercise 4.5. Design a MultiDim schema for the French horse race application given in Ex. 2.1. With respect to the races, the application must be able to display different statistics about the prizes won by owners, by trainers, by jockeys, by breeders, by horses, by sires (i.e., fathers), and by damsires (i.e., maternal grandfathers). With respect to the bets, the application must be able to display different statistics about the payoffs by type, by race, by racetrack, and by horses.

Exercise 4.6. In each of the dimensions of the multidimensional schema of Ex. 4.5, identify the hierarchies (if any) and determine its type.

Exercise 4.7. Design a MultiDim schema for the Formula One application given in Ex. 2.2. With respect to the races, the application must be able to display different statistics about the prizes won by drivers, by teams, by circuit, by Grand Prix, and by season.

Exercise 4.8. Consider a time dimension composed of two alternative hierarchies: (a) day, month, quarter, and year and (b) day, month, bimonth, and year. Design the conceptual schema of this dimension and show examples of instances.

Exercise 4.9. Consider the well-known Foodmart data warehouse whose conceptual schema is given in Fig. 4.22. Write using the OLAP operations the following queries[2].

  a. All measures for stores.
  b. All measures for stores in the states of California and Washington summarized at the state level.

----

[2] The queries of this exercise are based on a document written by Carl Nolan entitled "Introduction to Multidimensional Expressions (MDX)."

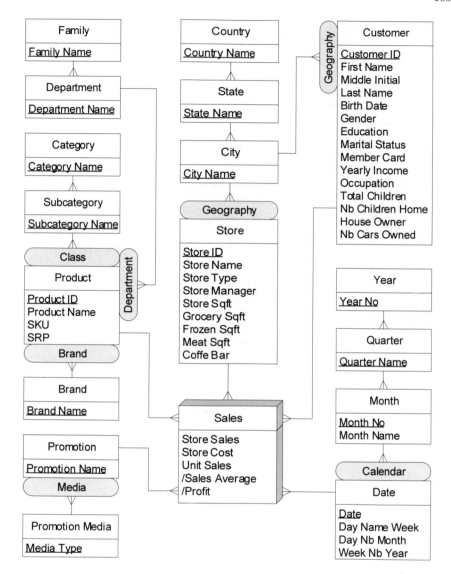

Fig. 4.22 Conceptual schema of the Foodmart cube

c. All measures for stores in the states of California and Washington summarized at the city level.

d. All measures, including the derived ones, for stores in the state of California summarized at the state and city levels.

e. Sales average in 2017 by store state and store type.

f. Sales profit in 2017 by store and semester.

g. Sales profit percentage in 2017 by store, quarter, and semester.

h. Sales profit by store for the first quarter of each year.
i. Unit sales by customer city and percentage of the unit sales of the city with respect to its state.
j. Unit sales by customer city and percentage of the unit sales of the city with respect to its country.
k. For promotions other than "No Promotion," unit sales and percentage of the unit sales of the promotion with respect to all promotions.
l. Unit sales by promotion, year, and quarter.
m. Unit sales by promotion and store, for stores in the states of California and Washington.
n. Sales profit by month and sales profit growth with respect to the previous month.
o. Sales profit by month and sales profit growth with respect to the same month of the previous year.
p. Sales profit by month and percentage profit growth with respect to the previous month.
q. For every month in 2017, unit sales and unit sales difference with respect to the opening month of the quarter.
r. Monthly year-to-date sales by product category.
s. Three-month moving average of the sales by product category.
t. Unit sales by product subcategory, customer state, and quarter.
u. Sales profit in 2017 by store type and store city, for cities whose unit sales in 2017 exceeded 25,000.
v. Sales profit in 2017 by store type and store city, for cities whose profit percentage in 2017 is less than the one of their state.
w. All measures for store cities between Beverly Hills and Spokane (in the USA) sorted by name regardless of the hierarchy.
x. All measures for store cities sorted by descending order of sales count regardless of the hierarchy.
y. All measures for the top-five store cities based on sales count.
z. All measures for the top-five store cities based on sales count and all measures for all the other cities combined.
aa. Store cities whose sales count accounts for 50% of the overall sales count.
bb. For store cities whose sales count accounts for 50% of the overall sales count, unit sales by store type.
cc. Unit sales and number of customers by product subcategory.
dd. Number of customers and number of female customers by store.
ee. For each product subcategory, maximum monthly unit sales in 2017 and the month when that occurred.
ff. For 2017 and by brand, total unit sales, average of monthly unit sales, and number of months involved in the computation of the average.

Chapter 5
Logical Data Warehouse Design

Conceptual models are useful to design database applications since they favor the communication between the stakeholders in a project. However, conceptual models must be translated into logical ones for their implementation on a database management system. In this chapter, we study how the conceptual multidimensional model studied in the previous chapter can be represented in the relational model. We start in Sect. 5.1 by describing the three logical models for data warehouses, namely, relational OLAP (ROLAP), multidimensional OLAP (MOLAP), and hybrid OLAP (HOLAP). In Sect. 5.2, we focus on the relational representation of data warehouses and study four typical implementations: the star, snowflake, starflake, and constellation schemas. In Sect. 5.3, we present the rules for mapping a conceptual multidimensional model (in our case, the MultiDim model) to the relational model. Section 5.4 discusses how to represent the time dimension. Sections 5.5 and 5.6 study how hierarchies, facts with multiple granularities, and many-to-many dimensions can be implemented in the relational model. Section 5.7 is devoted to the study of slowly changing dimensions, which arise when dimensions in a data warehouse are updated. In Sect. 5.8, we study how a data cube can be represented in the relational model and how it can be queried using SQL. Finally, to illustrate these concepts, we show in Sect. 5.9 how the Northwind data warehouse can be implemented in Analysis Services using both the multidimensional and the tabular models. For brevity, we refer to them, respectively, as Analysis Services Multidimensional and Analysis Services Tabular.

5.1 Logical Modeling of Data Warehouses

There are several approaches for implementing a multidimensional model, depending on how the data cube is stored. These are described next.

Relational OLAP (ROLAP) systems store multidimensional data in relational databases including SQL features and special access methods to

© Springer-Verlag GmbH Germany, part of Springer Nature 2022
A. Vaisman, E. Zimányi, *Data Warehouse Systems*, Data-Centric Systems
and Applications, https://doi.org/10.1007/978-3-662-65167-4_5

efficiently implement the OLAP operations. Further, in order to increase performance, aggregates are precomputed in relational tables (we will study aggregate computation in Chap. 8). These aggregates, together with indexing structures, take a large space from the database. The advantages of ROLAP systems rely on the fact that relational databases are well standardized and provide a large storage capacity. However, since OLAP operations must be performed on relational tables, this usually yields complex SQL queries.

Multidimensional OLAP (MOLAP) systems store data in specialized multidimensional data structures (e.g., arrays), which are combined with hashing and indexing techniques. Therefore, the OLAP operations can be implemented efficiently, since such operations are very natural and simple to perform. MOLAP systems generally provide less storage capacity than ROLAP systems. Furthermore, MOLAP systems are proprietary, which reduces their portability.

Hybrid OLAP (HOLAP) systems combine the two previous approaches in order to benefit from the storage capacity of ROLAP and the processing capabilities of MOLAP. For example, a HOLAP server may store large volumes of detailed data in a relational database, while aggregations are kept in a separate MOLAP store.

Current OLAP tools support a combination of the above models. Nevertheless, most of these tools rely on an underlying data warehouse implemented on a relational database management system. For this reason, in what follows, we study the ROLAP implementation in detail.

5.2 Relational Data Warehouse Design

One possible relational representation of the multidimensional model is the **star schema**, where there is one central **fact table** and a set of **dimension tables**, one for each dimension. An example is given in Fig. 5.1, where the fact table is depicted in gray and the dimension tables are depicted in white. The fact table contains the foreign keys of the related dimension tables, namely, ProductKey, StoreKey, PromotionKey, and DateKey, and the measures, namely, Amount and Quantity. As shown in the figure, **referential integrity** constraints are specified between the fact table and each of the dimension tables.

In a star schema, the dimension tables are, in general, not normalized. Therefore, there may contain redundant data, especially in the presence of hierarchies. This is the case for dimension Product in Fig. 5.1 since all products belonging to the same category will have redundant information for the attributes describing the category and the department. The same occurs in dimension Store with the attributes describing the city and the state.

On the other hand, fact tables are usually normalized: their key is the union of the foreign keys since this union functionally determines all the measures,

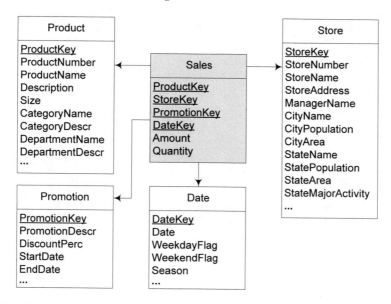

Fig. 5.1 An example of a star schema

while there is no functional dependency between the foreign key attributes. In Fig. 5.1, the fact table Sales is normalized and its key is composed of ProductKey, StoreKey, PromotionKey, and DateKey.

A **snowflake schema** avoids the redundancy of star schemas by normalizing the dimension tables. Therefore, a dimension is represented by several tables related by **referential integrity** constraints. In addition, as in the case of star schemas, referential integrity constraints also relate the fact table and the dimension tables at the finest level of detail.

An example of a snowflake schema is given in Fig. 5.2, where the fact table is the same as in Fig. 5.1. However, the dimensions Product and Store are now represented by normalized tables. For example, in the Product dimension, the information about categories has been moved to the table Category, and only the attribute CategoryKey remained in the original table. Thus, only the value of this key is repeated for each product of the same category, but the information about a category will only be stored once, in table Category. Normalized tables are easy to maintain and optimize storage space. However, performance is affected since more joins need to be performed when executing queries that require hierarchies to be traversed. For example, the query "Total sales by category" for the star schema in Fig. 5.1 reads in SQL as follows:

```
SELECT    CategoryName, SUM(Amount)
FROM      Product P, Sales S
WHERE     P.ProductKey = S.ProductKey
GROUP BY  CategoryName
```

while in the snowflake schema in Fig. 5.2 we need an extra join, as follows:

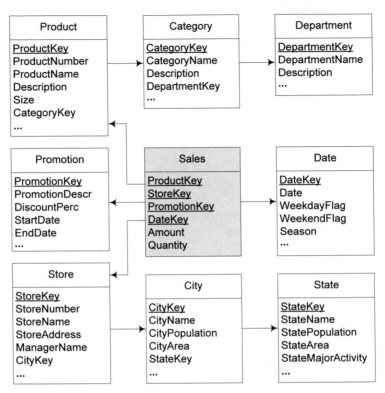

Fig. 5.2 An example of a snowflake schema

```
SELECT      CategoryName, SUM(Amount)
FROM        Product P, Category C, Sales S
WHERE       P.ProductKey = S.ProductKey AND P.CategoryKey = C.CategoryKey
GROUP BY CategoryName
```

A **starflake schema** is a combination of the star and the snowflake schemas, where some dimensions are normalized while others are not. We would have a starflake schema if we replace the tables Product, Category, and Department in Fig. 5.2, by the dimension table Product of Fig. 5.1, and leave all other tables in Fig. 5.2 (like dimension table Store) unchanged.

Finally, a **constellation schema** has multiple fact tables that share dimension tables. The example given in Fig. 5.3 has two fact tables Sales and Purchases sharing the Date and Product dimension. Constellation schemas may include both normalized and unnormalized dimension tables.

We will discuss further star and snowflake schemas when we study logical representation of hierarchies later in this chapter.

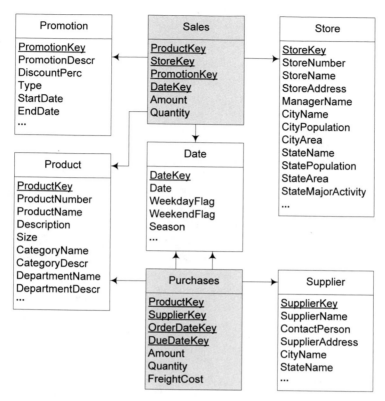

Fig. 5.3 An example of a constellation schema

5.3 Relational Representation of Data Warehouses

We define next a set of rules that are used to translate a multidimensional conceptual schema into a relational one. These rules are based on those given in Sect. 2.4.1, which translate an ER schema into the relational model.

Rule 1: A level L, provided it is not related to a fact with a one-to-one relationship, is mapped to a table T_L that contains all attributes of the level. A surrogate key may be added to the table, otherwise the identifier of the level will be the key of the table. Note that additional attributes will be added to this table when mapping relationships using Rule 3 below.

Rule 2: A fact F is mapped to a table T_F that includes as attributes all measures of the fact. Further, a surrogate key may be added to the table. Note that additional attributes will be added to this table when mapping relationships using Rule 3 below.

Rule 3: A relationship between either a fact F and a dimension level L, or between dimension levels L_P and L_C (standing for the parent and child levels, respectively), can be mapped in three different ways, depending on its cardinalities:

Rule 3a: If the relationship is one-to-one, the table corresponding to the fact (T_F) or to the child level (T_C) is extended with all the attributes of the dimension level or the parent level, respectively.

Rule 3b: If the relationship is one-to-many, the table corresponding to the fact (T_F) or to the child level (T_C) is extended with the surrogate key of the table corresponding to the dimension level (T_L) or the parent level (T_P), respectively, that is, there is a foreign key in the fact or child table pointing to the other table.

Rule 3c: If the relationship is many-to-many, a new table T_B (standing for bridge table) is created that contains as attributes the surrogate keys of the tables corresponding to the fact (T_F) and the dimension level (T_L), or the parent (T_P) and child levels (T_C), respectively. If the relationship has a distributing attribute, an additional attribute is added to the table to store this information.

In the above rules, surrogate keys are generated for each dimension level in a data warehouse. The main reason for this is to provide independence from the keys of the underlying source systems because such keys can change across time. Another advantage of this solution is that surrogate keys are usually represented as integers in order to increase efficiency, whereas keys from source systems may be represented in less efficient data types such as strings. Nevertheless, the keys coming from the source systems should also be kept in the dimensions to be able to match data from sources with data in the warehouse. Obviously, an alternative solution is to reuse the keys from the source systems in the data warehouse.

Notice that a fact table obtained by the mapping rules above will contain the surrogate key of each level related to the fact with a one-to-many relationship, one for each role that the level is playing. The key of the table is composed of the surrogate keys of all the participating levels. Alternatively, if a surrogate key is added to the fact table, the combination of the surrogate keys of all the participating levels becomes an alternate key.

As we will see in Sect. 5.5, more specialized rules are needed for mapping the various kinds of hierarchies that we studied in Chap. 4.

Applying the above rules to the Northwind conceptual data cube given in Fig. 4.1 yields the tables shown in Fig. 5.4. The Sales table includes eight foreign keys, that is, one for each level related to the fact with a one-to-many relationship. Recall from Chap. 4 that in **role-playing dimensions**, a dimension plays several roles. This is the case for the dimension Date where, in the relational model, each role will be represented by a foreign key. Thus, OrderDateKey, DueDateKey, and ShippedDateKey are foreign keys to the Date dimension table in Fig. 5.4. Note also that dimension Order is related to the fact with a one-to-one relationship. Therefore, the attributes of the dimension are included as part of the fact table. For this reason, such a dimension

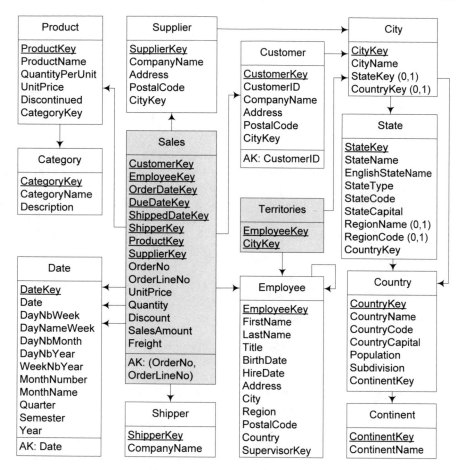

Fig. 5.4 Relational representation of the Northwind data warehouse in Fig. 4.1

is called a **fact** (or **degenerate**) **dimension**. The fact table also contains five attributes representing the measures UnitPrice, Quantity, Discount, Sales-Amount, and Freight. Finally, note that the many-to-many parent-child relationship between Employee and Territory is mapped to the table Territories, containing two foreign keys.

With respect to keys, in the Northwind data warehouse of Fig. 5.4 we have illustrated the two possibilities for defining the keys of dimension levels, namely, generating surrogate keys and keeping the database key as data warehouse key. For example, Customer has a surrogate key CustomerKey and a database key CustomerID. On the other hand, SupplierKey in Supplier is a database key. The choice of one among these two solutions is addressed in the ETL process that we will see in Chap. 9.

5.4 Time Dimension

Time information is present in almost every data warehouse. It is included both as foreign keys in fact tables, indicating the time when a fact took place, and as a time dimension, containing the aggregation levels, that is, the different ways in which facts can be aggregated across time.

In OLTP database applications, temporal information is usually derived from attributes of type DATE using the functions provided by the DBMS. For example, a typical OLTP application would not explicitly store whether a particular day corresponds to a weekend or to a holiday: this would be computed on the fly using appropriate functions. On the other hand, such information is stored in a data warehouse as attributes in the time dimension since OLAP queries are highly demanding, and there is no time to perform such computations each time a fact must be summarized. For example, a query like "Total sales during weekends," posed over the schema of Fig. 5.1, would be easily evaluated with the following SQL query:

```
SELECT  SUM(SalesAmount)
FROM    Date D, Sales S
WHERE   D.DateKey = S.DateKey AND D.WeekendFlag = 1
```

The **granularity** of the time dimension depends on application requirements. For example, if we are interested in monthly data, we would define the time dimension with a granularity that will correspond to a month. Thus, the time dimension table of a data warehouse spanning 5 years will have $5 \times 12 = 60$ tuples. On the other hand, if we are interested in more detailed data, we could define the time dimension with a granularity that corresponds to a second. In this case, in a data warehouse spanning 5 years we will have a time dimension with $5 \times 12 \times 30 \times 24 \times 3{,}600 = 155{,}520{,}000$ tuples. In order to avoid such a big dimension table, it is usually recommended to split the time dimension in two tables, one of date granularity containing all the dates covered by the time span of the data warehouse, and another table with granularity at the leves of seconds, containing all the seconds in a single day. In the previous example, a dimension Date covering 5 years will have $5 \times 365 + 1 = 1{,}825$ tuples and a dimension Time will have $24 \times 3{,}600 = 86{,}400$ tuples. Obviously, in this case the fact table requires two foreign keys for both time dimension tables. It is worth noting that the Time and Date dimensions can be (and in practice they are) populated automatically.

Finally, note that a time dimension may have more than one hierarchy (recall our calendar/fiscal year example in Fig. 4.7). Further, even if we use a single hierarchy we must be careful to satisfy the summarizability conditions. For example, a day aggregates correctly over a month and a year levels (a day belongs to exactly 1 month and 1 year), whereas a week may correspond to 2 different months, and thus the week level cannot be aggregated over the month level in a time dimension hierarchy.

5.5 Logical Representation of Hierarchies

The general mapping rules given in Sect. 5.3 do not capture the specific semantics of the various kinds of hierarchies described in Sect. 4.2. In addition, for some kinds of hierarchies, alternative logical representations exist. In this section, we study in detail the logical representation of hierarchies.

5.5.1 Balanced Hierarchies

As we have seen, in a conceptual multidimensional schema, the levels of dimension hierarchies are represented independently, and these levels are linked by parent-child relationships. Therefore, applying the mapping rules given in Sect. 5.3 to balanced hierarchies leads to **snowflake schemas** described before in this chapter: each level is represented as a separate table, which includes the key and the attributes of the level, as well as foreign keys for the parent-child relationships. For example, applying Rules 1 and 3b to the Categories hierarchy in Fig. 4.1 yields a snowflake structure with tables Product and Category shown in Fig. 5.5a.

Nevertheless, if **star schemas** are required, it is necessary to represent hierarchies using flat tables, where the key and the attributes of all levels forming a hierarchy are included in a single table. This structure can be obtained by denormalizing the tables that represent several hierarchy levels. As an example, the Date dimension of Fig. 4.1 can be represented in a single table containing all attributes, as shown in Fig. 5.5b.

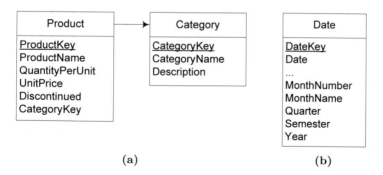

(a)   (b)

Fig. 5.5 Relations for a balanced hierarchy. (**a**) Snowflake structure; (**b**) Flat table

As we have seen in Sect. 5.2, **snowflake schemas** better represent hierarchical structures than star schemas, since every level can be easily distinguished and, further, levels can be reused between different hierarchies.

Additionally, in this representation specific attributes can be included in the different levels of a hierarchy. For example, the Product and Category tables in Fig. 5.5a have specific attributes. However, snowflake schemas are less performant for querying due to the joins that are needed for combining the data scattered in the various tables composing a hierarchy.

On the other hand, **star schemas** facilitate query formulation since fewer joins are needed for expressing queries, owing to denormalization. Additionally, much research has been done to improve system performance for processing star queries. However, star schemas have some drawbacks. For example, they do not model hierarchies adequately since the hierarchy structure is not clear. For example, for the Store dimension in Fig. 5.1, it is not clear which attributes can be used for hierarchies. As can also be seen in the figure, it is difficult to clearly associate attributes with their corresponding levels, making the hierarchy structure difficult to understand.

5.5.2 Unbalanced Hierarchies

Since unbalanced hierarchies do not satisfy the summarizability conditions (see Sect. 3.1.2), the mapping described in Sect. 5.3 may lead to the problem of excluding from the analysis the members of nonleaf levels that do not have an associated child. For instance, it may be the case in Fig. 4.2a that there are two fact tables associated with this dimension, one whose measures are associated with the ATM level and the other one containing measures at the Agency level. Aggregation of these measures up to higher levels can be safely done for those agencies that have ATMs and for those branches that have agencies. However, when we need to disaggregate information (i.e., drill down), for example, from Agency to ATM, we need to know which agencies have ATMs or not. Otherwise, OLAP tools wouldn't know what to do in the second case. Another problem would appear in star representations, where ATM cannot be defined as a primary key, since NULL values will appear for agencies with no ATM's.

To avoid the problems above, an unbalanced hierarchy can be transformed into a balanced one using placeholders (marked PH1, . . . , PHn in Fig. 5.6) in missing levels. Then, the logical mapping for balanced hierarchies may be applied. Note that when for a child member there are two or more missing consecutive parent levels, measure values must be repeated for aggregation purposes. For example, this would be the case for branch 2 in Fig. 5.6 where two placeholders are used for two consecutive missing levels. Finally, a special interface must be developed to hide placeholders from users. There are also situations when factual data in the same fact table come at different granularities. This case is addressed in Sect. 5.6.

Recall from Sect. 4.2.2 that **parent-child hierarchies** are a special case of unbalanced hierarchies. Mapping these hierarchies to the relational model

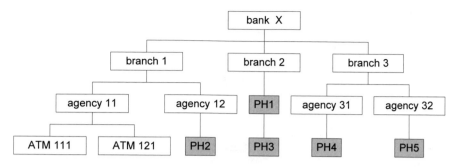

Fig. 5.6 Transforming the unbalanced hierarchy in Fig. 4.2b into a balanced one using placeholders

yields tables containing all attributes of a level, and an additional foreign key relating child members to their corresponding parent. For example, the table Employee in Fig. 5.4 shows the relational representation of the parent-child hierarchy in Fig. 4.1. As can be expected, operations over such a table are more complex. In particular, recursive queries are necessary for traversing a parent-child hierarchy. While recursive queries are supported in SQL and in MDX, this is not the case for DAX. As we will see in Sect. 5.9.2, it is thus necessary to flatten the hierarchical structure to a regular hierarchy made up of one column for each possible level of the hierarchy.

5.5.3 Generalized Hierarchies

Generalized hierarchies account for the case where dimension members are of different kinds, and each kind has a specific aggregation path. For example, in Fig. 4.4, customers can be either companies or persons, where companies are aggregated through the path Customer → Sector → Branch, while persons are aggregated through the path Customer → Profession → Branch.

As for balanced hierarchies, two approaches can be used for representing generalized hierarchies at the logical level: create a table for each level, leading to snowflake schemas, or create a single table for all the levels, where null values are used for attributes that do not pertain to specific members (e.g., tuples for companies will have null values in attributes corresponding to persons). A mix of these two approaches is also possible: create one table for the common levels and another table for the specific ones. Finally, we could also use separate fact and dimension tables for each path. In all these approaches we must keep metadata about which tables compose the different aggregation paths, while we need to specify additional constraints to ensure correct queries (e.g., to avoid grouping Sector with Profession in Fig. 4.4).

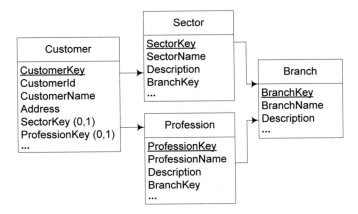

Fig. 5.7 Relations for the generalized hierarchy in Fig. 4.4

Applying the mapping described in Sect. 5.3 to the generalized hierarchy in Fig. 4.4 yields the relations shown in Fig. 5.7. Even though this schema clearly represents the hierarchical structure, it does not allow one to traverse only the common levels of the hierarchy (e.g., to go from Customer to Branch). To ensure this possibility, we must add the following mapping rule.

Rule 4: A table corresponding to a splitting level in a generalized hierarchy has an additional attribute which is a foreign key of the next joining level, provided it exists. The table may also include a discriminating attribute that indicates the specific aggregation path of each member.

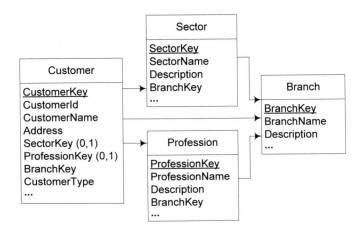

Fig. 5.8 Improved relational representation of the generalized hierarchy in Fig. 4.4

An example of the relations for the hierarchy in Fig. 4.4 is given in Fig. 5.8. The table **Customer** includes two kinds of foreign keys: one that indicates the next specialized hierarchy level (**SectorKey** and **ProfessionKey**), which is obtained by applying Rules 1 and 3b in Sect. 5.3; the other kind of foreign key corresponds to the next joining level (**BranchKey**), which is obtained by applying Rule 4 above. The discriminating attribute **CustomerType**, which can take the values **Person** and **Company**, indicates the specific aggregation path of members to facilitate aggregations. Finally, **check constraints** must be specified to ensure that only one of the foreign keys for the specialized levels may have a value, according to the value of the discriminating attribute.

```
ALTER TABLE Customer ADD CONSTRAINT CustomerTypeCK
      CHECK ( CustomerType IN ('Person', 'Company') )
ALTER TABLE Customer ADD CONSTRAINT CustomerPersonFK
      CHECK ( (CustomerType != 'Person') OR
      ( ProfessionKey IS NOT NULL AND SectorKey IS NULL ) )
ALTER TABLE Customer ADD CONSTRAINT CustomerCompanyFK
      CHECK ( (CustomerType != 'Company') OR
      ( ProfessionKey IS NULL AND SectorKey IS NOT NULL ) )
```

The schema in Fig. 5.8 allows choosing alternative paths for analysis. One possibility is to use the paths that include the specific levels, for example **Profession** or **Sector**. Another possibility is to only access the levels that are common to all members, for example, to analyze all customers, whatever their type, using the hierarchy **Customer** and **Branch**. As with the snowflake structure, one disadvantage of this structure is the need to apply join operations between several tables. However, an important advantage is the expansion of the analysis possibilities that it offers.

The mapping above can also be applied to **ragged hierarchies** since these hierarchies are a special case of generalized hierarchies. This is illustrated in Fig. 5.4 where the **City** level has two foreign keys to the **State** and **Country** levels. Nevertheless, since in a ragged hierarchy there is a unique path where some levels can be skipped, another solution is to embed the attributes of an optional level in the splitting level. This is also shown in Fig. 5.4, where the level **State** has two optional attributes corresponding to the **Region** level. Finally, another solution would be to transform the hierarchy at the instance level by including placeholders in the missing intermediate levels, as it is done for unbalanced hierarchies in Sect. 5.5.2. In this way, a ragged hierarchy would be converted into a balanced one.

5.5.4 Alternative Hierarchies

For alternative hierarchies, the traditional mapping to relational tables can be applied. This is shown in Fig. 5.9 for the conceptual schema in Fig. 4.7. Note that even though generalized and alternative hierarchies can be easily distinguished at the conceptual level (see Figs. 4.4a and 4.7), this distinction cannot be made at the logical level (compare Figs. 5.7 and 5.9).

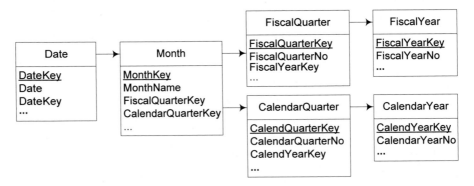

Fig. 5.9 Relations for the alternative hierarchy in Fig. 4.7

5.5.5 Parallel Hierarchies

As parallel hierarchies are composed of several hierarchies, their logical mapping consists in combining the mappings for the specific types of hierarchies. For example, Fig. 5.10 shows the result of applying this mapping to the schema shown in Fig. 4.9.

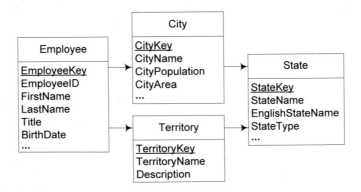

Fig. 5.10 Relations for the parallel dependent hierarchies in Fig. 4.10

Note that shared levels in parallel dependent hierarchies are represented in one table (**State**, in this example). Since these levels play different roles in each hierarchy, we can create views in order to facilitate queries and visualization.

For example, in Fig. 5.10 table **States** contains all states where an employee lives, works, or both. Therefore, aggregating along the path **Employee** → **City** → **State** will yield states where no employee lives. If we do not want these states in the result, we can create a view named **StateLives** containing only the states where at least one employee lives.

Finally, note also that both alternative and parallel dependent hierarchies can be easily distinguished at the conceptual level (Figs. 4.7 and 4.10); however, their logical representations (Figs. 5.9 and 5.10) look similar in spite of several characteristics that differentiate them, as explained in Sect. 4.2.5.

5.5.6 Nonstrict Hierarchies

Applying the mapping rules given in Sect. 5.3 to nonstrict hierarchies, creates relations for the levels and an additional relation, called a **bridge table**, for the many-to-many relationship between them. An example for the hierarchy in Fig. 4.13 is given in Fig. 5.11, where the bridge table **EmplSection** represents the many-to-many relationship. If the parent-child relationship has a distributing attribute (as in Fig. 4.13), it will be represented in the bridge table as an additional attribute, which stores the values required for measure distribution. However, this requires a special aggregation procedure that uses the distributing attribute.

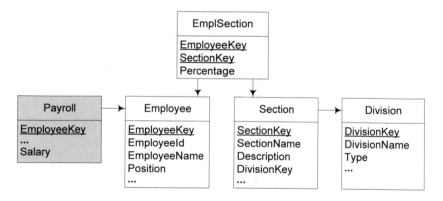

Fig. 5.11 Relations for the nonstrict hierarchy in Fig. 4.13

Recall from Sect. 4.2.6 that another solution is to transform a nonstrict hierarchy into a strict one by including an additional dimension in the fact, as shown in Fig. 4.14. Then, the corresponding mapping for a strict hierarchy can be applied. The choice between the two solutions may depend on various factors, explained next.

- Data structure and size: Bridge tables require less space than creating additional dimensions. In the latter case, the fact table grows if child members are related to many parent members. The additional foreign key in the fact table also increases the space required. In addition, for bridge tables, information about the parent-child relationship and distributing attribute (if it exists) must be stored separately.
- Performance and applications: For bridge tables, join operations, calculations, and programming effort are needed to aggregate measures correctly, while in the case of additional dimensions, measures in the fact table are ready for aggregation along the hierarchy. Bridge tables are thus appropriate for applications that have a few nonstrict hierarchies. They are also adequate when the information about measure distribution does not change with time. On the contrary, additional dimensions can easily represent changes in time of measure distribution.

Finally, yet another option consists in transforming the many-to-many relationship into a one-to-many one by defining a "primary" relationship, that is, to convert the nonstrict hierarchy into a strict one, to which the corresponding mapping for simple hierarchies is applied (as explained in Sect. 4.3.2).

5.6 Advanced Modeling Aspects

We discuss next how facts with multiple granularities, many-to-many dimensions, and links between facts can be represented in the relational model.

5.6.1 Facts with Multiple Granularities

Two approaches can be used for the logical representation of facts with multiple granularities. The first one consists in using multiple foreign keys, one for each alternative granularity, in a similar way as it was explained for generalized hierarchies in Sect. 5.5.3. The second approach consists in removing granularity variation at the instance level with the help of placeholders, in a similar way as explained for unbalanced hierarchies in Sect. 5.5.2.

Consider the example of Fig. 4.16, where measures are registered at multiple granularities. Figure 5.12 shows the relational schema resulting from the first solution above, where the Sales fact table is related to both the City and the State levels through referential integrity constraints. In this case, both attributes CityKey and StateKey are optional, and constraints must be specified to ensure that only one of the foreign keys may have a value.

Figure 5.13 shows an example of instances for the second solution above, where placeholders are used for facts that refer to nonleaf levels. There are

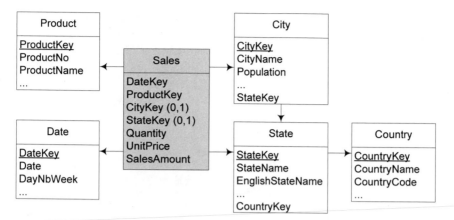

Fig. 5.12 Relations for the fact with multiple granularities in Fig. 4.16

two possible cases illustrated by the two placeholders in the figure. In the first case, a fact member points to a nonleaf member that has children. In this case, placeholder **PH1** represents all cities other than the existing children. In the second case, a fact member points to a nonleaf member without children. In this case, placeholder **PH2** represents all (unknown) cities of the state.

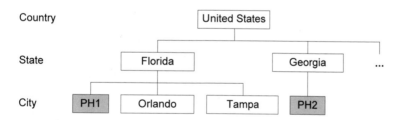

Fig. 5.13 Using placeholders for the fact with multiple granularities in Fig. 4.16

Obviously, in both solutions, the issue is to guarantee the correct summarization of measures. In the first solution, when aggregating at the state level, we need to perform a union of two subqueries, one for each alternative path. In the second solution, when aggregating at the city level, we obtain the placeholders in the result.

5.6.2 Many-to-Many Dimensions

The mapping to the relational model given in Sect. 5.3, applied to many-to-many dimensions, creates relations representing the fact, the dimension levels, and an additional bridge table representing the many-to-many relationship between the fact table and the dimension. Figure 5.14 shows the relational representation of the many-to-many dimension in Fig. 4.17. As can be seen, a bridge table BalanceClient relates the fact table Balance with the dimension table Client. Note also that a surrogate key was added to the Balance fact table so it can be used in the bridge table for relating facts with clients.

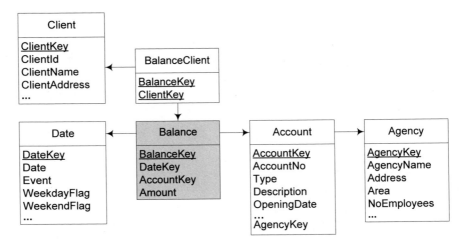

Fig. 5.14 Relations for the many-to-many dimension in Fig. 4.17

We have seen in Sect. 4.3.2 several solutions to decompose a many-to-many dimension according to the dependencies that hold on the fact table. In this case, after the decomposition, the traditional mapping to the relational model can be applied to the resulting decomposition.

5.6.3 Links between Facts

The logical representation of links between facts depends on their cardinalities. In the case of one-to-one or one-to-many cardinalities, the surrogate key of the fact with a cardinality one is added as a foreign key of the other fact. In the case of many-to-many cardinalities, a bridge table with foreign keys to the two facts is needed.

Consider the example of Fig. 4.21, where there is a many-to-many link between the Order and Delivery facts. Figure 5.15 shows the corresponding relational schema, where both facts have surrogate keys and the bridge table OrderDelivery relates the two facts. Examples of instances are given in Fig. 5.16. On the other hand, suppose that the link between the facts is one-to-many, that is, an order is delivered by only one delivery, while a delivery

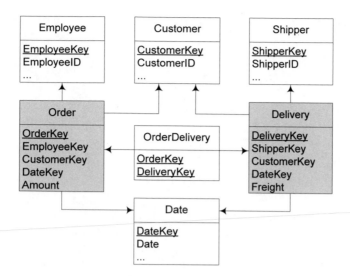

Fig. 5.15 Relations for the schema with a link between facts in Fig. 4.21

Order	Date	Customer	Employee	Amount
O1	1/5/2014	C1	E1	250.00
O2	1/5/2014	C1	E1	147.00
O3	3/5/2014	C1	E2	133.00
O4	5/5/2014	C2	E2	190.00

Order	Delivery
O1	D1
O3	D1
O2	D2
O2	D3
O4	D4

Delivery	Date	Customer	Shipper	Freight
D1	6/5/2014	C1	S3	25.00
D2	7/5/2014	C1	S2	30.00
D3	8/5/2014	C1	S2	27.00
D4	9/5/2014	C2	S1	50.00

Fig. 5.16 Examples of instances of the facts and their link in Fig. 5.15

may concern several orders. In this case, a bridge table is no longer needed and the DeliveryKey should be added to the Order fact table.

A link between fact tables is commonly used for combining the data from two different cubes through a join operation. In the example shown in Fig. 5.17, the information about orders and deliveries is combined to enable analysis of the entire sales process. Notice that only one copy of the CustomerKey is kept (since it is assumed that it is the same in both orders and deliveries), while the DateKeys of both facts are kept, and these are renamed OrderDateKey and DeliveryDateKey. Notice that since the relationship between the two facts is many-to-many, this may induce the double-counting problem to which we referred in Sect. 4.2.6.

Order	OrderDate	Customer	Employee	Amount	Delivery	DeliveryDate	Shipper	Freight
O1	1/5/2014	C1	E1	250.00	D1	6/5/2014	S3	25.00
O3	3/5/2014	C1	E2	133.00	D1	6/5/2014	S3	25.00
O2	1/5/2014	C1	E1	147.00	D2	7/5/2014	S2	30.00
O2	1/5/2014	C1	E1	147.00	D3	8/5/2014	S2	27.00
O4	5/5/2014	C2	E2	190.00	D4	9/5/2014	S1	50.00

Fig. 5.17 Drill-across of the facts through their link in Fig. 5.16

5.7 Slowly Changing Dimensions

So far, we have assumed that new data that arrives to the warehouse only corresponds to facts, which means dimensions are stable, and their data do not change. However, in many real-world situations, dimensions can change both at the structure and the instance level. Structural changes occur, for example, when an attribute is deleted from the data sources and therefore it is no longer available. As a consequence, this attribute should also be deleted from the dimension table. Changes at the instance level can be of two kinds. First, when a correction must be made to the dimension tables due to an error, the new data should replace the old one. Second, when the contextual conditions of an analysis scenario change, the contents of dimension tables must change accordingly. We cover these two latter cases in this section.

We introduce the problem by means of a simplified version of the Northwind data warehouse, where we consider a Sales fact table related only to the dimensions Date, Employee, Customer, and Product, and a SalesAmount measure. We assume a star (denormalized) representation of table Product, and thus category data are embedded in this table. Below, we show instances of the Sales fact table and the Product dimension table.

DateKey	EmployeeKey	CustomerKey	ProductKey	SalesAmount
t1	e1	c1	p1	100
t2	e2	c2	p1	100
t3	e1	c3	p3	100
t4	e2	c4	p4	100

ProductKey	ProductName	UnitPrice	CategoryName	Description
p1	prod1	10.00	cat1	desc1
p2	prod2	12.00	cat1	desc1
p3	prod3	13.50	cat2	desc2
p4	prod4	15.00	cat2	desc2

As we said above, new tuples will be entered into the Sales fact table as new sales occur. But also other updates are likely to occur. For example, when a new product starts to be commercialized by the company, a new tuple in Product must be inserted. Also, data about a product may be wrong, and in this case, the corresponding tuples must be corrected. Finally, the category of a product may change as a result of a new commercial or administrative policy. Assuming that these kinds of changes are not frequent, when the dimensions are designed so that they support them, they are called *slowly changing dimensions*.

In the scenario above, consider a query asking for the total sales per employee and product category, expressed as follows:

```
SELECT    E.EmployeeKey, P.CategoryName, SUM(SalesAmount)
FROM      Sales S, Product P
WHERE     S.ProductKey = P.ProductKey
GROUP BY E.EmployeeKey, P.CategoryName
```

This query would return the following table:

EmployeeKey	CategoryName	SalesAmount
e1	cat1	100
e2	cat1	100
e1	cat2	100
e2	cat2	100

Suppose now that, at an instant t after t4 (the date of the last sale shown in the fact table above), the category of product **prod1** changed to **cat2**, that means, there is a reclassification of the product with respect to its category. The trivial solution of updating the category of the product to **cat2** does not keep track of the previous category of a product. As a consequence, if the user poses the same query as above, and the fact table has not been changed in the meantime, she would expect to get the same result, but since all the sales occurred before the reclassification, she would get the following result:

EmployeeKey	CategoryName	SalesAmount
e1	cat2	200
e2	cat2	200

This result is incorrect since the products affected by the category change were already associated with sales data. Opposite to this, if the new category would be the result of an error correction (i.e., the actual category of **prod1** is **cat2**), this result would be correct. In the former case, obtaining the correct answer requires to guarantee the preservation of the results obtained when **prod1** had category **cat1**, and make sure that the new aggregations will be computed with the new category **cat2**.

Three basic ways of handling slowly changing dimensions have been proposed in the literature. The simplest one, called type 1, consists in overwriting the old value of the attribute with the new one, which implies that we lose the history of the attribute. This approach is appropriate when the modification is due to an error in the dimension data.

In the second solution, called type 2, the tuples in the dimension table are versioned, and a new tuple is inserted each time a change takes place. In our example, we would enter a new row for product **prod1** in the **Product** table with its new category cat2 so that all sales prior to t will contribute to the aggregation to cat1, while the ones that occurred after t will contribute to cat2. This solution requires to have a surrogate key in the dimension in addition to the business key so that all versions of a dimension member have different surrogate key but the same business key. In our example, we keep the business key in a column ProductID and the surrogate key in a column ProductKey. Furthermore, it also necessary to extend the table Product with two attributes indicating the validity interval of the tuple, let us call them From and To. The table Product would look like the following:

Product Key	Product ID	Product Name	UnitPrice	Category Name	Description	From	To
k1	p1	prod1	10.00	cat1	desc1	2010-01-01	2011-12-31
k11	p1	prod1	10.00	**cat2**	desc2	2012-01-01	9999-12-31
k2	p2	prod2	12.00	cat1	desc1	2010-01-01	9999-12-31
...	...	...	...	...	...	...	...

In the table above, the first two tuples correspond to the two versions of product prod1, with ProductKey values k1 and k11. The value 9999-12-31 in the To attribute indicates that the tuple is still valid; this is a usual notation in temporal databases. Since the same product participates in the fact table with as many surrogates as there are attribute changes, the business key keeps track of all the tuples that pertain to the same product. For example, the business key will be used when counting the number of different products sold by the company over specific time periods. Notice that since a new record is inserted every time an attribute value changes, the dimension can grow considerably, decreasing the performance during join operations with the fact table. More sophisticated techniques have been proposed to address this, and below we will comment on them.

In the type 2 approach, sometimes an additional attribute is added to explicitly indicate which is the current row. The table below shows an attribute denoted by RowStatus, telling which is the current value for product prod1.

Product Key	Product ID	Product Name	Unit Price	Category Name	Description	From	To	Row Status
k1	p1	prod1	10.00	cat1	desc1	2010-01-01	2011-12-31	Expired
k11	p1	prod1	10.00	**cat2**	desc2	2012-01-01	9999-12-31	Current
...	...	...	...	...	...	...	...	...

Let us consider a snowflake representation for the Product dimension where the categories are represented in a table Category, as given next.

Product Key	Product Name	Unit Price	Category Key
p1	prod1	10.00	c1
p2	prod2	12.00	c1
p3	prod3	13.50	c2
p4	prod4	15.00	c2

Category Key	Category Name	Description
c1	cat1	desc1
c2	cat2	desc2
c3	cat3	desc3
c4	cat4	desc4

The type 2 approach for a snowflake representation is handled in similar way as above, but now a surrogate key and two temporal attributes From and To must be added to both the Product and the Category tables. Assume that, as before, product prod1 changes its category to cat2. In the case of a solution of type 2, the Product table will be as shown below

Product Key	Product ID	Product Name	Unit Price	Category Key	From	To
k1	p1	prod1	10.00	l1	2010-01-01	2011-12-31
k11	p1	prod1	10.00	**l2**	2012-01-01	9999-12-31
k2	p2	prod2	12.00	l1	2010-01-01	9999-12-31
k3	p3	prod3	13.50	l2	2010-01-01	9999-12-31
k4	p4	prod4	15.00	l2	2011-01-01	9999-12-31

and the Category table remains unchanged. However, if the change occurs at an upper level in the hierarchy, this change needs to be propagated downward in the hierarchy. For example, suppose that the description of category cat1 changes, as reflected in the following table:

Category Key	Category ID	Category Name	Description	From	To
l1	c1	cat1	desc1	2010-01-01	2011-12-31
l11	c1	cat1	**desc11**	2012-01-01	9999-12-31
l2	c2	cat2	desc2	2010-01-01	9999-12-31
l3	c3	cat3	desc3	2010-01-01	9999-12-31
l4	c4	cat4	desc4	2010-01-01	9999-12-31

This change must be propagated to the Product table so that all sales prior to the change refer to the old version of category cat1 (with key l1), while the new sales must point to the new version (with key l11), as shown below:

Product Key	Product ID	Product Name	Unit Price	Category Key	From	To
k1	p1	prod1	10.00	l1	2010-01-01	2011-12-31
k11	p1	prod1	10.00	**l11**	2012-01-01	9999-12-31
k2	p2	prod2	12.00	l1	2010-01-01	2011-12-31
k21	p2	prod2	12.00	**l11**	2012-01-01	9999-12-31
k3	p3	prod3	13.50	l2	2010-01-01	9999-12-31
k4	p4	prod4	15.00	l2	2011-01-01	9999-12-31

The third solution to the problem of slowly changing dimensions, called type 3, consists in introducing an additional column for each attribute subject to change, which will hold the new value of the attribute. In our case, attributes CategoryName and Description changed since when product prod1 changes category from cat1 to cat2, the associated description of the category also changes from desc1 to desc2. The following table illustrates this solution:

Product Key	Product Name	UnitPrice	Category Name	New Category	Description	New Description
p1	prod1	10.00	**cat1**	**cat2**	**desc1**	**desc2**
p2	prod2	12.00	cat1		desc1	
p3	prod3	13.50	cat2		desc2	
p4	prod4	15.00	cat2		desc2	

Note that only the two last versions of the attribute can be represented in this solution and that the validity interval of the tuples is not stored.

It is worth noticing that it is possible to apply the three solutions above, or combinations of them, to the same dimension. For example, we may apply correction (type 1), tuple versioning (type 2), or attribute addition (type 3) for various attributes in the same dimension table.

In addition to these three classic approaches to handle slowly changing dimensions, more sophisticated (although more difficult to implement) solutions have been proposed. We briefly comment on them next.

The type 4 approach aims at handling very large dimension tables and attributes that change frequently. This situation can make the dimension tables to grow to a point that even browsing the dimension can become very slow. Thus, a new dimension, called a **minidimension**, is created to store the most frequently changing attributes. For example, assume that in the Product dimension there are attributes SalesRanking and PriceRange, which are likely to change frequently, depending on the market conditions. Thus, we will create a new dimension called ProductFeatures, with key ProductFeaturesKey, and the attributes SalesRanking and PriceRange, as follows:

Product FeaturesKey	Sales Ranking	Price Range
pf1	1	1-100
pf2	2	1-100
. . .	. . .	. . .
pf200	7	500-600

As can be seen, there will be one row in the minidimension for each unique combination of SalesRanking and PriceRange encountered in the data, not one row per product.

The key ProductFeaturesKey must be added to the fact table Sales as a foreign key. In this way, we prevent the dimension to grow with every change in the sales ranking score or price range of a product, and the changes are actually captured by the fact table. For example, assume that product prod1 initially has sales ranking 2 and price range 1-100. A sale of this product will be entered in the fact table with a value of ProductFeaturesKey equal to pf2. If later the sales ranking of the product goes up to 1, the subsequent sales will be entered with ProductFeaturesKey equal to pf1.

The type 5 approach is an extension of type 4, where the primary dimension table is extended with a foreign key to the minidimension table. In the current example, the Product dimension will look as follows:

Product Key	Product Name	UnitPrice	CurrentProduct FeaturesKey
p1	prod1	10.00	pf1
...	...	...	...

As can be seen, this allows us to analyze the current feature values of a dimension without accessing the fact table. The foreign key is a type 1 attribute, and thus, when any feature of the product changes, the current ProductFeaturesKey value is stored in the Product table. On the other hand, the fact table includes the foreign keys ProductKey and ProductFeaturesKey, where the latter points to feature values that were current *at the time of the sales*. However, the attribute CurrentProductFeaturesKey in the Product dimension would allow us to roll-up historical facts based on the current product profile.

The type 6 approach extends a type 2 dimension with an additional column with the current value of an attribute. For this, in the type 2 solution for the snowflake representation, where the Product dimension has a surrogate key ProductKey, a business key ProductID, and attributes From and To indicating the validity interval of the tuple, we add an attribute CurrentCategoryKey that contains the current value of the Category attribute as follows:

Product Key	Product ID	Product Name	Unit Price	Category Key	From	To	Current CategoryKey
k1	p1	prod1	10.00	l1	2010-01-01	2011-12-31	l11
k11	p1	prod1	10.00	l11	2012-01-01	9999-12-31	l11
k2	p2	prod2	12.00	l1	2010-01-01	9999-12-31	l1
k3	p3	prod3	13.50	l2	2010-01-01	9999-12-31	l2
k4	p4	prod4	15.00	l2	2011-01-01	9999-12-31	l2

In this case, the CategoryKey attribute can be used to group facts based on the category that was in effect when the facts occurred, while the CurrentCategoryKey attribute can be used to group facts based on the current category.

Finally, the type 7 approach delivers similar functionality as the type 6 solution in the case that there are many attributes in the dimension table for which we need to support both current and historical perspectives. In a type 6 solution that would require one additional column in the dimension table for each of such attributes, these columns will contain the current value of the attributes. Instead, a type 7 solution would add to the fact table an additional foreign key of the dimension table containing the natural key (ProductID in our example), provided it is a *durable* one. In our example, the Product dimension will be exactly the same as in the type 2 solution, but the fact table would look as follows:

DateKey	EmployeeKey	CustomerKey	ProductKey	ProductID	SalesAmount
t1	e1	c1	k1	p1	100
t2	e2	c2	k11	p1	100
t3	e1	c3	k3	p3	100
t4	e2	c4	k4	p4	100

The ProductKey column can be used for historical analysis based on the product values effective when the fact occurred, while the ProductID column

will be used for current values. In order to support current analysis we need
an additional view, called CurrentProduct, which keeps only current values of
the Product dimension as follows:

ProductID	ProductName	UnitPrice	CategoryKey
p1	prod1	10.00	l2
p2	prod2	12.00	l1
p3	prod3	13.50	l2
p4	prod4	15.00	l2

A variant of this approach uses the surrogate key as the key of the current
dimension, eliminating the need for two different foreign keys in the fact
table.

Several data warehouse platforms provide some support for slowly changing dimensions, typically type 1 to type 3. However, these solutions are not
satisfactory, since they require considerable programming effort for their correct manipulation. As we will see in Chap. 11, temporal data warehouses are
a more general solution to this problem since they provide built-in temporal
semantics to data warehouses.

5.8 Performing OLAP Queries with SQL

In this section, we briefly introduce the functionalities provided by SQL to
perform analytical queries.

A relational database is not the best data structure to hold multidimensional data. Consider a simple cube Sales, with two dimensions Product and
Customer, and a measure SalesAmount, as depicted in Fig. 5.18a. This data
cube contains all possible (2^2) aggregations of the cube cells, namely, Sales-
Amount by Product, by Customer, and by both Product and Customer, in
addition to the base nonaggregated data.

Figure 5.18b shows a relational fact table corresponding to Fig. 5.18a.
Computing all aggregations of a cube with n dimensions would require 2^n
GROUP BY statements, which is not very efficient. For this reason, the
GROUP BY clause is extended with the ROLLUP and CUBE operators. The
former computes group subtotals in the order given by a list of attributes.
The latter computes all totals of such a list. Over the grouped tuples, the
HAVING clause can be applied, as in a typical GROUP BY.

The syntax of both statements applied to our example above are

```
SELECT     ProductKey, CustomerKey, SUM(SalesAmount)
FROM       Sales
GROUP BY ROLLUP(ProductKey, CustomerKey)

SELECT     ProductKey, CustomerKey, SUM(SalesAmount)
FROM       Sales
GROUP BY CUBE(ProductKey, CustomerKey)
```

	c1	c2	c3	Total
p1	100	105	100	305
p2	70	60	40	170
p3	30	40	50	120
Total	200	205	190	595

ProductKey	CustomerKey	SalesAmount
p1	c1	100
p1	c2	105
p1	c3	100
p2	c1	70
p2	c2	60
p2	c3	40
p3	c1	30
p3	c2	40
p3	c3	50

(a)   (b)

Fig. 5.18 (a) A data cube with two dimensions, Product and Customer. (b) A fact table representing the same data

Figure 5.19 show the result of the GROUP BY ROLLUP and the GROUP BY CUBE queries above. In the case of roll-up, in addition to the detailed data, we can see the total amount by product and the overall total. For example, the total sales for product p1 is 305. If we also need the totals by customer, we would need the cube computation, performed by the second query.

ProductKey	CustomerKey	SalesAmount
p1	c1	100
p1	c2	105
p1	c3	100
p1	NULL	305
p2	c1	70
p2	c2	60
p2	c3	40
p2	NULL	170
p3	c1	30
p3	c2	40
p3	c3	50
p3	NULL	120
NULL	NULL	595

ProductKey	CustomerKey	SalesAmount
p1	c1	100
p2	c1	70
p3	c1	30
NULL	c1	200
p1	c2	105
p2	c2	60
p3	c2	40
NULL	c2	205
p1	c3	100
p2	c3	40
p3	c3	50
NULL	c3	190
p1	NULL	305
p2	NULL	170
p3	NULL	120
NULL	NULL	595

(a)   (b)

Fig. 5.19 Operators (a) GROUP BY ROLLUP and (b) GROUP BY CUBE

Actually, the ROLLUP and CUBE operators are simply shorthands for a more powerful operator, called GROUPING SETS, which is used to precisely specify the aggregations to be computed. For example, the GROUP BY ROLLUP query above can be written using GROUPING SETS as follows:

```
SELECT      ProductKey, CustomerKey, SUM(SalesAmount)
FROM        Sales
GROUP BY GROUPING SETS((ProductKey, CustomerKey), (ProductKey), ())
```

Analogously, the GROUP BY CUBE query would read:

```
SELECT      ProductKey, CustomerKey, SUM(SalesAmount)
FROM        Sales
GROUP BY GROUPING SETS((ProductKey, CustomerKey),
            (ProductKey), (CustomerKey), ())
```

A very common OLAP need is to compare detailed data with aggregate values. For example, we may need to compare the sales of a product to a customer against the maximum sales of this product to any customer. Thus, we could obtain the relevance of each customer with respect to the sales of the product. SQL provides the means to perform this through a feature called **window partitioning**. This query would be written as follows:

```
SELECT ProductKey, CustomerKey, SalesAmount, MAX(SalesAmount) OVER
       (PARTITION BY ProductKey) AS MaxAmount
FROM   Sales
```

The result of the query is given in Fig. 5.20. The first three columns are obtained from the initial Sales table. The fourth one is obtained as follows. For each tuple, a window is defined, called *partition*, containing all the tuples pertaining to the same product. The attribute SalesAmount is then aggregated over this group using the corresponding function (in this case MAX) and the result is written in the MaxAmount column. Note that the first three tuples, corresponding to product p1, have a MaxAmount of 105, that is, the maximum amount sold of this product to customer c2.

A second SQL feature to address OLAP queries is called **window ordering**. It is used to order the rows within a partition. This feature is useful, in particular, to compute rankings. Two common aggregate functions applied in this respect are ROW_NUMBER and RANK. For example, the next query shows how does each product rank in the sales of each customer. For this, we can partition the table by customer, and apply the ROW_NUMBER function as follows:

```
SELECT ProductKey, CustomerKey, SalesAmount, ROW_NUMBER() OVER
       (PARTITION BY CustomerKey ORDER BY SalesAmount DESC) AS RowNo
FROM   Sales
```

The result is shown in Fig. 5.21a. The first tuple, for example, was evaluated by opening a window with all the tuples of customer c1, ordered by the sales amount. We see that product p1 is the one most demanded by customer c1.

ProductKey	CustomerKey	SalesAmount	MaxAmount
p1	c1	100	105
p1	c2	105	105
p1	c3	100	105
p2	c1	70	70
p2	c2	60	70
p2	c3	40	70
p3	c1	30	50
p3	c2	40	50
p3	c3	50	50

Fig. 5.20 Sales of products to customers compared with the maximum amount sold for that product

Product Key	Customer Key	Sales Amount	RowNo
p1	c1	100	1
p2	c1	70	2
p3	c1	30	3
p1	c2	105	1
p2	c2	60	2
p3	c2	40	3
p1	c3	100	1
p3	c3	50	2
p2	c3	40	3

(a)

Product Key	Customer Key	Sales Amount	Rank
p1	c2	105	1
p1	c3	100	2
p1	c1	100	2
p2	c1	70	1
p2	c2	60	2
p2	c3	40	3
p3	c3	50	1
p3	c2	40	2
p3	c1	30	3

(b)

Fig. 5.21 (a) Ranking of products in the sales of customers; (b) Ranking of customers in the sales of products

We could instead partition by product, and study how each customer ranks in the sales of each product, using the function RANK.

```
SELECT ProductKey, CustomerKey, SalesAmount, RANK() OVER
       (PARTITION BY ProductKey ORDER BY SalesAmount DESC) AS Rank
FROM   Sales
```

As shown in the result given in Fig. 5.21b, the first tuple was evaluated opening a window with all the tuples with product p1, ordered by the sales amount. We can see that customer c2 is the one with highest purchases of p1, and customers c3 and c1 are in the second place, with the same ranking.

A third kind of feature of SQL for OLAP is **window framing**, which defines the size of the partition. This is used to compute statistical functions over time series, like moving averages. To give an example, let us assume that we add two columns Year and Month to the Sales table. The following query computes the 3-month moving average of sales by product.

```
SELECT ProductKey, Year, Month, SalesAmount, AVG(SalesAmount) OVER
          (PARTITION BY ProductKey ORDER BY Year, Month
          ROWS 2 PRECEDING) AS MovAvg3M
FROM    Sales
```

The result is shown in Fig. 5.22a. For each tuple, the query evaluator opens a window that contains the tuples pertaining to the current product. Then, it orders the window by year and month and computes the average over the current tuple and the preceding two ones, provided they exist. For example, in the first tuple, the average is computed over the current tuple (there is no preceding tuple), while in the second tuple, the average is computed over the current tuple and the preceding one. Finally, in the third tuple, the average is computed over the current tuple and the two preceding ones.

Product Key	Year	Month	Sales Amount	MovAvg3M
p1	2011	10	100	100
p1	2011	11	105	102.5
p1	2011	12	100	101.67
p2	2011	12	60	60
p2	2012	1	40	50
p2	2012	2	70	56.67
p3	2012	1	30	30
p3	2012	2	50	40
p3	2012	3	40	40

(a)

Product Key	Year	Month	Sales Amount	YTD
p1	2011	10	100	100
p1	2011	11	105	205
p1	2011	12	100	305
p2	2011	12	60	60
p2	2012	1	40	40
p2	2012	2	70	110
p3	2012	1	30	30
p3	2012	2	50	80
p3	2012	3	40	120

(b)

Fig. 5.22 (a) Three-month moving average of the sales per product (b) Year-to-date sum of the sales per product

As another example, the following query computes the year-to-date sum of sales by product.

```
SELECT ProductKey, Year, Month, SalesAmount, AVG(SalesAmount) OVER
          (PARTITION BY ProductKey, Year ORDER BY Month
          ROWS UNBOUNDED PRECEDING) AS YTD
FROM    Sales
```

The result is shown in Fig. 5.22b. For each tuple, the query evaluator opens a window that contains the tuples pertaining to the current product and year ordered by month. Unlike in the previous query, the aggregation function SUM is applied to all the tuples before the current tuple, as indicated by ROWS UNBOUNDED PRECEDING.

It is worth noting that queries that use window functions can be expressed without them, although the resulting queries are harder to read and may be less efficient. For example, the query above computing the year-to-date sales can be equivalently written as follows:

```
SELECT ProductKey, Year, Month, SalesAmount, AVG(SalesAmount) AS YTD
FROM   Sales S1, Sales S2
WHERE  S1.ProductKey = S2.ProductKey AND
       S1.Year = S2.Year AND S1.Month >= S2.Month
```

Of course, there are many other functions appropriate for OLAP provided by SQL, which the interested reader can find in the standard.

5.9 Defining the Northwind Data Warehouse in Analysis Services

In this section, we give an introduction to Analysis Services using the Northwind data warehouse. We consider a simplified version of the warehouse where the ragged geography hierarchy was transformed into a regular one. The reason for this was to simplify both the schema definition and the associated queries that we will show in Chap. 7. More precisely, we did not include sales data about cities that roll-up to the country level, and thus, we dropped the foreign key CountryKey in table City. Moreover, we did not consider the Region level. As a result, the hierarchy becomes balanced.

As stated in Sect. 3.5, Analysis Services comes in two modes, the multidimensional and tabular modes. The choice between these two modes depends on many factors. Regarding the *data model*, the multidimensional model has powerful capabilities for building advanced business intelligence applications. On the other hand, the tabular model is simpler to understand and quicker to build than the multidimensional model. However, the data volumes supported by the tabular model are smaller than those of the multidimensional model. Regarding the *query language*, each of these models has its own associated query language, MDX and DAX, respectively. Other important factors include performance, client tool support, and deployment platform.

We show next how to use Visual Studio to define the Northwind data warehouse using both a multidimensional and a tabular model.

5.9.1 Multidimensional Model

Data Sources

A data warehouse retrieves its data from one or several data stores. A **data source** contains connection information to a data store, which includes the location of the server, a login and password, a method to retrieve the data, and security permissions. Analysis Services supports multiple types of data sources. If the source is a relational database, then SQL is used by default to query the database. In our example, there is a single data source that connects to the Northwind data warehouse.

Data Source Views

A **data source view** (DSV) defines the relational schema that is used for populating an Analysis Services database. This schema is derived from the schemas of the various data sources. Indeed, some transformations are often needed in order to load data from sources into the warehouse. For example, common requirements are to select some columns from a table, to add a new derived column to a table, to restrict table rows on the basis of some specific criteria, and to merge several columns into a single one. These operations can be performed in the DSV by replacing a source table with a **named query** written in SQL or by defining a **named calculation**, which adds a derived column defined by an SQL expression. Further, if the source systems do not specify the primary keys and the relationships between tables using foreign keys, these can be defined in the DSV.

Analysis Services allows the user to specify friendly names for tables and columns. In order to facilitate visibility and navigation for large data warehouses, it also offers the possibility to define customizable views within a DSV, called **diagrams**, that show only certain tables.

The DSV, based on the Northwind data warehouse of Fig. 5.4 is given in Fig. 5.23 (recall that the ragged geography hierarchy was transformed into a regular one). We can see the Sales fact table and the associated dimension tables. The figure also shows several named calculations, which are identified by a special icon at the left of the attribute name. As we will see later, these named calculations are used for defining and browsing the dimensions. The calculations are given next.

- In the Employee dimension table, the named calculation EmployeeName combines the first and last name with the expression

  FirstName + ' ' + LastName

- In the Date dimension table, the named calculations FullMonth, FullQuarter, and FullSemester, are defined, respectively, by the expressions

  MonthName + ' ' + CONVERT(CHAR(4),Year)
  'Q' + CONVERT(CHAR(1), Quarter) + ' ' + CONVERT(CHAR(4), Year)
  'S' + CONVERT(CHAR(1), Semester) + ' ' + CONVERT(CHAR(4), Year)

  These calculations combine the month, quarter, or semester with the year.
- In the Sales fact table, the named calculation OrderLineDesc combines the order number and the order line using the expression

  CONVERT(CHAR(5),OrderNo) + ' - ' + CONVERT(CHAR(1),OrderLineNo)

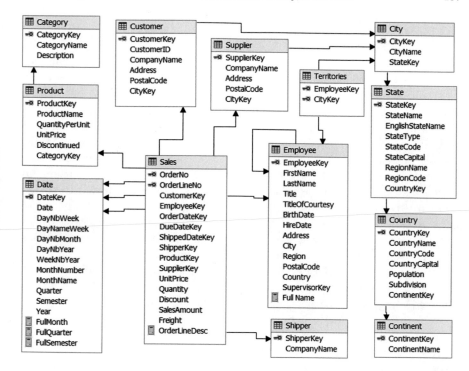

Fig. 5.23 The data source view for the Northwind data warehouse

Dimensions

Analysis Services supports several types of dimensions as follows:

- A **regular dimension** has a direct one-to-many link between a fact table and a dimension table. An example is the dimension Product.
- A **reference dimension** is indirectly related to the fact table through another dimension. An example is the Geography dimension, which is related to the Sales fact table through the Customer and Supplier dimensions. Reference dimensions can be chained together, for instance, one can define another reference dimension from the Geography dimension.
- In a **role-playing dimension**, a single fact table is related to a dimension table more than once. Examples are the dimensions OrderDate, DueDate, and ShippedDate, which all refer to the Date dimension. A role-playing dimension is stored once and used multiple times.
- A **fact dimension**, also referred to as **degenerate dimension**, is similar to a regular dimension but the dimension data are stored in the fact table. An example is the dimension Order.
- In a **many-to-many dimension**, a fact is related to multiple dimension members and a member is related to multiple facts. In the Northwind data warehouse, there is a many-to-many relationship between Employees and

Cities, which is represented in the bridge table Territories. This table must be defined as a fact table in Analysis Services, as we will see later.

Dimensions can be defined either from a DSV, which provides data for the dimension, or from preexisting templates provided by Analysis Services. An example of the latter is the time dimension, which does not need to be defined from a data source. Dimensions can be built from one or more tables.

In order to define dimensions, we need to discuss how hierarchies are handled in Analysis Services. In the next section, we provide a more detailed discussion on this topic. In Analysis Services, there are two types of hierarchies. **Attribute hierarchies** correspond to a single column in a dimension table, for instance, attribute ProductName in dimension Product. On the other hand, **multilevel** (or **user-defined**) **hierarchies** are derived from two or more attributes, each attribute being a level in the hierarchy, for instance Product and Category. An attribute can participate in more than one multilevel hierarchy, for instance, a hierarchy Product and Brand in addition to the previous one. Analysis Services supports three types of multilevel hierarchies, depending on how the members of the hierarchy are related to each other: balanced, ragged, and parent-child hierarchies. We will explain how to define these hierarchies in Analysis Services later in this section.

We illustrate how to define the different kinds of dimensions supported by Analysis Services using the Northwind data warehouse. We start with a **regular dimension**, namely, the Product dimension, shown in Fig. 5.24. The right pane defines the tables in the DSV from which the dimension is created. The attributes of the dimension are given in the left pane. Finally, the hierarchy Categories, composed of the Category and Product levels, is shown in the central pane. The attributes CategoryKey and ProductKey are used for defining these levels. However, in order to show friendly names when browsing the hierarchy, the NameColumn property of these attributes are set to CategoryName and ProductName, respectively.

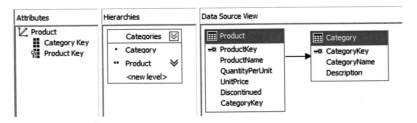

Fig. 5.24 Definition of the Product dimension

Figure 5.25 depicts some members of the Product dimension. As shown in the figure, the names of products and categories are displayed in the dimension browser. Notice that a member called Unknown is shown at the bottom of the figure. In fact, every dimension has an Unknown member. If a key error is

Fig. 5.25 Browsing the hierarchy of the Product dimension

encountered while processing a fact table, which means that a corresponding key cannot be found in the dimension, the fact value can be assigned to the Unknown member for that dimension. The Unknown member can be made visible or hidden using the dimension property UnknownMember. When set to be visible, the member is included in the results of the MDX queries.

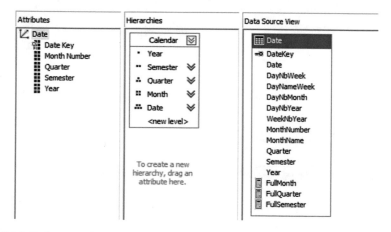

Fig. 5.26 Definition of the Date dimension

We next explain how to define the Date dimension. As shown in Fig. 5.26, the dimension has a hierarchy named Calendar, which is defined using the attributes Year, Semester, Quarter, Month, and Date. As can be seen, the last two attributes have been renamed in the hierarchy. To enable MDX time functions with time dimensions, the Type property of the dimension must be set to Time. Further, it is necessary to identify which attributes in a time dimension correspond to the typical subdivision of time. This is done by defining the Type property of the attributes of the dimension. Thus, the attributes DayNbMonth, MonthNumber, Quarter, Semester, and Year are, respectively, of type DayOfMonth, MonthOfYear, QuarterOfYear, HalfYearOfYear, and Year.

Attributes in hierarchies must have a one-to-many relationship to their parents in order to ensure correct roll-up operations. For example, a quarter must roll-up to its semester. In Analysis Services, this is stated by defining a key for each attribute composing a hierarchy. By default, this key is set to the attribute itself, which implies that, for example, years are unique. Nevertheless, in the Northwind data warehouse, attribute MonthNumber has values such as 1 and 2, and thus, a given value appears in several quarters. Therefore, it is necessary to specify that the key of the attribute is a combination of MonthNumber and Year. This is done by defining the KeyColumns property of the attribute, as shown in Fig. 5.27. Further, in this case, the NameColumn property must also be set to the attribute that is shown when browsing the hierarchy, that is, FullMonth. This should be done similarly for attributes Quarter and Semester.

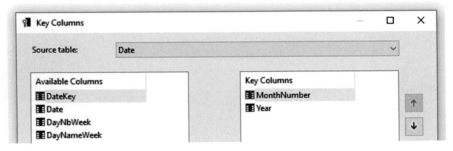

Fig. 5.27 Definition of the key for attribute MonthNumber in the Calendar hierarchy

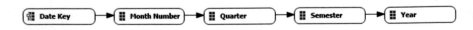

Fig. 5.28 Definition of the relationships in the Calendar hierarchy

These *relationships* between attributes for the Date dimension are given in Fig. 5.28, and correspond to the concept of functional dependencies. In Analysis Services, there are two types of relationships: flexible relationships, which can evolve over time (e.g., a product can be assigned to a new category), and rigid ones, which cannot (e.g., a month is always related to its year). The relationships shown in Fig. 5.28 are rigid, as indicated by the solid arrow head. Figure 5.29 shows some members of the Calendar hierarchy. As can be seen, the named calculations FullSemester (e.g., S2 1997), FullQuarter (e.g., Q2 1997), and FullMonth (e.g., January 1997) are displayed.

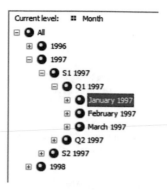

Fig. 5.29 Browsing the hierarchy in the Date dimension

The definition of the **fact dimension** Order follows similar steps than for the other dimensions, except that the *source table for the dimension is the fact table*. The key of the dimension will be composed of the combination of the order number and the line number. Therefore, the named calculation OrderLineDesc will be used in the NameColumn property when browsing the dimension. Also, we must indicate that this is a degenerate dimension when defining the cube. We will explain this later in this section.

Finally, in **many-to-many dimensions**, like in the case of City and Employee, we also need to indicate that the bridge table Territories is actually defined as a fact table, so Analysis Services can take care of the double-counting problem. This is also done when defining the cube.

Hierarchies

What we have generically called hierarchies in Chap. 4 and in the present one are referred to in Analysis Services as user-defined or multilevel hierarchies. Multilevel hierarchies are defined by means of dimension attributes, and these attributes may be stored in a single table or in several tables. Therefore, both the star and the snowflake schema representations are supported in Analysis Services Multidimensional. As we will see later in this chapter, this is not the case in Analysis Services Tabular.

Balanced hierarchies are supported by Analysis Services. Examples of these hierarchies are the Date and the Product dimensions.

Analysis Services does not support **unbalanced hierarchies**. We have seen in Sect. 5.5.2 several solutions to cope with them. On the other hand, Analysis Services supports **parent-child hierarchies**, which are a special

Fig. 5.30 Browsing the Supervision hierarchy in the Employee dimension

case of unbalanced hierarchies. An example is the Supervision hierarchy in the Employee dimension. As can be seen in Fig. 5.23, in the underlying dimension table the column SupervisorKey is a foreign key referencing EmployeeKey. When defining the dimension, the Usage property for the attributes of the dimension determines how they will be used. In our case, the value of such property will be Parent for the SupervisorKey attribute, will be Regular for all other attributes except EmployeeKey, and will be Key for this attribute. Figure 5.30 shows the members of the Supervision hierarchy, where the named calculation EmployeeName is displayed when browsing the hierarchy.

In parent-child hierarchies, the hierarchical structure between members is taken into account when measures are aggregated. Thus, for example, the total sales amount of an employee would be her personal sales amount plus the total sales amount of all employees under her in the organization. Each member of a parent-child hierarchy has a system-generated child member that contains the measure values directly associated to it, independently of its descendants. These are referred to as **data members**. The MembersWithData property of the parent attribute controls the visibility of data members: they are shown when the property is set to NonLeafDataVisible, while they are hidden when it is set to NonLeafDataHidden. We can seen in Fig. 5.30 that the data members are visible since both Andrew Fuller and Steven Buchanan appear twice in the hierarchy. The MembersWithDataCaption property of the parent attribute can be used to define a naming template for generating names of data members.

Analysis Services does not support **generalized hierarchies**. If the members differ in attributes and in hierarchy structure, the common solution is to define one hierarchy for the common levels and another hierarchy for each of the exclusive paths containing the specific levels. This is the case for most of the OLAP tools in the market. On the other hand, Analysis Services supports the particular case of **ragged hierarchies**. As we have already seen, in a ragged hierarchy, the parent of a member may be in a level which is not immediately above it. In a table corresponding to a ragged hierarchy, the missing members can be represented in various ways: with null values or empty strings, or they can contain the same value as their parent.

In Analysis Services, a ragged hierarchy is defined using all of its levels that is, the longest path. To support the display of ragged hierarchies, the HideMemberIf property of a level allows missing members to be hidden. The possible values for this property and their associated behaviors are as follows:

- Never: Level members are never hidden.
- OnlyChildWithNoName: A level member is hidden when it is the only child of its parent and its name is null or an empty string.
- OnlyChildWithParentName: A level member is hidden when it is the only child of its parent and its name is the same as the name of its parent.
- NoName: A level member is hidden when its name is empty.
- ParentName: A level member is hidden when its name is identical to that of its parent.

In order to display ragged hierarchies correctly, the MDX Compatibility property in the connection string from a client application must be set to 2. If it is set to 1, a placeholder member is exposed in a ragged hierarchy.

Regarding **alternative hierarchies**, in Analysis Services several hierarchies can be defined on a dimension, and they can share levels. For example, the hierarchy in Fig. 4.7 can be represented by two distinct hierarchies: a first one composed of Date → Month → CalendarQuarter → CalendarYear and another one composed of Date → Month → FiscalQuarter → FiscalYear.

Analysis Services supports **parallel hierarchies**, whether dependent or independent. Levels can be shared among the various component hierarchies.

Finally, to represent **nonstrict hierarchies** in Analysis Services, it is necessary to represent the corresponding bridge table as a fact table, as it was explained in Sect. 5.9.1. In the relational representation of the Northwind data warehouse given in Fig. 5.4, there is a many-to-many relationship between employees and cities represented by the table Territories. Such a table must be defined as a fact table in the corresponding multidimensional model. In this case, using the terminology of Analysis Services, the City dimension has a many-to-many relationship with the Sales measure group, through the Employee intermediate dimension and the Territories measure group.

Cubes

In Analysis Services, a cube is built from one or several DSVs. A cube consists of one or more dimensions from dimension tables and one or more **measure groups** from fact tables. A measure group is composed of a set of **measures**. The facts in a fact table are mapped as measures in a cube. Analysis Services allows multiple fact tables in a single cube. In this case, the cube typically contains multiple measure groups, one from each fact table.

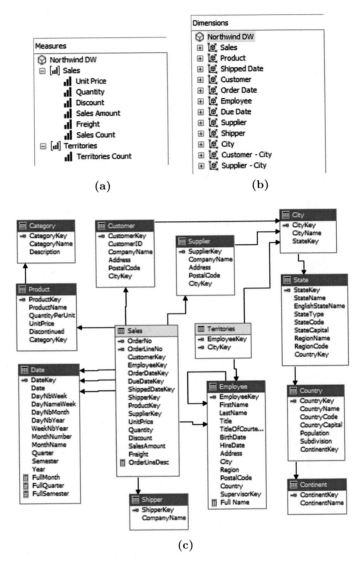

Fig. 5.31 Definition of the Northwind cube in Analysis Services Multidimensional. (**a**) Measure groups; (**b**) Dimensions; (**c**) Schema of the cube

Figure 5.31 shows the definition of the Northwind cube in Analysis Services. As can be seen in Fig. 5.31a, Analysis Services adds a new measure to each measure group, in our case Sales Count and Territories Count, which counts the number fact members associated with each member of each dimension. Thus, Sales Count would count the number of sales for each customer, supplier, product, and so on. Similarly, Territories Count would count the number of cities associated to each employee.

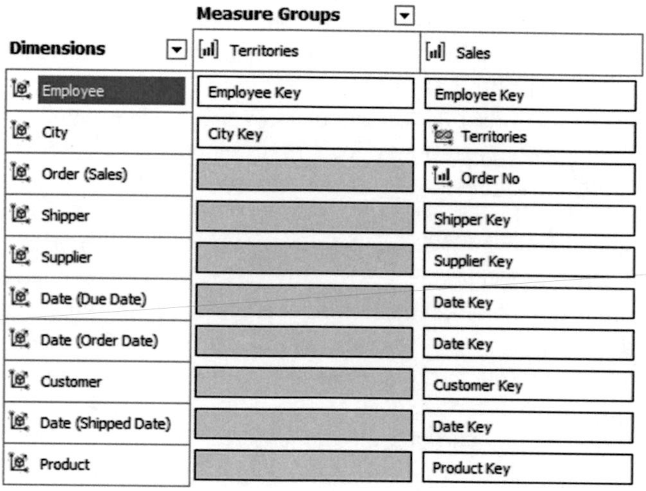

Fig. 5.32 Definition of the dimensions of the Northwind cube

Figure 5.32 shows the relationships between dimensions and measure groups in the cube. With respect to the Sales measure group, all dimensions except the last two are regular dimensions, and thus they do not have an icon to the left of the attribute relating the dimension and the measure group. On the other hand, Geography is a many-to-many dimension linked to the measure group through the Territories fact table. Finally, Order is a fact dimension linked to the measure group through the Order No attribute.

A measure group is stored in one or several **partitions**, each one defining its *storage mode*, which can be Multidimensional OLAP (MOLAP), Relational OLAP (ROLAP), or Hybrid OLAP (HOLAP). These storage modes, which we described in Sect. 5.1, affect the query and processing performance, storage requirements, and storage location of the partition and its parent measure group and cube.

Partitions provide a powerful and flexible mechanism for managing cubes, especially large ones. Typically, partitions are based on a time column. For example, a cube can contain a partition for each past year and also partitions for each quarter of the current year. In this way, only the current quarter partition needs to be processed when current information is added to the cube, which will improve processing performance. At the end of the year, the four quarterly partitions can be merged into a single one for the year and a new partition can be created for the first quarter of the new year.

Analysis Services supports the usual additive aggregation functions SUM, MIN, MAX, COUNT, and DISTINCT COUNT. It also supports **semiadditive**

measures, that is, measures that can be aggregated in some dimensions but not in others. Recall that we defined such measures in Sect. 3.1.2. Analysis Services provides several functions for semiadditive measures such as AverageOfChildren, FirstChild, LastChild, FirstNonEmpty, and LastNonEmpty.

The aggregation function associated to each measure must be defined with the AggregationFunction property. The default aggregation measure is SUM, and this is suitable for all measures in our example, except for Unit Price and Discount. Since these are semiadditive measures, their aggregation should be AverageOfChildren, which computes, for a member, the average of its children.

The FormatString property is used to state the format in which the measures will be displayed. For example, measure Unit Price is of type money, and thus, its format will be $\$\#\#\#,\#\#\#.00$, where a '#' displays a digit or nothing, a '0' displays a digit or a zero, and ',' and '.' are, respectively, thousand and decimal separators. The format string for measure Quantity will be $\#\#\#,\#\#0$. Finally, the format string for measure Discount will be 0.00%, where the percent symbol '%' specifies that the measure is a percentage and includes a multiplication by a factor of 100.

Further, we can define the default measure of the cube, in our case Sales Amount. As we will see in Chap. 6, if an MDX query does not specify the measure to be displayed, then the default measure will be used.

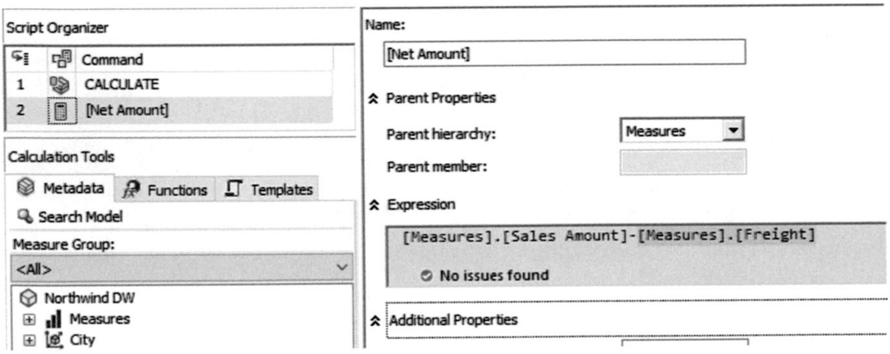

Fig. 5.33 Definition of the Net Amount derived measure

The derived measure **Net Amount** is defined as shown in Fig. 5.33. As can be seen in the figure, the measure will be a calculated member in the Measures dimension. The defining expression is the difference between the Sales Amount and the Freight measures.

Figure 5.34 shows an example of browsing the Northwind cube in Excel using the PivotTable tools. In the figure, the customer hierarchy is displayed on rows, the time hierarchy is displayed on columns, and the sales amount measure is displayed on cells. Thus, the figure shows the yearly sales of customers at different levels of the geography hierarchy, including the individual sales of a shop located in San Francisco.

Total Sales	Column Labels ▼			
Row Labels ▼	⊞ 2016	⊞ 2017	⊞ 2018	Grand Total
⊞ Europe	$113.290,89	$351.142,69	$219.090,18	$683.523,76
⊟ North America				
⊞ Canada	$7.283,08	$30.589,26	$9.539,48	$47.411,82
⊞ Mexico	$4.687,90	$12.700,83	$3.734,90	$21.123,63
⊟ United States				
⊞ Alaska	$4.675,80	$3.951,37	$4.792,89	$13.420,06
⊟ California				
⊟ San Francisco				
Let's Stop N Shop		$1.698,40	$1.378,07	$3.076,47
⊞ Idaho	$10.338,26	$56.241,08	$35.674,51	$102.253,85
⊞ Montana		$1.426,74	$326,00	$1.752,74
⊞ New Mexico	$9.923,78	$19.383,75	$19.982,55	$49.290,08
⊞ Oregon	$1.828,00	$15.150,98	$11.011,14	$27.990,11
⊞ Washington	$2.938,20	$10.810,46	$15.516,80	$29.265,46
⊞ Wyoming	$7.849,63	$2.475,00	$1.117,00	$11.441,63
⊞ South America	$29.034,32	$64.629,06	$60.942,88	$154.606,26
Grand Total	$191.849,87	$570.199,61	$383.106,38	$1.145.155,86

Fig. 5.34 Browsing the Northwind cube in Excel

5.9.2 Tabular Model

Data Sources

A tabular data model integrates data from one or several data sources, which can be relational databases, multidimensional databases, data feeds, text files, etc. Depending on the data source, specific connection and authentication information must be provided.

When importing data from a relational database, we can either choose the tables and views from which to import the data or write queries that specify the data to import. To limit the data in a table, it is possible to filter columns or rows that are not needed. A common best practice when defining a tabular model is to define database views that are used instead of tables for loading data into the model. Such views decouple the physical database structure from the tabular data model and, for instance, can combine information from several tables that corresponds to a single entity in the tabular data model. However, this requires appropriate access rights to create the views.

An essential question in a tabular model is to decide whether to use a snowflake dimension from the source data or denormalize the source tables into a single model table. Generally, the benefits of a single model table outweigh the benefits of multiple model tables, in particular since in the tabular model it is not possible to create a hierarchy that spans several tables, and also since it is more efficient from a performance viewpoint. However, the storage of redundant denormalized data can result in increased model storage size, particularly for very large dimension tables. Therefore, the optimal decision depends on the volume of data and the usability requirements.

When a data source contains a snowflake dimension that should be integrated into a single model table, this can be done either on the data source or in the tabular model. Denormalizing a dimension in a relational data source is typically done with a view. In our example, for the Product dimension we create a view ProductStar in the relational data warehouse as follows.

```
CREATE VIEW ProductStar AS
SELECT  P.ProductKey, P.ProductName, P.QuantityPerUnit, P.UnitPrice, P.Discontinued,
          C.CategoryName
FROM    Product P, Category C
WHERE  P.CategoryKey = C.CategoryKey;
```

Consider now the reference dimension Geography composed of the City, State, Country, and Continent levels, which is shared by the Customer, Supplier, and Employee dimensions. In the data warehouse we will create views CustomerStar and SupplierStar as follows.

```
CREATE VIEW CustomerStar AS
SELECT  U.CustomerKey, U.CustomerID, U.CompanyName, U.Address, U.PostalCode,
          C.CityName AS City, S.StateName AS State, Y.CountryName AS Country,
          N.ContinentName AS Continent
FROM    Customer U, City C, State S, Country Y, Continent N
WHERE  U.CityKey = C.CityKey AND C.StateKey = S.StateKey AND
          S.CountryKey = Y.CountryKey AND Y.ContinentKey = N.ContinentKey;
```

```
CREATE VIEW SupplierStar AS
SELECT  U.SupplierKey, U.CompanyName, U.Address, U.PostalCode,
          C.CityName AS City, S.StateName AS State, Y.CountryName AS Country,
          N.ContinentName AS Continent
FROM    Supplier U, City C, State S, Country Y, Continent N
WHERE  U.CityKey = C.CityKey AND C.StateKey = S.StateKey AND
          S.CountryKey = Y.CountryKey AND Y.ContinentKey = N.ContinentKey;
```

Obviously, it is essential to select the right attributes of the snowflake dimension to be included in the views. In the example above, we selected CityName, StateName, CountryName, and ContinentName, and thus, attributes such as StateCapital or Population will not be available in the tabular model and cannot be used for filtering.

On the other hand, the Employee dimension has a many-to-many relationship with the Geography reference dimension through the Territories bridge table. For this reason we create another view as follows.

```
CREATE VIEW EmployeeGeography AS
SELECT  C.CityKey, C.CityName AS City, S.StateName AS State,
          Y.CountryName AS Country, N.ContinentName AS Continent
FROM City C, State S, Country Y, Continent N
WHERE  C.StateKey = S.StateKey AND S.CountryKey = Y.CountryKey AND
          Y.ContinentKey = N.ContinentKey;
```

In the tabular model we will thus import the above views and we will rename the first three ones as Product, Customer, and Supplier. We also import the tables Employee, Territories, Sales, Date, and Shipper.

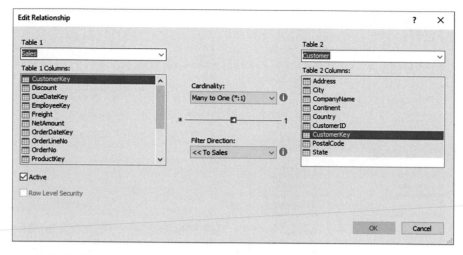

Fig. 5.35 Definition of a relationship in Analysis Services Tabular

Storage Modes

Analysis Services Tabular has two storage modes. By default, it uses an in-memory columnar database, referred to as **Vertipaq**, which stores a copy of the data read from the data source when the data model is refreshed. As we will analyze in Chap. 15, *in-memory* means that all the data reside in RAM whereas *columnar* means that the data of individual columns are stored independently from each other. In addition, data are compressed to reduce the scan time and the memory required. An alternative storage mode, referred to as **DirectQuery**, transforms a tabular model into a metadata layer on top of an external database. It converts a DAX query to a tabular model into one or more SQL queries to the external relational database, which reduces the latency between updates in the data source and the availability of such data in the analytical database. Which of the two storage modes to chose depends on the application requirements and the available hardware.

Relationships

When importing tables from a relational database, the import wizard infers relationships from foreign key constraints. However, this is not the case for the views we created above, which are not linked to the Sales table. We therefore need to create these relationships as shown in Fig. 5.35, where a relationship has several characteristics that define its cardinality, filter direction, and active state, which we describe below. Figure 5.36 shows the tabular model of the Northwind data warehouse after defining these relationships.

Relationships in a tabular model are based on a *single* column. At least one of the two tables involved in a relationship should use a column that

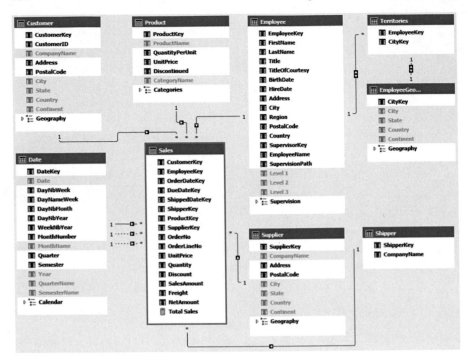

Fig. 5.36 Tabular model of the Northwind data warehouse in Analysis Services

has a unique value for each row of the table. This is usually the primary key of a table, but unlike in foreign keys, this can also be any candidate key. If a relationship is based on multiple columns, which is supported in foreign keys, they should be combined in a single column to create the corresponding relationship. This can be achieved for example through a calculated column that concatenates the values of the columns composing the relationship.

The **cardinality** of most relationships in a tabular model is one-to-many, where for each row of the table in the one side, called the **lookup table**, there are zero, one, or more rows in the other table, referred to as the **related table**. An example is the relationship between the Sales and Customer tables shown in Fig. 5.35. As shown in the figure, the cardinality may be many-to-one, one-to-many, and one-to-one. The latter option is when the columns in both sides of a relationship are candidate keys for the tables.

The uniqueness constraint in a relationship only affects the lookup table, whereas any value in the column of the related table that does not have a corresponding value in the lookup table will be mapped to a special blank row, which is automatically added to the lookup table to handle all the unmatched values in the related table. For example, such a special blank row would aggregate all the rows of the Sales table that do not have a corresponding row in the Customer table. This additional row exists only if there is at least one row in the Sales fact that does not exist in the Customer table. In a one-to-many relationship, the functions RELATEDTABLE and RELATED can be used in a row-related calculation of the, respectively, lookup and related tables.

In one-to-one relationships, both sides of the relationship have a unique-ness constraint in the column involved. However, it is not guaranteed that all values in one column are present in the other column. In one-to-one relationships, both tables can act as lookup tables and as related tables at the same time. For this reason, both functions RELATEDTABLE and RELATED can be used in row-related calculations for both tables.

Relationships in a tabular model are used for **filter propagation**, where a filter applied to any column of a table propagates through relationships to other tables following the filter direction of the relationships. The direction of a filter propagation is visible in the diagram view, as shown in Fig. 5.36. By default, a one-to-many relationship propagates the filter from the lookup table to the related table, which is referred to as a **unidirectional** relationship. For example, the relationship between Sales and Customer automatically propagates a filter applied to one or more of the columns of the Customer table to the Sales table. This can be modified by defining the relationship as **bidirectional**, which enables filter propagation in both directions. For example, as shown in Fig. 5.36, the two relationships linking the bridge table Territories are bidirectional. In addition, the filter propagation defined in a model can be modified in a DAX expression using the CROSSFILTER function. It is worth noting that a one-to-one relationship always has a bidirectional filter progagation. To change this behavior, the relationship type must be changed to one-to-many.

In a tabular model there can only be one **active** relationship between two tables. Consider for example the three role-playing dimensions between the Sales and the Date tables. As can be seen in Fig. 5.36, only one of the three relationships is active, which is the one defined by the OrderDate column and represented by the solid line; the other two are inactive, as represented by the dotted lines. An **inactive** relationship is not automatically used in a DAX expression unless it is activated by using the USERELATIONSHIP function. This function activates the relationship in the context of a single expression without altering the state of the relationships for other calculations and without modifying the underlying data model. More generally, there cannot be multiple paths between any two tables in the model. Therefore, when this happens, one or several relationships are automatically deactivated. This was one of the reasons for defining the views for the Customer and the Supplier in the relational database, which are then imported in the tabular model and used as normal tables. Otherwise it would not be possible to access, for example, both the countries of customers and the countries of suppliers without having to explictly write DAX expressions. However, this approach typically implies introducing data redundancy through denormalization.

Calculated Columns and Measures

A table in a data model can be extended with new columns, referred to as **calculated columns**. The content of such a column is defined by a DAX expression. For example, we can use a calculated column to define a column EmployeeName in the Employee table, which concatenates the first and last name of employees as follows.

Employee[EmployeeName] = Employee[FirstName] & " " & Employee[LastName]

This column can be created directly in Visual Studio using the grid view, where the expression is written in the formula textbox and the column is renamed after right-clicking on it. As another example, a calculated column can be used to define a measure NetAmount in the Sales table as follows.

Sales[NetAmount] = Sales[SalesAmount] - Sales[Freight]

A calculated column behaves like any other column. The DAX expression defining a calculated column operates in the context of the current row and cannot access other rows of the table. Calculated columns are computed during database processing and then stored in the model. This is by contrast with SQL, where calculated columns are computed at query time and do not use memory.

On the other hand, **measures** are used to aggregate values from many rows in a table. Suppose that we want to compute the percentage of the net amount with respect to the sales amount. We cannot use a calculated column for this. Indeed, although this would compute the right value at the row level, it would provide erroneous values when aggregating this measure since it would compute the sum of the ratios. Instead, we need to define a measure that computes the ratio on the aggregates as follows.

Sales[Net Amount %] := DIVIDE (SUM(Sales[NetAmount]), SUM(Sales[SalesAmount]))

A measure must be defined in a table. It is worth noting that in tabular models there is no notion of default aggregate function for measures as is the case for multidimensional models. The aggregate function of a measure must be defined explicitly in tabular models and in DAX queries.

Contrary to calculated columns, measures are evaluated in the context of a cell, which depends on the filters defined by the user in a report or a DAX query. Therefore, they are evaluated at query time and do not consume memory and disk space. Notice that some calculations, such as the net amount above, can be defined either as a calculated column or as measure. However, the choice between these two options is typically dictated by the computation mode, as in the case of the net amount percentage above, or depends on whether the calculated values must reflect user selections.

As another example, we can define a measure Total Sales as follows.

Sales[Total Sales] := SUM ([SalesAmount])

Figure 5.37 shows this measure by customer country in Power BI.

Fig. 5.37 Displaying the **Total Sales** measure by customer country in Power BI

Date Dimension

A tabular model requires a date dimension in order to enable time-related functions in DAX such as year-to-date aggregations. A date dimension is a table that has a column of the date data type with the following characteristics: It must have one record per day, it must cover at least the minimum and maximum dates in the date field to which it will be applied, but it may go beyond both ends, and it must have no gaps and thus, may include dates for which there are no facts recorded.

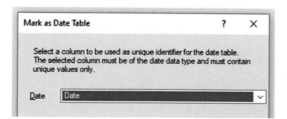

Fig. 5.38 Setting the **Date** table in the Northwind tabular model

Figure 5.38 shows how we specify this for the **Date** table in the Northwind example. We can also create calculated columns in this table as follows.

```
'Date'[SemesterName] = "S" & Date[Semester]
'Date'[QuarterName] = "Q" & Date[Quarter]
```

Hierarchies

Hierarchies are essential to enable the analysis of measures at various granularities. We create next a Calendar hierarchy for the Date dimension in
the Northwind data warehouse. We use the columns Date, MonthName,
QuarterName, SemesterName, and Year to define the hierarchy. As shown in
Fig. 5.39a, the columns may be renamed with user-friendly names. It is considered to be a good practice to hide columns participating in a hierarchy as
well as hiding columns that are used to sort other columns. This can be done
for example using the properties as shown in Fig. 5.39b.

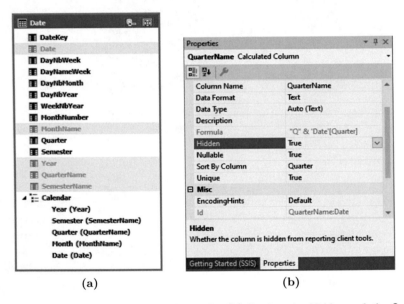

(a)   (b)

Fig. 5.39 (a) Defining the Calendar hierarchy (b) Setting the Hidden and the Sort by
Column properties

Parent-child hierarchies are currently not supported in the tabular model.
To handle such hierarchies, we must flatten them so that they are transformed
into ragged hierarchies made up of one column for each possible level of
the hierarchy. As shown in Fig. 4.3, in the Northwind data warehouse the
Supervision hierarchy has only three levels. We start by defining a calculated
column as follows.

SupervisionPath = PATH (Employee[EmployeeKey], Employee[SupervisorKey])

The above column uses the PATH function to obtain a delimited text with
the keys of all the supervisors of each row, starting from the topmost one.
For example, for the employee Michael Suyama with key 6 it will return the
value 2|5|6.

We then need to define three columns named Level 1, Level 2, and Level 3 for the levels. The Level 1 column is defined as follows.

```
Level 1 =
VAR LevelKey = PATHITEM ( Employee[EmployeePath], 1, INTEGER )
RETURN LOOKUPVALUE ( Employee[EmployeeName], Employee[EmployeeKey], LevelKey )
```

The PATHITEM function returns the employee key from the path at the position specified by the second argument counting from left to right, whereas the LOOKUPVALUE function returns the name of the employee whose key is equal to the value of the variable LevelKey. The other two columns are defined similarly by changing the value of the second argument of the PATHITEM function. Figure 5.40 shows these calculated columns, which should be hidden. A hierarchy named Supervision containing these three levels should be defined and the attribute Hide Members of the hierarchy should be set to Hide Blank Members to enable a proper visualization in client tools.

SupervisorKey	EmployeeName	SupervisionPath	Level 1	Level2	Level3
2	Nancy Davolio	2|1	Andrew Fuller	Nancy Davolio	
	Andrew Fuller	2	Andrew Fuller		
2	Janet Leverling	2|3	Andrew Fuller	Janet Leverling	
2	Margaret Peacock	2|4	Andrew Fuller	Margaret Peacock	
2	Steven Buchanan	2|5	Andrew Fuller	Steven Buchanan	
5	Michael Suyama	2|5|6	Andrew Fuller	Steven Buchanan	Michael Suyama
5	Robert King	2|5|7	Andrew Fuller	Steven Buchanan	Robert King
2	Laura Callahan	2|8	Andrew Fuller	Laura Callahan	
5	Anne Dodsworth	2|5|9	Andrew Fuller	Steven Buchanan	Anne Dodsworth

Fig. 5.40 Flattening the Supervision hierarchy in Analysis Services Tabular

5.10 Summary

In this chapter, we have studied the problem of logical design of data warehouses, specifically relational data warehouse design. Several alternatives were discussed: the star, snowflake, starflake, and constellation schemas. As in the case of operational databases, we provided rules for translating conceptual multidimensional schemas into logical schemas. Particular importance was given to the logical representation of the various kinds of hierarchies studied in Chap. 4. The problem of slowly changing dimensions was also addressed in detail. We then explained how the OLAP operations can be implemented in the relational model using SQL, and also reviewed the advanced features SQL provides to support OLAP queries. We concluded the chapter by showing how we can implement the Northwind data warehouse in Microsoft Analysis Services using both the multidimensional and the tabular models.

5.11 Bibliographic Notes

A comprehensive reference to data warehouse modeling can be found in the book by Kimball and Ross [129]. This work covers in particular the topic of slowly changing dimensions. The work by Jagadish et al. [119] discusses the uses of hierarchies in data warehousing. Complex hierarchies like the ones discussed in this chapter were studied, among other works, in [109, 112, 186]. The problem of summarizability is studied in the classic paper of Lenz and Shoshani [138], and in [110]. Following the ideas of Codd for the relational model, there have been attempts to define normal forms for multidimensional databases [137]. Regarding SQL, analytics and OLAP are covered in the books [45, 151]. There is a wide array of books on Analysis Services that describe in detail the functionalities and capabilities of this tool for both the multidimensional and the tabular models [108, 204, 205]. The works described in [116, 231] study data aggregation at different temporal granularities.

5.12 Review Questions

5.1 Describe the differences between relational OLAP (ROLAP), multidimensional OLAP (MOLAP), and hybrid OLAP (HOLAP).

5.2 Describe the differences between star schemas, snowflake schemas, starflake schemas, and constellation schemas.

5.3 Discuss the mapping rules for translating a MultiDim schema into a relational schema. Are these rules similar to those used for translating an ER schema into a relational schema?

5.4 Explain how a balanced hierarchy can be mapped into either normalized or denormalized tables. Discuss the advantages and disadvantages of these alternative mappings.

5.5 How do you transform at the logical level an unbalanced hierarchy into a balanced one?

5.6 Describe different approaches for representing generalized hierarchies at the logical level.

5.7 Is it possible to distinguish between generalized, alternative, and parallel dependent hierarchies at the logical level?

5.8 Explain how a nonstrict hierarchy can be represented in the relational model.

5.9 Describe with an example the various types of slowly changing dimensions. Analyze and discuss the pros and cons of each type.

5.10 Define the kinds of SQL/OLAP window functions: partitioning, window ordering, and window framing. Write, in English, queries of each class over the Northwind data warehouse.

5.11 Identify the kind of hierarchies that can be directly represented in Analysis Services Multidimensional and in Analysis Services Tabular.

5.12 Discuss how snowflake schemas are represented in Analysis Services Multidimensional and in Analysis Services Tabular.

5.13 Exercises

Exercise 5.1. Consider the data warehouse of the telephone provider given in Ex. 3.1. Draw a star schema diagram for the data warehouse.

Exercise 5.2. For the star schema obtained in the previous exercise, write in SQL the queries given in Ex. 3.1.

Exercise 5.3. Consider the data warehouse of the train application given in Ex. 3.2. Draw a snowflake schema diagram for the data warehouse with hierarchies for the train and station dimensions.

Exercise 5.4. For the snowflake schema obtained in the previous exercise, write in SQL the queries given in Ex. 3.2.

Exercise 5.5. Consider the university data warehouse described in Ex. 3.3. Draw a constellation schema for the data warehouse taking into account the different granularities of the time dimension.

Exercise 5.6. For the constellation schema obtained in the previous exercise, write in SQL the queries given in Ex. 3.3.

Exercise 5.7. Translate the MultiDim schema obtained for the French horse race application in Ex. 4.5 into the relational model.

Exercise 5.8. Translate the MultiDim schema obtained for the Formula One application in Ex. 4.7 into the relational model.

Exercise 5.9. Implement in Analysis Services a multidimensional model for the Foodmart data warehouse given in Fig. 5.41.

Exercise 5.10. Implement in Analysis Services a tabular model for the Foodmart data warehouse given in Fig. 5.41.

Exercise 5.11. The Research and Innovative Technology Administration (RITA)[1] coordinates the US Department of Transportation's (DOT) research programs. It collects several statistics about many kinds of transportation means, including the information about flight segments between airports summarized by month. It is possible to download a set of CSV files in ZIP format, one by year, ranging from 1990 up until now. These files include information about the scheduled and actually departured flights, the number of seats sold, the freight transported, and the distance traveled, among other ones. The mentioned web site describes all fields in detail.

Construct an appropriate data warehouse schema for the above application. Analyze the input data and motivate the choice of your schema.

---

[1] http://www.transtats.bts.gov/

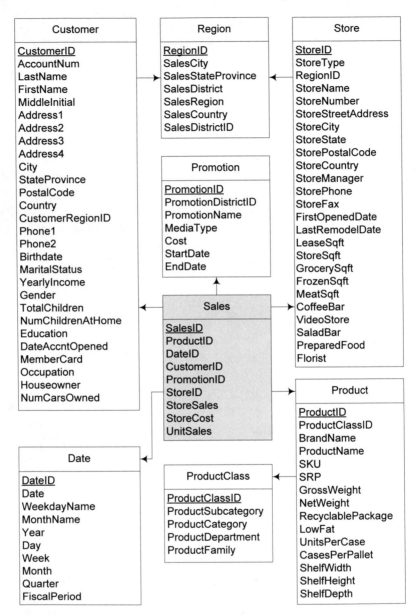

Fig. 5.41 Relational schema of the Foodmart data warehouse

Chapter 6
Data Analysis in Data Warehouses

In this chapter, we focus on data analysis in the context of data warehousing, that is, on the exploitation of the data collected in the warehouse to support decision making.

We start with an introduction to two languages that can be used for defining and querying data warehouses: MDX (MultiDimensional eXpressions) and DAX (Data Analysis eXpressions). MDX was defined by Microsoft in 1997 and was soon adopted by many OLAP tool providers, becoming a de facto standard. Despite of the success of Analysis Services and MDX, many users claimed that multidimensional cubes were hard to understand and manipulate. For this reason, Microsoft introduced in 2012 the tabular model and its associated language DAX, which have become widely popular since then. As we have seen in Chap. 5, from users' perspective, the underlying concepts of the tabular model are simpler than those of the multidimensional model both when designing models and when using them for analysis and reporting. Nevertheless, both the multidimensional and tabular models as well as their associated languages MDX and DAX will continue to coexist in the business intelligence world because each of them targets different application needs. For this reason, in this chapter we give an introduction of both languages, MDX in Sect. 6.1 and DAX in Sect. 6.2.

We continue this chapter describing two essential tools for data analysis. In Sect. 6.3 we discuss the notion of key performance indicators (KPIs), which are measurable values that evaluate how effectively an organization is achieving its key objectives. Finally, in Sect. 6.4, we explain how dashboards are used to display KPIs and other organizational information in a way that the managers can take timely and informed decisions.

All the topics above will be illustrated in Chap. 7 by applying them to the Northwind case study. We remark that this chapter is not intended to be a comprehensive presentation of these topics as there are many books entirely devoted to each one of them. We point at the end of the chapter to popular references in these domains.

© Springer-Verlag GmbH Germany, part of Springer Nature 2022
A. Vaisman, E. Zimányi, *Data Warehouse Systems*, Data-Centric Systems and Applications, https://doi.org/10.1007/978-3-662-65167-4_6

6.1 Introduction to MDX

Just as SQL is a language for manipulating relational databases, MDX is a language for defining and querying multidimensional databases. Although at first sight it may appear that MDX resembles SQL, they are significantly different from each other. While SQL operates over tables, attributes, and tuples, MDX works over data cubes, dimensions, hierarchies, and members.

MDX supports two distinct modes. On the one hand, it can be used as an expression language to design OLAP cubes, that is, to define and manipulate data in order to calculate values, to add business logic to the cubes, to define custom roll-ups and actions, to define security settings, and so on. On the other hand, it can be used as a query language to retrieve data from cubes. In this chapter and the following one, we address MDX as a query language.

6.1.1 Tuples and Sets

Two fundamental concepts in MDX are tuples and sets. We illustrate them using the example cube given in Fig. 6.1.

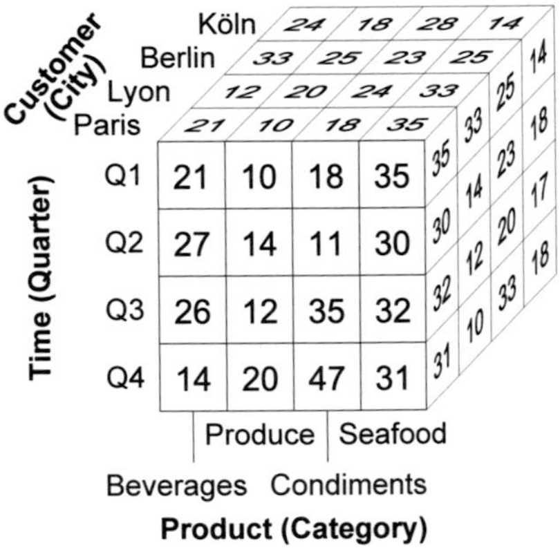

Fig. 6.1 A simple three-dimensional cube with one measure

A *tuple* identifies a cell in a multidimensional cube. It is defined by stating one member from one or several dimensions of the cube. For example, the cell in the top left corner with value 21 corresponds to the sales of beverages in Paris in the first quarter. To identify such cell, we just need to provide the coordinates of each dimension as follows:

(Product.Category.Beverages, Date.Quarter.Q1, Customer.City.Paris)

Notice that in the above expression we stated the coordinate for each of the three dimensions in the format Dimension.Level.Member. As we will see later, in MDX there are several ways to specify a member of a dimension. In particular, the order of the members is not significant, and the previous tuple can also be stated as follows:

(Date.Quarter.Q1, Product.Category.Beverages, Customer.City.Paris)

Since a tuple points to a single cell, then it follows that each member in the tuple must belong to a different dimension.

On the other hand, a *set* is a collection of tuples defined using the same dimensions. For example, the following set

{ (Product.Category.Beverages, Date.Quarter.Q1, Customer.City.Paris)
  (Product.Category.Beverages, Date.Quarter.Q1, Customer.City.Lyon) }

points to the previous cell with value 21 and the one behind it with value 12. It is worth noting that a set may have one or even zero tuples.

A tuple does not need to specify a member from every dimension. Thus, the tuple

(Customer.City.Paris)

points to the slice of the cube composed of the sixteen front cells of the cube, that is, the sales of product categories in Paris, while the tuple

(Customer.City.Paris, Product.Category.Beverages)

points to the four cells at the front and left of the cube, that is, the sales of beverages in Paris. If a member for a particular dimension is not specified, then the *default member* for the dimension is implied. Typically, the default member is the All member, which has the aggregated value for the dimension. However, as we will see later, the default member can be also the current member in the scope of a query.

Let us see now how tuples interact with hierarchies. Suppose that in our cube we have a hierarchy in the Customer dimension with levels Customer, City, State, and Country. In this case, the following tuple

(Customer.Country.France, Product.Category.Beverages, Date.Quarter.Q1)

uses the member France at the Country level and points to the single cell that holds the value for the total sales of beverages in France in the first quarter.

In MDX, measures act much like dimensions. Suppose that in our cube we have three measures UnitPrice, Discount, and SalesAmount. In this case, the Measures dimension, which exists in every cube, contains three members, and thus, we can specify the measure we want as in the following tuple.

(Customer.Country.France, Product.Category.Beverages, Date.Quarter.Q1,
Measures.SalesAmount)

If a measure is not specified, then a *default measure* will be used.

6.1.2 Basic Queries

The syntax of a typical MDX query is as follows:

```
SELECT  ⟨ axis specification ⟩
FROM    ⟨ cube ⟩
[ WHERE ⟨ slicer specification ⟩ ]
```

The axis specification states the axes of a query as well as the members selected for each of these axes. There can be up to 128 axes in an MDX query. Each axis is given a number: 0 for the x-axis, 1 for the y-axis, 2 for the z-axis, and so on. The first axes have predefined names, namely, COLUMNS, ROWS, PAGES, CHAPTERS, and SECTIONS. Otherwise, the axes can be referenced using the AXIS(number) or the number naming convention, where AXIS(0) corresponds to COLUMNS, AXIS(1) corresponds to ROWS, and so on. It is worth noting that query axes cannot be skipped, that is, a query that includes an axis must not exclude lower-numbered axes. For example, a query cannot have a ROWS axis without a COLUMNS axis.

The slicer specification on the WHERE clause is optional. If not specified, the query returns the default measure for the cube. Unless we want to display the Measures dimension, most queries have a slicer specification.

The simplest form of an axis specification consists in taking the members of the required dimension, including those of the Measures dimension, as follows:

```
SELECT [Measures].MEMBERS ON COLUMNS,
       [Customer].[Country].MEMBERS ON ROWS
FROM   Sales
```

This query displays all the measures for customers, summarized at the country level. In MDX the square brackets are optional, except for a name with embedded spaces, with numbers, or that is an MDX keyword, where they are required. In the following, we omit unnecessary square brackets.

The above query will show a row with only null values for countries that do not have customers. The next query uses the NONEMPTY function to remove such values.

```
SELECT Measures.MEMBERS ON COLUMNS,
       NONEMPTY(Customer.Country.MEMBERS) ON ROWS
FROM   Sales
```

Alternatively, the NON EMPTY keyword can be used as shown next.

```
SELECT Measures.MEMBERS ON COLUMNS,
       NON EMPTY Customer.Country.MEMBERS ON ROWS
FROM   Sales
```

Although in this case the use of the NONEMPTY *function* and the NON EMPTY *keyword* yields the same result, there are slight differences between both, which go beyond this introduction to MDX.

The above query displayed all measures that are stored in the cube. However, derived measures such as **Net Amount**, which we defined in Sect. 5.9.1, will not appear in the result. If we want this to happen, we should use the **ALLMEMBERS** keyword.

```
SELECT Measures.ALLMEMBERS ON COLUMNS,
       Customer.Country.MEMBERS ON ROWS
FROM   Sales
```

The **ADDCALCULATEDMEMBERS** function can also be used for this purpose.

6.1.3 Slicing

Consider now the query below, which shows all measures by year.

```
SELECT Measures.MEMBERS ON COLUMNS,
       [Order Date].Year.MEMBERS ON ROWS
FROM   Sales
```

To restrict the result to Belgium, we can write the following query.

```
SELECT Measures.MEMBERS ON COLUMNS,
       [Order Date].Year.MEMBERS ON ROWS
FROM   Sales
WHERE  (Customer.Country.Belgium)
```

The added condition tells the query to return the values of all measures for all years but only for customers who live in Belgium. Thus, we can see how the **WHERE** clause behaves different than in SQL.

Multiple members from *different* hierarchies can be added to the **WHERE** clause. The previous query can be restricted to customers who live in Belgium and who bought products in the category beverages as shown next.

```
SELECT Measures.MEMBERS ON COLUMNS,
       [Order Date].Year.MEMBERS ON ROWS
FROM   Sales
WHERE  (Customer.Country.Belgium, Product.Categories.Beverages)
```

To use multiple members from the *same* hierarchy, we need to include a set in the **WHERE** clause. For example, the following query shows the values of all measures for all years for customers who bought products in the category beverages and live in either Belgium or France.

```
SELECT Measures.MEMBERS ON COLUMNS,
       [Order Date].Year.MEMBERS ON ROWS
FROM   Sales
WHERE  ( { Customer.Country.Belgium, Customer.Country.France },
         Product.Categories.Beverages )
```

Using a set in the **WHERE** clause implicitly aggregates values for all members
in the set. In this case, the query shows aggregated values for Belgium and
France in each cell.

Consider now the following query, which requests the sales amount of
customers by country and by year.

```
SELECT  [Order Date].Year.MEMBERS ON COLUMNS,
        Customer.Country.MEMBERS ON ROWS
FROM    Sales
WHERE   Measures.[Sales Amount]
```

Here, we specified in the **WHERE** clause the measure to be displayed. If no
measure is stated, then the default measure is used.

The **WHERE** clause can combine measures and dimensions. For example,
the following query will show a result similar to the one given above, but now
with the figures restricted to the category beverages.

```
SELECT  [Order Date].Year.MEMBERS ON COLUMNS,
        Customer.Country.MEMBERS ON ROWS
FROM    Sales
WHERE   (Measures.[Sales Amount], Product.Category.[Beverages])
```

If a dimension appears in a slicer, it cannot be used in any axis in the
SELECT clause. We will see later that the **FILTER** function can be used to
filter members of dimensions appearing in an axis.

6.1.4 Navigation

The result of the query above contains aggregated values for all the years,
including the All column. The **CHILDREN** function can be used to display
only the values for the individual years (and not the All member) as follows:

```
SELECT  [Order Date].Year.CHILDREN ON COLUMNS, ...
```

The attentive reader may wonder why the member All does not appear in the
rows of the above result. The reason is that the expression

```
Customer.Country.MEMBERS
```

we used in the query is a shorthand notation for

```
Customer.Geography.Country.MEMBERS
```

and thus, it selects the members of the Country level of the Geography hierarchy of the Customer dimension. Since the All member is the topmost member
of the hierarchy, above the members of the Continent level, it is not a member
of the Country level and does not appear in the result. Let us explain this
further. As we have seen in Chap. 5, every attribute of a dimension defines
an attribute hierarchy. Thus, there is an All member in each hierarchy of a

dimension, for both the user-defined hierarchies and the attribute hierarchies. Since the dimension Customer has an attribute hierarchy Company Name, if in the above query we use the expression

Customer.[Company Name].MEMBERS

the result will contain the All member, in addition to the names of all the customers. Using CHILDREN instead will not show the All member.

It is also possible to select a single member or an enumeration of members of a dimension. An example is given in the following query.

```
SELECT [Order Date].Year.MEMBERS ON COLUMNS,
        { Customer.Country.France,Customer.Country.Italy } ON ROWS
FROM    Sales
WHERE Measures.[Sales Amount]
```

This expression queries the sales amount of customers by year summarized for France and Italy. In the above query, the set in the row axis could be also stated using expressions such as Customer.France, Customer.Geography.France, or Customer.Geography.Country.France. The latter expression uses fully qualified or unique names, namely, the dimension, hierarchy, and level to which the specific member belongs. When member names are uniquely identifiable, fully qualified member names are not required. Nevertheless, the use of unique names is recommended to remove any ambiguities.

The function CHILDREN may be used to retrieve the states of the countries above as follows:

```
SELECT [Order Date].Year.MEMBERS ON COLUMNS,
        { Customer.France.CHILDREN, Customer.Italy.CHILDREN } ON ROWS
FROM    Sales
WHERE Measures.[Sales Amount]
```

The MEMBERS and CHILDREN functions seen above do not provide the ability to drill down to a lower level in a hierarchy. For this, the function DESCENDANTS can be used. For example, the following query

```
SELECT [Order Date].Year.MEMBERS ON COLUMNS,
        DESCENDANTS(Customer.Germany, Customer.City) ON ROWS
FROM    Sales
WHERE Measures.[Sales Amount]
```

shows the sales amount for German cities

By default, the function DESCENDANTS displays only members at the level specified as its second argument. An optional third argument states whether to include or exclude descendants or children before and after the specified level as follows:

- SELF, which is the default, displays values for the City level as above.
- BEFORE displays values from the state to the Country levels.
- SELF_AND_BEFORE displays values from the City to the Country levels.

- **AFTER** displays values from the **Customer** level, since it is only level after **City**.
- **SELF_AND_AFTER** displays values from the **City** and **Customer** levels.
- **BEFORE_AND_AFTER** displays values from the **Country** to the **Customer** levels, excluding the former.
- **SELF_BEFORE_AFTER** displays values from the **Country** to the **Customer** levels.
- **LEAVES** displays values from the **City** level as above, since this is the only leaf level between **Country** and **City**. On the other hand, if **LEAVES** is used without specifying the level, as in the following query:

DESCENDANTS(Customer.Geography.Germany, ,LEAVES)

then the leaf level, that is, **Customer** will be displayed.

The **ASCENDANTS** function returns a set that includes a member and all of its ancestors. For example, the following query asks for the sales amount for the customer **Du monde entier** and all its ancestors in the **Geography** hierarchy, that is, at the **City**, **State**, **Country**, **Continent**, and **All** levels.

```
SELECT Measures.[Sales Amount] ON COLUMNS,
       ASCENDANTS(Customer.Geography.[Du monde entier]) ON ROWS
FROM   Sales
```

The function **ANCESTOR** can be used to obtain the result for an ancestor at a specified level, as shown next.

```
SELECT Measures.[Sales Amount] ON COLUMNS,
       ANCESTOR(Customer.Geography.[Du monde entier], Customer.Geography.State)
       ON ROWS
FROM   Sales
```

6.1.5 Cross Join

Although an MDX query can display up to 128 axes, most OLAP tools are only able to display two axes, that is, two-dimensional tables. In this case, the **CROSSJOIN** function can be used to combine several dimensions in a single axis. In order to obtain the sales amount for product categories by country and by quarter in a matrix format, we need to combine the customer and time dimensions in a single axis as shown next.

```
SELECT Product.Category.MEMBERS ON COLUMNS,
       CROSSJOIN(Customer.Country.MEMBERS,
       [Order Date].Calendar.Quarter.MEMBERS) ON ROWS
FROM   Sales
WHERE  Measures.[Sales Amount]
```

Alternatively, we can use the cross join operator '*' as shown next.

```
SELECT Product.Category.MEMBERS ON COLUMNS,
       Customer.Country.MEMBERS *
       [Order Date].Calendar.Quarter.MEMBERS ON ROWS
FROM   Sales
WHERE  Measures.[Sales Amount]
```

More than two cross joins can be applied, as shown in the following query.

```
SELECT Product.Category.MEMBERS ON COLUMNS,
       Customer.Country.MEMBERS * [Order Date].Calendar.Quarter.MEMBERS *
       Shipper.[Company Name].MEMBERS ON ROWS
FROM   Sales
WHERE  Measures.[Sales Amount]
```

6.1.6 Subqueries

As stated above, the **WHERE** clause applies a slice to the cube. This clause can be used to select the measures or the dimensions to be displayed. For example, the following query shows the sales amount for the beverages and condiments categories.

```
SELECT Measures.[Sales Amount] ON COLUMNS,
       [Order Date].Calendar.Quarter.MEMBERS ON ROWS
FROM   Sales
WHERE  { Product.Category.Beverages, Product.Category.Condiments }
```

Instead of using a slicer in the **WHERE** clause of above query, we can define a subquery in the **FROM** clause as follows:

```
SELECT Measures.[Sales Amount] ON COLUMNS,
       [Order Date].Calendar.Quarter.MEMBERS ON ROWS
FROM   ( SELECT { Product.Category.Beverages,
                  Product.Category.Condiments } ON COLUMNS
         FROM   Sales )
```

This query displays the sales amount for each quarter in a subquery which only mentions the beverages and condiments product categories. As we can notice, different from SQL, in the outer query we can mention attributes that are not selected in the subquery.

Nevertheless, there is a fundamental difference between using the **WHERE** clause and using subqueries. When we include the product category hierarchy in the **WHERE** clause it cannot appear on any axis, but this is not the case in the subquery approach as the following query shows.

```
SELECT Measures.[Sales Amount] ON COLUMNS,
       [Order Date].Calendar.Quarter.MEMBERS * Product.Category.MEMBERS
       ON ROWS
FROM   ( SELECT { Product.Category.Beverages, Product.Category.Condiments }
                  ON COLUMNS
         FROM   Sales )
```

The subquery may include more than one dimension, as shown next.

```
SELECT  Measures.[Sales Amount] ON COLUMNS,
        [Order Date].Calendar.Quarter.MEMBERS * Product.Category.MEMBERS
        ON ROWS
FROM    ( SELECT ( { Product.Category.Beverages, Product.Category.Condiments },
                  { [Order Date].Calendar.[Q1 2017],
                    [Order Date].Calendar.[Q2 2017] } ) ON COLUMNS
        FROM   Sales )
```

We can also nest several subquery expressions, which are used to express complex multistep filtering operations, as it is done in the following query, which asks for the sales amount by quarter for the top two selling countries for the beverages and condiments product categories.

```
SELECT  Measures.[Sales Amount] ON COLUMNS,
        [Order Date].Calendar.[Quarter].Members ON ROWS
FROM    ( SELECT TOPCOUNT(Customer.Country.MEMBERS, 2,
                Measures.[Sales Amount]) ON COLUMNS
        FROM ( SELECT { Product.Category.Beverages,
                       Product.Category.Condiments } ON COLUMNS
              FROM   Sales ) )
```

This query uses the TOPCOUNT function, which sorts a set in descending order with respect to the expression given as third parameter and returns the specified number of elements with the highest values. Notice that although we could have used a single nesting, the expression above is easier to understand.

6.1.7 Calculated Members and Named Sets

Calculated members are new members in a dimension or new measures that are defined using the WITH clause in front of the SELECT statement

```
WITH MEMBER Parent.MemberName AS ⟨ expression ⟩
```

where Parent is the parent of the new calculated member and MemberName is its name. Similarly, named sets are used to define new sets as follows:

```
WITH SET SetName AS ⟨ expression ⟩
```

Calculated members and named sets defined using the WITH clause as above remain within the scope of a query. To make them visible within the scope of a session and thus visible to all queries in that session, or within the scope of a cube, a CREATE statement must be used. In the sequel, we will only show examples of calculated members and named sets defined within queries. Calculated members and named sets are computed at run time and thus, there is no penalty in the processing of the cube or in the number of aggregations to be stored.

The most common use of calculated members is to define a new measure that relates already defined measures. For example, a measure that calculates the percentage profit of sales can be defined as follows:

```
WITH MEMBER Measures.[Profit%] AS
        (Measures.[Sales Amount] - Measures.[Freight]) / (Measures.[Sales Amount]),
        FORMAT_STRING = '#0.00%'
SELECT { [Sales Amount], Freight, [Profit%] } ON COLUMNS,
        Customer.Country ON ROWS
FROM    Sales
```

Here, FORMAT_STRING specifies the display format to use for the new calculated member. In the format expression above, a '#' displays a digit or nothing, while a '0' displays a digit or a zero. The use of the percent symbol '%' specifies that the calculation returns a percentage and includes a multiplication by a factor of 100.

We can also create a calculated member in a dimension, as shown next.

```
WITH MEMBER Product.Categories.[All].[Meat & Fish] AS
        Product.Categories.[Meat/Poultry] + Product.Categories.[Seafood]
SELECT { Measures.[Unit Price], Measures.Quantity, Measures.Discount,
        Measures.[Sales Amount] } ON COLUMNS,
        Category.ALLMEMBERS ON ROWS
FROM    Sales
```

The query above creates a calculated member equal to the sum of the Meat/Poultry and Seafood categories. Being a child of the All member of the hierarchy Categories of the Product dimension, it will thus belong to the Category level.

In the following query, we define a named set Nordic Countries composed of the countries Denmark, Finland, Norway, and Sweden.

```
WITH SET [Nordic Countries] AS
        { Customer.Country.Denmark, Customer.Country.Finland,
        Customer.Country.Norway, Customer.Country.Sweden }
SELECT Measures.MEMBERS ON COLUMNS,
        [Nordic Countries] ON ROWS
FROM    Sales
```

In the above example, the named set is defined by enumerating its members and thus, it is a static name set even if defined in the scope of a session or a cube, since its result must not be reevaluated upon updates of the cube. On the contrary, a *dynamic* named set is evaluated any time there are changes to the scope. As an example of a dynamic named set, the following query displays several measures for the top five selling products.

```
WITH SET TopFiveProducts AS
        TOPCOUNT ( Product.Categories.Product.MEMBERS, 5,
        Measures.[Sales Amount] )
SELECT { Measures.[Unit Price], Measures.Quantity, Measures.Discount,
        Measures.[Sales Amount] } ON COLUMNS,
        TopFiveProducts ON ROWS
FROM    Sales
```

6.1.8 Relative Navigation

It is often necessary to relate the value of a member to the values of
other members in a hierarchy. MDX has many methods that can be applied to a member to traverse a hierarchy, the most common ones are PRE-
VMEMBER, NEXTMEMBER, CURRENTMEMBER, PARENT, FIRSTCHILD,
and LASTCHILD. Suppose we want to compute the sales of a member of the
Geography hierarchy as a percentage of the sales of its parent, as shown in
the following query.

```
WITH MEMBER Measures.[Percentage Sales] AS
        (Measures.[Sales Amount], Customer.Geography.CURRENTMEMBER) /
        (Measures.[Sales Amount], Customer.Geography.CURRENTMEMBER.PARENT),
        FORMAT_STRING = '#0.00%'
SELECT { Measures.[Sales Amount], Measures.[Percentage Sales] } ON COLUMNS,
        NON EMPTY DESCENDANTS(Customer.Europe, Customer.Country,
        SELF_AND_BEFORE) ON ROWS
FROM    Sales
```

The CURRENTMEMBER function in the WITH clause, returns the current
member along a dimension during an iteration, while the PARENT function
returns the parent of a member. In the SELECT clause, the measures for European countries are displayed. The expression defining the calculated member
can be abbreviated as follows:

```
(Measures.[Sales Amount]) / (Measures.[Sales Amount],
        Customer.Geography.CURRENTMEMBER.PARENT)
```

where the current hierarchy member is used by default if not specified.

The problem with the above calculated measure is that it works well for
all members of the Geography hierarchy, at any level, except for the All member, since it does not have a parent. Therefore, we must add a conditional
expression in the definition of the measure as follows:

```
WITH MEMBER Measures.[Percentage Sales] AS
        IIF((Measures.[Sales Amount],
        Customer.Geography.CURRENTMEMBER.PARENT)=0, 1,
        (Measures.[Sales Amount]) / (Measures.[Sales Amount],
        Customer.Geography.CURRENTMEMBER.PARENT)),
        FORMAT_STRING = '#0.00%'
SELECT ...
```

The IIF function has three parameters: the first one is a Boolean condition,
the second one is the value returned if the condition is true, and the third
one is the value returned if the condition is false. Thus, since the All member
has no parent, the value of the measure sales amount for its parent will be
equal to 0, and in this case a value of 1 will be given for the percentage sales.

The GENERATE function iterates through the members of a set, using a
second set as a template for the resultant set. Suppose we want to display the
sales amount by category for all customers in Belgium and France. To avoid

enumerating in the query all customers for each country, the **GENERATE** function can be used as follows:

```
SELECT  Product.Category.MEMBERS ON COLUMNS,
        GENERATE({Customer.Belgium, Customer.France},
        DESCENDANTS(Customer.Geography.CURRENTMEMBER, Customer))
        ON ROWS
FROM    Sales
WHERE   Measures.[Sales Amount]
```

The **PREVMEMBER** function can be used to show growth over a time period. The following query displays net amount and the incremental change from the previous time member for all months in 2016.

```
WITH MEMBER Measures.[Net Amount Growth] AS
        (Measures.[Net Amount]) -
        (Measures.[Net Amount], [Order Date].Calendar.PREVMEMBER),
        FORMAT_STRING = '$###,##0.00; $-###,##0.00'
SELECT { Measures.[Net Amount], Measures.[Net Amount Growth] } ON COLUMNS,
        DESCENDANTS([Order Date].Calendar.[2016], [Order Date].Calendar.[Month])
        ON ROWS
FROM    Sales
```

The format expression above defines two formats, the first one for positive numbers and the second one for negative numbers. Using **NEXTMEMBER** in the expression above would show net amount for each month compared with those of the following month. Since the Northwind cube contains sales data starting from July 2016, the growth for the first month cannot be measured, and thus it would be equal to the net amount. In this case, a value of zero is used for the previous period that is beyond the range of the cube.

In the query above, instead of the **PREVMEMBER** function we can use the **LAG(n)** function, which returns the member located a specified number of positions preceding a specific member along the member dimension. If the number given is negative, a subsequent member is returned, if it is zero the current member is returned. Thus, **PREV**, **NEXT**, and **CURRENT** can be replaced with **LAG(1)**, **LAG(-1)**, and **LAG(0)**, respectively. A similar function called **LEAD** exists, such that **LAG(n)** is equivalent to **LEAD(-n)**.

6.1.9 Time-Related Calculations

Time period analysis is an essential component of business intelligence applications. For example, one could want to examine the sales of a month or quarter compared to those of the same month or quarter last year. MDX provides a powerful set of time series functions for time period analysis. While their most common use is with a time dimension, most of them can also be used with any other dimension.

The **PARALLELPERIOD** function is used to compare values of a specified member with those of a member in the same relative position in a prior period. For example, one would compare values from one quarter with those of the same quarter in the previous year. In the previous query, we used the **PREVMEMBER** function to compute the growth with respect to the previous month. The **PARALLELPERIOD** function can be used to compute the growth with respect to the same period in the previous year, as shown next.

```
WITH MEMBER Measures.[Previous Year] AS
        (Measures.[Net Amount], PARALLELPERIOD([Order Date].Calendar.Quarter, 4)),
        FORMAT_STRING = '$###,##0.00'
MEMBER Measures.[Net Amount Growth] AS
        Measures.[Net Amount] - Measures.[Previous Year],
        FORMAT_STRING = '$###,##0.00; $-###,##0.00'
SELECT { [Net Amount], [Previous Year], [Net Amount Growth] } ON COLUMNS,
        [Order Date].Calendar.Quarter ON ROWS
FROM    Sales
```

Here, the **PARALLELPERIOD** function selects the member that is four quarters (i.e., a year) prior to the current quarter. Since the Northwind cube contains sales data starting from July 2016, the above query will show for the first four quarters a null value for measure **Previous Year** and the same value for the measures **Net Amount** and **Net Amount Growth**.

The functions **OPENINGPERIOD** and **CLOSINGPERIOD** return, respectively, the first or last sibling among the descendants of a member at a given level. For example, the difference between the sales quantity of a month and that of the opening month of the quarter can be obtained as follows:

```
WITH MEMBER Measures.[Quantity Difference] AS
        (Measures.[Quantity]) - (Measures.[Quantity],
        OPENINGPERIOD([Order Date].Calendar.Month,
        [Order Date].Calendar.CURRENTMEMBER.PARENT))
SELECT { Measures.[Quantity], Measures.[Quantity Difference] } ON COLUMNS,
        [Order Date].Calendar.[Month] ON ROWS
FROM    Sales
```

In deriving the calculated member **Quantity Difference**, the opening period at the month level is taken for the quarter to which the month corresponds. If **CLOSINGPERIOD** is used instead, the query will show sales based on the final month of the specified season,

The **PERIODSTODATE** function returns a set of periods (members) from a specified level starting with the first period and ending with a specified member. For example, the following expression defines a set containing all the months up to and including June 2017.

```
PERIODSTODATE([Order Date].Calendar.Year, [Order Date].Calendar.[June 2017])
```

Suppose now that we want to define a calculated member that displays year-to-date information, for example, the monthly year-to-date sales. For this, in addition to **PERIODSTODATE** we need to use the **SUM** function, which returns the sum of a numeric expression evaluated over a set. For example, the sum of sales amount for Italy and Greece can be displayed with the following expression.

SUM({Customer.Country.Italy, Customer.Country.Greece}, Measures.[Sales Amount])

In the expression below, the measure to be displayed is the sum of the current time member over the year level.

SUM(PERIODSTODATE([Order Date].Calendar.Year,
    [Order Date].Calendar.CURRENTMEMBER), Measures.[Sales Amount])

Similarly, by replacing **Year** by **Quarter** in the above expression we can obtain quarter-to-date sales. For example, the following query shows year-to-date and quarter-to-date sales.

```
WITH MEMBER Measures.YTDSales AS
        SUM(PERIODSTODATE([Order Date].Calendar.Year,
        [Order Date].Calendar.CURRENTMEMBER), Measures.[Sales Amount])
        MEMBER Measures.QTDSales AS
        SUM(PERIODSTODATE([Order Date].Calendar.Quarter,
        [Order Date].Calendar.CURRENTMEMBER), Measures.[Sales Amount])
SELECT { Measures.[Sales Amount], Measures.YTDSales, Measures.QTDSales }
        ON COLUMNS, [Order Date].Calendar.Month.MEMBERS ON ROWS
FROM    Sales
```

As the Northwind data warehouse contains sales data starting in July 2016, the value of both **YTDSales** and **QTDSales** for August 2016 is the sum of **Sales Amount** of July and August 2016. On the other hand, the value of **YTDSales** for December 2016 is the sum of **Sales Amount** from July to December 2016, while the value of **QTDSales** for December 2016 is the sum of **Sales Amount** from October to December 2016.

The xTD (YTD, QTD, MTD, and WTD) functions refer to year-, quarter-, month-, and week-to-date periods. They are only applicable to a time dimension (which was not the case for the other functions we have seen so far). The xTD functions are equivalent to the PeriodsToDate function with a level specified. YTD specifies a year level, QTD specifies a quarter level, and so on. For example, in the query above, the measure YTDSales can be defined instead by the following expression:

SUM(YTD([Order Date].Calendar.CURRENTMEMBER), Measures.[Sales Amount])

Moving averages are used to solve very common business problems. They are well suited to track the behavior of temporal series, such as financial indicators or stock market data. As these data change very rapidly, moving averages are used to smooth out the variations and discover general trends. However, choosing the period over which smoothing is performed is essential, because if the period is too long the average will be flat and will not be useful to discover any trend, whereas a too short period will show too many peaks and troughs to highlight general trends.

The **LAG** function we have seen in the previous section, combined with the range operator ':', helps us to write moving averages in MDX. The range operator returns a set of members made of two given members and all the members in between. Thus, for computing the 3-month moving average of the number of orders we can write the following query:

```
WITH MEMBER Measures.MovAvg3M AS
        AVG([Order Date].Calendar.CURRENTMEMBER.LAG(2):
        [Order Date].Calendar.CURRENTMEMBER,
        Measures.[Order No]), FORMAT_STRING = '###,##0.00'
SELECT { Measures.[Order No], Measures.MovAvg3M } ON COLUMNS,
        [Order Date].Calendar.Month.MEMBERS ON ROWS
FROM    Sales
WHERE  (Measures.MovAvg3M)
```

The **AVG** function returns the average of an expression evaluated over a set. The **LAG(2)** function obtains the month preceding the current one by 2 months. The range operator returns the set containing the 3 months over which the average of the number of orders is computed. Since the Northwind cube contains sales data starting from July 2016, the average for this month would be equal to the number of orders, as there are no prior data, while the average for August 2016 will be computed from the data from July and August 2016. From September 2006 onward, the average will be computed from the current month and the prior 2 months.

6.1.10 Filtering

As its name suggests, filtering is used to reduce the number of axis members that are displayed. This is to be contrasted with slicing, as specified in the **WHERE** clause, since slicing does not affect selection of the axis members, but rather the values that go into them.

We have already seen the most common form of filtering, where the members of an axis that have no values are removed with the **NON EMPTY** clause. The **FILTER** function filters a set according to a specified condition. Suppose we want to show sales amount in 2017 by city and by product category. If one were only interested in top-performing cities, defined by those whose sales amount exceeds $25,000, a filter would be defined as follows:

```
SELECT Product.Category.MEMBERS ON COLUMNS,
        FILTER(Customer.City.MEMBERS, (Measures.[Sales Amount],
        [Order Date].Calendar.[2017]) > 25000) ON ROWS
FROM    Sales
WHERE  (Measures.[Sales Amount], [Order Date].Calendar.[2017])
```

As another example, the following query shows customers that in 2017 had profit margin below the one of their city.

```
WITH MEMBER Measures.[Profit%] AS
        (Measures.[Sales Amount] - Measures.[Freight]) / (Measures.[Sales Amount]),
        FORMAT_STRING = '#0.00%'
MEMBER Measures.[Profit%City] AS
        (Measures.[Profit%], Customer.Geography.CURRENTMEMBER.PARENT),
        FORMAT_STRING = '#0.00%'
SELECT { Measures.[Sales Amount], Measures.[Freight], Measures.[Net Amount],
        Measures.[Profit%], Measures.[Profit%City] } ON COLUMNS,
        FILTER(NONEMPTY(Customer.Customer.MEMBERS),
        (Measures.[Profit%]) < (Measures.[Profit%City])) ON ROWS
FROM    Sales
WHERE [Order Date].Calendar.[2017]
```

Here, Profit% computes the profit percentage of the current member, and Profit%City applies Profit% to the parent of the current member, that is, the profit of the state to which the city belongs.

6.1.11 Sorting

In cube queries, all the members in a dimension have a hierarchical order. For example, consider the query below:

```
SELECT Measures.MEMBERS ON COLUMNS,
        Customer.Geography.Country.MEMBERS ON ROWS
FROM    Sales
```

In the above queries, the countries are displayed in the hierarchical order determined by the **Continent** level (the topmost level of the **Geography** hierarchy), that is, first the European countries, then the North American countries, and so on. If we wanted the countries sorted by their name, we can use the **ORDER** function, whose syntax is given next.

```
ORDER(Set, Expression [, ASC | DESC | BASC | BDESC])
```

The expression can be a numeric or string expression. The default sort order is **ASC**. The 'B' prefix indicates that the hierarchical order can be broken. The hierarchical order first sorts members according to their position in the hierarchy, and then it sorts each level. The nonhierarchical order sorts members in the set independently of the hierarchy. In the previous query, the set of countries can be ordered regardless of the hierarchy in the following way:

```
SELECT Measures.MEMBERS ON COLUMNS,
        ORDER(Customer.Geography.Country.MEMBERS,
        Customer.Geography.CURRENTMEMBER.NAME, BASC) ON ROWS
FROM    Sales
```

Here, the property **NAME** returns the name of a level, dimension, member, or hierarchy. A similar property, **UNIQUENAME**, returns the corresponding unique name. The answer to this query will show the countries in alphabetical order, that is, Argentina, Australia, Austria, and so on.

It is often the case that the ordering is based on an actual measure. To sort the query above based on the sales amount, we can proceed as follows:

```
SELECT Measures.MEMBERS ON COLUMNS,
        ORDER(Customer.Geography.Country.MEMBERS,
        Measures.[Sales Amount], BDESC) ON ROWS
FROM    Sales
```

Sorting on multiple criteria is difficult to express in MDX. Unlike in SQL, the ORDER function allows a *single* expression for sorting. Suppose, for instance, that we want to analyze the sales amount by continent and category that we want to order the result first by continent name and then by category name. For this we need to use the GENERATE function.

```
SELECT Measures.[Sales Amount] ON COLUMNS,
        NON EMPTY GENERATE(
        ORDER( Customer.Geography.Continent.ALLMEMBERS,
        Customer.Geography.CURRENTMEMBER.NAME, BASC ),
        ORDER( { Customer.Geography.CURRENTMEMBER } *
        Product.Categories.Category.ALLMEMBERS,
        Product.Categories.CURRENTMEMBER.NAME, BASC ) ) ON ROWS
FROM    Sales
```

In the first argument of the GENERATE function, we sort the continents in ascending order of their name. In the second argument, we cross join the current continent with the categories sorted in ascending order of their name.

6.1.12 Top and Bottom Analysis

When displaying information such as the best-selling cities based on sales amount, a usual requirement is to limit the query to, say, the top three. The HEAD function returns the first members in the set based on the number that one requests. A similar function TAIL returns a subset from the end of the set. The query "Top three best-selling store cities" is expressed as follows:

```
SELECT Measures.MEMBERS ON COLUMNS,
        HEAD(ORDER(Customer.Geography.City.MEMBERS,
        Measures.[Sales Amount], BDESC), 3) ON ROWS
FROM    Sales
```

The function TOPCOUNT can also be used to answer the previous query.

```
SELECT Measures.MEMBERS ON COLUMNS,
        TOPCOUNT(Customer.Geography.City.MEMBERS, 3,
        Measures.[Sales Amount]) ON ROWS
FROM    Sales
```

As a more elaborate example, suppose that we want to display the top three cities based on sales amount together with their combined sales, and the combined sales of all the other cities. This can be written as follows:

```
WITH SET SetTop3Cities AS TOPCOUNT(
        Customer.Geography.City.MEMBERS, 3, [Sales Amount])
MEMBER Customer.Geography.[Top 3 Cities] AS
        AGGREGATE(SetTop3Cities)
MEMBER Customer.Geography.[Other Cities] AS
        (Customer.[All]) - (Customer.[Top 3 Cities])
SELECT Measures.MEMBERS ON COLUMNS,
        { SetTop3Cities, [Top 3 Cities], [Other Cities], Customer.[All] } ON ROWS
FROM    Sales
```

The query starts by selecting the three best-selling cities and denotes this set SetTop3Cities. Then, it adds two members to the Geography hierarchy. The first one, called Top 3 Cities, contains the aggregation of the measures of the elements in the set SetTop3Cities. The other member, called Other Cities, contains the difference between the measures of the member Customer.[All] and the measures of the member Top 3 Cities. The AGGREGATE function aggregates each measure using the aggregation operator specified for each measure. Thus, for measures Unit Price and Discount the average is used, while for the other measures the sum is applied.

Other functions exist for top filter processing. The TOPPERCENT and TOPSUM functions return the top elements whose cumulative total is at least a specified percentage or a specified value, respectively. For example, the next query displays the list of cities whose sales count accounts for 30% of all the sales.

```
SELECT Measures.[Sales Amount] ON COLUMNS,
        { TOPPERCENT(Customer.Geography.City.MEMBERS, 30,
        Measures.[Sales Amount]), Customer.Geography.[All] } ON ROWS
FROM    Sales
```

There is also an analogous series of BOTTOM functions, returning the bottom items in a list. For example, in the above query we could use the BOTTOMSUM function to obtain the bottom cities whose cumulative sales amount is less than, say, $10,000.

6.1.13 Aggregation Functions

MDX provides many aggregation functions. We have seen already the SUM and AVG functions. Other functions, like MEDIAN, MAX, MIN, VAR, and STDDEV compute, respectively, the median, maximum, minimum, variance, and standard deviation of tuples in a set based on a numeric value. For example, the following query analyzes each product category to see the total, maximum, minimum, and average sales amount for a 1-month period in 2017.

```
WITH MEMBER Measures.[Maximum Sales] AS
        MAX(DESCENDANTS([Order Date].Calendar.Year.[2017],
        [Order Date].Calendar.Month), Measures.[Sales Amount])
MEMBER Measures.[Minimum Sales] AS
        MIN(DESCENDANTS([Order Date].Calendar.Year.[2017],
        [Order Date].Calendar.Month), Measures.[Sales Amount])
MEMBER Measures.[Average Sales] AS
        AVG(DESCENDANTS([Order Date].Calendar.Year.[2017],
        [Order Date].Calendar.Month), Measures.[Sales Amount])
SELECT { [Sales Amount], [Maximum Sales], [Minimum Sales], [Average Sales] }
        ON COLUMNS,
        Product.Categories.Category.MEMBERS ON ROWS
FROM   Sales
```

Our next query computes the maximum sales by category as well as the month in which they occurred.

```
WITH MEMBER Measures.[Maximum Sales] AS
        MAX(DESCENDANTS([Order Date].Calendar.Year.[2017],
        [Order Date].Calendar.Month), Measures.[Sales Amount])
MEMBER Measures.[Maximum Period] AS
        TOPCOUNT(DESCENDANTS([Order Date].Calendar.Year.[2017],
        [Order Date].Calendar.Month), 1, Measures.[Sales Amount]).ITEM(0).NAME
SELECT { [Maximum Sales], [Maximum Period] } ON COLUMNS,
        Product.Categories.Category.MEMBERS ON ROWS
FROM   Sales
```

Here, the TOPCOUNT function obtains the tuple corresponding to the maximum sales amount. Then, the ITEM function retrieves the first member from the specified tuple, and the NAME function obtains the name of this member.

The COUNT function counts the number of tuples in a set. It has an optional parameter, with values INCLUDEEMPTY or EXCLUDEEMPTY, which states whether to include or exclude empty cells. For example, the COUNT function can be used to compute the number of customers that purchased a particular product category. This can be done by counting the number of tuples obtained by joining the sales amount and customer names. Excluding empty cells is necessary to restrict the count to those customers for which there are sales in the corresponding product category as shown below.

```
WITH MEMBER Measures.[Customer Count] AS
        COUNT({Measures.[Sales Amount] *
        [Customer].[Company Name].MEMBERS}, EXCLUDEEMPTY)
SELECT { Measures.[Sales Amount], Measures.[Customer Count] } ON COLUMNS,
        Product.Category.MEMBERS ON ROWS
FROM   Sales
```

6.2 Introduction to DAX

DAX (Data Analysis Expressions) is a functional language used to perform calculations on a tabular model. As already seen in Sect. 5.9.2, the tabular model is composed of tables, columns, and relationships. An important characteristic of DAX is that the existing relationships between tables, typically those represented by referential integrity, are *implicitly* used in queries. This is different from SQL, where join terms must be *explicitly* used when combining data from two tables. The fact that relationships are implicit in DAX makes queries easier to write for users. In addition, a DAX expression is evaluated in a particular context, in which filters on the tables are automatically applied. More precisely, this means that an aggregation does not necessarily include all the rows of a table, but only those that appear active in the current evaluation context. It is important to stress that understanding context and context changes is one of the most difficult aspects of DAX.

6.2.1 Expressions

DAX is a typed language that supports the following **data types**: integer numbers, floating-point numbers, currency (a fixed decimal number with four digits of fixed precision that is stored as an integer), datetimes, Boolean, string, and binary large object (BLOB). The type system determines the resulting type of an expression based on the terms used in it.

Functions are used to perform calculations on a data model. Most functions have input arguments, or parameters, and these may be required or optional. A function returns a value when it is executed, which may be a single value or a table. DAX provides multiple functions to perform calculations, including date and time functions, logical functions, statistical functions, mathematical and trigonometric functions, financial functions, etc.

DAX provides several types of **operators**, namely, arithmetic (+, -, *, /), comparison (=, <>, >, etc.), text concatenation (&), and logical operators (&& and ||||, corresponding to logical and and logical or). Operators are overloaded, that is, an operator behaves differently depending on its arguments.

Expressions are constructed with elements of a data model (such as tables, columns, or measures), functions, operators, or constants. They are used to define measures, calculated columns, calculated tables, or queries. An expression for a measure or a calculated column must return a scalar value, such as a number or a string, while an expression for a calculated table or a query must return a table. Recall that we have already used DAX expressions for defining measures and calculated columns when we defined the tabular model for the Northwind case study in Sect. 5.9.2.

A table in a data model includes both columns and measures. These can be referenced in an expression for example as 'Sales'[Quantity], where the

quotes can be omited if the table name does not start with a number, does
not contain spaces, and is not a reserved word like **Date** or **Sum**. In addition,
the table name can be omitted if the expression is written in the same context
as the table that includes the referenced column or measure. However, it is
common practice to write the table name for a column reference, such as the
example above, and omit the table name for a measure reference, such as
[Sales Amount]. This improves readability and maintainability, since column
and measure references have different calculation semantics.

Measures are used to aggregate values from multiple rows in a table. An
example is given next, which uses the **SUM** aggregate function.

Sales[Sales Amount] := SUM(Sales[SalesAmount])

DAX requires a measure to be defined in a table, which is table **Sales** in this
case. The above expression is just a shortcut for an iterator function **SUMX**
with two arguments, the table to scan and an expression to evaluate for every
row of the table, as in the following example.

Sales[Total Cost] := SUMX(Sales, Sales[Quantity] * Sales[UnitCost])

A measure can reference other measures as shown next.

Sales[Margin] := [Sales Amount] - [Total Cost]
Sales[Margin %] := [Margin] / [Sales Amount]

Other aggregation functions include **MIN, MAX, COUNT, AVERAGE**, and
STDDEV, all of which have a corresponding iterator function with an **X** suffix.
The first argument of many aggregation functions is a table expression, as in
the above examples. However, a table expression may include a table function.
For example, the **FILTER** function reads rows from a table expression and
returns a table that has only the rows that sastisfy the logical condition in
the second argument, as in the following example.

SUMX (FILTER (Sales, Sales[UnitPrice] >= 10), Sales[Quantity] * Sales[UnitPrice])

Calculated columns are derived by an expression and can be used like
any other column. An example is given next.

Employee[Age] = INT(YEARFRAC(Employee[BirthDate], TODAY()))

Here, **TODAY** returns the current date, **YEARFRAC** returns the year fraction
representing the number of days between two dates, and **INT** rounds a number
down to the nearest integer. Calculated columns are computed during database processing and stored into the model. This contrasts with SQL, where
calculated columns are computed at query time and do not use memory. As
a consequence, computing complex calculated columns in DAX is done at
process time and not query time, resulting in a better user experience.

Variables can be used to avoid repeating the same subexpression. The
following example classifies customers according to their total sales.

```
Customer[Class] =
    VAR TotalSales = SUM( Sales[SalesAmount] )
RETURN
    SWITCH( TRUE, TotalSales > 1000, "A", TotalSales > 100, "B", "C" )
```

Here, **SWITCH** returns different results depending on the value of an expression. Variables can be of any scalar data type, including tables.

Calculated tables are derived by an expression and are materialized in the model. A typical scenario for using a calculated table is to generate a Date table when it is not available in the data sources. In the example shown next, we assume that the Sales table contains a column OrderDate.

```
Date =
    VAR MinYear = YEAR( MIN( Sales[OrderDate] ) )
    VAR MaxYear = YEAR( MAX( Sales[OrderDate] ) )
RETURN
ADDCOLUMNS(
    FILTER(
        CALENDARAUTO(),
        YEAR( [Date] ) >= MinYear && YEAR( [Date] ) <= MaxYear ),
    "Year", YEAR( [Date] ), "Month Name", FORMAT( [Date], "mmmm" ),
    "Month Number", MONTH( [Date] ) )
```

The **CALENDARAUTO** function searches in all dates of the data model and returns a table with a single column named Date containing all the dates from the first day of the year of the minimum date to the last day of the year of the maximum date. Since this may include irrelevant dates, such as customers' birth dates, the **FILTER** function fixes the date range to the years in the existing transactions of the Sales table. Finally, the **ADDCOLUMNS** function returns a table with new columns specified by the expressions.

6.2.2 Evaluation Context

A DAX expression is evaluated inside a **context**, which is the environment under which the formula is evaluated. The evaluation context has two different components. The **filter context** is the set of filters that identifies the active rows in a table, while the **row context** is the single row that is active in a table for evaluating column references.

For analyzing the filter context, consider Fig. 6.2. Each cell of the PivotTable evaluates the expression independently from the other cells. In a given cell, because the category name is on the rows and the year is on the columns, each row of the PivotTable can only see the subset of the rows of the Sales table that concerns the products of that category and that year. This is the set of filters applied to the database prior to the formula evaluation. The only case where no filtering happens is in the grand total, where the entire database is visible. It is worth noting that any filter applied to a table

Total Sales	Column Labels ▼			
Row Labels ▼	⊞2016	⊞2017	⊞2018	Grand Total
⊞Beverages	$41.934,68	$91.831,81	$103.437,42	$237.203,91
⊞Condiments	$14.781,46	$46.105,02	$30.642,33	$91.528,81
⊞Confections	$29.094,55	$81.585,99	$51.763,37	$162.443,91
⊞Dairy Products	$38.781,09	$109.431,14	$72.945,07	$221.157,31
⊞Grains/Cereals	$9.129,92	$50.323,62	$21.417,04	$80.870,58
⊞Meat/Poultry	$27.949,06	$74.609,43	$36.869,69	$139.428,18
⊞Produce	$12.257,62	$53.154,27	$24.804,25	$90.216,14
⊞Seafood	$17.921,49	$63.158,33	$41.227,21	$122.307,02
Grand Total	$191.849,87	$570.199,61	$383.106,38	$1.145.155,86

Fig. 6.2 Displaying the Sales Amount measure in a PivotTable

automatically propagates to other tables in the data model by following the filter propagation directions, as specified in the relationships existing between the tables. For example, the filter propagation directions can be seen in the tabular model given in Fig. 5.36.

We explain now the row context. Consider the calculated column NetAmount defined by the following expression.

Sales[NetAmount] = Sales[SalesAmount] - Sales[Freight]

This expression is valid only when it is possible to identify a notion of "current row" in the Sales table from which the value of the columns are obtained. Thus, the row context is active for expressions defining a calculated column, the argument executed in an iterator function (such as the functions with an X suffix such as SUMX), or the filter expression for a security role. A row context does not propagate automatically to other tables, although it can be propagated to another table by using the RELATED function.

The functions CALCULATE and CALCULATETABLE modify a filter context before executing an expression. The main difference between the two functions is that the former returns a single value whereas the latter returns a table. For example, the CALCULATE function requires a first argument which is an expression that may be followed by a set of filter expressions (if any) as in the following example

CALCULATE(SUM(Sales[SalesAmount]), Product[Category] = "Beverages",
    Product[UnitPrice] > 10)

In this case, the CALCULATE function procedes as follows: (1) saves the current filter context, (2) evaluates each filter argument and produces for each of them the list of valid values for the column, (3) uses the new condition to replace the existing filters in the model, (4) computes the expression of the first argument in the new filter context, and (5) restores the original filter context and returns the computed result.

Another task performed by the CALCULATE function is to transform any existing row context into an equivalent filter context. For example, in the following expression

SUMX(Product, CALCULATE(SUM(Sales[SalesAmount])))

the row context in **Product** is transformed into an equivalent filter context which automatically propagates to the **Sales** table through the existing relationship in the data model between **Product** and **Sales**.

6.2.3 Queries

A **query** is an expression that returns a table. The syntax is as follows:

```
[ DEFINE
    { MEASURE ⟨ tableName ⟩ [ ⟨ name ⟩ ] = ⟨ expression ⟩ }
    { VAR ⟨ name ⟩ = ⟨ expression ⟩ } ]
EVALUATE ⟨ table ⟩
[ ORDER BY { ⟨ expression ⟩ [ {ASC | DESC} ] } [ , ... ]
[ START AT { ⟨ value ⟩ | ⟨ parameter ⟩ } [ , ... ] ] ]
```

The most basic query is defined by an **EVALUATE** statement containing a table expression. An example is as follows.

```
EVALUATE
SUMMARIZECOLUMNS( Customer[Country], 'Date'[Year], "Total Sales", [Total Sales] )
ORDER BY [Country], [Year]
```

The **SUMMARIZECOLUMNS** function returns a summary table aggregated by customer country and by year showing the **Total Sales** measure. Recall from Sect. 5.9.2 that we defined this measure in the tabular model. The optional **ORDER BY** clause sorts the result. Alternatively, we could use

```
ORDER BY [Total Sales] DESC
```

to sort the result of the above query in descending order of total sales. An optional **START AT** keyword, which is used inside an **ORDER BY** clause, can be used to define the value at which the query results begin.

The optional **DEFINE** clause is used to define measures or variables that are local to the query. Definitions can reference other definitions that appear before or after the current definition. The next example displays all measures by category and supplier.

```
DEFINE
    MEASURE Sales[Sales Amount] = SUM( [SalesAmount] )
    MEASURE Sales[Freight] = SUM( [Freight] )
    MEASURE Sales[Avg Unit Price] = AVERAGE( [UnitPrice] )
    MEASURE Sales[Quantity] = SUM( [Quantity] )
    MEASURE Sales[Avg Discount] = AVERAGE( [Discount] )
EVALUATE
SUMMARIZECOLUMNS(
    Product[CategoryName], Supplier[CompanyName], "Sales Amount", [Sales Amount],
    "Freight", [Freight], "Avg Unit Price", [Avg Unit Price],
    "Quantity", [Quantity], "Avg Discount", [Avg Discount] )
ORDER BY [CategoryName], [CompanyName]
```

Notice that not all the measures above are additive, which is why we used the **AVERAGE** aggregate function for Unit Price and Discount.

Consider now the next query, which shows the total, minimum, and maximum sales amount by country and category.

```
DEFINE
    MEASURE Sales[Sales Amount] = SUM( [SalesAmount] )
    MEASURE Sales[Min Amount] = MIN( [SalesAmount] )
    MEASURE Sales[Max Amount] = MAX( [SalesAmount] )
EVALUATE
SUMMARIZECOLUMNS(
    Customer[Country], Product[CategoryName], "Sales Amount", [Sales Amount],
    "Min Amount", [Min Amount], "Max Amount", [Max Amount] )
ORDER BY [Country]
```

The above query will not show the rows without sales for a country and a category. Recall that to achieve this in MDX we need to explicitly add the **NON EMPTY** keyword. If we want to show the rows without sales we need to explicitly replace the measures with a zero value as shown next.

```
MEASURE Sales[Sales Amount] =
    IF( ISBLANK( SUM( [SalesAmount] ) ), 0, SUM( [SalesAmount] ) )
```

In DAX, **BLANK** denotes the absence of a value, which corresponds to the **NULL** value in SQL although it behaves differently, and **ISBLANK** returns true if the expression passed as argument is **BLANK**. The above expression uses the **IF** function, which returns the value passed in the second or the third argument depending on whether the expression in the first argument is true.

The **ROLLUP** function computes subtotals over grouping columns. The next query asks for the sales by customer state and country.

```
DEFINE
    MEASURE Sales[Sales Amount] = SUM( [SalesAmount] )
EVALUATE
SUMMARIZE(
    Customer, ROLLUP( Customer[Country], Customer[State] ),
    "Sales Amount", [Sales Amount] )
ORDER BY [Country], [State]
```

Note that the **ROLLUP** function must be used with the **SUMMARIZE** function, which is similar to the **SUMMARIZECOLUMNS** function introduced above.

6.2.4 Filtering

Filtering is an essential operation in data analysis, and this is especially the case in data warehouses, where we need to obtain insight from huge volumes of data. Consider the next query, which computes the sales amount by category and quarter.

```
DEFINE
    MEASURE Sales[Sales Amount] = SUM( [SalesAmount] )
EVALUATE
SUMMARIZECOLUMNS(
    Product[CategoryName], 'Date'[Year], 'Date'[Quarter], "Sales Amount", [Sales Amount] )
ORDER BY [CategoryName], [Year], [Quarter]
```

Suppose that in the above query we would like to focus only on sales to European customers. This can be done as follows.

```
DEFINE
    MEASURE Sales[Sales Amount] = SUM( [SalesAmount] )
EVALUATE
SUMMARIZECOLUMNS(
    Product[CategoryName], 'Date'[Year], 'Date'[Quarter],
    FILTER( Customer, Customer[Continent] = "Europe" ),
    "Sales Amount", [Sales Amount] )
ORDER BY [CategoryName], [Year], [Quarter]
```

The FILTER function returns the rows of a table that satisfy a condition. In this case, the result of the query will have the same number of rows as the previous one without a filter, although the aggregated values will only consider sales to European customers. On the other hand, the following query focuses only on the beverages and condiments categories.

```
DEFINE
    MEASURE Sales[Sales Amount] = SUM( [SalesAmount] )
EVALUATE
SUMMARIZECOLUMNS(
    Product[CategoryName], 'Date'[Year], 'Date'[Quarter],
    FILTER( Product, Product[CategoryName] IN { "Condiments", "Beverages" } ),
    "Sales Amount", [Sales Amount] )
ORDER BY [CategoryName], [Year], [Quarter]
```

In this case, the resulting table will display only rows pertaining to one of the two categories. Notice that several filters can be applied at the same time as shown in the next query.

```
DEFINE
    MEASURE Sales[Sales Amount] = SUM( [SalesAmount] )
EVALUATE
SUMMARIZECOLUMNS(
    Product[CategoryName], 'Date'[Year], 'Date'[Quarter],
    FILTER( Customer, Customer[Continent] = "Europe" ),
    FILTER( Product, Product[CategoryName] IN { "Condiments", "Beverages" } ),
    FILTER( 'Date', 'Date'[Year] = 2017 ),
    "Sales Amount", [Sales Amount] )
ORDER BY [CategoryName], [Year], [Quarter]
```

Consider again the roll-up query of the previous section, which asks for the sales by customer state and country. Using filtering we can restrict that query to only European customers as shown next.

```
DEFINE
    MEASURE Sales[Sales Amount] = SUM( [SalesAmount] )
EVALUATE
SUMMARIZE(
    FILTER( Customer, Customer[Continent] = "Europe" ),
    ROLLUP( Customer[Country], Customer[State] ),
    "Sales Amount", [Sales Amount] )
ORDER BY [Country], [State]
```

Consider now the following query, which displays the percentage profit of sales for Nordic countries.

```
DEFINE
    MEASURE Sales[Sales Amount] = SUM( [SalesAmount] )
    MEASURE Sales[Freight] = SUM( [Freight] )
    MEASURE Sales[Profit %] = ( [Sales Amount] - [Freight] )/ [Sales Amount]
EVALUATE
SUMMARIZECOLUMNS(
    Customer[Country],
    FILTER( Customer, Customer[Country] IN
        { "Denmark", "Finland", "Norway", "Sweden" } ),
    "Sales Amount", [Sales Amount], "Freight", [Freight], "Profit %", [Profit %] )
ORDER BY [Country]
```

The filter above, like all the previous ones, is *static* in the sense that it always shows the aggregate values for the given countries. Suppose now that we would like to display only the countries with an overall sales amount greater than $25,000. In this case, the filter would be *dynamic*, since different countries will be shown depending on the contents of the database.

```
DEFINE
    MEASURE Sales[Sales Amount] = SUM( [SalesAmount] )
    MEASURE Sales[Freight] = SUM( [Freight] )
    MEASURE Sales[Profit %] = ( [Sales Amount] - [Freight] ) / [Sales Amount]
EVALUATE
FILTER(
    SUMMARIZECOLUMNS(
        Customer[Country], "Sales Amount", [Sales Amount], "Freight", [Freight],
        "Profit %", [Profit %] ),
    [Sales Amount] > 25000 )
ORDER BY [Sales Amount] DESC
```

As another example of dynamic filtering, suppose we want to show sales amount in 2018 by city and by product category for top-performing cities in 2017, defined as those whose overall sales amount in 2017 exceeds $25,000. This can be written as follows.

```
DEFINE
    MEASURE Sales[Sales Amount] = SUM( [SalesAmount] )
EVALUATE
SUMMARIZECOLUMNS(
    Customer[City], Product[CategoryName],
    FILTER( 'Date', 'Date'[Year] = 2018 ),
```

```
    FILTER(
        SUMMARIZECOLUMNS(
            Customer[City], FILTER( 'Date', 'Date'[Year] = 2017 ),
            "Sales Amount", Sales[Sales Amount] ),
        [Sales Amount] > 25000 ),
    "Sales Amount", Sales[Sales Amount] )
ORDER BY [City], [CategoryName]
```

The inner **SUMMARIZECOLUMNS** aggregates sales in 2017 by city, while the outer one aggregates sales in 2018 by city and category for the top-performing cities in 2017.

The **FILTER** function can also be used for defining measures, as in the next query, which compares the overall sales with the European sales by category.

```
DEFINE
    MEASURE Sales[World Sales] = SUM( [SalesAmount] )
    MEASURE Sales[European Sales] =
        CALCULATE( SUM( [SalesAmount] ),
            FILTER( Customer, Customer[Continent] = "Europe" ) )
    MEASURE Sales[Sales %] = [European Sales] / [World Sales]
EVALUATE
SUMMARIZECOLUMNS(
    Product[CategoryName], "World Sales", [World Sales],
    "European Sales", [European Sales], "Sales %", [Sales %] )
ORDER BY [CategoryName]
```

Recall from Sect. 6.2.2 that the **CALCULATE** function evaluates an expression in a context modified by filters, in this case restricted to European customers. As a more elaborate example, the following query classifies orders in three categories according to their total sales amount and displays by month the total number of orders as well as the number of orders per category.

```
DEFINE
MEASURE Sales[Sales Amount] = SUM( Sales[SalesAmount] )
MEASURE Sales[Order Count] = DISTINCTCOUNT( Sales[OrderNo] )
MEASURE Sales[Order Count A] =
    COUNTROWS(
        FILTER( VALUES( Sales[OrderNo] ), CALCULATE( [Sales Amount] <= 1000 ) ) )
MEASURE Sales[Order Count B] =
    COUNTROWS(
        FILTER( VALUES( Sales[OrderNo] ),
            CALCULATE( [Sales Amount] > 1000 && [Sales Amount] <= 10000 ) ) )
MEASURE Sales[Order Count C] =
    COUNTROWS(
        FILTER( VALUES( Sales[OrderNo] ), CALCULATE( [Sales Amount] > 10000 ) ) )
EVALUATE
SUMMARIZECOLUMNS( 'Date'[MonthNumber], 'Date'[Year],
    "Order Count", [Order Count], "Order Count A", [Order Count A],
    "Order Count B", [Order Count B], "Order Count C", [Order Count C] )
ORDER BY [Year], [MonthNumber]
```

Function **DISTINCTCOUNT** counts the number of distinct values, while function **COUNTROWS** counts the number of rows in a table.

6.2.5 Hierarchy Handling

As we have seen in Sect. 5.9.2, hierarchies can be defined in a tabular data model. However, as opposed to MDX, which provides functions for relative navigation such as accessing the parent or the children of the current member, hierarchies in DAX are somehow difficult to manipulate, given the limited available functions provided for this purpose. Further, we already mentioned that DAX does not currently support parent-child hierarchies.

Assume a traditional business scenario where we want to compare a measure for a member with that of its parent. For example, the following query computes the ratio of the sales of a city with those of its country.

```
DEFINE
    MEASURE Sales[Sales Amount] = SUM( [SalesAmount] )
    MEASURE Sales[Sales Amount %] = SUM( [SalesAmount] ) /
        CALCULATE( SUM( Sales[SalesAmount] ), ALL( Customer[City] ) )
EVALUATE
SUMMARIZECOLUMNS(
    Customer[City], Customer[Country], "Sales Amount", [Sales Amount],
    "Sales Amount %", FORMAT( [Sales Amount %], "Percent" ) )
ORDER BY [Country], [City]
```

The **ALL** function removes any filter from the customer city column. Since the customer country is used in the **SUMMARIZECOLUMNS** function as a grouping column, this has the effect of setting a context filter, so the ratio is computed for all cities of that country. If we remove this column, the ratio would instead be computed with respect to all cities. The query also shows the **FORMAT** function, which formats output values, in this case percentages.

If we would like to restrict the above query so that it only shows data for European cities, this can be done by adding a filter as follows.

```
DEFINE
    MEASURE Sales[Sales Amount] = SUM( [SalesAmount] )
    MEASURE Sales[Sales Amount %] = SUM( [SalesAmount] ) /
        CALCULATE( SUM( Sales[SalesAmount] ), ALLSELECTED( Customer[City] ) )
EVALUATE
SUMMARIZECOLUMNS(
    Customer[City], Customer[Country],
    FILTER( Customer, Customer[Continent] = "Europe" ),
    "Sales Amount", [Sales Amount], "Sales Amount %", [Sales Amount %] )
ORDER BY [Country], [City]
```

Notice that we used the **ALLSELECTED** function, which removes any context filters from the customer city column while keeping explicit filters. Using **ALL** instead would give the wrong results. This is just an example of the complexities of context changes, whose explanation goes beyond this introduction to DAX.

The following query shows the customers that in 2017 had profit margins below that of their city.

```
DEFINE
    MEASURE Sales[Sales Amount] = SUM( [SalesAmount] )
    MEASURE Sales[Net Amount] = SUM( [SalesAmount] ) - SUM( [Freight] )
    MEASURE Sales[Profit %] = [Net Amount] / [Sales Amount]
    MEASURE Sales[Profit % City] =
        CALCULATE( [Profit %], ALL( Customer[CompanyName] ) )
EVALUATE
FILTER(
    SUMMARIZECOLUMNS(
        Customer[CompanyName], Customer[City],FILTER( 'Date', 'Date'[Year] = 2017 ),
        "Sales Amount", [Sales Amount], "Net Amount", [Net Amount],
        "Profit %", [Profit %], "Profit % City", [Profit % City] ),
    NOT ISBLANK([Profit %]) && [Profit %] < [Profit % City] )
ORDER BY [CompanyName]
```

With the **SUMMARIZECOLUMNS** function we compute the profit margin
of the customers and those of their corresponding city. The resulting table
is then passed on to the **FILTER** function, which, in addition to testing the
condition of the query with respect to the profit margin, also uses the negated
ISBLANK function to ensure that the customer actually has sales in 2017. This
is necessary because blanks are replaced by zero in comparisons in DAX.

6.2.6 Time-Related Calculations

DAX provides a set of functions, referred to as time intelligence functions,
that enable time-related calculations such as year to date, same period last
year, period growth, etc. As we have seen in Sect. 5.9.2, an important requirement for such functions is that the data model must contain a date dimension.
It is important to note that the time intelligence functions only work with a
standard Gregorian calendar. Performing such calculations with a fiscal calendar or using periods based on weeks requires rewriting the inherent logic of
the time intelligence functions using functions like **FILTER** and **CALCULATE**.
In this section we only cover calculations using a standard calendar.

We start by illustrating the calculations that compare the value of a measure with respect to the value a number of periods forward or back in time.
For example, the next query compares net amount values from one quarter
with those of the same quarter in the previous year.

```
DEFINE
    MEASURE Sales[Net Amount] = SUM( [NetAmount] )
    MEASURE Sales[Net Amount PY] =
        CALCULATE( [Net Amount], PARALLELPERIOD('Date'[Date], -4, Quarter ) )
    MEASURE Sales[Net Amount Growth] = [Net Amount] - [Net Amount PY]
EVALUATE
SUMMARIZECOLUMNS(
    'Date'[Quarter], 'Date'[Year], "Net Amount", [Net Amount],
    "Net Amount PY", [Net Amount PY], "Net Amount Growth", [Net Amount Growth] )
ORDER BY [Year], [Quarter]
```

The **PARALLELPERIOD** function above shifts the dates four quarters (that is, one year) back in time. The above query could be written by using the **DATEADD** function. Nevertheless, the two functions are not equivalent, since **PARALLELPERIOD** returns full periods at the month, quarter, and year granularity, while **DATEADD** also works at the day granularity. Notice also that since the Northwind cube contains sales data starting from July 2016, for the first four quarters the value of **Net Amount PY** will be blank and thus, the values of **Net Amount** and **Net Amount Growth** will be equal.

As another example, the following query computes the difference between the sales quantity of a month and that of the opening month of the quarter.

```
DEFINE
    MEASURE Sales[Total Qty] = SUM( [Quantity] )
    MEASURE Sales[Total Qty SoQ Diff] =
        VAR SoQ = STARTOFQUARTER( 'Date'[Date] )
    RETURN
        [Total Qty] - CALCULATE( SUM( [Quantity] ),
            DATESBETWEEN( 'Date'[Date], SoQ, ENDOFMONTH( SoQ ) ) )
EVALUATE
SUMMARIZECOLUMNS(
    'Date'[MonthName], 'Date'[Year], 'Date'[MonthNumber], "Total Qty", [Total Qty],
    "Total Qty SoQ Diff", [Total Qty SoQ Diff] )
ORDER BY [Year], [MonthNumber]
```

The functions **STARTOFQUARTER** and **ENDOFMONTH** return, respectively, the begining date of the quarter and the end date of the month, while **DATESBETWEEN** returns the dates between two given dates.

Another very common business scenario is to compute time period to date calculations. For this purpose, DAX provides the **TOTALYTD**, **TOTALQTD**, and **TOTALMTD** functions, which correspond to year, quarter, and month periods. As an example, the following query computes the year- and quarter-to-date sales.

```
DEFINE
    MEASURE Sales[Sales Amount] = SUM( [SalesAmount] )
    MEASURE Sales[Sales Amount YTD] =
        TOTALYTD( SUM( [SalesAmount] ), 'Date'[Date] )
    MEASURE Sales[Sales Amount QTD] =
        TOTALQTD( SUM( [SalesAmount] ), 'Date'[Date] )
EVALUATE
SUMMARIZECOLUMNS(
    'Date'[MonthName], 'Date'[Year], 'Date'[MonthNumber],
    "Sales Amount", [Sales Amount], "Sales Amount YTD", [Sales Amount YTD],
    "Sales Amount QTD", [Sales Amount QTD] )
ORDER BY [Year], [MonthNumber]
```

As mentioned in Sect. 6.1.9, moving averages are a common technique used to remove the effect of peaks and drops in a measure in order to display trends. The following query shows the three-month moving average of the number of orders.

```
DEFINE
    MEASURE Sales[No Orders] = DISTINCTCOUNT( Sales[OrderNo] )
    MEASURE Sales[MovAvg3M] =
        CALCULATE(
            AVERAGEX( VALUES( 'Date'[MonthNumber] ), [No Orders] ),
            DATESINPERIOD( 'Date'[Date], MAX( 'Date'[Date] ), -3, MONTH ) )
EVALUATE
SUMMARIZECOLUMNS(
    'Date'[MonthName], 'Date'[Year], 'Date'[MonthNumber],
    "No Orders", [No Orders], "MovAvg3M", [MovAvg3M] )
ORDER BY [Year], [MonthNumber]
```

The **DISTINCTCOUNT** function counts the number of distinct order numbers. The **VALUES** function returns a single-column table of month number values without duplicates, which is used in the **AVERAGEX** function to compute the average of the number of orders. The **DATESINPERIOD** function returns all the dates between the maximum date in the current context and three months before.

Another common time-related question asks for the time when something occurred. The following query displays the last order date for each customer.

```
DEFINE
    MEASURE Customer[Last Order Date] =
        MAXX( ADDCOLUMNS( Sales, "Order Date", RELATED( 'Date'[Date] ) ),
            [Order Date] )
EVALUATE
SUMMARIZECOLUMNS (
    Customer[CompanyName],
    "Last Order Date", FORMAT( [Last Order Date], "yyyy-mm-dd" ) )
ORDER BY [CompanyName]
```

The **ADDCOLUMNS** function adds to the **Sales** table a new column containing the order date using the **RELATED** function. Recall from Sect. 5.9.2 that in the tabular model the active relationship between tables **Sales** and **Date** is based on the order date. If we want instead to obtain the last shipped date of customers, this can be done as shown next.

```
DEFINE
    MEASURE Customer[Last Shipped Date] =
        MAXX( ADDCOLUMNS( Sales, "Shipped Date",
            LOOKUPVALUE( 'Date'[Date], 'Date'[DateKey], Sales[ShippedDateKey] ) ),
            [Shipped Date] )
EVALUATE
SUMMARIZECOLUMNS (
    Customer[CompanyName],
    "Last Shipped Date", FORMAT( [Last Shipped Date], "yyyy-mm-dd" ) )
ORDER BY [CompanyName]
```

The **LOOKUPVALUE** function searches for the date value in table **Date** that corresponds to the shipped date key value in table **Sales**.

All the measures we have seen until now use the active relationships between the **Date** and the **Sales** table. The following query uses the function

USERELATIONSHIP to compare the monthly sales amount as of the order date and as of the due date.

```
DEFINE
    MEASURE Sales[SalesByOrderDate] = SUM ( Sales[SalesAmount] )
    MEASURE Sales[SalesByDueDate] =
        CALCULATE (
            SUM ( Sales[SalesAmount] ),
            USERELATIONSHIP ( Sales[DueDateKey], 'Date'[DateKey] ) )
EVALUATE
SUMMARIZECOLUMNS (
    'Date'[MonthNumber], 'Date'[Year], "SalesByOrderDate", Sales[SalesByOrderDate],
    "SalesByDueDate", Sales[SalesByDueDate] )
ORDER BY [Year], [MonthNumber]
```

6.2.7 Top and Bottom Analysis

A common analysis scenario is to display the n topmost or bottommost elements of an ordered list. The following query displays the three top-performing cities with respect to the sales amount.

```
DEFINE
    MEASURE Sales[Sales Amount] = SUM( [SalesAmount] )
EVALUATE
TOPN( 3,
    SUMMARIZECOLUMNS( Customer[City], "Sales Amount", [Sales Amount] ),
    [Sales Amount], DESC )
ORDER BY [Sales Amount] DESC
```

Here we use the TOPN function, which returns a given number of top rows according to a specified expression.

As a more elaborate example, the next query displays the top three cities based on sales amount together with their combined sales, the combined sales of all the other cities, and the overall sales of all cities.

```
DEFINE
MEASURE Sales[Sales Amount] = SUM( [SalesAmount] )
    VAR Top3Cities =
        TOPN( 3,
            SUMMARIZECOLUMNS( Customer[City], "Sales Amount", [Sales Amount] ),
            [Sales Amount], DESC )
    VAR TotalTop3Cities =
        ROW("City", "Top 3 Cities",
            "Sales Amount", CALCULATE( [Sales Amount], Top3Cities ) )
    VAR AllCities =
        ROW("City", "All Cities",
            "Sales Amount", CALCULATE( [Sales Amount] ) )
    VAR OtherCities =
        ROW("City", "Other Cities",
            "Sales Amount", CALCULATE( [Sales Amount] ) -
```

```
        CALCULATE( [Sales Amount], Top3Cities ) )
EVALUATE
UNION( Top3Cities, TotalTop3Cities, OtherCities, AllCities)
ORDER BY [Sales Amount]
```

Table Top3Cities uses the TOPN function to select from the result of the SUM-MARIZECOLUMNS function the three rows with the highest sales amount values. Table TotalTop3Cities uses the ROW function to compute a single-row table aggregating the sales amount value of the top three cities. Table AllCities computes a single-row table containing the overall sales amount of all cities. Table OtherCities computes a single-row table that subtracts the overall sales amount of the top-three cities from the overall sales amount of all cities. Finally, the main query uses the UNION function to form the union of all the previously computed partial results.

Ranking is another essential analytics requirement. DAX provides the RANKX function for this purpose. For example, the following query ranks the customer countries with respect to the sales amount figures.

```
DEFINE
    MEASURE Sales[Sales Amount] = SUM ( [SalesAmount] )
EVALUATE
ADDCOLUMNS(
    SUMMARIZECOLUMNS( Customer[Country], "SalesAmount", [Sales Amount] ),
    "Country Rank", RANKX( ALL( Customer[Country] ), [Sales Amount] ) )
ORDER BY [Country Rank]
```

Suppose now that we want to add product categories to the ranking of the previous query. There are two possible ways to interpret this, which are illustrated by the two different rankings computed in the next query.

```
DEFINE
    MEASURE Sales[Sales Amount] = SUM ( [SalesAmount] )
    MEASURE Sales[Category Rank] =
        RANKX( ALL( Product[CategoryName] ), [Sales Amount] )
    MEASURE Sales[Country Rank] =
        RANKX( ALL( Customer[Country] ), [Sales Amount] )
EVALUATE
SUMMARIZECOLUMNS(
    Customer[Country], Product[CategoryName], "SalesAmount", [Sales Amount],
    "Category Rank", [Category Rank], "Country Rank", [Country Rank] )
ORDER BY [Country], [Category Rank]
```

The first ranking, Category Rank, computes for each country the rank of the categories. For example, that would give as result that in Argentina the category with the highest sales is confections. The columns stated in the ORDER BY clause above allow us to visualize this. On the other hand, Country Rank computes for each category the rank of the countries. For example, that would give as result that for the category confections the country with highest sales is United States. In order to better visualize this second ranking, the ORDER BY in the above query should be changed as follows.

ORDER BY [CategoryName], [Country Rank]

   Another common analysis requirement is to compute the best or the n topmost values within a group. As an example, we can obtain for each country its best category by modifying the above query as follows.

```
DEFINE
    MEASURE Sales[Sales Amount] = SUM ( [SalesAmount] )
    MEASURE Sales[Category Rank] =
        RANKX( ALL( Product[CategoryName] ), [Sales Amount] )
EVALUATE
SELECTCOLUMNS(
    FILTER (
        SUMMARIZECOLUMNS(
            Customer[Country], Product[CategoryName], "SalesAmount", [Sales Amount],
            "Category Rank", [Category Rank] ),
        [Category Rank] = 1 ),
    "Country", [Country], "Best Category", [CategoryName],
    "SalesAmount", [Sales Amount] )
ORDER BY [Country]
```

The **FILTER** function selects the best category for each country, while the **SELECTCOLUMNS** function projects out the rank column and renames the column with the best category.

6.2.8 Table Operations

DAX provides several functions for combining tables. Consider the following query, which lists and counts the cities assigned to employees.

```
DEFINE
    MEASURE Employee[Nb Cities] = COUNT( EmployeeGeography[City] )
    MEASURE Employee[Cities] =
        CONCATENATEX( VALUES( EmployeeGeography[City] ), [City], ", " )
EVALUATE
FILTER(
    SUMMARIZECOLUMNS(
        Employee[EmployeeName], "Nb Cities", [Nb Cities], "Cities", [Cities] ),
    [EmployeeName] <> BLANK() )
ORDER BY [EmployeeName]
```

Here, **COUNT** counts the number of cities, while **CONCATENATEX** returns a string that concatenates all the cities separated by commas.

   Suppose now that we want to know the number of customers and the number of suppliers of each country. Remember from Sect. 5.9.2 that in the tabular model we defined star dimensions for the **Customer** and **Supplier** tables, each one materializing the shared **Geography** hierarchy. Therefore, from DAX's perspective, the countries of the customers and of the suppliers are unrelated and we cannot leverage any relationship between the two for filtering these measures according to the current context in the main query.

This brings us to the concept of **data lineage**. In DAX, every column in a table, including derived ones, is associated with a tag that identifies the original column in the data model from which its values originated. To solve the above query, we could use the function TREATAS, as shown next.

```
DEFINE
    MEASURE Sales[Nb Customers] = COUNT( Customer[CompanyName] )
    MEASURE Sales[Nb Suppliers] =
        CALCULATE( COUNT(Supplier[CompanyName] ),
            TREATAS( VALUES( Customer[Country] ), Supplier[Country] ) )
EVALUATE
SUMMARIZECOLUMNS(
    Customer[Country], "Nb Customers", [Nb Customers], "Nb Suppliers", [Nb Suppliers] )
ORDER BY [Country]
```

The function TREATAS modifies the data lineage and makes customer countries behave as supplier countries when calculating the measure. Thus, by using customer country as a grouping column in SUMMARIZECOLUMNS, we obtain the number of suppliers for that country.

As said above, in the tabular model there is not a single table containing all countries, instead countries are associated to customers, suppliers, and employees independently. We need to use set operations to combine the countries appearing in three different tables. DAX provides the following set operations: UNION, INTERSECT, and EXCEPT, the latter one being the set difference. For example, the following query computes the union without duplicates of the customer and supplier countries.

```
EVALUATE
DISTINCT( UNION( VALUES( Customer[Country] ), VALUES( Supplier[Country] ) ) )
ORDER BY [Country]
```

As shown in the query, the UNION function keeps duplicate values, which are removed with the DISTINCT function. It is worth mentioning that the result of the union above has no data lineage.

DAX provides the following functions for performing various kinds of joins: NATURALINNERJOIN, NATURALLEFTOUTERJOIN, and CROSSJOIN. The first two functions join the tables on common columns of the same name, while the last function performs a Cartesian product.

NATURALINNERJOIN and NATURALLEFTOUTERJOIN only join columns from the same source table. In order to join two columns with the same name that have no relationship, it is necessary to either use the TREATAS function explained above or to write the column using an expression that breaks the data lineage. This is shown in the next query, which computes the number of customers and suppliers for all customer and supplier countries.

```
DEFINE
    MEASURE Sales[Nb Customers] = COUNT( Customer[CompanyName] )
    MEASURE Sales[Nb Suppliers] = COUNT( Supplier[CompanyName] )
    VAR T1 =
        SELECTCOLUMNS(
```

```
        SUMMARIZECOLUMNS(
            Customer[Country], "Nb Customers", [Nb Customers] ),
        "Country", [Country] & "", "Nb Customers", [Nb Customers] )
    VAR T2 =
        SELECTCOLUMNS(
            SUMMARIZECOLUMNS(
                Supplier[Country], "Nb Suppliers", [Nb Suppliers] ),
            "Country", [Country] & "", "Nb Suppliers", [Nb Suppliers] )
EVALUATE
DISTINCT(
    UNION(
        NATURALLEFTOUTERJOIN( T1, T2 ),
        SELECTCOLUMNS(
            NATURALLEFTOUTERJOIN( T2, T1 ),
            "Country", [Country], "Nb Customers", [Nb Customers],
            "Nb Suppliers", [Nb Suppliers] ) ) )
ORDER BY [Country]
```

We compute in tables T1 and T2, respectively, the number of customers and suppliers per country. In order to combine these tables, we need to break the data lineage by concatenating the country names with an empty string. Notice that there is no function for performing a full outer join in DAX. Therefore, we compute the union without duplicates of the left and right outer joins, where the latter is obtained by inverting the arguments of the left outer join and reordering the attributes with the SELECTCOLUMNS function.

The next query uses the CROSSJOIN function to compute the sales amount between customer countries and supplier countries.

```
DEFINE
    MEASURE Sales[Sales Amount] = SUM ( Sales[SalesAmount] )
EVALUATE
ADDCOLUMNS(
    CROSSJOIN( VALUES( Customer[Country] ), VALUES( Supplier[Country] ) ),
    "Sales Amount", [Sales Amount] )
ORDER BY [Country], [Country]
```

As in the Northwind data warehouse customers come from 20 countries and suppliers come from 15 countries, the result has 300 rows, where some country combinations do not have sales amount figures.

6.3 Key Performance Indicators

Managers typically use reporting tools to display statistics in order to monitor the performance of an organization. These reports, for example, display the monthly sales by employee for the current year, the sales amount by month also during the current year, the top ten orders or the top ten employees (according to the sales figures achieved), and so on. However, these reports lack a lot of crucial information. For example, how are sales performing against expected figures? What are the sale goals for employees? What is the sales trend? To obtain this information, business users must define a collection of indicators and display them timely in order to alert when things are getting out of the expected path. For example, they can devise a sales indicator that shows the sales over the current analysis period (e.g., quarter), and how these sales figures compare against an expected value or company goal. Indicators of this kind are called key performance indicators (KPIs).

KPIs are complex measurements used to estimate the effectiveness of an organization in carrying out their activities, and to monitor the performance of their processes and business strategies. KPIs are traditionally defined with respect to a business strategy and business objectives, delivering a global overview of the company status. They are usually included in dashboards and reports (which will be discussed below), providing a detailed view of each specific area of the organization. Thus, business users can assess and manage organizational performance using KPIs. To support decision making, KPIs typically have a current value which is compared against a target value, a threshold value and a minimum value. All these values are usually normalized, to facilitate interpretation.

6.3.1 Classification of Key Performance Indicators

There have been many proposals of classification of KPIs. The simplest one is to classify them according to the industry in which they are applied. In this way, we have, for instance, agriculture KPIs, education and training KPIs, finance KPIs, and so on. Another simple classification is based on the functional area where they are applied. Thus, we have accounting KPIs, corporate services KPIs, finance KPIs, human resources KPIs, and so on.

KPIs can be also classified along the time dimension, depending on whether they consider the future, the present, or the past.

- Leading KPIs reflect expectations about what can happen in the future. An example is *expected demand.*
- Coincident KPIs reflect what is currently happening. An example is *number of current orders.*
- Lagging KPIs reflect what happened in the past. Examples include *customer satisfaction* or *earnings before interest and taxes.*

Another way to classify KPIs refers to whether the indicator measures characteristics of the input or the output of a process.

- Input KPI measure resources invested in or used to generate business results. Examples include *headcount* or *cost per hour.*
- Output KPIs reflect the overall results or impact of the business activity to quantify performance. An example is *customer retention.*

KPIs can be classified depending on whether they are measurable or not.

- Qualitative KPIs measure a descriptive characteristic, an opinion, or a property. An example is *customer satisfaction measured through surveys*, where even if survey data are quantitative, the measures are based on a subjective interpretation of a customer's opinions.
- Quantitative KPIs measure characteristics obtained through a numerical expression. These are the most common kinds of KPIs. An example is *units per man-hour*.

KPIs can be also classified based on the organizational level they target.

- Strategic KPIs are typically reported to senior levels in the organization, and at less regular intervals than the corresponding operational indicators. They have a medium- or long-term time scope.
- Operational KPIs are focused at lower levels in the organization, and are reported more frequently than strategic indicators. They usually have a short-term time scope.

The last classification we give is based on the issues addressed by a KPI.

- Process KPIs refer to the efficiency or productivity of a business process. Examples are *sales growth* or *shipping efficiency*.
- Quality KPIs, which describe the quality of the production. Examples are *number of production interruptions* or *customer satisfaction*.
- Context KPIs are not directly influenced by the processes of the organization. Examples are *size of market* or *number of competitors*.

There are many other classifications of KPIs in the literature, although the list we have given above covers the most common ones.

6.3.2 Defining Key Performance Indicators

In order to define an appropriate set of indicators for an organization, we need to identify the sources from which we can obtain relevant information. These sources can be classified into primary, secondary, and external, as follows:

- Primary sources.
  - Front-line employees. They are at the core of the value chain and know what are the important factors to achieve the operational goals.
  - Managers. They provide their perspective across the value chain and their strategic knowledge.
  - Board. It defines the organizational goals and suggest specific KPIs that are highly prioritized and sometimes nonnegotiable.
  - Suppliers and customers. They bring an external perspective to what should be measured and improved.

- Secondary sources. These include strategic development plan, annual business/strategic plan, annual reports, internal operational reports, and competitor review reports.
- External sources. These include social media and discussion forums, expert advice, and information about related organizations and competitors such as annual reports and catalogs.

When the sources have been identified, we can follow the steps below in order to define the indicators for the problem at hand.

1. Assemble a (preferably small) team.
2. Categorize potential metrics to assess the business from many different perspectives. For example, we may want to define metrics that capture how the organization is performing from a financial perspective, from a customer's perspective, and with respect to employee's expectations.
3. Brainstorm possible metrics to discuss many possible measures before deciding the final set.
4. Prioritize the initially defined metrics. In order to do this, for each metric we must:

   - Give its precise definition.
   - Define if the indicator is leading or lagging. It is recommended to have a balanced number of leading and lagging metrics.
   - Verify if the metric is likely to have a relevant impact.
   - Check if the metric is linked to a specific set of business processes that we can drill into if it deviates from the desired values.
   - Check if we have at least one to two metrics for each key category defined in the second step.

5. Perform a final filter on metrics. This consists in checking if the metric definition is unambiguous and clear to people not on the core team, if we have credible data to compute the metric, and making sure that achieving the metrics will lead to achieving our goals.
6. Set targets for the selected metrics. This is a crucial step since it is one of the biggest challenges in KPI definition. For this, historical information can be used as a guide against which the core team can look at industry benchmarks, and economic conditions.

Finally, we give a set of conditions that a KPI must satisfy in order to be potentially useful. The conditions below consolidate a collection of good practices usually found in the literature.

- The metric must be specific and unambiguous, that means, the definition of the indicator must be clear and easily understandable. In addition, the definition must precisely specify how the metric will be computed. In the Northwind case, for instance, an indicator called Sales Performance could be defined as the total value of the SalesAmount attribute in the Sales fact table, computed over the current quarter, divided by the value of the attribute for the same period last year. This ratio is then compared against an expected sales growth value set as a company goal.

- The indicator must be clearly owned by a department or company office, that means, there must be an individual or a group that must be made clearly accountable for keeping the indicator on track.
- The metric must be measurable, which means all elements must be quantifiable.
- The indicator can be produced timely. To be useful for decision making, we must be able to produce a KPI at regular predefined intervals, in a way such that it can be analyzed together with other KPIs in the set of indicators.
- The indicator must be aligned with the company goals. KPIs should lead to the achievement of the global company goals. For example, a global goal can be to grow 10% per year.
- The number of KPIs must remain manageable, and decision makers must not be overwhelmed by a large number of indicators.

We will apply the above guidelines to define a collection of indicators for the Northwind case study in Sect. 7.5.

6.4 Dashboards

The most popular visualization tools in business intelligence are **dashboards**, which are collections of multiple visual components (such as charts or KPIs) on a single view. A classic definition due to Stephen Few states that a dashboard is a "display of the most important information needed to achieve one or more objectives, consolidated and arranged on a single screen so the information can be monitored at a glance."

Dashboards enable organizations to effectively measure, monitor, and manage business performance. Dashboards are used to visualize organizational data and utilize different performance measurement models to identify and implement measures for all levels in the organization. There is an extensive practitioner-oriented literature on dashboards, although there is a lack of academic literature. In this section, we characterize dashboards and give some practical hints for their design.

Dashboards help to make fact-based decisions, using the right data, delivered reliably in an easily accessed and perceivable form. Note that decision makers require data in context to manage performance over time. Thus, although the current status of business is important, decision makers require comparisons of current values to past performance and to future objectives. We must also take into account that the time horizon and scope of data needed differ significantly based on the roles in the organization. An executive, focused on achieving enterprise-wide strategic goals, requires a high-level view across different lines of business and covering months or years. Business managers, on the other hand, must achieve daily or weekly performance goals, and require not only a narrower time frame and kind of data, but also, if current rates are off-target, the ability to quickly investigate the amount and cause of variation of a parameter. Business analysts have a much broader set of needs. Rather than knowing what they are looking for, they often approach performance data with ad hoc questions, therefore they may require a time frame ranging between just a few hours up to many weeks.

6.4.1 Types of Dashboards

A well-known classification of dashboards proposes three high-level categories: strategic, operational, and analytical.

Strategic dashboards provide a quick overview of the status of an organization, assisting executive decisions such as the definition of long-term goals. Strategic dashboards, therefore, do not require real-time data: the focus is not on what is going on right now but in the past performance. Strategic dashboard data may be quantitative or qualitative. For instance, in the Northwind case study, the sales manager wants trend data on revenues and sales. Qualitatively, a human resource manager may want the top ten and worst ten salesmen. Because of their broad time horizon, strategic dashboards should have an interface that quickly guides decision makers to the answers they seek, telling if the indicator is on track.

Operational dashboards are designed to monitor the company operations. Monitoring operations requires more timely data, tracking constantly changing activities that could require immediate attention. Operational dashboards require a simple view to enable rapid visual identification of measures that are going away from the goals and require immediate action. Thus, the design of these kinds of dashboards must be very simple to avoid mistakes. The timeliness of operational data can vary. If things are on track, periodic snapshots may be sufficient. However, if a measure deviates from the goal, operational managers may want real-time data to see if the variance is an anomaly or a trend.

Analytical dashboards support interaction with the data, such as drilling-down into the underlying details, to enable the exploration needed to make sense of it, that means, not just to see what is going on but to examine the causes. Therefore, analytical dashboards support exploratory data analysis.

6.4.2 Guidelines for Dashboard Design

In order to design a dashboard that complies with the needs of the intended audience, the visual elements and interactions must be carefully chosen. Factors such as placement, attention, cognitive load, and interactivity contribute greatly to the effectiveness of a dashboard.

A dashboard is meant to be viewed at a glance, so that the the visual elements to be shown must be arranged in a display that can be viewed all at once in a screen, without having to scroll or navigate through multiple pages, minimizing the effort of viewing information. In addition, important information must be noticed quickly. From a designer's viewpoint, it is crucial to know who the users of the dashboard will be and what their goals are, in order to define to which of the categories we defined above the dashboard belongs. This information is typically obtained through user interviews.

To design a dashboard that can be effective and usable for its audience, we need to choose data visualizations that convey the information clearly, are easy to interpret, avoid excessive use of space, and are attractive and legible. For example, dashboards may provide the user with visualizations that allow data comparison. Line graphs, bar charts, and bullet bars are effective visual metaphors to use for quick comparisons. Analytical dashboards should provide interactivity, such as filtering or drill-down exploration. A scatter plot can provide more detail behind comparisons by showing patterns created by individual data points.

Operational dashboards should display any variations that would require action in a way that is quickly and easily noticeable. KPIs are used for effectively showing the comparison and drawing attention to data that indicate that action is required. A KPI must be set up to show where data falls within a specified range, so if a value falls below or above a threshold the visual element utilizes color coding to draw attention to that value. Typically, red is used to show when performance has fallen below a target, green indicates good performance, and yellow can be used to show that no action is required. If multiple KPIs are used in a dashboard, the color coding must be used consistently for the different KPIs, so a user does not have to go through the extra work of decoding color codes for KPIs that have the same meaning. For example, we must use the same shade of red for all KPIs on a dashboard that show if a measure is performing below a threshold.

We must avoid including distracting tools in a dashboard, like motion and animations. Also, using too many colors, or colors that are too bright, is distracting and must be avoided. Dashboard visualization should be easy to interpret and self-explanatory. Thus, only important text (like graph titles, category labels, or data values) should be placed on the dashboard. While a dashboard may have a small area, text should not be made so small that it is difficult to read. A good way to test readability is through test users.

We will apply the above guidelines to define a dashboard for the Northwind case study in Sect. 7.6.

6.5 Summary

The first part of this chapter was devoted to querying data warehouses. For this, we used three different languages, MDX, DAX, and SQL. Both MDX and DAX can be used as an expression language for defining, respectively, multidimensional and tabular models, as well as a query language for extracting data from them. In this chapter, we limited ourselves to their use as a query language and introduced the main functionalities of MDX and DAX through examples. We continued by studying Key Performance Indicators, We gave a classification of them and provided guidelines for their definition. The chapter finished with the study of dashboards. We characterized different types of dashboards, and gave guidelines for their definition.

6.6 Bibliographic Notes

MDX was first introduced in 1997 by Microsoft as part of the OLE DB for OLAP specification. After the commercial release of Microsoft OLAP Services in 2018 and Microsoft Analysis Services in 2005, MDX was adopted by the wide range of OLAP vendors, both at the server and the client side. The latest version of the OLE DB for OLAP specification was issued by Microsoft in 1999. In Analysis Services 2005 Microsoft added some MDX extensions like subqueries. There are many books about MDX, a recent one is [189]. MDX is also covered, although succinctly, in general books covering OLAP tools, such as [108].

Self-service business intelligence is an approach to data analytics that enables business users to access and work with corporate information in order to create personalized reports and analytical queries on their own, without the involvement of IT specialists. In order to realize this vision, Microsoft introduced the Business Intelligence Semantic Model (BISM), which we introduced in Chap. 3. The BISM supports two models, the traditional multidimensional model and a new tabular model. The tabular model was designed to be simpler and easier to understand by users familiar with Excel and the relational data model. In addition, Microsoft has created a new query language to query the tabular model. This language, called DAX (Data Analysis Expressions), is a new functional language that is an extension of the formula language in Excel. In this chapter, we covered DAX, despite being, at the time of writing, only supported by Microsoft tools. Books entirely devoted to the tabular model and DAX are [204, 205], although these topics are also covered in the book [108] already cited above. Data analysis with Power BI and also with Excel is covered in [74].

The field of visual analytics has produced a vast amount of research results (see for example the work by Andrienko et al. [9]). However, most of the books on KPIs and dashboards are oriented to practitioners. A typical reference on

KPIs is the book by Parmenter [183]. Scientific articles on KPIs are, e.g., [21, 28, 58, 61]. Dashboard design is studied in depthby Few, a specialist in data visualization [75]. Practical real-world cases are presented in [260]. The design and implementation of dashboards for Power BI is covered in[170]. Finally, Microsoft Reporting Services is described (among other books) in [242]

6.7 Review Questions

6.1 Describe what is MDX and what it is used for. Describe the two modes supported by MDX.

6.2 Define what are tuples and sets and MDX.

6.3 Describe the basic syntax of MDX queries and describe the several clauses that compose an MDX query. Which clauses are required and which are optional?

6.4 Describe conceptually how an MDX query is executed by specifying the conceptual order of executing the different clauses composing the query.

6.5 Define the slicing operation in MDX. How does this operation differ from the filtering operation specified in SQL in the **WHERE** clause?

6.6 Why is navigation essential for querying multidimensional databases? Give examples of navigation functions in MDX and exemplify their use in common queries.

6.7 What is a cross join in MDX? For which purpose is a cross join needed? Establish similarities and differences between the cross join in MDX and the various types of join in SQL.

6.8 What is subcubing in MDX? Does subcubing provide additional expressive power to the language?

6.9 Define calculated members and named sets. Why are they needed for? State the syntax for defining them in an MDX query.

6.10 Why time series analysis is important in many business scenarios? Give examples of functionality that is provided by MDX for time series analysis.

6.11 What is filtering and how does this differ from slicing?

6.12 How you do sorting in MDX? What are the limitations of MDX in this respect?

6.13 Give examples of MDX functions that are used for top and bottom analysis. How do they differ from similar functions provided by SQL?

6.14 Describe the main differences between MDX and SQL.

Chapter 7
Data Analysis in the Northwind Data Warehouse

This chapter provides a practical overview of the data analysis topics presented in Chap. 6, namely, querying, key performance indicators, and dashboards. These topics are illustrated in the Northwind case study using several Microsoft tools: Analysis Services, Reporting Services, and Power BI.

The begining of the chapter is devoted to the topic of querying data warehouses. For this, we revisit the queries already presented in Sect. 4.4, which address representative data analysis needs. In Sect. 7.1 we query the multidimensional database using MDX, in Sect. 7.2 we query the tabular database using DAX, and in Sect. 7.3 we query the relational data warehouse using SQL. This allows us to compare the main features of these languages in Sect. 7.4. We continue the chapter by defining in Sect. 7.5 a set of key performance indicators for the Northwind case study and implement them in the multidimensional and tabular models. Finally, we conclude the chapter by defining in Sect. 7.6 a dashboard for the Northwind case study.

7.1 Querying the Multidimensional Model in MDX

Query 7.1. *Total sales amount per customer, year, and product category.*

```
SELECT  [Order Date].Year.CHILDREN ON COLUMNS,
        NON EMPTY Customer.[Company Name].CHILDREN *
        Product.[Category Name].CHILDREN ON ROWS
FROM    Sales
WHERE   Measures.[Sales Amount]
```

Here, we display the years on the column axis and we use a cross join of the **Customer** and **Category** dimensions to display both dimensions in the row axis. We use the **CHILDREN** function instead of **MEMBERS** to prevent displaying the All members of the three dimensions involved in the query. The **NON EMPTY** keyword is used to avoid displaying customers that never ordered articles from a particular category. Finally, we state the measure to be displayed as a slicer in the **WHERE** clause.

Query 7.2. *Yearly sales amount for each pair of customer country and supplier countries.*

```
SELECT  [Order Date].Year.MEMBERS ON COLUMNS,
        NON EMPTY Customer.Country.MEMBERS *
        Supplier.Country.MEMBERS ON ROWS
FROM    Sales
WHERE   Measures.[Sales Amount]
```

In this query, we use a cross join of the **Customer** and **Supplier** dimensions to display the pair of countries from both dimensions in the row axis.

Query 7.3. *Monthly sales by customer state compared to those of the previous year.*

```
WITH MEMBER Measures.[Previous Year] AS
        (Measures.[Sales Amount],
        PARALLELPERIOD([Order Date].Calendar.Month,12)),
        FORMAT_STRING = '$###,##0.00'
SELECT { Measures.[Sales Amount], Measures.[Previous Year] } ON COLUMNS,
        NON EMPTY ORDER(Customer.Geography.State.MEMBERS,
        Customer.Geography.CURRENTMEMBER.NAME, BASC) *
        [Order Date].Calendar.Month.MEMBERS ON ROWS
FROM    Sales
```

In this query, we do a cross join of the **Customer** and **Order Date** dimensions to display the states and months on the row axis. We use the **ORDER** function to sort the states of the customers in alphabetical order irrespective of the **Geography** hierarchy. The calculated measure **Previous Year** computes the sales amount of the same month of the previous year for the current state and month using the **PARALLELPERIOD** function. The format for displaying the new measure is also defined.

Query 7.4. *Monthly sales growth per product, that is, total sales per product compared to those of the previous month.*

```
WITH MEMBER Measures.[Previous Month] AS
        (Measures.[Sales Amount],
        [Order Date].Calendar.CURRENTMEMBER.PREVMEMBER),
        FORMAT_STRING = '$###,##0.00'
MEMBER Measures.[Sales Growth] AS
        (Measures.[Sales Amount]) - (Measures.[Previous Month]),
        FORMAT_STRING = '$###,##0.00; $-###,##0.00'
SELECT { Measures.[Sales Amount], Measures.[Previous Month],
        Measures.[Sales Growth] } ON COLUMNS,
        NON EMPTY ORDER(Product.Categories.Product.MEMBERS,
        Product.Categories.CURRENTMEMBER.NAME, BASC) *
        [Order Date].Calendar.Month.MEMBERS ON ROWS
FROM    Sales
```

In this query, we do a cross join of the **Product** and **Order Date** dimensions to display the products and months on the row axis. The calculated measure **Previous Month** computes the sales amount of the previous month of the current category and month, while the calculated measure **Sales Growth** computes the difference of the sales amount of the current month and the one of the previous month.

Query 7.5. *Three best-selling employees.*

```
SELECT Measures.[Sales Amount] ON COLUMNS,
       TOPCOUNT(Employee.[Full Name].CHILDREN, 3,
       Measures.[Sales Amount]) ON ROWS
FROM   Sales
```

Here, we use the **TOPCOUNT** function to find the three employees who have the highest value of the sales amount measure. We use the **CHILDREN** function instead of **MEMBERS** since otherwise the All member will appear in the first position, as it contains the total sales amount of all employees.

Query 7.6. *Best-selling employee per product and year.*

```
WITH MEMBER Measures.[Top Sales] AS
       MAX([Order Date].Calendar.CURRENTMEMBER *
       Employee.[Full Name].CHILDREN, Measures.[Sales Amount])
MEMBER Measures.[Top Employee] AS
       TOPCOUNT([Order Date].Calendar.CURRENTMEMBER *
       Employee.[Full Name].CHILDREN, 1, Measures.[Sales Amount]).
       ITEM(0).ITEM(1).NAME
SELECT { Measures.[Top Sales], Measures.[Top Employee] } ON COLUMNS,
       ORDER(Product.Categories.Product.MEMBERS,
       Product.Categories.CURRENTMEMBER.NAME,BASC) *
       [Order Date].Calendar.Year.MEMBERS ON ROWS
FROM   Sales
```

The calculated measure **Top Sales** computes the maximum value of sales amount for the current year among all employees. The calculated measure **Top Employee** uses the function **TOPCOUNT** to obtain the tuple composed of the current year and the employee with highest sales amount. The **ITEM** function retrieves the first member of the specified tuple. Since such member is a combination of year and employee, **ITEM** applied again to obtain the employee. Finally, the **NAME** function retrieves the name of the employee.

Query 7.7. *Countries that account for top 50% of the sales amount.*

```
SELECT Measures.[Sales Amount] ON COLUMNS,
       { Customer.Geography.[All],
       TOPPERCENT([Customer].Geography.Country.MEMBERS, 50,
       Measures.[Sales Amount]) } ON ROWS
FROM   Sales
```

In this query, we use the **TOPPERCENT** function for selecting the countries whose cumulative total is equal to the specified percentage. We can see in the answer below, that the sum of the values for the three listed countries slightly exceeds 50% of the sales amount.

Query 7.8. *Total sales and average monthly sales by employee and year.*

```
WITH MEMBER Measures.[Avg Monthly Sales] AS
        AVG(DESCENDANTS([Order Date].Calendar.CURRENTMEMBER,
        [Order Date].Calendar.Month),Measures.[Sales Amount]),
        FORMAT_STRING = '$###,##0.00'
SELECT { Measures.[Sales Amount], Measures.[Avg Monthly Sales] } ON COLUMNS,
        Employee.[Full Name].CHILDREN *
        [Order Date].Calendar.Year.MEMBERS ON ROWS
FROM    Sales
```

In this query, we cross join the **Employee** and **Order Date** dimensions to display the employee name and the year on the row axis. The calculated measure **Avg Monthly Sales** computes the average of sales amount of the current employee for all months of the current year.

Query 7.9. *Total sales amount and discount amount per product and month.*

```
WITH MEMBER Measures.[TotalDisc] AS
        Measures.Discount * Measures.Quantity * Measures.[Unit Price],
        FORMAT_STRING = '$###,##0.00'
SELECT { Measures.[Sales Amount], [TotalDisc] } ON COLUMNS,
        NON EMPTY ORDER(Product.Categories.Product.MEMBERS,
        Product.Categories.CURRENTMEMBER.NAME, BASC) *
        [Order Date].Calendar.Month.MEMBERS ON ROWS
FROM    Sales
```

In this query, we cross join the **Product** and **Order Date** dimensions to display the product and the month on the row axis. The calculated measure **TotalDisc** multiplies the discount, quantity, and unit price measures to compute the total discount amount of the current product and month.

Query 7.10. *Monthly year-to-date sales for each product category.*

```
WITH MEMBER Measures.YTDSales AS
        SUM(PERIODSTODATE([Order Date].Calendar.[Year],
        [Order Date].Calendar.CURRENTMEMBER),
        Measures.[Sales Amount]), FORMAT_STRING = '###,##0.00'
SELECT DESCENDANTS([Order Date].[2016], [Order Date].[Month])
        ON COLUMNS, Product.[Category].MEMBERS ON ROWS
FROM    Sales
WHERE (Measures.YTDSales)
```

Here, we use the **PERIODSTODATE** function in order to select all months of the current year up to the current month. Then, the **SUM** function is applied to obtain the year-to-date aggregate value of the measure **Sales Amount**.

Query 7.11. *Moving average over the last 3 months of the sales amount by product category.*

```
WITH MEMBER Measures.MovAvg3M AS
            AVG([Order Date].Calendar.CURRENTMEMBER.LAG(2):
            [Order Date].Calendar.CURRENTMEMBER,
            Measures.[Sales Amount]), FORMAT_STRING = '$###,##0.00'
SELECT [Order Date].Calendar.Month.MEMBERS ON COLUMNS,
        Product.[Category].MEMBERS ON ROWS
FROM    Sales
WHERE  (Measures.MovAvg3M)
```

Here, we use the **LAG** function and the range operator ':' to construct the set composed of the current month and its preceding 2 months. Then, we take the average of the measure **Sales Amount** over these 3 months.

Query 7.12. *Personal sales amount made by an employee compared with the total sales amount made by herself and her subordinates during 2017.*

```
WITH MEMBER Measures.[Personal Sales] AS
            (Employee.Supervision.DATAMEMBER, [Measures].[Sales Amount]),
            FORMAT_STRING = '$###,##0.00'
SELECT { Measures.[Personal Sales], Measures.[Sales Amount] } ON COLUMNS,
        ORDER(Employee.Supervision.MEMBERS - Employee.Supervision.[All],
        Employee.Supervision.CURRENTMEMBER.NAME, BASC) ON ROWS
FROM    Sales
WHERE  [Order Date].Calendar.Year.[2017]
```

In this query, we use the parent-child hierarchy **Supervision** of the **Employee** dimension. In such a hierarchy, each employee has personal sales amount values. As we have seen in Sect. 5.9.1 such value is kept in system-generated child members. This value can be accessed in MDX using the keyword **DATAMEMBER** as shown in the calculated measure **Personal Sales** of the above query. Furthermore, the value of the total sales amount for an employee at the lower level of the hierarchy (i.e., without subordinates) is equal to its personal sales. For employees with subordinates, the value of the measure is the sum of her personal sales and those of her subordinates. Notice that in this query we removed the member **All** from the set of members of the **Supervision** hierarchy, using the set difference operator denoted by '-'. If in the query above we replace **Employee.Supervision.MEMBERS** with **Employee.Supervision.CHILDREN**, we will obtain only the first line of the answer corresponding to Andrew Fuller. As can be seen, parent-child hierarchies behave to this respect differently from user-defined hierarchies.

It is worth remarking that the personal sales amount made by an employee can also be obtained with the following query, which exploits the attribute hierarchy [Full Name] instead of the parent-child hierarchy **Supervision**.

```
SELECT Measures.[Sales Amount] ON COLUMNS,
        Employee.[Full Name].CHILDREN ON ROWS
FROM    Sales
WHERE  [Order Date].Calendar.Year.[2017]
```

Query 7.13. *Total sales amount, number of products, and sum of the quantities sold for each order.*

```
WITH MEMBER Measures.[NbProducts] AS
        COUNT(NONEMPTY([Order].[Order No].CURRENTMEMBER *
        [Order].[Order Line].MEMBERS))
SELECT { Measures.[Sales Amount], NbProducts, Quantity } ON COLUMNS,
        [Order].[Order No].CHILDREN ON ROWS
FROM    Sales
```

In this query, we use the fact (or degenerate) dimension Order, which is defined from the fact table Sales in the data warehouse. The dimension has two attributes, the order number and the order line, and the order number is displayed on the rows axis. In the calculated measure NbProducts, a cross join is used to obtain the order lines associated to the current order. By counting the elements in this set, we can obtain the number of distinct products of the order. Finally, the measures Sales Amount, NbProducts, and Quantity are displayed on the column axis.

Query 7.14. *For each month, total number of orders, total sales amount, and average sales amount by order.*

```
WITH MEMBER Measures.AvgSales AS
        Measures.[Sales Amount]/Measures.[Order No],
        FORMAT_STRING = '$###,##0.00'
SELECT { Measures.[Order No], [Sales Amount], AvgSales } ON COLUMNS,
        NON EMPTY [Order Date].Calendar.Month.MEMBERS ON ROWS
FROM    Sales
```

This query displays the months of the Order Date dimension on the row axis, and the measures Order No, Sales Amount, and AvgSales on the column axis, the latter being a calculated measure. For Sales Amount, the roll-up operation computes the sum of the values in a month. For the Order No measure, since in the cube definition the aggregate function associated to the measure is DistinctCount, the roll-up operation computes the number of orders within a month. Notice that for computing the average in the calculated measure AvgSales we divided the two measures Sales Amount and Order No. If we used instead AVG(Measures.[Sales Amount]), the result obtained will correspond to the Sales Amount. Indeed, the average will be applied to a set containing as only element the measure of the current month.

Query 7.15. *For each employee, total sales amount, number of cities, and number of states to which she is assigned.*

```
WITH MEMBER NoCities AS
        Measures.[Territories Count]
MEMBER NoStates AS
        DISTINCTCOUNT(Employee.[Full Name].CURRENTMEMBER *
        City.Geography.State.MEMBERS)
SELECT { Measures.[Sales Amount], Measures.NoCities, Measures.NoStates }
        ON COLUMNS, Employee.[Full Name].CHILDREN ON ROWS
FROM    Sales
```

Here, we exploit the many-to-many relationship between employees and cities through the bridge table **Territories**. We assume that we are using Analysis Services and thus, we make use of the **Territories Count** measure that is automatically added to each measure when it is created, as explained in Sect. 5.9.1. We rename this measure as **NoCities** at the beginning of the query. Then, for the **NoStates** calculated measure, we perform a cross join that obtains the states to which the current employee is related and apply **DISTINCTCOUNT** to the result, in order to compute the number of states for such employee. Notice that a similar approach can be used to obtain the number of cities if the measure **Territories Count** does not exist in the cube. Finally, the **SELECT** clause displays the measures.

7.2 Querying the Tabular Model in DAX

In this section, we revisit the queries of the previous section in DAX.

Query 7.1. *Total sales amount per customer, year, and product category.*

```
DEFINE
    MEASURE Sales[Sales Amount] = SUM( [SalesAmount] )
EVALUATE
SUMMARIZECOLUMNS(
    Customer[CompanyName], 'Date'[Year], Product[CategoryName],
    "Sales Amount", [Sales Amount] )
ORDER BY [CompanyName], [Year], [CategoryName]
```

After defining the measure **Sales Amount**, we aggregate it per customer, year, and product category with the function **SUMMARIZECOLUMNS**.

Query 7.2. *Yearly sales amount for each pair of customer and supplier countries.*

```
DEFINE
    MEASURE Sales[Sales Amount] = SUM( [SalesAmount] )
EVALUATE
SUMMARIZECOLUMNS(
    Customer[Country], Supplier[Country], 'Date'[Year],
    "Sales Amount", [Sales Amount] )
ORDER BY Customer[Country], Supplier[Country], [Year]
```

In this query, we define the measure **Sales Amount** as before and aggregate it for each pair of customer and supplier countries and per year.

Query 7.3. *Monthly sales by customer state compared to those of the previous year.*

```
DEFINE
    MEASURE Sales[Sales Amount] = SUM( [SalesAmount] )
    MEASURE Sales[Sales Amount PY] =
        CALCULATE( [Sales Amount], DATEADD('Date'[Date], -1, YEAR ) )
EVALUATE
SUMMARIZECOLUMNS(
    Customer[State], 'Date'[MonthName], 'Date'[Year], 'Date'[MonthNumber],
    "Sales Amount", [Sales Amount], "Sales Amount PY", [Sales Amount PY] )
ORDER BY [State], [Year], [MonthNumber]
```

In this query, we define the measure **Sales Amount** as before and we define the measure **Sales Amount PY** by using the DATEADD function. We then aggregate both measures by customer state and month. The above query requires that the data model defines the **Date** table as the reference table for time-intelligence calculations. Alternatively, we can define the measure using standard DAX functions as shown next.

```
MEASURE Sales[Sales Amount PY] =
    CALCULATE( [Sales Amount],
        FILTER( ALL( 'Date' ),
            'Date'[MonthNumber] = MAX( 'Date'[MonthNumber] ) &&
            'Date'[Year] = MAX( 'Date'[Year] ) - 1 ) )
```

Here, we define the measure by filtering all the dates up to those in the current month in the previous year.

Query 7.4. *Monthly sales growth per product, that is, total sales per product compared to those of the previous month.*

```
DEFINE
    MEASURE Sales[Sales Amount] = SUM( [SalesAmount] )
    MEASURE Sales[Sales Amount PM] =
        CALCULATE( [Sales Amount], DATEADD('Date'[Date], -1, MONTH ) )
    MEASURE Sales[Sales Growth] = [Sales Amount] - [Sales Amount PM]
EVALUATE
SUMMARIZECOLUMNS(
    Product[ProductName], 'Date'[MonthName], 'Date'[Year], 'Date'[MonthNumber],
    "Sales Amount", [Sales Amount], "Sales Amount PM", [Sales Amount PM],
    "Sales Growth", [Sales Growth] )
ORDER BY [ProductName], [Year], [MonthNumber]
```

We define measure **Sales Amount** as before, measure **Sales Amount PM** by using the DATEADD function, and measure **Sales Growth** as the difference between the previous two measures. We then aggregate these measures by product and month.

Query 7.5. *Three best-selling employees.*

```
DEFINE
    MEASURE Sales[Sales Amount] = SUM( [SalesAmount] )
EVALUATE
TOPN( 3,
    SUMMARIZECOLUMNS(
        Employee[EmployeeName], "Sales Amount", [Sales Amount] ),
    [Sales Amount], DESC )
ORDER BY [Sales Amount] DESC
```

Here, we use the **TOPN** function to find the three employees who have the highest value of the **Sales Amount** measure. Recall that in Sect. 5.9.2 we defined the calculated column **EmployeeName** as the concatenation of the first name and last name of employees.

Query 7.6. *Best-selling employee per product and year.*

```
DEFINE
    MEASURE Sales[Sales Amount] = SUM( [SalesAmount] )
    MEASURE Sales[Employee Rank] =
        RANKX( ALL( Employee[EmployeeName] ), [Sales Amount] )
EVALUATE
FILTER(
    SUMMARIZECOLUMNS(
        Product[ProductName], 'Date'[Year], Employee[EmployeeName],
        "Top Sales", IF( [Employee Rank] = 1, [Sales Amount], BLANK() ) ),
    [Top Sales] <> BLANK () )
ORDER BY [ProductName], [Year]
```

The **Employee Rank** measure uses the **RANKX** function to rank the employees according to the **Sales Amount** measure. In the function **SUMMARIZECOLUMNS**, the column **Top Sales** is defined, which has values only for those employees who are ranked first. Finally, the **FILTER** function keeps the rows having a non-blank **Top Sales** column.

Query 7.7. *Countries that account for top 50% of the sales amount.*

```
DEFINE
    MEASURE Sales[Sales Amount] = SUM( [SalesAmount] )
    MEASURE Sales[Country Sales] =
        CALCULATE( [Sales Amount], ALL( Customer[Country] ) )
    MEASURE Sales[Perc Sales] = [Sales Amount] / [Country Sales]
    MEASURE Sales[Cumul Sales] =
        CALCULATE( [Sales Amount],
            FILTER(
                ADDCOLUMNS(
                    ALL( Customer[Country] ), "Sales", [Sales Amount] ),
                [Sales Amount] >=
                    MINX( VALUES ( Customer[Country] ), [Sales Amount] ) ) )
    MEASURE Sales[Cumul Perc] = [Cumul Sales] / [Sales Amount]
```

```
VAR Total =
    SUMMARIZECOLUMNS(
        Customer[Country], "Sales Amount", [Sales Amount],
        "Perc Sales", [Perc Sales], "Cumul Sales", [Cumul Sales],
        "Cumul Perc", [Cumul Perc] )
EVALUATE
FILTER( Total,
    RANKX( Total, [Cumul Sales], , ASC ) <=
        COUNTROWS( FILTER( Total, [Cumul Perc] < 0.5 ) ) + 1 )
ORDER BY [Cumul Perc]
```

As can be guessed from the above query, in DAX there is no equivalent
to the MDX function **TOPPERCENT**. Measure **Sales Amount** is defined as
before, measure **Sales Amount** computes the overall sales amount, measure
Perc Sales computes the percentage of sales over the overall sales amount, and
measures **Cumul Sales** and **Cumul Perc** compute the cumulative version of the
corresponding measure. In measure **Cumul Sales**, function **ADDCOLUMNS**
computes a table associating to each city its sales amount, and function
FILTER selects in this table the cities whose sales amount are greater or equal
than the minimum sales amount value for all the cities in the current context.
Finally, the temporary table **Total** aggregates all the previous measures. In the
main query, the **COUNTROWS** function determines the number of countries
whose cumulative percentage is less than 0.5, which is combined with the
result of the **RANKX** function to write the expression in the **FILTER** function
to select the required countries.

Query 7.8. *Total sales and average monthly sales by employee and year.*

```
DEFINE
    MEASURE Sales[Sales Amount] = SUM( [SalesAmount] )
    MEASURE Sales[Avg Monthly Sales] = [Sales Amount] /
        COUNTROWS(
            FILTER(
                SUMMARIZE(
                    FILTER( ALL( 'Date' ), 'Date'[Year] = MAX( 'Date'[Year] ) ),
                    'Date'[MonthNumber], "Monthly Sales", [Sales Amount] ),
                [Sales Amount] > 0 ) )
EVALUATE
SUMMARIZECOLUMNS(
    Employee[EmployeeName], 'Date'[Year], "Sales Amount", [Sales Amount],
    "Avg Monthly Sales", [Avg Monthly Sales] )
ORDER BY [Full Name], [Year]
```

To compute the **Avg Monthly Sales** measure, we start by computing the
monthly sales with the **SUMMARIZE** function; we use the **FILTER** function
to select the months where there were any sales, and then count the number
of remaining months with the **COUNTROWS** function. In the main query,
the function **SUMMARIZECOLUMNS** performs the aggregation of these measures.

Query 7.9. *Total sales amount and discount amount per product and month.*

```
DEFINE
    MEASURE Sales[Sales Amount] = SUM( [SalesAmount] )
    MEASURE Sales[Total Discount] =
        SUMX( Sales, Sales[Quantity] * Sales[Discount] * Sales[UnitPrice] )
EVALUATE
SUMMARIZECOLUMNS(
    'Product'[ProductName], 'Date'[MonthName], 'Date'[Year], 'Date'[MonthNumber],
    "Sales Amount", [Sales Amount], "Total Discount", [Total Discount] )
ORDER BY [ProductName], [Year], [MonthNumber]
```

We compute the Total Discount measure by multiplying the quantity, the discount, and the unit price. This measure is then used in the SUMMA-RIZECOLUMNS function in the main query.

Query 7.10. *Monthly year-to-date sales for each product category.*

```
DEFINE
    MEASURE Sales[Sales Amount] = SUM( [SalesAmount] )
    MEASURE Sales[YTDSales] = TOTALYTD ( SUM( [SalesAmount] ), 'Date'[Date] )
EVALUATE
SUMMARIZECOLUMNS(
    Product[CategoryName], 'Date'[MonthName], 'Date'[Year], 'Date'[MonthNumber],
    "Sales Amount", [Sales Amount], "YTDSales", [YTDSales] )
ORDER BY [CategoryName], [Year], [MonthNumber]
```

In the measure YTDSales, we use the TOTALYTD function to aggregate the measure Sales Amount for all dates of the current year up to the current date.

Query 7.11. *Moving average over the last 3 months of the sales amount by product category.*

```
DEFINE
    MEASURE Sales[Sales Amount] = SUM( [SalesAmount] )
    MEASURE Sales[MovAvg3M] =
        CALCULATE(
            AVERAGEX( VALUES ( 'Date'[YearMonth] ), [Sales Amount] ),
            DATESINPERIOD( 'Date'[Date], MAX( 'Date'[Date] ), -3, MONTH ) )
EVALUATE
SUMMARIZECOLUMNS(
    Product[CategoryName], 'Date'[MonthName], 'Date'[Year], 'Date'[MonthNumber],
    "Sales Amount", [Sales Amount], "MovAvg3M", [MovAvg3M] )
ORDER BY [CategoryName], [Year], [MonthNumber]
```

Here, we use the DATESINPERIOD function to select all the dates three months before the current one. These will be used as context for the CALCU-LATE function. The AVERAGEX function computes the Sales Amount measure for each YearMonth value (in the context of the measure it is at most three values), and these are then averaged.

Query 7.12. *Personal sales amount made by an employee compared with the total sales amount made by herself and her subordinates during 2017.*

```
DEFINE
    MEASURE Sales[Sales Amount] = SUM( [SalesAmount] )
    MEASURE Sales[Subordinates Sales] =
        CALCULATE( [Sales Amount],
            FILTER( ALL( Employee ),
                PATHCONTAINS( Employee[SupervisionPath],
                    SELECTEDVALUE( Employee[EmployeeKey] ) ) ) )
EVALUATE
SUMMARIZECOLUMNS(
    Employee[EmployeeName], FILTER( 'Date', 'Date'[Year] = 2017 ),
    "Personal Amount", [Sales Amount], "Subordinates Amount", [Subordinates Sales] )
ORDER BY [EmployeeName]
```

In this query, we exploit the parent-child hierarchy **Supervision** of the **Employee** dimension. Recall from Sect. 5.9.2 that we defined a derived column **SupervisionPath**, obtaining a delimited text with the keys of all the supervisors of each row. The measure **Subordinate Sales** uses the function **SELECTEDVALUE** to select the employee key of the current filter context, which is passed to the **PATHCONTAINS** function to select those employees having the given employee in their supervision hierarchy. In the main query we aggregate the measures filtering the year to 2017.

Query 7.13. *Total sales amount, number of products, and sum of the quantities sold for each order.*

```
DEFINE
    MEASURE Sales[Sales Amount] = SUM( [SalesAmount] )
    MEASURE Sales[NbProducts] = COUNTROWS( VALUES ( Sales[ProductKey] ) )
    MEASURE Sales[Quantity] = SUM( Sales[Quantity] )
EVALUATE
SUMMARIZECOLUMNS(
    Sales[OrderNo], "Sales Amount", [Sales Amount], "NbProducts", [NbProducts],
    "Quantity", [Quantity] )
ORDER BY [OrderNo]
```

This query addresses the fact dimension **Order**, which is defined from the fact table **Sales**. In the measure **NbProducts** we use the function **COUNTROWS** to obtain the number of distinct products of the order. The measure **Quantity** aggregates the quantity values for the products. Finally, the main query shows the requested measures.

Query 7.14. *For each month, total number of orders, total sales amount, and average sales amount by order.*

```
DEFINE
    MEASURE Sales[Sales Amount] = SUM( [SalesAmount] )
    MEASURE Sales[Nb Orders] = COUNTROWS( SUMMARIZE( Sales, Sales[OrderNo] ) )
    MEASURE Sales[AvgSales] = DIVIDE ( [Sales Amount], [Nb Orders] )
```

```
EVALUATE
SUMMARIZECOLUMNS(
    'Date'[MonthName], 'Date'[Year], 'Date'[MonthNumber], "Nb Orders", [Nb Orders],
    "Sales Amount", [Sales Amount], "AvgSales", [AvgSales] )
ORDER BY [Year], [MonthNumber]
```

The measure Nb Orders computes the number of orders while the measure AvgSales divides the measure Sales Amount by the previous measure.

Query 7.15. *For each employee, total sales amount, number of cities, and number of states to which she is assigned.*

```
DEFINE
    MEASURE Sales[Sales Amount] = SUM( [SalesAmount] )
    MEASURE Sales[NoCities] =
        CALCULATE( COUNTROWS( Territories ),
            CROSSFILTER( Territories[EmployeeKey], Employee[EmployeeKey], BOTH ) )
    MEASURE Sales[NoStates] =
        CALCULATE( COUNTROWS( VALUES( EmployeeGeography[State] ),
            CROSSFILTER( Territories[EmployeeKey], Employee[EmployeeKey], BOTH ) ) ),
EVALUATE
FILTER(
    SUMMARIZECOLUMNS(
        Employee[FirstName], Employee[LastName], "Sales Amount", [Sales Amount],
        "NoCities", [NoCities], "NoStates", [NoStates] ),
    [FirstName] <> BLANK() )
ORDER BY [FirstName], [LastName]
```

In this query, we need to traverse the many-to-many relationship between employees and cities represented by the table Territories. As shown in Fig. 5.36, the relationship between Territories and Employees is defined as unidirectional, while the relationship between Territories and EmployeeGeography is bidirectional. This means that a filter from EmployeeGeography propagates to the Employee table, but this is not the case for a filter defined in the Employee table. Therefore, to define the measures NoCities and NoStates, we need to use the CROSSFILTER function to make the relationship bidirectional during the evaluation of the query. Then, in the NoCities measure, the COUNTROWS function counts the number of rows of the Territories table, while for the NoStates measure we count the number of values of the State column. Finally, in the main query, after aggregating the values with the SUMMARIZECOLUMNS function, we need to remove the line that contains all blanks excepted for the total number of states with the FILTER function.

7.3 Querying the Relational Data Warehouse in SQL

Given the schema of the Northwind data warehouse in Fig. 5.4, we revisit the queries of the previous sections in SQL. This is of particular importance because some OLAP tools automatically translate MDX or DAX queries into SQL and send them to a relational server.

To simplify month-related computations, we create the next two views.

```
CREATE VIEW YearMonth AS
        SELECT DISTINCT Year, MonthNumber, MonthName
        FROM    Date
CREATE VIEW YearMonthPM AS
        WITH YearMonthPrevMonth AS (
                SELECT Year, MonthNumber, MonthName,
                        LAG(Year * 100 + MonthNumber) OVER (ORDER BY
                        Year * 100 + MonthNumber) AS PrevMonth
                FROM    YearMonth )
        SELECT Year, MonthNumber, MonthName, PrevMonth / 100 AS PM_Year,
                PrevMonth % 100 AS PM_MonthNumber
        FROM    YearMonthPrevMonth
```

View YearMonth contains all the year and months from the Date dimension. View YearMonthPM associates with each year and month in the Date dimension the same month of the previous year. For this, table YearMonth-PrevMonth uses the LAG window function to associate each month with the previous one represented by a numerical expression in the format YYYYMM. For example, the expression associated with January 2017 would be 201612. Finally, the main query splits this expression into the year and the month.

Query 7.1. *Total sales amount per customer, year, and product category.*

```
SELECT     C.CompanyName, D.Year, A.CategoryName,
           SUM(SalesAmount) AS SalesAmount
FROM       Sales S, Customer C, Date D, Product P, Category A
WHERE      S.CustomerKey = C.CustomerKey AND S.OrderDateKey = D.DateKey AND
           S.ProductKey = P.ProductKey AND P.CategoryKey = A.CategoryKey
GROUP BY C.CompanyName, D.Year, A.CategoryName
ORDER BY C.CompanyName, D.Year, A.CategoryName
```

Here, we join the fact table with the involved dimension tables and aggregate the results by company, year, and category.

Query 7.2. *Yearly sales amount for each pair of customer country and supplier countries.*

```
SELECT     CO.CountryName AS Country, SO.CountryName AS Country,
           D.Year, SUM(SalesAmount) AS SalesAmount
FROM       Sales F, Customer C, City CC, State CS, Country CO,
           Supplier S, City SC, State SS, Country SO, Date D
WHERE      F.CustomerKey = C.CustomerKey AND C.CityKey = CC.CityKey AND
           CC.StateKey = CS.StateKey AND CS.CountryKey = CO.CountryKey AND
           F.SupplierKey = S.SupplierKey AND S.CityKey = SC.CityKey AND
           SC.StateKey = SS.StateKey AND SS.CountryKey = SO.CountryKey AND
           F.OrderDateKey = D.DateKey
GROUP BY CO.CountryName, SO.CountryName, D.Year
ORDER BY CO.CountryName, SO.CountryName, D.Year
```

Here, the tables of the geography dimension are joined twice with the fact table to obtain the countries of the customer and the supplier.

Query 7.3. *Monthly sales by customer state compared to those of the previous year.*

```
WITH StateMonth AS (
            SELECT     DISTINCT StateName, Year, MonthNumber, MonthName
            FROM       Customer C, City Y, State S, YearMonth M
            WHERE      C.CityKey = Y.CityKey AND Y.StateKey = S.StateKey ),
      SalesStateMonth AS (
            SELECT     StateName, Year, MonthNumber,
                       SUM(SalesAmount) AS SalesAmount
            FROM       Sales F, Customer C, City Y, State S, Date D
            WHERE      F.CustomerKey = C.CustomerKey AND
                       C.CityKey = Y.CityKey AND Y.StateKey = S.StateKey AND
                       F.OrderDateKey = D.DateKey
            GROUP BY S.StateName, D.Year, D.MonthNumber )
SELECT     S.StateName, S.MonthName, S.Year, M1.SalesAmount,
           M2.SalesAmount AS SalesAmountPY
FROM       StateMonth S LEFT OUTER JOIN SalesStateMonth M1 ON
           S.StateName = M1.StateName AND
           S.Year = M1.Year AND
           S.MonthNumber = M1.MonthNumber
           LEFT OUTER JOIN SalesStateMonth M2 ON
           S.StateName = M2.StateName AND
           S.Year - 1 = M2.Year AND
           S.MonthNumber = M2.MonthNumber
WHERE      M1.SalesAmount IS NOT NULL OR M2.SalesAmount IS NOT NULL
ORDER BY S.StateName, S.Year, S.MonthNumber
```

The query starts by defining a table StateMonth makes the Cartesian product of the all the customer states and all months in the view YearMonth. Then, table SalesStateMonth computes the monthly sales by state. Finally, the main query performs twice a left outer join of the table StateMonth with the table SalesStateMonth to compute the result.

Query 7.4. *Monthly sales growth per product, that is, total sales per product compared to those of the previous month.*

```
WITH ProdYearMonthPM AS (
            SELECT     DISTINCT ProductName, Year, MonthNumber, MonthName,
                       PM_Year, PM_MonthNumber
            FROM       Product, YearMonthPM ),
      SalesProdMonth AS (
            SELECT     ProductName, Year, MonthNumber,
                       SUM(SalesAmount) AS SalesAmount
            FROM       Sales S, Product P, Date D
            WHERE      S.ProductKey = P.ProductKey AND S.OrderDateKey = D.DateKey
            GROUP BY ProductName, Year, MonthNumber )
SELECT     P.ProductName, P.MonthName, P.Year, S1.SalesAmount,
           S2.SalesAmount AS SalesPrevMonth, COALESCE(S1.SalesAmount,0) -
           COALESCE(S2.SalesAmount,0) AS SalesGrowth
```

```
FROM        ProdYearMonthPM P LEFT OUTER JOIN SalesProdMonth S1 ON
            P.ProductName = S1.ProductName AND
            P.Year = S1.Year AND
            P.MonthNumber = S1.MonthNumber LEFT OUTER JOIN SalesProdMonth S2
            ON P.ProductName = S2.ProductName AND
            P.PM_Year = S2.Year AND
            P.PM_MonthNumber = S2.MonthNumber
ORDER BY ProductName, P.Year, P.MonthNumber
```

Table ProdYearMonthPM computes the Cartesian product of the Product table with the view YearMonthPM. Table SalesProdMonth computes the monthly sales by product. Finally, the main query performs twice a left outer join of the table ProdYearMonthPM with the table SalesProdMonth to compute the result.

Query 7.5. *Three best-selling employees.*

```
SELECT      TOP(3) E.FirstName + ' ' + E.LastName AS EmployeeName,
            SUM(S.SalesAmount) AS SalesAmount
FROM        Sales S, Employee E
WHERE       S.EmployeeKey = E.EmployeeKey
GROUP BY E.FirstName, E.LastName
ORDER BY SalesAmount DESC
```

We group the sales by employee and apply the SUM aggregation to each group. The result is then sorted in descending order of the aggregated sales and the TOP function is used to obtain the first three tuples.

Query 7.6. *Best-selling employee per product and year.*

```
WITH SalesProdYearEmp AS (
            SELECT      P.ProductName, D.Year, SUM(S.SalesAmount) AS SalesAmount,
                        E.FirstName + ' ' + E.LastName AS EmployeeName
            FROM        Sales S, Employee E, Date D, Product P
            WHERE       S.EmployeeKey = E.EmployeeKey AND
                        S.OrderDateKey = D.DateKey AND
                        S.ProductKey = P.ProductKey
            GROUP BY P.ProductName, D.Year, E.FirstName, E.LastName )
SELECT      ProductName, Year, EmployeeName AS TopEmployee,
            SalesAmount AS TopSales
FROM        SalesProdYearEmp S1
WHERE       S1.SalesAmount = (
            SELECT      MAX(SalesAmount)
            FROM        SalesProdYearEmp S2
            WHERE       S1.ProductName = S2.ProductName AND S1.Year = S2.Year )
ORDER BY ProductName, Year
```

The table SalesProdYearEmp computes the yearly sales by product and employee. In the query, we select the tuples of this table such that the total sales equals the maximum total sales for the product and the year.

Query 7.7. *Countries that account for top 50% of the sales amount.*

```
WITH TotalSales AS (
            SELECT      SUM(SalesAmount) AS SalesAmount
            FROM        Sales),
      SalesCountry AS (
            SELECT      CountryName, SUM(SalesAmount) AS SalesAmount
            FROM        Sales S, Customer C, City Y, State T, Country O
            WHERE       S.CustomerKey = C.CustomerKey AND
                        C.CityKey = Y.CityKey AND Y.StateKey = T.StateKey AND
                        T.CountryKey = O.CountryKey
            GROUP BY CountryName ),
      CumulSalesCountry AS (
            SELECT      S.*, SUM(SalesAmount) OVER (ORDER BY SalesAmount DESC
                        ROWS UNBOUNDED PRECEDING) AS CumulSales
            FROM        SalesCountry S )
SELECT      C.CountryName, C.SalesAmount, C.SalesAmount / T.SalesAmount AS
            PercSales, C.CumulSales, C.CumulSales / T.SalesAmount AS CumulPerc
FROM        CumulSalesCountry C, TotalSales T
WHERE       CumulSales <= (
            SELECT      MIN(CumulSales) FROM CumulSalesCountry
            WHERE       CumulSales >= (
                        SELECT 0.5 * SUM(SalesAmount) FROM SalesCountry ) )
ORDER BY SalesAmount DESC
```

The table **SalesCountry** aggregates the sales by country. In the table **Cumul-SalesCountry**, for each row in the previous table, we define a window containing all the rows sorted in decreasing value of sales amount, and compute the sum of the current row and all the preceding rows in the window. Finally, in the main query, we have to select the countries in **CumulSalesCountry** whose cumulative sales amount is less or equal than the minimum value that is higher or equal to the 50% of the total sales amount.

Query 7.8. *Total sales and average monthly sales by employee and year.*

```
WITH MonthlySalesEmp AS (
            SELECT      E.FirstName + ' ' + E.LastName AS EmployeeName,
                        D.Year, D.MonthNumber, SUM(SalesAmount) AS SalesAmount
            FROM        Sales S, Employee E, Date D
            WHERE       S.EmployeeKey = E.EmployeeKey AND
                        S.OrderDateKey = D.DateKey
            GROUP BY E.FirstName, E.LastName, D.Year, D.MonthNumber )
SELECT      EmployeeName, Year, SUM(SalesAmount) AS SalesAmount,
            AVG(SalesAmount) AS AvgMonthlySales
FROM        MonthlySalesEmp
GROUP BY EmployeeName, Year
ORDER BY EmployeeName, Year
```

Table **MonthlySalesEmp** computes the monthly sales by employee. In the query, we group the tuples of this table by employee and year, and the **SUM** and **AVG** functions are applied to obtain, respectively, the total yearly sales and the average monthly sales.

Query 7.9. *Total sales amount and discount amount per product and month.*

```
SELECT    P.ProductName, D.Year, D.MonthNumber,
          SUM(S.SalesAmount) AS SalesAmount,
          SUM(S.UnitPrice * S.Quantity * S.Discount) AS TotalDisc
FROM      Sales S, Date D, Product P
WHERE     S.OrderDateKey = D.DateKey AND S.ProductKey = P.ProductKey
GROUP BY  P.ProductName, D.Year, D.MonthNumber
ORDER BY  P.ProductName, D.Year, D.MonthNumber
```

Here, we group the sales by product and month. Then, the SUM aggregation function is used to obtain the total sales and the total discount amount.

Query 7.10. *Monthly year-to-date sales for each product category.*

```
WITH SalesCategoryMonth AS (
          SELECT    CategoryName, Year, MonthNumber,
                    SUM(SalesAmount) AS SalesAmount
          FROM      Sales S, Product P, Category C, Date D
          WHERE     S.OrderDateKey = D.DateKey AND
                    S.ProductKey = P.ProductKey AND
                    P.CategoryKey = C.CategoryKey
          GROUP BY CategoryName, Year, MonthNumber ),
      CategorySales AS (
          SELECT    DISTINCT CategoryName
          FROM      SalesCategoryMonth ),
      CategoryMonth AS (
          SELECT    *
          FROM      CategorySales, YearMonth )
SELECT    C.CategoryName, C.MonthName, C.Year, SalesAmount, SUM(SalesAmount)
          OVER (PARTITION BY C.CategoryName, C.Year ORDER BY
          C.MonthNumber ROWS UNBOUNDED PRECEDING) AS YTDSalesAmount
FROM      CategoryMonth C LEFT OUTER JOIN SalesCategoryMonth S ON
          C.CategoryName = S.CategoryName AND C.Year = S.Year AND
          C.MonthNumber = S.MonthNumber
ORDER BY CategoryName, Year, C.MonthNumber
```

This query follows an approach similar to Query 7.4 so that the year-to-date aggregation is computed over all the months, including those for which there are no sales for a category. Table SalesCategoryMonth aggregates the sales amount by category and month. Table CategorySales collects all categories in the previous table. Table CategoryMonth computes the Cartesian product of the previous table with the YearMonth view defined at the beginning of this section containing all the months in the Date dimension. In the main query, we perform a left outer join of the previous table with SalesCategoryMonth and, for each row in the result, define a window containing all the rows with the same category and year, sort the rows in the window by month, and compute the sum of the current row and all the preceding rows in the window.

Query 7.11. *Moving average over the last 3 months of the sales amount by product category.*

```
WITH SalesCategoryMonth AS ( ... ),
     CategorySales AS ( ... ),
     CategoryMonth AS ( ... )
SELECT    C.CategoryName, C.MonthName, C.Year, SalesAmount,
          AVG(SalesAmount) OVER (PARTITION BY C.CategoryName ORDER BY
          C.Year, C.MonthNumber ROWS 2 PRECEDING) AS MovAvg3M
FROM      CategoryMonth C LEFT OUTER JOIN SalesCategoryMonth S ON
          C.CategoryName = S.CategoryName AND C.Year = S.Year AND
          C.MonthNumber = S.MonthNumber
ORDER BY CategoryName, Year, C.MonthNumber
```

This query is a variation of the previous one and it defines the same temporary tables, which are not repeated here. In the query, we perform a left outer join of the CategoryName table with the SalesCategoryMonth table and for each row of the result, we define a window containing all the tuples with the same category, order the tuples in the window by year and month, and compute the average of the current row and the two preceding ones.

Query 7.12. *Personal sales amount made by an employee compared with the total sales amount made by herself and her subordinates during 2017.*

```
WITH Supervision AS (
          SELECT    EmployeeKey, SupervisorKey
          FROM      Employee
          WHERE     SupervisorKey IS NOT NULL
          UNION ALL
          SELECT    E.EmployeeKey, S.SupervisorKey
          FROM      Supervision S, Employee E
          WHERE     S.EmployeeKey = E.SupervisorKey ),
     SalesEmp2017 AS (
          SELECT    EmployeeKey, SUM(S.SalesAmount) AS PersonalSales
          FROM      Sales S, Date D
          WHERE     S.OrderDateKey = D.DateKey AND D.Year = 2017
          GROUP BY EmployeeKey ),
     SalesSubord2017 AS (
          SELECT    SupervisorKey AS EmployeeKey,
                    SUM(S.SalesAmount) AS SubordinateSales
          FROM      Sales S, Supervision U, Date D
          WHERE     S.EmployeeKey = U.EmployeeKey AND
                    S.OrderDateKey = D.DateKey AND D.Year = 2017
          GROUP BY SupervisorKey )
SELECT    FirstName + ' ' + LastName AS EmployeeName, S1.PersonalSales,
          COALESCE(S1.PersonalSales + S2.SubordinateSales, S1.PersonalSales)
          AS PersSubordSales
FROM      Employee E JOIN SalesEmp2017 S1 ON E.EmployeeKey = S1.EmployeeKey
          LEFT OUTER JOIN SalesSubord2017 S2 ON
          S1.EmployeeKey = S2.EmployeeKey
ORDER BY EmployeeName
```

Table Supervision computes with a recursive query the transitive closure of the supervision relationship. Table SalesEmp2017 computes the total sales by employee, while table **SalesSubord2017** computes the total sales of the subordinates of an employee. The main query computes the left outer join of the two latter tables while aggregating in the **SELECT** clause the personal sales and the subordinates sales. The **COALESCE** function takes into account the case where an employee has no subordinates.

Query 7.13. *Total sales amount, number of products, and sum of the quantities sold for each order.*

```
SELECT     OrderNo, SUM(SalesAmount) AS SalesAmount,
           MAX(OrderLineNo) AS NbProducts, SUM(Quantity) AS Quantity
FROM       Sales
GROUP BY OrderNo
ORDER BY OrderNo
```

Recall that the **Sales** fact table contains both the order number and the order line number, which constitute a fact dimension. In the query, we group the sales by order number, and then we apply the **SUM** and **MAX** aggregation functions to obtain the requested values.

Query 7.14. *For each month, total number of orders, total sales amount, and average sales amount by order.*

```
WITH OrderAgg AS (
           SELECT     OrderNo, OrderDateKey, SUM(SalesAmount) AS SalesAmount
           FROM       Sales
           GROUP BY OrderNo, OrderDateKey )
SELECT     Year, MonthNumber, COUNT(OrderNo) AS NoOrders,
           SUM(SalesAmount) AS SalesAmount, AVG(SalesAmount) AS AvgAmount
FROM       OrderAgg O, Date D
WHERE      O.OrderDateKey = D.DateKey
GROUP BY Year, MonthNumber
ORDER BY Year, MonthNumber
```

Table **OrderAgg** computes the sales amount of each order. Note that we also need to keep the key of the time dimension, which will be used in the main query to join the fact table and the time dimension table. Then, grouping the tuples by year and month, we compute the aggregated values requested.

Query 7.15. *For each employee, total sales amount, number of cities, and number of states to which she is assigned.*

```
SELECT     FirstName + ' ' + LastName AS EmployeeName,
           SUM(SalesAmount) / COUNT(DISTINCT CityName) AS TotalSales,
           COUNT(DISTINCT CityName) AS NoCities,
           COUNT(DISTINCT StateName) AS NoStates
FROM       Sales F, Employee E, Territories T, City C, State S
WHERE      F.EmployeeKey = E.EmployeeKey AND E.EmployeeKey = T.EmployeeKey AND
           T.CityKey = C.CityKey AND C.StateKey = S.StateKey
GROUP BY FirstName, LastName
ORDER BY EmployeeName
```

The Territories table captures the many-to-many relationship between employees and cities. The above query joins the five tables and groups the result by employee. In the SELECT clause we sum the SalesAmount measure and divide it by the number of distinct CityName assigned to an employee in table Territories. This solves the double-counting problem studied in Sect. 4.2.6.

If an attribute Percentage in table Territories states the percentage of time an employee is assigned to each city, the query above will read:

```
SELECT  FirstName + ' ' + LastName AS EmployeeName,
        SUM(SalesAmount) * T.Percentage AS TotalSales,
        COUNT(DISTINCT CityName) AS NoCities,
        COUNT(DISTINCT StateName) AS NoStates
FROM    Sales F, Employee E, Territories T, City C, State S
WHERE ...
```

We can see that the sum of the SalesAmount measure is multiplied by the percentage to account for the double-counting problem.

7.4 Comparison of MDX, DAX, and SQL

In the preceding sections, we used MDX, DAX, and SQL for querying the Northwind data warehouse. In this section, we compare these languages.

At a first glance, the syntax of the three languages looks similar. Also their functionality is similar since, indeed, we expressed the same set of queries in the three languages. However, there are some fundamental differences between SQL, MDX, and DAX, which we discuss next.

The main difference between SQL, MDX, and DAX is the ability of MDX to reference multiple dimensions. Although it is possible to use SQL exclusively to query cubes, MDX provides commands that are designed specifically to retrieve multidimensional data with almost any number of dimensions. For DAX, being based in the tabular model, it is naturally harder to handle multiple dimensions and hierarchies, as we have discussed in Chap. 6. In some sense this is similar to SQL, given that the latter refers to only two dimensions, columns and rows. Nevertheless, this fundamental difference between the three languages somehow disappears since for most OLAP tools it is difficult to display a result set using more than two dimensions (although of course, different line formats, colors, etc., are used for this). We have seen in our example queries the use of the cross join operator to combine several dimensions in one axis when we needed to analyze measures across more than two dimensions in MDX, for instance. In SQL, the SELECT clause is used to define the column layout for a query. However, in MDX the SELECT clause is used to define several axis dimensions. The approach in DAX is different, since there is no SELECT clause, of course.

In SQL, the WHERE clause is used to *filter* the data returned by a query, whereas in MDX, the WHERE clause is used to provide a *slice* of the data returned by a query. While the two concepts are similar, they are not equivalent. In an SQL query, the WHERE clause contains an arbitrary list of items which may or may not be returned in the result set, in order to narrow down the scope of the data that are retrieved. In MDX, however, the concept of a slice implies a reduction in the number of dimensions, and thus, each member in the WHERE clause must identify a distinct portion of data from a different dimension. Furthermore, unlike in SQL, the WHERE clause in MDX cannot filter what is returned on an axis of a query. To filter what appears on an axis of a query, we can use functions such as FILTER, NONEMPTY, and TOPCOUNT. This is also the approach in DAX, where the values that we do not want to display are filtered out using the FILTER clause, and there is no WHERE clause whatsoever, and there is no notion of slicing either.

We next compare the queries over the Northwind data warehouse as expressed in MDX in Sect. 7.1, DAX in Sect 7.2, and SQL in Sect. 7.3.

Consider Query 7.1. A first observation is that, in SQL, the joins between tables must be explicitly indicated in the query, whereas they are implicit in MDX and DAX. Also, in SQL, an inner join will remove empty combinations, whereas in MDX and DAX, NON EMPTY and ISBLANK, respectively, must be specified to achieve this. On the other hand, outer joins are needed in SQL if we want to show empty combinations.

Furthermore, in SQL the aggregations needed for the roll-up operations must be explicitly stated through the GROUP BY and the aggregation functions in the SELECT clause, while in MDX the aggregation functions are stated in the cube definition and they are automatically performed upon roll-up operations, and in DAX this is done when the measures are computed with the MEASURE statement. Finally, in SQL the display format must be stated in the query, while in MDX this is stated in the cube definition, and in DAX in the model definition.

Consider now the comparison of measures of the current period with respect to those of a previous period, such as the previous month or the same month in the previous year. An example is given in Query 7.3. In MDX this can be done with calculated members using the WITH MEMBER clause. In SQL a temporary table is defined in the WITH clause in which the aggregations needed for the roll-up operation are performed for each period, and an outer join is needed in the main query to obtain the measure of the current period together with that of a previous period. Nevertheless, as shown in Query 7.4, obtaining the previous month in SQL is somehow complex since we must account for two cases depending on whether the previous month is in the same year or in the previous year. In this sense, the approach of DAX is similar to that in MDX, and the MEASURE statement computes the sales in the previous period (like MDX does using WITH). Therefore, either in DAX or in MDX this computation looks simpler and more flexible, although it requires more semantics to be included in the query languages, which makes them more cryptic for non-expert users.

Consider now top and bottom performance analysis, an example of which is given in Query 7.5. In MDX, this can be obtained with functions such as TOPCOUNT, in DAX with the TOPN, whereas in SQL this can be achieved with the TOP function. The three queries then are expressed in a very simple way. Nevertheless, there is a fundamental difference between the three approaches when it comes to computing cumulative sums, which is clearly shown in Query 7.7. In MDX, the function TOPPERCENT sorts a set in descending order, and returns a set of tuples with the highest values whose cumulative total is equal to or greater than a specified percentage. This makes the query very easy to express. In SQL, stating TOP(n) PERCENT will return the percentage of the total number of tuples in the answer, and therefore the computation must be crafted in a different way, using window functions to compute the running sum. The query turns out to be very complex in DAX, since there is no function equivalent to MDX's TOPPERCENT and there is no notion of window functions either; therefore the query is built basically though a sequence of measure computations and filtering.

Query 7.8 is an example of aggregate manipulation at several granularities. In MDX this is done by starting at the finer granularity, and obtaining the coarser granularity through the ASCENDANTS function. In SQL the finer granularity is computed in a temporary table and the coarser granularity is obtained by aggregating the temporary table in the main query. DAX follows a similar approach, although through the computation of measures, and aggregating at coarser granularity using the SUMMARIZECOLUMNS function.

Let us consider period-to-date calculations and moving averages, as exemplified in Queries 7.10 and 7.11. In MDX, the function PERIODSTODATE is used for the former and LAG is used for the latter. In DAX, TOTALYTD and AVERAGEX are used, respectively. These functionalities make these queries very concise to compute (provided that the user has enough expertise with the languages). On the other hand, in SQL these are obtained by using window functions; therefore queries in this case are more ad hoc.

Query 7.12 is an example of aggregation in parent-child hierarchies. As can be seen, this is easily expressed in MDX, while a complex recursive query is needed to obtain similar functionality in SQL. In DAX, although the query looks simple, it requires the previous computation of a measure Supervision-Path to override the lack of hierarchy handling of the tabular model. Thus, we can say that the power of the dimensional approach of MDX is fully exploited when addressing recursive queries.

Queries 7.13 and 7.14 show examples of manipulation of fact dimensions, since they mention the dimension Order. Although this can be expressed quite succinctly in MDX, it is not immediate to understand how to achieve such a result. The corresponding queries in SQL are easier to write. DAX can also handle fact dimensions quite naturally, as can be seen in these queries.

Finally, Query 7.15 is an example of manipulating many-to-many dimensions. The SQL version needs to deal with the double-counting problem while aggregating the measure, although the query remains quite simple. The MDX query handles the problem naturally through the use of the bridge table when the cube was created. DAX in this case requires extra handling because of the limitations imposed by the directionality of the relationships between the employees and the territories they are assigned to.

To conclude, Table 7.1 summarizes some of the advantages and disadvantages of the three languages.

Table 7.1 Comparison of MDX, DAX, and SQL

	Pros	**Cons**
M D X	• Expressive multidimensional model comprising facts, dimensions, hierarchies, measure groups • Simple navigation within time dimension and hierarchies • Easy to express business-related requests • Fast, due to the existence of aggregations	• Extra effort for designing a cube and setting up aggregations • Steep learning curve: manipulating an n-dimensional space • Hard-to-grasp concepts: current context, execution phases, etc. • Some operations are difficult to express, such as ordering on multiple criteria
D A X	• Simple model with tables joined implicitly through relationships • Similar syntax as Excel functions aiming at self-service BI • Built-in time-related calculations • Fast, due to in-memory, compressed columnar storage	• Steep learning curve • Hard-to-grasp concepts, e.g., evaluation contexts • Single functionality can be achieved in multiple ways • Limited model, e.g., hierarchies in a single table, at most one active relationship between two entities • Limited functionality for handling hierarchies
S Q L	• Large user base • Simple model using two-dimensional tables • Standardized language supported by multiple systems • Easy-to-understand semantics of queries • Various ways to relate tables: joins, derived tables, correlated queries, common table expressions, etc.	• Tables must be joined explicitly in queries • No concept of row ordering and hierarchies: navigating dimensions may be complex • Analytical queries and time-related computations may be difficult to express • Analytical queries may be costly

7.5 KPIs for the Northwind Case Study

Recall that we discussed in Sect. 6.3 various categories of key performance
indicators (KPIs). We give next examples of indicators that may be appropriate for the Northwind company. These KPIs address the requirements of
several departments that are responsible for monitoring them. For example,
the sales department wants to monitor sales performance and order activity.
The marketing department wants to follow shipping efficiency as an indirect
way of estimating customer satisfaction. The human resources department
wants to measure how sales employees are performing to estimate the end-
of-year bonuses. Therefore, we propose the following KPIs:

1. *Sales performance.* Measures the monthly sales amount with respect to
   the same month of the previous year. *The goal consists in achieving 15%
   growth year over year.*
2. *Number of orders.* Measures the number of orders submitted per month.
   The goal is to achieve a 5% monthly increase. Note that if we also compute this KPI weekly, we can have an idea of how orders are evolving
   within the current period, and can take corrective measures in order to
   achieve the monthly goal.
3. *Shipping efficiency.* Measures the delay in the shipping of orders and thus,
   it is a measure of customer satisfaction. It is computed as the monthly
   average of the difference between the order and the shipped dates. *The
   goal is that the difference between the two dates takes a value less than 7.*
4. *Shipping costs.* Measures the relative cost of shipping with respect to the
   sales amount. It is computed monthly as the quotient between the freight
   costs and the total sales amount for the current month. *The goal is that
   the shipping cost does not exceed 5% of the sales amount.*
5. *Sales quota.* Measures the percentage of employees reaching their sales
   quota at the end of the year. An employee's sales quota is computed as
   a 15% increase over last year's sales. It is computed monthly, to see how
   this number is evolving during the current year. *The goal is that at least
   75% of the employees reach their quota.*

We next show how we can define KPIs using Microsoft Analysis Services
in both the multidimensional and tabular models.

7.5.1 KPIs in Analysis Services Multidimensional

In a multidimensional model, a cube may have a collection of KPIs. Only the
metadata for the KPIs are stored in the cube, and a set of MDX functions is
available for retrieving KPI values from cubes using these metadata.

Each KPI has five predefined properties, namely, the *value*, the *goal*, the
status, the *trend*, and the *weight*. These are MDX expressions that return

numeric values from a cube. The expressions for the status and the trend should return a value between −1 and 1. This value is used to display a graphical indicator of the KPI property. The weight controls the contribution of the KPI to its parent KPI, if it has one. Analysis Services creates hidden calculated members on the **Measures** dimension for each KPI property above, although they can be used in an MDX expression.

We show next how to implement the *Sales performance* KPI defined in the previous section. Recall that we want to monitor the monthly sales amount with respect to the goal of achieving 15% growth year over year. Let us now give more detail about what the users want. The performance is considered satisfactory if the actual sales amount is at least 95% of the goal. If the sales amount is within 85–95% of the goal, there should be an alert. If the sales amount drops under 85% of the goal, immediate actions are needed to change the trend. These alerts and calls to action are commonly associated with the use of KPIs. We are also interested in the trends associated with the sales amount; if the sales amount is 20% higher than expected, this is great news and should be highlighted. Similarly, if the sales amount is 20% lower than expected, then we have to deal immediately with the situation.

The MDX query that computes the goal of the KPI is given next:

```
WITH MEMBER Measures.SalesPerformanceGoal AS
        CASE
            WHEN ISEMPTY(PARALLELPERIOD([Order Date].Calendar.Month, 12,
                [Order Date].Calendar.CurrentMember))
            THEN Measures.[Sales Amount]
            ELSE 1.15 * ( Measures.[Sales Amount],
                PARALLELPERIOD([Order Date].Calendar.Month, 12,
                [Order Date].Calendar.CurrentMember) )
        END, FORMAT_STRING = '$###,##0.00'
SELECT { [Sales Amount], SalesPerformanceGoal } ON COLUMNS,
        [Order Date].Calendar.Month.MEMBERS ON ROWS
FROM    Sales
```

The **CASE** statement sets the goal to the actual monthly sales if the corresponding month of the previous year is not included in the time frame of the cube. Since the sales in the Northwind data warehouse started in July 2016, this means that the goal until June 2017 is set to the actual sales.

We can use Visual Studio to define the above KPI, which we name **Sales Performance**. For this, we need to provide MDX expressions for each of the above properties as follows:

- **Value:** The measure defining the KPI is [Measures].[Sales Amount].
- **Goal:** The goal to increase 15% over last year's sales amount is given by

  FORMAT(CASE ... END, '$###,##0.00')

  where the **CASE** expression is as in the query above.
- **Status:** We select the traffic light indicator for displaying the status of the KPI. Therefore, the corresponding MDX expression must return a value

between -1 and 1. The KPI browser displays a red traffic light when the status is -1, a yellow traffic light when the status is 0, and a green traffic light when the status is 1. The MDX expression is given next:

```
CASE
    WHEN KpiValue("Sales Performance") / KpiGoal("Sales Performance") >= 0.95
    THEN 1
    WHEN KpiValue("Sales Performance") / KpiGoal("Sales Performance") < 0.85
    THEN -1
    ELSE 0
END
```

The KpiValue and KpiGoal functions above retrieve, respectively, the actual and the goal values of the given KPI. The expression computes the status by dividing the actual value by the goal value. If it is 95% or more, the value of the status is 1, if it is less than 85%, the value of the status is -1, otherwise, the value is 0.

- Trend: Among the available graphical indicators, we select the status arrow. The associated MDX expression is given next:

```
CASE
    WHEN ( KpiValue("Sales Performance") - KpiGoal("Sales Performance") ) /
        KpiGoal("Sales Performance") > 0.2
    THEN 1
    WHEN ( KpiValue("Sales Performance") - KpiGoal("Sales Performance") ) /
        KpiGoal("Sales Performance") <= -0.2
    THEN -1
    ELSE 0
END
```

This expression computes the trend by subtracting the goal from the value, then dividing by the goal. If there is a shortfall of 20% or more the value of the trend is -1, if there is a surplus of 20% or more the value of the trend is 1, otherwise, the value is 0.

- Weight: We leave it empty.

Figure 7.1 shows the KPI for November and December 2017. As can be seen, where the figures for the month of December achieved the goal, this was not the case for the month of November.

Now that the KPI is defined, we can issue an MDX query such as the next one to display the KPI.

```
SELECT { Measures.[Sales Amount], Measures.[Sales Performance Goal],
        Measures.[Sales Performance Trend] } ON COLUMNS,
        { [Order Date].Calendar.Month.[November 2017],
        [Order Date].Calendar.Month.[December 2017] } ON ROWS
FROM    Sales
```

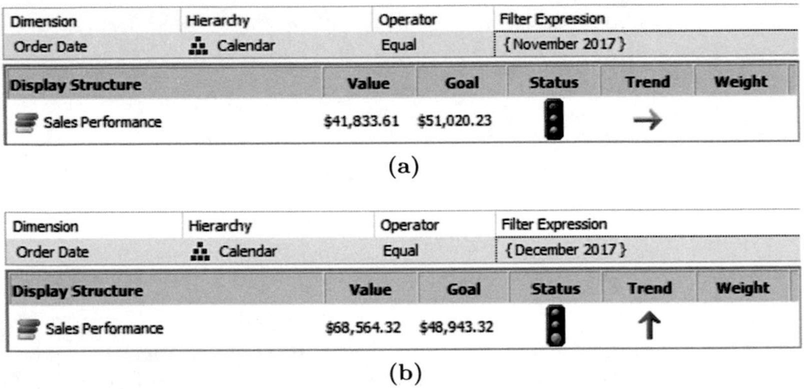

Dimension	Hierarchy	Operator	Filter Expression
Order Date	⚏ Calendar	Equal	{ November 2017 }

Display Structure	Value	Goal	Status	Trend	Weight
🖥 Sales Performance	$41,833.61	$51,020.23	🚦	→	

(a)

Dimension	Hierarchy	Operator	Filter Expression
Order Date	⚏ Calendar	Equal	{ December 2017 }

Display Structure	Value	Goal	Status	Trend	Weight
🖥 Sales Performance	$68,564.32	$48,943.32	🚦	↑	

(b)

Fig. 7.1 Display of the Sales Performance KPI. (a) November 2017; (b) December 2017

7.5.2 KPIs in Analysis Services Tabular

In the tabular model, a KPI is always based on a measure. However, in contrast with the multidimensional model, when a KPI is defined, the measure itself becomes the value of the KPI. However, it is still possible to use and reference the measure in DAX.

A KPI has three additional properties: the *goal*, the *status*, and the *trend*. In our example, the goal of Sales Performance is to increase 15% over last year's sales amount. The status is a value describing how the actual value of the KPI compares with the goal. Finally, the trend is a value describing how the measure is changing over time. The last two properties are typically transformed into a visual representation.

We now implement the Sales Performance KPI in Tabular. The following DAX query defines the target, the status, and the trend of the KPI.

```
DEFINE
    MEASURE Sales[Sales Target] =
        VAR SalesAmountPY = CALCULATE( [Sales Amount],
            PARALLELPERIOD( 'Date'[Date], -12, MONTH) )
    RETURN
        IF( ISBLANK(SalesAmountPY), [Sales Amount], SalesAmountPY * 1.15 )
    MEASURE Sales[Sales Status] =
        SWITCH( TRUE,
            [Sales Amount] / [Sales Target] >= 0.95, 1,
            [Sales Amount] / [Sales Target] < 0.85, -1,
            0 )
    MEASURE Sales[Sales Trend] =
        SWITCH( TRUE,
            ( [Sales Amount] - [Sales Target] ) / [Sales Target] >= 0.2, 1,
            ( [Sales Amount] - [Sales Target] ) / [Sales Target] < -0.2, -1,
            0 )
EVALUATE
SUMMARIZECOLUMNS(
```

```
'Date'[MonthNumber], 'Date'[Year],
"Sales Amount", FORMAT( [Sales Amount], "$###,##0.00" ),
"Sales Target", FORMAT( [Sales Target], "$###,##0.00" ),
"Sales Status", [Sales Status], "Sales Trend", [Sales Trend] )
ORDER BY [Year], [MonthNumber]
```

In the **Sales Target** measure, the variable **SalesAmountPY** computes the sales amount in the previous year, so that the target is set to the sales amount if there is no value for the previous year, otherwise the target is set to a 15% increase of the sales amount in the previous year. The **Sales Status** measure returns a value of 1 if the ratio between the actual value and the target value of the KPI is 95% or more, it is −1 if this ratio is less than 85%, and 0 otherwise. Finally, the **Sales Trend** measure returns a value of 1 if the difference between the actual value and the target value divided by the latter is 20% or more, it is −1 if this ratio is less than 20%, and 0 otherwise.

Now that we have defined the DAX expressions for the KPI, we can use them to display the KPI in PowerBI Desktop. For this we need to install the Tabular Editor so that we can define the KPI in the model. In the Tabular Editor we need to transform the **Sales Amount** measure into a KPI as shown in Fig. 7.2. The values can then be visualized as shown in Fig. 7.3.

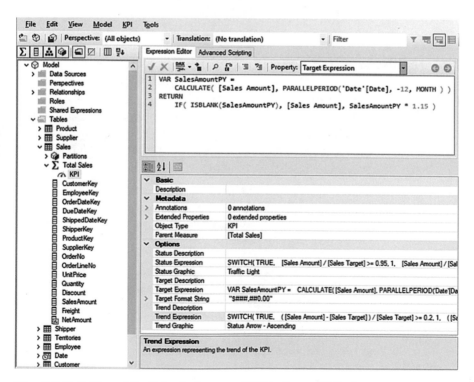

Fig. 7.2 Definition of the **Sales Performance** KPI in Power BI Desktop

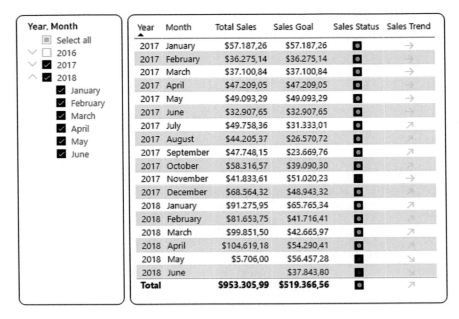

Fig. 7.3 Display of the Sales Performance KPI in Power BI Desktop

7.6 Dashboards for the Northwind Case Study

In this section, we show how to define a dashboard for the Northwind case study. Since the database contains sales until May 5, 2018, we assume that we are currently at that date.

We want to display in a dashboard a group of indicators to monitor the performance of several sectors of the company. The dashboard will contain:

- A graph showing the evolution of the *total sales per month*, together with the total sales in the same month for the previous year.
- A gauge monitoring the *percentual variation of total sales* in the last month with respect to the same month for the previous year. The goal is to obtain a 5% increase.
- Another graph conveying the *shipping costs*. The graph reports, monthly, the total freight cost with respect to the total sales. The goal is that the shipping costs must be less than the 5% of the sales amount.
- A gauge showing the year-to-date shipping costs to sales ratio. This is the KPI introduced in Sect. 6.3.
- A table analyzing the performance of the sales force of the company. It will list the three employees with the poorest sales performance as a percentage of their target sales as of the current date. For each one of them, we compute the total sales and the percentage with respect to the

expected yearly sales quota. Employees are expected to increase their sales 5% each year.

We illustrate next how to build this dashboard in Microsoft Reporting Services and Power BI.

7.6.1 Dashboards in Reporting Services

Reporting Services is a server-based reporting platform that provides reporting functionality for a wide range of data sources. Its three main components are the *client*, the *report server*, and the *report databases*. Visual Studio is typically used as the client, in particular for defining the dashboard. The report server performs functions such as authentication, report and data processing, report rendering, scheduling, and delivery. Finally, there are three databases in Reporting Services. The data source is the origin of the data that will populate the reports, and can correspond to various data providers, such as SQL Server and Oracle databases. The other two databases, called **ReportServer** and **ReportServerTempDB**, store metadata about the reports.

Reporting Services provides multiple objects that can be included in a dashboard. These include various chart types, report objects such as gauges (typically used with KPIs), images, maps, data bars, sparklines, and indicators. These can be put together with tabular data, as we will show below.

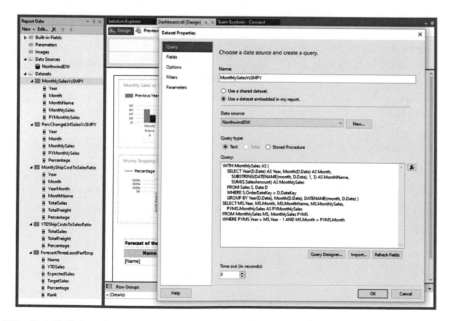

Fig. 7.4 Defining the Northwind dashboard in Reporting Services using Visual Studio

Figure 7.4 shows the definition of the Northwind dashboard using Visual Studio. As shown in the left of the figure, the data source is the Northwind data warehouse. There are five datasets, one for each element of the dashboard. Each dataset has an associated SQL query and a set of fields, which correspond to the columns returned by the SQL query. The query shown in the dialog box corresponds to the top left chart of the report. Figure 7.5 shows the resulting dashboard. We explain below its different components.

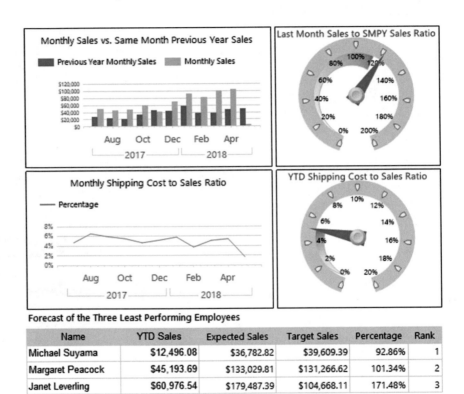

Forecast of the Three Least Performing Employees

Name	YTD Sales	Expected Sales	Target Sales	Percentage	Rank
Michael Suyama	$12,496.08	$36,782.82	$39,609.39	92.86%	1
Margaret Peacock	$45,193.69	$133,029.81	$131,266.62	101.34%	2
Janet Leverling	$60,976.54	$179,487.39	$104,668.11	171.48%	3

Fig. 7.5 Dashboard of the Northwind case study in Reporting Services

The top left chart shows the monthly sales together with those of the same month of the previous year. The SQL query is given next.

```
WITH MonthlySales AS (
        SELECT    Year(D.Date) AS Year, Month(D.Date) AS Month,
                  SUBSTRING(DATENAME(month, D.Date), 1, 3) AS MonthName,
                  SUM(S.SalesAmount) AS MonthlySales
        FROM      Sales S, Date D
        WHERE     S.OrderDateKey = D.DateKey
        GROUP BY Year(D.Date), Month(D.Date), DATENAME(month, D.Date) )
SELECT MS.Year, MS.Month, MS.MonthName, MS.MonthlySales,
        PYMS.MonthlySales AS PreviousYearMonthlySales
FROM    MonthlySales MS, MonthlySales PYMS
WHERE  PYMS.Year = MS.Year - 1 AND MS.Month = PYMS.Month
```

In the above query, table **MonthlySales** computes the monthly sales amount. Notice that the column **MonthName** computes the first three letters of the month name, which is used for the labels of the x-axis of the chart. Then, the main query joins table **MonthlySales** twice to obtain the result.

The top right gauge shows the percentage of the last month's sales with respect to the sales in the same month of the previous year. Recall that the last order in the database was placed on May 5, 2018, and thus we would like to show the figures for the last complete month, that is April 2018. The gauge defines a range (shown at the interior of the scale) with a gradient from white to light blue and ranging from 0% to 115%. This corresponds to the KPI targeting a 15% increase of the monthly sales amount with respect to the same month of the previous year. The query for the gauge is given next:

```
WITH MonthlySales AS (
        SELECT Year(D.Date) AS Year, Month(D.Date) AS Month,
               SUM(S.SalesAmount) AS MonthlySales
        FROM    Sales S, Date D
        WHERE S.OrderDateKey = D.DateKey
        GROUP BY Year(D.Date), Month(D.Date) ),
     LastMonth AS (
        SELECT Year(MAX(D.Date)) AS Year, Month(MAX(D.Date)) AS MonthNumber
        FROM    Sales S, Date D
        WHERE S.OrderDateKey = D.DateKey )
SELECT MS.Year, MS.Month,
        MS.MonthlySales,
        PYMS.MonthlySales AS PYMonthlySales,
        (MS.MonthlySales - PYMS.MonthlySales) / PYMS.MonthlySales AS Percentage
FROM    LastMonth L, YearMonthPM Y, MonthlySales MS, MonthlySales PYMS
WHERE  L.Year = Y.Year AND L.MonthNumber = Y.MonthNumber AND
        Y.PM_Year = MS.Year AND Y.PM_MonthNumber = MS.Month AND
        PYMS.Year = MS.Year - 1 AND MS.Month = PYMS.Month
```

Table **MonthlySales** computes the monthly sales amount as in the previous query. Table **LastMonth** computes the year and month of the last order. Finally, the main query performs a join of **LastMonth** with the view **YearMonthPM** to obtain the previous month of the last order; the additional joins obtain the sales of that month and the sales of the same month of the previous year.

The query for the middle left chart, which shows the shipping costs with respect to the total sales by month is given next.

```
SELECT    Year(D.Date) AS Year, Month(D.Date) AS Month,
          SUBSTRING(DATENAME(mm, D.Date), 1, 3) AS MonthName,
          SUM(S.SalesAmount) AS TotalSales, SUM(S.Freight) AS TotalFreight,
          SUM(S.Freight) / SUM(S.SalesAmount) AS Percentage
FROM      Sales S, Date D
WHERE     S.OrderDateKey = D.DateKey
GROUP BY Year(D.Date), Month(D.Date), DATENAME(mm, D.Date)
ORDER BY Year, Month, DATENAME(mm, D.Date)
```

Here we compute the total sales and the total freight cost by month, and the percentage of the former comprised by the latter.

The gauge in the middle right of Fig. 7.5 shows the year-to-date shipping costs to sales ratio. The range of the gauge reflects the KPI used for monitoring shipping costs, targeted at remaining below 5% of the sales amount. The corresponding query is given next.

```
WITH LastMonth AS (
        SELECT Year(MAX(D.Date)) AS Year, Month(MAX(D.Date)) AS Month
        FROM    Sales S, Date D
        WHERE S.OrderDateKey = D.DateKey )
SELECT SUM(S.SalesAmount) AS TotalSales, SUM(S.Freight) AS TotalFreight,
        SUM(S.Freight) / SUM(S.SalesAmount) AS Percentage
FROM    LastMonth L, YearMonthPM Y, Sales S, Date D
WHERE L.Year = Y.Year AND L.Month = Y.MonthNumber AND
        S.OrderDateKey = D.DateKey AND Year(D.Date) = Y.PM_Year AND
        Month(D.Date) <= Y.PM_MonthNumber
```

As for the previous gauge, we use **LastMonth** and **YearMonthPM** to compute the requested value for the last complete month, that is April 2018.

Finally, the query for the bottom table showing the three lowest-performing employees is given next:

```
WITH LastDay AS (
        SELECT Year(MAX(Date)) AS Year, DATEPART(dy, MAX(Date)) AS DayNbYear
        FROM    Sales S, Date D
        WHERE S.OrderDateKey = D.DateKey ),
     TgtSales AS (
        SELECT S.EmployeeKey, SUM(S.SalesAmount) * 1.05 AS TargetSales
        FROM    Sales S, Date D, LastDay L
        WHERE S.OrderDateKey = D.DateKey AND Year(D.Date) = L.Year - 1
        GROUP BY S.EmployeeKey ),
     ExpSales AS (
        SELECT S.EmployeeKey, SUM(S.SalesAmount) AS YTDSales,
                SUM(S.SalesAmount) * 365 / L.DayNbYear AS ExpectedSales
        FROM    Sales S, Date D, LastDay L
        WHERE S.OrderDateKey = D.DateKey AND Year(D.Date) = L.Year
        GROUP BY S.EmployeeKey, L.DayNbYear )
SELECT TOP(3) FirstName + ' ' + LastName AS Name, YTDSales, ExpectedSales,
        TargetSales, ExpectedSales/TargetSales AS Percentage,
        RANK() OVER (ORDER BY ExpectedSales/TargetSales) AS Rank
```

```
FROM    TgtSales T, ExpSales S, Employee E
WHERE T.EmployeeKey = S.EmployeeKey AND S.EmployeeKey = E.EmployeeKey
ORDER BY Percentage
```

Table LastDay computes the year and the day-of-the-year number of the last order (124 for May 4, 2018 in our example). Table TgtSales computes the target sales that employees must achieve for the current year, as a 5% increase of the sales amount for the previous year. Table ExpSales computes the year-to-date sales as well as the expected sales obtained by multiplying the latter by a factor accounting for the number of days remaining in the year. Finally, in the main query we join the last two tables with the Employee table, compute the expected percentage, and display the three lowest-performing employees.

7.6.2 Dashboards in Power BI

In this section, we show how the dashboard of the previous section can be implemented in Power BI. Figure 7.6 shows the resulting dashboard. We explain next the DAX queries for various components.

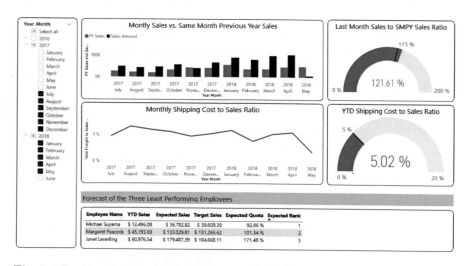

Fig. 7.6 Dashboard of the Northwind case study in Power BI

The top left chart shows the monthly sales compared with those of the same month in the previous year. The required measures are given next.

```
[Sales Amount] = SUM ( [SalesAmount] )
[PY Sales] = CALCULATE( [Sales Amount], SAMEPERIODLASTYEAR( 'Date'[Date] ) )
```

The top right gauge shows the percentage change in sales between the last month and the same month in the previous year. The required measures are given next.

```
[LastOrderDate] = CALCULATE( MAX( 'Date'[Date] ), FILTER( ALL( 'Sales' ), TRUE ) )
[LM Sales] =
    VAR LastOrderEOMPM = CALCULATE ( MAX ( 'Date'[YearMonth] ),
        FILTER ( 'Date', 'Date'[Date] = EOMONTH ( [LastOrderDate], -1 ) ) )
    RETURN
        CALCULATE ( [Sales Amount],
            FILTER( ALL( 'Date' ), 'Date'[YearMonth] = LastOrderEOMPM ) )
[LMPY Sales] =
    VAR LastOrderEOMPY = CALCULATE ( MAX ( 'Date'[YearMonth] ),
        FILTER ( 'Date', 'Date'[Date] = EOMONTH ( [LastOrderDate], -13 ) ) )
    RETURN
        CALCULATE ( [Sales Amount],
            FILTER( ALL( 'Date' ), 'Date'[YearMonth] = LastOrderEOMPY ) )
[Perc Change Sales] = DIVIDE([LM Sales] - [LMPY Sales], [LMPY Sales], 0)
[Perc Change Sales Min] = 0.0
[Perc Change Sales Max] = 2.0
[Perc Change Sales Target] = 1.15
```

LastOrderDate computes the date of the last order. LM Sales computes the sales of the month preceding the last order date, while LMPY Sales computes the sales of the same month in the previous year. For this, we use the EOMONTH function, which computes the last day of the month, a specified number of months in the past or in the future. Perc Change Sales uses the two previous measures to compute the percentage change. In addition to this, we also set the minumum, maximum, and target values for the gauge.

Next, we show the measures for the middle left chart, which displays the shipping costs with respect to the total sales by month.

```
[Total Freight] = SUM( [Freight] )
[Total Freight to Sales Ratio] = DIVIDE( [Total Freight], [Sales Amount], 0 )
```

The middle right gauge shows the year-to-date shipping costs to sales ratio. In addition to computing this measure, we need set the minimum, maximum, and target values for the gauge as given next.

```
[YTD Freight] = CALCULATE( [Total Freight],
    FILTER( 'Date', 'Date'[Year] = MAX( 'Date'[Year] ) ) )
[YTD Sales] = CALCULATE( [Sales Amount],
    FILTER( 'Date', 'Date'[Year] = MAX( 'Date'[Year] ) ) )
[YTD Freight to Sales Ratio] = DIVIDE( [YTD Freight], [YTD Sales], 0 )
[Freight to Sales Ratio Min Value] = 0.0
[Freight to Sales Ratio Max Value] = 0.2
[Freight to Sales Ratio Target Value] = 0.05
```

Finally, the measures for the bottom table showing the forecast of the three lowest-performing employees at the end of the year is given next:

```
[LastOrderDayNbYear] = CALCULATE( MAX ( 'Date'[DayNbYear] ),
    FILTER ( ALL ( 'Sales' ), TRUE ),
    FILTER ( 'Date', 'Date'[Year] = MAX ( 'Date'[Year] ) ) )
[Expected Sales] = [YTD Sales] * DIVIDE( 365, [LastOrderDayNbYear], 1 )
[Target Sales] = CALCULATE( [Sales Amount] * 1.05,
    FILTER(ALL('Date'), 'Date'[Year] = MAX ('Date'[Year] ) - 1))
[Expected Quota] = DIVIDE( [Expected Sales], [Target Sales], 0 )
[Quota Rank] = RANKX( FILTER( ALLSELECTED( Employee ),
    [EmployeeName] <> "" ), [Expected Quota], , ASC )
```

The first measure computes the day-of-the-year number for the last order date (124 for May 4, 2018 in our example). The expected sales are obtained by multiplying the year-to-date sales by a factor accouting for the number of days remaining until the end of the year. The target sales are computed as a 5% increase of the previous year's sales, while the expected quota is computed as the ratio between the expected sales and the target sales. Finally, the last measure computes the rank of the employees with respect to the expected quota. Notice that the filter to display only three employees is done in the Power BI interface.

7.7 Summary

The first part of this chapter was devoted to illustrating how MDX, DAX, and SQL can be used for querying data warehouses. For this, we addressed a series of queries to the Northwind data warehouse. We concluded the first part of the chapter by comparing the expressiveness of MDX, DAX, and SQL, highlighting the advantages and disadvantages of these languages. We continued the chapter by illustrating how to define KPIs for the Northwind case study in both Analysis Services Multidimensional and Tabular. Finally, we concluded the chapter by illustrating how to create dashboards for the Northwind case study using Microsoft Reporting Services and Power BI.

7.8 Review Questions

7.1 What are key performance indicators or KPIs? What are they used for? Detail the conditions a good KPI must satisfy.

7.2 Define a collection of KPIs using an example of an application domain that you are familiar with.

7.3 Explain the notion of dashboard. Compare the different definitions for dashboards.

7.4 What types of dashboards do you know? How would you use them?

7.5 Comment on the dashboard design guidelines.

7.6 Define a dashboard using an example of an application domain that you are familiar with.

7.9 Exercises

Exercise 7.1. Using the multidimensional model for the Foodmart data warehouse defined in Ex. 5.9, write in MDX the queries given in Ex. 4.9.

Exercise 7.2. Using the tabular model for the Foodmart data warehouse defined in Ex. 5.10, write in DAX the queries given in Ex. 4.9.

Exercise 7.3. Using the relational schema of the Foodmart data warehouse in Fig. 5.41, write in SQL the queries given in Ex. 4.9.

Exercise 7.4. Implement in Analysis Services Multidimensional the KPIs defined in Sect. 7.5 for the Northwind data warehouse.

Exercise 7.5. Implement in Analysis Services Tabular the KPIs defined in Sect. 7.5 for the Northwind data warehouse.

Exercise 7.6. The Foodmart company wants to define a set of KPIs based on its data warehouse. The finance department wants to monitor the overall performance of the company stores, to check the percentage of the stores accountable for 85% of the total sales. The sales department wants to monitor the evolution of the sales cost. It also wants to measure the monthly rate of new customers. Propose KPIs that can help the departments in these tasks. Define these KPIs together with the goals that they are aimed to evaluate.

Exercise 7.7. Define in Analysis Services Multidimensional the KPIs of Ex. 7.6.

Exercise 7.8. Define in Analysis Services Tabular the KPIs of Ex. 7.6.

Exercise 7.9. Using the Foodmart data warehouse, define in Reporting Services a dashboard to display the best five customers (regarding sales amount) for the last year, the best five selling products for the last year, the evolution in the last 2 years of the product sales by family, and the evolution in the last 2 years of the promotion sales against nonpromoted sales.

Exercise 7.10. Implement in Power BI a dashboard corresponding to the one in the previous exercise.

Part II
Implementation and Deployment

Chapter 8
Physical Data Warehouse Design

Physical design of data warehouses is crucial to ensure adequate query response time. There are typically three common techniques for improving performance in data warehouse systems: materialized views, indexing, and partitioning. A materialized view is a view that is physically stored in a database, which enhances query performance by precalculating costly operations such as joins and aggregations. With respect to indexing, traditional techniques used in OLTP systems are not appropriate for multidimensional data. Thus, alternative indexing mechanisms are used in data warehouses, typically bitmap and join indexes. Finally, partitioning divides the contents of a relation into several files, typically based on a range of values of an attribute.

In this chapter, we focus on a relational implementation of the data warehouse and the associated data cubes. We first give in Sect. 8.1 an introduction to the problems stated above. Then, in Sect. 8.2, we study the problem of computing and maintaining materialized views. In Sect. 8.3, we study the data cube maintenance problem, and discuss in detail the classic algorithms in the field. Section 8.4 studies efficient ways of computing and materializing the data cube. Section 8.5 studies data warehouse indexing techniques in detail, while Sect. 8.6 discusses how indexes are used to evaluate typical data warehouse queries. Section 8.7 overviews partitioning issues while Sect. 8.8 reviews the basic ideas of parallel query processing and illustrates them in PostgreSQL. Section 8.9 studies physical design support in SQL Server and in Analysis Services, while Sect. 8.10 briefly discusses query optimization in Analysis Services.

© Springer-Verlag GmbH Germany, part of Springer Nature 2022
A. Vaisman, E. Zimányi, *Data Warehouse Systems*, Data-Centric Systems
and Applications, https://doi.org/10.1007/978-3-662-65167-4_8

8.1 Physical Modeling of Data Warehouses

In this section, we give an overview of the three classic techniques for improving data warehouse performance: materialized views, indexing, and partitioning. Later in the chapter we study these techniques in detail.

As we studied in Chap. 2, a **view** in the relational model is just a query that is stored in the database with an associated name, and which can then be used like a normal table. This query can involve base tables (i.e., tables physically stored in the database) and/or other views. A **materialized view** is a view that is physically stored in a database. Materialized views enhance query performance by precalculating costly operations such as joins and aggregations and storing the results in the database. In this way, queries that only need to access materialized views will be executed faster. Obviously, the increased query performance is achieved at the expense of storage space.

A typical problem of materialized views is **updating** since all modifications to the underlying base tables must be propagated into the view. Whenever possible, updates to materialized views are performed in an incremental way, avoiding to recalculate the whole view from scratch. This implies capturing the modifications to the base tables and determining how they influence the content of the view. Much research work has been done in the area of view maintenance. We study the most classic ones in this chapter.

In a data warehouse, given that the number of aggregates grows exponentially with the number of dimensions and hierarchies, normally not all possible aggregations can be precalculated and materialized. Thus, an important problem in designing a data warehouse is the **selection of materialized views**. The goal is to select an appropriate set of views that minimizes the total query response time and the cost of maintaining the selected views, given a limited amount of resources such as storage space or materialization time. Many algorithms have been designed for selection of materialized views and currently some commercial DBMSs provide tools that tune the selection of materialized views on the basis of previous queries to the data warehouse.

Once the views to be materialized have been defined, the queries addressed to a data warehouse must be rewritten in order to best exploit such views to improve query response time. This process, known as **query rewriting**, tries to use the materialized views as much as possible, even if they only partially fulfill the query conditions. Selecting the best rewriting for a query is a complex process, in particular for queries involving aggregations. Many algorithms have been proposed for query rewriting in the presence of materialized views. These algorithms impose various restrictions on the given query and the potential materialized views so that the rewriting can be done.

A drawback of the materialized view approach is that it requires one to anticipate the queries to be materialized. However, data warehouse queries are often ad hoc and cannot always be anticipated. As queries which are not precalculated must be computed at run time, indexing methods are required to ensure effective query processing. Traditional indexing techniques for OLTP systems are not appropriate for multidimensional data. Indeed, most OLTP transactions access only a small number of tuples, and the indexing techniques used are designed for this situation. Since data warehouse queries typically access a large number of tuples, alternative indexing mechanisms are needed.

Two common types of indexes for data warehouses are bitmap indexes and join indexes. **Bitmap indexes** are a special kind of index, particularly useful for columns with a low number of distinct values (i.e., low cardinality attributes), although several compression techniques eliminate this limitation. On the other hand, **join indexes** materialize a relational join between two tables by keeping pairs of row identifiers that participate in the join. In data warehouses, join indexes relate the values of dimensions to rows in the fact table. For example, given a fact table Sales and a dimension Client, a join index maintains for each client a list of row identifiers of the tuples recording the sales to this client. Join indexes can be combined with bitmap indexes, as we will see in this chapter.

Partitioning is a mechanism used in relational databases to improve the efficiency of queries. It consists in dividing the contents of a relation into several files that can be more efficiently processed in this way. For example, a table can be partitioned such that the most often used attributes are stored in one partition, while other less often used attributes are kept in another partition. Another partitioning scheme in data warehouses is based on time, where each partition contains data about a particular time period, for instance, a year or a range of months.

In the following sections we study these techniques in detail.

8.2 Materialized Views

We know that a view is a derived relation defined in terms of base relations or other views, by means of the CREATE VIEW statement in SQL. A view is recomputed every time it is invoked. A materialized view, on the other hand, is a view that is physically stored in the database. This improves query performance, playing the role of a cache which can be directly accessed without looking into the base relations. But this benefit has a counterpart. When the base relations are updated, the materialized views derived from them also need to be updated. The process of updating a materialized view in response to changes in the base relations is called **view maintenance**. Under certain conditions, it is possible to compute changes to the view caused by changes in the underlying relations without recomputing the entire view from scratch. This is called **incremental view maintenance**. As this problem is central to data warehousing, we will describe it with some detail.

The view maintenance problem can be analyzed through four dimensions:

- Information: Refers to the information available for view maintenance, like integrity constraints, keys, access to base relations, and so on.

- Modification: Refers to the kinds of modifications that can be handled by the maintenance algorithm, namely, insertions, deletions, and updates, the latter are usually treated as deletions followed by insertions.
- Language: Refers to the language used to define the view, most often SQL. Aggregation and recursion are also issues in this dimension.
- Instance: Refers to whether or not the algorithm works for every instance of the database, or for a subset of all instances.

For example, consider a relation Sales(ProductKey, CustomerKey, Quantity) and a materialized view TopProducts that keeps the products for which at least one customer ordered more than 150 units. The view TopProducts is defined as follows:

TopProducts $= \pi_{ProductKey}(\sigma_{Quantity>150}(Sales))$.

It is clear that inserting a tuple like (p2, c3, 110) in the table Sales would have no effect on the view, since the tuple does not satisfy the view condition. However, the insertion of the tuple (p2, c3, 160) would possibly modify the view. An algorithm can easily update it without accessing the base relation, basically adding the product if it is not already in the view.

Let us now analyze the deletion of a tuple from Sales, for example, (p2, c3, 160). We cannot delete p2 from the view until checking if p2 has not been ordered by some other customer in a quantity greater than 150, which requires to scan the relation Sales.

In summary, although in some cases insertion can be performed just accessing the materialized view, deletion *always* requires further information.

Consider now a view FoodCustomers which includes a join. The view contains the customers that ordered at least one product in the food category (we use the simplified and denormalized Product dimension defined in Sect. 5.7).

FoodCustomers $= \pi_{CustomerKey}(\sigma_{CategoryName='Food'}(Product) * Sales)$

If we insert the tuple (p3, c4, 170) in table Sales, we cannot know if c4 will be in the view FoodCustomers (of course assuming that it is not in the view already) unless we check in the base relations whether or not p3 is in the food category.

The above examples show the need of characterizing the kinds of view maintenance problems in terms of the kind of update and of the operations in the view definition. Two main classes of algorithms for view maintenance have been studied in the database literature:

- Algorithms using full information, which means the views and the base relations.
- Algorithms using partial information, namely, the materialized views and the key constraints.

8.2.1 Algorithms Using Full Information

Three kinds of views are addressed by these algorithms: nonrecursive views, outer-join views, and recursive views. In this section, we discuss the first two kinds and omit the discussion on recursive views, which is beyond the scope of this book.

The basic algorithm for nonrecursive views (which may include join, union, negation, and aggregation) is the **counting algorithm**. This algorithm counts the number of alternative derivations that every tuple in the view has. In this way, if we delete a tuple in a base relation, we can check whether or not we should delete it from the view. To study this kind of view, let us consider the relation FoodCustomers introduced above. The view is created as follows:

```
CREATE VIEW FoodCustomers AS (
        SELECT DISTINCT CustomerKey
        FROM    Sales S, Product P
        WHERE  S.ProductKey = P.ProductKey AND P.CategoryName = 'Food' )
```

An instance of relation Sales is depicted in Fig. 8.1a; the view FoodCustomers over this instance is shown in Fig. 8.1b. We added a column Count indicating the number of possible derivations for each tuple. For example, $(c2, 2)$ means that customer $c2$ bought two products from the category food. Further, we suppose that the only products of the category food are $p1$ and $p2$ and the tuples shown are the only ones concerning these products.

ProductKey	CustomerKey	Quantity
p1	c1	20
p1	c2	100
p2	c2	50
. . .	. . .	. . .

CustomerKey	Count
c1	1
c2	2

CustomerKey	Count
c1	1
c2	1

(a)   (b)   (c)

Fig. 8.1 An example of the counting algorithm: (a) Instance of the Sales relation; (b) View FoodCustomers, including the number of possible derivations of each tuple; (c) View FoodCustomers after the deletion of $(p1, c2, 100)$

Suppose that we delete tuple $(p1, c2, 100)$ from Sales. Although $c2$ in FoodCustomers is derived from the deleted tuple, it has also an alternative derivation, through $(p2, c2, 50)$. Thus, deleting $(p1, c2, 100)$ does not prevent $c2$ to be in the view. The counting algorithm computes a relation $\Delta^-(\text{FoodCustomers})$ which contains the tuples that can be derived from $(p1, c2, 100)$, and therefore affected by the deletion of such tuple, and adds a -1 to each tuple. In this example, $\Delta^-(\text{FoodCustomers})$ will contain the tuples

$\{(c2, -1)\}$. Analogously, for dealing with insertions, Δ^+(FoodCustomers) extends the tuples with a 1. The updated view (shown in Fig. 8.1c) is obtained by joining Δ^-(FoodCustomers) with the materialized view FoodCustomers using the attribute CustomerKey, and subtracting Δ^-(FoodCustomers).Count from FoodCustomers.Count. We can see that, since c2 has two possible derivations (Fig. 8.1b), it will not be removed from the view, we will only eliminate one possible derivation. If later the tuple (p2, c2, 50) gets deleted, c2 will be also eliminated from the view. On the contrary, c1 would be deleted together with (p1, c1, 20).

We analyze now views defined with an outer join. Let us consider two relations Product(ProdID, ProdName, ShipID) and Shipper(ShipID, ShipName) as depicted, respectively, in Fig. 8.2a,b. An example of outer join view is as follows:

```
CREATE VIEW ProductShipper AS (
        SELECT P.ProdID, P.ProdName, S.ShipID, S.ShipName
        FROM    Product P FULL OUTER JOIN Shipper S ON
                P.ShipID = S.ShipID )
```

This view is depicted in Fig. 8.2d. A modification Δ(Product) to a relation Product consists in insertions Δ^+(Product) and deletions Δ^-(Product). As usual, updates are considered as deletions followed by insertions. View maintenance is tackled by rewriting the full outer join as either left or right outer joins as indicated below, depending on whether we tackle the updates of the left or the right table of the full outer join. Then, we merge the result with the view to be updated.

```
SELECT P.ProdID, P.ProdName, S.ShipID, S.ShipName
FROM    Δ(Product) P LEFT OUTER JOIN Shipper S ON P.ShipID = S.ShipID

SELECT P.ProdID, P.ProdName, S.ShipID, S.ShipName
FROM    Product P RIGHT OUTER JOIN Δ(Shipper) S ON P.ShipID = S.ShipID
```

The first query computes the effect on the view of the changes to Product, and the second one does the same with the changes to Shipper. Consider the two relations Product and Shipper in Fig. 8.2a,b, as well as Δ^+(Product) in Fig. 8.2c containing the tuples inserted in Product. When we insert a matching tuple like (p3, MP3, s2), the projection of the left outer join with Shipper would be (p3, MP3, s2, DHL). In this case, the algorithm should also delete (NULL, NULL, s2, DHL) (because (s2, DHL) now has a matching tuple), together with adding (p3, MP3, s2, DHL). For the tuple (p4, PC, NULL) is inserted into Product, the left outer join between (p4, PC, NULL) and Shipper, yields (p4, PC, NULL, NULL), which is inserted into the view. Figure 8.2e shows the final state of the view.

ProdID	ProdName	ShipID
p1	TV	s1
p2	Tablet	NULL

(a)

ShipID	ShipName
s1	Fedex
s2	DHL

(b)

ProdID	ProdName	ShipID
p3	MP3	s2
p4	PC	NULL

(c)

ProdID	ProdName	ShipID	ShipName
p1	TV	s1	Fedex
p2	Tablet	NULL	NULL
NULL	NULL	s2	DHL

(d)

ProdID	ProdName	ShipID	ShipName
p1	TV	s1	Fedex
p2	Tablet	NULL	NULL
p3	MP3	s2	DHL
p4	PC	NULL	NULL

(e)

Fig. 8.2 An example of maintenance of a full outer join view. (**a**) Table Product; (**b**) Table Shipper; (**c**) Δ^+(Product); (**d**) View ProductShipper; (**e**) Resulting view after the insertions

8.2.2 Algorithms Using Partial Information

It is not always possible to maintain a view using only partial information. A view is called **self-maintainable** if it can be maintained using only the view and key constraints. This is important for data warehouses because we do not want to access base data to update summary tables. Further, we say that a view is self-maintainable with respect to a modification type T to a base relation R if the view can be self-maintained for all instances of the database in response to all modifications of type T over R.

As an example, consider again the view FoodCustomers defined above.

FoodCustomers $= \pi_{\text{CustomerKey}}(\sigma_{\text{CategoryName}=\text{'Food'}}(\text{Product}) * \text{Sales})$

Suppose that c3 is in the view and we delete the tuple (p1, c3, 100) from the relation Sales. We could not delete c3 from the view without checking if this customer ordered another food product. If in the base relations we find that there is another tuple in Sales of the form (p, c3, q), such that p is in the food category, then c3 will remain in the view. Thus, the view FoodCustomers is not self-maintainable with respect to deletions on Sales. Analogously, this view is not self-maintainable with respect to insertions into any of the two base relations, because for any tuple inserted, for example, into Sales, we must check if the product is in the food category (except if c3 is already in the view, in which case nothing should be done).

We say an attribute is **distinguished** in a view V if it appears in the SELECT clause of the view definition. An attribute A belonging to a relation R is **exposed** in a view V if A is used in a predicate in V. We briefly present some well-known results in view maintenance theory.

- A select-project-join view is not self-maintainable with respect to insertions.
- A select-project-join view is self-maintainable with respect to deletions in a relation R if the key attributes from each occurrence of R in the join are either included in the view or equated to a constant in the view definition. Note that none of these conditions are satisfied in the example above.
- A left or full outer join view V defined using two relations R and S such that the keys of R and S are distinguished and all exposed attributes of R are distinguished is self-maintainable with respect to all types of modifications in S.

Consider again the outer join view defined in the previous section, and the instances of Fig. 8.2.

```
CREATE VIEW ProductShipper AS (
        SELECT P.ProdID, P.ProdName, S.ShipID, S.ShipName
        FROM    Product P FULL OUTER JOIN Shipper S ON
                P.ShipID = S.ShipID )
```

Since this view satisfies the third condition above, it is self-maintainable with respect to all types of modifications in Product. Let us first compute the projection of the view over Shipper, expressed as

Proj_Shipper= $\pi_{ShipID,ShipName}$(Product $\bowtie$ Shipper),

shown in Fig. 8.3a. Notice that the tuple (NULL, NULL) is excluded from this projection. The tables Δ^+(Product) and Δ^-(Product) denoting, respectively, the tuples inserted and deleted from Product, are shown in Fig. 8.3b,c. Since the view is self-maintainable, we can join these delta tables with Proj_Shipper instead of Shipper, thus avoiding to access the base relations. The joins between delta tables and Proj_Shipper are shown in Fig. 8.3d,e. Finally, the result of both joins is merged with the original view and the side effects are addressed. For example, when inserting (p3, MP3, s2, DHL), we must delete (NULL, NULL, s2, DHL). Analogously, when deleting (p1, TV, s1, Fedex), we must insert (NULL, NULL, s1, Fedex). Figure 8.3f shows the final result.

8.3 Data Cube Maintenance

In data warehouses, materialized views that include aggregate functions are called *summary tables*. We now discuss how summary tables can be maintained with minimum access to the base data, while keeping maximum data availability. The problem can be stated as follows: as data at the sources are added or updated, the summary tables that depend on these data must be also updated. Then, two options arise: to recompute the summary tables from scratch or to apply incremental view maintenance techniques to avoid such

ShipID	ShipName
s1	Fedex
s2	DHL

(a)

ProdID	ProdName	ShipID
p3	MP3	s2
p4	PC	NULL

(b)

ProdID	ProdName	ShipID
p1	TV	s1

(c)

ProdID	ProdName	ShipID	ShipName
p3	MP3	s2	DHL
p4	PC	NULL	NULL

(d)

ProdID	ProdName	ShipID	ShipName
p1	TV	s1	Fedex

(e)

ProdID	ProdName	ShipID	ShipName
p2	Tablet	NULL	NULL
p3	MP3	s2	DHL
p4	PC	NULL	NULL
NULL	NULL	s1	Fedex

(f)

Fig. 8.3 An example of self-maintenance of a full outer join view. (a) Proj_Shipper; (b) Δ^+(Product); (c) Δ^-(Product); (d) Δ^+(Product) ⋈ Proj_Shipper; (e) Δ^-(Product) ⋈ Proj_Shipper; (f) Final result

recomputation. Note that since summary tables remain unavailable to the data warehouse users while they are maintained, we need to reduce the time invested in their updating. In this section, we explain a representative summary table maintenance algorithm called the **summary-delta algorithm**, although many other techniques (like the ones that maintain many versions of the summary tables) exist in the literature.

Analogously to the definition of self-maintainable views, we say that an aggregate function is **self-maintainable** if the new value of the function can be computed solely from the old values and from changes to the base data. Aggregate functions must be distributive in order to be self-maintainable. The five classic aggregate functions in SQL are self-maintainable with respect to insertions, but not to deletions. In fact, **MAX** and **MIN** are not, and cannot be made, self-maintainable with respect to deletions.

The summary-delta algorithm has two main phases called propagate and refresh. The main advantage of this approach is that the propagate phase can be performed in parallel with data warehouse operations, only the refresh phase requires taking the warehouse offline. The basic idea is to create in the propagate phase a so-called *summary-delta table* that stores the net changes to the summary table due to changes in the source data. Then, during the refresh phase, these changes are applied to the summary table.

We will explain the algorithm with a simplified version of the Sales fact table in the Northwind case study, whose schema we show next.

Sales(ProductKey, CustomerKey, DateKey, Quantity)

Consider a view DailySalesSum defined as follows:

```
CREATE VIEW DailySalesSum AS (
        SELECT    ProductKey, DateKey, SUM(Quantity) AS SumQuantity,
                  COUNT(*) AS Count
        FROM      Sales
        GROUP BY ProductKey, DateKey )
```

The Count attribute is added in order to maintain the view in the presence of deletions, as we will explain later. In the propagate phase, we define two tables, Δ^+(Sales) and Δ^-(Sales), which store the insertions and deletions to the fact table, and a view where the net changes to the summary tables are stored. The latter is called a summary-delta table, which in this example is created as follows:

```
CREATE VIEW SD_DailySalesSum(ProductKey, DateKey,
              SD_SumQuantity, SD_Count) AS
        WITH Temp AS (
            ( SELECT ProductKey, DateKey,
                       Quantity AS _Quantity, 1 AS _Count
              FROM   Δ⁺(Sales) )
            UNION ALL
            ( SELECT ProductKey, DateKey,
                      -1 * Quantity AS _Quantity, -1 AS _Count
              FROM   Δ⁻(Sales) ) )
        SELECT ProductKey, DateKey, SUM(_Quantity), SUM(_Count)
        FROM Temp
        GROUP BY ProductKey, DateKey
```

In the temporary table Temp of the view definition, we can see that for each tuple in Δ^+(Sales) we store a 1 in the _Count attribute, while for each tuple in Δ^-(Sales) we store a -1. Analogously, the Quantity attribute values are multiplied by 1 or -1 depending if they are retrieved from Δ^+(Sales) or Δ^-(Sales), respectively. Then, in the main SELECT clause, the SD_SumQuantity attribute contains the net sum of the quantity for each combination of ProductKey and DateKey, while SD_Count contains the net number of tuples in the view corresponding to such combination.

During the refresh phase, we apply to the summary table the net changes stored in the summary-delta table. Below we give a general scheme of the refresh algorithm valid when the aggregate function is SUM.

```
Refresh Algorithm
INPUT: Summary-delta table SD_DailySalesSum
    Summary table DailySalesSum
OUTPUT: Updated summary table DailySalesSum
BEGIN
    For each tuple T in SD_DailySalesSum DO
        IF NOT EXISTS (
              SELECT *
              FROM   DailySalesSum D
```

```
                WHERE  T.ProductKey = D.ProductKey AND
                       T.DateKey = D.DateKey)
            INSERT T INTO DailySalesSum
        ELSE
            IF EXISTS (
                    SELECT *
                    FROM   DailySalesSum D
                    WHERE  T.ProductKey = D.ProductKey AND
                           T.DateKey = D.DateKey AND
                           T.SD_Count + D.Count = 0)
                DELETE T FROM DailySalesSum
            ELSE
                UPDATE DailySalesSum
                SET SumQuantity = SumQuantity + T.SD_SumQuantity,
                    Count = Count + T.SD_Count
                WHERE ProductKey = T.ProductKey AND
                      DateKey = T.DateKey
END
```

For each tuple T in the summary-delta table, the algorithm checks if T is already in the view. If not, it is inserted. If T is in the view and all the occurrences of a (ProductKey, DateKey) combination are deleted (T.SD_Count + D.Count = 0), then T is deleted from the view. Otherwise, the tuple in the view corresponding to T is updated with the new sum and the new count.

Figure 8.4 shows an example using the SUM aggregate function. Figure 8.4a shows the original DailySalesSum table, Fig. 8.4b,c shows the tables containing the changes to DailySalesSum, and Fig. 8.4d shows the summary-delta table. Finally, the result of the view update is shown in Fig. 8.4e. For instance, the tuple (p4, c2, t4, 100) has been inserted, as depicted in Δ^+(Sales) (Fig. 8.4b). The tuple (p4, t4, 100, 1) in Fig. 8.4d tells the net result of the combination (p4, t4) that has to be used to update the DailySalesSum view, which yields the tuple (p4, t4, 200, 16) depicted in Fig. 8.4e.

Figure 8.5 shows an example using the MAX aggregate function. As can be seen in Fig. 8.5a, in the view DailySalesMax we need an additional column that counts the number of tuples *that have the maximum value*, instead of counting the number of tuples that have the same combination of ProductKey and DateKey as was the case for the SUM. The view can be created as follows:

```
CREATE VIEW DailySalesMax(ProductKey, DateKey, MaxQuantity, Count) AS (
        SELECT ProductKey, DateKey, MIN(Quantity), COUNT(*)
        FROM   Sales S1
        WHERE Quantity = (
                SELECT MAX(Quantity)
                FROM   Sales S2
                WHERE S1.ProductKey = S2.ProductKey AND
                      S1.DateKey = S2.DateKey )
        GROUP BY ProductKey, DateKey )
```

Figure 8.5b shows the summary-delta table. As can be seen, we need a column for keeping the maximum value in the tuples inserted or deleted, as well as another column counting the number of insertions or deletions of tuples

Product Key	Date Key	Sum Quantity	Count
p2	t2	100	10
p3	t3	100	20
p4	t4	100	15
p5	t5	100	2
p6	t6	100	1

(a)

Product Key	Customer Key	Date Key	Quantity
p1	c1	t1	150
p2	c1	t2	200
p2	c2	t2	100
p4	c2	t4	100
p6	c5	t6	200

(b)

Product Key	Customer Key	Date Key	Quantity
p2	c1	t2	10
p5	c2	t5	10
p6	c5	t6	100

(c)

Product Key	Date Key	SD_Sum Quantity	SD_Count
p1	t1	150	1
p2	t2	290	1
p4	t4	100	1
p5	t5	-10	-1
p6	t6	100	0

(d)

Product Key	Date Key	Sum Quantity	Count
p1	t1	150	1
p2	t2	390	11
p3	t3	100	20
p4	t4	200	16
p5	t5	90	1
p6	t6	200	1

(e)

Fig. 8.4 An example of the propagate and refresh algorithm with aggregate function SUM. (a) Original view DailySalesSum; (b) Δ^+(Sales); (c) Δ^-(Sales); (d) Summary-delta table SD_DailySalesSum; (e) View DailySalesSum after update

having the maximum value. Thus, the first four tuples in the summary-delta table correspond to insertions, while the last three correspond to deletions since the count value is negative. The view for creating the summary-delta table is given next.

```
CREATE VIEW SD_DailySalesMax(ProductKey, DateKey,
            SD_MaxQuantity, SD_Count) AS (
        SELECT ProductKey, DateKey, Quantity, COUNT(*)
        FROM   Δ⁺(Sales) S1
        WHERE Quantity = (
                SELECT MAX(Quantity)
                FROM   Δ⁺(Sales) S2
                WHERE S1.ProductKey = S2.ProductKey AND
                        S1.DateKey = S2.DateKey )
        GROUP BY ProductKey, DateKey
                UNION ALL
```

Product Key	Date Key	Max Quantity	Count
p2	t2	150	4
p3	t3	100	5
p4	t4	50	6
p5	t5	150	5
p6	t6	100	3
p7	t7	100	2

(a)

Product Key	Date Key	SD_Max Quantity	SD_Count
p1	t1	100	2
p2	t2	100	2
p3	t3	100	2
p4	t4	100	2
p5	t5	100	-2
p6	t6	100	-2
p7	t7	100	-2

(b)

Product Key	Date Key	Max Quantity	Count
p1	t1	100	2
p2	t2	150	4
p3	t3	100	7
p4	t4	100	2
p5	t5	150	5
p6	t6	100	1
p7	t7	?	?

(c)

Fig. 8.5 An example of the propagate and refresh algorithm with aggregate function MAX. (**a**) Original view DailySalesMax; (**b**) Summary-delta table SD_DailySalesMax; (**c**) Updated view DailySalesMax

```
SELECT ProductKey, DateKey, Quantity, -1 * COUNT(*)
FROM    Δ⁻(Sales) S1
WHERE Quantity = (
         SELECT MAX(Quantity)
         FROM    Δ⁻(Sales) S2
         WHERE S1.ProductKey = S2.ProductKey AND
               S1.DateKey = S2.DateKey )
GROUP BY ProductKey, DateKey )
```

Finally, Fig. 8.5c shows the view after the update. Let us consider first the insertions. The tuple for p1 in the summary-delta table does not have a corresponding tuple in the view, and thus, it is inserted in the view. The tuple for p2 in the summary-delta table has a maximum value smaller than that in the view so the view is not modified. The tuple for p3 in the summary-delta table has a quantity value equal to the maximum in the view so the maximum value remains the same and the counter is increased to 7. The tuple for p4 in the summary-delta table has a maximum value greater than the maximum in the view, and thus, the view must be updated with the new maximum and the new counter.

Now consider the deletions. The tuple for p5 in the summary-delta table has a quantity value smaller than the maximum in the view so the view is not modified. The tuple for p6 in the summary-delta table has a quantity value equal to the maximum in the view but with a greater count value. In this case, we decrease the counter in the view to 1. The tuple for p7 illustrates why the MAX function is not self-maintainable with respect to deletions. The maximum value and the counter in the summary-delta table are equal to those value in the view. There are two possible cases. If there are other tuples in the base table with the same combination (p7, t7) we must obtain the new maximum value and the new count from the base tables. This case is depicted in Fig. 8.5c. Otherwise, if there are no other tuples in the base table with the same combination (p7, t7), we must simply delete the tuple from the view.

The algorithm for refreshing the view DailySalesMax from the summary-delta table SD_DailySalesMax is left as an exercise.

8.4 Computation of a Data Cube

In Chap. 5, we have explained how the data cube could be computed by means of an SQL query, where the all value is represented by the null value. This requires performing the UNION of 2^n GROUP BY queries, one for each possible aggregation. Computing the whole data cube in this way from the base fact and dimension tables would be unacceptable in real-life applications unless an adequate strategy is applied. Thus, several optimization techniques have been proposed for this. We study next some of them in order to convey the main idea.

The optimization methods start with the notion of **data cube lattice**. In this lattice, each node represents a possible aggregation of the fact data, where there is an edge from node i to node j if j can be computed from i and the number of grouping attributes of i is the number of attributes of j plus one. For instance, given an aggregate view by CustomerKey and ProductKey of the Sales table of the previous section, we can compute the total sales amount by customer directly from this view, without computing it from the base table. In what follows, to avoid overloading figures, we will work with the lattice depicted in Fig. 8.6, corresponding to a four-dimensional data cube, with dimensions A, B, C, and D. In this lattice, an edge from ABC to AB means that the summary table AB can be computed from ABC. We do not include in the lattice the transitive edges, for example, edges like ABCD → AB.

The simplest optimizations for computing the cube lattice are

- Smallest-parent: Computes each view from the smallest previously computed one. In the lattice of Fig. 8.6, AB can be computed from ABC, ABD, or ABCD. This method chooses the smallest of them.
- Cache-results: Caches in memory an aggregation from which other ones can be computed.
- Amortize-scans: Computes in memory as many aggregations as possible, reducing the amount of table scans.

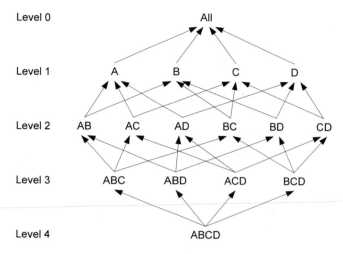

Fig. 8.6 A data cube lattice

- Share-sorts: Applies only to methods based on sorting and aims at sharing costs between several aggregations.
- Share-partitions: These are specific to algorithms based on hashing. When the hash table is too large to fit in main memory, data are partitioned and aggregation is performed for each partition that fits in memory. The partitioning cost can be shared across multiple aggregations.

Note that these methods can be contradictory. For instance, share-sorts would induce to prefer AB to be derived from ABC, while ABD could be its smallest parent. Sophisticated cube computation methods try to combine together some of these simple optimization techniques to produce an efficient query evaluation plan. We explain below a method based on sorting. Methods based on hashing follow a similar rationale. Note that most of these algorithms require the estimation of the sizes of each aggregate view in the lattice.

8.4.1 PipeSort Algorithm

The **PipeSort algorithm** gives a global strategy for computing the data cube, which includes the first four optimization methods specified above. The algorithm includes cache-results and amortize-scans strategies by means of computing nodes with common prefixes in a single scan. This is called pipelined evaluation in database query optimization. In this way, we could compute ABCD, ABC, AB, and A in a single scan because the attribute order in the view is the sorting order in the file. For example, in the base table below,

with a single scan of the first five tuples we can compute the aggregations
$(a1, b1, c1, 200)$, $(a1, b1, c2, 500)$, $(a1, b1, 700)$, $(a1, b2, 400)$, and $(a1, 1100)$.

A	B	C	D	
a1	b1	c1	d1	100
a1	b1	c1	d2	100
a1	b1	c2	d1	200
a1	b1	c2	d1	300
a1	b2	c1	d1	400
a2	b1	c1	d1	100
a2	b1	c2	d2	400
...	...	...	...	...

The input of the algorithm is a data cube lattice in which each edge e_{ij},
where node i is the parent of node j, is labeled with two costs, $S(e_{ij})$ and
$A(e_{ij})$. $S(e_{ij})$ is the cost of computing j from i if i is not sorted. $A(e_{ij})$ is
the cost of computing j from i if i is already sorted. Thus, $A(e_{ij}) \leq S(e_{ij})$.
In addition, we consider the lattice organized into levels, where each level k
contains views with exactly k attributes, starting from All, where $k = 0$. This
data structure is called a *search lattice*.

The output of the algorithm is a subgraph of the search lattice such that
each node has exactly one parent from which it will be computed in a certain
mode, that is, sorted or not (note that in the search lattice, each node, except
All, has more than one parent). If the attribute order of a node j is a prefix of
the order of its parent i, then j can be computed from i without sorting the
latter, and in the resulting graph, the edge will have cost $A(e_{ij})$. Otherwise,
i has to be sorted to compute j and the edge will have cost $S(e_{ij})$. Note that
for any node i in an output graph there can be at most one outgoing edge
marked A, and many outgoing edges marked S. The goal of the algorithm is
to find an output graph representing an execution plan such that the sum of
the costs labeling the edges is minimum.

To obtain the minimum cost output graph, the algorithm proceeds level
by level, starting from level 0 until level $N - 1$, where N is the number of
levels in the search lattice. We find the best way of computing the nodes in
each level k from the nodes in level $k + 1$, reducing the problem to a *weighted
bipartite matching* problem as follows. Consider a pair $(k, k+1)$ of levels. The
algorithm first transforms the level $k + 1$ by making k copies of each one of
its nodes. Thus, each node in level $k+1$ will have $k+1$ children, that is, $k+1$
outgoing edges. All original edges have cost $A(e_{ij})$ and all replicated edges
have cost $S(e_{ij})$. Therefore, this transformed graph induces a bipartite graph
(because there are edges between nodes in different levels but not between
nodes in the same level). Finally, we compute the minimum cost matching
such that each node j in level k will be matched to some node i in level $k+1$.
If j is connected to i by an $A()$ edge, then j determines the attribute order
in which i will be sorted during its computation. If, instead, j is connected
to i by an $S()$ edge, i will be sorted in order to compute j.

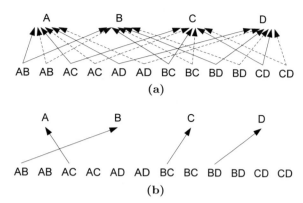

Fig. 8.7 Minimum bipartite matching between two levels in the cube lattice

As an example, consider in Fig. 8.7 the graph constructed as indicated above, for the levels 1 and 2 of the lattice in Fig. 8.6. Edges of type $A(e_{ij})$ are represented with solid lines, while edges of type $S(e_{ij})$ with dashed lines. Note that in Fig. 8.7a we have added a copy of each node at level 2. In Fig. 8.7b, we can see that all the views will be computed at a cost $A(e_{ij})$. For example, A will be computed from AC, B from BA, and so on.

The matching above is performed N times, where N is the number of grouping attributes, generating an evaluation plan. The heuristics is that if for every pair of levels the cost is minimum, the same occurs for the whole plan. The output lattice gives a sorting order to compute each node. As a result, the PipeSort algorithm induces the following evaluation strategy: in every chain such that a node in level k is a prefix of node in level $k + 1$ (in the output graph), all aggregations can be computed in a pipeline.

The general scheme of the PipeSort algorithm is given next.

PipeSort Algorithm
INPUT: A search lattice with the $A()$ and $S()$ edges costs
OUTPUT: An evaluation plan to compute all nodes in the search lattice
BEGIN
    For level $k = 0$ to level $N - 1$
        Generate-Plan($k + 1 \rightarrow k$);
        For each node i in level $k + 1$
            Fix the sort order of i as the order of the level k node
            connected to i by an $A()$ edge;
    Generate-Plan($k + 1 \rightarrow k$);
    Create k additional copies of each level $k + 1$ node;
    Connect each copy node to the same set of level k nodes as the original node;
    Assign cost $A(e_{ij})$ to edges e_{ij} from the original nodes and cost $S(e_{ij})$
        to edges from the copy nodes;
    Find the minimum cost matching on the transformed level $k + 1$ with level k;
END

Figure 8.8 shows an evaluation plan for computing the cube lattice of Fig. 8.6 using the PipeSort algorithm. The minimum cost sort plan will first sort the base fact table in CBAD order and compute CBA, CB, C, and All aggregations in a pipelined fashion. Then, we sort the base fact table in the BADC order and proceed as above to compute aggregates BAD, BA, and A. We continue in the same way with ACDB and DBCA. Note how the views in level 1 (A, B, C, and D) are computed from the views in level 2 in the way that was indicated by the bipartite graph matching in Fig. 8.7.

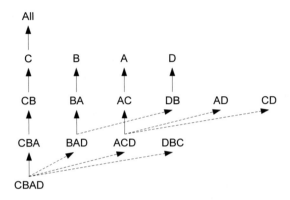

Fig. 8.8 Evaluation plan for computing the cube lattice in Fig. 8.6

8.4.2 Cube Size Estimation

We have already said that algorithms like PipeSort, and most algorithms computing summary tables, require knowing the size of each aggregate. However, in general this is not known in advance. Thus, we need to accurately predict the sizes of the different aggregates. There are three classic methods for this, although a wide array of statistical techniques could be used. The first of these methods is purely analytical, the second is based on sampling, and the last one on probabilistic counting.

The **analytical algorithm** is based on a result by Feller from 1957, stating that choosing r elements (which we can assume are the tuples in a relation) randomly from a set of n elements (which are all the different values a set of attributes can take), the expected number of distinct elements obtained is $n - n \times (1 - \frac{1}{n})^r$. This assumes that data are uniformly distributed. If it turns out not to be the case, and data present some skew, we will be overestimating the size of the data cube. For instance, let us suppose a relation R(ProductKey, CustomerKey, DateKey). If we want to estimate the size of the aggregation over ProductKey and CustomerKey, we should know the number of different values of each attribute. Then, $n = |ProductKey| \times |CustomerKey|$, and r is the number of tuples in R. The main advantage of this method is its simplicity and performance. The obvious drawback of the algorithm is that it does not consult the database, and the results can be used only when we know that data are uniformly distributed.

The basic idea of the **sampling-based algorithm** is to take a random subset of the database and compute the cube over this subset. Let D be the database, S the sample, and $Cube(S)$ the size of the cube computed from S. The size of the cube will be estimated as $Cube(S) \times \frac{|D|}{|S|}$. This method is simple and fast, and it has been reported that it provides satisfactory results over real-world data sets.

The **probabilistic counting algorithm** is based on the following observation: suppose we want to compute the number of tuples of the aggregation of sales by product category and shipper. We would first aggregate along the dimension Product, to generate product categories, and count the number of distinct shippers generated by this operation. For example, for the set of product-shipper pairs $\{(p1, s1), (p2, s1), (p3, s2), (p4, s4), (p5, s4)\}$, if p1 and p2 correspond to category c1, and the rest to category c2, the aggregation will have three tuples: $\{(c1, s1), (c2, s2), (c2, s4)\}$. In other words, c1 yields only one value of shipper, and c2 yields two distinct values of shipper. Thus, estimating the number of *distinct* tuples in a group (in this case, shippers by category), we can estimate the number of *tuples* in that group. This idea is used to estimate the size of a data cube by means of counting the number of distinct elements in a multiset as proposed in a well-known algorithm by Flajolet and Martin, performing this for all possible combinations of the hierarchies in the cube. The algorithm estimates the sizes of the aggregations in a cube at the cost of scanning the whole database once. However, this is cheaper than actually computing the cube, and it is proved that the error has a bound. Details of this algorithm fall beyond the scope of this book.

8.4.3 Partial Computation of a Data Cube

Generally speaking, three alternatives exist to implement a data warehouse: materialize the whole data cube (as studied in the previous section), materialize a selected portion of the cube, and not materializing any aggregation at all. Materializing the whole cube has not only the drawback of the storage space required, but also the cost of refreshing the summary tables. On the other hand, it implies that any possible aggregate query will match a summary table, thus the cost of answering the query would just be a table scan which, in addition, will often be of a small size. The "no materialization" approach is likely to be inefficient in most real-world situations. It follows that a good trade-off between these options can be to materialize only a portion of the views in the data cube. The main problem in this case is to decide which views are going to be materialized. Notice that once we decide which are the views to materialize, we can apply the techniques for cube computation and maintenance already studied in this chapter. Actually, the problem could be stated in many ways:

- How many views must we materialize to get reasonable performance?
- Given a certain amount of storage space, which views should we materialize in order to minimize the average query cost?
- If we can assume an X% performance degradation with respect to a fully materialized data cube, how much space do we save?

We next explain the classic **view selection algorithm**, which is a greedy algorithm that finds, given a cube lattice, the best set of views to materialize under a certain criterion. Although the set of views returned by the algorithm may not always be the optimal one, we have chosen this algorithm as representative of a class of algorithms that aim at solving the same problem.

The algorithm makes use of a lattice that takes into account two kinds of dependencies between nodes. The first kind of dependency accounts for the case in which the attributes of a view are included in those of another view. For example, in the lattice representing the possible aggregations of the fact table Sales(ProductKey, CustomerKey, DateKey), there is a dependency between the node (ProductKey, CustomerKey) and the node (ProductKey), stating that the latter can be computed from the former since {ProductKey} ⊆ {ProductKey, CustomerKey} holds. The second kind of dependency accounts for hierarchies. For example, given a hierarchy Month → Year, if we have an aggregation over Month, we can use it to compute the aggregation over Year without going down to the fact table. Thus, the dependency lattice represents a relation $v_i \preceq v_j$ between the views such that a view v_i can be answered using v_j. For simplicity, and without loss of generalization, in the examples of this section we only consider the case in which the attributes of a view are included in those of another view.

The view selection algorithm is based on calculating the costs of computing the views in the lattice. A linear cost model with the following characteristics is assumed:

- The cost of answering a view v from a materialized view v_m is the number of rows in v_m.
- All queries are identical to some view in the dependency lattice.

The algorithm also requires knowing the expected number of rows for each view in the lattice. Finally, it is assumed that the lowest node in the lattice (typically, the base fact table) is always materialized.

The goal of the algorithm is to minimize the time taken to evaluate a view, constrained to materialize a fixed number of views regardless of the space available, a problem known to be NP-complete. The greedy algorithm we present below uses a heuristic that selects a sequence of views such that each choice in this sequence is the best, given what was selected before.

Let us call $C(v)$ the cost of view v, k the number of views to materialize, and S a set of materialized views. The benefit of materializing a view v not in S, relative to the materialized views already in S is denoted by $B(v, S)$, and it is computed as follows:

View Materialization Benefit Algorithm
INPUT: A lattice L, each view node labeled with its expected number of rows
    A node v, not yet selected to materialize
    A set S containing the nodes already selected to materialize
OUTPUT: The benefit of materializing v given S
BEGIN
    For each view $w \preceq v$, $w \notin S$, Bw is computed by
        Let u be the view of least cost in S such that $w \preceq u$
        If $C(v) < C(u)$, $Bw = C(u) - C(v)$, otherwise $Bw = 0$
    $B(v, S) = \sum_{w \preceq v} Bw$
END

The algorithm above works as follows. Given a view w (not yet materialized), let us denote u the (materialized) view of minimum cost from which w can be computed. Given a candidate view v selected for materialization, for each view w that depends on v, the benefit of materializing w (denoted by Bw) is computed as the difference between the costs of v and u. If computing w from v is more expensive than doing it from u ($C(v) > C(u)$), materializing the candidate view does not benefit the computation of w ($Bw = 0$). The algorithm iterates over all views w, and finally, the benefit of materializing v is the sum of all individual benefits ($\sum_{w \preceq v} Bw$).

The view selection algorithm computes, in each iteration, the view v whose materialization gives the maximum benefit. This algorithm is given next.

View Selection Algorithm
INPUT: A lattice L, each view node v labeled with its expected number of rows
    The number of views to materialize, k
OUTPUT: The set of views to materialize
BEGIN
    $S = \{$The bottom view in $L\}$
    FOR $i = 1$ TO k DO
        Select a view v not in S such that $B(v, S)$ is maximized
        $S = S \cup \{v\}$
    END DO
    S is the selection of views to materialize
END

The set S contains the views already materialized. In each one of the k iterations, the algorithm computes the benefit produced by the materialization of each of the views not yet in S. The one with the maximum benefit is added to S, and a new iteration begins.

Let us apply the algorithm to the lattice in Fig. 8.9. In addition to the node label, beside each node we indicate the cost of the view that the node represents. Assume that we can materialize three views and that the bottom view is already materialized.

Let us show how to select the first view to materialize. We need to compute the benefit of materializing each view, knowing that $S = \{ABC\}$. We start

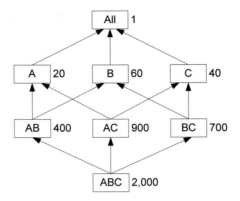

Fig. 8.9 Dependency lattice. Initially, the only view materialized is ABCD

with node AB, which is a good candidate, since it offers a cost reduction of 1,600 units for each view that depends on it. For example, node A depends on AB. Currently, computing A has cost 2,000, since this is performed from ABC. If we materialize AB, the cost of computing A will drop to 400.

The benefit of materializing AB given S is given by

$$B(\mathsf{AB}, S) = \sum_{w \preceq \mathsf{AB}} Bw.$$

Thus, for each view w covered by AB, we compute $C(\mathsf{ABC}) - C(\mathsf{AB})$, because ABC is the only materialized view when the algorithm begins. That is, $C(\mathsf{ABC}) - C(\mathsf{AB})$ is the benefit of materializing AB for each view covered by AB. For example, to compute B without materializing AB, we would need to scan ABC at cost 2,000. With AB being materialized this reduces to 400. The same occurs with all the views that have a path to All that passes through AB, that is, A, B, All, and AB itself. For C, AC, and BC, the materialization of AB is irrelevant. Then,

$$B(\mathsf{AB}, S) = 1,600 + 1,600 + 1,600 + 1,600 = 6,400.$$

In an analogous way,

$$B(\mathsf{BC}, S) = \sum_{w \preceq \mathsf{BC}} Bw = 1,300 \times 4 = 5,200,$$

which is the benefit of materializing BC for the computation of B, C, All, and BC itself. If we continue in this fashion, we will find that AB is the view to materialize because it yields the maximum benefit. Thus, when we start the second iteration we have $S = \{\mathsf{ABC}, \mathsf{AB}\}$.

We now explain the second iteration. The benefit of materializing BC is $B(\mathsf{BC}, S) = \sum_{w \preceq \mathsf{BC}} Bw = 1,300 + 1,300 = 2,600$, corresponding to C and BC itself since materializing BC has no effect on the nodes that reach All through AB because they can be computed from AB at a cost of 400. For example, B can be computed from AB at cost 400, therefore materializing BC yields no benefit for the computation of B. On the other hand, the benefit of materializing B is $B(B, S) = \sum_{w \preceq B} Bw = 340 \times 2$ since both B and All can be computed from AB at a cost $Bw = 400 - 60$ each. Also note that the benefit of materializing C is $B(C, S) = \sum_{w \preceq C} Bw = 1,960 + 400 - 40 = 2,320$ since the benefit for computing All is just $400 - 40$ because All can be computed from AB at a cost of 400. We will eventually choose BC in the second iteration with a benefit of $2,600$.

Finally, the three views to materialize will be AB, BC, and AC, with a total benefit of 10,100. The following table shows the complete computation. Each cell in the table shows the benefit of selecting a given view in an iteration.

View	First Iteration	Second Iteration	Third Iteration
AB	**1,600 × 4 = 6,400**		
AC	1,100 × 4 = 4,400	1,100 × 2 = 2,200	**1,100 × 1 = 1,100**
BC	1,300 × 4 = 5,200	**1,300 x 2 = 2,600**	
A	1,980 × 2 = 3,960	380 × 2 = 760	380 × 2 = 760
B	1,940 × 2 = 3,880	340 × 2 = 680	340 × 2 = 680
C	1,960 × 2 = 3,920	1,960 + (400 - 40) = 2,320	660 + 360 = 1,020
All	1,999 × 1 = 1,999	399 × 1 = 399	399 × 1 = 399

It can be proved that the benefit of this greedy algorithm is at least 63% of the benefit of the optimal algorithm. On the other hand, even this is a classic algorithm, pedagogically interesting for presenting the problem, a clear drawback is that it does not consider the frequency of the queries over each view. Thus, in our example, even though the sum of the benefit is maximum, nothing is said about the frequency of the queries asking for A or B. This drawback has been addressed in several research papers.

8.5 Indexes for Data Warehouses

A major concern in database management systems (DBMSs) is to provide fast access to data. Given a query, a relational DBMS attempts to choose the best possible access path to the data. A popular way to speed data access is known as indexing. An index provides a quick way to locate data of interest. Almost all the queries asking for data that satisfy a certain condition are answered with the help of some index.

As an example, consider the following SQL query:

```
SELECT *
FROM    Employee
WHERE EmployeeKey = 1234
```

Without an index on attribute EmployeeKey, we should perform a complete scan of table Employee (unless it is ordered), whereas with the help of an index over such attribute, a single disk block access will do the job since this attribute is a key for the relation.

Although indexing provides advantages for fast data access, it has a drawback: almost every update on an indexed attribute also requires an index update. This suggests that database administrators should be careful on defining indexes because their proliferation can lead to bad updating performance.

The most popular indexing technique in relational databases is the B^+-tree. All major vendors provide support for some variation of B^+-tree indexes. A B^+-tree index is a multilevel structure containing a root node and pointers to the next lower level in a tree. The lowest level is formed by the leaves of the tree, which in general contain a record identifier for the corresponding data. Often, the size of each node equals the size of a block, and each node holds a large number of keys, so the resulting tree has a low number of levels and the retrieval of a record can be very fast. This works well if the attribute being indexed is a key of the file or if the number of duplicate values is low.

We have seen that queries submitted to an OLAP system are of a very different nature than those of an OLTP system. Therefore, new indexing strategies are needed for OLAP systems. Some indexing requirements for a data warehouse system are as follows:

- Symmetric partial match queries: Most OLAP queries involve partial ranges. An example is the query "Total sales from January 2006 to December 2010." As queries can ask for ranges over any dimension, all the dimensions of the data cube should be symmetrically indexed so that they can be searched simultaneously.
- Indexing at multiple levels of aggregation: Since summary tables can be large or queries may ask for particular values of aggregate data, summary tables must be indexed in the same way as base nonaggregated tables.
- Efficient batch update: As already said, updates are not so critical in OLAP systems, which allows more columns to be indexed. However, the refreshing time of a data warehouse must be taken into account when designing the indexing schema. Indeed, the time needed for reconstructing the indexes after the refreshing extends the downtime of the warehouse.
- Sparse data: Typically, only 20% of the cells in a data cube are nonempty. The indexing schema must thus be able to deal efficiently with sparse and nonsparse data.

Bitmap indexes and join indexes are commonly used in data warehouse systems to cope with these requirements. We study these indexes next.

8.5.1 Bitmap Indexes

Consider the table Product in Fig. 8.10a. For clarity, we assume a simplified example with only six products. We show next how to build a bitmap index

on attributes QuantityPerUnit and UnitPrice. There are, respectively, four and
five possible values for these attributes in table Product. We create a bit vector
of length 6 (the number of rows in Product) for each possible attribute value,
as shown in Fig. 8.10b,c. In a position i of vector j, there is a '1' if the
product in row i has the value in the label of column j, and a '0' otherwise.
For example, in the first row of the table in Fig. 8.10b there is a '1' in the
vector with label 25, indicating that the corresponding product (p1) has a
value 25 in attribute QuantityPerUnit. Note that we have included the product
key in the first column of the bitmap index to facilitate the reading, although
this column is not part of the index.

ProductKey	ProductName	QuantityPerUnit	UnitPrice	Discontinued	CategoryKey
p1	prod1	25	60	No	c1
p2	prod2	45	60	Yes	c1
p3	prod3	50	75	No	c2
p4	prod4	50	100	Yes	c2
p5	prod5	50	120	No	c3
p6	prod6	70	110	Yes	c4

(a)

	25	45	50	70
p1	1	0	0	0
p2	0	1	0	0
p3	0	0	1	0
p4	0	0	1	0
p5	0	0	1	0
p6	0	0	0	1

(b)

	60	75	100	110	120
p1	1	0	0	0	0
p2	1	0	0	0	0
p3	0	1	0	0	0
p4	0	0	1	0	0
p5	0	0	0	0	1
p6	0	0	0	1	0

(c)

Fig. 8.10 An example of bitmap indexes for a Product dimension table. (a) Product
dimension table; (b) Bitmap index for attribute QuantityPerUnit; (c) Bitmap
index for attribute UnitPrice

Now, assume the query "Products with unit price equal to 75." A query
processor will just need to know that there is a bitmap index over UnitPrice in
Product, and look for the bit vector with a value of 75. The vector positions
where a '1' is found indicate the positions of the records that satisfy the
query, in this case, the third row in the table.

For queries involving a search range, the process is a little bit more involved. Consider the query "Products having between 45 and 55 pieces per
unit, and with a unit price between 100 and 200." To compute this query, we
first look for the index over QuantityPerUnit, and the bit vectors with labels
between 45 and 55. There are two such vectors, with labels 45 and 50. The
products having between 45 and 55 pieces per unit are the ones correspond-

	45	50	OR1
p1	0	0	0
p2	1	0	1
p3	0	1	1
p4	0	1	1
p5	0	1	1
p6	0	0	0

(a)

	100	110	120	OR2
p1	0	0	0	0
p2	0	0	0	0
p3	0	0	0	0
p4	1	0	0	1
p5	0	0	1	1
p6	0	1	0	1

(b)

	OR1	OR2	AND
p1	0	0	0
p2	1	0	0
p3	1	0	0
p4	1	1	1
p5	1	1	1
p6	0	1	0

(c)

Fig. 8.11 Finding the products having between 45 and 55 pieces per unit and with a unit price between 100 and 200. (**a**) OR for QuantityPerUnit; (**b**) OR for UnitPrice; (**c**) AND operation

ing to an OR operation between these vectors. Then we look for the index over UnitPrice and the bit vectors with labels between 100 and 200. There are three such vectors, with labels 100, 110, and 120. The products having unit price between 100 and 200 are, again, the ones corresponding to an OR operation between these vectors. We obtain the two vectors labeled OR1 and OR2 in Fig. 8.11a,b, respectively. Finally, an AND between these two vectors, shown in Fig. 8.11c, gives the rows satisfying both conditions. The result is that products p4 and p5 satisfy the query.

The operation just described is the main reason of the high performance achieved by bitmapped indexing in the querying process. When performing AND, OR, and NOT operations, the system will just perform a bit comparison, and the resulting bit vector is obtained at a very low CPU cost.

The above example suggests that the best opportunities for these indexes are found where the cardinality of the attributes being indexed is low. Otherwise, we will need to deal with large indexes composed of a large number of sparse vectors, and the index can become space inefficient. Continuing with our example, assume that the Product table contains 100,000 rows. A bitmapped index on the attribute UnitPrice will occupy $100,000 \times 6/8$ bytes $= 0.075$ MB. A traditional B-tree index would occupy approximately $100,000 \times 4 = 0.4$ MB (assume 4 bytes are required to store a record identifier). It follows that the space required by a bitmapped index is proportional to the number of entries in the index and to the number of rows, while the space required by traditional indexes depends strongly on the number of records to be indexed. OLAP systems typically index attributes with low cardinality. Therefore, one of the reasons for using bitmap indexes is that they occupy less space than B$^+$-tree indexes, as shown above.

There are two main reasons that make bitmap indexes not adequate in OLTP environments. First, these systems are subject to frequent updates, which are not efficiently handled by bitmap indexes. Second, in database systems locking occurs at page level and not at the record level. Thus, concurrency can be heavily affected if bitmap indexes are used for operational systems, given that a locked page would lock a large number on index entries.

8.5.2 Bitmap Compression

As we have seen, bitmap indexes are typically sparse: the bit vectors have a few '1's among many '0's. This characteristic makes them appropriate for compression. We have also seen that even without compression, for low cardinality attributes bitmap outperforms B^+-tree in terms of space. In addition, bitmap compression allows indexes to support high-cardinality attributes. The downside of this strategy is the overhead of decompression during query evaluation. Given the many textbooks on data compression, and the high number of compression strategies, we next just give the idea of a simple and popular strategy, called run-length encoding (RLE). Many sophisticated techniques are based on RLE, as we comment on the bibliographic notes section of this chapter.

Run-length encoding is very popular for compressing black and white and grayscale images since it takes advantage of the fact that the bit value of an image is likely to be the same as the one of its neighboring bits. There are many variants of this technique, most of them based on how they manage decoding ambiguity. The basic idea is the following: if a bit of value v occurs n consecutive times, replace these occurrences with the number n. This sequence of bits is called a run of length n.

In the case of bitmap indexes, since the bit vectors have a few '1's among many '0's, if a bit of value '0' occurs n consecutive times, we replace these occurrences with the number n. The '1's are written as they come in the vector. Let us analyze the following sequence of bits: 0000000111000000000011. We have two runs of lengths 7 and 10, respectively, three '1's in between, and two '1's at the end. This vector can be trivially represented as the sequence of integers 7,1,1,1,10,1,1. However, this encoding can be ambiguous since we may not be able to distinguish if a '1' is an actual bit or the length of a run. Let us see how we can handle this problem. Let us call j the number of bits needed to represent n, the length of a run. We can represent the run as a sequence of $j - 1$ '1' bits, followed by a '0', followed by n in binary format. In our example, the first run, 0000000, will be encoded as 110111, where the first two '1's correspond to the $j - 1$ part, '0' indicates the component of the run, and the last three '1's are the number 7 (the length of the run) in binary format.

Finally, the bitmap vector above is encoded as **110011111111**1**010101**, where the encoding is indicated in boldface and the actual bits of the vector are indicated in normal font. Note that since we know the length of the array, we could get rid of the trailing '1's to save even more space.

8.5.3 Join Indexes

It is a well-known fact that join is one of the most expensive database operations. Join indexes are particularly efficient for join processing in decision-support queries since they take advantage of the star schema design, where, as we have seen, the fact table is related to the dimension tables by foreign keys, and joins are typically performed on these foreign keys.

RowID Product	Product Key	Product Name	...	Discontinued	...
1	p1	prod1	...	No	...
2	p2	prod2	...	Yes	...
3	p3	prod3	...	No	...
4	p4	prod4	...	Yes	...
5	p5	prod5	...	No	...
6	p6	prod6	...	Yes	...

(a)

RowID Sales	Product Key	Customer Key	Date Key	Sales Amount
1	p1	c1	t1	100
2	p1	c2	t1	100
3	p2	c2	t2	100
4	p2	c2	t3	100
5	p3	c3	t3	100
6	p4	c3	t4	100
7	p5	c4	t5	100

(b)

RowID Sales	RowID Product
1	1
2	1
3	2
4	2
5	3
6	4
7	5

(c)

Yes	No
0	1
0	1
1	0
1	0
0	1
1	0
0	1

(d)

Fig. 8.12 An example of a join and a bitmap join indexes: (**a**) Product dimension table, (**b**) Sales fact table, (**c**) Join index, (**d**) Bitmap join index on attribute Discontinued

The main idea of join indexes consists in precomputing the join as shown in Fig. 8.12. Consider the dimension table Product and the fact table Sales from the Northwind data warehouse. We can expect that many queries require a join between both tables using the foreign key. Figure 8.12a depicts table Product, with an additional attribute RowIDProd, and Fig. 8.12b shows table Sales extended with an additional attribute RowIDSales. Figure 8.12c shows the corresponding join index, basically a table containing pointers to the matching rows. This structure can be used to efficiently answer queries requiring a join between tables Product and Sales.

A particular case of join index is the *bitmap join index*. Suppose now that a usual query asks for total sales of discontinued products. In this case, a bitmap join index can be created on table Sales over the attribute Discontinued, as shown in Fig. 8.12d. As can be seen, the sales pertaining to discontinued products (products p2 and p4) have a '1' in the bit vector labeled 'Yes'. At first sight, this may appear to be strange because attribute Discontinued does not belong to Sales. Actually what happens is that the index points to the tuples in Sales that store sales of discontinued products. This is done by precomputing the join between both tables through the attribute ProductKey, and then creating a bitmap index on Sales for each possible value of the attribute Discontinued ('Yes' or 'No'). A query like the one above will be answered straightforwardly, since we have precomputed the join between the two tables and the bitmap over the attribute Discontinued.

In the next section, we will show how bitmap and join indexes are used in query evaluation.

8.6 Evaluation of Star Queries

Queries over star schemas are called **star queries** since they make use of the star schema structure, joining the fact table with the dimension tables. For example, a typical star query over our simplified Northwind example in Sect. 8.3 would be "Total sales of discontinued products, by customer name and product name." This query reads in SQL:

```
SELECT    C.CustomerName, P.ProductName, SUM(S.SalesAmount)
FROM      Sales S, Customer C, Product P
WHERE     S.CustomerKey = C.CustomerKey AND
          S.ProductKey = P.ProductKey AND P.Discontinued = 'Yes'
GROUP BY C.CustomerName, P.ProductName
```

We will study now how this query is evaluated by an engine using the indexing strategies studied above.

An efficient evaluation of our example query would require the definition of a B^+-tree over the dimension keys CustomerKey and ProductKey, and bitmap indexes on Discontinued in the Product dimension table and on the foreign key columns in the fact table Sales. Figure 8.13a,c,d shows the Product and Customer dimension tables and the Sales fact table, while the bitmap indexes are depicted in Fig. 8.13b,e,f.

Let us describe how this query is evaluated by an OLAP engine. The first step consists in obtaining the record numbers of the records that satisfy the condition over the dimension, that is, Discontinued = 'Yes'. As shown in the bitmap index (Fig. 8.13b), such records are the ones with ProductKey values p2, p4, and p6. We then access the bitmap vectors with these labels in Fig. 8.13f, thus performing a join between Product (Fig. 8.13a) and Sales. Only the vectors labeled p2 and p4 match the search since there is no fact record for product p6. The third, fourth, and sixth rows in the fact table are the answer since they are the only ones with a '1' in the corresponding vectors in Fig. 8.13f. We then obtain the key values for the CustomerKey (c2 and c3)

Product Key	Product Name	...	Discontinued	...
p1	prod1	...	No	...
p2	prod2	...	Yes	...
p3	prod3	...	No	...
p4	prod4	...	Yes	...
p5	prod5	...	No	...
p6	prod6	...	Yes	...

Yes	No
0	1
1	0
0	1
1	0
0	1
1	0

(a)   (b)

Customer Key	Customer Name	Address	Postal Code	...
c1	cust1	35 Main St.	7373	...
c2	cust2	Av. Roosevelt 50	1050	...
c3	cust3	Av. Louise 233	1080	...
c4	cust4	Rue Gabrielle	1180	...

(c)

Product Key	Customer Key	Date Key	Sales Amount
p1	c1	t1	100
p1	c2	t1	100
p2	c2	t2	100
p2	c2	t3	100
p3	c3	t3	100
p4	c3	t4	100
p5	c4	t5	100

c1	c2	c3	c4
1	0	0	0
0	1	0	0
0	1	0	0
0	1	0	0
0	0	1	0
0	0	1	0
0	0	0	1

p1	p2	p3	p4	p5	p6
1	0	0	0	0	0
1	0	0	0	0	0
0	1	0	0	0	0
0	1	0	0	0	0
0	0	1	0	0	0
0	0	0	1	0	0
0	0	0	0	1	0

Yes	No
0	1
0	1
1	0
1	0
0	1
1	0
0	1

(d)   (e)   (f)   (g)

Fig. 8.13 An example of evaluation of star queries with bitmap indexes: (**a**) Product table, (**b**) Bitmap for Discontinued, (**c**) Customer table, (**d**) Sales fact table, (**e**) Bitmap for CustomerKey, (**f**) Bitmap for ProductKey, and (**g**) Bitmap join index for Discontinued

using the bitmap index in Fig. 8.13e. With these values we search in the B^+-tree index over the keys in tables Product and Customer to find the names of the products and the customer satisfying the query condition. Note that this performs the join between the dimensions and the fact table. As we can see in Figs. 8.10a and 8.13c, the records correspond to the names cust2, cust3, prod2, and prod4, respectively. Finally, the query answer is (cust2, prod2, 200) and (cust3, prod4, 100).

Note that the last join with Customer would not be needed if the query would have been of the following form:

```
SELECT    S.CustomerKey, P.ProductKey, SUM(SalesAmount)
FROM      Sales S, Product P
WHERE     S.ProductKey = P.ProductKey AND P.Discontinued = 'Yes'
GROUP BY S.CustomerKey, P.ProductKey
```

The query above only mentions attributes in the fact table **Sales**. Thus, the only join that needs to be performed is the one between **Product** and **Sales**.

We illustrate now the evaluation of star queries using bitmap join indexes. We have seen that the main idea is to create a bitmap index over a fact table using an attribute belonging to a dimension table, precomputing the join between both tables and building a bitmap index over the latter. Figure 8.13g shows the bitmap join index between **Sales** and **Product** over the attribute **Discontinued**. Finding the facts corresponding to sales of discontinued products, as required by the query under study, is now straightforward: we just need to find the vector labeled 'Yes', and look for the bits set to '1'. During query evaluation, this avoids the first step described in the previous section, when evaluating the query with bitmap indexes. This is done at the expense of the cost of (off-line) precomputation.

Note that this strategy can reduce dramatically the evaluation cost if in the **SELECT** clause there are no dimension attributes, and thus we do not need to join back with the dimensions using the B^+-tree as explained above. Thus, the answer for the alternative query above would just require a simple scan of the **Sales** table, in the worst case.

8.7 Partitioning

Partitioning consists in dividing a table into smaller ones (called *partitions*) to better support the management and processing of large volumes of data. From an application perspective, a partitioned table is *identical* to a nonpartitioned table and thus, partitioning is transparent for writing SQL statements. Partitioning can be applied to tables as well as to indexes. Further, a partitioned index can be defined over an unpartitioned table, and vice versa, a partitioned table may have unpartitioned indexes defined over it.

There are two ways of partitioning a table. **Horizontal partitioning** splits a table into smaller ones having the same structure as the full table, but fewer records. For example, if some queries only require the most recent data, a fact table can be horizontally partitioned according to some time frame, for example, years. An advantage of horizontal partitioning is that refreshing the data warehouse is more efficient since only the last partition must be accessed. On the other hand, **vertical partitioning** splits the attributes of a table into groups that are independently stored. In this case, a key of the relation must be kept in all partitions to be able to reconstruct the tuples. For example, a table can be partitioned such that the most often used attributes are stored in one partition, while other less often used attributes are kept in another partition. In this way, more records can be brought into main memory with a single operation, reducing the processing time. Column-store database systems (which are studied in Chap. 15) are based on this technique.

There are several *horizontal* partitioning strategies in database systems. Given n partitions, **round-robin partitioning**, assigns the i-th tuple in insertion order to partition i mod n. This strategy is good for parallel sequential access. However, accessing an individual tuple based on a predicate requires accessing the entire relation. **Hash partitioning** applies a hash function to some attribute to assign tuples to partitions. The hash function should distribute rows among partitions in a uniform fashion, yielding partitions of about the same size. This strategy allows exact-match queries on the distributing attribute to be processed by exactly one partition. **Range partitioning** assigns tuples to partitions based on ranges of values of some attribute. The temporal dimension is a natural candidate for range partitioning. For example, when partitioning a table by a date column, a January 2021 partition will only contain rows from that month. This strategy can deal with non-uniform data distributions and can support both exact-match queries and range queries. **List partitioning** assigns tuples to partitions by specifying a list of values of some attribute. In this way, data can be organized in an ad hoc fashion. Finally, **composite partitioning** combines the basic data distribution methods above. For example, a table can be range partitioned, and each partition can be further subdivided using hash partitioning.

Partitioning database tables into smaller ones improves query performance. This is especially true when parallel processing is applied (as we will see in Sect. 8.8) or when a table is distributed across different servers (as we will see in Sect. 15.3). There are two classic techniques for improving query performance using partitioning. **Partition pruning** enables a smaller subset of the data to be accessed when queries refer to data located in only some of the partitions. For example, a Sales fact table in a warehouse can be partitioned by month. A query requesting orders for a single month only needs to access the partition corresponding to that month instead of accessing all the table, greatly reducing query response time. The performance of **joins** can also be enhanced by using partitioning. This occurs when the two tables to be joined are partitioned on the join attributes or, in the case of foreign-key joins, when the reference table is partitioned on its primary key. In these cases, a large join is broken into smaller joins that occur between each of the partitions, producing significant performance gains, which can be improved by taking advantage of parallel execution.

Partitioning also facilitates administrative tasks, since tables and indexes are partitioned into smaller, more manageable pieces. In this way, maintenance operations can be performed on the partitions. For example, a database administrator may back up just a single partition of a table instead of the whole table. In the case of indexes, partitioning is advised, for example, in order to perform maintenance on parts of the data without invalidating the entire index. In addition, partitioned database tables and indexes induce high data availability. For example, if some partitions of a table become unavailable, it is possible that most of the other partitions of the table remain online and available, in particular if partitions are allocated to various different devices. In this way, applications can continue to execute queries and transactions that do not need to access the unavailable partitions. Even during normal operation, since each partition can be stored in a separate tablespace, backup and recovery operations can be performed over individual partitions, independently of each other. Thus, the active parts of the database can be made available sooner than in the case of an unpartitioned table.

8.8 Parallel Processing

Parallel query processing is defined as the transformation of queries into execution plans that can be efficiently executed in parallel on a multiprocessor computer. Efficient execution is crucial for high performance, for example, query response time or query throughput. It is obtained by exploiting efficient parallel execution techniques and query optimization which selects the most efficient parallel execution plan among all equivalent plans.

There are two main forms of parallelism that are based on how data is placed physically on disk or in memory. **Interquery parallelism** consists of processing several queries in parallel, while **intraquery parallelism** consists in executing specific steps of a single query in parallel. These forms of parallelism can obviously be combined.

Parallel algorithms for efficient database query processing are designed to take advantage of data partitioning. This requires a trade-off between parallelism and communication costs. The goal of parallel algorithms for relational algebra operators is to maximize the degree of parallelism, taking into account that not all operations in a program can be parallelized. For example, highly sequential algorithms are not good for parallelization. The Quicksort algorithm is an example of this, while, on the other hand, the sort-merge algorithm is appropriate for parallel execution, and it is abundantly used in shared-nothing architectures.

Given two partitioned relations, there are three parallel join algorithms, which are based on their non-parallel versions: the *parallel sort-merge join algorithm*, the *parallel nested-loop algorithm*, and the *parallel hash-join algorithm*. The first one simply sorts both relations on the join attribute using a parallel merge sort, and joins them using a merge-like operation done by a single node. The parallel nested-loop algorithm computes the Cartesian product of two relations, in parallel, thus supporting any kind of join predicates besides the classic equijoin. Finally, the parallel hash-join algorithm only supports equijoin. The basic idea is to partition two relations R and S into the same number p of mutually exclusive fragments R_i and S_i such that the join between R and S is equal to the union of the joins between R_i and S_i. Each join between R_i and S_i is performed in parallel. Of course, the algorithms above are the basis for actual implementations which exploit main memory and multicore processors.

We next explain parallel processing in a representative system like PostgreSQL. PostgreSQL achieves interquery parallelism through multiple connections, typically in a multiuser setting, but also by processing the same query on different partitions, which is essential for OLAP queries. It also allows parallel query processing in a single connection, which means that a single process can have multiple threads to process a query, taking advantage of multicore processors. This allows intraquery parallelism.

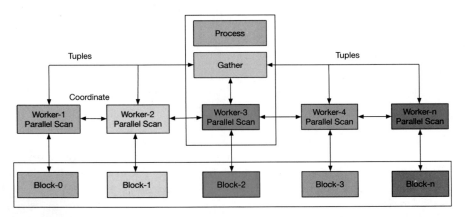

Fig. 8.14 A parallel query plan in PostgreSQL

A parallel query plan in PostgreSQL has three main components, shown in Fig. 8.14: Process, Gather, and Workers. Without parallelism, Process handles the overall query execution. When a query (or some part of it) can be parallelized, Process adds a Gather node as root of the subtree of the parallelizable part of the query plan. Together with the Gather node, a set of Workers are allocated. The Workers are threads that run in parallel. Query execution starts at the Process level and all the serial parts of the plan are run by it. The relation's blocks are divided among the threads such that the access to the relation remains sequential. The Workers coordinate and communicate using shared memory, and once they complete their work, the results are passed on to the Process, so the partial results can be put together.

There are three main kinds of parallel computation in PostgreSQL. A *sequential scan* is a scan of a table in which a sequence of blocks is evaluated one after the other. This is an obvious candidate for parallel computation. Index pages can also be scanned in parallel: a Worker scans the B-tree and upon reaching the leaf node, it scans the block and tells a waiting Worker to scan the next block. *Parallel aggregation* is computed using a divide-and-conquer strategy: multiple Workers calculate the part of an aggregate before the final values based on these calculations are calculated by the coordinator. PartialAggregate nodes are added to a plan tree, and each of these nodes takes the output from one Worker. These outputs are then sent to a FinalizeAggregate node that combines the aggregates from the PartialAggregate ones. Finally, *parallel merge join* is also supported. Here, a table joins with other tables performing an inner loop hash or merge. Parallelism is not supported for the inner loop. Parallelism occurs when each Worker executes the inner loop as a whole. The result of each join is sent to the Gather node to produce the final results.

PostgreSQL also allows users to define **partitions** declaratively. Partitioning improves the performance of both queries and bulk loads, since they are done over smaller tables, but also increases parallel processing. Tables are partitioned using a list of columns or expressions that define a *partition key*. We explain next the various kinds of partitioning supported, using a table Employee(EmpNbr, Position, Salary) as example.

A *list partition* holds predefined values of the partition key. A default partition holds the values that are not part of any specified partition. A partition for each position is created as follows (only one partition is shown).

```
CREATE TABLE EmployeeManager PARTITION OF Employee
        FOR VALUES IN ('Manager');
```

A *range partition* holds values of the partition key within a range. Both minimum and maximum values of the range need to be specified, where the minimum value is inclusive and the maximum value is exclusive. Below we show how three partitions on salary ranges are created.

```
CREATE TABLE EmployeeSalaryLow PARTITION OF Employee
        FOR VALUES FROM (MINVALUE) TO (50000);
CREATE TABLE EmployeeSalaryMiddle PARTITION OF Employee
        FOR VALUES FROM (50000) TO (100000);
CREATE TABLE EmployeeSalaryHigh PARTITION OF Employee
        FOR VALUES FROM (100000) TO (MAXVALUE);
```

A *hash partition* is created using a modulus and a remainder for each partition. Each partition holds the rows for which the hash value of the partition key divided by the given modulus produces the given remainder. An example is as follows (only one partition is shown):

```
CREATE TABLE EmployeeHash1 PARTITION OF Employee
        WITH (modulus 3, remainder 0);
```

Finally, a *multilevel partition* is created by partitioning an already partitioned table. For example, we can combine the range and list partitioning above as shown next:

```
CREATE TABLE EmployeeSalaryLow PARTITION OF Employee
        FOR VALUES FROM (MINVALUE) TO (50000)
        PARTITION BY LIST (Position);
```

```
CREATE TABLE EmployeeSalaryLow_Manager PARTITION OF EmployeeSalaryLow
      FOR VALUES IN ('Manager');
```

Table partitions are used by PostgreSQL for query processing. Consider, for example, the following query:

```
SELECT AVG(Salary)
FROM   Employee;
```

The query plan devised by the query optimizer is as follows, according to the architecture shown in Fig. 8.14.

```
Finalize Aggregate
      Gather
      Workers Planned: 4
            Partial Aggregate
            Parallel Append
                  Parallel Seq Scan on EmployeeSalaryHigh
                  Parallel Seq Scan on EmployeeSalaryMiddle
                  Parallel Seq Scan on EmployeeSalaryLow
```

The optimizer first defines how many Workers the query requires. In the example above, we have eight cores available, although only four are needed, since more may cause a decrease in performance. The **Parallel** Append causes the Workers to spread out across the partitions. For example, one of the partitions may end up being scanned by two Workers, and the other two partitions are attended by one Worker each. When the engine has finished with a given partition, the Worker(s) allocated to it are spread out across the remaining partitions, so that the total number of Workers per partition is kept as even as possible.

8.9 Physical Design in SQL Server and Analysis Services

In this section, we discuss how the theoretical concepts studied in this chapter are applied in Microsoft SQL Server. We start with the study of how materialized views are supported in these tools. We then introduce a novel kind of index provided by SQL Server called column-store index. Then, we study partitioning, followed by a description of how the three types of multidimensional data representation introduced in Chap. 5, namely, ROLAP, MOLAP, and HOLAP, are implemented in Analysis Services.

8.9.1 Indexed Views

In SQL Server, materialized views are called indexed views. Basically, an indexed view consists in the creation of a unique clustered index on a view, thus precomputing and materializing such view. We have seen that this is a mandatory optimization technique in data warehouse environments.

When we create an indexed view, it is essential to verify that the view and the base tables satisfy the many conditions required by the tool. For example, the definition of an indexed view must be deterministic, meaning that all expressions in the SELECT, WHERE, and GROUP BY clauses are deterministic. For instance, the DATEADD function is deterministic because it always returns the same result for any given set of argument values for its three parameters. On the contrary, GETDATE is not deterministic because it is always invoked with the same argument, but the value it returns changes each time it is executed. Also, indexed views may be created with the SCHEMABIND-ING option. This indicates that the base tables cannot be modified in a way that would affect the view definition. For example, the following statement creates an indexed view computing the total sales by employee over the Sales fact table in the Northwind data warehouse.

```
CREATE VIEW EmployeeSales WITH SCHEMABINDING AS (
        SELECT    EmployeeKey, SUM(UnitPrice * OrderQty * Discount)
                  AS TotalAmount, COUNT(*) AS SalesCount
        FROM      Sales
        GROUP BY EmployeeKey )
CREATE UNIQUE CLUSTERED INDEX CI_EmployeeSales ON
        EmployeeSales (EmployeeKey)
```

An indexed view can be used in two ways: when a query explicitly references the indexed view and when the view is not referenced in a query but the query optimizer determines that the view can be used to generate a lower-cost query plan.

In the first case, when a query refers to a view, the definition of the view is expanded until it refers only to base tables. This process is called view expansion. If we do not want this to happen, we can use the NOEXPAND hint, which forces the query optimizer to treat the view like an ordinary table with a clustered index, preventing view expansion. The syntax is as follows:

```
SELECT EmployeeKey, EmployeeName, ...
FROM   Employee, EmployeeSales WITH (NOEXPAND)
WHERE ...
```

In the second case, when the view is not referenced in a query, the query optimizer determines when an indexed view can be used in a given query execution. Thus, existing applications can benefit from newly created indexed views without changing those applications. Several conditions are checked to determine if an indexed view can cover the entire query or a part of it, for example, (1) the tables in the FROM clause of the query must be a superset of the tables in the FROM clause of the indexed view; (2) the join conditions in the query must be a superset of the join conditions in the view; and (3) the aggregate columns in the query must be derivable from a subset of the aggregate columns in the view.

8.9.2 Partition-Aligned Indexed Views

If a partitioned table is created in SQL Server and indexed views are built on this table, SQL Server automatically partitions the indexed view by using the same partition scheme as the table. An indexed view built in this way is called a partition-aligned indexed view. The main feature of such a view is that the database query processor automatically maintains it when a new partition of the table is created, without the need of dropping and recreating the view. This improves the manageability of indexed views.

We show next how we can create a partition-aligned indexed view on the Sales fact table of the Northwind data warehouse. To facilitate maintenance, and for efficiency reasons, we decide to partition this fact table by year. This is done as follows.

To create a partition scheme, we need first to define the partition function. We want to define a scheme that partitions the table by year, from 2016 through 2018. The partition function is called PartByYear and takes as input an attribute of integer type, which represents the values of the surrogate keys for the Date dimension.

```
CREATE PARTITION FUNCTION [PartByYear] (INT)
AS RANGE LEFT FOR VALUES (184, 549, 730);
```

Here, 184, 549, and 730 are, respectively, the surrogate keys representing the dates 31/12/2016, 31/12/2017, and 31/12/2018. These dates are the boundaries of the partition intervals. RANGE LEFT means that the records with values less or equal than 184 will belong to the first partition, the ones greater than 184 and less or equal than 549 to the second, and the records with values greater than 730 to the third partition.

Once the partition function has been defined, the partition scheme is created as follows:

```
CREATE PARTITION SCHEME [SalesPartScheme]
        AS PARTITION [PartByYear] ALL to ( [PRIMARY] );
```

Here, PRIMARY means that the partitions will be stored in the primary filegroup, that is, the group that contains the startup database information. Filegroup names can be used instead (can be more than one). ALL indicates that all partitions will be stored in the primary filegroup.

The Sales fact table is created as a partitioned table as follows:

```
CREATE TABLE Sales (CustomerKey INT, EmployeeKey INT,
        OrderDateKey INT, ...) ON SalesPartScheme(OrderDateKey)
```

The statement ON SalesPartScheme(OrderDateKey) tells that the table will be partitioned following the SalesPartScheme and the partition function will have OrderDateKey as argument.

Now we create an indexed view over the Sales table, as explained in Sect. 8.9.1. We first create the view.

```
CREATE VIEW SalesByDateProdEmp WITH SCHEMABINDING AS (
        SELECT    OrderDateKey, ProductKey, EmployeeKey, COUNT(*) AS Cnt,
                  SUM(SalesAmount) AS SalesAmount
        FROM      Sales
        GROUP BY OrderDateKey, ProductKey, EmployeeKey )
```

Finally, we materialize the view.

```
CREATE UNIQUE CLUSTERED INDEX UCI_SalesByDateProdEmp
        ON SalesByDateProdEmp (OrderDateKey, ProductKey, EmployeeKey)
        ON SalesPartScheme(OrderDateKey)
```

Since the clustered index was created using the same partition scheme, this is a partition-aligned indexed view.

8.9.3 Column-Store Indexes

SQL Server provides column-store indexes, which store data by column. In a sense, column-store indexes work like a vertical partitioning commented above, and can dramatically enhance performance for certain kinds of queries. The same concepts that were explained for bitmap indexes and their use in star-join evaluation also apply to column-store indexes. We will provide a detailed study of this kind of indexes in Chap. 15.

We now show how a column-store index is defined. For this, suppose there is a materialized view Sales2012 that selects from the Sales fact table the data pertaining to 2012. Suppose that many queries request the attributes DueDateKey, EmployeeKey, and SalesAmount. In order to speed up access to the Sales2012 view, we can define a column-store index over it as follows:

```
CREATE NONCLUSTERED COLUMNSTORE INDEX CSI_Sales2012
        ON Sales2012 (DueDateKey, EmployeeKey, SalesAmount)
```

Column-store indexes have important limitations. One of them is that a table over which a column-store index is defined cannot be updated. Thus, we cannot define the index over the original Sales fact table since it is subject to updates, and create instead the index over a view.

Bitmap indexes are not supported in SQL Server. Instead, SQL Server provides **bitmap filters**, which are bitmaps created at execution time by the query processor to filter values on tables. Bitmap filtering can be introduced in the query plan after optimization, or it can be introduced dynamically by the query optimizer during the generation of the query plan. The latter is called optimized bitmap filter and can significantly improve the performance of data warehouse queries that use star schemas by removing nonqualifying rows from the fact table early in the query plan. Note that this is completely different from defining a bitmap index like we explained above, and which is supported by other database systems like Oracle and Informix.

8.9.4 Partitions in Analysis Services

In Analysis Services, a partition is a container for a portion of the data of a measure group. Defining a partition requires to specify:

- Basic information, like name of the partition, the storage mode, and the processing mode.
- Slicing definition, which is an MDX expression specifying a tuple or a set.
- Aggregation design, which is a collection of aggregation definitions that can be shared across multiple partitions.

The data for the partitions of a measure group must be mutually exclusive, otherwise these data would be considered more than once. Every measure group has at least one partition, created when the measure group is defined. This initial partition is based on a single fact table in the data source view of the cube. When there are multiple partitions for a measure group, each partition can reference a different table in either the data source view or in the underlying relational data source for the cube. Also, more than one partition in a measure group can reference the same table.

Analogously to what we explained in the previous section for database tables, partitions allow large data cubes to be managed efficiently, for example, by distributing source and aggregate data of a cube across multiple hard disks and multiple servers. This improves performance of queries, loads, and cube maintenance. For example, if we partition the data in the Northwind cube by year, only the last partition will be processed when current information is added to the cube. Partitions can later be merged. For example, at the end of a year, the quarterly partitions can be merged into a single partition for the year and a new partition created for the first quarter of the new year. Thus, partitions can be configured, added, or dropped by the database administrator. Each partition is stored in a separate set of files. Aggregate data of each partition can be stored on either the instance of Analysis Services where the partition is defined or on another instance.

Finally, the storage mode of each partition can be configured independently of other partitions, for example, using any combination of source data location, storage mode, and aggregation design. We study this feature next.

ROLAP Storage

In the **ROLAP** storage mode, the aggregations of a partition are stored in indexed views in the relational database specified as the data source of the partition. The indexed views in the data source are accessed to answer queries. In the ROLAP storage, the query response time and the processing time are generally slower than with the MOLAP or HOLAP storage modes (see below). However, ROLAP enables users to view data in real time and can save storage space when working with large data sets that are infrequently queried, such as purely historical data.

If a ROLAP partition has its source data stored in SQL Server, Analysis Services tries to create indexed views to store aggregations. When these views cannot be created, aggregation tables are not created. Indexed views for aggregations can be created if several conditions hold in the ROLAP partition and the tables in it. The more relevant ones are as follows:

- The partition cannot contain measures that use the MIN or MAX aggregate functions.
- Each table in the ROLAP partition must be used only once.
- All table names in the partition schema must be qualified with the owner name, for example, [dbo].[Customer].
- All tables in the partition schema must have the same owner.
- The source columns of the partition measures must not be nullable.

MOLAP Storage

In the **MOLAP** storage mode, both the aggregations and a copy of the source data are stored in a multidimensional structure. Such structures are highly optimized to maximize query performance. Since a copy of the source data resides in the multidimensional structure, queries can be processed without accessing the source data of the partition.

Note however that data in a MOLAP partition reflect the most recently processed state of a partition. Thus, when source data are updated, objects in the MOLAP storage must be reprocessed to include the changes and make them available to users. Changes can be processed from scratch or, if possible, incrementally, as explained in Sect. 8.2. This update can be performed without taking the partition or cube offline. However, if structural changes to OLAP objects are performed, the cube must be taken offline. In these cases, it is recommended to update and process cubes on a staging server.

HOLAP Storage

The **HOLAP** storage mode combines features of MOLAP and ROLAP modes. Like MOLAP, in HOLAP the aggregations of the partition are stored in a multidimensional data structure. However, like in ROLAP, HOLAP does not store a copy of the source data. Thus, if queries only access summary data of a partition, HOLAP works like MOLAP very efficiently. Queries that need to access unaggregated source data must retrieve it from the relational database and therefore will not be as fast as if it were stored in a MOLAP structure. However, this can be solved if the query can use cached data, that is, data that are stored in main memory rather than on disk.

In summary, partitions stored as HOLAP are smaller than the equivalent MOLAP partitions since they do not contain source data. On the other hand, they can answer faster than ROLAP partitions for queries involving summary data. Thus, this mode tries to capture the best of both worlds.

Defining Partitions in Analysis Services

We show next how MOLAP, ROLAP, and HOLAP partitions over measure groups can be defined in Analysis Services.

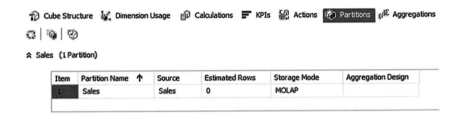

Fig. 8.15 Initial partition for the Sales measure group

Figure 8.15 shows a unique initial partition for the Sales measure group in a data cube created from the Northwind cube. As we can see, this is a MOLAP partition. Assume now that, for efficiency reasons, we want to partition this measure group by year. Since in the Northwind data warehouse we have data from 2016, 2017, and 2018, we will create one partition for each year. We decided that the first two ones will be MOLAP partitions, and the last one, a ROLAP partition. To define the limits for the partitions, the Analysis Services cube wizard creates an SQL query template, shown in Fig. 8.16, which must be completed in the **WHERE** clause with the key range corresponding to each partition. To obtain the first and last keys for each period, a query such as the following one must be addressed to the data warehouse.

```
SELECT MIN(DateKey), MAX(DateKey)
FROM    Date
WHERE Date >= '2017-01-01' AND Date <= '2017-12-31'
```

The values obtained from this query can then be entered in the wizard for defining the partition for 2017.

Figure 8.17 shows the three final partitions of the measure group Sales. Note that in that figure the second partition is highlighted. Figure 8.18 shows the properties of such partition, in particular the ROLAP storage mode. This dialog box also can be used to change the storage mode.

8.10 Query Performance in Analysis Services

We now briefly describe how query performance can be enhanced in Analysis Services through several techniques.

The first step must be to optimize cube and measure group design. For this, many of the issues studied in this book apply. For example, it is suggested to

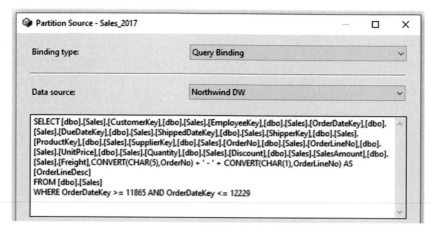

Fig. 8.16 Template query that defines a partition

Fig. 8.17 Final partitions for the Sales measure group

use cascading attribute relationships, like Day → Month → Quarter → Year, and define user hierarchies of related attributes within each dimension. These are called natural hierarchies. The reason for this is that attributes participating in natural hierarchies are materialized on disk and are automatically considered to be aggregation candidates. Redundant relationships between attributes must be removed to assist the query execution engine in generating an appropriate query plan. Also, the cube space must be kept as small as possible, only including measure groups that are needed. Measures that are queried together must be allocated to the same measure group since if a query retrieves measures from multiple measure groups it will require multiple storage engine operations. Large sets of measures that are not queried together must be placed into separate measure groups. Large parent-child hierarchies must be avoided, because in these hierarchies aggregations are created only for the key attribute and the top attribute. Thus, queries asking for cells at intermediate levels are calculated at query time and can be slow for large parent-child dimensions. Many-to-many dimension performance must be optimized, since it requires a run-time join between the data measure group and

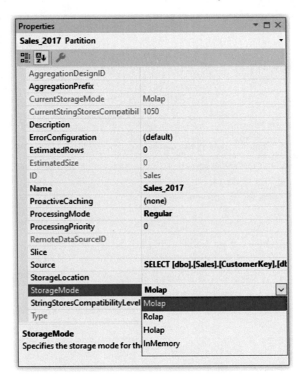

Fig. 8.18 Storage mode for the Sales_2017 partition

the intermediate measure group. Also, if possible, the size of the intermediate
fact table underlying the intermediate measure group must be reduced.

Aggregations are also used by Analysis Services to enhance query performance. Thus, the most efficient aggregations for the query workload must
be selected to reduce the number of records that the storage engine needs
to scan on disk to evaluate a query. When designing aggregations, we must
evaluate the benefits that aggregations provide when querying, against the
time it takes to create and refresh such aggregations. Moreover, unnecessary
aggregations can worsen query performance. A typical example is the case
when a summary table matches an unusual query. This can make the summary table to be moved into the cache to be accessed faster. Since this table
will be rarely used afterwards, it can deallocate a more useful table from the
cache (which has a limited size), with the obvious negative effect on query.
Summarizing, we must avoid designing a large number of aggregations since
they may reduce query performance.

The Analysis Services aggregation design algorithm does not automatically
consider every attribute for aggregation. Consequently, we must check the
attributes that are considered for aggregation and determine if we need to
suggest additional aggregation candidates, for example, because we detected

that most user queries not resolved from cache are resolved by partition reads rather than aggregation reads. Analysis Services uses the Aggregation Usage property to determine which attributes it should consider for aggregation. This property can take one of four values: full (every aggregation for the cube must include this attribute), none (no aggregation uses the attribute), unrestricted (the attribute must be evaluated), and default (a rule is applied to determine if the attribute must be used). The administrator can use this property to change its value for influencing its use for aggregation.

As we have explained, partitions enable Analysis Services to access less data to answer a query when it cannot be answered from the data cache or from aggregations. Data must be partitioned matching common queries. Analogously to the case of measure groups, we must avoid partitioning in a way that requires most queries to be resolved from many partitions. It is recommended by the vendor that partitions contain at least 2 million and at most 20 million records. Also, each measure group should contain less than 2,000 partitions. A separate ROLAP partition must be selected for real-time data and this partition must have its own measure group.

We can also optimize performance by writing efficient MDX queries and expressions. For this, run-time checks in an MDX calculation must be avoided. For example, using CASE and IF functions that must be repeatedly evaluated during query resolution will result in a slow execution. In that case, it is recommended to rewrite the queries using the SCOPE function. If possible, Non_Empty_Behavior must be used to enable the query execution engine to use the bulk evaluation mode. In addition, EXISTS rather than filtering on member properties should be used since this enables bulk evaluation mode. Too many subqueries must be avoided if possible. Also, if possible, a set must be filtered before using it in a cross join to reduce the cube space before performing such cross join.

The cache of the query engine must be used efficiently. First, the server must have enough memory to store query results in memory for reuse in subsequent queries. We must also define calculations in MDX scripts because these have a global scope that enables the cache related to these queries to be shared across sessions with the same security permissions. Finally, the cache must be warmed by executing a set of predefined queries using any tool.

Other techniques are similar to the ones used for tuning relational databases, like tuning memory and processor usage. For details, we refer the reader to the Analysis Services documentation.

8.11 Summary

In this chapter, we studied the problem of physical data warehouse design. We focused on three techniques: view materialization, indexing, and partitioning. For the former, we studied the problem of incremental view maintenance, that is, how and when a view can be updated without recomputing it from scratch. In addition, we presented algorithms that compute efficiently the data cube when all possible views are materialized. Also, we showed that when full materialization is not possible, we can estimate which is the best set to be chosen for materialization given a set of constraints. We then studied two typical indexing schemes used in data warehousing, namely, bitmap and join indexes, and how they are used in query evaluation. Finally, we discussed partitioning techniques and strategies, aimed at enhancing data warehouse performance and management. The last three sections of the chapter were devoted to study physical design and query performance in Analysis Services, showing how the theoretical concepts studied in the first part of the chapter are applied over real-world tools.

8.12 Bibliographic Notes

A general book about physical database design is [140], while physical design for SQL Server is covered, for instance, in [56, 227]. Most of the topics studied in this chapter have been presented in classic data warehousing papers. Incremental view maintenance has been studied in [95, 96]. The summary table algorithm is due to Mumick et al. [159]. The PipeSort algorithm, as well as other data cube computation techniques, is discussed in detail in [3]. The view selection algorithm was proposed in a classic paper by Harinarayan et al. [100]. Bitmap indexes were first introduced in [173] and bitmap join indexes in [172]. A study of the joint usage of indexing, partitioning, and view materialization in data warehouses is reported in [25]. A book on indexing structures for data warehouses is [123]. A study on index selection for data warehouses can be found in [85], while [223] surveys bitmap indices for data warehouses. A popular bitmap compression technique, based of run-length encoding, is WAH (Word Align Hybrid) [266]. The PLWAH (Position List Word Align Hybrid) bitmap compression technique [223] was proposed as a variation of the WAH scheme, and it is reported to be more efficient than the former, particularly in terms of storage. Rizzi and Saltarelli [198] compare view materialization against indexing for data warehouse design. Finally, a survey of view selection methods is [146].

8.13 Review Questions

8.1 What is the objective of physical data warehouse design? Specify different techniques that are used to achieve such objective.

8.2 Discuss advantages and disadvantages of using materialized views.

8.3 What is view maintenance? What is incremental view maintenance?

8.4 Discuss the kinds of algorithms for incremental view maintenance, that is, using full and partial information.

8.5 What are self-maintainable aggregate functions and views.

8.6 Explain briefly the main idea of the summary-delta algorithm for data cube maintenance.

8.7 How is data cube computation optimized? What are the kinds of optimizations that algorithms are based on?

8.8 Explain the idea of the PipeSort algorithm.

8.9 How can we estimate the size of a data cube?

8.10 Explain the algorithm for selecting a set of views to materialize. Discuss its limitations. How can they be overridden?

8.11 Compare B^+-tree indexes, hash indexes, bitmap indexes, and join indexes with respect to their use in databases and data warehouses.

8.12 How do we use bitmap indexes for range queries?

8.13 Explain run length encoding.

8.14 Describe a typical indexing scheme in a star and snowflake schemas.

8.15 How are bitmap indexes used during query processing?

8.16 How do join indexes work in query processing? Explain for which kinds of queries they are efficient.

8.17 Explain and discuss horizontal and vertical data partitioning.

8.18 Discuss different horizontal partitioning strategies. When would you use each of them?

8.19 Explain two techniques for increasing query performance taking advantage of partitioning.

8.20 Explain how parallel query processing is implemented in PostgreSQL.

8.21 Discuss the characteristics of storage modes in Analysis Services.

8.22 How do indexed views compare with materialized views?

8.14 Exercises

Exercise 8.1. In the Northwind database, consider the relations

Employee(EmpID, FirstName, LastName, Title, ...)
Orders(OrderID, CustID, EmpID, OrderDate, ...).

Consider further a view

EmpOrders(EmpID, Name, OrderID, OrderDate)

computed from the full outer join of tables Employee and Orders, where Name is obtained by concatenating FirstName and LastName.

Define the view EmpOrders in SQL. Show an example of instances for the relations and the corresponding view. By means of examples, show how the view EmpOrders must be modified upon insertions and deletions in table Employee. Give the SQL command to compute the delta relation of the view from the delta relations of table Employee. Write an algorithm to update the view from the delta relation.

Exercise 8.2. Consider a relation Connected(CityFrom, CityTo, Distance), which indicates pairs of cities that are directly connected and the distance between them, and a view OneStop(CityFrom, CityTo), which computes the pairs of cities $(c1, c2)$ such that $c2$ can be reached from $c1$ passing through exactly one intermediate stop. Answer the same questions as those of the previous exercise.

Exercise 8.3. Consider the following tables

Store(<u>StoreID</u>, City, State, Manager)
Order(<u>OrderID</u>, StoreID, Date)
OrderLine(<u>OrderID, LineNo</u>, ProductID, Quantity, Price)
Product(<u>ProductID</u>, ProductName, Category, Supplier)
Part(<u>PartID</u>, PartName, ProductID, Quantity)

and the following views

- ParisManagers(Manager) that contains managers of stores located in Paris.
- OrderProducts(OrderID, ProductCount) that contains the number of products for each order.
- OrderSuppliers(OrderID, SupplierCount) that contains the number of suppliers for each order.
- OrderAmount(OrderID, StoreID, Date, Amount) which adds to the table Order an additional column that contains the total amount of each order.
- StoreOrders(StoreID, OrderCount) that contains the number of orders for each store.
- ProductPart(ProductID, ProductName, PartID, PartName) that is obtained from the full outer join of tables Product and Part.

Define the above views in SQL. For each of them, determine whether the view is self-maintainable with respect to insertions and deletions. Give examples illustrating the cases that are not self-maintainable.

Exercise 8.4. Consider the following tables

Professor(<u>ProfNo</u>, ProfName, Laboratory)
Supervision(<u>ProfNo,StudNo</u>)
PhDStudent(<u>StudNo</u>, StudName, Laboratory)

and a view ProfPhdStud(ProfNo, ProfName, StudNo, StudName) computed from the outer joins of these three relations.

Determine whether the view is self-maintainable. Write the SQL command for creating the view. Show a possible instance of the tables and the corresponding view. Give a delta table composed of insertions to and deletions from the table Supervision and show how the view is computed from these delta tables.

Exercise 8.5. By means of examples, explain the propagate and refresh algorithm for the aggregate functions AVG, MIN, and COUNT. For each aggregate function, write the SQL command that creates the summary-delta table from the tables containing the inserted and deleted tuples in the fact table, and write the algorithm that refreshes the view from the summary-delta table.

Exercise 8.6. Suppose that a cube Sales(A, B, C, D, Amount) has to be fully materialized. The cube contains 64 tuples. Sorting takes the typical $n\log(n)$ time. Every GROUP BY with k attributes has 4×2^k tuples.

a. Compute the cube using the PipeSort algorithm.
b. Compute the gain of applying the PipeSort compared to the cost of computing all the views from scratch.

Exercise 8.7. Consider the graph in Fig. 8.19, where each node represents a view and the numbers are the costs of materializing the view. Assuming that the bottom of the lattice is materialized, determine using the View Selection Algorithm the five views to be materialized first.

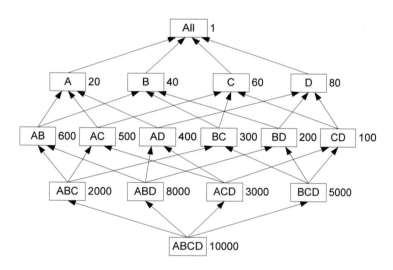

Fig. 8.19 A data cube lattice

Exercise 8.8. Consider the data cube lattice of a three-dimensional cube with dimensions A, B, and C. Extend the lattice to take into account the hierarchies $A \to A_1 \to All$ and $B \to B_1 \to B_2 \to All$. Since the lattice is complex to draw, represent it by giving the list of nodes and the list of edges.

Exercise 8.9. Consider an n-dimensional cube with dimensions $D_1, D_2, \ldots, D_n$. Suppose that each dimension D_i has a hierarchy with n_i levels. Compute the number of nodes of the corresponding data cube lattice.

Exercise 8.10. Modify the algorithm for selecting views to materialize in order to consider the probability that each view has to completely match a given query. In other words, consider that you know the distribution of the queries, so that view A has probability $P(A)$ to match a query, view B has probability $P(B)$, etc.

a. How would you change the algorithm to take into account this knowledge?
b. Suppose that in the lattice of Fig. 8.9, the view ABC is already materialized. Apply the modified algorithm to select four views to be materialized given the following probabilities for the views: $P(\mathsf{ABC}) = 0.1$, $P(\mathsf{AB}) = 0.1$, $P(\mathsf{AC}) = 0.2$, $P(\mathsf{BC}) = 0.3$, $P(\mathsf{A})) = 0.05$, $P(\mathsf{B}) = 0.05$, $P(\mathsf{C}) = 0.1$, and $P(\mathsf{All}) = 0.1$.
c. Answer the same question as in (b) but now with the probabilities as follows: $P(\mathsf{ABC}) = 0.1$, $P(\mathsf{AB}) = 0.05$, $P(\mathsf{AC}) = 0.1$, $P(\mathsf{BC}) = 0$, $P(\mathsf{A}) = 0.2$, $P(\mathsf{B}) = 0.1$, $P(\mathsf{C}) = 0.05$, and $P(\mathsf{All}) = 0.05$. Compare the results.

Exercise 8.11. Given the Employee table below, show how a bitmap index on attribute Title would look like. Compress the bitmap values using run-length encoding.

Employee Key	Employee Name	Title	Address	City	Department Key
e1	Peter Brown	Dr.	...	Brussels	d1
e2	James Martin	Mr.	...	Wavre	d1
e3	Ronald Ritchie	Mr.	...	Paris	d2
e4	Marco Benetti	Mr.	...	Versailles	d2
e5	Alexis Manoulis	Mr.	...	London	d3
e6	Maria Mortsel	Mrs.	...	Reading	d3
e7	Laura Spinotti	Mrs.	...	Brussels	d4
e8	John River	Mr.	...	Waterloo	d4
e9	Bert Jasper	Mr.	...	Paris	d5
e10	Claudia Brugman	Mrs.	...	Saint-Denis	d5

Exercise 8.12. Given the Sales table below and the Employee table from Ex. 8.11, show how a join index on attribute EmployeeKey would look like.

RowID Sales	Product Key	Customer Key	Employee Key	Date Key	Sales Amount
1	p1	c1	e1	d1	100
2	p1	c2	e3	d1	100
3	p2	c2	e4	d2	100
4	p2	c3	e5	d2	100
5	p3	c3	e1	d3	100
6	p4	c4	e2	d4	100
7	p5	c4	e2	d5	100

Exercise 8.13. Given the Department table below and the Employee table from Ex. 8.11, show how a bitmap join index on attribute DeptKey would look like.

Department Key	Department Name	Location
d1	Management	Brussels
d2	Production	Paris
d3	Marketing	London
d4	Human Resources	Brussels
d5	Research	Paris

Exercise 8.14. Consider the tables Sales in Ex. 8.12, Employee in Ex. 8.11, and Department in Ex. 8.13.

a. Propose an indexing scheme for the tables, including any kind of index you consider it necessary. Discuss possible alternatives according to several query scenarios. Discuss the advantages and disadvantages of creating the indexes.

b. Consider the query:

```
SELECT    E.EmployeeName, SUM(S.SalesAmount)
FROM      Sales S, Employee E, Department D
WHERE     S.EmployeeKey = E.EmployeeKey AND
          E.DepartmentKey = D.DepartmentKey AND
          ( D.Location = 'Brussels' OR D.Location = 'Paris' )
GROUP BY E.EmployeeName
```

Explain a possible query plan that uses the indexes defined in (a).

Chapter 9
Extraction, Transformation, and Loading

Extraction, transformation, and loading (ETL) processes extract data from internal and external sources of an organization, transform these data, and load them into a data warehouse. Since ETL processes are complex and costly, it is important to reduce their development and maintenance costs. Modeling ETL processes at a conceptual level is a way to achieve this goal. However, existing ETL tools have their own specific language to define ETL processes, and there is no agreed-upon conceptual model to specify such processes. In this chapter, we study the design of ETL processes using a conceptual approach, based on the Business Process Modeling Notation (BPMN), a de facto standard for specifying business processes. The model provides a set of primitives that cover the requirements of frequently used ETL processes. BPMN provides a conceptual and implementation-independent specification of ETL processes, hiding technical details and allowing designers to focus on essential characteristics of such processes. Finally, ETL processes expressed in BPMN can be translated into executable specifications for ETL tools. As an alternative to using such tools, we also show how an extended relational algebra can be used to implement ETL processes, which can be then automatically translated into SQL scripts to be executed over any RDBMS.

The chapter starts with a brief introduction of BPMN in Sect. 9.1. Then, in Sect. 9.2, we explain how we can use BPMN for ETL conceptual modeling. In Sect. 9.3, we apply these concepts to the Northwind case study. We design a conceptual model for the ETL process that loads the Northwind data warehouse used in the previous chapters with data extracted from the Northwind operational database and other sources. Finally, after providing in Sect. 9.4 a brief overview of Microsoft Integration Services, we show in Sect. 9.5 how the ETL conceptual model can be implemented in this tool. The chapter concludes in Sect. 9.6 explaining the relational algebra implementation of ETL processes and its translation into SQL, which is illustrated with the implementation of the Norwthind ETL.

© Springer-Verlag GmbH Germany, part of Springer Nature 2022
A. Vaisman, E. Zimányi, *Data Warehouse Systems*, Data-Centric Systems and Applications, https://doi.org/10.1007/978-3-662-65167-4_9

9.1 Business Process Modeling Notation

A **business process** is a collection of related activities or tasks in an organization whose goal is to produce a specific service or product. In a business
process, a task can be performed by software systems, humans, or a combination of these. Business process modeling is the activity of representing the
business processes of an organization so that the current processes may be
analyzed and improved.

Many techniques have been proposed to model business processes. Traditional ones include Gantt charts, flowcharts, PERT diagrams, and data flow
diagrams. However, the problem with these techniques is the lack of a formal
semantics. On the other hand, formal techniques such as Petri Nets have a
well-defined semantics but are difficult to understand by business users and,
further, do not have the expressiveness to represent some typical situations
that arise in real-world settings. These reasons motivated the development
of BPMN, a de facto standard for modeling business processes. The current
version of the standard is BPMN 2.0.[1]

BPMN provides a graphical notation for defining, understanding, and communicating the business processes of an organization. The rationale behind
BPMN is to define a language that is usable by the business community, is
constrained to support the modeling concepts that are applicable to business
processes, and is useful in clearly describing complex processes. BPMN is
defined using the Unified Modeling Language (UML). In addition, a precise
semantics of the language and an execution semantics are also defined.

BPMN aims at tackling two conflicting requirements, namely, providing
a simple mechanism for creating business process models and handling the
complexity inherent to them. For this reason, the graphical aspects of the
notation are organized into categories, so that the reader of a BPMN diagram can easily recognize the basic types of elements and understand the
diagram. Within the basic categories of elements, additional variation and information can be added to support the requirements for complexity without
dramatically changing the basic layout of the diagram.

BPMN provides four basic categories of elements, namely, flow objects,
connecting objects, swimlanes, and artifacts. These are described next.

Flow objects are the main elements for defining a business process. There
are three types of flow objects: activities, gateways, and events. An **activity**
is a work performed during a process. Activities can be either single tasks
or subprocesses, and thus, they can be atomic or nonatomic. Figure 9.1a
shows how a task is represented. A **subprocess** is an encapsulated process
whose details we want to hide. Figure 9.1b shows that there are two ways of
representing a subprocess: collapsed and expanded.

Gateways are used to control the sequence of activities in a process depending on *conditions*. It is worth noting that BPMN does not state how

---

[1] http://www.omg.org/spec/BPMN/2.0/

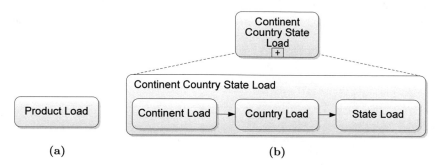

(a)   **(b)**

Fig. 9.1 Activities: **(a)** Single task; **(b)** Collapsed and expanded subprocess

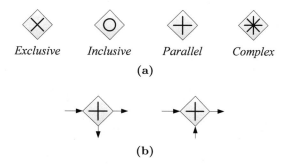

(b)

Fig. 9.2 **(a)** Different types of gateways; **(b)** Splitting and merging gateways

these conditions must be written; this is left to the modeler. Gateways are represented by diamond shapes. BPMN defines several types of gateways, shown in Fig. 9.2a, which are distinguished by the symbol used inside the diamond shape. All these types can be *splitting* or *merging* gateways, as shown in Fig. 9.2b, depending on the number of ingoing and outgoing branches. An *exclusive gateway* models an exclusive OR decision, that is, depending on a condition, the gateway activates exactly one of its outgoing branches. It can be represented as an empty diamond shape or a diamond shape with an 'X' inside. A default flow (see below) can be defined as one of the outgoing flows, if no other condition is true. An *inclusive gateway* triggers or merges one or more flows. In a *splitting* inclusive gateway, any combination of outgoing flows can be triggered. However, a default flow cannot be included in such a combination. In a *merging* inclusive gateway, any combination can be chosen to continue the flow. A *parallel gateway* allows the synchronization between outgoing and incoming flows. A *splitting* parallel gateway is analogous to an AND operation: the incoming flow triggers one or more outgoing parallel flows. On the other hand, a *merging* parallel gateway synchronizes the flow merging all the incoming flows into a single outgoing one. Finally, *complex gateways* can represent complex conditions. For example, a merging complex gateway can model that when three out of five flows are completed, the process can continue without waiting for the completion of the other two.

Fig. 9.3 Examples of events

Fig. 9.4 Error handling: canceled and compensated activities

Events (see Fig. 9.3) represent something that happens that affects the sequence and timing of the workflow activities. Events may be internal or external to the task into consideration. There are three types of events, which can be distinguished depending on whether they are drawn with a single, a double, or a thick line. *Start* and *end* events indicate the beginning and ending of a process, respectively. *Intermediate* events include time, message, cancel, and terminate events. *Date* events can be used to represent situations when a task must wait for some period of time before continuing. *Message* events can be used to represent communication, for example, to send an e-mail indicating that an error has occurred. They can also be used for triggering a task, for example, a message may indicate that an activity can start. *Cancel* events listen to the errors in a process and notify them either by an explicit action like sending a message, as in the canceled activity shown in Fig. 9.4, or by an implicit action to be defined in the next steps of the process development. *Compensation* events can be employed to recover errors by launching specific compensation activities, which are linked to the compensation event with the association connecting object (Fig. 9.5), as shown in Fig. 9.4. Finally, *terminate* events stop the entire process, including all parallel processes.

Connecting objects are used to represent how objects are connected. There are three types of connecting objects, as illustrated in Fig. 9.5.

A **sequence flow** represents a sequencing constraint between flow objects. It is the basic connecting object in a workflow. It states that if two activities are linked by a sequence flow, the target activity will start only when the

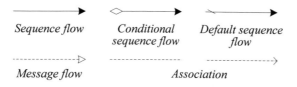

Fig. 9.5 Connecting objects

source one has finished. If multiple sequence flows outgo from an activity, all of them will be activated after its execution. In case there is a need to control a sequence flow, it is possible to add a condition to the sequence flow by using the **conditional sequence flow**. A sequence flow may be set as the **default flow** in case of many outgoing flows. For example, as explained above, in an exclusive or an inclusive gateway, if no other condition is true, then the default flow is followed. Note that sequence flows can replace splitting and merging gateways. For example, an exclusive gateway splitting into two paths could be replaced by two conditional flows, provided the conditions are *mutually exclusive*. Inclusive gateways could be replaced by conditional flows, even when the former constraint does not apply.

A **message flow** represents the sending and receiving of messages between organizational boundaries (i.e., pools, explained below). A message flow is the only connecting object able to get through the boundary of a pool and may also connect to a flow object within that pool.

An **association** relates artifacts (like annotations) to flow objects (like activities). We give examples below. An association can indicate directionality using an open arrowhead, for example, when linking the compensation activity in case of error handling.

Fig. 9.6 Activity and subprocess loops

A **loop** (see Fig. 9.6) represents the repeated execution of a process for as long as the underlying looping condition is true. This condition must be evaluated for every loop iteration and may be evaluated at the beginning or at the end of the iteration. In the example of Fig. 9.7, we represent a task of an ETL process that connects to a server. At a high abstraction level, the subprocess activity hides the details. It has the loop symbol attached (a curved arrow), indicating that the subprocess is executed repeatedly until an ending condition is reached. When we expand the subprocess, we can see what happens within it: the server waits for 3 minutes (this waiting task is represented by the time event). If the connection is not established, the

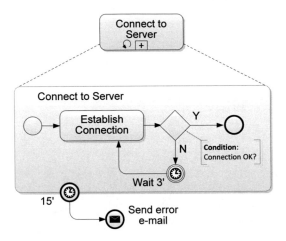

Fig. 9.7 An example of a subprocess loop

request for the connection is launched again. After 15 minutes (another time event), if the connection was not reached, the task is stopped and an error e-mail is sent (a message event).

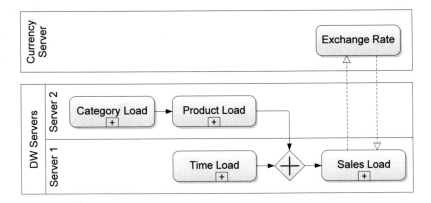

Fig. 9.8 Swimlanes: pool and lanes

A **swimlane** (see Fig. 9.8) is a structuring object that comprises **pools** and **lanes**. Both of them are used to define process boundaries. Only messages are allowed between two pools, not sequence flows. In other words, a workflow must be contained in only one pool. However, a pool may be subdivided into several lanes, which represent roles or services in the enterprise. Lanes within a pool do not have any special constraint, and thus sequence flows may cross a lane freely. We give an example in the next section.

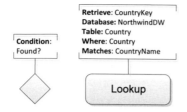

Fig. 9.9 BPMN artifacts: annotations

Artifacts are used to add information to a diagram. There are three types of artifacts. A **data object** represents either data that are input to a process, data resulting from a process, data that needs to be collected, or data that needs to be stored. A **group** organizes tasks or processes that have some kind of significance in the overall model. A group does not affect the flow in the diagram. **Annotations** are used to add extra information to flow objects. For example, an annotation for an activity in an ETL process can indicate a gateway condition or the attributes involved in a lookup task, as shown in Fig. 9.9. Annotations may be associated to both activities and subprocesses in order to describe their semantics.

9.2 Conceptual ETL Design Using BPMN

There is no standard conceptual model for defining ETL processes. Each existing ETL tool provides its own model, often too detailed since it takes into consideration many implementation issues. In this section, we show how BPMN can be customized for designing ETL processes at a conceptual level. We describe how the BPMN constructs introduced in the previous sections can be used to define the most common ETL tasks. We also introduce a BPMN-based notation for ETL. The most obvious advantage of using a conceptual approach for designing ETL processes is the ability to replicate the same process with different tools. We will illustrate this fact by describing in Sect. 9.3 the conceptual model of the ETL process that loads the Northwind data warehouse. Then, in Sect. 9.5 we will show how this conceptual model can be implemented in SQL Server Integration Services.

A key point of the approach we present here is the perception of ETL processes as a combination of control and data tasks, where **control tasks** orchestrate groups of tasks and **data tasks** detail how input data are transformed and output data are produced. For example, the overall process of populating a data warehouse is a control task composed of multiple subtasks, while populating a fact or dimension table is a data task. Therefore, control tasks can be considered as workflows where arrows represent the precedence between tasks, while data tasks represent data flows where records are transferred through the arrows. Given the discussion above, designing ETL processes using business process modeling tools appears natural. We present next the conceptual model for ETL processes based on BPMN.

Control tasks represent the orchestration of an ETL process, independently of the data flowing through such process. Such tasks are represented by means of the constructs described in Sect. 9.1. For example, gateways are used to control the sequence of activities in an ETL process. The most used types of gateways in an ETL context are exclusive and parallel gateways. Events are another type of objects often used in control tasks. For instance, a cancelation event can be used to represent the situation when an error occurs and may be followed by a message event that sends an e-mail to notify the failure.

Swimlanes can be used to organize ETL processes according to several strategies, namely, by *technical architecture* (such as servers to which tasks are assigned), by *business entities* (such as departments or branches), or by *user profiles* (such as manager, analyst, or designer) that give special access rights to users. For example, Fig. 9.8 illustrates the use of swimlanes for the Northwind ETL process (we will explain in detail this process later in this chapter). The figure shows some of the subprocesses that load the Product dimension table, the Date dimension table, and the Sales fact table (represented as compound activities with subprocesses); it also assumes their distribution between Server 1 and Server 2. Each one of these servers is considered as a lane contained inside the pool of data warehouse servers. We can also see that a swimlane called Currency Server contains a web service that receives an input currency (like US dollars), an amount, and an output currency (like euros) and returns the amount equivalent in the output currency. This could be used in the loading of the Sales fact table. Thus, flow messages are exchanged between the Sales Load activity, and the Exchange Rate task which is performed by the web service. These messages go across both swimlanes.

Data tasks represent activities typically carried out to manipulate data, such as input data, output data, and data transformation. Since such data manipulation operations occur *within* an activity, data tasks can be considered as being at a lower abstraction level than control tasks. Recall that arrows in a data task represent not only a precedence relationship between its activities but also the flow of data records between them.

Data tasks can be classified into row and rowset operations. **Row operations** apply transformations to the data on a row-by-row basis. In contrast, **rowset operations** deal with a set of rows. For example, updating the value of a column is a row operation, while aggregation is a rowset operation. Data tasks can also be classified (orthogonally to the previous classification) into **unary** or ***n*-ary data tasks**, depending of the number of input flows.

Figure 9.10 shows examples of unary row operations: Input Data, Insert Data, Add Columns, and Convert Columns. Note the annotations linked to the tasks by means of association flows. The annotations contain metadata that specify the parameters of the task. For example, in Fig. 9.10a, the annotation tells that the data is read from an Excel file called Date.xls. Similarly, the

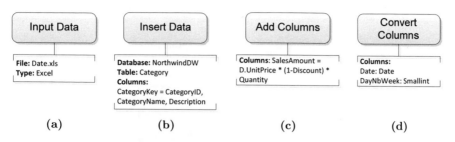

Fig. 9.10 Unary row operations

annotation in Fig. 9.10b tells that the task inserts tuples in the table **Category** of the **NorthwindDW** database, where column **CategoryKey** is obtained from the **CategoryID** in the flow. Further, new records will be appended to the table. The task in Fig. 9.10c adds a column named **SalesAmount** to the flow whose value is computed from the expression given. Here, it is supposed that the values of the columns appearing in the expression are taken from the current record. Finally, Fig. 9.10d converts the columns **Date** and **DayNbWeek** (e.g., read from an Excel file as strings) into a **Date** and a **Smallint**, respectively.

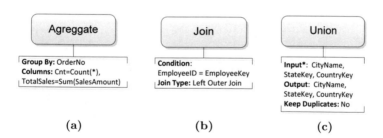

Fig. 9.11 Rowset operations: (a) **Aggregate** (unary); (b) **Join** (binary); (c) **Union** (*n*-ary)

Figure 9.11 shows three rowset operations: **Aggregate** (unary), **Join** (binary), and **Union** (*n*-ary). These operations receive a set of rows to process altogether, rather than operating row by row. Again, annotations complement the diagram information. For example, in the case of the **Union** task, the annotation tells the name of the input and output columns and informs if duplicates must be kept. Note that the case of the union is a particular one: if duplicates are retained, then it becomes a row operation since it can be done row by row. If duplicates are eliminated, then it becomes a rowset operation because sorting is involved in the operation.

A common data task in an ETL process is the lookup, which checks if some value is present in a file, based on a single or compound search key.

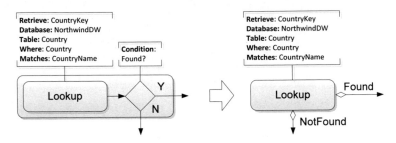

Fig. 9.12 Shorthand notation for the lookup task

Typically, a lookup is immediately followed by an exclusive gateway with a branching condition. For conciseness, we use a shorthand for these two tasks and replace this by two conditional flows, as shown in Fig. 9.12.

Table 9.1 defines the various ETL tasks and their annotations. The annotations between brackets, as in [Group By], are optional, while the annotations suffixed with an asterisk, as in Input*, can be repeated several times. Finally, the annotations separated by a vertical bar, as in Table | Query, are exclusive, one of which must be provided. In Appendix A, we give the BPMN notation for these ETL tasks.

9.3 Conceptual Design of the Northwind ETL Process

In this section, using the concepts explained in the previous ones, we present a conceptual model of the ETL process that loads the Northwind data warehouse from the operational database and other sources. Later, in Sect. 9.5, we show how this model can be implemented in Microsoft Integration Services.

The operational data reside in a relational database, whose logical schema is shown in Fig. 2.4. These data must be mapped to a data warehouse, whose schema is given in Fig. 5.4. In addition to the operational database, some other files are needed for loading the data warehouse. We next describe these files, as well as the requirements of the process.

First, an Excel file called Date.xls contains the data needed for loading the Date dimension table. The time interval of this file covers the dates contained in the table Orders of the Northwind operational database.

We can see in Fig. 5.4 that in the Northwind data warehouse the dimension tables Customer, Supplier, and Employee share the geographic hierarchy starting at the City level. Data for the hierarchy State → Country → Continent are loaded from an XML file called Territories.xml that begins as shown in Fig. 9.13a. A graphical representation of the schema of the XML file is shown in Fig. 9.13b, where rectangles represent elements and rounded rectangles represent attributes. The cardinalities of the relationships are also indicated.

Table 9.1 Annotations of the ETL tasks in BPMN

Add Columns: adds new derived columns to the flow	
Columns	List of Col=Expr computing the value of a new column Col added to the output flow from expression Expr
Add Columns: adds new columns to the flow obtained from an SQL query	
Columns	List of column names added to the output flow
Database	Name of the database
Query	SQL query
Aggregate: adds new columns to the flow computed by aggregating values from the input flow, possibly after grouping the records	
[Group By]	List of column names from the input flow that are used for grouping. These columns are the only ones from the input flow that are also in the output flow
Columns	List of Col1=AgFct(Col2) or Col1=AgFct(*), where a new column Col1 in the output flow will be assigned the value AgFct(Col2) or AgrFct(*)
Convert Columns: changes the type of columns from the flow	
Columns	List of Col:Type, where column Col in the input flow is converted to type Type in the output flow
Delete Data: deletes tuples from a database corresponding to records in the flow	
Database	Name of the database
Table	Name of the table
Where	List of column names from the input flow
Matches	List of attribute names from the table
Difference: computes the difference of two flows	
Input*	List of column names from the two input flows. Input* is used if the column names are the same for both flows, otherwise Input1 and Input2 are used, each flow defining the column names
Output	List of column names from the output flow
Drop Columns: drops columns from the flow	
Columns	List of column names from the input flow that are removed from the output flow
Input Data: inserts records into the flow obtained from a file	
File	Name of the file
Type	Type of the file, such as Text, CSV, Excel, or XML
[Columns]	Name of the columns or XPath expressions
Input Data: inserts records into the flow obtained from a database	
Database	Name of the database
Table | Query	Name of the table or SQL query
[Columns]	Name of the columns
Insert Data: inserts records from the flow into a file	
File	Name of the file
Type	Type of the file
[Columns]	Name of the columns
[Options]	Headers if column names are put in the first line of the file; either Empty or Append depending on whether the file is emptied before inserting the new tuples, the latter is the default

Table 9.1 Annotations of the ETL tasks in BPMN (cont.)

Insert Data: inserts tuples into a database corresponding to records in the flow	
Database	Name of the database
Table	Name of the table
[Columns]	List of Col or Col = Expr, where column Col in the database either takes the values for the same column of the flow or takes the values from the expression Expr
[Options]	Either Empty or Append depending on whether the table is emptied before inserting the new tuples, the latter is the default
Intersection: computes the intersection of two flows	
Input*	List of column names from the two input flows. Input* is used if the column names are the same for both flows, otherwise Input1 and Input2 are used, each flow defining the column names
Output	List of column names from the output flow
Join: computes the join of two flows	
Condition	List of Col1 op Col2, where Col1 belongs to the first input flow, Col2 to the second flow, and op is a comparison operator
[Join Type]	Either Inner Join, Left Outer Join, Right Outer Join, or Full Outer Join, the first one is the default
Lookup: adds columns to the flow obtained by looking up data from a database	
Retrieve	List of column names added to the output flow
Database	Database name
Table | Query	Name of the table or SQL query
Where	List of column names from the input flow
Matches	List of attribute names from the lookup table or SQL query
Lookup: replaces column values of the flow with values obtained by looking up data from a database	
Replace	List of column names from the input flow whose values are replaced in the output flow
Database	Database name
Table | Query	Name of the table or SQL query
Where	List of column names from the input flow
Matches	List of attribute names from the lookup table or description of an SQL query
Multicast: produces several output flows from an input flow	
Input	List of column names from the input flow
Output*	List of column names from each output flow. Output* is used if the column names are the same for all flows, otherwise Output1, . . . , Outputn are used, each flow defining the column names
Distinct: removes duplicate records from the flow	
(None)	This task does not have any annotation
Rename Columns: changes the name of columns from the flow	
Columns	List of Col->NewCol where column Col from the input flow is renamed NewCol in the output flow
Sort: sorts the records of the flow	
Columns	List of column names from the input flow, where for each of them, either ASC or DESC is specified, the former being the default

Table 9.1 Annotations of the ETL tasks in BPMN (cont.)

Union: computes the union of two or more flows	
Input*	List of column names from each input flow. Input* is used if the column names are the same for all flows. Otherwise Input1, ..., Inputn are used, each flow defining the column names
Output	List of column names from the output flow
[Keep Duplicates]	Either Yes or No, the former is the default
Update Columns: replaces column values from the flow	
Columns	List of Col=Expr computing the new value of column Col from the input flow from expression Expr
[Condition]	Boolean condition that the records in the input flow must satisfy in order to be updated. If not specified all records are updated
Update Columns: replaces column values from the flow	
Columns	List of column names from the input flow whose values are changed in the output flow
Database	Name of the database
Query	SQL Query
[Condition]	Boolean condition that the records in the input flow must satisfy in order to be updated. If not specified all records are updated
Update Data: update tuples of a database corresponding to records in the flow	
Database	Name of the database
Table	Name of the table
Columns	List of Attr=Expr computing the new value of attribute Attr in the table from expression Expr
Where	List of column names from the input flow
Matches	List of attribute names from the table

Notice that type is an attribute of State that contains, for example, the value state for Austria. However, for Belgium it contains the value province (not shown in the figure). Notice also that EnglishStateName, RegionName, and RegionCode are optional, as indicated by the cardinality 0..1.

It is worth noting that the attribute Region of tables Customers and Suppliers in the Northwind database contains in fact a state or province name (e.g., Québec), or a state code (e.g., CA). Similarly, the attribute Country contains a country name (e.g., Canada) or a country code (e.g., USA). To identify to which state or province a city belongs, a file called Cities.txt is used. The file contains three fields separated by tabs and begins as shown in Fig. 9.14a, where the first line contains field names. In the case of cities located in countries that do not have states, as it is the case of Singapore, a null value is given for the second field. The above file is also used to identify to which state the city in the attribute TerritoryDescription of table Territories in the Northwind database corresponds. A temporary table in the data warehouse, called TempCities, will be used for storing the contents of this file. The structure of the table is given in Fig. 9.14b.

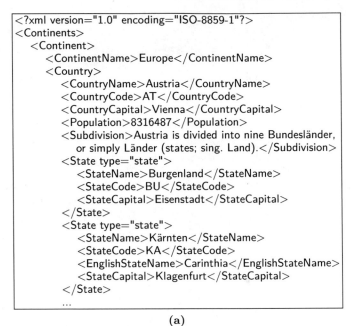

```
<?xml version="1.0" encoding="ISO-8859-1"?>
<Continents>
   <Continent>
      <ContinentName>Europe</ContinentName>
      <Country>
         <CountryName>Austria</CountryName>
         <CountryCode>AT</CountryCode>
         <CountryCapital>Vienna</CountryCapital>
         <Population>8316487</Population>
         <Subdivision>Austria is divided into nine Bundesländer,
            or simply Länder (states; sing. Land).</Subdivision>
         <State type="state">
            <StateName>Burgenland</StateName>
            <StateCode>BU</StateCode>
            <StateCapital>Eisenstadt</StateCapital>
         </State>
         <State type="state">
            <StateName>Kärnten</StateName>
            <StateCode>KA</StateCode>
            <EnglishStateName>Carinthia</EnglishStateName>
            <StateCapital>Klagenfurt</StateCapital>
         </State>
         ...
```

(a)

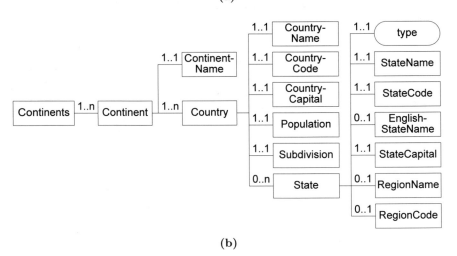

(b)

Fig. 9.13 (a) Beginning of the file Territories.xml; (b) XML Schema of the file

It is worth noting that the keys of the operational database are reused in the data warehouse as surrogate keys for all dimensions except for dimension Customer. In this dimension, the key of the operational database is kept in the attribute CustomerID, while a new surrogate key is generated during the ETL process.

City → State → Country	TempCities
Aachen → North Rhine-Westphalia → Germany	City
Albuquerque → New Mexico → USA	State
Anchorage → Alaska → USA	Country
Ann Arbor → Michigan → USA	
Annecy → Haute-Savoie → France	
...	

(a)   (b)

Fig. 9.14 (a) Beginning of the file Cities.txt; and (b) Associated table TempCities

In addition, for the Sales table in the Northwind data warehouse, the following transformations are needed:

- The attribute OrderLineNo must be generated in ascending order of ProductID (in the operational database there is no order line number).
- The attribute SalesAmount must be calculated taking into account the unit price, the discount, and the quantity.
- The attribute Freight, which in the operational database is related to the whole order, must be evenly distributed among the lines of the order.

Figure 9.15 provides a general overview of the whole ETL process. The figure shows the control tasks needed to perform the transformation from the operational database and the additional files presented above, and the loading of the transformed data into the data warehouse. We can see that the process starts with a start event, followed by activities (with subprocesses) that can be performed in parallel (represented by a splitting parallel gateway) which populate the dimension hierarchies. Finally, a parallel merging gateway synchronizes the flow, meaning that the loading of the Sales fact table (activity Sales Load) can only start when all other tasks have been completed. If the process fails, a cancelation event is triggered and an error message in the form of an e-mail is dispatched.

Figure 9.16 shows the task that loads the Category table in the data warehouse. It is composed of an input data task and an insertion data task. The former reads the table Categories from the operational database. The latter loads the table Category in the data warehouse, where the CategoryID attribute in the Categories table is mapped to the CategoryKey attribute in the Category table. Similarly, Fig. 9.17 shows the task that loads the Date table from an Excel file. It is similar to the previously explained task, but includes a conversion of columns, which defines the data types of the attributes of the target table Date in the data warehouse, and the addition of a column DateKey initialized with null values so the database can generate surrogate keys for this attribute. We do not show the task that loads the TempCities table, shown in Fig. 9.14b, since it is similar to the one that loads the Categories table just described, except that the data is input from a file instead of a database.

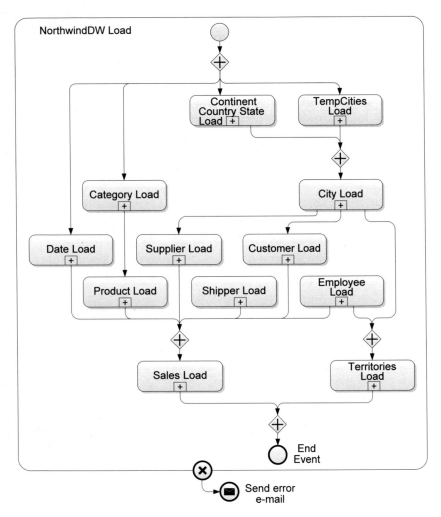

Fig. 9.15 Overall view of the conceptual ETL process for the Northwind data warehouse

The control task that loads the tables composing the hierarchy State → Country → Continent is depicted in Fig. 9.18a. As can be seen, this requires a sequence of data tasks. Figure 9.18b shows the data task that loads the Continent table. It reads the data from the XML file using the following XPath expression:

<Continents>/<Continent>/<ContinentName>

Then, a new column is added to the flow in order to be able to generate the surrogate key for the table in the data warehouse.

Figure 9.18c shows the task that loads the Country table. It reads the data from the XML file using the following XPath expressions:

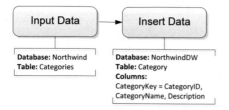

Fig. 9.16 Load of the Category dimension table

Fig. 9.17 Load of the Date dimension table

```
<Continents>/<Continent>/<Country>/*
<Continents>/<Continent>/<ContinentName>
```

In this case, we need to read from the XML file not only the attributes of Country, but also the ContinentName to which a country belongs. For example, when reading the Country element corresponding to Austria we must also obtain the corresponding value of the element ContinentName, that is, Europe. Thus, the flow is now composed of the attributes CountryName, CountryCode, CountryCapital, Population, Subdivision, State, and ContinentName (see Fig. 9.13b). The ContinentName value is then used in a lookup task for obtaining the corresponding ContinentKey from the data warehouse. Finally, the data in the flow is loaded into the warehouse. We do not show the task that loads the State table since it is similar to the one that loads the Country table just described.

The process that loads the City table is depicted in Fig. 9.19. The first task is an input data task over the table TempCities. Note that the final goal is to populate a table with a state key and a country key, one of which is null depending on whether the country is divided into states or not. Thus, the first exclusive gateway tests whether State is null or not (recall that this is the optional attribute). In the first case, a lookup obtains the CountryKey. In the second case, we must match (State, Country) pairs in TempCities to values in the State and Country tables. However, as we have explained, states and countries can come in many forms, thus we need three lookup tasks, as shown in the annotations in Fig. 9.19. The three lookups are as follows:

- The first lookup process records where State and Country correspond, respectively, to StateName and CountryName. An example is state Loire and country France.

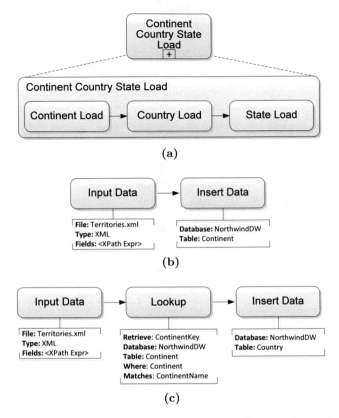

Fig. 9.18 Load of the tables for the State → Country → Continent hierarchy. (**a**) Associated control task; (**b**) Load of the Continent table; (**c**) Load of the Country table

- The second lookup process records where State and Country correspond, respectively, to EnglishStateName and CountryName. An example is state Lower Saxony, whose German name is Niedersachsen, together with country Germany.
- Finally, the third lookup process records where State and Country correspond, respectively, to StateName and CountryCode. An example is state Florida and country USA.

The SQL query associated to these lookups is as follows:

```
SELECT S.*, CountryName, CountryCode
FROM   State S JOIN Country C ON S.CountryKey = C.CountryKey
```

Finally, a union is performed with the results of the four flows, and the table is populated with an insert data task. Note that in the City table, if a state was not found in the initial lookup (Input1 in Fig. 9.19), the attribute State will be null; on the other hand, if a state was found it means that the city will

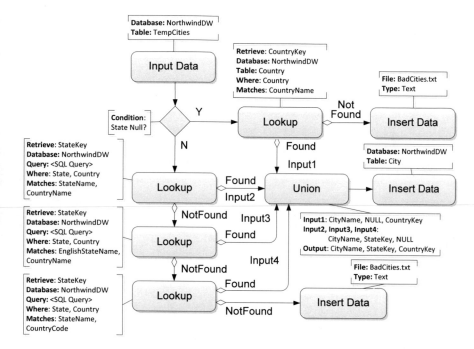

Fig. 9.19 Load of the City dimension table

have an associated state, therefore, the Country attribute will be null (Inputs2, Input3, and Input4 in the figure). Records for which the state and/or country are not found are stored into a BadCities.txt file.

Figure 9.20 shows the conceptual ETL process for loading the Customer table in the data warehouse. The input table Customers is read from the operational database using an input data task. Recall that the Region attribute in this table corresponds actually to a state name or a state code. Since this attribute is optional, the first exclusive gateway checks whether this attribute is null or not. If Region is null, a lookup checks if the corresponding (City, Country) pair matches a pair in TempCities, and retrieve the State attribute from the latter, creating a new column. Since the value State just obtained may be null for countries without states, another exclusive gateway tests whether State is null, in which case a lookup obtains the CityKey by matching values of City and Country in a lookup table defined by the following SQL query:

```
SELECT CityKey, CityName, CountryName
FROM   City C JOIN Country T ON C.CountryKey = T.CountryKey
```

Then, we send the obtained records to a union task in order to load them in the data warehouse.

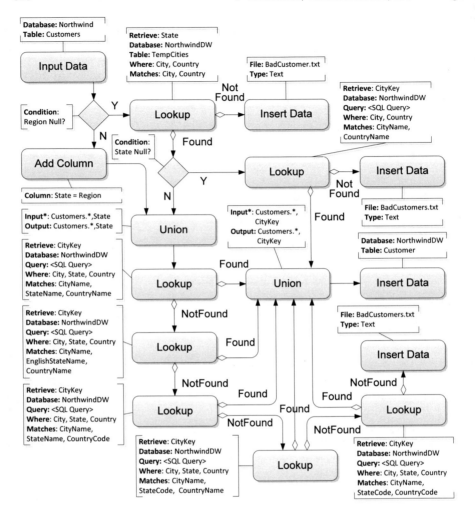

Fig. 9.20 Load of the Customer dimension table

Returning back to the first exclusive gateway, if the **Region** attribute is non-null, we add a new column **State** initialized with the values of column **Region** and we make the union of these records with ones having a value of **State** different from null obtained in the first lookup.

Then, in a similar way as the task that loads the **City** table, five lookup tasks are needed, where each one tries to match a couple of values of **State** and **Country** to values in the lookup table built as a join between the **City**, **State**, and **Country** tables as follows:

```
SELECT  C.CityKey, C.CityName, S.StateName, S.EnglishStateName,
        S.StateCode, T.CountryName, T.CountryCode
FROM    City C JOIN State S ON C.StateKey = S.StateKey
```

      JOIN Country T ON S.CountryKey = T.CountryKey

Two additional cases are needed with respect to the City Load task:

- The fourth lookup process records where State and Country correspond, respectively, to StateCode and CountryName. An example is state BC and country Canada.
- The fifth lookup process records where State and Country correspond, respectively, to StateCode and CountryCode. An example is state AK and country USA.

Finally, we perform the union of all flows, add the column CustomerKey for the surrogate key initialized to null, and write to the target table by means of an insert data task. We omit the description of the ETL process that loads the Supplier table, since it is similar to the one that loads the Customer table just described.

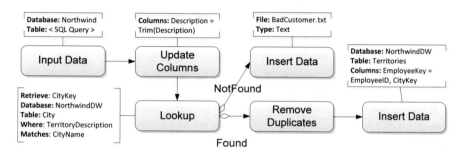

Fig. 9.21 Load of the Territories bridge table

    Figure 9.21 depicts the process for loading the Territories bridge table. The input table is the following SQL query:

SELECT E.*, TerritoryDescription
FROM   EmployeeTerritories E JOIN Territories T ON E.TerritoryID = T.TerritoryID

Then, an update column task is applied to remove the leading spaces (with operation trim) from the attribute TerritoryDescription. The city key is then obtained with a lookup over the table City in the data warehouse, which adds the attribute CityKey to the flow. The data flow continues with a task that removes duplicates in the assignment of employees to cities. Indeed, in the Northwind operational database New York appears twice in the Territories table with different identifiers, and employee number 5 is assigned to both of these versions of New York in the EmployeeTerritories table. Finally, after removing duplicates, we populate the Territories table with an insert data task, where the column EmployeeID in the flow is associated with the attribute EmployeeKey in the data warehouse.

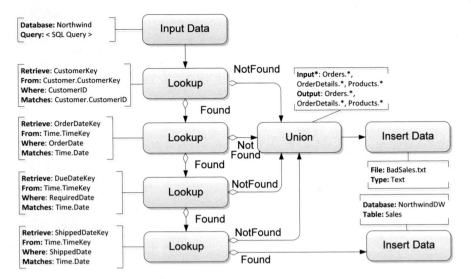

Fig. 9.22 Load of the Sales fact table

Figure 9.22 shows the conceptual ETL process for loading the Sales fact table. This task is performed once all the other tasks loading the dimension tables have been done. The process starts with an input data task that obtains data from the operational database by means of the SQL query below:

```
SELECT  O.CustomerID, EmployeeID AS EmployeeKey, O.OrderDate,
        O.RequiredDate AS DueDate, O.ShippedDate,
        ShipVia AS ShipperKey, P.ProductID AS ProductKey,
        P.SupplierID AS SupplierKey, O.OrderID AS OrderNo,
        ROW_NUMBER() OVER (PARTITION BY D.OrderID
        ORDER BY D.ProductID) AS OrderLineNo,
        D.UnitPrice, Quantity, Discount,
        D.UnitPrice * (1-Discount) * Quantity AS SalesAmount,
        O.Freight/COUNT(*) OVER (PARTITION BY D.OrderID) AS Freight
FROM    Orders O, OrderDetails D, Products P
WHERE   O.OrderID = D.OrderID AND D.ProductID = P.ProductID
```

A sequence of lookups follows, which obtains the missing foreign keys for the dimension tables. Finally, the fact table is loaded with the data retrieved.

9.4 SQL Server Integration Services

In this section, we introduce Integration Services, a component of SQL Server that is used to perform data migration tasks, and in particular ETL processes. Then, in next section, we implement the conceptual ETL design for the Northwind data warehouse given in Sect. 9.3 using this tool.

In Integration Services, a *package* is basically a workflow containing a collection of tasks executed in an orderly fashion. A package consists of a *control flow* and, optionally, one or more *data flows*. Integration Services provides three different types of control flow elements:

- *Tasks*, which are individual units of work that provide functionality to a package.
- *Containers*, which group tasks logically into units of work, and are also used to define variables and events. Examples of containers are the **Sequence Container** and the **For Loop Container**.
- *Precedence constraints*, which connect tasks, containers, and executables in order to define the order in which these are executed within the workflow of a package.

A control flow orchestrates the order of execution of package components according to the precedence constraints defined. Among the many different kinds of tasks supported by Integration Services, there are *data flow tasks* (which run data flows to extract data, apply column level transformations, and load data), *data preparation tasks* (which copy files and directories, download files and data, profile data for cleansing, and so on), *Analysis Services tasks* (which create, modify, delete, and process Analysis Services objects), and *workflow tasks* (which communicate with other processes to run packages, send and receive messages, send e-mail messages, and so on).

Creating a control flow in Integration Services requires the following steps:

- *Adding containers* that implement repeating workflows in a package.
- *Adding tasks* of the kinds mentioned above. If the package has to work with data (which is most of the times the case), the control flow must include at least one data flow task.
- *Connecting containers and tasks* using precedence constraints. Tasks or containers can be joined in a control flow dragging their connectors from one item to another. A connector between two items represents a precedence constraint, which specifies that the first one must be executed successfully before the next one in the control flow can run.
- *Adding connection managers*, which are needed when a task requires a connection to a data source.

A *data flow* extracts data into memory, transforms them, and writes them to a destination. Integration Services provides three different types of data flow components as follows:

- *Sources*, which extract data from data stores like tables and views in relational databases, files, and Analysis Services databases. Integration Services can connect with OLE DB data sources, like SQL Server, Oracle, or DB2. Also, sources can be Excel files, flat files, and XML files, among other ones.

- *Transformations*, which modify, summarize, and clean data. These transformations can split, divert, or merge the flow. Examples of transformations are **Conditional Split**, **Copy Column**, and **Aggregate**.
- *Destinations*, which load data into data stores or in-memory data sets.

Creating a data flow includes the following steps:

- *Adding one or more sources* to extract data from files and databases, and add connection managers to connect to these sources.
- *Adding the transformations* to satisfy the package requirements.
- *Connecting data flow components*.
- *Adding one or more destinations* to load data into data stores.
- *Configuring error outputs* on components.
- *Including annotations* to document the data flow.

We illustrate all these concepts in Sect. 9.5 when we study the implementation of the Northwind ETL process in Integration Services.

9.5 The Northwind ETL Process in Integration Services

In this section, we show an implementation in Integration Services of the ETL process that loads the Northwind data warehouse. We compare this implementation with the conceptual design presented in Sect. 9.3 and show how to translate the constructs of the conceptual ETL language into the equivalent ones in Integration Services. In our implementation, the Northwind operational database and the Northwind data warehouse are located on an SQL Server database.

Figure 9.23 shows the overall ETL process. It is composed of one sequence container task (the one with the blue arrow in the left) and eleven data flow tasks. All of these tasks are connected by precedence constraints, represented by green arrows. The reader can compare this representation with the one in Fig. 9.15. Note that gateways are not present, but the semantics of the corresponding arrows is quite similar: no task can start until all precedent tasks have finished.

Several data flow tasks are simple. For example, the task that loads the **Category** table is given in Fig. 9.24a (compare with Fig. 9.16), where the data flow tasks are an OLE DB Source task that reads the entire table from the operational database, and an OLE DB Destination task that receives the output from the previous task and stores it in the data warehouse. Similar data flows are used for loading the **Product**, **Shipper**, and **Employee** tables.

Another straightforward task is the data flow that loads the **Date** dimension table, shown in Fig. 9.24b. After loading the source Excel file, a data conversion transformation is needed to convert the data types from the Excel file into the data types of the database. We can also see that this is very similar to the conceptual specification depicted in Fig. 9.17, except that the

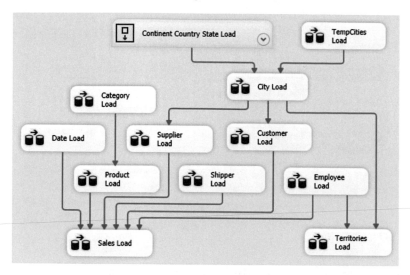

Fig. 9.23 Overall view of the ETL process in Integration Services

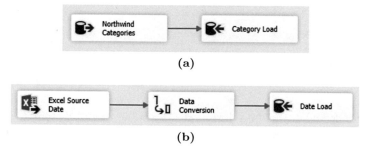

(a)

(b)

Fig. 9.24 Load of the Category (a) and the Date (b) dimension tables

addition of the surrogate key column is implicit in the Date Load task. We further explain this next.

As explained in Sect. 9.3, in some tables, the keys of the operational database are reused as surrogate keys in the data warehouse, while in other tables a surrogate key must be generated in the data warehouse. Therefore, the mapping of columns in the OLE DB Destination tasks should be done in one of the ways shown in Fig. 9.25. For example, for table Category (Fig. 9.25a) we reuse the key in the operational database (CategoryID) as key in the data warehouse (CategoryKey). On the other hand, for table Customer (Fig. 9.25b), the CustomerID key in the operational database is kept in the CustomerID column in the data warehouse, and a new value for CustomerKey is generated during the insertion in the data warehouse.

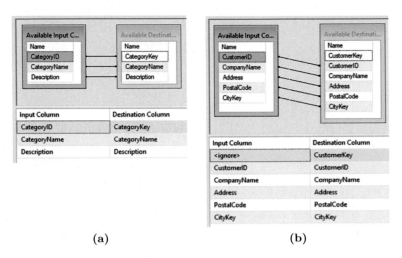

| (a) | (b) |

Fig. 9.25 Mappings of the source and destination columns, depending on whether the key in the operational database is reused in the data warehouse

Fig. 9.26 Load of the TempCities table

Figure 9.26 shows the data flow used for loading the table TempCities from the text file Cities.txt. A data conversion transformation is needed to convert the default types obtained from the text file into the database types.

Figure 9.27a shows the data flow that loads the hierarchy composed of the Continent, Country, and State tables. This is the Integration Services equivalent to the conceptual control flow defined in Fig. 9.18a. A Sequence Container is used for the three data flows that load the tables of the hierarchy. Since Continent is the highest level in the hierarchy, we first need to produce a key for it, so it can be later referenced from the Country level. The data flow for loading the table Continent is given in Fig. 9.27b. With respect to the conceptual model given in Fig. 9.18b, a data conversion is needed to convert the data types from the XML file into the data types of the database. For example, the ContinentName read from the XML file is by default of length 255 and it must be converted into a string of length 20. Finally, the Continent table is loaded, and a ContinentKey is automatically generated.

The data flow that loads the table Country is given in Fig. 9.27c. With respect to the conceptual model given in Fig. 9.18b, a merge join transformation is needed to obtain for a given Country the corresponding ContinentName. A data conversion transformation is needed to convert the data types from the XML file into the data types of the database. Then, a lookup transforma-

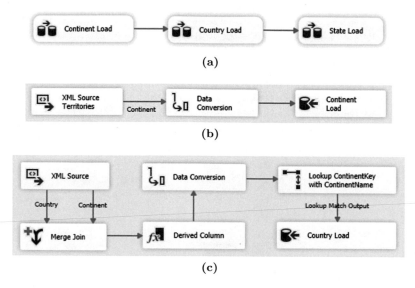

(a)

(b)

(c)

Fig. 9.27 (a) Load of the tables for the Continent → Country → State hierarchy; (b) Load of the Continent dimension table; (c) Load of the Country dimension table

tion is needed to obtain, from the database, the ContinentKey corresponding to the ContinentName. This attribute is also added to the flow. Finally, the Country table is loaded analogously to the Continent table above. Notice that the data flow that loads the table State is similar, therefore we omit it.

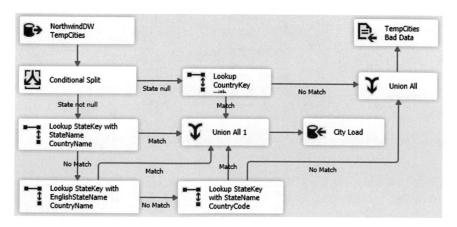

Fig. 9.28 Load of the City dimension table

Figure 9.28 shows the data flow for loading the City table. It corresponds to conceptual model in Fig. 9.19. The data flow needs to associate to each city in the TempCities table either a StateKey or a CountryKey, depending on whether or not the corresponding country is divided into states. For this, the conditional split tests if the State is null or not. In the first case, a lookup is needed for obtaining the CountryKey. This will obtain, for example, the country key for Singapore, which has no states. In the second case, as explained in Sect. 9.3, three lookup tasks are needed, where a couple of values of State and Country in TempCities must be matched with either StateName and CountryName, EnglishStateName and CountryName, or StateName and CountryCode. Since this process is similar to the one in the conceptual design, we do not repeat it here. Finally, a union of the four flows is performed (note that this task is named Union All 1 since there cannot exists two tasks with the same name), and the City table is loaded.

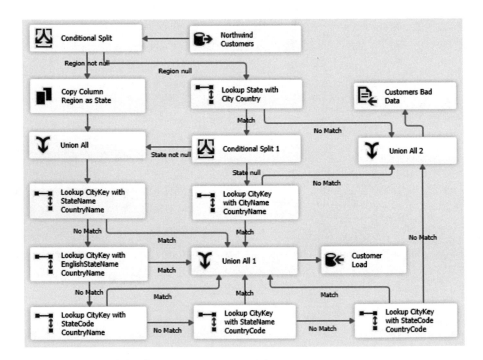

Fig. 9.29 Load of the Customer dimension table

The task that loads the Customer table is shown in Fig. 9.29, while its conceptual specification is given in Fig. 9.20. It starts with a conditional split since some customers have a null value in Region (which actually holds state values). In this case, a lookup adds a column State by matching City and Country from Customers with City and Country from TempCities. Since the value State just obtained may be null for countries without states, another conditional split (called Conditional Split 1) is needed. If State is null, then a lookup tries to find a CityKey by means of matching values of City and Country. The SQL query of the lookup task, as in Sect. 9.3, is as follows:

```
SELECT CityKey, CityName, CountryName
FROM   City C JOIN Country T ON C.CountryKey = T.CountryKey
```

On the other hand, for customers that have a nonnull Region, the values of this column are copied into a new column State. Analogously to the loading of City, we must perform five lookup tasks in order to retrieve the city key. Since this process is analogous to the one in the conceptual design given in Sect. 9.3, we do not repeat the details here. Finally, we perform the union of all flows and load the data into the warehouse. A similar data flow task is used for loading the Supplier dimension table.

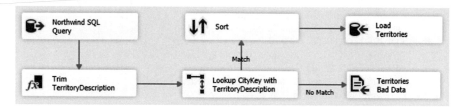

Fig. 9.30 Load of the Territories bridge table

The data flow that loads the Territories bridge table is shown in Fig. 9.30. This data flow is similar to the conceptual design of Fig. 9.21. It starts with an OLE DB Source task consisting in an SQL query that joins the EmployeeTerritories and the Territories table as in Sect. 9.3. It continues with a derived column transformation that removes the trailing spaces in the values of TerritoryDescription. Then, a lookup transformation searches the corresponding values of CityKey in City. The data flow continues with a sort transformation that removes duplicates in the assignment of employees to territories, as described in Sect. 9.3. Finally, the data flow finishes by loading the data warehouse table.

Fig. 9.31 Load of the Sales fact table

Finally, the data flow that loads the Sales table is shown in Fig. 9.31. The first OLE DB Source task includes an SQL query that combines data from the operational database and the data warehouse, as follows:

```
SELECT ( SELECT CustomerKey FROM dbo.Customer C
          WHERE C.CustomerID = O.CustomerID) AS CustomerKey,
        EmployeeID AS EmployeeKey,
        ( SELECT DateKey FROM dbo.Date D
          WHERE D.Date = O.OrderDate) AS OrderDateKey,
        ( SELECT DateKey FROM dbo.Date D
          WHERE D.Date = O.RequiredDate) AS DueDateKey,
        ( SELECT DateKey FROM dbo.Date D
          WHERE D.Date = O.ShippedDate) AS ShippedDateKey,
        ShipVia AS ShipperKey, P.ProductID AS ProductKey,
        SupplierID AS SupplierKey, O.OrderID AS OrderNo,
        CONVERT(INT, ROW_NUMBER() OVER (PARTITION BY D.OrderID
          ORDER BY D.ProductID)) AS OrderLineNo,
        D.UnitPrice, Quantity, Discount,
        CONVERT(MONEY, D.UnitPrice * (1-Discount) * Quantity) AS SalesAmount,
        CONVERT(MONEY, O.Freight/COUNT(*) OVER
          (PARTITION BY D.OrderID)) AS Freight
FROM    Northwind.dbo.Orders O, Northwind.dbo.OrderDetails D,
        Northwind.dbo.Products P
WHERE O.OrderID = D.OrderID AND D.ProductID = P.ProductID
```

The above query obtains data from both the Northwind operational database and the Northwind data warehouse in a single query. This is possible to do in Integration Services but not in other platforms such as in PostgreSQL. Thus, the above query performs the lookups of surrogate keys from the data warehouse in the inner queries of the SELECT clause. However, if these surrogate keys are not found, null values are returned in the result. Therefore, a conditional split transformation task selects the records obtained in the previous query with a null value in the lookup columns and stores them in a flat file. The correct records are loaded in the data warehouse.

Compare the above query with the corresponding one in the conceptual specification in Fig. 9.22. While the above query implements all the necessary lookups, in the conceptual design we have chosen to implement the lookups in individual tasks, which conveys information in a clearer way. Therefore, the conceptual design is more appropriate to communicate the process steps in an intuitive way but also gives us the flexibility to choose the implementation that is more appropriate for the application needs.

9.6 Implementing ETL Processes in SQL

As an alternative approach to using an ETL tool, in this section we show how conceptual ETL processes specified in BPMN can be implemented in SQL.

We illustrate this approach using SQL scripts for PostgreSQL, although a similar approach can be used for any platform.

The basic idea for implementing BPMN ETL processes in SQL is to implement each control task with an SQL procedure and each data task with an SQL statement. Obviously, we can leverage the expressive power of SQL and, whenever possible, optimize the SQL scripts by merging several BPMN tasks into a single SQL procedure or statement.

We start by implementing the overall ETL process depicted in Fig. 9.15 with the following procedure.

```
DROP FUNCTION IF EXISTS NorthwindDWLoad();
CREATE FUNCTION NorthwindDWLoad()
RETURNS VOID LANGUAGE plpgsql AS $$
BEGIN
        PERFORM ContinentCountryStateLoad(); PERFORM TempCitiesLoad();
        PERFORM CategoryLoad(); PERFORM CityLoad();
        PERFORM DateLoad(); PERFORM SupplierLoad();
        PERFORM CustomerLoad(); PERFORM ProductLoad();
        PERFORM ShipperLoad(); PERFORM EmployeeLoad();
        PERFORM SalesLoad(); PERFORM TerritoriesLoad();
END; $$;
```

As we can see, the overall ETL process is divided into several procedures that correspond to the tasks in the BPMN specification.

The loading of the State → Country → Continent hierarchy in SQL (corresponding to Fig. 9.18) is given next.

```
DROP FUNCTION IF EXISTS ContinentCountryStateLoad();
CREATE FUNCTION ContinentCountryStateLoad()
RETURNS VOID LANGUAGE plpgsql AS $$
BEGIN
        -- Input XML file
        DROP TABLE IF EXISTS TerritoriesInput;
        CREATE TEMPORARY TABLE TerritoriesInput AS
        SELECT xml_import('D:/InputFiles/Territories.xml') AS data;
        -- Load Continent
        INSERT INTO Continent(ContinentName)
        SELECT unnest(xpath('/Continents/Continent/ContinentName/text()', data)::text[])
        FROM TerritoriesInput;
        -- Load Country
        INSERT INTO Country(CountryName, CountryCode, CountryCapital, Population,
                Subdivision, ContinentKey)
        WITH CountriesInput AS (
                SELECT xmltable.*
                FROM TerritoriesInput, XMLTABLE(
                        '//Continents/Continent/Country' PASSING data COLUMNS
                        CountryName varchar(40) PATH 'CountryName',
                        CountryCode varchar(3) PATH 'CountryCode',
                        CountryCapital varchar(40) PATH 'CountryCapital',
                        Population integer PATH 'Population',
                        Subdivision text PATH 'Subdivision',
                        ContinentName varchar(20) PATH '../ContinentName') )
```

```
    SELECT CountryName, CountryCode, CountryCapital, Population, Subdivision, (
        SELECT ContinentKey C FROM Continent C
        WHERE C.ContinentName = I.ContinentName)
    FROM CountriesInput I;
    -- Load State
    INSERT INTO State (StateName, EnglishStateName, StateType, StateCode,
        StateCapital, RegionName, RegionCode, CountryKey)
    WITH StatesInput AS (
        SELECT xmltable.*
        FROM TerritoriesInput, XMLTABLE(
            '//Continents/Continent/Country/State' PASSING data COLUMNS
            StateName varchar(40) PATH 'StateName',
            EnglishStateName varchar(40) PATH 'EnglishStateName',
            StateType varchar(40) PATH '@type',
            StateCode char(3) PATH 'StateCode',
            StateCapital varchar(40) PATH 'StateCapital',
            RegionName varchar(40) PATH 'RegionName',
            RegionCode varchar(3) PATH 'RegionCode',
            CountryName varchar(40) PATH '../CountryName') )
    SELECT StateName, EnglishStateName, StateType, StateCode, StateCapital,
        RegionName, RegionCode, (
        SELECT CountryKey C FROM Country C
        WHERE C.CountryName = I.CountryName)
    FROM StatesInput I;
END; $$ ;
```

We start by calling the procedure xml_import, which parses the XML file into the temporary table TerritoriesInput. We then import the Continent, Country, and State elements from the XML file into the corresponding tables. For the Continent table, the path expression returns an array of text values, which is converted into a set of rows with the function unnest in order to be inserted into the table. Recall that the primary key ContinentKey is generated automatically. Loading the Country table requires all attributes of Country and its associated ContinentName to be input into the temporary table CountriesInput. The main query then performs a lookup of the ContinentKey with the nested SELECT clause. Loading the State table is done similarly as for the Country table.

The loading of the City table (corresponding to Fig. 9.19) is given next.

```
DROP FUNCTION IF EXISTS CityLoad();
CREATE FUNCTION CityLoad()
RETURNS VOID AS $$
BEGIN
        -- Drop temporary tables
        DROP TABLE IF EXISTS StateCountry;
        -- Insert cities without state
        INSERT INTO City (CityName, CountryKey)
        SELECT City, CountryKey
        FROM TempCities, Country
        WHERE State IS NULL AND Country = CountryName;
        -- Insert non-matching tuples into error table
        INSERT INTO BadCities (City, State, Country)
```

```
SELECT City, State, Country
FROM TempCities
WHERE State IS NULL AND NOT EXISTS (
        SELECT * FROM City WHERE StateKey IS NULL AND City = CityName );
-- Create lookup table
CREATE TEMPORARY TABLE StateCountry AS
SELECT * FROM State S NATURAL JOIN Country C;
-- Insert cities with state
INSERT INTO City (CityName, StateKey)
SELECT City, StateKey
FROM TempCities, StateCountry
WHERE (State = StateName AND Country = CountryName) OR
        (State = EnglishStateName and Country = CountryName) OR
        (State = StateName and Country = CountryCode);
-- Insert non-matching tuples into error table
INSERT INTO BadCities (City, State, Country)
SELECT City, State, Country
FROM TempCities
WHERE State IS NOT NULL AND NOT EXISTS (
        SELECT * FROM City
        WHERE StateKey IS NOT NULL AND City = CityName );
END; $$;
```

After dropping the temporary table needed by the procedure, we start by
loading the tuples from TempCities without state into the City table, where a
join with Country is performed to retrieve the CountryKey column. We then
insert into the BadCities table the tuples for which no matching country has
been found. We continue loading the tuples with a state. For this, the temporary table StateCountry stores a natural join of the State and Country tables.
Recall from Fig. 9.19 that three lookups are needed to obtain the StateKey
from various join conditions involving StateName, EnglishStateName, Country-
Name, and CountryCode. The subsequent INSERT combines the three lookups
into a *single* one. It retrieves the StateKey value by matching the State and
Country pairs in TempCities to their corresponding values in StateCountry.
Finally, the tuples for which no correspondence has been found in the last
INSERT are stored in the BadCities table.

The loading of the Customer table (refer to Fig. 9.20) is given next.

```
DROP FUNCTION IF EXISTS CustomerLoad();
CREATE FUNCTION CustomerLoad()
RETURNS VOID LANGUAGE plpgsql AS $$
BEGIN
        -- Drop temporary tables
        DROP TABLE IF EXISTS CustomerInput, CC, CSC;
        -- Input customer data from the operational database
        CREATE TEMPORARY TABLE CustomerInput AS
        SELECT *
        FROM dblink('dbname=Northwind port=5432 user=postgres password=postgres',
                'SELECT CustomerID, CompanyName, Address, City, Region, PostalCode,
                Country FROM Customers') AS CustomerInput(CustomerID varchar(5),
                CompanyName varchar(40), Address varchar(60), City varchar(15),
                State varchar(40), PostalCode varchar(20), Country varchar(15));
```

```
-- Lookup State from TempCities
UPDATE CustomerInput C
SET State = T.State FROM TempCities T
WHERE C.State IS NULL AND C.City = T.City AND C.Country = T.Country;
-- Create lookup table for cities without state
CREATE TEMPORARY TABLE CC AS
SELECT * FROM City NATURAL JOIN Country;
-- Insert customers without state
INSERT INTO Customer
SELECT CustomerID, CompanyName, Address, PostalCode, CityKey
FROM CustomerInput, CC
WHERE State IS NULL AND City = CityName AND Country = CountryName;
-- Create lookup table for cities with state
CREATE TEMPORARY TABLE CSC AS
SELECT C.CityKey, C.CityName, S.*, O.CountryName, O.CountryCode
FROM City C, State S, Country O
WHERE C.StateKey = S.StateKey AND S.CountryKey = O.CountryKey;
-- Insert customers with state
INSERT INTO Customer
SELECT CustomerID, CompanyName, Address, PostalCode, CityKey
FROM CustomerInput, CSC
WHERE State IS NOT NULL AND
(City = CityName AND State = StateName AND Country = CountryName) OR
(City = CityName AND State = EnglishStateName AND Country = CountryName) OR
(City = CityName AND State = StateName AND Country = CountryCode) OR
(City = CityName AND State = StateCode AND Country = CountryName) OR
(City = CityName AND State = StateCode AND Country = CountryCode);
-- Insert non-matching tuples into error table
INSERT INTO BadCustomers
SELECT * FROM CustomerInput WHERE CustomerID NOT IN
      ( SELECT CustomerID FROM Customer );
END; $$;
```

Recall that the Region column in the Customers table corresponds to one of the columns StateName, EnglishStateName, or StateCode in the State table. Also, the Country column in the Customers table corresponds to one of the columns CountryName or CountryCode in the Country table. We begin reading customer data from the operational database and looking up missing State values from the TempCities table. We continue by loading the tuples without State. A natural join of City and Country is stored in table CC, which is used as a lookup table for finding the CityKey for tuples, which are then inserted into the Customer table. Recall that CustomerKey is a surrogate key in table Customer while the CustomerID column is also kept. Then, we load the tuples with State. A natural join of City, State, and Country is stored in table CSC. The next INSERT performs in a *single* lookup for the CityKey the five lookups in Fig. 9.20. Each disjunction in the join condition tries to match the values of the City, State, and Country columns in CustomerInput to their corresponding values in columns of CSC. Finally, we insert in the BadCustomers table the tuples from CustomerInput for which a match was not found.

Finally, the loading of the Sales fact table (see Fig. 9.22) is shown next.

```
DROP FUNCTION IF EXISTS SalesLoad();
CREATE FUNCTION SalesLoad()
RETURNS VOID LANGUAGE plpgsql AS $$
BEGIN
        -- Drop temporary tables
        DROP TABLE IF EXISTS ODP, SalesInput;
        -- Input sales data from operational database
        CREATE TEMPORARY TABLE ODP AS
        SELECT *
        FROM dblink('dbname=Northwind port=5432 user=postgres password=postgres',
                'SELECT O.OrderID, O.CustomerID, O.EmployeeID, O.OrderDate,
                O.RequiredDate, O.ShippedDate, O.ShipVia, O.Freight, D.ProductID,
                D.UnitPrice, D.Quantity, D.Discount, P.SupplierID FROM Orders O,
                OrderDetails D, Products P WHERE O.OrderID = D.OrderID AND
                D.ProductID = P.ProductID') AS Orders(OrderID integer,
                CustomerID varchar(10), EmployeeID integer, OrderDate date,
                RequiredDate date, ShippedDate date, ShipVia integer, Freight money,
                ProductID integer, UnitPrice money, Quantity integer, Discount real,
                SupplierID integer);
        -- Lookup values
        CREATE TEMPORARY TABLE SalesInput AS
        SELECT O.*, ( SELECT CustomerKey FROM Customer C
                WHERE C.CustomerID = O.CustomerID) AS CustomerKey,
                ( SELECT DateKey FROM Date D
                WHERE D.Date = O.OrderDate) AS OrderDateKey,
                ( SELECT DateKey FROM Date D
                WHERE D.Date = O.RequiredDate) AS DueDateKey,
                ( SELECT DateKey FROM Date D
                WHERE D.Date = O.ShippedDate) AS ShippedDateKey,
                ROW_NUMBER() OVER (PARTITION BY O.OrderID
                ORDER BY O.ProductID) AS OrderLineNo,
                UnitPrice * (1-Discount) * Quantity AS SalesAmount,
                Freight/COUNT(*) OVER (PARTITION BY OrderID) AS FreightPP
        FROM ODP O;
        -- Insert matching tuples
        INSERT INTO Sales
        SELECT CustomerKey, EmployeeID AS EmployeeKey, OrderDateKey, DueDateKey,
                ShippedDateKey, ShipVia AS ShipperKey, ProductID AS ProductKey,
                SupplierID AS SupplierKey, OrderID AS OrderNo, OrderLineNo, UnitPrice,
                Quantity, Discount, SalesAmount, FreightPP
        FROM SalesInput
        WHERE CustomerKey IS NOT NULL AND EmployeeID IS NOT NULL AND
                OrderDateKey IS NOT NULL AND DueDateKey IS NOT NULL
                AND ShippedDateKey IS NOT NULL AND ShipVia IS NOT NULL AND
                ProductID IS NOT NULL AND SupplierID IS NOT NULL;
        -- Insert non-matching tuples into error table
        INSERT INTO BadSales
        SELECT OrderID, CustomerID, EmployeeID, OrderDate, RequiredDate, ShippedDate,
                ShipVia, Freight, ProductID, UnitPrice, Quantity, Discount, SupplierID
        FROM SalesInput
        WHERE CustomerKey IS NULL OR EmployeeID IS NULL OR OrderDateKey IS
                NULL OR DueDateKey IS NULL OR ShippedDateKey IS NULL OR
                ShipVia IS NULL OR ProductID IS NULL OR SupplierID IS NULL;
END; $$;
```

Recall that the keys of the operational database are also keys in the data warehouse for all dimensions except for Customer and Date, whose keys are, respectively, CustomerKey and DateKey. We start with a query to the tables Orders, OrderDetails, and Products of the operational database. Then, we perform lookups to retrieve the CustomerKey, OrderDateKey, DueDateKey, and ShippedDateKey columns as well as compute new columns SalesAmount, OrderLineNo, and FreightPP. Finally, the tuples with all required columns are inserted into the Sales fact table after a renaming operation and the erroneous ones are inserted into the BadSales table.

9.7 Summary

In this chapter, we have presented a detailed study of ETL processes, a key component of a data warehousing architecture. We have shown the usefulness of producing a conceptual model of ETL processes, independent of any implementation. In this way, deploying the model in different tools is possible. Further, information can be shared and distributed in a language that can be easily understood by the stakeholders. The conceptual model for ETL processes is based on the BPMN standard, relying on the assumption that ETL processes are similar to business processes. We illustrated the design and implementation of ETL processes with a complete example based on the Northwind case study. Thus, the reader can have a clear idea of the usual tasks that must be performed while implementing such processes. We provided three versions of the Northwind ETL process, a conceptual one using BPMN and an implementation in Microsoft Integration Services. We described the differences between the three versions of this ETL process, taking into account implementation considerations in the two platforms chosen. In the last part of this chapter, we proposed relational algebra as a language to specify ETL processes at the conceptual level, illustrating the process using, again, the loading of the Northwind Data Warehouse, comparing this specification against the conceptual specification based on BPMN, and explaining how standard SQL code can be straightforwardly produced from this specification.

9.8 Bibliographic Notes

A classic reference for ETL is the book by Kimball and Caserta [128]. Various approaches for designing, optimizing, and automating ETL processes have been proposed in the last few years. A survey of ETL technology can be found in [253]. Simitsis et al. [254] represent ETL processes as a graph where nodes match to transformations, constraints, attributes, and data stores, and edges correspond to data flows, inter-attribute relations, compositions, and concurrent candidates. An approach for mapping conceptual ETL design to logical ETL design was proposed in [218].

This chapter is based on previous work on using BPMN as a conceptual model for ETL processes, performed by the authors and collaborators, e.g., [66, 67]. An introduction to business process modeling and an overview of BPMN 2.0 are provided in [245]. The relational algebra specification for ETL processes was first proposed by Santos et al. [208, 209]. The approach of implementing BPMN specifications for ETL process into relational algebra and in SQL has been developed in [17, 18].

The book [52] describes in detail Microsoft Integration Services. All existing ETL tools provide their own language for specifying ETL processes. Their languages differ considerably in many respects, in particular since they are based on different paradigms and have different expression power. That was the reason that motivated us to devise a conceptual model for ETL processes that can then be implemented in various implementation platforms.

9.9 Review Questions

9.1 What is a business process? Why do we need to model business processes?

9.2 Describe and classify the main constructs of BPMN.

9.3 What is the difference between an exclusive and an inclusive gateway?

9.4 Can we model splitting of flows without gateways? Are there cases where this is not possible?

9.5 Give examples of the use of the several kinds of BPMN events.

9.6 What is a default flow? When should we use it?

9.7 Discuss why should we or should we not need a conceptual design phase for ETL processes.

9.8 Why is BPMN appropriate for modeling ETL processes? Do you think that there are situations where this is not the case?

9.9 Explain the rationale of the methodology studied in the chapter. What are control tasks? What are data tasks?

9.10 What is the main difference between the diagrams for ETL design proposed in this chapter and the typical BPMN diagram?

9.11 Discuss the advantages and disadvantages of representing, in Integration Services, a sequence of tasks as a single SQL query (see an example in Sect. 9.5).

9.12 Compare the BPMN and the SQL specifications of ETL processes. For this comparison, use the ETL process of the Northwind data warehouse.

9.10 Exercises

Exercise 9.1. Design the conceptual ETL schema for loading the Product dimension of the Northwind data warehouse.

Exercise 9.2. In the Northwind data warehouse, suppose that surrogate keys CategoryKey and ProductKey are added, respectively, to the Category and the Product tables, while the operational keys are kept in attributes CategoryID and ProductID. Modify the conceptual ETL schema obtained in Ex. 9.1 to take into account this situation.

Exercise 9.3. Modify the conceptual ETL schema obtained in Ex. 9.2 to take into account a refresh scenario in which products obtained from the operational database may be already in the Product dimension in the data warehouse. Use a type 1 solution for the slowly changing dimension by which the attribute values obtained from the operational database are updated in the data warehouse.

Exercise 9.4. Modify the conceptual ETL schema obtained in Ex. 9.3 by using a type 2 solution for the slowly changing dimension Product by which for the products that have changed the value of the To attribute for the current record is set to the current date and a new record is inserted in the dimension with a null value in that attribute.

Exercise 9.5. Design the conceptual ETL schema for loading the Supplier dimension of the Northwind data warehouse.

Exercise 9.6. Implement in Integration Services the ETL processes defined in Exs. 9.1 and 9.5.

Exercise 9.7. Implement in SQL the ETL processes defined in Exs. 9.1 and 9.5.

Exercise 9.8. Implement in SQL the ETL process loading the Territories bridge table of the Northwind data warehouse, whose conceptual schema is given in Fig. 9.21.

Exercise 9.9. Implement in SQL the conceptual schemas of Exs. 9.1 and 9.5.

Exercise 9.10. Given the operational database of the French horse race application obtained in Ex. 2.1 and the associated data warehouse obtained in Ex. 4.5, design the conceptual ETL schema that loads the data warehouse from the operational database.

Exercise 9.11. Given the operational database of the Formula One application obtained in Ex. 2.2 and the associated data warehouse obtained in Ex. 4.7, design the conceptual ETL schema that loads the data warehouse from the operational database.

Exercise 9.12. Given the source database in Ex. 5.11 and the schema of your solution, implement in Integration Services the ETL schema that loads the AirCarrier data warehouse from the sources.

Chapter 10
A Method for Data Warehouse Design

Even though there is an abundant literature in the area of software development, few publications have been devoted to the development of data warehouses. Most of them are written by practitioners based on their experience in building data warehouses. On the other hand, the scientific community has proposed a variety of approaches, which in general target a specific conceptual model and are too complex to be used in real-world environments. As a consequence, there is still a lack of a methodological framework to guide developers in the various stages of the data warehouse development process.

In this chapter, building over several existing approaches, we describe a general method for data warehouse design. We use the Northwind case study to illustrate the methodology. In Sect. 10.1, we present the existing approaches to data warehouse design. Then, in Sect. 10.2, we refer to the various phases that make up the data warehouse design process. Analogously to traditional database design, the methodology includes the phases of requirements specification, conceptual design, logical design, and physical design. The subsequent sections are devoted to more detailed descriptions of each design phase. In Sect. 10.3, we describe three different approaches to requirements specification. These approaches differ in which is the driving force for specifying requirements: users, source systems, or both. Section 10.4 covers conceptual design for data warehouses. In Sects. 10.5 and 10.6, we briefly describe the logical and physical design phases for data warehouses, extensively covered in Chaps. 5 and 8. We just provide this description to give a complete self-contained vision of the method. Section 10.7 highlights the advantages and disadvantages of the three approaches.

10.1 Approaches to Data Warehouse Design

A wide variety of approaches have been proposed for designing data warehouses. They differ in several aspects, such as whether they target data ware-

© Springer-Verlag GmbH Germany, part of Springer Nature 2022
A. Vaisman, E. Zimányi, *Data Warehouse Systems*, Data-Centric Systems and Applications, https://doi.org/10.1007/978-3-662-65167-4_10

houses or data marts, the various phases that make up the design process, and the methods used for performing requirements specification and data warehouse design. This section highlights some of the essential characteristics of the current approaches according to these aspects.

A data warehouse includes data about an entire organization that help users at high management levels to take strategic decisions. However, these decisions may also be taken at lower organizational levels related to specific business areas, in which case only a subset of the data contained in a data warehouse is required. This subset is typically contained in a **data mart** (see Sect. 3.4), which has a similar structure to a data warehouse but is smaller in size. Data marts can be physically collocated with the data warehouse or they can have their own separate platform.

Like in operational databases (see Sect. 2.1), there are two major methods for the design of a data warehouse and its related data marts:

- **Top-down design:** The requirements of users at different organizational levels are merged before the design process begins, and one schema for the entire data warehouse is built. Then, separate data marts are tailored according to the characteristics of each business area or process.
- **Bottom-up design:** A separate schema is built for each data mart, taking into account the requirements of the decision-making users responsible for the corresponding specific business area or process. Later, these schemas are merged in a global schema for the entire data warehouse.

The choice between the top-down and the bottom-up approach depends on many factors, such as the professional skills of the development team, the size of the data warehouse, the users' motivation for having a data warehouse, and the financial support, among other things. The development of an enterprise-wide data warehouse using the top-down approach may be overwhelming for many organizations in terms of cost and duration. It is also a challenging activity for designers because of its size and complexity. On the other hand, the smaller size of data marts allows the return of the investment to be obtained in a shorter time period and facilitates the development processes. Further, if the user motivation is low, the bottom-up approach may deliver a data mart faster and at less cost, allowing users to quickly interact with OLAP tools and create new reports; this may lead to an increase in users' acceptance level and improve the motivation for having a data warehouse. Nevertheless, the development of these data marts requires a global data warehouse framework to be established so that the data marts are built considering their future integration into a whole data warehouse. Without this global framework, such integration difficult and costly in the long term.

There is no consensus on the phases that should be followed for data warehouse design. Some authors consider that the traditional phases of developing operational databases described in Chap. 2, that is, requirements specification, conceptual design, logical design, and physical design, can also be used in developing data warehouses. Other authors ignore some of these phases, especially the conceptual design phase. Several approaches for data warehouse design have been proposed based on whether the business goals, the source systems, or a combination of these are used as the driving force. We next present these approaches, which we study in detail in the next sections.

The **business-driven approach** requires the identification of key users that can provide useful input about the organizational goals. Users play a fundamental role during requirements analysis and must be actively involved in the process of discovering relevant facts and dimensions. Users from different levels of the organization must be selected. Then, various techniques, such as interviews or facilitated sessions, are used to specify the information requirements. Consequently, the specification obtained will include the requirements of users at all organizational levels, aligned with the overall business goals. This is also called analysis- or requirements-driven approach.

In the **data-driven approach**, the data warehouse schema is obtained by analyzing the underlying source systems. Some of the proposed techniques require conceptual representations of the operational source systems, most of them based on the entity-relationship model, which we studied in Chap. 2. Other techniques use a relational schema to represent the source systems. These schemas should be normalized, to facilitate the extraction of facts, measures, dimensions, and hierarchies. In general, the participation of users is only required to confirm the correctness of the derived structures, or to identify some facts and measures as a starting point for the design of multidimensional schemas. After creating an initial schema, users can specify their information requirements.

The **business/data-driven** approach is a combination of the business- and data-driven approaches, which takes into account what are the business needs from the users and what the source systems can provide. Ideally, these two components should match, that is, all information that the users require for business purposes should be supplied by the data included in the source systems. This approach is also called top-down/bottom-up analysis.

These approaches, originally proposed for the requirements specification phase, are adapted to the other data warehouse design phases in the method that we explain in the next section.

10.2 General Overview of the Method

We next describe a general method for data warehouse design that encompasses various existing approaches from both research and practitioners. The method is based on the assumption that data warehouses are a particular type of databases dedicated to analytical purposes. Therefore, their design should follow the traditional database design phases, as shown in Fig. 10.1. Nevertheless, there are significant differences between the design phases for databases and data warehouses, which stem from their different nature, as explained in Chap. 3. Note that although the various phases in Fig. 10.1 are depicted consecutively, actually there are multiple interactions between them, especially if an iterative development process is adopted in which the system is developed in incremental versions with increased functionality.

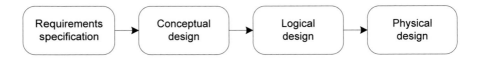

Fig. 10.1 Phases in data warehouse design

The phases in Fig. 10.1 may be applied to define either the overall data warehouse schema or the schemas of the individual data marts. From now on, we shall use the term "data warehouse" to mean that the concepts that we are discussing apply also to data marts if not stated otherwise.

For all the phases in Fig. 10.1, the specification of business and technical metadata is in continuous development. These include information about the data warehouse and data source schemas, and the ETL processes. For example, the metadata for a data warehouse schema may provide information such as aliases used for various elements, abbreviations, currencies for monetary attributes or measures, and metric systems. The elements of the source systems should also be documented similarly. This could be a difficult task if conceptual schemas for these systems do not exist. The metadata for the ETL processes should consider several elements, such as the frequency of data refreshment. Data in a fact table may be required on daily or monthly basis, or after some specific event (e.g., after finishing a project). Therefore, users should specify a data refreshment strategy that corresponds to their business needs.

To illustrate the proposed method, we will use a hypothetical scenario concerning the design of the Northwind data warehouse we have been using as example throughout this book. We assume that the company wants to analyze its sales along dimensions like customers, products, geography, and so on in order to optimize the marketing strategy, for example, detecting customers that potentially could increase their orders, or sales regions that are underperforming. To be able to conduct the analytical process, Northwind decided to implement a data warehouse system.

10.3 Requirements Specification

The requirements specification phase is one of the earliest steps in system development and entails significant problems if it is faulty or incomplete.

Not much attention has been paid to the requirements analysis phase in data warehouse development, and many projects skip this phase; instead, they concentrate on technical issues, such as database modeling or query performance. As a consequence, many data warehouse projects fail to meet user needs and do not deliver the expected support for decision making.

Requirements specification determines *which* data should be available and *how* these data should be organized. In this phase, the queries of interest for the users are also determined. This phase should lead the designer to discover the essential elements of a multidimensional schema, like the facts and their associated dimensions, which are required to facilitate future data manipulation and calculations. We will see that requirements specification for decision support and operational systems differ significantly from each other. The requirements specification phase establishes a foundation for all future activities in data warehouse development; in addition, it has a major impact on the success of data warehouse projects since it directly affects the technical aspects, as well as the data warehouse structures and applications.

We present next a general framework for the requirements specification phase. Although we separate the phases of requirements specification and conceptual design for readability purposes, these phases often overlap. In many cases, as soon as initial requirements have been documented, an initial conceptual schema starts to be sketched. As the requirements become more complete, so does the conceptual schema. For each one of the three approaches above, we first give a general description and then explain in more detail the various steps; finally, we apply each approach to the Northwind case study. We do not indicate the various iterations that may occur between steps. Our purpose is to provide a general framework to which details can be added and that can be tailored to the particularities of a specific data warehouse project.

10.3.1 Business-Driven Requirements Specification

In the business-driven approach, the driving force for developing the conceptual schema are the business needs of users. These requirements express the organizational goals and needs that the data warehouse is expected to address to support the decision-making process.

The steps in the business-driven approach to requirements specification are shown in Fig. 10.2 and described next.

Identify Users

Users at various hierarchical levels in the organization should be considered when analyzing requirements. *Executive users* at the top organizational level typically require global, summarized information. They help in understanding high-level objectives and goals, and the overall business vision. *Management*

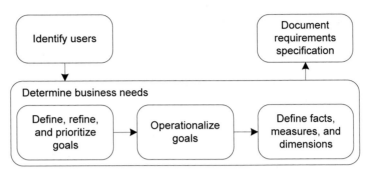

Fig. 10.2 Steps for requirements specification in the business-driven approach

users may require more detailed information pertaining to a specific area of the organization. They provide more insight into the business processes or the tactics used for achieving the business goals. Finally, *professional users* are responsible for a specific section or set of services and may demand specific information related to their area of interest. Furthermore, the identification of potential users should also consider different entities in a horizontal division of the organization (e.g., departments). This will help in providing an overall view of the project and its scope.

Determine Business Needs

Business needs help developers understand what data should be available to respond to the users' expectations on the data warehouse system. This phase should eventually discover a collection of facts, measures, dimensions, and hierarchies. The process includes several steps, as follows.

Define, Refine, and Prioritize Goals The starting point in determining business needs is the consideration of the business goals. Successful data warehouse projects assume that the goals of the company are the same for everyone and that the entire company will therefore be pursuing the same direction. Therefore, a clear specification of goals is essential to guide user needs and convert them into data elements. Since users at several different management levels participate in requirements specification, business needs may be expressed considering both general and specific goals. The latter should be aligned with the general ones to ensure a common direction of the overall development. The goal-gathering process is conducted by means of interviews and brainstorming sessions, among other ones. The list of goals should be analyzed to detect redundancies and dependencies. For example, some goals could be combined because of their similarity, discarded because of their inconsistency, or considered as subgoals of other ones. This analysis may require additional interaction with the users to set the final list of goals.

Operationalize Goals Once the goals have been defined and prioritized, we need to make them concrete. Thus, for each goal identified in the previous step, a collection of representative queries must be defined through interviews with the users. These queries capture **functional requirements**, which define the operations and activities that a system must be able to perform.

Each user is requested to provide, in natural language, a list of queries needed for her daily task. Initially, the vocabulary can be unrestricted. However, certain terms may have different meanings for different users. The analyst must identify and disambiguate them. For example, a term like "the best customer" should be expressed as "the customer with the highest total sales amount." A document is then produced, where for each goal there is a collection of queries, and each query is associated with a user.

The process continues with query analysis and integration. Here, users review and consolidate the queries in the document above, to avoid misunderstandings or redundancies. The frequency of the queries must also be estimated. Finally, a prioritization process is carried out. Since we worked with different areas of the organization, we must unify all requirements from these areas and define priorities between them. A possible priority hierarchy can be *areas → users → queries of the same user*. Intuitively, the idea is that the requirement with the least priority in an area prevails over the requirement with the highest priority in the area immediately following in importance the previous one. Obviously, other criteria could also be used. This is a cyclic process, which results in a final document containing consistent, nonredundant queries.

In addition to the above, **nonfunctional requirements** should also be elicited and specified. These are criteria that can be used to judge the operation of a system rather than specific behavior. Thus, a list of nonfunctional requirements may be associated to each query, for example, required response time and accuracy.

Define Facts, Measures, and Dimensions In this step, the analyst tries to identify the underlying facts and dimensions from the queries above. This is typically a manual process. For example, in the documentation of this step, we can find a query "Name of top five customers with monthly average sales higher than $1,500." This query includes the following data elements: customer name, month, and sales. We should also include information about which data elements will be aggregated and the functions that must be used. If possible, this step should also specify the granularities required for the measures, and information about whether they are additive, semiadditive, or nonadditive (see Sect. 3.1).

Document Requirements Specification

The information obtained in the previous step should be documented. The documentation delivered is the starting point for the **technical** and **business metadata** (see Sect. 3.4). Therefore, this document should include all elements required by the designers and also a dictionary of the terminology, organizational structure, policies, and constraints of the business, among other things. For example, the document could express in business terms what the candidate measures or dimensions actually represent, who has access to them, and what operations can be done. Note that this document will not be final since additional interactions could be necessary during the conceptual design phase in order to refine or clarify some aspects.

Application to the Northwind Case Study

We now apply the business-driven approach to produce a requirements specification for the Northwind data warehouse. We do not include all details about each step; we illustrate only the essential aspects of the method.

We start with the first step, which is **Identify Users**. In this example, three groups of users were identified:

1. Executive: The members of the board of directors of the Northwind company, who define the overall company goals.
2. Management: Managers at departmental levels, for example, marketing, regional sales, and human resources.
3. Professional: Professional personnel who implement the indications of the management. Examples are marketing executive officers.

We continue with the second step, which is **Determine Business Needs**. This step starts with the specification of the goals. We will just address the general goal: *increase the overall company sales by 10% yearly*. This goal can be decomposed into *subgoals*:

1. Increase sales in underperforming regions.
2. For customers buying below their potential, increase their orders (in number of orders and individual order amount).
3. Increase sales of products selling below the company expectations.
4. Take action on employees performing below their expected quota.

In the next step, further sessions with the users are carried out to understand their demands in more detail, and operationalize the goals and subgoals. As we explained above, the queries can be expressed in free natural language. Then, the terms must be aligned with a data dictionary or common vocabulary during a process of cleansing, disambiguation, and prioritization. Below, we give some examples of the queries that operationalize the goals above. We show the queries already expressed in a common vocabulary that we assume has been previously defined in a data dictionary. We omit here the process of prioritizing queries and users. We then identify potential dimensions, hierarchy levels, and measures. To facilitate reading, we use different fonts for dimensions, hierarchy levels, and *measures*.

1. Increase sales in underperforming regions:

   a. Five best- and worst-selling (measured as total *sales* amount) pairs of customer and supplier countries.
   b. Countries, states, and cities whose customers have the highest total *sales* amount.
   c. Five best- and worst-selling (measured as total *sales* amount) products by customer country, state, and city.

2. For customers buying below their potential, increase their orders (in number of orders and individual order amount):

   a. Monthly *sales* by customer compared to the corresponding *sales* (for the same customer) of the previous year.
   b. Total number of orders by customer, time period (e.g., year), and product.
   c. Average *unit price* per customer.

3. Increase sales of products selling below the company expectations:

   a. Monthly *sales* for each product category for the current year.
   b. Average *discount* percentage per product and month.
   c. Average *quantity* ordered per product.

4. Take action on employees performing below their expected quota:

   a. Best-selling employee per product per year with respect to *sales* amount.
   b. Average monthly *sales* by employee and year.
   c. Total *sales* by an employee and her subordinates during a certain time period.

Table 10.1 shows, for each query, which are the candidate dimensions, measures, and hierarchies. If priorities are considered, they will be associated with each query; it is also usual that each query is associated with the users that proposed it. In the first column from the left of the table, dimension and measure names are distinguished by their fonts. Thus, for instance, Employee is a dimension while *Quantity* is a measure. The table displays summarized information in the sense that a check mark is placed if a query mentions at least one level of one hierarchy in the second column from the left. Note that Table 10.1 includes more hierarchy levels than the ones referenced in the goals and subgoals above. We assume that these have been discovered by means of the analysis of other queries not shown here. Actually, the complete design includes more dimensions and measures not displayed here for the sake of clarity. For example, we do not show the information related to the shipping of products. Also, regarding the Date dimension, note that we did not identify the three roles it plays in the Northwind data warehouse, that is, as an order date, a shipped date, or a due date. We just consider the order date role.

Table 10.1 Multidimensional elements for the analysis scenarios of the Northwind case study obtained using the business-driven approach

Dimensions and measures	Hierarchies and levels	Analysis scenarios											
		1a	1b	1c	2a	2b	2c	3a	3b	3c	4a	4b	4c
Employee	**Supervision** Subordinate → Supervisor **Territories** Employee ⇆ City → State → Country → Continent	–	–	–	–	–	–	–	–	–	✓	✓	✓
Date	**Calendar** Day → Month → Quarter → Semester → Year	–	–	–	✓	✓	✓	✓	✓	–	✓	✓	✓
Product	**Categories** Product → Category	–	–	✓	–	✓	–	✓	✓	✓	✓	–	–
Customer	**Geography** Customer → City → State → Country → Continent	✓	✓	✓	✓	✓	✓	–	–	–	–	–	–
Supplier	**Geography** Supplier → City → State → Country → Continent	✓	–	–	–	–	–	–	–	–	–	–	–
Quantity	–	–	–	–	–	–	–	–	–	✓	–	–	–
Discount	–	–	–	–	–	–	–	–	✓	–	–	–	–
SalesAmount	–	✓	✓	✓	✓	–	–	✓	–	–	✓	✓	✓
UnitPrice	–	–	–	–	–	–	✓	–	–	–	–	–	–

Table 10.1 does not only show the dimensions but also candidate hierarchies, inferred from the queries above and company documentation. For example, in dimension **Employee**, we can see that there are two candidate hierarchies: **Supervision** and **Territories**. The former can be inferred, among other sources of information, from Requirement 4c, which suggests that users are interested in analyzing together employees and their supervisors as a sales force. The **Territories** hierarchy is derived from the documentation of the company processes, which state that employees are assigned to a given number of cities and a city may have many employees assigned to it. In addition, users informed that they are interested in analyzing total sales along a geographic dimension. Note that following the previous description, the hierarchy will be nonstrict. Requirements 1a–c suggest that customers are organized geographically and that this organization is relevant for analysis. Thus, **Geography** is a candidate hierarchy to be associated with customers. The same occurs with suppliers. The hierarchy **Categories** follows straightforwardly from Requirement 3a. The remaining hierarchies are obtained analogously.

Finally, the last step is **Document Requirements Specification**. The information compiled is included in the specification of the user requirements. For example, it can contain summarized information as presented in Table 10.1 and also more descriptive parts that explain each element. The requirements specification document also contains the business metadata. For the Northwind case study, there are various ways to obtain these metadata, for example, by interviewing users or administrative staff, or accessing the existing company documentation. We do not detail this document here.

10.3.2 Data-driven Requirements Specification

The data-driven approach is based on the data available at the source systems. It aims at identifying all multidimensional schemas that can be implemented starting from the available operational databases. These databases are analyzed exhaustively in order to discover the elements that can represent facts with associated dimensions, hierarchies, and measures leading to an initial data warehouse schema.

Fig. 10.3 Steps for requirements specification in the data-driven approach

We briefly describe next the steps in this approach to requirements specification, depicted in Fig. 10.3. As with the business-driven approach, we do not show the various iterations that could be required before the final data warehouse schema is developed.

Identify Source Systems

The aim of this step is to determine the existing operational systems that can be data providers for the warehouse. External sources are not considered at this stage; they can be included later on when the need for additional information has been identified.

This step relies on system documentation, preferably represented using the entity-relationship model or relational tables. However, in many situations, this representation may be difficult to obtain, for example, when the data sources include implicit structures that are not declared through the data definition language of the database, redundant and denormalized structures have been added to improve query response time, the database has not been well designed, or the databases reside on legacy systems whose inspection is a difficult task. In such situations, **reverse engineering** processes can be applied. These processes are used to rebuild the logical and conceptual schemas of source systems whose documentation is missing or outdated.

It is important not only to identify the data sources but also to assess their quality. Moreover, it is often the case where the same data are available from more than one source. Reliability, availability, and update frequency of these sources may differ from each other. Thus, data sources must be analyzed to assess their suitability to satisfy nonfunctional requirements. For this, meetings with data producers are carried out, where the set of data sources, the quality of their data, and their availability must be documented. At the end of the whole requirements specification process, ideally we will have for each data element the best data source for obtaining it.

Apply Derivation Process

There are many techniques to derive multidimensional elements from operational databases. All these techniques require that the operational databases are represented using either the entity-relationship or the relational model.

Facts and their associated measures are determined by analyzing the existing documentation or the structure of the databases. Facts and measures are associated with elements that are frequently updated. If the operational databases are relational, they may correspond to tables and attributes, respectively. If the operational databases are represented using the entity-relationship model, facts could be entity or relationship types, while measures may be attributes of these elements. An alternative option is to involve users who understand the operational systems and can help to determine what data can be considered as measures. Identifying facts and measures is the most important aspect of this approach since these form the basis for constructing multidimensional schemas.

Various procedures can be applied to derive dimensions and hierarchies. These procedures may be automatic, semiautomatic, or manual. The former two require knowledge about the specific conceptual models that are used for the initial schema and its subsequent transformations. The process of discovering a dimension or a leaf level of a hierarchy usually starts from identifying the static (not frequently updated) elements that are related to the facts. Then, a search for other hierarchy levels is carried out. Starting with a leaf level of a hierarchy, every relationship in which it participates is revised. Unlike automatic or semiautomatic procedures, manual procedures allow designers to find hierarchies embedded within the same entity or table, for example, to find city and province attributes in a customer or employee entity type. However, either the presence of system experts who understand the data in the operational databases is required or the designer must have good knowledge about the business domain and the underlying systems.

Document Requirements Specification

Like in the business-driven approach, the requirements specification phase should be documented. The documentation should describe those elements of the source systems that can be considered as facts, measures, dimensions, and hierarchies. This will be contained in the **technical metadata**. Further, it is desirable to involve at this stage a domain expert who can help in defining business terminology for these elements and in indicating, for example, whether measures are additive, semiadditive, or nonadditive.

Application to the Northwind Case Study

We illustrate next the data-driven approach for the Northwind case study.

We start with the first step, which is **Identify Source Systems**. We assume that the entity-relationship schema of the operational database, shown in Fig. 2.1, is available and data of appropriate quality can be obtained. We skip the step of identifying the source systems, except for the geographic data, which were obtained from external sources (typically web-based), to complement the Customers, Employees, and Suppliers tables.

We continue with the second step, which is **Apply Derivation Process**. We chose a manual derivation process to provide a more general solution, although automatic or semiautomatic methods could have also been applied.

We start by identifying candidate facts. In the schema of Fig. 2.1, we can distinguish the many-to-many relationship type OrderDetails, with attributes that represent numeric data. This is a clear candidate to be a fact in a multidimensional schema. Candidate measures for this fact are the attributes UnitPrice, Quantity, and Discount. An order in Orders is associated with many products through the relationship type OrderDetails. Since users have expressed that they are interested in individual sales rather than in the whole content of an order, a fact should be associated with an order line. Thus, the products in OrderDetails may be subsumed in the Orders table so that each record in the latter now becomes a fact. We call this fact Sales. A sales fact is associated with a unique employee (in entity type Employees), shipper (in entity type Shippers), and customer (in entity type Customers). In addition, it is associated with three dates: the order date, the required date, and the shipped date. These are potential dimensions, analyzed below.

Since each sales fact is associated with an order line, we may also envision a dimension Order, with a one-to-one relationship with the fact Sales. Thus, Order is a candidate to be a fact or degenerate dimension (see Chap. 3), which can be used, for example, to determine the average sales amount of an order or the average number of items in an order.

The other many-to-many relationship type in the schema is EmployeeTerritories. Since it does not have associated attributes, initially we can consider it as candidate to be a nonstrict hierarchy rather than a fact.

We now analyze potential dimensions and hierarchies. We start with the time dimension. Users have indicated that for decision making, a granularity at the level of day will suffice, and analysis by month, quarter, semester, and year are needed. The former defines, on the one hand, a Date dimension and, on the other hand, the hierarchy Date → Month → Quarter → Semester →

Year. We call this hierarchy Calendar. We mentioned that each sales fact is associated with three dates, thus yielding three roles for the Date dimension, namely, OrderDate and ShippedDate (for the attribute with that name in the operational database) and DueDate (for the RequiredDate attribute).

In addition to the Date dimension, we have seen that a sales fact is associated with three other potential dimensions: Employee, Customer, and Supplier, derived from the respective many-to-one relationship types with the Orders table. A careful inspection of these geographic data showed that the data sources were incomplete. Thus, external data sources need to be checked (like Wikipedia[1] and GeoNames[2]) to complete the data. This analysis also shows that we need several different kinds of hierarchies to account for all possible political organizations of countries. Further, the term territories in the database actually refers to cities, and this is the name we will adopt in the requirements process. Also, in the one-to-many relationship type Belongs, between Territories and Regions, we consider the latter as a candidate to be a dimension level, yielding a candidate hierarchy City → Region.

In light of the above, we define a hierarchy, called Geography, composed of the levels City → State → Region → Country. But this hierarchy should also allow other paths to be followed, like City → Country (for cities that do not belong to any state) and State → Country (for states that do not belong to any region). This will be discussed in the conceptual design phase. This hierarchy will be shared by the Customer and Supplier dimensions and will also be a part of the Employee dimension via the Territories hierarchy. Note that the latter is a nonstrict hierarchy, while Geography is a strict one.

The Products entity type induces the Product dimension, mentioned before. The Categories entity type and the HasCategory relationship type allow us to derive a hierarchy Product → Category, which we call Categories.

Finally, the entity type Employees is involved in a one-to-many recursive relationship type called ReportsTo. This is an obvious candidate to be a parent-child hierarchy, which we call Supervision.

Table 10.3 summarizes the result of applying the derivation process. We included the cardinalities of the relationship between the dimensions and the fact Sales. The term Employee ⇆ City indicates a many-to-many relationship between the Employee and City levels. All other relationships are many-to-one.

We conclude with the last step, which is **Document Requirements Specification**. Similarly to the business-driven approach, all information specified in the previous steps is documented here. This documentation includes a detailed description of the source schemas that serve as a basis for identifying the elements in the multidimensional schema. It may also contain elements in the source schema for which it is not clear whether they can be used as attributes or hierarchies in a dimension. For example, we considered that the address of employees will not be used as a hierarchy. If the

---

[1] http://www.wikipedia.org

[2] http://www.geonames.org

Table 10.2 Multidimensional elements in the Northwind case study obtained using the data-driven approach

Facts	Measures	Dimensions and cardinalities		Hierarchies and levels
Sales	UnitPrice	Product	1:n	**Categories**
	Quantity			Product → Category
	Discount	Supplier	1:n	**Geography**
				Supplier → City → State →
				Region → Country
		Customer	1:n	**Geography**
				Supplier → City → State →
				Region → Country
		Employee	1:n	**Supervision**
				Subordinate → Supervisor
				Territories
				Employee ⇆ City → State →
				Region → Country
		OrderDate	1:n	**Calendar**
				Date → Month → Quarter →
				Semester → Year
		DueDate	1:n	**Calendar** (as above)
		ShippedDate	1:n	**Calendar** (as above)
		Order	1:1	

source schemas use attributes or relation names with unclear semantics, the corresponding elements of the multidimensional schema must be renamed, specifying clearly the correspondences between the old and new names.

10.3.3 Business/Data-driven Requirements Specification

The business/data-driven approach to requirements specification combines both of the previously described approaches, which can be used in parallel to achieve an optimal design. As illustrated in Fig. 10.4, two types of activities can be distinguished: one that corresponds to business needs (as described in Sect. 10.3.1) and another that represents the steps involved in creating a multidimensional schema from operational databases (as described in Sect. 10.3.2). Each type of activity results in the identification of elements for the initial multidimensional schema.

Table 10.3 Multidimensional elements in the Northwind case study obtained using the data-driven approach

Facts

- Sales
  - Measures: UnitPrice, Quantity, Discount
  - Dimensions and cardinalities: Product (1:n), Supplier (1:n), Customer (1:n), Employee (1:n), OrderDate (1:n), DueDate (1:n), ShippedDate (1:n), Order (1:1)

Dimensions and hierarchies

- Product
  - Categories: Product → Category
- Supplier
  - Geography: Supplier → City → State → Region → Country
- Customer
  - Geography: Customer → City → State → Region → Country
- Employee
  - Supervision: Subordinate → Supervisor
  - Territories: Employee ⇆ City → State → Region → Country
- OrderDate
  - Calendar: Date ⇆ Month → Quarter → Semester → Semester
- DueDate
  - Calendar: same as above
- ShippedDate
  - Calendar: same as above

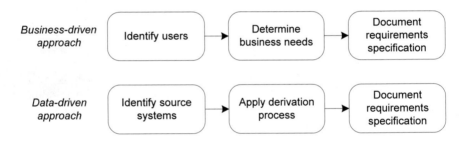

Fig. 10.4 Steps for requirements specification in the business/data-driven approach

10.4 Conceptual Design

Independently of whether the business-driven or the data-driven approach has been used, the requirements specification phase should eventually provide the necessary elements for building the initial conceptual data warehouse schema. The purpose of this schema is to represent a set of data requirements in a clear and concise manner that can be understood by the users. In the following, we detail the various steps of the conceptual-design phase and show examples of their execution. We use the MultiDim model described in Chap. 4 to define the conceptual schemas, although other conceptual models that provide an abstract representation of a data warehouse schema can also be used.

10.4.1 Business-Driven Conceptual Design

The design of a conceptual schema is an iterative process composed of three steps, shown in Fig. 10.5, namely, the development of the initial schema, the verification that the data in this schema are available in the source systems, and the mapping between the data in the schema and the data in the sources. In the case of missing data items, modification of the schema must be performed, which may lead to changes in the mappings. Finally, note that data can be directly obtained from the sources, or can be derived from one or many sources. We next detail the three steps above.

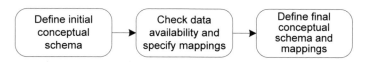

Fig. 10.5 Steps for conceptual design in the business-driven approach

Develop Initial Conceptual Schema

Well-specified business requirements lead to clearly distinguishable multi-dimensional elements, that is, facts, measures, dimensions, and hierarchies. We have shown this in Tables 10.1 and 10.3 that result from the business- and data-driven requirements specification, respectively. Therefore, a first approximation to the conceptual schema can be developed. This schema should be validated against its potential use for analytical processing. This can be done by first revising the list of queries and analytical scenarios and also by consulting the users directly. Designers should be aware of the features of the multidimensional model in use and pose additional questions to clarify any aspect that may remain unclear. During this step, the refinement of the conceptual schema may require several iterations with the users.

Check Data Availability and Specify Mappings

The data in the source systems determines whether the proposed conceptual schema can be transformed into logical and physical schemas and be fed with the data required for analysis. All elements included in the conceptual schema are checked against the data items in the source systems. This process can be time-consuming if the underlying source systems are not documented, are denormalized, or are legacy systems. The result of this step is a specification of the mappings for all elements of the multidimensional schema that match data in the source systems. If transformations are needed, the specification also includes a description them. Note that in data warehouse design it is crucial to determine data availability at an early stage, to avoid developing logical and physical schemas for which the required data may not be available.

Develop Final Conceptual Schema and Mappings

The initial schema could be considered as the final one if data in the source systems exist for all elements of the conceptual schema. However, if this is not the case, a new iteration with the users is required, to modify their requirements. according to the availability of data. As a result, a new schema should be developed and presented to the users for acceptance. The changes to the schema may require modification of existing mappings.

Application to the Northwind Case Study

We start with the first phase, which is **Develop Initial Schema**. Based on the user requirements, we developed the initial conceptual diagram shown in Fig. 4.1. As described in the requirements phase, the main focus of analysis refers to sales figures. This is represented at the conceptual level by the Sales fact in Fig. 4.1. Given that the source data are organized into orders, we need to transform orders data into sales facts during the ETL process. For example, the schema in Fig. 4.1 includes the measures Quantity, UnitPrice, Discount, SalesAmount, Freight, and NetAmount. The first three measures are obtained directly from the sources, while the others must be computed during the ETL process. SalesAmount is computed from Quantity, UnitPrice, and Discount. Also, since in the operational database Freight is associated with a complete order rather than with an order line, in the data warehouse it must be distributed proportionally across the articles in the corresponding order.

Finally, NetAmount is a derived measure, computed over the data cube. Note the difference between a measure that is computed during the ETL process (SalesAmount) and a derived attribute, which is computed from the data cube (NetAmount). In addition, we specify the aggregate function to be applied to each measure. For example, average is applied to the measures UnitPrice and Discount. Note that the measures Freight and NetAmount are not included in Table 10.1 since they do not follow from Requirements 1a–4c, which only represent a portion of the actual set of requirements.

The Sales fact is defined between the Product, Supplier, Customer, Employee, and Date dimensions. Since the orders are associated with different time instants, the Date level participates in the Sales fact with the roles Order-Date, DueDate, and ShippedDate. According to the requirements summarized in Table 10.1, the Date dimension contains four aggregation levels, where most of the scenarios include aggregation over time. Dimension Product is related to the parent level Category with a one-to-many cardinality, defining a strict hierarchy.

Also, following Table 10.1, geographic data are transformed in dimension levels used in the hierarchies for the Customer, Supplier, and Employee dimensions. These hierarchies share the levels City, State, Region, Country, and Continent, and are manually constructed (using the external data sources) taking into account the administrative divisions of the countries we want to represent. In addition, the many-to-many relationship between Employee and City, defines a nonstrict hierarchy. This relationship was discovered analyzing the content of the source database in the requirements phase.

Finally, for human resource management (Columns 4a–4c in Table 10.1), we need to analyze sales by employee supervisors. Thus, in dimension Employee, we defined a recursive hierarchy called Supervision.

We continue with the second step, which is **Check Data Availability and Specify Mappings**. The next step in the method is to check the availability of data in the source systems for all elements included in the data warehouse schema. In our example, the logical schema of the data source is depicted in Fig. 2.1, thus facilitating the task of specifying mappings. In the absence of a conceptual representation of the source systems, their logical structures can be used instead. Table 10.4 shows an example of a table that specifies the way in which source tables and attributes of the operational databases are related to the levels and attributes of the data warehouse. The rightmost column indicates whether a transformation is required. For example, data representing the ProductName, QuantityPerUnit, and UnitPrice of products in the operational database can be used without any transformation in the data warehouse for the corresponding attributes of the Product level. Note that Table 10.4 is just a simplification of the information that should be collected. Additional documentation should be delivered that includes more detailed specification of the required mappings and transformations.

Table 10.4 Data transformation between sources and the data warehouse

Source table	Source attribute	DW level	DW attribute	Transformation
Products	ProductName	Product	ProductName	—
Products	QuantityPerUnit	Product	QuantityPerUnit	—
Products	UnitPrice	Product	UnitPrice	—
...	...	...	...	...
Customers	CustomerID	Customer	CustomerID	✓
Customers	CompanyName	Customer	CompanyName	—
...	...	...	...	...
Orders	OrderID	Order	OrderNo	✓
Orders		Order	OrderLineNo	✓
Orders	OrderDate	Date	—	✓
...	...	...	...	...

We continue with the third step, which is **Develop Final Conceptual Schema and Mappings**. Revision and additional consultation with users are required in order to adapt the multidimensional schema to the content of the data sources. When this has been done, the final schema and the corresponding mappings are developed. In our example, some of the issues found in the revision process were:

- We need to create and populate the dimension Date. The time interval of this dimension must cover the dates contained in the table Orders of the Northwind operational database.
- The dimensions Customer and Suppliers share the geographic hierarchy starting with City. However, this information is incomplete in the operational database. Therefore, the data for the hierarchy State, Country, and Continent must be obtained from an external source.

Metadata for the source systems, the data warehouse, and the ETL processes are also developed in this step. This includes the specification of transformations and the abstract descriptions of various features mentioned earlier. For example, for each source system, access information must be specified (e.g., login, password). Also, for each element in the source schemas (e.g., the entity and relationship types), we specify name, alias, a description of its semantics in the application domain, and so on. The elements of the data warehouse schema are also described by names and aliases and, additionally, include information about data granularity, policies for the preservation of data changes (i.e., whether they are kept or discarded upon updates), loading frequencies, and the purging period, among other things.

10.4.2 Data-driven Conceptual Design

In this approach, the initial data warehouse is developed once the operational schemas have been analyzed. Since not all facts will be of interest for the purpose of decision support users must identify which facts are important. Users can also refine the existing hierarchies since some of these are sometimes "hidden" in an entity type or a table. Thus, the initial data warehouse schema is modified until it becomes the final version accepted by the users.

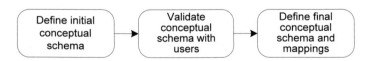

Fig. 10.6 Steps for conceptual design in the data-driven approach

The conceptual-design phase consists of three steps, shown in Fig. 10.6. We discuss next these steps.

Develop Initial Schema

Since the multidimensional elements have been identified in the requirements specification phase, the development of an initial data warehouse conceptual schema is straightforward. The usual practice for these kinds of schemas is to use names for the various schema elements that facilitate user understanding. However, in some cases, users are familiar with the technical names used in the source systems. Therefore, designers should develop a dictionary of names to facilitate communication with the users.

Validate Conceptual Schema with Users

The schema was obtained starting from the data sources. Thus, at this point, the participation of the users has been minimal, consisting of responding only to specific inquiries from the designer. In this step, users are incorporated in a more active role. Most of the time, these users belong to the professional or administrative level, because of their knowledge of the underlying systems. The initial schema is examined in detail, and it is possible that it requires some modification for several reasons: (1) it may contain more elements than those required for the analysis purposes of the decision-making users; (2) some elements may require transformation (e.g., attributes into hierarchies); and (3) some elements could be missing even though they exist in the source systems (e.g., owing to confusing names). Note that the inclusion of new elements may require further interaction with the source systems.

Develop Final Conceptual Schema and Mappings

Users' recommendations about changes are incorporated into the initial schema, leading to a final conceptual schema that should be approved by the users. In this stage, an abstract specification of mappings and transformations (if required) between the data in the source systems and the data in the data warehouse is defined.

During all the above steps of the conceptual-design phase, a specification of the business, technical, and ETL metadata should be developed, following the same guidelines as those described for the business-driven approach.

Application to the Northwind Case Study

We start with the first step, which is **Develop Initial Schema**. The requirements elicitation phase discussed in Sect. 10.3.2 resulted in the multidimensional elements depicted in Table 10.3, namely, the facts, dimensions, and hierarchies inferred from the analysis of the operational database (Fig. 2.1). This led to the multidimensional schema shown in Fig. 4.1.

We start with the second step, which is **Validate Conceptual Schema with Users**. The initial data warehouse schema as presented in Fig. 4.1 should be delivered to the users. In this way, they can assess its appropriateness for the analysis needs. This can lead to the modification of the schema, either by removing schema elements that are not needed for analysis or by specifying missing elements. Recall that in the data-driven approach, during the requirements elicitation the users have not participated, thus changes to the initial conceptual schema will likely be needed.

The next step is **Develop Final Conceptual Schema and Mappings**. The modified schema is finally delivered to the users. Given that the operational schema of the Northwind database is very simple, the mapping between the source schema and the final data warehouse schema is almost straightforward. The implementation of such a mapping was described in Chap. 9, thus we do not repeat it here. Further, since we already have the schemas for the source system and the data warehouse, we can specify metadata in a similar way to that described for the business-driven approach above.

10.4.3 Business/Data-driven Conceptual Design

In this approach, two activities are performed, targeting both the business requirements of the data warehouse and the exploration of the source systems feeding the warehouse. This leads to the creation of two data warehouse schemas (Fig. 10.7). The schema obtained from the business-driven approach identifies the structure of the data warehouse as it emerges from the business requirements. The data-driven approach results in a data warehouse schema that can be extracted from the existing operational databases. After both initial schemas have been developed, they must be matched. Several aspects should be considered in this matching process, such as the terminology used and the degree of similarity between the two solutions for each multidimensional element, for example, between dimensions, levels, attributes, or hierarchies. Some solutions for this have been proposed in academic literature, although they are highly technical and complex to implement.

An ideal situation arises when both schemas cover the same analysis aspects, that is, the users' needs are covered by the data in the operational systems and no other data are needed to expand the analysis. In this case, the schema is accepted, and mappings between elements of the source systems and the data warehouse are specified. Additionally, documentation is developed following the guidelines studied for the business- and data-driven approaches. This documentation contains metadata about the data warehouse, the source systems, and the ETL process. Nevertheless, in real-world

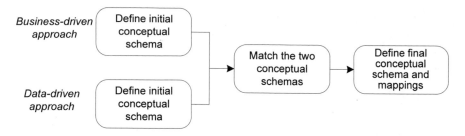

Fig. 10.7 Steps for conceptual design in the business/data-driven approach

situations, it is seldom the case that both schemas will cover the same aspects of analysis. Two situations may occur:

1. Users require less information than what the operational databases can provide. In this case, we must determine whether users may consider new aspects of analysis or whether to eliminate from the schema those facts that are not of their interest. Therefore, another iteration of the business- and data-driven approaches is required, where either new users will be involved or a new initial schema will be developed.
2. Users require more information than what the operational databases can provide. In this case, the users may reconsider their needs and limit them to those proposed by the business-driven solution. Alternatively, users may require the inclusion of external sources or legacy systems not con-sidered in the previous iteration. Thus, new iterations of the business- and data-driven approaches may again be needed.

10.5 Logical Design

Figure 10.8 illustrates the steps of the logical design phase. First, the trans-formation of the conceptual multidimensional schema into a logical schema is developed. Then, the ETL processes are specified, considering the mappings and transformations indicated in the previous phase. We shall refer next to these two steps.

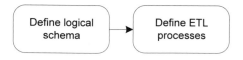

Fig. 10.8 Steps for logical design

10.5.1 Logical Schemas

After the conceptual design phase has been completed, it is necessary to apply mapping rules to the resulting conceptual schema in order to generate a logical schema. These mapping rules depend on the conceptual model used. In Sect. 5.3, we described some general mapping rules that translate the MultiDim conceptual model into the relational model. In this section, we apply these rules to the conceptual multidimensional schemas developed in the previous phase. As explained in Sect. 5.2, the logical representation of a data warehouse is often based on the relational data model using specific structures such as star and snowflake schemas.

We comment next on some design decisions taken when transforming the schema shown in Fig. 4.1 into relational tables, as shown in Fig. 5.4.

First, considering users' business needs, query performance, and data reuse, we must decide whether a star (denormalized) or a snowflake (normalized) representation will be used. In Sect. 5.2, we have discussed the advantages and disadvantages of these schemas for representing dimensions with hierarchies. The following decisions were taken in our case study.

Given that the Calendar hierarchy is only used in the Date dimension, for performance reasons we denormalize these hierarchies and include them in a single table instead of mapping every level to a separate table, thus choosing a star representation for the Date dimension.

The hierarchies Territories, Geography (for customers), and Geography (for suppliers) in Fig. 4.1 share the levels City, State, Region, Country, and Continent. To favor the reuse of existing data, we use the *snowflake representation* for this hierarchy. Note that we must consider that the hierarchy City → State → Region → Country → Continent is a ragged one (Sect. 4.2). In Chap. 5 we explained that mapping a ragged hierarchy to the relational model, can be performed embedding all the data of the parent level in the child one (a denormalized mapping) or creating a table for each level and an optional foreign key referencing the potential parent levels. In our example, since most of the countries do not have regions, we embedded attributes RegionName and RegionCode in the State table as optional one, since the other alternative would imply the inclusion of optional foreign keys that would be null most of the time. Each other level above was represented in a separate table. For example, in the City table, we have embedded StateKey and CountryKey as optional foreign keys. Then, if a city does directly belong to a country, we can reference the country without traversing the intermediate levels.

Territories is a nonstrict hierarchy (Sect. 4.2.6) since it contains a many-to-many relationship between the Employee and City levels. We use a bridge table for representing this relationship in the relational model. Thus, we create the table Territories, which references the Employee and the City tables.

In a similar way, we define tables for the other hierarchies and levels. Finally, the fact table is created containing all measures included in the conceptual schema and referencing all participating dimensions.

10.5.2 ETL Processes

During the conceptual design phase, we identified the mappings required between the sources and the data warehouse. We also specify some transformations that could be necessary in order to match user requirements with the data available in the source systems. However, before implementing the ETL processes, several additional tasks must be specified in more detail.

In the logical design phase, all transformations of the source data should be considered. Some of them can be straightforward, for example, the separation of addresses into their components (e.g., street, city, postal code) or the extraction of date components (e.g., month and year). Note that the transformation may depend on the logical model. For example, in the relational model, each component of a department address will be represented as a separate attribute.

Other transformations may require further decisions, for instance, whether to recalculate measure values to express them in euros or dollars or to use the original currency and include the exchange rate. It should be clear that in real situations, complex data transformations may be required. Further, since the same data can be included in different source systems, the issue of inconsistencies may arise, and an appropriate strategy for resolving them must be devised. Also, developers should design the necessary data structures for all elements for which users want to keep changes, as explained in Sect. 5.7.

A preliminary sequence of execution for the ETL processes should also be determined. This ensures that all data will be transformed and included, with their consistency being checked. We do not explain here the ETL design for the Northwind data warehouse since it was studied in detail in Chap. 9.

10.6 Physical Design

As with the logical-design phase, we should consider two aspects in the physical-design phase: one related to the implementation of the data warehouse schema and another that considers the ETL processes. This is illustrated in Fig. 10.9.

In Chaps. 8 and 9 we have studied, respectively, physical data warehouse design and ETL processes, therefore we do not extend further in this topic here.

Fig. 10.9 Steps for physical design

10.7 Characterization of the Various Approaches

In this section, we summarize the three approaches to data warehouse development. We also discuss the many aspects that must be considered before choosing one of those approaches for a specific data warehouse project.

10.7.1 Business-Driven Approach

The business-driven approach requires the intensive participation of users from different organizational levels. In particular, the support of executive-level users is important in order to define business goals and needs. The identification of key users for requirements specification is a crucial task. It is necessary to consider several aspects:

- Users should be aware of the overall business goals to avoid situations where the requirements represent the personal perceptions of users according to their role in the organization or business unit.
- Users who would dominate the requirements specification process should be avoided or tempered in order to ensure that the information needs of different users will be considered.
- Users must be available and agree to participate during the whole process of requirements gathering and conceptual design.
- Users must have an idea of what a data warehouse system and an OLAP system can offer. If this is not the case, they should be instructed by means of explanations, demonstrations, or prototypes.

The development team requires highly qualified professionals. For example, a project manager should have very strong moderation and leadership skills. A good knowledge of information-gathering techniques and business process modeling is also required. It is important that data warehouse designers should be able to communicate with and to understand nonexpert users in order to obtain the required information and, later on, to present and describe the proposed multidimensional schema to them. This helps to avoid the situation where users describe the requirements for the data warehouse system using business terminology and the data warehouse team develops the system using a more technical viewpoint difficult for the users to understand.

Advantages of the business-driven approach are

- It provides a comprehensive and precise specification of the needs of stakeholders from their business viewpoint.
- It facilitates, through the effective participation of users, a better understanding of the facts, dimensions, and the relationships between them.
- It promotes the acceptance of the system if there is continuous interaction with potential users and decision makers.

- It enables the specification of long-term strategic goals.

However, some disadvantages of this approach can play an important role in determining its usability for a specific data warehouse project:

- The specification of business goals can be a difficult process, and its result depends on the techniques applied and the skills of the developer team.
- Requirements specification not aligned with business goals may produce a complex schema that does not support the decision processes at all organizational levels.
- The duration of the project tends to be longer than the duration of the data-driven approach. Thus, the cost of the project can also be higher.
- The user requirements might not be satisfied by the information existing in the source systems.

10.7.2 Data-driven Approach

In this approach, the participation of the users is not explicitly required. They are involved only sporadically, either to confirm the correctness of the structures derived or to identify facts and measures as a starting point for creating multidimensional schemas. Typically, users come from the professional or the administrative organizational level since data are represented at a low level of detail. Also, this approach requires highly skilled and experienced designers. Besides the usual modeling abilities, they should have enough business knowledge to understand the business context and its needs. They should also have the capacity to understand the structure of the underlying operational databases.

The data-driven method has several advantages:

- It ensures that the data warehouse reflects the underlying relationships in the data.
- It ensures that the data warehouse contains all necessary data from the beginning.
- It simplifies the ETL processes since data warehouses are developed on the basis of existing operational databases.
- It reduces the user involvement required to start the project.
- It facilitates a fast and straightforward development process, provided that well-structured and normalized operational systems exist.
- It allows automatic or semiautomatic techniques to be applied if the operational databases are represented using the entity-relationship model or normalized relational tables.

However, it is important to consider the following disadvantages before choosing this approach:

- Only business needs reflected in the underlying source data models can be captured.
- The system may not meet users' expectations since the company's goals and the user requirements are not reflected at all.
- The method may not be applied when the logical schemas of the underlying operational systems are hard to understand or the data sources reside on legacy systems.
- Since it relies on existing data, this approach cannot be used to address long-term strategic goals.
- The inclusion of hierarchies may be difficult since they may be hidden in various structures, for example, in generalization relationships.
- It is difficult to motivate end users to work with large schemas developed for and by specialists.
- The derivation process can be difficult without knowledge of the users' needs since, for instance, the same data can be considered as a measure or as a dimension attribute.

10.7.3 Business/Data-driven Approach

As this approach combines the business-driven and data-driven approaches, the recommendations regarding users and the development team given above should also be considered here. The business/data-driven approach has several important advantages:

- It generates a feasible solution, supported by the existing data sources, which better reflects the users' goals.
- It alerts about missing data in the operational databases that are required to support the decision-making process.
- If the source systems offer more information than what the business users initially demand, the analysis can be expanded to include new aspects not yet considered.

However, this approach has the following disadvantages:

- The development process is complicated since two schemas are required, one obtained from the definition of the business requirements and another derived from the underlying source systems.
- The integration process to determine whether the data sources cover the user requirements may need complex techniques.

10.8 Summary

In this chapter, we have presented a general method for the design of data warehouses. Our proposal is close to the classic database design method and is composed of the following phases: requirements specification, conceptual design, logical design, and physical design. For the requirements specification and conceptual design phases we have proposed three different approaches: (1) the business-driven approach, which focuses on business needs; (2) the data-driven approach, which develops the data warehouse schema on the basis of the data of the underlying operational databases, typically represented using the entity-relationship or the relational model; and (3) the business/data-driven approach, which combines the first two approaches, matching the users' business needs with the availability of data. The next phases of the method presented correspond to those of classic database design. Therefore, a mapping from the conceptual model to a logical model is specified, followed by the definition of physical structures. The design of these structures should consider the specific features of the target DBMS with respect to the particularities of data warehouse applications.

10.9 Bibliographic Notes

Given the lack of consensus about a data warehouse design methodology, we comment first some *classic approaches* to this topic. Golfarelli and Rizzi [84] present a data warehouse design method composed of the following steps: analysis of the information system, requirements specification, conceptual design workload refinement and schema validation, logical design, and physical design. This method corresponds to the one used in traditional database design, extended with an additional phase of workload refinement in order to determine the expected data volume. Luján-Mora and Trujillo [142] propose a method for data warehouse design based on UML. This proposal deals with all data warehouse design phases from the analysis of the operational data sources to the final implementation, including the ETL processes. Jarke et al. [120] introduced the DWQ (Data Warehouse Quality) design method for data warehouses, which consists of six steps and focuses in data quality concepts.

Regarding requirements specification following the *business-driven approach*, Mazón et al. [150] propose to include business goals in data warehouse requirements analysis. These requirements are then transformed into a multidimensional model. Kimball et al. [129, 130] base their data warehouse development strategy on choosing the core business processes to model. Then, business users are interviewed to introduce the data warehouse team to the company's goals and to understand the users' expectations of the data warehouse. Even though this approach lacks formality, it has been applied in many data warehouse projects.

There are several methods for requirements analysis based on the *data-driven approach*: Böhnlein and Ulbrich-vom Ende [34] propose a method to derive logical data warehouse structures from the conceptual schema of operational systems. Golfarelli et al. [83] present a graphical conceptual model for data warehouses called the Dimensional Fact Model and proposed a semiautomatic process for building conceptual schemas from operational entity-relationship (ER) schemas. Cabibbo and Torlone [40] present a design method that starts from an existing ER schema and derives a multidimensional schema. They also provide an implementation in terms of relational tables and multidimensional arrays. Paim et al. [178] propose a method for requirements specification which consists of three phases: requirements planning, specification, and validation. Paim and Castro [179] later extended this method by including nonfunctional requirements, such as performance and accessibility. Vaisman [244] propose a method for the specification of functional and nonfunctional requirements that integrates the concepts of requirements engineering and data quality. This method refers to the mechanisms for collecting, analyzing, and integrating requirements. Users are also involved in order to determine the expected quality of the source data. Then, data sources are selected using quantitative measures to ensure data quality. The outcome of this method is a set of documents and a ranking of the operational data sources that should satisfy the users requirements according to various quality parameters.

As for the *combination* of approaches, Bonifati et al. [35] introduce a method for the identification and design of data marts, which consists of three general parts: top-down analysis, bottom-up analysis, and integration. The top-down analysis emphasizes the user requirements and requires precise identification and formulation of goals. On the basis of these goals, a set of ideal star schemas is created. On the other hand, the bottom-up analysis aims at identifying all the star schemas that can be implemented using the available source systems. This analysis requires to represent the source systems using the ER model. The final integration phase is used to match the ideal star schemas with realistic ones based on the existing data. Elamin et al. [68] introduces a method denoted *SSReq* to generate star schemas from business users'. This is, like the previous one, a mixed approach that produces star schemas from both data sources and business requirements. The method has three steps: (a) Business requirements elicitation; (b) Requirements normalization, which takes the requirements to a format that eliminates redundancy; and (c) Generation of the star schemas.

We now comment on some *miscellaneous* proposals that do not fit in the classification above. In [161], the authors propose a method covering the full requirements engineering cycle for data warehouses, based on the Goal-Oriented Requirements Engineering (GORE) approach. A book that covers the overall requirements engineering for data warehouses is [192]. The rationale is that requirements engineering should be integrated into agile development. Therefore, rather than restricting incremental and iterative development to the design and implementation tasks, the authors propose to extend it to the requirements engineering task as well. A recent technique for requirements-driven data warehouse design based on enhanced pivot tables is given in [26]. Also [211] describes a methodology to transform the constellation schema of a data warehouse by integrating fact data into a dimension. The methodology is aimed at solving the problems of dimensions containing numerical data and facts containing categorical data.

Given the wide spectrum of design methologies commented above, Di Tria el al. [237] designed a collection of metrics for evaluating the quality of multidimensional schemas with respect to the effort spent in the design process and the automation degree of the methodology. They based on mixed methodologies that combine data- and business-driven approaches, since the authors' claim is that these methodologies are the only ones that can ensure the multidimensional schema is consistent with both, data sources and user business goals. In [238], the same authors extend this methodology for data warehouse design in a big data context.

From the *practitioner's perspective*, two recent methodological developments are described next.

Data Vault, developed by Daniel Linstedt, is a modeling method that aims at providing long-term historical storage of data coming in from multiple operational systems. In this sense, it could be classified as data-driven. It emphasizes, in particular, the need to trace where all the data in the database came from. This requires that every row in a data vault must be accompanied by record source and load date attributes, enabling to trace values back to the source. The latest version of Data Vault 2.0 is described in [141].

The Unified Star Schema, developed by Bill Inmon and Francesco Puppini, is an agile an resilient approach for designing analytics applications. To achieve self-service BI, we translate the traditional constellation schema, that is, a set of star schemas joint via conformed dimensions, by one super star where all the tables (both fact and dimensions) are joined via one big auxiliary table called Bridge. This approach is described in [118].

10.10 Review Questions

10.1 What are the similarities and the differences between designing a database and designing a data warehouse?

10.2 Compare the top-down and the bottom-up approaches for data warehouse design. Which of the two approaches is more often used? How does the design of a data warehouse and of a data mart differ?

10.3 Discuss the various phases in data warehouse design, emphasizing the objective of each phase.

10.4 Summarize the main characteristics of the business-driven, data-driven, and business/data-driven approaches for requirements specification. How do they differ from each other? What are their respective advantages and disadvantages? Identify in which situations one approach would be preferred over the others.

10.5 Using an application domain that you are familiar with, illustrate the various steps in the business-driven approach for requirements specification. Identify at least two different users, each one with a particular business goal.

10.6 Using the application domain of Question 10.5, illustrate the various steps in the data-driven approach for requirements specification. Define an excerpt of an ER schema from which some multidimensional elements can be derived.

10.7 Compare the steps for conceptual design in the business-driven, data-driven, and business/data-driven approaches.

10.8 Develop a conceptual multidimensional schema for the application domain of Question 10.5 using among the three approaches the one that you know best.

10.9 Illustrate the different aspects of the logical design phase by translating the conceptual schema developed in Question 10.8 into the relational model.

10.10 Describe several aspects that are important to consider in the physical design phase of data warehouses.

10.11 Exercises

Exercise 10.1. Consider the train application described in Ex. 3.2. Using the business-driven approach, write the requirements specifications that would result in the MultiDim schema obtained in Ex. 4.3.

Exercise 10.2. Consider the French horse race application described in Ex. 2.1. Using the data-driven approach, write the requirements specifications in order to produce the MultiDim schema obtained in Ex. 4.5.

Exercise 10.3. Consider the Formula One application described in Ex. 2.2. Using the business/data-driven approach, write the requirements specifications in order to produce the MultiDim schema obtained in Ex. 4.7.

Exercise 10.4. The ranking of universities has become an important factor in establishing the reputation of a university at the international level. Our university wants to determine what actions it should take to improve its position in the rankings. To simplify the discussion, we consider only the ranking by *The Times*. The evaluation criteria in this ranking refer to the two main areas of activities of universities, namely, research and education. However, a closer analysis shows that 60% of the criteria are related to research activities (peer review and citation/faculty scores) and 40% to the university's commitment to teaching. Therefore, we suppose that the decision-making users chose initially to analyze the situation related to research activities. To be able to conduct the analysis process, it was decided to implement a data warehouse system.

Universities are usually divided into faculties representing general fields of knowledge (e.g., medicine, engineering, sciences, and so on). These faculties comprise several departments dedicated to more specialized domains; for example, the faculty of engineering may include departments of civil engineering, mechanical engineering, and computer engineering, among others. University staff (e.g., professors, researchers, teaching assistants, administrative staff, and so on) are administratively attached to departments. In addition, autonomous structures called research centers support multidisciplinary research activities. University staff from various faculties or departments may belong to these research centers. Research projects are conducted by one or several research bodies, which may be either departments or research centers. The research department is the administrative body that coordinates all research activities at the university. It serves as a bridge between high-level executives (e.g., the Rector and the research council of the university) and researchers, as well as between researchers and external organizations, whether industrial or governmental. For example, the research department is responsible for the evaluation of research activities, for the development of strategic research plans, for promoting research activities and services, for managing intellectual property rights and patents, and for technology transfer and creation of spin-offs, among other things. In particular, the establishment of strategic research areas is based on the university's core strengths and ambitions, taking into account long-term potential and relevance. These areas are the focus of institutional initiatives and investments. On the basis of the institutional research strategy, faculties, departments, and research centers establish their own research priorities.

Suppose the university has *one general goal*: to improve its ranking considering the strategic research areas established at the university. This goal is decomposed into two subgoals related to improving the scores in two evaluation criteria of *The Times* ranking: the peer review and the citation per faculty criteria. The peer review criterion (40% of the ranking score) is based on interviewing selected academics from various countries to name the top institutions in the areas and subjects about which they feel able to make an informed judgment. The citation per faculty criterion (20% of the ranking score) refers to the numbers of citations of academic papers generated by staff members.

Determining the activities that could improve these evaluation criteria required the participation of users at various organizational levels. Interviews with users allowed us to conclude that, in the first step, information related to international conferences, projects, and publications was necessary to better understand the participation of the university's staff in international forums.

Participation in *international conferences* helps the university's staff to meet international colleagues working in the same or a similar area. In this way, not only can new strategic contacts be established (which may lead to international projects), but also the quality of the university's research can be improved.

Further, *international projects* promote the interaction of the university staff with peers from other universities working in the same area and thus could help to *improve the peer review score*. There are several sources of funding for research projects: the university, industry, and regional, national, and international institutions. Independently of the funding scheme, a project may be considered as being international when it involves participants from institutions in other countries.

Finally, knowledge about the international publications produced by the university's staff is essential for assessing the *citation per faculty criterion*. Publications can be of several types, namely, articles in conference proceedings or in journals, and books.

Based on the description above, we ask you to

a. Produce a requirements specification for the design of the data warehouse using the *business-driven approach*. For this, you must

   - Identify users.
   - For each goal and subgoal, write a set of queries that these users would require. Refine and prioritize these queries.
   - Define facts, measures, and dimensions based on these queries.
   - Infer dimension hierarchies.
   - Build a table summarizing the information obtained.

b. Produce a conceptual schema, using the *business-driven approach* and the *top-down design*. Discuss data availability conditions and how they impact on the design. Identify and specify the necessary mappings.

c. Produce a conceptual schema, using the *business-driven approach*, and the *bottom-up design*. For this, you must build three data marts: one for the analysis of conferences, another one for the analysis of publications, and the third one for the analysis of research projects. Then, merge the three of them, and compare the schema produced with the one obtained through the top-down approach above.

d. Produce a requirements specification for the design of the data warehouse using the *data-driven approach*, given the entity-relationship schema of the operational database in Fig. 10.10. For this, you must

   - Explain how the facts, measures, dimensions, and hierarchies are derived.
   - Summarize in a table the information obtained.

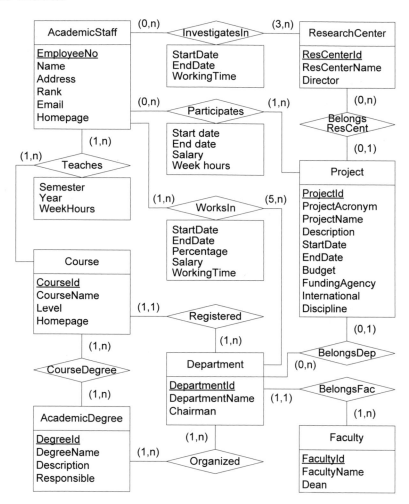

Fig. 10.10 Excerpt from the ER schema of the operational database in the university application

Part III
Advanced Topics

Chapter 11
Temporal and Multiversion Data Warehouses

The data warehouses studied so far in this book assumed that only facts and their measures evolve in time. However, dimension data may also vary in time; for instance, a product may change its price or its category. The most popular approach for tackling this issue in the context of relational databases is the so-called slowly changing dimensions one, which we have studied in Chap. 5. An alternative approach is based on the field of temporal databases. Such databases provide mechanisms for managing information that varies over time. The combination of temporal databases and data warehouses leads to *temporal data warehouses*, which are studied in the first part of this chapter.

While temporal data warehouses address the evolution of *data*, another situation that may arise is that the *schema* of a data warehouse evolves. To cope with this issue, the data in the warehouse can be modified to comply with the new version of the schema. However, this is not always possible nor desirable in many real-world situations, and therefore, it is necessary to maintain several versions of a data warehouse. This leads to *multiversion data warehouses*, which are studied in the second part of this chapter.

Section 11.1 introduces some concepts related to temporal databases, and how to query such databases using standard SQL. In Sect. 11.2, we present a temporal extension of the conceptual multidimensional model we use in this book. Section 11.3 presents the mapping of our temporal multidimensional model into the relational model, while Sect. 11.4 discusses various implementation considerations in this respect. In Sect. 11.5, we address the issue of querying a temporal data warehouse in SQL. Sect. 11.6 compares temporal data warehouses with slowly changing dimensions and provides an alternative implementation of the temporal Northwind data warehouse using slowly changing dimensions. In Sect. 11.7, we study conceptual modeling of multiversion data warehouses, while logical design of multiversion data warehouses is presented in Sect. 11.8. We conclude in Sect. 11.9 illustrating how to query a multiversion data warehouse.

© Springer-Verlag GmbH Germany, part of Springer Nature 2022
A. Vaisman, E. Zimányi, *Data Warehouse Systems*, Data-Centric Systems and Applications, https://doi.org/10.1007/978-3-662-65167-4_11

11.1 Manipulating Temporal Information in SQL

Temporal databases are databases that represent and manage information that varies over time. In addition to storing current data, temporal databases allow previous or future data to be stored, as well as the time when the changes in this data occurred or will occur. Thus, they enable users to know the evolution of information as required in many application domains.

Time can be represented in a database in various ways. Most approaches assume a discrete model of time where the instants in the time line are isomorphic (that is, structurally equivalent) to the natural numbers. We follow this approach in this chapter. The time line is then represented by a sequence of nondecomposable, consecutive time periods of identical duration, called **chronons**, which correspond to the smallest time unit that the system is able to represent. Consecutive chronons can be grouped into larger units called **granules**, such as seconds, minutes, or days. **Granularity** represents the time unit used for specifying the duration of a granule.

There are several ways of interpreting the time frame associated with the information contained in a temporal database. **Valid time** (VT) specifies the period of time in which an assertion is true in the modeled reality; for example, it captures the period when a specific salary was paid to an employee. Valid time is usually provided by the user. **Transaction time** (TT) indicates the period of time in which an assertion is stored in the database. The transaction time of an assertion begins at the time when it is inserted or updated, and ends when the fact is deleted or updated. Transaction time is generated by the database system. Valid time and transaction time can be combined to define **bitemporal time** (BT). This indicates both when a fact is true in reality and when it is current in the database.

Current DBMSs provide limited support for dealing with time-varying data: many of them only provide data types for encoding dates or timestamps. Although the most recent versions of the SQL standard provide temporal support, this has not yet been fully implemented in most DBMSs and therefore in many cases traditional SQL must be used for querying time-varying data. However, as we will show in this section, this is a challenging task.

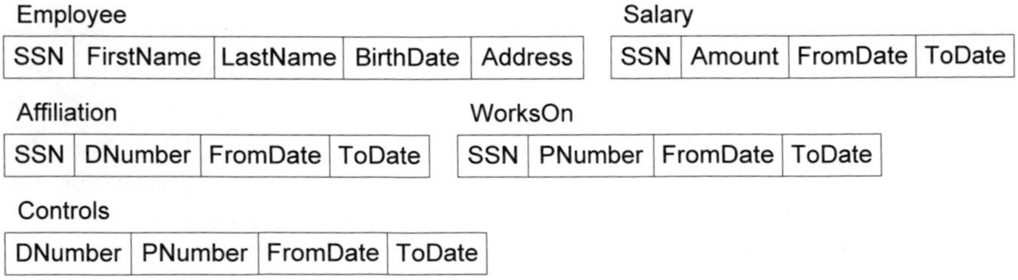

Employee

SSN	FirstName	LastName	BirthDate	Address

Salary

SSN	Amount	FromDate	ToDate

Affiliation

SSN	DNumber	FromDate	ToDate

WorksOn

SSN	PNumber	FromDate	ToDate

Controls

DNumber	PNumber	FromDate	ToDate

Fig. 11.1 Example of a temporal database schema

Figure 11.1 shows an example of a temporal database schema. Table Employee is nontemporal, while the other tables are valid-time temporal tables. The columns FromDate and ToDate indicate when the information in the corresponding row is valid, for instance, the period of time during which an employee is affiliated to a department. Since a data type for representing periods is not available in SQL, a period is encoded in two columns of type Date. The problem with this solution is that columns with such a particular semantics are encoded in SQL in the same way as columns such as BirthDate, which is also of type Date, but has a different semantics.

SSN	DNumber	FromDate	ToDate
123456789	D1	2002-01-01	2003-06-01
123456789	D2	2003-06-01	9999-12-31
333444555	D2	2003-10-01	2004-01-01
333444555	D3	2004-01-01	9999-12-31

Fig. 11.2 An example of an instance of table Affiliation

Figure 11.2 shows a possible instance of table Affiliation, where a closed-open representation [FromDate,ToDate) for periods is used. For instance, the first two rows state that the employee worked in department D1 from 2002-01-01 until (but not including) 2003-06-01, the date at which she began working in D2. Also, a special date 9999-12-31 denotes currently valid rows. Thus, the second row states that the employee is currently working in department D2.

We show next how to use SQL to extend the relational algebra operators we have seen in Sect. 2.4.3 to cope with time-varying information.

Temporal Projection

Given the table Affiliation of Fig. 11.2, suppose that we want to obtain the periods of time in which an employee has worked for the company, independently of the department. Figure 11.3a shows the result of projecting out attribute DNumber from the table of Fig. 11.2. As can be seen, the resulting table is redundant. The first two rows are **value equivalent**, that is, they are equal on all their columns except for FromDate and ToDate, and in addition, the time periods of these rows meet. The situation is similar for the last two rows. Therefore, the result of the projection should be as given in Fig. 11.3b. This process of combining several value-equivalent rows into one provided that their time periods overlap is called **coalescing**.

Coalescing is a complex and costly operation in SQL, as shown next.

SSN	FromDate	ToDate
123456789	2002-01-01	2003-06-01
123456789	2003-06-01	9999-12-31
333444555	2003-10-01	2004-01-01
333444555	2004-01-01	9999-12-31

SSN	FromDate	ToDate
123456789	2002-01-01	9999-12-31
333444555	2003-10-01	9999-12-31

(a)   (b)

Fig. 11.3 Projecting out attribute DNumber from the table in Fig. 11.2. (a) Initial result; (b) Coalescing the result

```
SELECT DISTINCT F.SSN, F.FromDate, L.ToDate
FROM    Affiliation F, Affiliation L
WHERE F.SSN = L.SSN AND F.FromDate < L.ToDate AND NOT EXISTS (
        SELECT *
        FROM    Affiliation C
        WHERE F.SSN = C.SSN AND F.FromDate < C.FromDate AND
                C.FromDate <= L.ToDate AND NOT EXISTS (
                SELECT *
                FROM    Affiliation C1
                WHERE F.SSN = C1.SSN AND C1.FromDate < C.FromDate AND
                        C.FromDate <= C1.ToDate ) )
        AND NOT EXISTS (
        SELECT *
        FROM    Affiliation E
        WHERE F.SSN = E.SSN AND
                ( (E.FromDate < F.FromDate AND F.FromDate <= E.ToDate)
                OR (E.FromDate <= L.ToDate AND L.ToDate < E.ToDate) ) )
```

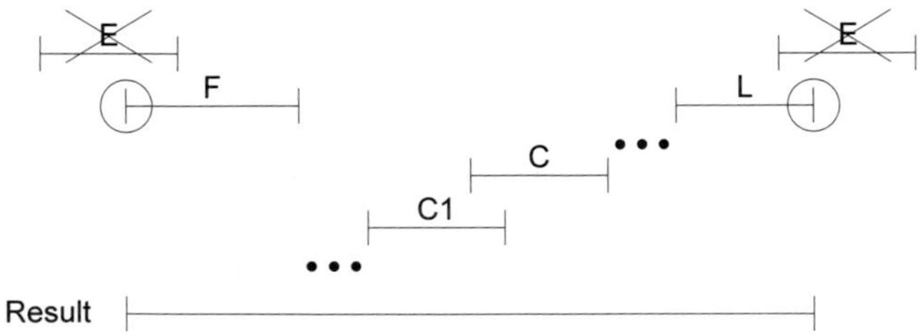

Fig. 11.4 Coalescing value-equivalent rows

Consider the diagram in Fig. 11.4. To coalesce value-equivalent rows we select the period [FromDate, ToDate) obtained from two rows F(irst) and L(ast) such that there is no gap during the period, that is, for every row C valid within the selected period there is another row C1 that can extend C to the left. This is implemented by the first and second NOT EXISTS predicates. The third NOT EXISTS predicate ensures that no other row E can extend the selected period to the left or to the right.

Temporal Join

Recall from Fig. 11.1 that tables **Salary** and **Affiliation** keep, respectively, the evolution of the salary and the affiliation of employees. To determine the joint evolution across time of salary and affiliation, a temporal join of these tables is needed. Given one row from each table whose validity periods intersect, a temporal join returns the salary and affiliation values together with the intersection of the two validity periods. As illustrated in Fig.11.5, there are four cases in which two periods may intersect.

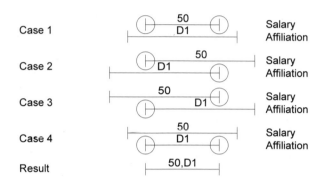

Fig. 11.5 Various cases for temporal join

Expressing a temporal join in SQL requires four **SELECT** statements and complex inequality predicates verifying that the validity periods of the rows to be combined intersect, as follows.

```
-- Case 1
SELECT S.SSN, Amount, DNumber, S.FromDate, S.ToDate
FROM   Salary S, Affiliation A
WHERE  S.SSN = A.SSN AND A.FromDate < S.FromDate AND S.ToDate <= A.ToDate
-- Case 2
UNION ALL
SELECT S.SSN, Amount, DNumber, S.FromDate, A.ToDate
FROM   Salary S, Affiliation A
WHERE  S.SSN = A.SSN AND S.FromDate >= A.FromDate AND
       S.FromDate < A.ToDate AND A.ToDate < S.ToDate
-- Case 3
UNION ALL
SELECT S.SSN, Amount, DNumber, A.FromDate, S.ToDate
FROM   Salary S, Affiliation A
WHERE  S.SSN = A.SSN AND A.FromDate >= S.FromDate AND
       A.FromDate < S.ToDate AND S.ToDate < A.ToDate
-- Case 4
UNION ALL
SELECT S.SSN, Amount, DNumber, A.FromDate, A.ToDate
FROM   Salary S, Affiliation A
WHERE  S.SSN = A.SSN AND A.FromDate > S.FromDate AND A.ToDate < S.ToDate
```

The above query assumes that there are no duplicate rows in the tables: at each point in time an employee has one salary and one affiliation. The UNION ALL is used since the query does not generate duplicates and this is more efficient than using UNION. It is worth noting that the result of this query must be coalesced.

A temporal join can be written in a single statement using either a CASE statement or functions. Suppose that in SQL Server we write two functions MinDate and MaxDate as follows.

```
CREATE FUNCTION MinDate(@one DATE, @two DATE)
        RETURNS DATE
BEGIN
        RETURN CASE WHEN @one < @two THEN @one ELSE @two END
END
CREATE FUNCTION MaxDate(@one DATE, @two DATE)
        RETURNS DATE
BEGIN
        RETURN CASE WHEN @one > @two THEN @one ELSE @two END
END
```

These functions return, respectively, the minimum and the maximum of their two arguments. They allow us to write the temporal join as follows.

```
SELECT S.SSN, Amount, DNumber, dbo.MaxDate(S.FromDate, A.FromDate) AS FromDate,
        dbo.MinDate(S.ToDate, A.ToDate) AS ToDate
FROM    Salary S, Affiliation A
WHERE   S.SSN = A.SSN AND
        dbo.MaxDate(S.FromDate, A.FromDate) < dbo.MinDate(S.ToDate, A.ToDate)
```

The two functions are used in the SELECT clause for constructing the intersection of the corresponding validity periods. The condition in the WHERE clause ensures that the two validity periods overlap.

Temporal Difference

The difference is expressed in SQL using either EXCEPT or NOT EXISTS. Suppose that we want to list the employees who work on a single project. If the table WorksOn is nontemporal, this can be expressed as follows

```
SELECT W1.EmployeeKey
FROM   WorksOn W1
WHERE NOT EXISTS (
        SELECT *
        FROM   WorksOn W2
        WHERE W1.EmployeeKey = W2.EmployeeKey AND
              W1.PNumber <> W2.PNumber )
```

Now suppose that we want to find out the periods of time when employees worked on a single project. Expressing a temporal difference in SQL requires the four possible cases shown in Fig. 11.6 to be considered. These cases show

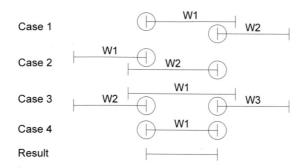

Fig. 11.6 Various cases for temporal difference

an employee working on one, two, or three projects W1, W2, and W3 such
that she is not involved in any other project.

The temporal difference can be expressed in SQL as follows.

```
-- Case 1
SELECT W1.EmployeeKey, W1.FromDate, W2.FromDate
FROM   WorksOn W1, WorksOn W2
WHERE  W1.EmployeeKey = W2.EmployeeKey
       W1.FromDate < W2.FromDate AND W2.FromDate < W1.ToDate AND
       NOT EXISTS (
       SELECT *
       FROM   WorksOn W3
       WHERE  W1.EmployeeKey = W3.EmployeeKey AND
              W1.FromDate < W3.ToDate AND W3.FromDate < W2.FromDate )
UNION
-- Case 2
SELECT W1.EmployeeKey, W1.ToDate, W2.ToDate
FROM   WorksOn W1, WorksOn W2
WHERE  W1.EmployeeKey = W2.EmployeeKey
       W2.FromDate < W1.ToDate AND W1.ToDate < W2.ToDate AND
       NOT EXISTS (
       SELECT *
       FROM   WorksOn W3
       WHERE  W1.EmployeeKey = W3.EmployeeKey
              W1.ToDate < W3.ToDate AND W3.FromDate < W2.ToDate )
UNION
-- Case 3
SELECT W1.EmployeeKey, W2.ToDate, W3.FromDate
FROM   WorksOn W1, WorksOn W2, WorksOn W3
WHERE  W1.EmployeeKey = W2.EmployeeKey AND
       W1.EmployeeKey = W3.EmployeeKey AND
       W2.ToDate < W3.FromDate AND W1.FromDate < W2.ToDate AND
       W3.FromDate < W1.ToDate AND NOT EXISTS (
       SELECT *
       FROM   WorksOn W3
       WHERE  W1.EmployeeKey = W3.EmployeeKey AND
              W2.ToDate < W3.ToDate AND W3.FromDate < W3.FromDate )
UNION
```

```
-- Case 4
SELECT EmployeeKey, FromDate, ToDate
FROM   WorksOn W1
WHERE  NOT EXISTS (
         SELECT *
         FROM   WorksOn W3
         WHERE  W1.EmployeeKey = W3.EmployeeKey AND
                W1.FromDate < W3.ToDate AND W3.FromDate < W1.ToDate )
```

The above query assumes that the table WorksOn is coalesced. Furthermore, its result must be coalesced.

Temporal Aggregation

SQL provides aggregate functions such as SUM, COUNT, MIN, MAX, and AVG. These are used for answering queries such as "compute the maximum salary" or "compute the maximum salary by department." The temporal version of these queries requires a three-step process: (1) split the time line into periods of time during which all values are constant, (2) compute the aggregation over these periods, and (3) coalesce the result.

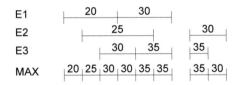

Fig. 11.7 Evolution of the maximum salary

Suppose that we want to compute the evolution over time of the maximum salary. Figure 11.7 shows a diagram where table Salary has three employees E1, E2, and E3, as well as the result of the temporal maximum. Computing the temporal maximum in SQL is done as follows.

```
WITH SalChanges(Day) AS (
         SELECT    FromDate
         FROM      Salary
         UNION
         SELECT    ToDate
         FROM      Salary ),
     SalPeriods(FromDate, ToDate) AS (
         SELECT    P1.Day, P2.Day
         FROM      SalChanges P1, SalChanges P2
         WHERE     P1.Day < P2.Day AND NOT EXISTS (
                   SELECT *
                   FROM    SalChanges P3
                   WHERE  P1.Day < P3.Day AND P3.Day < P2.Day ) ),
     TempMax(MaxSalary, FromDate, ToDate) AS (
         SELECT    MAX(Amount), P.FromDate, P.ToDate
```

```
FROM      Salary S, SalPeriods P
WHERE     S.FromDate <= P.FromDate AND P.ToDate <= S.ToDate
GROUP BY P.FromDate, P.ToDate )
-- Coalescing the table TempMax above
SELECT DISTINCT F.MaxSalary, F.FromDate, L.ToDate
FROM   TempMax F, TempMax L
WHERE ...
```

Table SalChanges gathers the dates at which a salary change occurred, while table SalPeriods constructs the periods from such dates. Table TempMax computes the temporal maximum on these periods. Finally, table TempMax is coalesced in the main query as explained for the temporal projection above. We refer to the bibliographic section at the end of the chapter for references that show how to compute more complex temporal aggregations.

Temporal Division

The division is needed to answer queries such as "List the employees who work on *all* projects controlled by the department to which they are affiliated." As we have seen in Sect. 2.4.3, since SQL does not provide the division operation, the above query should be rephrased as follows: "List the employees such that there is no project controlled by the department to which they are affiliated on which they do not work." The latter query can be expressed in SQL with two nested NOT EXISTS predicates as follows.

```
SELECT SSN
FROM   Affiliation A
WHERE NOT EXISTS (
        SELECT *
        FROM   Controls C
        WHERE A.DNumber = C.DNumber AND NOT EXISTS (
                SELECT *
                FROM   WorksOn W
                WHERE C.PNumber = W.PNumber AND A.SSN = W.SSN ) )
```

Consider now the temporal version of the above query. As in the case of temporal aggregation, a three-step process is needed: (1) split the time line into periods of time during which all values are constant, (2) compute the division over these periods, and (3) coalesce the result.

Four cases arise depending on whether the tables Affiliation, Controls, and WorksOn are temporal or not. Here we consider the case when Controls and WorksOn are temporal but Affiliation is not. The bibliographic section at the end of the chapter provides further references that study the other cases.

Figure 11.8 shows possible values in the three tables and the result of the temporal division. At the top it is shown that employee E is affiliated to department D; C1 and C2 represent two rows of Controls relating department D with projects P1 and P2; and W1, W2 represent two rows of WorksOn relating employee E with projects P1 and P2. Finally, Result shows the periods for which the division must be calculated and the corresponding result (where ✓

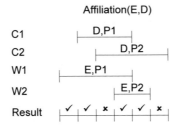

Fig. 11.8 Periods in which employee E works on all projects controlled by the department D to which she is affiliated

represents true and ✗ represents false). Notice that, in this example, employees may work on projects controlled by departments which are not the one to which they are affiliated, as shown in W1 when employee E starts to work on project P1. The query computing the temporal division is as follows.

```
WITH ProjChanges(SSN, Day) AS (
        SELECT SSN, FromDate
        FROM    Affiliation A, Controls C
        WHERE A.DNumber = C.DNumber
        UNION
        SELECT SSN, ToDate
        FROM    Affiliation A, Controls C
        WHERE A.DNumber = C.DNumber
        UNION
        SELECT SSN, FromDate
        FROM    WorksOn
        UNION
        SELECT SSN, ToDate
        FROM    WorksOn ),
     ProjPeriods(SSN, FromDate, ToDate) AS (
        SELECT P1.SSN, P1.Day, P2.Day
        FROM    ProjChanges P1, ProjChanges P2
        WHERE P1.SSN = P2.SSN AND P1.Day < P2.Day AND NOT EXISTS (
                SELECT *
                FROM    ProjChanges P3
                WHERE P1.SSN = P3.SSN AND P1.Day < P3.Day AND
                        P3.Day < P2.Day ) ),
     TempDiv(SSN, FromDate, ToDate) AS (
        SELECT DISTINCT P.SSN, P.FromDate, P.ToDate
        FROM    ProjPeriods P, Affiliation A
        WHERE P.SSN = A.SSN AND NOT EXISTS (
                SELECT *
                FROM    Controls C
                WHERE A.DNumber = C.DNumber AND
                        C.FromDate <= P.FromDate AND P.ToDate <= C.ToDate
                AND NOT EXISTS (
                SELECT *
                FROM    WorksOn W
                WHERE C.PNumber = W.PNumber AND
```

```
                          P.SSN = W.SSN AND
                          W.FromDate <= P.FromDate AND
                          P.ToDate <= W.ToDate ) ) )
-- Coalescing the table TempDiv above
SELECT DISTINCT SSN, FromDate, ToDate
FROM   TempDiv F, TempDiv L
WHERE ...
```

Table ProjChanges extracts for each employee the day when her department starts or finishes controlling a project, as well as the day when she starts or finishes working on a project. Table ProjPeriods constructs the periods from the above days, while table TempDiv computes the division on these periods. Notice how the query computing the latter table generalizes the query given at the beginning of this section computing the nontemporal version of the division. Finally, the main query coalesces the TempDiv table.

11.2 Conceptual Design of Temporal Data Warehouses

In this section, we present the temporal extension of the MultiDim model. The graphical notation of the model is described in Appendix A. The temporal features of the model allow us to represent changes at the *instance level*, such as adding new products or changing the association between products and categories. Changes at the *schema level*, such as adding a new level to a hierarchy or deleting measures, are *not* considered here, since they require schema versioning mechanisms, which are covered from Sect. 11.7 on.

11.2.1 Time Data Types

Temporal databases associate a **temporal extent** with real-world phenomena. This temporal extent may represent either events or states. **Events** correspond to phenomena occurring at a particular instant, for example the time at which a sale occurred. **States** represent phenomena that span time, such as the duration of a project. The **time data types** shown in Fig. 11.9 are used to specify the temporal extent of real-world phenomena.

An Instant denotes a single point in time according to a specific granularity. It has no duration. An instant may take a special value **now**, which indicates the current time. Instants are used to represent events.

A Period denotes a set of successive instants enclosed between two instants. Periods are used to represent states.

SimpleTime is a generic type that generalizes the Instant and Period data types. It is an abstract type and thus, when a value associated with SimpleTime is created, the specific subtype (either Instant or Period) must be

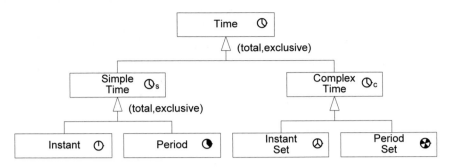

Fig. 11.9 Time data types

specified. A SimpleTime can represent, for example, the time (with a granularity of day) at which an event such as a conference occurs, where one-day conferences are represented by an Instant and other conferences, spanning two or more days, are represented by a Period.

An InstantSet is a set of instants, which can represent, for example, the instants at which car accidents have occurred at a particular location.

A PeriodSet is a set of periods that represent discontinuous durations, as in the case of a project that was interrupted during a lapse of time.

A ComplexTime denotes any heterogeneous set of temporal values that may include instants and periods.

Finally, Time is the most generic time data type, meaning "this element has a temporal extent" without any commitment to a specific time data type. It is an abstract type that can be used, for example, to represent the lifespan of projects, where it may be either a Period or a PeriodSet.

We allow empty temporal values, that is, values that represent an empty set of instants. This is needed, in particular, to express the fact that the intersection of two temporal values is empty.

11.2.2 Synchronization Relationships

Synchronization relationships[1] specify how two temporal values relate to each other. They allow one to determine, for example, whether two events occur simultaneously or whether one precedes the other. These relationships generalize the well-known Allen's temporal predicates for periods and are defined on the basis of the concepts of exterior, interior, and boundary. Intuitively, the **exterior** of a temporal value is composed of all the instants of the underlying time frame that do not belong to the temporal value. The

---

[1] These are usually called *temporal relationships*, but here we use this term for relationships that have temporal support.

interior of a temporal value is composed of all its instants that do not belong to the boundary. The **boundary** of a temporal value is the interface between its interior and exterior and it is defined for the various time data types as follows. An instant has an empty boundary. The boundary of a period consists of its start and end instants. The boundary of a ComplexTime value is (recursively) defined as the union of the boundaries of its components that do not intersect with other components.

We describe next the most commonly used synchronization relationships; the associated icons are given in Fig. 11.10.

⊢⊣ Meets	⊢⊣ Overlaps/Intersects
⊢⊣ Contains/Inside	⊢⊣ Covers/CoveredBy
⊔ Equals	⊢⊣ Disjoint
⊢ Starts	⊣ Finishes
⟵ Precedes	⟶ Succeeds

Fig. 11.10 Icons for the various synchronization relationships

Meets: Two temporal values meet if they intersect in an instant but their interiors do not. Note that two temporal values may intersect in an instant but not meet.

Overlaps: Two temporal values overlap if their interiors intersect and their intersection is not equal to either of them.

Contains/Inside: Contains and Inside are symmetric predicates: a Contains b if and only if b Inside a. A temporal value contains another one if the interior of the former includes all instants of the latter.

Covers/CoveredBy: These are symmetric predicates: a Covers b if and only if b CoveredBy a. A temporal value covers another one if the former includes all instants of the latter. Thus, the former contains the latter but without the restriction that the boundaries of the temporal extents do not intersect. As a particular case, the two temporal values may be equal.

Disjoint/Intersects: Disjoint and Intersects are inverse predicates: when one applies, the other does not. Two temporal values are disjoint if they do not share any instant.

Equals: Two temporal values are equal if every instant of the first value belongs also to the second and conversely.

Starts/Finishes: A temporal value starts another one if the first instants of the two values are equal. Similarly, a temporal value finishes another one if the last instants of the two values are equal.

Precedes/Succeeds: A temporal value precedes another one if the last instant of the former is before the first instant of the latter. Similarly, a temporal value succeeds another one if the first instant of the former is later than the last instant of the latter.

11.2.3 A Conceptual Model for Temporal Data Warehouses

We now extend the MultiDim model that we have seen in Chap. 4 with temporal features. The model provides support for the temporality types we have seen in Sect. 11.1, namely, **valid time** (VT) and **transaction time** (TT). Furthermore, it adds the notion of **lifespan** (LS), which captures the time during which an object or relationship exists. For example, a lifespan can be used to represent the duration of a project or the duration during which an employee has worked on a project. The lifespan of an object or relationship may be seen as the valid time of the related fact stating that the object or relationship exists. Therefore, we use valid time for attributes and lifespan for objects and relationships as a whole.

These temporality types can be combined for a single schema element, for example, a level can have an associated lifespan and a transaction time. Valid time and lifespan are typically used to analyze measures taking into account changes in dimension data. On the other hand, transaction time is used in traceability applications, for example for fraud detection, where the time when changes to data occurred are required for analysis purposes.

Even though most real-world phenomena vary over time, storing their evolution in time may not be necessary for an application. Therefore, the choice of the data elements for which the data warehouse keeps track of their evolution in time depends on application requirements and the availability of this information in source systems. The MultiDim model allows users to specify which schema elements require temporal support.

Figure 11.11 shows the conceptual schema of the temporal Northwind data warehouse. It assumes that changes in data related to products and employees are kept for analysis purposes, as indicated by the various pictograms included in the schema. On the other hand, it assumes that we are not interested in keeping track of changes to customer data, since this dimension does not include any temporal support. As can be seen in the figure, the MultiDim model allows both temporal and conventional (nontemporal) levels, attributes, parent-child relationships, hierarchies, and dimensions. The definitions of the conventional elements of the model remain the same as those presented in Chap. 4.

A **temporal level** keeps track of the lifespan of its members. The schema in Fig. 11.11 includes three temporal levels (indicated by the temporal symbols to the left of the level name): Product, Category, and Employee. These levels are used to track changes in a member as a whole, for example inserting or deleting a product or a category. Notice that the temporal symbols for the Product and Category levels are different. The ✪ symbol represents a noncontinuous lifespan; for example, a product may cease to be sold, and return to the catalog later. On the other hand, the ◐ symbol represents a

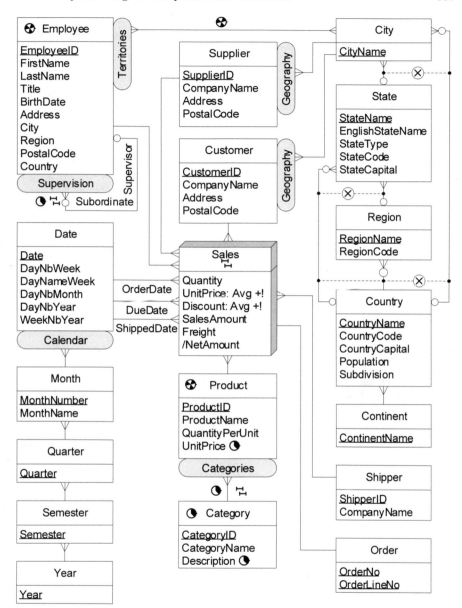

Fig. 11.11 Conceptual schema of the temporal Northwind data warehouse

continuous lifespan; for example, a closed category cannot be sold again. The usual levels without temporality are called **conventional levels**.

A **temporal attribute** keeps track of the changes in its values and the time when they occur. For instance, the temporality for UnitPrice in the

Product level indicates that the history of changes in this attribute is kept. As shown in Fig. 11.12, a level may be temporal independently of the fact that it has temporal attributes.

Fig. 11.12 Types of temporal support for a level. (**a**) Temporal level; (**b**) Temporal level with a temporal attribute; (**c**) Conventional level with a temporal attribute

Some temporal models impose constraints on temporal attributes and the lifespan of their corresponding levels. A typical constraint is that the valid time of the attribute values must be covered by the lifespan of their level. The MultiDim model does not impose such constraints a priori. This allows one to model, for example, the case where a product does not belong to a store's catalog but it is on sale on a trial basis. For this product, the valid time of its temporal attributes may not be within the product's lifespan. On the other hand, if required, temporal integrity constraints may be explicitly defined using the synchronization relationships given in Sect. 11.2.2.

We assume time-invariant (or permanent) identifiers for members. In Fig. 11.12, ProductID is the identifier of the Product level and it is assumed that this attribute does not change. On the contrary, if the attribute values change and we must keep track of their evolution, we should use a new surrogate identifier for the level and make ProductID a temporal attribute.

A **temporal parent-child relationship** keeps track of the time frame associated with the links relating a child and a parent member. For example, in Fig. 11.11 the temporal symbol in the relationship linking Product and Category indicates that the assignments of products to categories may evolve in time and that this evolution will be stored.

Recall that **cardinalities** in parent-child relationships constrain the minimum and the maximum number of members in one level that can be related to a member in another level. There are two possible interpretations of cardinalities in temporal parent-child relationships. The **instant cardinality** is valid at every time instant, whereas the **lifespan cardinality** is valid over the member's entire lifespan. In the MultiDim model, the cardinalities shown in the schema represent instant cardinalities, while lifespan cardinalities are represented as annotations to the schema to avoid overloading them. Thus, in Fig. 11.11, the instant cardinality between Product and Category levels is one-to-many. This indicates that a product belongs to only one category at any time instant, but may belong to many categories over its lifespan, that is, its lifespan cardinality will be many-to-many. On the other hand, if the lifespan cardinality is many-to-one, that would mean that a product is assigned to a single category throughout its lifespan.

A **temporal hierarchy** is a hierarchy that has at least one temporal level or one temporal parent-child relationship. Thus, temporal hierarchies can combine temporal and conventional levels. Similarly, a **temporal dimension** is a dimension that has at least one temporal hierarchy. The usual dimensions and hierarchies without temporality are called **conventional dimensions** and **conventional hierarchies**.

Two temporal levels related in a hierarchy define a **synchronization constraint**, which we studed in Sect. 11.2.2. To represent them, we use the pictograms shown in Fig. 11.10. By default we assume the overlaps synchronization constraint, which indicates that the lifespans of a child member and its parent member overlap. For example, in Fig. 11.11 the lifespan of each product overlaps the lifespan of its corresponding category, that is, at each point in time a valid product belongs to a valid category. As we shall see in Sect. 11.2.4, other synchronization relationships may exist.

A **temporal fact** links one or more temporal levels and may involve a synchronization relationship: this is indicated by an icon in the fact. For example, the temporal fact Sales in Fig. 11.11 relates two temporal levels: Product and Employee. The overlaps synchronization icon in the fact indicates that a product is related to an employee in an instance of the fact provided that their lifespans overlap. If a synchronization icon is not included in a fact, there is no particular synchronization constraint on its instances.

A **temporal measure** keeps track of the changes in its values and the time when they occur. For instance, in Fig. 11.18a, the temporality for the measure InterestRate indicates that the history of changes in this measure is kept. As seen in the figure, a fact may be temporal independently of whether it has temporal measures.

Notice that in the MultiDim model, the temporal support for dimensions, hierarchies, levels, and measures differs from the traditional temporal support for facts, where the latter are related explicitly to a time dimension.

In the next section we elaborate on the temporal components of the MultiDim model. For simplicity, we only discuss valid time and lifespan; the results may be generalized to transaction time.

11.2.4 Temporal Hierarchies

Given two related levels in a hierarchy, the levels, the relationship between them, or both may be temporal. We study these situations next.

Figure 11.13a shows an example of temporal levels associated with a conventional relationship. In this case, the relationship only keeps *current* links

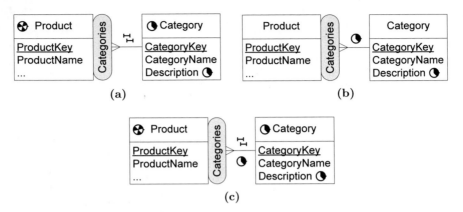

Fig. 11.13 Various cases of temporal support for relationships, depending on whether the levels and/or the relationship are temporal or not.

between products and categories. To ensure correctness of roll-up and drill-down operations, a product may be related to a category provided that both are currently valid. As a consequence, the lifespans of a child member and its associated parent member must overlap, as indicated by the icon of the synchronization relationship in the figure. By default we assume the **overlaps** synchronization relationship between related temporal levels. Nevertheless, other synchronization relationships may be specified. For example, if a product is related to a single category throughout its lifespan, then the lifespan of a product must be covered by the lifespan of its associated category.

Consider now Fig. 11.13b where a temporal relationship links conventional levels. In this case, the levels keep only *current* members while the relationship keeps the history of links between them. To avoid dangling references, upon deletion of a member of the related levels all its links must also be deleted. This means that if a category is deleted, then all the history of assignments of products to that category will also be deleted. The situation is similar if a product is deleted. If we need to keep the *complete* history of the links, then the levels should also be temporal, as explained next.

Figure 11.13c shows a temporal relationship relating temporal levels. To ensure correctness of roll-up and drill-down operations, the lifespan of a relationship instance must be covered by the intersection of the lifespans of the participating objects. This means that if a product and a category are related by a relationship then both the product and the category must exist throughout the lifespan of the relationship. Furthermore, the instant cardinalities imply that a child member must be related to a parent member throughout the child's lifespan, and that a parent member must have assigned at least one child member throughout the parent's lifespan. This means that the lifespan of a child member is equal to the union of the lifespans of all its links to a parent member, and the lifespan of a parent member is equal to the union of the lifespans of all its links to a child member.

11.2.5 Temporal Facts

In temporal data warehouses, a fact may be related to one or several temporal levels. Furthermore, a fact is typically linked to a time dimension, which associates a time frame to the fact instances and their measures. In this case, synchronization constraints may restrict the time frame of a fact instance and the lifespans of the related members.

Consider the schema in Fig. 11.11, with two temporal dimensions **Product** and **Employee**. Furthermore, the **Sales** fact is related to the **Date** dimension through three roles **OrderDate**, **DueDate**, and **ShippedDate**. In this case, a constraint could state that a product can be ordered only if it is currently valid. This would imply that, for each fact instance, the date of the associated **Date** member is included in the lifespan of the associated product. A similar constraint could state that an employee can only be involved in a sale during her lifespan. On the other hand, it may be the case that when a product is discontinued all its orders which are not yet delivered should be processed. In this case, the due date and the shipped date of a sale could be later than the end of the lifespan of the associated product.

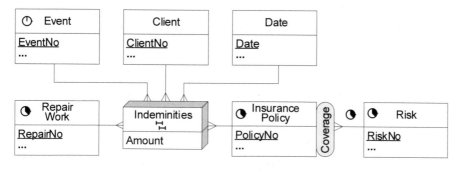

Fig. 11.14 Schema for analysis of indemnities paid by an insurance company

Consider now the schema in Fig. 11.14, used by an insurance company to analyze the indemnities paid for insurance policies covering various risks. The lifespan in **InsurancePolicy** states the validity of the policy, the lifespan in **Event** states the instant at which the event occurred, and the lifespan in **RepairWork** states the period of time when the work was done. Finally, the **Date** dimension associated with the fact states the date at which the payment corresponding to an indemnity is made. A typical constraint states that there is an indemnity for an event provided it occurred within the lifespan of its related insurance policy. However, a client may decide to terminate an insurance policy after an event has occurred; therefore the repair work and the payment of indemnities would be done after the end of the policy.

11.3 Logical Design of Temporal Data Warehouses

We now explain how a conceptual temporal multidimensional schema is translated into a relational schema. This translation is based on the rules given in Sect. 5.3. As an example, Fig. 11.15 shows the relational representation of the temporal Northwind conceptual schema given in Fig. 11.11.

Rule 1: A level L, provided it is not related to a fact by a one-to-one relationship, is mapped to a table T_L that contains all conventional attributes of the level. A surrogate key *must* be added to the table as primary key to cope with temporal attributes and temporal relationships.

If the level is temporal, the mapping of its lifespan depends on its type (see Fig. 11.9). Events (that is Instant or InstantSet) are represented with a single attribute AtDate, while states (that is Period or PeriodSet) are represented with two attributes FromDate and ToDate. For Instant or Period, the attribute(s) are added to the table T_L, while for InstantSet or PeriodSet, the attribute(s) are placed in an additional table $T_{L_{LS}}$, which also contains the primary key of the level.

A temporal *attribute* A of a level L is mapped to a table T_{L_A} storing the evolution of its values. This table contains the primary key of the level and either an attribute AtDate or two attributes FromDate and ToDate depending on whether its temporality represent events or states. The primary key of T_{L_A} is composed of the primary key of the level and either AtDate or FromDate.

Note that additional attributes will be added to the table T_L when mapping relationships using Rule 3 below.

Rule 2: A fact F is mapped to a table T_F that includes all conventional measures of the fact. A surrogate key *must* be added to the table to cope with temporal measures. The mapping of temporal measures is done in a similar way to temporal attributes above using the surrogate key of the fact. Note that additional attributes will be added to this table when mapping relationships using Rule 3 below.

Rule 3: A conventional relationship between either a fact F and a dimension level L, or between dimension levels L_P and L_C (standing for the parent and child levels, respectively), can be mapped in three different ways, depending on its cardinalities:

Rule 3a: If the relationship is one-to-one, the table corresponding to the fact (T_F) or to the child level (T_C) is extended with all the attributes of the dimension level or the parent level, respectively.

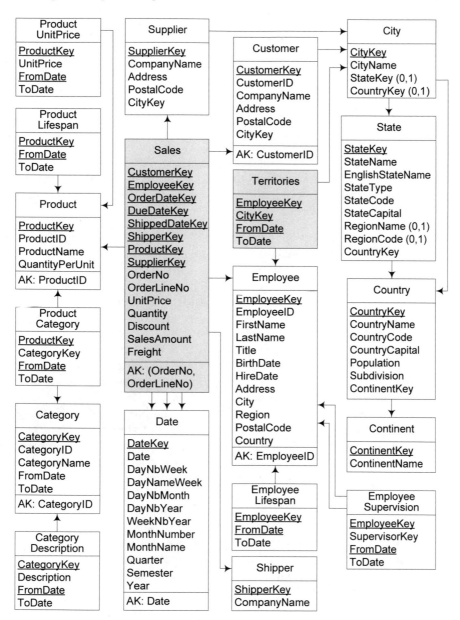

Fig. 11.15 Relational schema of the temporal Northwind data warehouse in Fig. 11.11

Rule 3b: If the relationship is one-to-many, the table corresponding to the fact (T_F) or to the child level (T_C) is extended with the surrogate key of the table corresponding to the dimension level (T_L) or the parent level (T_P), respectively, that is, there is a foreign key in the fact or child table pointing to the other table.

Rule 3c: If the relationship is many-to-many, a new bridge table T_B is created, containing as attributes the surrogate keys of the tables corresponding to the fact (T_F) and the dimension level (T_L), or the parent (T_P) and child levels (T_C), respectively. The key of the table is the combination of the two surrogate keys. If the relationship has a distributing attribute, an additional attribute is added to the table.

If the relationship is temporal, we can only use Rule 3c above independently of the cardinalities. In addition, two attributes FromDate and ToDate must be added to the table T_B, and the key of the table is composed of the combination of the surrogate keys and FromDate.

The above rules suppose that the temporal features have a day granularity and thus, the columns AtDate, FromDate, and ToDate are of type Date. If the granularity were timestamp instead, then the corresponding columns are called AtTime, FromTime, and ToTime, and they are of type Timestamp. Notice also that the above rules have not considered the synchronization constraints present in the schema. As we will see in Sect. 11.4.3, a set of triggers must ensure that these constraints are satisfied.

For example, as shown in Fig. 11.15, the level Product is mapped to the table with the same name, its temporal attribute UnitPrice is mapped to the table ProductUnitPrice, and its lifespan is stored in table ProductLifespan, since, as indicated by the corresponding icon in Fig. 11.11, the lifespan of products is not continuous. On the other hand, the lifespan of categories is stored in the attributes FromDate and ToDate of table Category, since, as indicated by the corresponding icon, the lifespan of categories is continuous. Regarding temporal parent-child relationships, table ProductCategory represents the relationship between products and categories, while EmployeeSupervision represents the relationship between employees and their supervisors.

As we have seen in this section, the relational representation of temporal data warehouses produces a significant number of tables, which may cause performance issues owing to the multiple join operations required for reassembling this information. In addition, as we will show in the next section, the resulting relational schema has to be supplemented with many integrity constraints that encode the underlying semantics of time-varying data.

11.4 Implementation Considerations

11.4.1 Period Encoding

As we have seen in Sect. 11.1, a closed-open representation of periods is commonly used for facilitating the manipulation of temporal information in standard SQL. For temporal data warehouses, this concerns (1) the lifespan of levels and relationships, (2) the values of temporal attributes, and (3) the temporal extent of facts that represent states.

For example, in Fig. 11.15, the periods in tables ProductLifespan, ProductUnitPrice, and ProductCategory will be encoded using an closed-open representation. Notice that even if the Sales fact is related by several roles to the Date dimension, the fact represents events. On the other hand, consider the example given in Fig. 11.16a, which is used to analyze the balance of bank accounts. In this case, the Balance fact represents states, as indicated by the roles FromDate and ToDate. Thus, the corresponding table Balance shown in Fig. 11.16b will use a closed-open representation for the periods defined by the columns FromDateKey and ToDateKey.

11.4.2 Tables for Temporal Roll-Up

To enable temporal roll-up operations, a set of tables associated with each granularity of the time dimension must be defined. For example, in Fig. 11.11, the granularities of the Date dimension are day, month, quarter, semester, and year. The tables associated with these granularities are as follows.

```
CREATE TABLE Month(Year, MonthNumber, FromDate, ToDate, NoDays) AS
        SELECT    Year, MonthNumber, MIN(Date), DateAdd(month, 1, MIN(Date)),
                  DateDiff(day, MIN(Date), DateAdd(month, 1, MIN(Date)))
        FROM      Date
        GROUP BY Year, MonthNumber;
CREATE TABLE Quarter(Year, Quarter, FromDate, ToDate, NoDays) AS
        SELECT    Year, Quarter, MIN(Date), DateAdd(month, 3, MIN(Date)),
                  DateDiff(day, MIN(Date), DateAdd(month, 3, MIN(Date)))
        FROM      Date
        GROUP BY Year, Quarter;
CREATE TABLE Semester(Year, Semester, FromDate, ToDate, NoDays) AS
        SELECT    Year, Semester, MIN(Date), DateAdd(month, 6, MIN(Date)),
                  DateDiff(day, MIN(Date), DateAdd(month, 6, MIN(Date)))
        FROM      Date
        GROUP BY Year, Semester;
CREATE TABLE Year(Year, FromDate, ToDate, NoDays) AS
        SELECT    Year, MIN(Date), DateAdd(year, 1, MIN(Date)),
                  DateDiff(day, MIN(Date), DateAdd(year, 1, MIN(Date)))
        FROM      Date
        GROUP BY Year;
```

These tables compute, for each granularity, the beginning and end dates in a closed-open representation as well as the number of days in the period. Such tables are needed to roll-up measures through the time dimension. Note that these tables can be defined as views to ensure that when the Date is updated, e.g., to expand the underlying time frame of the data warehouse, they contain up-to-date information. However, declaring these tables as views will make more complex the work of the query optimizer when executing OLAP queries.

11.4.3 Integrity Constraints

The tables that implement a temporal data warehouse must be complemented with multiple integrity constraints that enforce the inherent semantics of time. As we have seen in Chap. 2, current relational DBMSs provide a set of predefined integrity constraints such as not null attributes, keys, and referential integrity. All other integrity constraints are typically implemented using triggers. In this section, we discuss the issue of enforcing temporal integrity constraints using SQL Server as the target implementation platform.

Consider the tables for the Product dimension in Fig. 11.15, that is, the tables Product, ProductLifespan, ProductUnitPrice, ProductCategory, Category, and CategoryDescription. Several constraints must be defined on the above tables to verify the temporal constraints. We give below the constraints for products; similar constraints must be enforced for categories.

```
ALTER TABLE ProductLifespan ADD CONSTRAINT AK_ProductKey_ToDate
        UNIQUE (ProductKey, ToDate);
ALTER TABLE ProductLifespan ADD CONSTRAINT ValidPeriod
        CHECK (FromDate < ToDate);
```

The first constraint complements the primary key of the table to ensure that in the lifespan of a product there are no two tuples with the same value of ToDate. The second constraint ensures that the periods are well constructed. In addition, we need the following trigger to ensure that all periods defining the lifespan of a product are disjoint.

```
CREATE TRIGGER ProductLifespan_OverlappingPeriods ON ProductLifespan
AFTER INSERT, UPDATE AS
IF EXISTS (
      SELECT *
      FROM   INSERTED P1
      WHERE 1 < (
              SELECT COUNT(*)
              FROM   ProductLifespan P2
              WHERE P1.ProductKey = P2.ProductKey AND
                    P1.FromDate < P2.ToDate AND P2.FromDate < P1.ToDate ) )
BEGIN
      RAISERROR ('Overlapping periods in lifespan of product', 1, 1)
      ROLLBACK TRANSACTION
END
```

The condition in the **WHERE** clause ensures that two periods denoted by **P1** and **P2** for the same product overlap. Since this condition is satisfied if **P1** and **P2** are the same tuple, the value of **COUNT(*)** in the inner query must be greater than 1 to ensure that two *distinct* periods overlap.

Suppose now that a constraint states that the time frame of the temporal attribute **UnitPrice** must be included in the lifespan of **Product**, or in other words, the evolution of the attribute values is only kept while a product is in the catalog. The following trigger ensures this constraint.

```
CREATE TRIGGER ProductUnitPrice_PeriodInLifespan ON ProductUnitPrice
AFTER INSERT, UPDATE AS
IF EXISTS (
      SELECT *
      FROM   INSERTED P1
      WHERE  NOT EXISTS (
             SELECT *
             FROM   ProductLifespan P2
             WHERE  P1.ProductKey = P2.ProductKey AND
                    P2.FromDate <= P1.FromDate AND
                    P1.ToDate <= P2.ToDate ) )
BEGIN
      RAISERROR ('Period of unit price is not contained in lifespan of product', 1, 1)
      ROLLBACK TRANSACTION
END
```

The condition in the **WHERE** clause ensures that the period of the attribute value denoted by **P1** is included in the lifespan of its product denoted by **P2**.

As said in Sect. 11.2.4, in temporal parent-child relationships the lifespan of a relationship instance must be covered by the intersection of the lifespans of the participating members. The following triggers ensure this constraint for the relationship between products and categories.

```
CREATE TRIGGER ProductCategory_LifespanInProduct_1 ON ProductCategory
AFTER INSERT, UPDATE AS
IF EXISTS (
      SELECT *
      FROM   INSERTED PC
      WHERE  NOT EXISTS (
             SELECT *
             FROM   ProductLifespan P
             WHERE  PC.ProductKey = P.ProductKey AND
                    P.FromDate <= PC.FromDate AND PC.ToDate <= P.ToDate ) )
BEGIN
      RAISERROR ('Lifespan of relationship is not contained in lifespan of product', 1, 1)
      ROLLBACK TRANSACTION
END
CREATE TRIGGER ProductCategory_LifespanInProduct_2 ON ProductLifespan
AFTER UPDATE, DELETE AS
IF EXISTS (
      SELECT *
      FROM   ProductCategory PC
      WHERE  PC.ProductKey IN ( SELECT ProductKey FROM DELETED )
```

```
                    AND NOT EXISTS (
                    SELECT *
                    FROM    ProductLifespan P
                    WHERE  PC.ProductKey = P.ProductKey AND
                              P.FromDate <= PC.FromDate AND PC.ToDate <= P.ToDate ) )
BEGIN
            RAISERROR ('Lifespan of relationship is not contained in lifespan of product', 1, 1)
            ROLLBACK TRANSACTION
END
```

Similar triggers should also be added for categories.

To ensure correctness of roll-up and drill-down operations, in temporal hierarchies a child member must be related to a parent member throughout the child's lifespan. This amounts to saying that the lifespan of a child member is equal to the union of the lifespans of its links to all parent members. In the case of products, we can define a view ProductLifespanLinks that computes the periods during which a product is associated with any category by performing a temporal projection of the table ProductCategory as shown in Sect. 11.1. Then, the following query displays the products whose lifespan is not equal to the union of the lifespans of their links.

```
SELECT P.ProductKey
FROM    ProductLifespan P
WHERE  NOT EXISTS (
            SELECT *
            FROM    ProductLifespanLinks L
            WHERE  P.FromDate = L.FromDate AND P.ToDate = L.ToDate )
UNION
SELECT P.ProductKey
FROM    ProductLifespanLinks L
WHERE  NOT EXISTS (
            SELECT *
            FROM    ProductLifespan P
            WHERE  P.FromDate = L.FromDate AND P.ToDate = L.ToDate )
```

Since the lifespan of products is discontinuous, the above query ensures that every period composing the lifespan is found in the links and vice versa.

Synchronization constraints restrict the lifespan of related objects. Consider in Fig. 11.11 the synchronization constraint between Product and Category, which checks that the lifespans of a product and its associated category overlap. A trigger that ensures this constraint is given next.

```
CREATE TRIGGER ProductOverlapsCategory ON ProductCategory
    AFTER INSERT, UPDATE AS
IF EXISTS (
    SELECT *
    FROM    INSERTED PC
    WHERE  NOT EXISTS (
                SELECT *
                FROM    ProductLifespan P, CategoryLifespan C
                WHERE  P.ProductKey = PC.ProductKey AND
                          C.CategoryKey = PC.CategoryKey AND
```

                              P.FromDate < C.ToDate AND C.FromDate < P.ToDate))
BEGIN
              RAISERROR ('Lifespans of product and category do not overlap', 1, 1)
              ROLLBACK TRANSACTION
END

Facts associated with states may impose additional constraints. Consider
the example given in Fig. 11.16a, used to analyze the balance of bank accounts. Ensuring that at each point in time a bank account has only one
balance amounts to saying that for a given account there cannot be two facts
with overlapping periods. The following trigger ensures this constraint.

```
CREATE TRIGGER Balance_OverlappingPeriods ON Balance
AFTER INSERT, UPDATE AS
IF EXISTS (
        SELECT *
        FROM    INSERTED B1
        WHERE 1 < (
                SELECT COUNT(*)
                FROM    Balance B2
                WHERE B1.AccountNo = B2.AccountNo AND
                      B1.FromDate < B2.ToDate AND B2.FromDate < B1.ToDate ) )
BEGIN
        RAISERROR ('Overlapping periods in balance of an account', 1, 1)
        ROLLBACK TRANSACTION
END
```

In the above trigger, the condition in the WHERE clause ensures that the two
periods denoted by the facts B1 and B2 for the same account overlap, which
constitutes a violation of the constraint.

Enforcing temporal integrity constraints is a complex and costly operation.
We have given examples of triggers that monitor sometimes the insert and
update operations, sometimes the update and delete operations. Additional
triggers must be introduced to monitor all potential insert, update, and delete
operations in all involved tables.

11.4.4 Measure Aggregation

The temporal algebra operators shown in Section 11.1 must be applied
for *conventional* (nontemporal) data warehouses when aggregating measures
along the time dimension for facts representing states (see Sect. 11.2.1). Further, the aggregation must distinguish between **atelic** and **telic** measures.
Atelic measures satisfy the **downward inheritance property** while telic
measures do not. This means that if an atelic measure has a given value during a time period p, it has the same value in any subperiod of p. An example
of an atelic measure is the balance of bank accounts, since if an account has
a balance of $100 in a time period, then the account has the same balance

at any instant included in that period. An example of a telic measure is the distance traveled by a vehicle during a period, since the distance traveled in a subperiod will be less than the total distance.

Consider the example in Fig. 11.16a, which is used for analyzing bank accounts. The fact **Balance** represents temporal states, as indicated by the two links **FromDate** and **ToDate** to the **Date** dimension. As stated above, the measure **Amount** is atelic. Figure 11.16b shows three tables of the corresponding relational schema. The top of Fig. 11.16c shows values for the association of accounts A1, A2, and A3 with branches B1 and B2 in table **Account**. Then, the figure shows values for the **Amount** measure in table **Balance**. The values of **Amount** by branch and month are shown at the bottom.

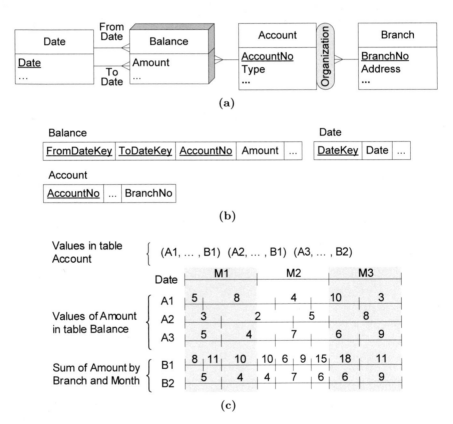

Fig. 11.16 Aggregation of an atelic state measure. (**a**) Excerpt of a schema for analyzing bank accounts; (**b**) Three tables of the corresponding relational schema; (**c**) Aggregation of **Amount** by branch and month

The query that aggregates **Amount** by branch and month is as follows:

```
WITH BalanceByMonth(BranchNo, Amount, FromDate, ToDate) AS (
        SELECT      BranchNo, Amount, dbo.MaxDate(D1.Date, M.FromDate) AS
                    FromDate, dbo.MinDate(D2.Date, M.ToDate) AS ToDate
        FROM        Balance B, Account A, Date D1, Date D2, Month M
        WHERE       B.AccountNo = A.AccountNo AND
                    B.FromDateKey = D1.DateKey AND
                    B.ToDateKey = D2.DateKey AND
                    dbo.MaxDate(D1.Date, M.FromDate) <
                    dbo.MinDate(D2.Date, M.ToDate) ),
    AmountChanges(BranchNo, Day) AS (
        SELECT      BranchNo, FromDate
        FROM        BalanceByMonth
        UNION
        SELECT      BranchNo, ToDate
        FROM        BalanceByMonth ),
    AmountPeriods(BranchNo, FromDate, ToDate) AS (
        SELECT      P1.BranchNo, P1.Day, P2.Day
        FROM        AmountChanges P1, AmountChanges P2
        WHERE       P1.BranchNo = P2.BranchNo AND P1.Day < P2.Day AND
                    NOT EXISTS (
                    SELECT *
                    FROM    AmountChanges P3
                    WHERE P1.BranchNo = P3.BranchNo AND
                        P1.Day < P3.Day AND P3.Day < P2.Day ) ),
    TempSum(BranchNo, SumAmount, FromDate, ToDate) AS (
        SELECT      B.BranchNo, SUM(Amount), P.FromDate, P.ToDate
        FROM        BalanceByMonth B, AmountPeriods P
        WHERE       B.BranchNo = P.BranchNo AND
                    B.FromDate <= P.FromDate AND P.ToDate <= B.ToDate
        GROUP BY B.BranchNo, P.FromDate, P.ToDate )
-- Coalescing the table TempSum above
SELECT DISTINCT F.BranchNo, F.SumAmount, F.FromDate, L.ToDate
FROM    TempSum F, TempSum L
WHERE ...
```

Table BalanceByMonth contains the result of a temporal join of tables Month (defined in Sect. 11.4.2) and Balance. This allows us to split the periods in the fact table by month and to associate these periods with branches. Then, the temporal aggregation of table BalanceByMonth must be performed using the approach shown in Sect. 11.1.

Consider now the example in Fig. 11.17a, which is used for analyzing deliveries. Measures NoKm and FuelCons in the fact Delivery are telic measures. Figure 11.17b shows three tables of the corresponding relational schema. The top of Fig. 11.17c shows how vehicles V1, V2, and V3 are associated with fleets F1 and F2 in table Vehicle. Next, the figure shows values for the measure NoKm for vehicles V1, V2, and V3 in table Delivery. The aggregated values of the measure by fleet and month are shown at the bottom of Fig. 11.17c. For example, the value 30 for V3 is proportionally divided between months M1 and M2. As can be seen, the measures must be divided by month.

The query that aggregates NoKm by fleet and month is as follows:

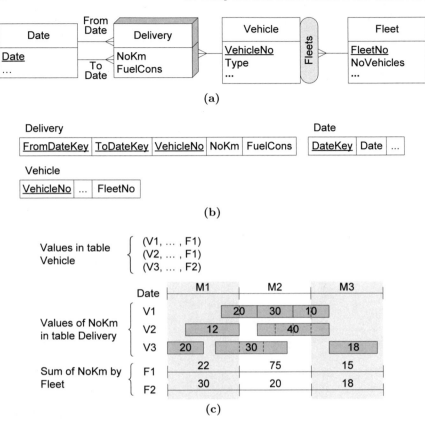

Fig. 11.17 Aggregation of a telic state measure. (**a**) Excerpt of a schema for analyzing deliveries; (**b**) Three tables of the corresponding relational schema; (**c**) Aggregation of NoKm by fleet and month

```
SELECT    V.FleetNo, M.Year, M.MonthNumber, SUM(NoKm *
          DateDiff(day, dbo.MaxDate(D1.Date, M.FromDate),
          dbo.MinDate(D2.Date, M.ToDate)) /
          DateDiff(day, D1.Date, D2.Date) ) AS NoKm
FROM      Delivery D, Vehicle V, Date D1, Date D2, Month M
WHERE     D.VehicleNo = V.VehicleNo AND D.FromDateKey = D1.DateKey AND
          D.ToDateKey = D1.DateKey AND
          dbo.MaxDate(D1.Date, M.FromDate) < dbo.MinDate(D2.Date, M.ToDate)
GROUP BY V.FleetNo, M.Year, M.MonthNumber
ORDER BY V.FleetNo, M.Year, M.MonthNumber
```

The above query performs a temporal join of tables Delivery and Month. This allows us to split the periods in the fact table by month and to aggregate the measure by month and fleet. Then, the SELECT clause computes the percentage of measure NoKm pertaining to a particular fleet and month. This is obtained by multiplying the value of the measure by the duration in days of the intersection between the periods associated with the measure and the month, divided by the duration of the period associated with the measure.

Obviously, the discussion above also applies for *temporal* data warehouses. For example, suppose the schemas in Figs. 11.16a and 11.17a are temporal, where the parent-child relationships that associate accounts to branches and vehicles to fleets are temporal. In this case, the above SQL queries that aggregate measures Amount and NoKm must be extended to take into account the temporal parent-child relationships. These queries are left as an exercise.

11.4.5 Temporal Measures

Figure 11.18a shows a schema for analyzing bank loans. The loan fact has measures Amount, RateType, and InterestRate, where the latter is a **slowly changing measure**, that is, the value of the measure may change during the duration of the fact. Indeed, depending on the value of the RateType, the InterestRate may be fixed throughout the whole duration of the loan, or can be variable and thus re-evaluated periodically (for example, every year) according to market conditions. As shown in Fig. 11.18b, the evolution of the interest rate for loans is kept in table LoanInterestRate.

If the interest rate of loans only changes by month, the following query computes the time-weighted average of the measure InterestRate by branch.

```
WITH LoanRateDuration AS (
        SELECT    *, DateDiff(mm, StartDate, EndDate) AS Duration
        FROM      LoanInterestRate ),
     LoanDuration AS (
        SELECT    LoanKey, DateDiff(mm, D1.Date, D2.Date) AS Duration
        FROM      Loan L, Date D1, Date D2
        WHERE     L.StartDateKey = D1.DateKey AND L.EndDateKey = D2.DateKey
        GROUP BY LoanKey ),
     LoanAvgInterestRate AS (
        SELECT R.LoanKey, SUM(R.InterestRate * R.Duration) / MAX(L.duration)
        FROM LoanRateDuration R, LoanDuration L
        WHERE R.LoanKey = L.LoanKey
        GROUP BY R.LoanKey )
SELECT    B.BranchID, AVG(InterestRate) AS AvgInterestRate
FROM      Loan L, LoanAvgInterestRate A, Branch B
WHERE     L.LoanKey = A.LoanKey AND L.BranchKey = B.BranchKey
GROUP BY B.BranchID
ORDER BY B.BranchID
```

As can be seen, computing the time-weighted average requires computation of the number of months during which the interest rate does not change. For example, if the interest rate is 2% from January to March and 4% from April to December, the time-weighted average would be $(2\% \times 3 + 4\% \times 9) = 3.1666\%$.

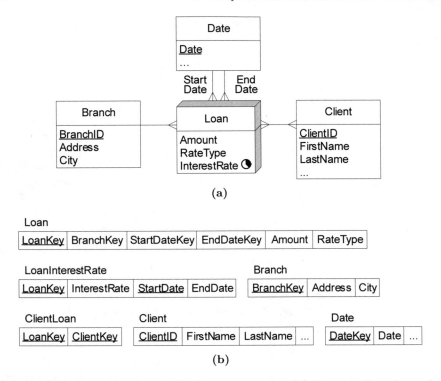

Fig. 11.18 An example of a slowly changing measure. (a) Excerpt of a schema for analyzing bank loans; (b) Tables of the corresponding relational schema

11.5 Querying the Temporal Northwind Data Warehouse in SQL

In this section, we show examples of queries addressed to the temporal Northwind data warehouse. These queries implement the temporal version of the OLAP operations studied in Sect. 3.2. They also illustrate the temporal relational operations studied in Sect. 11.1.

Query 11.1. *Total sales amount per customer, year, and product category.*

```
SELECT    C.CompanyName, D.Year, A.CategoryName,
          SUM(SalesAmount) AS SalesAmount
FROM      Sales S, Customer C, Date D, Product P, ProductCategory PC, Category A
WHERE     S.CustomerKey = C.CustomerKey AND S.OrderDateKey = D.DateKey AND
          S.ProductKey = P.ProductKey AND P.ProductKey = PC.ProductKey AND
          PC.CategoryKey = A.CategoryKey AND
          PC.FromDate <= D.Date AND D.Date < PC.ToDate
GROUP BY  C.CompanyName, D.Year, A.CategoryName
```

This query is the temporal version of Query 7.1. It implements a temporal roll-up taking into account that the assignment of products to categories varies over time. These assignments are stored in table ProductCategory. The last line of the WHERE clause ensures that products are rolled up to the category they were associated to *at the order date*. Queries with this interpretation are called **temporally consistent queries**. If, instead, we want products to be rolled up to their *current* category, in the last line of the WHERE clause, D.Date should be replaced by GetDate(). The situation is similar if we want products to be rolled up to the category they were associated to at a particular date (e.g., 1/1/2017). Queries with this interpretation are called **time-slice queries** because they extract the state of the data warehouse at a particular point in time. As a result, the sales of products that are not valid at time t will not be aggregated in the result. For example, if we want products to be rolled up to their current category, sales of discontinued products will not satisfy the above condition in the WHERE clause.

Query 11.2. *Monthly year-to-date sales for each product category.*

```
WITH SalesByCategoryMonth AS (
           SELECT    CategoryName, Year, MonthNumber, MonthName,
                     SUM(SalesAmount) AS SalesAmount
           FROM      Sales S, Product P, ProductCategory PC, Category C, Date D
           WHERE     S.OrderDateKey = D.DateKey AND
                     S.ProductKey = P.ProductKey AND
                     P.ProductKey = PC.ProductKey AND
                     PC.CategoryKey = C.CategoryKey AND
                     PC.FromDate <= D.Date AND D.Date < PC.ToDate
           GROUP BY CategoryName, Year, MonthNumber, MonthName )
SELECT     CategoryName, MonthName + ' ' + CAST(Year AS CHAR(4)) AS Month,
           SUM(SalesAmount) OVER (PARTITION BY CategoryName, Year
           ORDER BY MonthNumber ROWS UNBOUNDED PRECEDING)
           AS YTDSalesAmount
FROM       SalesByCategoryMonth
ORDER BY CategoryName, Year, MonthNumber
```

This query is the temporal version of Query 7.10. It implements a temporal roll-up. The temporary table aggregates the sales amount by category and month, where a product is rolled up to the category that was valid at the order date. The main query computes the monthly year-to-date sales.

Query 11.3. *For each employee, total sales amount of products she sold with unit price greater than $30 at the time of the sale.*

```
SELECT    FirstName + ' ' + LastName AS EmployeeName,
          SUM(SalesAmount), AS SalesAmount
FROM      Sales S, Date D, Employee E, Product P, ProductUnitPrice U
WHERE     S.OrderDateKey = D.DateKey AND S.EmployeeKey = E.EmployeeKey AND
          S.ProductKey = P.ProductKey AND P.ProductKey = U.ProductKey AND
          U.FromDate <= D.Date AND D.Date < U.ToDate AND U.UnitPrice > 30
GROUP BY FirstName + ' ' + LastName
ORDER BY FirstName + ' ' + LastName
```

This query implements a temporal selection taking into account that the unit price of products varies over time. These values are stored in table **ProductUnitPrice**. The query selects the price of a product at the order date and verifies that it is greater than \$30. Then, the query aggregates the result by employee to compute the total sales amount.

Query 11.4. *For each product and month, list the unit price and the total sales amount at that price.*

```
SELECT    P.ProductName, M.Year, M.MonthNumber, U.UnitPrice,
          SUM(SalesAmount) AS SalesAmount,
          dbo.MaxDate(M.FromDate, U.FromDate) AS FromDate,
          dbo.MinDate(M.ToDate, U.ToDate) AS ToDate
FROM      Sales S, Date D, Product P, ProductUnitPrice U, Month M
WHERE     S.OrderDateKey = D.DateKey AND S.ProductKey = P.ProductKey AND
          P.ProductKey = U.ProductKey AND
          dbo.MaxDate(M.FromDate, U.FromDate) <
          dbo.MinDate(M.ToDate, U.ToDate) AND
          dbo.MaxDate(M.FromDate, U.FromDate) <= D.Date AND
          D.Date < dbo.MinDate(M.ToDate, U.ToDate)
GROUP BY P.ProductName, U.UnitPrice, M.FromDate, U.FromDate, M.ToDate, U.ToDate
ORDER BY P.ProductName, dbo.MaxDate(M.FromDate, U.FromDate)
```

This query performs a temporal join of the tables **ProductUnitPrice** and **Month** to split the months according to the variation of the unit price of products. Combining this with a traditional join of the other tables we compute the total sales amount in the periods obtained.

Query 11.5. *Average unit price by category as of January 1st, 2017.*

```
SELECT    C.CategoryName, AVG(UnitPrice) AS AvgUnitPrice
FROM      Product P, ProductUnitPrice PU, ProductCategory PC, Category C
WHERE     P.ProductKey = PC.ProductKey AND PC.CategoryKey = C.CategoryKey AND
          P.ProductKey = PU.ProductKey AND
          PC.FromDate <= '2017-01-01' AND '2017-01-01' < PC.ToDate AND
          PU.FromDate <= '2017-01-01' AND '2017-01-01' < PU.ToDate
GROUP BY C.CategoryName
```

This is a time-slice query that performs a temporal roll-up of products to categories and obtains the unit price of products at the given date. Note that the query does not involve the fact table, only the tables of the **Product** dimension. The query performs a join of the tables and extracts the tuples of these tables that were valid at the requested date. If instead the query asks for the *current* average price by category, then in the last two lines of the **WHERE** clause above we should replace '2017-01-01' by **GetDate()**.

Query 11.6. *Personal sales amount made by an employee compared with the total sales amount made by herself and her subordinates during 2017.*

```
WITH Supervision AS (
         SELECT     EmployeeKey, SupervisorKey, FromDate, ToDate
         FROM       EmployeeSupervision
         WHERE      SupervisorKey IS NOT NULL
         UNION ALL
         SELECT     E.EmployeeKey, S.SupervisorKey,
                    dbo.MaxDate(S.FromDate, E.FromDate) AS FromDate,
                    dbo.MinDate(S.ToDate, E.ToDate) AS ToDate
         FROM       Supervision S, EmployeeSupervision E
         WHERE      S.EmployeeKey = E.SupervisorKey AND
                    dbo.MaxDate(S.FromDate, E.FromDate) <
                    dbo.MinDate(S.ToDate, E.ToDate) ),
     SalesEmp2017 AS (
         SELECT     EmployeeKey, SUM(S.SalesAmount) AS PersonalSales
         FROM       Sales S, Date D
         WHERE      S.OrderDateKey = D.DateKey AND D.Year = 2017
         GROUP BY EmployeeKey ),
     SalesSubord2017 AS (
         SELECT     SupervisorKey AS EmployeeKey,
                    SUM(S.SalesAmount) AS SubordinateSales
         FROM       Sales S, Supervision U, Date D
         WHERE      S.EmployeeKey = U.EmployeeKey AND
                    S.OrderDateKey = D.DateKey AND D.Year = 2017 AND
                    U.FromDate <= D.Date AND D.Date < U.ToDate
         GROUP BY SupervisorKey )
SELECT     FirstName + ' ' + LastName AS EmployeeName, S1.PersonalSales,
           COALESCE(S1.PersonalSales + S2.SubordinateSales, S1.PersonalSales)
           AS PersSubordSales
FROM       Employee E JOIN SalesEmp2017 S1 ON E.EmployeeKey = S1.EmployeeKey
           LEFT OUTER JOIN SalesSubord2017 S2 ON
           S1.EmployeeKey = S2.EmployeeKey
ORDER BY EmployeeName
```

This query is the temporal version of Query 7.12. It expresses a recursive temporal roll-up taking into account that the assignment of employees to supervisors varies over time. Table Supervision computes the temporal transitive closure of the supervision relationship using a temporal join of the EmployeeSupervision table and the recursive view Supervision. Table SalesEmp2017 computes the personal sales of employees during 2017, while table SalesSubord2017 computes the sales of employees' subordinates during 2017. The main query uses a left outer join to take into account employees who have no supervisor in 2017. After that, the COALESCE function adds to the personal sales of employees the sales of their subordinates, if any.

Query 11.7. *Total sales amount by supervisor.*

```
WITH Supervisors AS (
            SELECT      SupervisorKey AS EmployeeKey, FromDate, ToDate
            FROM        EmployeeSupervision
            WHERE       SupervisorKey IS NOT NULL ),
      SupervisorsCoalesced AS (
            -- Coalescing the table Supervisors above
            ... ),
SELECT      FirstName + ' ' + LastName AS EmployeeName,
            SUM(SalesAmount) AS Total, FromDate, ToDate
FROM        Sales S, Date D, Employee E, SupervisorsCoalesced U
WHERE       S.OrderDateKey = D.DateKey AND S.EmployeeKey = E.EmployeeKey AND
            E.EmployeeKey = U.EmployeeKey AND
            U.FromDate <= D.Date AND D.Date < U.ToDate
GROUP BY FirstName + ' ' + LastName, FromDate, ToDate
ORDER BY FirstName + ' ' + LastName, FromDate
```

This query computes a temporal projection. Table **Supervisors** computes the periods during which a supervisor supervised at least one employee. This table is coalesced in table **SupervisorsCoalesced**. Finally, the main query computes the total sales of employees during the periods they were supervisors.

Query 11.8. *For each employee and supervisor pair, list the number of days that the supervision lasted.*

```
WITH EmpSup AS (
            SELECT E.FirstName + ' ' + E.LastName AS EmployeeName,
                   U.FirstName + ' ' + U.LastName AS SupervisorName,
                   DateDiff(day, S.FromDate, dbo.MinDate(GetDate(), S.ToDate))
                   AS NoDays
            FROM   EmployeeSupervision S, Employee E, Employee U
            WHERE  S.EmployeeKey = E.EmployeeKey AND
                   S.SupervisorKey = U.EmployeeKey )
SELECT      EmployeeName, SupervisorName, SUM(NoDays) AS NoDays
FROM        EmpSup
GROUP BY EmployeeName, SupervisorName
ORDER BY EmployeeName, SupervisorName
```

This query uses the **DateDiff** function to compute the number of days in a period. The function **MinDate** obtains the minimum date between the current date (obtained with the function **GetDate**) and the **ToDate** of a period. In this way, if the period associated with a supervision ends in the future (as is the case when the supervision is current), then the number of days will be computed from the beginning of the period until the current date.

Query 11.9. *Total sales amount for employees during the time they were assigned to only one city.*

```
WITH EmpOneCity(EmployeeKey, FromDate, ToDate) AS (
            -- Case 1
            SELECT T1.EmployeeKey, T1.FromDate, T2.FromDate
```

```
        FROM    Territories T1, Territories T2
        WHERE   T1.EmployeeKey = T2.EmployeeKey AND
                T1.FromDate < T2.FromDate AND T2.FromDate < T1.ToDate AND
                NOT EXISTS (
                SELECT *
                FROM    Territories T3
                WHERE   T1.EmployeeKey = T3.EmployeeKey AND
                        T1.FromDate < T3.ToDate AND
                        T3.FromDate < T2.FromDate )
        UNION
        -- Case 2
        SELECT T1.EmployeeKey, T2.ToDate, T1.ToDate
        FROM    Territories T1, Territories T2
        WHERE   T1.EmployeeKey = T2.EmployeeKey AND
                T1.FromDate < T2.ToDate AND T2.ToDate < T1.ToDate AND
                NOT EXISTS (
                SELECT *
                FROM    Territories T3
                WHERE   T1.EmployeeKey = T3.EmployeeKey AND
                        T2.ToDate < T3.ToDate AND T3.FromDate < T1.ToDate )
        UNION
        -- Case 3
        SELECT T1.EmployeeKey, T2.ToDate, T3.FromDate
        FROM    Territories T1, Territories T2, Territories T3
        WHERE   T1.EmployeeKey = T2.EmployeeKey AND
                T1.EmployeeKey = T3.EmployeeKey AND
                T2.ToDate < T3.FromDate AND T1.FromDate < T2.ToDate AND
                T3.FromDate < T1.ToDate AND NOT EXISTS (
                SELECT *
                FROM    Territories T4
                WHERE   T1.EmployeeKey = T4.EmployeeKey AND
                        T2.ToDate < T4.ToDate AND T4.FromDate < T3.FromDate )
        UNION
        -- Case 4
        SELECT EmployeeKey, FromDate, ToDate
        FROM    Territories T1
        WHERE   NOT EXISTS (
                SELECT *
                FROM    Territories T2
                WHERE   T1.EmployeeKey = T2.EmployeeKey AND
                        T1.CityKey <> T2.CityKey AND
                        T1.FromDate < T2.ToDate AND T2.FromDate < T1.ToDate ) ),
    EmpOneCityCoalesced(EmployeeKey, FromDate, ToDate) AS (
        -- Coalescing the table EmpOneCity above
        ... )
SELECT    FirstName + ' ' + LastName AS EmployeeName,
          SUM(SalesAmount) AS SalesAmount
FROM      Sales S, Date D, Employee E, EmpOneCity O
WHERE     S.OrderDateKey = D.DateKey AND S.EmployeeKey = E.EmployeeKey AND
          E.EmployeeKey = O.EmployeeKey AND O.FromDate <= D.Date AND
          D.Date < O.ToDate
GROUP BY FirstName + ' ' + LastName
ORDER BY FirstName + ' ' + LastName
```

This query performs a temporal difference to obtain the periods during which an employee is assigned to a single city. In table **EmpOneCity**, the four inner queries after the **NOT EXISTS** predicate verify that no other assignment overlaps the period during which an employee is assigned to a single city. Table **EmpOneCityCoaslesced** coalesces the previous table. Finally, the main query selects the sales whose order date belongs to the period when the employee is assigned to a single city. Then, it groups the results by employee to compute the total sales amount.

Query 11.10. *For each employee, compute the total sales amount and number of cities to which she is assigned.*

```
WITH CityChanges(EmployeeKey, Day) AS (
        SELECT      EmployeeKey, FromDate
        FROM        Territories
        UNION
        SELECT      EmployeeKey, ToDate
        FROM        Territories ),
    CityPeriods(EmployeeKey, FromDate, ToDate) AS (
        SELECT      T1.EmployeeKey, T1.Day, T2.Day
        FROM        CityChanges T1, CityChanges T2
        WHERE       T1.EmployeeKey = T2.EmployeeKey AND
                    T1.Day < T2.Day AND NOT EXISTS (
                    SELECT *
                    FROM    CityChanges T3
                    WHERE   T1.EmployeeKey = T3.EmployeeKey AND
                            T1.Day < T3.Day AND T3.Day < T2.Day ) ),
    CityCount(EmployeeKey, NoCities, FromDate, ToDate) AS (
        SELECT      P.EmployeeKey, COUNT(CityKey), P.FromDate, P.ToDate
        FROM        Territories T, CityPeriods P
        WHERE       T.EmployeeKey = P.EmployeeKey AND
                    T.FromDate <= P.FromDate AND P.ToDate <= T.ToDate
        GROUP BY P.EmployeeKey, P.FromDate, P.ToDate ),
    CityCountCoalesced(EmployeeKey, NoCities, FromDate, ToDate) AS (
        -- Coalescing the table CityCount above
        ... )
SELECT FirstName + ' ' + LastName AS EmployeeName,
        SUM(SalesAmount) AS TotalSales, NoCities,
        dbo.MaxDate(C.FromDate, S.FromDate) AS FromDate,
        dbo.MinDate(C.ToDate, S.ToDate) AS ToDate
FROM    Sales F, Date D, Employee E, CityCountCoalesced C, StateCountCoalesced S
WHERE F.OrderDateKey = D.DateKey AND F.EmployeeKey = E.EmployeeKey AND
        F.EmployeeKey = C.EmployeeKey AND F.EmployeeKey = S.EmployeeKey AND
        dbo.MaxDate(C.FromDate, S.FromDate) < dbo.MinDate(C.ToDate, S.ToDate)
        AND dbo.MaxDate(C.FromDate, S.FromDate) <= D.Date AND
        D.Date < dbo.MinDate(C.ToDate, S.ToDate)
GROUP BY FirstName + ' ' + LastName, dbo.MaxDate(C.FromDate, S.FromDate),
        dbo.MinDate(C.ToDate, S.ToDate), NoCities
ORDER BY FirstName + ' ' + LastName, dbo.MaxDate(C.FromDate, S.FromDate)
```

This query is a temporal version of Query 7.15. It computes a temporal count considering that the assignment of employees to cities varies over time.

Therefore, the result of the query must include the period during which an employee is assigned to a given number of cities. Table CityChanges computes for each employee the days when her assignment to a city starts or ends, and thus her number of cities could change on those days. Table CityPeriods computes the periods from the days in the table CityChanges. Table CityCount counts the number of cities assigned to an employee for each of the periods of the table CityPeriods. Table CityCountCoalesced coalesces the table CityCount since there may be adjacent periods in the latter table that have the same number of cities. Finally, the main query performs a temporal join of the tables, keeping the city and state count, and a traditional join of the other three tables and verifies that the order date is included in the period to be output. Then, the query groups the result by employee and period to obtain the total sales amount. Notice that in this query the double-counting problem (see Sect. 4.2.6) does not arise since a sales fact is joined to a single period in the table resulting from the temporal join of CityCountCoalesced and StateCountCoalesced; this is verified in the last two lines of the WHERE clause.

Query 11.11. *Total sales per category, for categories in which all products have a price greater than $7.*

```
WITH CatUnitPrice(CategoryKey, UnitPrice, FromDate, ToDate) AS (
        SELECT      P.CategoryKey, U.UnitPrice,
                    dbo.MaxDate(P.FromDate, U.FromDate),
                    dbo.MinDate(P.ToDate, U.ToDate)
        FROM        ProductCategory P, ProductUnitPrice U
        WHERE       P.ProductKey = U.ProductKey AND
                    dbo.MaxDate(P.FromDate, U.FromDate) <
                    dbo.MinDate(P.ToDate, U.ToDate) ),
    CatChanges(CategoryKey, Day) AS (
        SELECT      CategoryKey, FromDate
        FROM        CatUnitPrice
        UNION
        SELECT      CategoryKey, ToDate
        FROM        CatUnitPrice
        UNION
        SELECT      CategoryKey, FromDate
        FROM        Category
        UNION
        SELECT      CategoryKey, ToDate
        FROM        Category ),
    CatPeriods(CategoryKey, FromDate, ToDate) AS (
        SELECT      P1.CategoryKey, P1.Day, P2.Day
        FROM        CatChanges P1, CatChanges P2
        WHERE       P1.CategoryKey = P2.CategoryKey AND
                    P1.Day < P2.Day AND NOT EXISTS (
                    SELECT *
                    FROM    CatChanges P3
                    WHERE P1.CategoryKey = P3.CategoryKey AND
                          P1.Day < P3.Day AND P3.Day < P2.Day ) ),
    TempDiv(CategoryKey, FromDate, ToDate) AS (
```

```
SELECT      P.CategoryKey, P.FromDate, P.ToDate
FROM        CatPeriods P
WHERE       NOT EXISTS (
            SELECT *
            FROM    CatUnitPrice U
            WHERE P.CategoryKey = U.CategoryKey AND
                  U.UnitPrice <= 7 AND
                  U.FromDate <= P.FromDate AND
                  P.ToDate <= U.ToDate ) ),
TempDivCoalesced(CategoryKey, FromDate, ToDate) AS (
-- Coalescing the table TempDiv above
... )
SELECT      CategoryName, SUM(SalesAmount) AS Total, U.FromDate, U.ToDate
FROM        Sales S, Date D, ProductCategory P, Category C, TempDivCoalesced U
WHERE       S.OrderDateKey = D.DateKey AND S.ProductKey = P.ProductKey AND
            P.CategoryKey = C.CategoryKey AND C.CategoryKey = U.CategoryKey AND
            U.FromDate <= D.Date AND D.Date < U.ToDate AND
            P.FromDate <= D.Date AND D.Date < P.ToDate
GROUP BY CategoryName, U.FromDate, U.ToDate
ORDER BY CategoryName, U.FromDate
```

This query performs a temporal division. Table CatUnitPrice computes the temporal join of tables ProductCategory and ProductUnitPrice in order to obtain, for each category, the prices of its products with their associated period. Table CatChanges computes, for each category, the days on which there is a change in unit price or category assignment of one of its products. Table CatPeriods computes the periods from the table CatChanges. Table TempDiv selects the tuples in CatPeriods where there is no product in the category with unit price less than or equal to $7 in the period. Table TempDivCoalesced coalesces the table TempDiv. Finally, the main query computes for each tuple of the table TempDivCoalesced the total sales amount for the category that occurred during the period.

11.6 Temporal Data Warehouses versus Slowly Changing Dimensions

We have seen in Chap. 5 that slowly changing dimensions have been proposed as an approach to cope with dimensions that evolve over time. In this section, we compare the approach for temporal data warehouses we have presented in this chapter with slowly changing dimensions. We only consider type 2 slowly changing dimensions, since this is the most-used approach.

Figure 11.19 shows the relational representation of the temporal Northwind conceptual schema given in Fig. 11.11 using type 2 slowly changing dimensions. In the schema, tables Product, Category, Territories, and Employee are the only temporal tables. Thus, for example, information about products, their lifespan, unit price, and category are kept in table Product, while these are kept in four separate tables in the schema of Fig. 11.15.

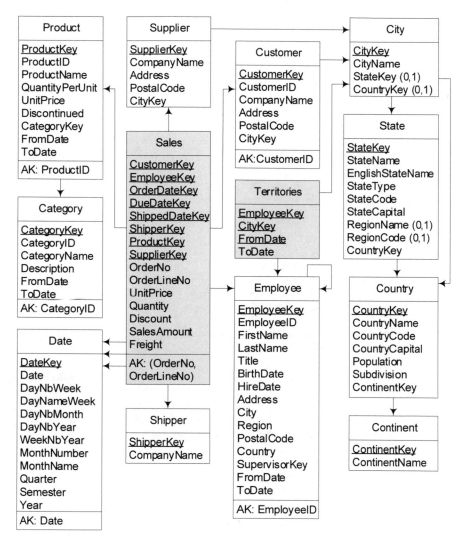

Fig. 11.19 Relational schema of the temporal Northwind data warehouse in Fig. 11.11 using type 2 slowly changing dimensions

We revisit next some queries of the previous section with this version of the temporal Northwind data warehouse. To facilitate our discussion, the schema in Fig. 11.15 is referred to as the temporal version while the schema in Fig. 11.19 is referred to as the SCD (slowly changing dimension) version.

Query 11.1. *Average unit price by category as of January 1st, 2017.*

```
SELECT    C.CategoryName, AVG(UnitPrice) AS AvgUnitPrice
FROM      Product P, Category C
WHERE     P.CategoryKey = C.CategoryKey AND
          P.FromDate <= '2017-01-01' AND '2017-01-01' < P.ToDate AND
          C.FromDate <= '2017-01-01' AND '2017-01-01' < C.ToDate
GROUP BY C.CategoryName
```

Since the evolution of products is kept in a single-table, this query performs a join of two tables, whereas the previous version of the query requires a join of four tables to obtain the unit price and the category of products.

Query 11.2. *Total sales amount per customer, year, and product category.*

```
SELECT    C.CompanyName, D.Year, A.CategoryName,
          SUM(SalesAmount) AS SalesAmount
FROM      Sales S, Customer C, Date D, Product P, Category A
WHERE     S.CustomerKey = C.CustomerKey AND S.OrderDateKey = D.DateKey AND
          S.ProductKey = P.ProductKey AND P.CategoryKey = A.CategoryKey AND
          P.FromDate <= D.Date AND D.Date < P.ToDate
GROUP BY C.CompanyName, D.Year, A.CategoryName
```

The previous version of the query had an additional join with table **Product-Category** to select the category of a product valid at the order date.

Query 11.9. *For each product, list the name, unit price, and total sales amount by month.*

```
WITH ProdUnitPrice(ProductID, UnitPrice, FromDate, ToDate) AS (
          SELECT    ProductID, UnitPrice, FromDate, ToDate
          FROM      Product ),
      ProdUnitPriceCoalesced AS (
          -- Coalescing the table ProdUnitPrice above
          ... ),
SELECT    P.ProductName, U.UnitPrice, SUM(SalesAmount)
          AS SalesAmount,
          dbo.MaxDate(M.FromDate, U.FromDate) AS FromDate,
          dbo.MinDate(M.ToDate, U.ToDate) AS ToDate
FROM      Sales S, Date D, Product P, ProdUnitPriceCoalesced U, Month M
WHERE     S.OrderDateKey = D.DateKey AND S.ProductKey = P.ProductKey AND
          P.ProductID = U.ProductID AND dbo.MaxDate(M.FromDate, U.FromDate) <
          dbo.MinDate(M.ToDate, U.ToDate) AND
          dbo.MaxDate(M.FromDate, U.FromDate) <= D.Date AND
          D.Date < dbo.MinDate(M.ToDate, U.ToDate)
GROUP BY P.ProductName, U.UnitPrice, M.FromDate, U.FromDate, M.ToDate, U.ToDate
ORDER BY P.ProductName, dbo.MaxDate(M.FromDate, U.FromDate)
```

This query requires a temporal projection of the **Product** table to compute the **ProductUnitPrice** table that is available in the temporal version.

Query 11.11. *Total sales per category, for categories in which all products have a price greater than $7.*

```
WITH CatUnitPrice(CategoryID, UnitPrice, FromDate, ToDate) AS (
        SELECT    DISTINCT CategoryID, UnitPrice, P.FromDate, P.ToDate
        FROM      Product P, Category C
        WHERE     P.CategoryKey = C.CategoryKey),
    CatUnitPriceCoalesced(CategoryID, UnitPrice, FromDate, ToDate) AS (
        -- Coalescing the table CatUnitPrice above
        ... ),
    CatLifespan(CategoryID, FromDate, ToDate) AS (
        SELECT DISTINCT CategoryID, FromDate, ToDate
        FROM Category C ),
    CatLifespanCoalesced AS (
        -- Coalescing the table CatLifespan above
        ... ),
    CatChanges(CategoryID, Day) AS (
        SELECT    CategoryID, FromDate
        FROM      CatUnitPriceCoalesced
        UNION
        SELECT    CategoryID, ToDate
        FROM      CatUnitPriceCoalesced
        UNION
        SELECT    CategoryID, FromDate
        FROM      CatLifespanCoalesced
        UNION
        SELECT    CategoryID, ToDate
        FROM      CatLifespanCoalesced ),
    CatPeriods(CategoryID, FromDate, ToDate) AS (
        -- As in the previous version of this query
        ... ),
    TempDiv(CategoryID, FromDate, ToDate) AS (
        SELECT    P.CategoryID, P.FromDate, P.ToDate
        FROM      CatPeriods P
        WHERE     NOT EXISTS (
                  SELECT *
                  FROM    CatUnitPriceCoalesced U
                  WHERE   P.CategoryID = U.CategoryID AND
                          U.UnitPrice <= 7 AND
                          U.FromDate <= P.FromDate AND
                          P.ToDate <= U.ToDate ) ),
    TempDivCoalesced(CategoryKey, FromDate, ToDate) AS (
        -- Coalescing the table TempDiv above
        ... )
SELECT ... -- As in the previous version of this query
```

In the previous version of this query, a temporal join between tables ProductCategory and ProductUnitPrice is needed for computing the CatUnitPrice temporary table while in this version, this information is available in table Product. Nevertheless, if other attributes of products were temporal (e.g., QuantityPerUnit), the SCD version would require a temporal projection of the Product table to obtain the joint evolution of the unit price and category independently of the evolution of the other temporal attributes.

We compare the temporal (Fig. 11.15) and the SCD (Fig. 11.19) versions of the schema with respect to querying using the **Product** dimension. As we have seen, information about products, their lifespan, unit price, and category are kept in a single-table **Product** in the SCD version, while these are kept in four separate tables in the temporal version. Therefore, to obtain the lifespan, the unit price, or the category of products, a temporal projection (with coalescing) of table **Product** is required in the SCD version, while this information is already present in the temporal version. As has been said, coalescing is a complex and costly operation. On the other hand, for operations such as temporal slice or temporal roll-up, the SCD version requires fewer joins, since in the temporal version we have to join the **Product** table with the **ProductUnitPrice** or the **ProductCategory** tables. As has been said, temporal join is a relatively simple operation that can be efficiently implemented.

In conclusion, regardless the version of the logical schema, querying temporal data warehouses requires complex SQL queries to express temporal algebraic operations. Further, such queries are very inefficient. The only way to solve this problem is for the DBMS to enable such temporal operations to be expressed natively in SQL, as has been suggested by many researchers in the temporal database community. Similarly, MDX and DAX should also be extended with temporal versions of the OLAP operators.

11.7 Conceptual Design of Multiversion Data Warehouses

In this chapter, we have studied so far *temporal* data warehouses, which keep track of the evolution of their *instances*. However, the schema of a data warehouse may also evolve, for example, to cope with new analytical requirements or to reflect changes in the modeled reality. This brings about the need for *multiversion data warehouses*, which keep track of the evolution of their *schema* so that the various versions of the schema and their data are kept. This will be the topic of the remainder of this chapter. Obviously, multiversion and temporal data warehouses can be combined to keep the evolution of *both* the schema and their instances. This requires the mechanisms studied in this chapter to be combined into a single framework.

As the schema of a data warehouse evolves, two possible cases can be envisaged. In the first case, the existing data can be modified to comply with the new version of the schema: This implies removing data that are no longer needed and adding new data that were not previously collected. In the second case, the two versions of the schema and their data should be maintained. New data will be added according to the new schema, while previous data entered with the previous schema are kept for analysis purposes. Thus, users and applications can continue working with the previous version of the schema, while new users and applications can target the new version of the schema.

We illustrate the need for multiversion data warehouses using a scenario for the Northwind case study. Figure 11.20a shows the conceptual schema of the initial version of the Northwind data warehouse. This version of the schema has a restricted scope compared to the schema given in Fig. 4.1, which we have used throughout the book. Indeed, this initial version only considers sales and does not consider shipments. Further, there is no Supplier dimension; this information is defined as a hierarchy in the Product dimension. On the other hand, there is a new dimension Store, which is related to the Geography hierarchy also used by the Customer and Employee dimensions.

Figure 11.20b shows the second version of the Northwind data warehouse. A Shipper dimension has been added, together with a ShippedDate role to the Date dimension, and a Freight measure. Further, the attributes of the Store level has been modified: the attribute StoreSqft has been removed, and a new attribute Manager has been added.

Finally, Fig. 11.20c shows the third version of the Northwind data warehouse. Here, the Store level has been removed while keeping the remaining levels of the dimension starting from City. On the other hand, the hierarchy Supplier in the Product dimension has been removed and transformed into a new dimension which is linked to the Geography hierarchy.

We define next our multiversion data warehouse model. Its main characteristics are that (1) the warehouse keeps all data loaded into it throughout its lifespan, and (2) the data are available using any schema version.

A *multiversion data warehouse* is a collection of *data warehouse versions*, where each of them is a traditional data warehouse. Each version is composed of a schema version and an instance version. A *schema version* describes the structure of the data within a time period, while an *instance version* represents the warehouse data using a particular schema version. We consider a linear versioning model where at a given time instant only one data warehouse version is current. New data are loaded using the current version and a new version is derived by applying changes to the current version. Each version is associated with the transaction time period during which it was current. The end of the period for the current version is set to UC (until-changed).

Figure 11.21 shows the time line for the various data warehouse versions given in Fig. 11.20. Suppose that the initial version V_1 shown in Fig. 11.20a was created at time T_1. The associated period for V_1 is set to $[T_1, UC)$. Later, at time T_2, version V_2 shown in Fig. 11.20b was derived from V_1 with associated period $[T_2, UC)$ and the period for V_1 was changed to $[T_1, T_2)$. Finally, at time T_3, version V_3 shown in Fig. 11.20c was derived from V_2 with associated period $[T_3, UC)$ and the period for V_2 was changed to $[T_2, T_3)$.

As we have seen, schema changes in dimensions and/or facts create a new data warehouse version. We consider the following changes to a *dimension*: adding or deleting an attribute in a level, changing the domain of an attribute, and adding or deleting a level in a hierarchy. The possible changes to a *fact* are: adding or deleting a dimension, changing the granularity of a dimension, adding or deleting a measure, and changing the domain of a measure. In

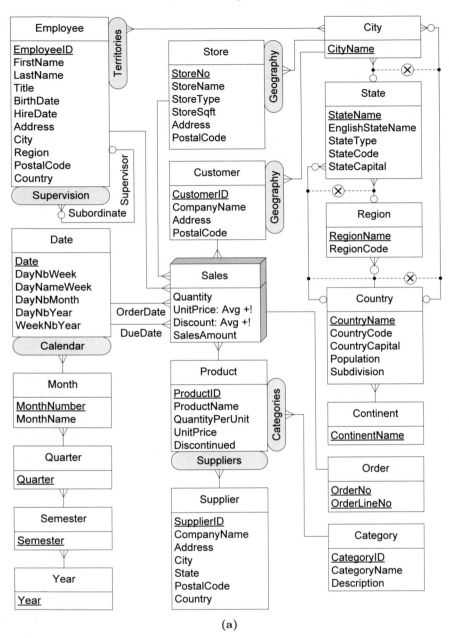

(a)

Fig. 11.20 Conceptual schemas of the multiversion Northwind data warehouse. (a) Initial version V_1

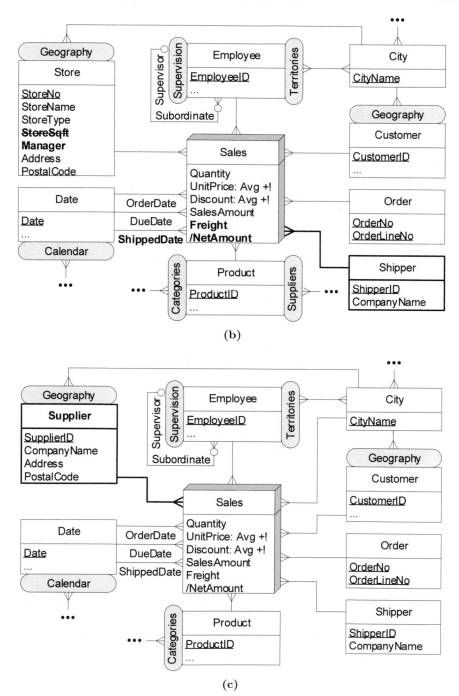

Fig. 11.20 Conceptual schemas of the multiversion Northwind data warehouse (cont.)
(**b**) Second version V_2 (excerpt); (**c**) Third version V_3 (excerpt)

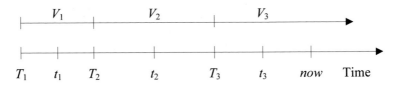

Fig. 11.21 Time line for the creation of the data warehouse versions in Fig. 11.20

certain cases, a change in a dimension also requires changes in a fact. For example, adding or removing a level at the lowest granularity of a hierarchy may also require changing the granularity in the related facts.

StoreID	StoreName	StoreType	StoreSqft	...
s1	Store 1	Grocery	200	...
s2	Store 2	Supermarket	300	...
s3	Store 3	Supermarket	500	...

(a)

StoreID	StoreName	StoreType	~~StoreSqft~~	Manager	...
s1	Store 1	Grocery	~~200~~		...
s2	Store 2	Supermarket	~~300~~		...
s3	Store 3	Supermarket	~~500~~		...
s4	Store 4	Grocery		Johnson	...

(b)

StoreID	StoreName	StoreType	StoreSqft	~~Manager~~	...
s1	Store 1	Grocery	200		...
s2	Store 2	Supermarket	300		...
s3	Store 3	Supermarket	500		...
s4	Store 4	Grocery		~~Johnson~~	...

(c)

Fig. 11.22 Contents of the versions of the Store dimension. (a) Store in V_1 at time t_1; (b) Store in V_2 at time t_2; (c) Store in V_1 at time t_2

We explain next with the help of examples the mechanisms required to make all data available using any schema version. Figure 11.22a shows the state of level Store at time t_1 in V_1. After the derivation of version V_2, Fig. 11.22b shows the state of level Store at time t_2 when a new store member s4 has been added to the current version. The shaded and crossed out column represents the fact that when deriving version V_2 from V_1, the data warehouse must retain the values of the deleted attribute for the existing store members. However, when accessing the store members using version V_1, the user should be able to access all the members stored in V_1 and V_2, including the new store s4. As attribute Manager does not exist in V_1, it is not available in

V_1 at t_2, as shown in Fig. 11.22c. Similarly, as attribute StoreSqft does not exist in V_2, the value of the attribute for s4 is not available in V_1.

(a)

CustomerID	...	StoreID	...	SalesAmount
c1	...	s1	...	20
c1	...	s2	...	15
c2	...	s3	...	18

(b)

CustomerID	...	StoreID	ShipperID	...	SalesAmount	Freight	NetAmount
c1	...	s1		...	20		
c1	...	s2		...	15		
c2	...	s3		...	18		
c3	...	s4	p1	...	9	1	8

(c)

CustomerID	...	~~StoreID~~	ShipperID	SupplierID	...	SalesAmount	Freight	NetAmount
~~c1~~	...	~~s1~~		~~u1~~	...	~~20~~		
~~c1~~	...	~~s2~~		~~u1~~	...	~~15~~		
c1	...			u1	...	35		
c2	...	~~s3~~		u2	...	18		
c3	...	~~s4~~	p1	u2	...	9	1	8
c4	...		p2	u3	...	25	5	20

(d)

CustomerID	...	StoreID	~~ShipperID~~	~~SupplierID~~	...	SalesAmount	~~Freight~~	~~NetAmount~~
c1	...	s1		~~u1~~	...	20		
c1	...	s2		~~u1~~	...	15		
c2	...	s3		~~u2~~	...	18		
c3	...	s4	~~p1~~	~~u2~~	...	9	~~1~~	~~8~~
c4	...		~~p2~~	~~u3~~	...	25	~~5~~	~~20~~

Fig. 11.23 Contents of the versions of the Sales fact. (**a**) Sales in V_1 at time t_1; (**b**) Sales in V_2 at time t_2; (**c**) Sales in V_3 at time t_3; (**d**) Sales in V_1 at time t_3

Consider now Fig. 11.23a, which shows the state of the Sales fact in version V_1 at time t_1. After the first schema change, Fig. 11.23b shows the state of the fact in V_2 at time t_2 where the last fact member is added to the current version. The figure shows the new dimension Shipper and the new measures Freight and NetAmount. As the shipper information is not available for the previous facts, they roll-up to an unknown shipper. Consider now Fig. 11.23c, which shows the state of the fact in V_3 at time t_3 where the last member is added to the current version. The figure shows a new dimension Supplier. Since in the previous versions level Product rolled-up to level Supplier, it is possible to obtain the SupplierID values for the existing fact members. For this, the fact members related to the same supplier should be aggregated provided that the value of the other dimensions are the same. For example, as the first two fact members are related to the same supplier u1 and the values of the other dimensions are the same, these fact members are combined and represented as a single member in the new version of the fact. If the user accesses fact Sales in V_1 at time t_3, the value of StoreID for the last fact member will not be available as this attribute is not present in the new version of the fact. This situation is depicted in Fig. 11.23d.

Notice that in some cases default values can be used instead of null values for information that was not captured in a particular version. Suppose that in version V_2 the Sales fact has an additional dimension Promotion and that the measure Discount is not in V_1. If there were no promotions or discounts in version V_1, instead of having null values for the facts introduced in V_1, these facts can be related to a member 'No Promotion' in the Promotion dimension and have a value 0 for Discount. This will allow the data warehouse to better capture the application semantics.

11.8 Logical Design of Multiversion Data Warehouses

Figure 11.24 shows the logical schemas of the three versions of the Northwind data warehouse given in Fig. 11.20. In the figures, the tables that changed from the previous version are shown with all their attributes, while the tables that did not change from the previous version are shown with only their primary key. Since any of these schemas can be used to address the data warehouse, a user must chose one of them prior to any interaction with it. After that, she can use the data warehouse like a traditional one. We describe next two approaches to implement such a multiversion data warehouse.

In the *single-table version* (STV) approach, the newly added attributes are appended to the existing ones and the deleted attributes are not dropped from the table. A default or null value is stored for unavailable attributes. This approach is preferred for dimension tables since they usually have fewer records as compared to the number of records in the fact tables. Figure 11.25 shows the state of the Store table after the first schema change where attribute Manager is added and StoreSqft is deleted. Records s1, s2, and s3 have null values for attribute Manager because its value is unknown for these records. Since attribute StoreSqft has been deleted, all newly added records such as s4 will have null values for it, which may result in a space overhead in the presence of a huge amount of dimension data.

The members of level Store in versions V_1 and V_2 can be accessed using the following views.

```
CREATE VIEW StoreV1 AS
        SELECT StoreKey, StoreName, StoreType, StoreSqft, Address, PostalCode, CityKey
        FROM    Store
```

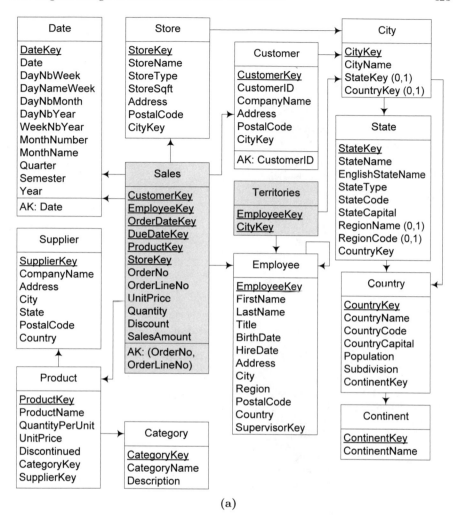

(a)

Fig. 11.24 Logical schemas of the multiversion Northwind data warehouse. (a) Initial version V_1

```
CREATE VIEW StoreV2 AS
        SELECT StoreKey, StoreName, StoreType, Manager, Address, PostalCode, CityKey
        FROM   Store
```

These views select the columns pertaining to each version of the Store level.

On the other hand, in the *multiple-table version* (MTV) approach, each change in the schema of a table produces a new version. This approach is preferred for fact tables since they typically contain many more records than dimension tables and records are added to them more frequently. Figure 11.26 illustrates this approach for the Sales fact table. As can be seen, records are

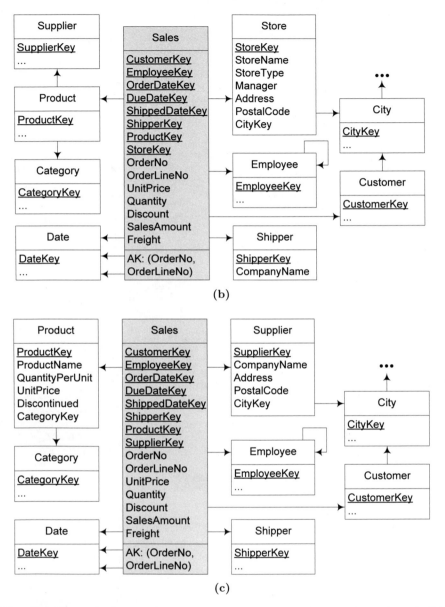

Fig. 11.24 Logical schemas of the multiversion Northwind data warehouse (cont.). (**b**) Second version V_2 (excerpt); (**c**) Third version V_3 (excerpt)

added to the version of the fact table that is current at the time of the insertion. An advantage of the MTV approach over the STV one is that it does not require null values in the new or deleted columns, and thus it prevents the storage space overhead. On the other hand, a disadvantage of

StoreKey	StoreName	StoreType	StoreSqft	Manager	...	CityKey
s1	Store 1	Grocery	200		...	t1
s2	Store 2	Supermarket	300		...	t1
s3	Store 3	Supermarket	500		...	t2
s4	Store 4	Grocery		Johnson	...	t2

Fig. 11.25 Table storing all versions of the Store level in the STV approach.

CustomerKey	...	StoreKey	...	SalesAmount
c1	...	s1	...	20
c1	...	s2	...	15
c2	...	s3	...	18

(a)

CustomerKey	...	StoreKey	ShipperKey	...	SalesAmount	Freight
c3	...	s4	p1	...	9	1

(b)

CustomerKey	...	CityKey	ShipperKey	SupplierKey	...	SalesAmount	Freight
c4	...	t3	p2	u1	...	25	2

(c)

Fig. 11.26 Tables storing the versions of the Sales fact in the MTV approach. (**a**) Table SalesT1 for V_1; (**b**) Table SalesT2 for V_2; (**c**) Table SalesT3 for V_3

the MTV approach is that the views needed for accessing the data of a fact table require gathering the records stored in several tables. Depending on the size of the fact table and the number of existing versions, these operations may negatively impact query performance.

For example, the following view returns the fact members in version V_1.

```
CREATE VIEW SalesV1 AS
        SELECT CustomerKey, EmployeeKey, OrderDateKey, DueDateKey, ProductKey,
                StoreKey, OrderNo, OrderLineNo, UnitPrice, Quantity, Discount,
                SalesAmount
        FROM   SalesT1
        UNION ALL
        SELECT CustomerKey, EmployeeKey, OrderDateKey, DueDateKey, ProductKey,
                StoreKey, OrderNo, OrderLineNo, UnitPrice, Quantity, Discount,
                SalesAmount
        FROM   SalesT2
        UNION ALL
        SELECT CustomerKey, EmployeeKey, OrderDateKey, DueDateKey, ProductKey,
                NULL, OrderNo, OrderLineNo, UnitPrice, Quantity, Discount,
                SalesAmount
        FROM   SalesT3
```

This view selects the columns pertaining to version V_1 of the Sales fact. Notice that all facts stored in table SalesT3 will have a null value for StoreKey. The view that returns the fact members in version V_2 is similar.

Finally, the view that returns the fact members in version V_3 is as follows.

```
CREATE VIEW SalesV3 AS
        SELECT CustomerKey, EmployeeKey, OrderDateKey, DueDateKey, NULL, NULL,
               S.ProductKey, P.SupplierKey,
               CASE WHEN COUNT(*) = 1 THEN MAX(OrderNo) ELSE NULL END,
               CASE WHEN COUNT(*) = 1 THEN MAX(OrderLineNo) ELSE NULL
               END, AVG(S.UnitPrice), SUM(Quantity), AVG(Discount),
               SUM(SalesAmount), NULL
        FROM   SalesT1 S JOIN Store T ON S.StoreKey = T.StoreKey JOIN
               Product P ON S.ProductKey = P.ProductKey
        GROUP BY CustomerKey, EmployeeKey, OrderDateKey, DueDateKey,
               S.ProductKey, P.SupplierKey
        UNION ALL
        SELECT CustomerKey, EmployeeKey, OrderDateKey, DueDateKey,
               ShippedDateKey, ShipperKey, S.ProductKey, P.SupplierKey,
               CASE WHEN COUNT(*) = 1 THEN MAX(OrderNo) ELSE NULL END,
               CASE WHEN COUNT(*) = 1 THEN MAX(OrderLineNo) ELSE NULL
               END, AVG(S.UnitPrice), SUM(Quantity), AVG(Discount),
               SUM(SalesAmount), SUM(Freight)
        FROM   SalesT2 S JOIN Store T ON S.StoreKey = T.StoreKey JOIN
               Product P ON S.ProductKey = P.ProductKey
        GROUP BY CustomerKey, EmployeeKey, OrderDateKey, DueDateKey,
               ShippedDateKey, ShipperKey, S.ProductKey, P.SupplierKey
        UNION ALL
        SELECT CustomerKey, EmployeeKey, OrderDateKey, DueDateKey,
               ShippedDateKey, ShipperKey, ProductKey, SupplierKey, OrderNo,
               OrderLineNo, UnitPrice, Quantity, Discount, SalesAmount, Freight
        FROM   SalesT3
```

Recall that dimension Supplier was added to the fact in V_3 while in versions V_1 and V_2 it was a level in dimension Product. Therefore, the fact members stored in tables SalesT1 and SalesT2 must be aggregated with respect to the Supplier level of the Product dimension. In addition to aggregating the measures, we must take care of how to display the OrderNo and OrderLineNo values. The CASE statement in the SELECT clause does this. For facts that are not aggregated, that is, the count of the group is equal to 1, the values of OrderNo and OrderLineNo are displayed (although a MAX function must be used to comply with the SQL syntax). Aggregated facts will have several values for OrderNo and OrderLineNo and therefore, a null value is displayed.

11.9 Querying the Multiversion Northwind Data Warehouse in SQL

As already said, to query a multiversion data warehouse, the user must first specify which version of the warehouse she wants to use. Then, thanks to the views defined on the warehouse, querying is done in a similar way to traditional data warehouses. However, the SQL code for a user query may vary across versions. Further, a user query may not be valid in all versions. Also, the result of a query may only be partial since it requires information which is not available throughout the overall lifespan of the data warehouse. We discuss these issues with the help of examples.

Query 11.12. *Compute the yearly sales amount per supplier country.*
This query is valid in all schema versions. The query for V_1 is as follows.

```
SELECT    SO.CountryName AS SupplierCountry, D.Year,
          SUM(SalesAmount) AS SalesAmount
FROM      SalesV1 F, Product P, Supplier S, City SC, State SS, Country SO, Date D
WHERE     F.ProductKey = P.ProductKey AND P.SupplierKey = S.SupplierKey AND
          S.CityKey = SC.CityKey AND SC.StateKey = SS.StateKey AND
          SS.CountryKey = SO.CountryKey AND F.OrderDateKey = D.DateKey
GROUP BY SO.CountryName, D.Year
ORDER BY SO.CountryName, D.Year
```

On the other hand, the query for V_3 is as follows.

```
SELECT    SO.CountryName AS SupplierCountry, D.Year,
          SUM(SalesAmount) AS SalesAmount
FROM      SalesV3 F, Supplier S, City SC, State SS, Country SO, Date D
WHERE     F.SupplierKey = S.SupplierKey AND
          S.CityKey = SC.CityKey AND SC.StateKey = SS.StateKey AND
          SS.CountryKey = SO.CountryKey AND F.OrderDateKey = D.DateKey
GROUP BY SO.CountryName, D.Year
ORDER BY SO.CountryName, D.Year
```

The differences between the above queries (which are underlined) come from the fact that in V_1 suppliers are represented as a hierarchy in the **Product** dimension, while in V_3 they are represented as a dimension in the **Sales** fact. Therefore, the joins must be implemented differently in the two queries above.

Query 11.13. *Total sales amount and total freight by category and year.*
Since the **Freight** measure was introduced in version V_2 of the schema, this query cannot be answered in V_1. The query for V_3 is as follows.

```
SELECT    CategoryName, D.Year, SUM(SalesAmount) AS SalesAmount,
          SUM(Freight) AS Freight
FROM      SalesV3 F, Product P, Category C, Date D
WHERE     F.ProductKey = P.ProductKey AND P.CategoryKey = C.CategoryKey AND
          F.OrderDateKey = D.DateKey
GROUP BY CategoryName, D.Year
ORDER BY CategoryName, D.Year
```

Suppose that version V_2 was implemented on January 1st, 2017. Then, the sales facts previous to that date will have a null value for **Freight**.

Query 11.14. *Total sales amount by category for stores that have more than 30,000 square feet.*

This query can only be answered in V_1 since the attribute **StoreSqft** only exists in that version. The query is as follows.

```
SELECT      CategoryName, SUM(SalesAmount) AS SalesAmount
FROM        SalesV1 F, Product P, Category C, Store S
WHERE       F.ProductKey = P.ProductKey AND P.CategoryKey = C.CategoryKey AND
            F.StoreKey = S.StoreKey AND StoreSqft > 30000
GROUP BY CategoryName
ORDER BY CategoryName
```

This query illustrates that data introduced in later versions is also available in V_1. However, stores introduced in V_2 or V_3 have a null value for **StoreSqft** and sales introduced in V_3 have no associated **Store**. Due to these reasons, the result of this query will be partial since the information required by the query is not available throughout the lifespan of the data warehouse.

11.10 Summary

In this chapter, after introducing basic concepts of temporal databases, we presented a temporal extension of the MultiDim model. It supports several temporality types, namely, valid time, transaction time, and lifespan. Temporal levels associate a time frame with their members. Temporal attributes keep track of the evolution of their values. Temporal relationships keep track of the evolution of the links between parent and child members. The model distinguishes between instant and lifespan cardinalities, which indicate the number of members of one level that can be related to members of another level at any time instant and over the lifespan of the member, respectively. We have discussed three cases of temporal hierarchies, depending on whether the levels and/or the relationships between them are temporal or not, and discussed how to aggregate measures when levels are related by temporal relationships. We also explained how to translate the temporal MultiDim model into the relational model and discussed several implementation considerations. We then showed examples of SQL queries over a temporal data warehouse. We also compared temporal data warehouses against the slowly changing dimensions approach, traditionally used in data warehouses for coping with dimensions that vary over time.

Finally, we studied multiversion data warehouses, separating this problem from that of temporal data warehouses. Distinguishing concerns and dealing with each problem separately allows us to provide practical and efficient solutions for each of them. As we have stated, the problem of dealing with both multiversion data warehouses and temporal data warehouses can be solved by combining these solutions. We proposed a conceptual multiversion data warehouse model and provided a logical implementation of it using the single-table approach for dimension tables and the multiple-table approach for fact tables. We showed how views can be used as an efficient mechanism for accommodating warehouse data across versions, and finally, we addressed several issues that arise when querying multiversion data warehouses in SQL.

11.11 Bibliographic Notes

Research on temporal databases started at the beginning of the 1990s [229]. A temporal extension of SQL called TSQL2 [220] was proposed by Snodgrass and some of its features are part of the SQL standard [133] and have also been incorporated into major DBMSs such as SQL Server, DB2, Oracle, and Teradata. We refer to [221, 276] for a detailed explanation of how to deal with temporal aspects in traditional SQL. Books covering temporal data in relational databases and in SQL are [55, 121]. Extensions of relational DBMSs for supporting temporal queries have been proposed in [60]. The difference between telic and atelic facts has been analyzed, e.g., in [232]. Conceptual models that represent temporal information in the ER model (e.g., [71]) or UML (e.g., [41]) have been proposed. Conceptual models that represent both spatial and temporal features have also been proposed (e.g., [127, 182]).

The addition of temporal features to data warehouses, leading to temporal data warehouses, has been studied by several authors. Although many of the proposed solutions cover *schema evolution* and *data evolution* simultaneously, as we have shown in this chapter, these are different problems that require specific solutions. Obviously, the two approaches can be combined to allow the coexistence of different versions of the schema and instances. Surveys on temporal and multiversion data warehouses can be found in [87, 147]. This chapter is based on previous work from the authors [4, 5, 51, 145].

Challenging problems abound in temporal data warehouses, concerning temporality types (e.g., [1]), querying (e.g., [154]), multidimensional aggregation (e.g., [33]), correct aggregation in the presence of changes (e.g., [65, 82]), materialization of temporal views (e.g., [268]), multidimensional schema evolution (e.g., [32, 65]), and logical representation of temporal data warehouses (e.g., [31, 113]), etc. Slowly changing measures are defined in [89].

Representative approaches to schema versioning are [30, 65, 158]). The one presented in [264] distinguishes between real and alternative schema versions, the latter are used for exploratory analysis. This work also studies querying multiversion data warehouses. In [248] is presented a temporal model supporting historical dimensions and fact table versioning. A temporal query language is also proposed. In [197] is described a prototype implementation that manages schema versions using graph-based metamodels and performs data transformations between schema versions. A join index for multiversion data warehouses is presented in [49]. Automated support for the database schema evolution process is described in [53, 103]. The two approaches studied in this chapter to implement multiversion databases, namely, the single-table and multiple-table versions, are discussed in [259]. A third approach, called the partial multiple-table version is also discussed. The evolution of ETL processes in the presence of evolution of the schema of data sources and/or the data warehouse has been studied in [181, 262].

11.12 Review Questions

11.1 What are temporal databases? Discuss different ways of interpreting the time frame associated with the facts in a temporal database.

11.2 Describe the various time data types, giving for each one of them an example of its use.

11.3 Define the various synchronization relationships in terms of the boundary, interior, and exterior of temporal values.

11.4 Comment on the support that current DBMSs and SQL provide for representing and querying time-varying data.

11.5 Illustrate with examples the temporality types of the MultiDim model.

11.6 Discuss with an example the various situations when a level, one of its attributes, or both are temporal.

11.7 Explain the difference between instant and lifespan cardinalities.

11.8 Explain how to ensure correctness of roll-up operations when the related levels and/or the parent-child relationship are temporal.

11.9 Explain the role of synchronization relationships in temporal facts.

11.10 Discuss the mapping rules for translating a temporal MultiDim schema into a relational one.

11.11 Illustrate with examples the relational mapping of a level depending on the temporality of the level and/or its attributes.

11.12 Discuss different options that can be used for mapping a temporal relationship into the relational model.

11.13 How are measures mapped into the relational model? How does the mapping differ when measures represent states or events?

11.14 How can the various temporal constraints included in a conceptual multidimensional schema be represented in a logical schema?

11.15 State the difference between telic and atelic measures. Illustrate with examples how these types of measures influence measure aggregation.

11.16 With the help of an example, discuss the differences between the two relational implementations of a temporal data warehouse.

11.17 What are multiversion data warehouses? How do they differ from temporal data warehouses?

11.18 Give an example scenario that motivates the need to maintain several versions of a data warehouse.

11.19 Describe with the scenario of the previous question the model for multiversion data warehouses presented in this chapter.

11.20 How is a time frame associated to the versions of a data warehouse?

11.21 What possible changes may occur in a multidimensional schema?

11.22 Compare the two approaches for implementing a multiversion data warehouse, identifying their advantages and disadvantages.

11.23 Why are views needed for multiversion data warehouses? Give two examples of views that differ significantly in their complexity.

11.24 Describe the various issues that be must taken into account when querying a multiversion data warehouse.

11.13 Exercises

Exercise 11.1. Using the example schema in Fig. 11.1, write an SQL query expressing the maximum salary by department.

Exercise 11.2. An insurance company uses the following temporal database

- Client(<u>ClientNo</u>, FirstName, LastName, Address, TelNo)
- Car(<u>PlateNo</u>, Model, Year, ClientNo, <u>FromDate</u>, ToDate)
  ClientNo references Client.ClientNo
- Policy(<u>PolicyNo</u>, PolicyType, PlateNo, Amount, FromDate, ToDate)
  PlateNo references Car.PlateNo
- Accident(<u>AccNo</u>, PlateNo, Location, Description, DateTime)
  PlateNo references Car.PlateNo
- Repair(<u>AccNo</u>, Description, Cost, <u>FromDate</u>, ToDate)
  AccNo references Accident.AccNo

where

- Table Client contains the persons that have a car covered by an insurance policy
- Table Car contains information describing cars. The temporality describes the period during which a client owns a car.
- Table Policy contains information about car insurance policies. The temporality describes the period during which a policy covers a car.
- Table Accident contains information about the accidents involving cars. The temporality describes the instant at which an accident happened.
- Table Repair contains information about the repairs made to cars after an accident. The temporality describes the period of time during which the repair was made. Notice that a repair may be performed several months after an accident, even if the insurance policy has expired meanwhile.

Write in standard SQL the following queries.

a. Number of accidents that were not covered by an insurance policy.
b. Name and address of clients such that one of their insurance policies expired last month.
c. Name and address of clients such that all the cars they currently own are covered by an insurance policy.
d. For each insurance policy, number and total cost of all their repairs.
e. For accidents that occurred in 2014, average time that clients waited for the corresponding repairs.
f. Periods of time in which clients had at least one car.
g. For each car, insurance policies that have covered it.
h. Time during which cars were not covered by any insurance policy.
i. Total cost of repairs for each insurance policy.
j. Number of cars owned by clients.
k. Clients who never had an accident involving any of their cars during the time the cars were covered by an insurance policy.

Exercise 11.3. Design a temporal MultiDim schema for an application domain that you are familiar with. Illustrate in it the following concepts: temporal dimension, temporal level, temporal attribute, temporal fact relationship, temporal hierarchy, temporal parent-child relationship, instant cardinality, and synchronization relationship.

Exercise 11.4. Consider the conceptual schema for the university application obtained in the solution of Ex. 4.4. Extend the conceptual schema to keep the following information.

- The lifecycles of courses, professors, departments, and projects.
- The evolution of dean and number of students for departments.
- The evolution of status for professors.
- The evolution of the affiliation of professors to departments.
- The evolution of teaching.

Exercise 11.5. Translate the temporal MultiDim schema obtained for the university application in the previous exercise into the relational model.

Exercise 11.6. In the relational schema obtained for Ex. 11.5, enforce the following integrity constraints.

a. The intervals defining the lifespan of a professor are disjoint.
b. The time frame of the temporal attribute Status is included in the lifespan of Professor.
c. The lifespan of the relationship between professors and departments is covered by the intersection of the lifespans of the participating members.
d. The lifespan of a professor is equal to the union of the lifespans of her links to all departments.

 e. The lifespans of a professor and a department participating in a roll-up relationship overlap.
 f. Professors participate in teaching only during their lifespan.
 g. At each point in time a professor teaches at most four courses.

Exercise 11.7. Translate the schema in Fig. 11.27 into the relational model and write the SQL query that computes the average quantity by category, branch, and month.

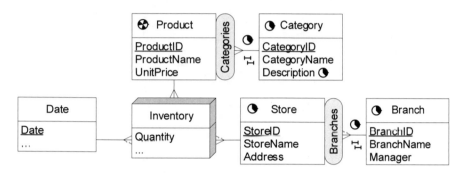

Fig. 11.27 A schema for analyzing inventories

Exercise 11.8. Translate the schema in Fig. 11.28 into the relational model and write the SQL query that computes the average dosage of drugs by diagnosis and age group.

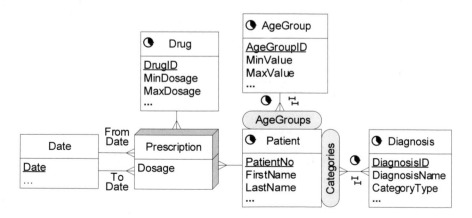

Fig. 11.28 A schema for analyzing prescriptions

Exercise 11.9. Translate the schema in Fig. 11.29 into the relational model and write the SQL query that computes the total cost by department and month from the measures TotalDays and DailyRate.

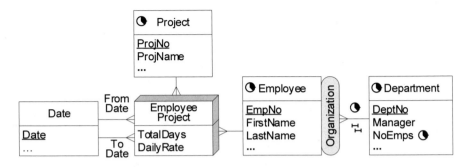

Fig. 11.29 A schema for analyzing the assignment of employees to projects

Exercise 11.10. Consider the conceptual schema given in Fig. 11.30, which is used for analyzing car insurance policies. Translate the conceptual schema into a relational one and write the following SQL queries.

  a. Number of policies by coverage as of January 1st, 2015.
  b. Total policy amount per coverage and month.
  c. Monthly year-to-date policy amount for each coverage.
  d. Number of policies sold by an employee in 2014 compared with the number of policies sold by herself and her subordinates in 2014.
  e. For each policy type, number of days of its lifespan compared with the number of days that it contained the coverage "Personal Injury".
  f. For each customer, total policy amount for current policies covering vehicles with appraised value at the begining of the policy greater than $10,000.
  g. For each vehicle, give the periods during which it was covered by a policy.
  h. Total policy amount for policies with coverages "Collision" or "Personal Injury".
  i. For each employee, monthly number of policies sold by month and department.
  j. For each vehicle, total policy amount in the periods during which the vehicle was assigned to only one driver.
  k. Monthly number of policies by customer.
  l. Total amount for policy types during the periods in which all their coverages have a limit greater than $7,000.

Exercise 11.11. Consider the conceptual schema of the Foodmart cube given in Fig. 4.22. Imagine a scenario of schema evolution and define three versions of the schema, the last one being the one in Fig. 4.22. Make sure to

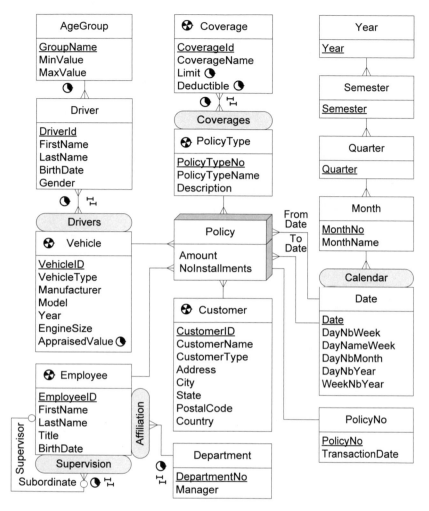

Fig. 11.30 A conceptual schema for analyzing car insurance policies

consider adding and removing the following concepts across versions: dimensions, measures, level attributes, and hierarchies.

Exercise 11.12. Translate into the relational model the conceptual schemas of the multiversion Foodmart cube obtained in Ex. 11.11.

Exercise 11.13. Given the data warehouse obtained as answer in Ex. 11.12, create the views for accessing the content of the warehouse in the various versions.

Exercise 11.14. Write in SQL the following queries for the data warehouse obtained as answer in Ex. 11.12. For each query, determine in which versions

it is valid, in which versions it gives full or partial information, and compare
the SQL queries for the versions in which it is valid.

a. All measures for stores.
b. All measures for stores in the states of California and Washington summarized at the sales region level.
c. By store, monthly average of the number of days between the order date
   and the shipped date.
d. Sales average in 2017 by store state and store type.
e. Sales profit in 2017 by store and semester.
f. For promotions other than "No Promotion," unit sales and percentage of
   the unit sales of the promotion with respect to all promotions.
g. Unit sales and number of promotion cities by promotion and quarter.
h. Unit sales by promotion and sales district.
i. Monthly cost by promotion.
j. Store sales and number of customers by month and sales region.
k. Monthly year-to-date sales by product brand.
l. Store districts whose sales count accounts for 50% of the overall sales
   count.

Chapter 12
Spatial and Mobility Data Warehouses

A vast amount of information stored in databases has a spatial or location component. However, this information is usually represented in a nonspatial manner (that is, using solely the place name). Nevertheless, it is well known that including spatial data in the analysis process can help to reveal patterns that are difficult to discover otherwise.

The first part of this chapter is devoted to *spatial data warehouses*, which are data warehouses that contain spatial data. They focus on the analysis of *static objects*, that is, objects whose spatial features do not change (or change exceptionally) across time. However, many applications require the analysis of the so-called *moving objects*, that is, objects that change their position in space and time. Mobility analysis can be applied, for example, in traffic management, which requires to analyze traffic flows to capture their characteristics. Other applications aim at tracking the position of persons recorded by the electronic devices they carry, like smartphones, in order to analyze their behavior. Extending data warehouses to cope with mobility data leads to *mobility data warehouses*, which we study in the second part of this chapter.

Section 12.1 introduces some background concepts related to spatial databases and presents a spatial extension of the conceptual multidimensional model we use in this book. In Sect. 12.2, we discuss implementation considerations for spatial data focusing in PostGIS, the spatial extension of PostgreSQL, an open-source relational DBMS. Section 12.3 presents the relational representation of spatial data warehouses while Sect. 12.4 discusses the implementation of topological constraints. In Sect. 12.5, we address analytical queries to spatial data warehouses expressed in SQL. We then continue in Sect. 12.6 motivating mobility data analysis. In Sect. 12.7, we define temporal types, which provide a way to represent values that evolve over time, while in Sect. 12.8 we describe the implementation of these types in MobilityDB, a mobility database based on PostgreSQL and PostGIS. Mobility data warehouses are defined in Sect. 12.9, and Sect. 12.10 is devoted to querying mobility data warehouses.

© Springer-Verlag GmbH Germany, part of Springer Nature 2022
A. Vaisman, E. Zimányi, *Data Warehouse Systems*, Data-Centric Systems and Applications, https://doi.org/10.1007/978-3-662-65167-4_12

12.1 Conceptual Design of Spatial Data Warehouses

Spatial databases have been used for several decades for storing and manipulating the spatial properties of real-world phenomena. There are two complementary ways of consider these phenomena. **Discrete phenomena** correspond to recognizable objects with an associated spatial extent. Examples are bus stops, roads, and states, whose spatial extents are represented, respectively, by a point, a line, and a surface. **Continuous phenomena** vary over space (and possibly time) and associate to each point within their spatial and/or temporal extent a value that characterizes the phenomenon at that point. Examples include temperature, soil composition, and elevation. These concepts are not mutually exclusive. In fact, many phenomena may be viewed alternatively as discrete or continuous. For example, while a road is a discrete entity, the speed limit and the number of lanes may vary from one position to another of the road.

In this section, we present the spatial extension of the MultiDim model. The graphical notation of the model is described in Appendix A. We start by describing next the data types for representing, at a conceptual level, discrete and continuous phenomena.

12.1.1 Spatial Data Types

Spatial data types are used to represent the spatial extent of real-world objects. At the conceptual level, we use the spatial data types shown in Fig. 12.1. These data types provide support for two-dimensional features.

Point represents zero-dimensional geometries denoting a single location in space. A point can be used to represent, for instance, a village in a country.

Line represents one-dimensional geometries denoting a set of connected points defined by a continuous curve in the plane. A line can be used to represent, for instance, a road in a road network. A line is closed if it has no identifiable extremities (i.e., its start point is equal to its end point).

OrientedLine represents lines whose extremities have the semantics of a start point and an end point (the line has a given direction from the start point to the end point). It can be used to represent, for instance, a river in a hydrographic network.

Surface represents two-dimensional geometries denoting a set of connected points that lie inside a boundary formed by one or more disjoint closed lines. If the boundary consists of more than one closed line, one of the closed lines contains all the others, and the latter represent holes in the surface defined by the former line. In simpler words, a surface may have holes but no islands (no exterior islands and no islands within a hole).

SimpleSurface represents surfaces without holes. For example, the extent of a lake without islands may be represented by a simple surface.

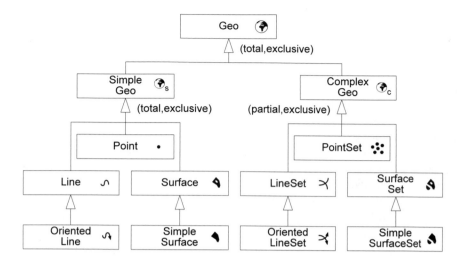

Fig. 12.1 Spatial data types

SimpleGeo is a generic spatial data type that generalizes the types Point, Line, and Surface. SimpleGeo is an abstract type, that is, it is never instantiated as such: Upon creation of a SimpleGeo value, it is necessary to specify which of its subtypes characterizes the new element. A SimpleGeo value can be used, for instance, to represent cities, whereas a small city may be represented by a point and a bigger city by a simple surface.

Several spatial data types are used to describe spatially homogeneous sets. PointSet represents sets of points, for instance, tourist points of interest. LineSet represents sets of lines, for example, a road network. OrientedLineSet represents a set of oriented lines, for example, a river and its tributaries. SurfaceSet and SimpleSurfaceSet represent sets of surfaces with or without holes, respectively, for example, administrative regions.

ComplexGeo represents any heterogeneous set of geometries that may include sets of points, sets of lines, and sets of surfaces. ComplexGeo may be used to represent a water system consisting of rivers (oriented lines), lakes (surfaces), and reservoirs (points). ComplexGeo has PointSet, LineSet, OrientedLineSet, SurfaceSet, and SimpleSurfaceSet as subtypes.

Finally, Geo is the most generic spatial data type, generalizing the types SimpleGeo and ComplexGeo; its semantics is "this element has a spatial extent" without any commitment to a specific spatial data type. Like SimpleGeo, Geo is an abstract type. It can be used, for instance, to represent the administrative regions of a country, which may be either a Surface or a SurfaceSet.

It is worth noting that empty geometries are allowed, that is, geometries representing an empty set of points. This is needed in particular to express the fact that the intersection of two disjoint geometries is also a geometry, although it may be an empty one.

12.1.2 Topological relationships

Topological relationships specify how two spatial values relate to each
other. They they can be used to test, for instance, whether two states have
a common border, a highway crosses a state, or a city is located in a state.
Topological relationships are defined based on the boundary, the interior, and
the exterior of spatial values. The **exterior** of a spatial value is composed
of all the points of the underlying space that do not belong to itself. The
interior of a spatial value is composed of all its points that do not belong to
the boundary. The **boundary** of a spatial value is the interface between its
interior and exterior. It is defined for the various spatial data types as follows.
A point has an empty boundary, and its interior is equal to the point. The
boundary of a line is given by its extreme points, provided that they can be
distinguished (e.g., a closed line has no boundary). The boundary of a surface
is given by the enclosing closed line and those of its holes.

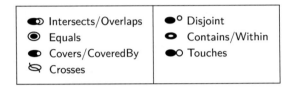

Fig. 12.2 Icons for the various topological relationships

We describe next the topological relationships; the associated icons are
given in Fig. 12.2.

Intersects/Disjoint: Intersects and Disjoint are inverse relationships: When one
    applies, the other does not. Two geometries are disjoint if the interior and
    the boundary of one object intersects only the exterior of the other object.
Equals: A geometry equals another one if they share the same set of points.
Overlaps: Two geometries overlap if the interior of each one intersects both
    the interior and the exterior of the other one.
Contains/Within: Contains and Within are symmetric relationships: a Contains
    b if and only if b Within a. A geometry contains another one if the inner
    object is located in the interior of the other object and the boundaries of
    the two objects do not intersect.
Touches: Two geometries touch each other if they intersect but their interiors
    do not.
Covers/CoveredBy: Covers and CoveredBy are symmetric relationships: a Cov-
    ers b if and only if b CoveredBy a. A geometry covers another one if it
    includes all points of the other, inner geometry. This means that the first
    geometry contains the inner one, as defined previously, but without the
    restriction that the boundaries of the geometries do not intersect.

Crosses: One geometry crosses another if they intersect and the dimension of this intersection is less than the greatest dimension of the geometries.

12.1.3 Continuous Fields

Continuous fields represent phenomena that change continuously in space and/or time. Examples are altitude and temperature, where the former varies only in space and the latter varies in both space and time. At a *conceptual level*, a continuous field is defined as a partial function that assigns to each point in a spatial and/or temporal extent a value of a domain. Hence, a value of a field type representing altitude is a function f : point $\rightarrow$ real. Similary, a value of field type representing temperature is a function f : point, instant $\rightarrow$ real.

Continuous fields are partial functions since they could be undefined at some points in space. Consider, for example, a field defining the altitude in Belgium. Since there are several enclaves and exclaves between Belgium, the Netherlands, and Germany, the altitude of an enclave of Germany within Belgium will be undefined.

Field types have associated operations. For a detailed description, we refer the reader to the references provided at the end of this chapter.

12.1.4 A Conceptual Model of Spatial Data Warehouses

We explain next the spatial extension of the MultiDim model. For this, we use as example the GeoNorthwind data warehouse, which is the Northwind data warehouse extended with spatial types. As shown in the schema in Fig. 12.3, pictograms are used to represent spatial information.

A **spatial level** is a level for which the application needs to store spatial characteristics. A spatial level is represented using the icon of its associated **geometry** to the right of the level name, which is represented using one of the spatial data types described in Sect. 12.1.1. For example, in Fig. 12.3, City and State are spatial levels, while Product and Date are nonspatial levels.

A **spatial attribute** is an attribute whose domain is a spatial data type. For example, CapitalGeo is a spatial attribute of type point, while Elevation is a spatial attribute of type field of reals. Attributes representing continuous fields are identified by the 'f(◈)' pictogram.

A level may be spatial independently of the fact that it has spatial attributes. For example, as shown in Fig. 12.4, depending on application re-

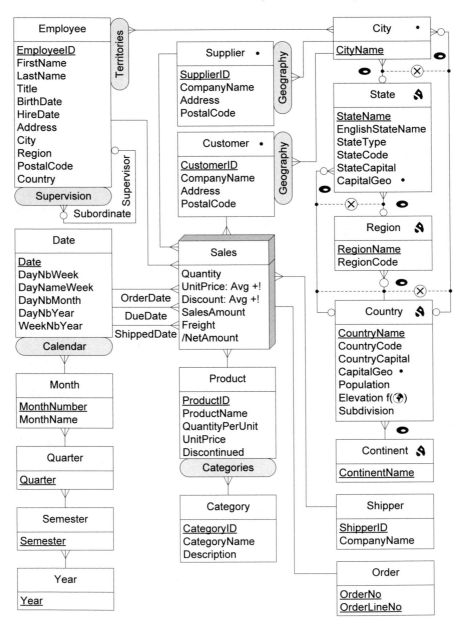

Fig. 12.3 Conceptual schema of the GeoNorthwind data warehouse

quirements, a level such as State may be spatial or not and may have spatial
attributes such as CapitalGeo.

Fig. 12.4 Examples of levels with spatial characteristics. (a) Spatial level; (b) Spatial level with a spatial attribute; (c) Nonspatial level with a spatial attribute

A **spatial hierarchy** is a hierarchy that includes at least one spatial level. Similarly, a **spatial dimension** is a dimension that includes at least one spatial level. For example, Fig. 12.3 shows two spatial hierarchies in the Supplier and Customer dimensions, which share the levels from City to Continent. All hierarchy types we have discussed in Sect. 4.2 apply also to spatial hierarchies.

Two spatial levels related in a spatial hierarchy may involve a **topological constraint**, expressed using the topological relationships given in Sect. 12.1.2. They are represented using the pictograms shown in Fig. 12.2. For example, in Fig. 12.3, the geometry of each state is covered by the one of its region or country, depending on which level a state rolls up to. Note that in Fig. 12.3, there is no topological constraint between the Supplier and City levels since the location of the supplier is obtained from its address through geocoding and the location of the city corresponds to the center of the city.

A **spatial fact** is a fact that relates several levels, two or more of which are spatial. A spatial fact may also have associated a **topological constraint** that must be satisfied by the related spatial levels: An icon in the fact indicates the topological relationship used for specifying the constraint. In the GeoNorthwind data warehouse, the Sales fact does not impose any constraint between its spatial dimensions Supplier and Customer. On the other hand, consider Fig. 12.5, which is used for the analysis of highway maintenance costs. The spatial fact Maintenance relates two spatial levels: County and Segment. This fact includes an Overlaps topological constraint, indicating that a segment and a county related to a fact member must overlap.

A **spatial measure** is a measure represented by a spatial data type. Note that numeric measures can be calculated using spatial operations. For example, in Fig. 12.5, Length is a numerical measure that represents the length of the part of a highway segment that belongs to a county, while CommonArea is a spatial measure that represents the geometry of the common part.

Various aggregation functions can be used for aggregating spatial measures along hierarchies. Examples of *spatial distributive* functions include convex hull, spatial union, and spatial intersection. Examples of *spatial algebraic*

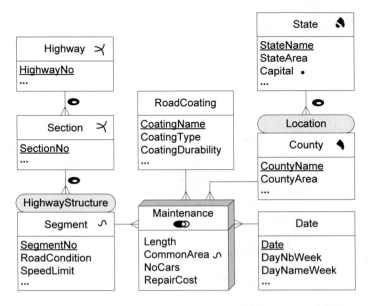

Fig. 12.5 A spatial data warehouse for analyzing the maintenance of highways

functions are the center of n points and the center of gravity. Finally, examples of *spatial holistic* functions are equipartition and nearest-neighbor. By default, the MultiDim model uses sum for aggregating numerical measures and spatial union for aggregating spatial measures. For example, in Fig. 12.5, when users roll-up from the County to the State level, for each state the measure Length of the corresponding counties will be summed, while the CommonArea measure will be a LineSet resulting from the spatial union of the lines representing highway segments for the corresponding counties.

Spatial measures allow richer analysis than nonspatial measures do. Consider Fig. 12.6, which is used for analyzing the locations of road accidents according to insurance categories (e.g., full vs. partial coverage). The schema includes a spatial measure representing the locations of accidents. Spatial union can be used to roll-up to the InsuranceCategory level to display the accident locations corresponding to each category represented as a set of points. Other aggregation functions can also be used, such as the center of n points. On the other hand, Fig. 12.7 shows an alternative schema for the analysis of road accidents. This schema has no spatial measure: the focus of analysis has been changed to the amount of insurance payments according to the various geographic locations as reflected by the spatial dimension Location.

We compare Figs. 12.6 and 12.7 with respect to the different analyses that can be performed when a location is represented as a spatial measure or as a spatial hierarchy. In Fig. 12.6, the locations of accidents can be aggregated (by using spatial union) when a roll-up operation over the Date or Insurance hierarchies is executed. However, this aggregation cannot be done with

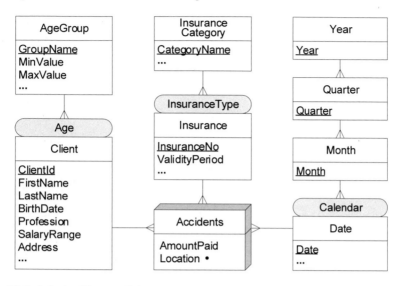

Fig. 12.6 A fact with a spatial measure

the schema in Fig. 12.7. The dimensions are independent, and traversing a hierarchy along one of them does not aggregate data in another hierarchy. Further, an analysis of the amounts of insurance payments made in different geographic zones is not supported in Fig. 12.6 since in this case only the exact locations of the accidents are known.

12.2 Implementation Considerations for Spatial Data

The discrete and continuous approaches that we presented in Sect. 12.1 are used to represent spatial data at a *conceptual* level. Two common implementations of these models are, respectively, the vector model and the raster model. In this section, we study how these models are implemented in PostGIS, a spatial extension of the open-source DBMS PostgreSQL.

12.2.1 Spatial Reference Systems

The Earth is a complex surface whose shape and dimension cannot be described with mathematical formulas. There are two main reference surfaces to approximate the shape of the Earth: the geoid and the ellipsoid.

The **geoid** is a reference model for the surface of the Earth that coincides with the mean sea level and its imaginary extension through the continents.

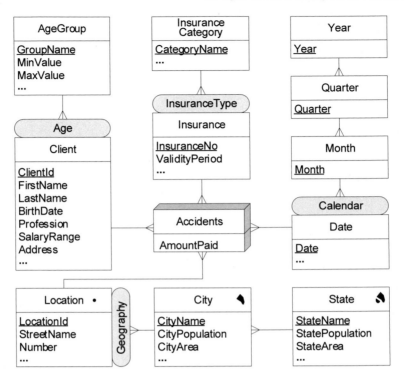

Fig. 12.7 A variant of the schema in Fig. 12.6

It is used in geodesy to measure precise surface elevations. However, the geoid is not practical to produce maps. The **ellipsoid** is a mathematical surface that approximates the geoid. The most common reference ellipsoid is the one defined by the World Geodetic System in 1984, usually referred to as WGS 84. This ellipsoid is used by the Global Positioning System (GPS). Nevertheless, different regions of the world use different reference ellipsoids, minimizing the differences between the geoid and the ellipsoid.

The ellipsoid is used to measure the location of points of interest using latitude and longitude. These are measures of the angles (in degrees) from the center of the Earth to a point on the Earth's surface. *Latitude* measures angles in the North–South direction, while *longitude* measures angles in the East–West direction. While an ellipsoid approximates the shape of the Earth, a **datum** defines where on the Earth to anchor the ellipsoid.

To produce a map, the curved reference surface of the Earth, approximated by an ellipsoid, must be transformed into the flat plane of the map by means of a **map projection**. Thus, a point on the reference surface of the Earth with geographic coordinates expressed by latitude and longitude is transformed into Cartesian coordinates representing positions on the map plane. However, as a map projection necessarily causes deformations, different projections are used for different purposes, depending on which information is preserved, namely, shapes and angles, area, distance, or directions. These four features are conflicting (e.g., it is not possible to preserve both shapes and angles as well as area), and thus, the importance placed on each of these features dictates the choice of a particular projection.

A **spatial reference system** (SRS) assigns coordinates in a mathematical space to a location in real-world space. An SRS defines at least the units of measure of the underlying coordinate system (such as degrees or meters), the maximum and minimum coordinates (referred to as the bounds), whether data are planar or spheroid, and projection information for transforming the data to other SRSs. Two geometries need to be in the same SRS to be manipulated. Otherwise, they must be transformed into a common one. SRSs are in general good for only a specific region of the globe. There are numerous SRSs, each one is identified by a spatial reference system identifier (SRID).

12.2.2 Vector Model

The spatial data types given in Sect. 12.1.1 describe spatial features at a conceptual level, without taking into account their implementation. The **vector model** provides a collection of data types for representing spatial objects into the computer. Thus, for example, while at a conceptual level a linear object is defined as an infinite collection of points, at the implementation level such a line must be approximated using points, lines, and curves as primitives.

The standard ISO/IEC 13249 SQL/MM is an extension of SQL for managing multimedia and application-specific packages. Part 3 of the standard is devoted to spatial data. It defines how zero-, one-, or two-dimensional spatial data values are represented on a two-dimensional ($\mathbb{R}^2$), three-dimensional ($\mathbb{R}^3$) or four-dimensional ($\mathbb{R}^4$) coordinate space. We describe next the spatial data types defined by SQL/MM, which are used and extended in PostGIS.

Figure 12.8 shows the type hierarchy defined in the SQL/MM standard for geometric features. ST_Geometry is the root of the hierarchy, which is an abstract type. ST_Point represents zero-dimensional geometries. ST_Curve is an abstract type representing one-dimensional geometries. Several subtypes of ST_Curve are defined according to type of interpolation function used. For example, ST_LineString and ST_CircularString represent line segments defined by a sequence of points using linear, respectively, circular interpolation, while ST_Circle represents circles defined by three noncollinear points.

ST_Surface is an abstract type representing two-dimensional geometries composed of simple surfaces consisting of a single patch whose boundary is specified by one exterior ring and zero or more interior rings if the surface has holes. In ST_CurvePolygon, the boundaries are any curve, while in ST_Polygon, the boundaries are linear strings. ST_Triangle represents poly-

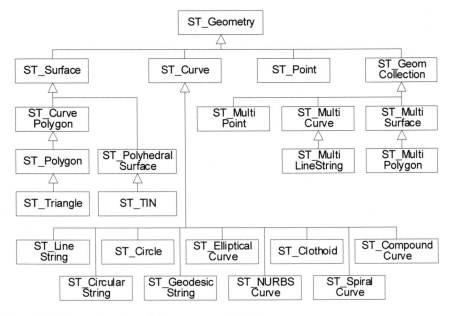

Fig. 12.8 Hierarchy of spatial types in SQL/MM

gons composed of three linear strings. ST_PolyhedralSurface represents surfaces formed by stitching together simple surfaces along their boundaries,
while ST_TIN represents polyhedral surfaces composed only of triangles.

ST_GeomCollection represents collections of zero or more ST_Geometry
values. ST_MultiPoint represents a collection of single points, not necessarily
distinct (i.e., a bag of points). Similarly, ST_MultiCurve represents a bag
of ST_Curve and ST_MultiLineString a bag of ST_LineString. The types
ST_MultiSurface and ST_MultiPolygon represent, respectively, sets of curve
polygons and sets of polygons with linear boundaries.

The standard also defines corresponding spatial methods and functions.
These can be grouped in several categories.

There are methods that retrieve properties or measures from a geometry.
Examples are ST_Boundary for retrieving the boundary of a geometry and
ST_Length for the length of a line string of a multiline string.

There are also methods that convert between geometries and external data
formats. Three external data formats are supported: well-known text representation (WKT), well-known binary representation (WKB), and Geography
Markup Language (GML). For example, function ST_LineFromGML returns
a line value from its GML representation.

There are methods that compare two geometries with respect to their
spatial relation. These are ST_Equals, ST_Disjoint, ST_Within, ST_Touches,
ST_Crosses, ST_Intersects, ST_Overlaps, and ST_Contains. All these methods return a Boolean value.

There are also methods that generate new geometries from other ones. The newly generated geometry can be the result of a set operation on two geometries (e.g., ST_Difference, ST_Intersection, ST_Union) or can be calculated by some algorithm applied to a single geometry (e.g., ST_Buffer).

To conclude this section, it is important to remark that several DBMSs, such as SQL Server and PostGIS, provide two kinds of data types: the **geometry** data type and the **geography** data type. The former is the most used one. It represents a feature in the Euclidean space. All spatial operations over this type use units of the Spatial Reference System the geometry is in. The **geography** data type uses geodetic (i.e., spherical) coordinates instead of Cartesian (i.e., planar) coordinates. This type allows storing data in longitude/latitude coordinates. However, the functions for manipulating **geography** values (e.g., distance and area) are more complex and take more time to execute. Furthermore, current systems typically provide fewer functions defined on **geography** than there are on **geometry**.

12.2.3 Raster Model

The continuous fields presented in Sect. 12.1.3 are used to represent spatio-temporal phenomenon at a conceptual level. They are represented at a logical level by **coverages**. The ISO 19123:2005 standard provides an abstract model of coverages which is concretized by the OGC Coverage Implementation Schema in various implementations such as spatio-temporal regular and irregular grids, point clouds, and general meshes. A coverage consists of four components, described next.

The **domain set** defines the spatial and/or temporal extent for the coverage, where the coordinates are expressed with respect to a Coordinate Reference System (CRS). In the case of spatio-temporal coverages, as in a time-series of satellite images, the CRS combines a spatial reference system such as WGS 84 and a temporal coordinate system such as ISO 8601, which represents dates and times in the Gregorian calendar. The spatial extent is defined by a set of geometric objects, which may be extended to the convex hull of these objects. Commonly used domains include point sets, grids, and collections of closed rectangles. The geometric objects may exhaustively partition the domain, and thereby form a tessellation as in the case of a grid or a Triangulated Irregular Network (TIN). Coverage subtypes may be defined in terms of their domains. The **range set** is the set of stored values of the coverage. The **range type** describes the type of the range set values. In the case of images, it corresponds to the pixel data type, which often consists of one or more fields (also referred to as bands or channels). However, since coverages often model many associated functions sharing the same domain, the range type can be any record type. As example, a coverage that assigns to each point in a city at a particular date and time the temperature, pressure, humidity, and wind velocity will define the range type as a record of four fields. Finally, the **metadata** component represents an extensible slot for storing any kind of application-specific metadata structures.

Coverages can be of two types. A **discrete coverage** has a domain defined by a finite collection of geometric objects. A discrete coverage maps each geometric object to a single record of attribute values. An example is a coverage that maps a set of polygons to the soil type found within each polygon. On the other hand, in a **continuous coverage** both the domain and the range may take infinitely many different values. In most cases, a continuous coverage is associated with a discrete coverage that provides a set of control values to be used as a basis for evaluating the continuous coverage. Evaluation of the continuous coverage at other positions is done by interpolating between the geometry and value pairs of the control set. For example, a continuous coverage representing the temperature in a city at a particular date and time would be associated with a discrete coverage that holds the temperature values observed at a set of weather stations, from which the temperature at any point within the city would be calculated. As another example, a triangulated irregular network involves interpolation of values within a triangle composed of three neighbouring point and value pairs.

The most popular coverage type is the regular grid, which supports the **raster model**. This model is structured as an array of cells, where each cell represents the value of an attribute for a real-world location. In PostGIS, the raster data type can be used for storing raster data in a binary format. Rasters are composed of bands, also called channels. Although rasters can have many bands, they are normally limited to four, each one storing integers. For example, a picture such as a JPEG, PNG, or TIFF is generally composed of one to four bands, expressed as the typical red green blue alpha (RGBA) channels. A pixel in raster data is generally modeled as a rectangle with a value for each of its bands. Each rectangle in a raster has a width and a height, both representing units of measure (such as meters or degrees) of the geographic space in the corresponding SRS. We describe next some of the functions provided by PostGIS to manipulate raster data. Please refer to the PostGIS documentation for the full set of functions

Several functions allow to query the properties of a raster. For example, the function ST_BandNoDataValue returns the value used in a band to represent cells whose values are unknown, referred to as no data. Function ST_Value returns the value in a location of the raster for a given band.

Other functions convert between rasters and external data formats. For example, the function ST_AsJPEG returns selected bands of the raster as a single JPEG image. Analogously, the function ST_AsBinary return the binary representation of the raster.

Another group of functions converts between rasters and vector formats. The function ST_AsRaster converts a geometry to a RASTER. To convert a raster to a polygon, the function ST_Polygon is used. The function

ST_Envelope returns the minimum bounding box of the extent of the raster, represented as a polygon.

Other functions compare two rasters or a raster and a geometry with respect to their spatial relation. For example, function ST_Intersects returns true if two raster bands intersect or if a raster intersects a geometry.

Finally, another group of functions generates new rasters or geometries from other ones. For example, ST_Intersection takes two rasters as arguments and returns another raster. Also, the ST_Union function returns the union of a set of raster tiles into a single raster composed of one band. The extent of the resulting raster is the extent of the whole set.

12.3 Logical Design of Spatial Data Warehouses

In this section, we explain how a conceptual multidimensional schema is translated into a relational schema in the presence of spatial data. For example, Fig. 12.9 shows the relational representation of the GeoNorthwind conceptual schema given in Fig. 12.3. In the figure, the spatial attributes are written in boldface for better readability.

A first consideration that must be taken into account is whether a geometry (i.e., planar) or a geography (i.e., spherical) spatial type is used for representing the spatiality of levels and attributes. The choice depends on the expected extent of the spatial data warehouse. If the spatial extent of the data is relatively small, for example, is local to a state or a county, then the geometry type can be used. On the other hand, if the data span the globe or a large continental area, then the geography type should be considered.

Furthermore, the abstract spatial types presented in Sect. 12.1.1 must be mapped into corresponding spatial types provided by the implementation platform at hand. For instance, while at the conceptual level the Line data type in Fig. 12.1 represents arbitrary curves, such curves can only be approximated with one of the subtypes of the ST_Curve data type in Fig. 12.8. In addition, current systems differ in the set of spatial types provided. For instance, while PostGIS provides types similar to those of the SQL/MM standard presented in Sect. 12.2.2, Oracle provides a unique data type SDO_Geometry that must be parameterized for defining different types of geometries.

We generalize next the rules given in Sect. 5.3 for coping with spatial features.

Rule 1: A level L, provided it is not related to a fact with a one-to-one relationship, is mapped to a table T_L that contains all attributes of the level. A surrogate key may be added to the table, otherwise the identifier of the level will be the key of the table. For each spatial attribute, a spatial data type must be chosen to store its spatial extent. If the level is spatial, an additional attribute of a spatial data type is added to represent

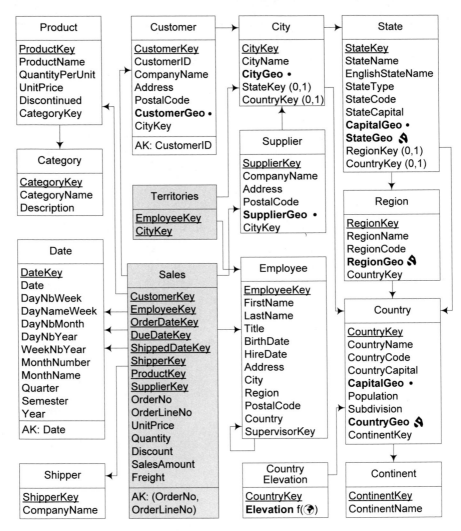

Fig. 12.9 Logical representation of the GeoNorthwind data warehouse in Fig. 12.3

the spatial extent of its members. Note that additional attributes will be added to this table when mapping relationships using Rule 3 below.

Rule 2: A fact F is mapped to a table T_F that includes as attributes all measures of the fact. Further, a surrogate key may be added to the table. Spatial measures must be mapped to attributes having a spatial type. In addition, if the fact has an associated topological constraint, a trigger may be added to ensure that the constraint is satisfied for all fact members. Note that additional attributes will be added to this table when mapping relationships using Rule 3 below.

Rule 3: A relationship between either a fact F and a dimension level L or between dimension levels L_P and L_C (standing for the parent and child levels, respectively) can be mapped in three different ways, depending on its cardinalities:

Rule 3a: If the relationship is one-to-one, the table corresponding to the fact (T_F) or to the child level (T_C) is extended with all the attributes of the dimension level or the parent level, respectively.

Rule 3b: If the relationship is one-to-many, the table corresponding to the fact (T_F) or to the child level (T_C) is extended with the surrogate key of the table corresponding to the dimension level (T_L) or the parent level (T_P), respectively, that is, there is a foreign key in the fact or child table pointing to the other table.

Rule 3c: If the relationship is many-to-many, a new table T_B (standing for bridge table) is created that contains as attributes the surrogate keys of the tables corresponding to the fact (T_F) and the dimension level (T_L) or the parent (T_P) and child levels (T_C), respectively. If the relationship has a distributing attribute, an additional attribute is added to the table to store this information.

Further, spatial attributes in the relationship must be mapped to attributes having a spatial data type. If the relationship has an associated topological constraint, a trigger may be added to ensure that the constraint is satisfied by all instances of the relationship.

We illustrate the rules above by mapping the State level shown in Fig. 12.9. The PostGIS definition for this table is given next, where the definition of some columns is elided for readability:

```
CREATE TABLE State (
        StateKey INTEGER PRIMARY KEY NOT NULL,
        StateName VARCHAR (30) NOT NULL,
        ...
        CapitalGeo geography(Point, 4326),
        StateGeo geography(MultiPolygon, 4326),
        ...
        CONSTRAINT CapitalInState CHECK(ST_Covers(StateGeo, CapitalGeo)))
```

To account for the implicit geometry indicated by a pictogram in the conceptual schema, a column StateGeo of type MultiPolygon is used for storing the geometry of states. Further, the spatial attribute CapitalGeo of type Point is used for storing the geometry of the capital cities of states. Both spatial columns are defined in the WGS84 SRS, whose identifier in PostGIS is 4326. Finally, notice that a **check constraint** ensures that the geometry of a state covers the geometry of its capital.

Figure 12.9 illustrates an alternative mapping of spatial attributes. Here, the raster attribute Elevation is not included in table Country, but it is placed instead in another table CountryElevation. This is done for optimization reasons: Raster data could be voluminous and therefore slow down significantly queries involving the Country level. Moreover, most of those queries will not require the elevation information. Notice that this approach can be used for all spatial attributes. The table CountryElevation can be created as follows:

```
CREATE TABLE CountryElevation (
        CountryKey INTEGER, Elevation RASTER,
        FOREIGN KEY (CountryKey) REFERENCES Country(CountryKey));
```

The table contains a foreign key to the Country dimension table and an attribute of the RASTER data type. This attribute will store a raster that covers the spatial extent of each country.

As another example, applying the above rules to the spatial fact Maintenance given in Fig. 12.5 will result in a table that contains the surrogate keys of the four dimensions Segment, RoadCoating, County, and Date, as well as the corresponding referential integrity constraints. Further, the table contains attributes for the measures Length and CommonArea, where the latter is a spatial attribute. The table can be created as follows:

```
CREATE TABLE Maintenance (
        SegmentKey INTEGER NOT NULL,
        RoadCoatingKey INTEGER NOT NULL,
        CountyKey INTEGER NOT NULL,
        DateKey INTEGER NOT NULL,
        Length INTEGER NOT NULL,
        CommonArea geometry(LINESTRING, 4326),
        FOREIGN KEY (SegmentKey) REFERENCES Segment(SegmentKey),
        /* Other foreign key constraints */ );
```

As an example of mapping of spatial hierarchies, Fig. 12.9 shows the mapping of the relationship between the Region and Country levels in Fig. 12.3. We see that the Region table includes an attribute CountryKey referencing the parent level Country.

12.4 Topological Constraints

In this section, we study how a topological constraint in a fact or between two spatial levels is mapped to the relational model. These constraints restrict either the geometries of spatial members related to a fact or the geometry of children members with respect to the geometry of their associated parent member. For example, the spatial fact Maintenance in Fig. 12.5 has an Overlaps relationship that states that a segment and a county related in a fact member must overlap. Similarly, in Fig. 12.3, a CoveredBy relationship exists between the Region and Country levels, which indicates that the geometry of a region is covered by the geometry of a country.

The trigger that enforces the topological constraint in the spatial fact Maintenance can be written as follows:

```
CREATE OR REPLACE FUNCTION SegmentOverlapsCounty()
RETURNS TRIGGER AS $$
    DECLARE
        SegmentGeo geometry;
        CountyGeo geometry;
    BEGIN
        /* Retrieve the geometries of the associated segment and county */
        SegmentGeo = (SELECT S.SegmentGeo FROM Segment S
            WHERE NEW.SegmentKey = S.SegmentKey);
        CountyGeo = (SELECT C.CountyGeo FROM County C
            WHERE NEW.CountyKey = C.CountyKey);
        /* Raise error if the topological constraint is violated */
        IF NOT ST_OVERLAPS(SegmentGeo, CountyGeo) THEN
            RAISE EXCEPTION 'The segment and the county must overlap';
        END IF;
        RETURN NEW;
    END;
$$ LANGUAGE plpgsql;

CREATE TRIGGER SegmentOverlapsCounty
BEFORE INSERT OR UPDATE ON Maintenance
FOR EACH ROW EXECUTE PROCEDURE SegmentOverlapsCounty();
```

Notice that in the above example, the topological constraint involves only two spatial levels. It is somewhat more complex to enforce a topological constraint that involves more than two spatial dimensions.

A topological constraint between spatial levels can be enforced either at each insertion of a child member or after the insertion of all children members. The choice among these two solutions depends on the kind of topological constraint. For example, a topological constraint stating that a region is located inside the geometry of its country can be enforced each time a city is inserted, while a topological constraint stating that the geometry of a country is the spatial union of all its composing regions must be enforced after all of the regions and the corresponding country have been inserted.

As an example of the first solution, a trigger can be used to enforce the CoveredBy topological constraint between the Region and Country levels in Fig. 12.3. This trigger should raise an error if the geometry of a region member is not covered by the geometry of its related country member. Otherwise, it should insert the new data into the Country table. The trigger is as follows:

```
CREATE OR REPLACE FUNCTION RegionInCountry()
RETURNS TRIGGER AS $$
    DECLARE
        CountryGeo geometry;
    BEGIN
        /* Retrieve the geometry of the associated country */
        CountryGeo = (SELECT C.CountryGeo FROM Country C
            WHERE NEW.CountryKey = C.CountryKey);
        /* Raise error if the topological constraint is violated */
        IF NOT ST_COVERS(CountryGeo, NEW.RegionGeo) THEN
            RAISE EXCEPTION 'A region cannot be outside its country';
```

```
     END IF;
     RETURN NEW;
  END;
$$ LANGUAGE plpgsql;

CREATE TRIGGER RegionInCountry
BEFORE INSERT OR UPDATE ON Region
FOR EACH ROW EXECUTE PROCEDURE RegionInCountry();
```

In the second solution, child members are inserted without activating a trigger. When all children members have been inserted, the verification is performed. For the GeoNorthwind case study, suppose that the geometries of Region partition the geometry of Country. When all regions of a country have been inserted into the warehouse, the following query can be used to look for countries whose regions do not partition the geometry of the country.

```
SELECT CountryKey, CountryName
FROM   Country C
WHERE  NOT ST_EQUALS(C.CountryGeo,
        (SELECT ST_UNION(R.RegionGeo)
         FROM Region R WHERE R.CountryKey = C.CountryKey))
```

12.5 Querying the GeoNorthwind Data Warehouse in SQL

Analogously to what we did in Chap. 7, we show next how spatial multidimensional queries can also be expressed in SQL.

Query 12.1. *Total sales in 2017 to customers located in cities that are within an area whose extent is a polygon drawn by the user.*

```
SELECT    C.CompanyName AS CustomerName, SUM(S.SalesAmount) AS SalesAmount
FROM      Sales S, Customer C, City Y, Date D
WHERE     S.CustomerKey = C.CustomerKey AND C.CityKey = Y.CityKey AND
          S.OrderDateKey = D.DateKey AND D.Year = 2017 AND
          ST_Covers(ST_GeographyFromText('POLYGON(
          (200.0 50.0,300.0 50.0, 300.0 80.0, 200.0 80.0, 200.0 50.0))'), Y.CityGeo)
GROUP BY C.CompanyName
```

The above query uses the spatial predicate ST_Covers to filter customer cities according to their location. The polygon given as argument to the ST_GeomFromText function will be defined by the user with the mouse in a graphical interface showing a map.

Query 12.2. *Total sales to customers located in a state that contains the capital city of the country.*

```
SELECT    C.CompanyName AS CustomerName, SUM(S.SalesAmount) AS SalesAmount
FROM      Sales S, Customer C, City Y, State A, Country O
WHERE     S.CustomerKey = C.CustomerKey AND C.CityKey = Y.CityKey AND
          Y.StateKey = A.StateKey AND A.CountryKey = O.CountryKey AND
          ST_Covers(A.StateGeo, O.CapitalGeo)
GROUP BY  C.CompanyName
```

The above query uses the function **ST_Covers** to verify that the geometry of a state covers the geometry of the capital of its country.

Query 12.3. *Spatial union of the states in the USA where at least one customer placed an order in 2017.*

```
SELECT ST_Union(DISTINCT A.StateGeo::Geometry)
FROM   Sales S, Customer C, City Y, State A, Country O, Date D
WHERE  S.CustomerKey = C.CustomerKey AND C.CityKey = Y.CityKey AND
       Y.StateKey = A.StateKey AND A.CountryKey = O.CountryKey AND
       O.CountryName = 'United States' AND S.OrderDateKey = D.DateKey AND
       D.Year = 2017
```

Here, the function **ST_Union** performs the spatial union of all the states in the USA that satisfy the query condition. The second argument of the function states the name of the property (i.e., **StateGeo**) containing the geometries that will be aggregated. Notice that we use **StateGeo::Geometry** to convert the geographies to geometries prior to applying the spatial union.

Query 12.4. *Distance between the customers' locations and the capital of the state in which they are located.*

```
SELECT    C.CompanyName AS CustomerName,
          ST_Distance(C.CustomerGeo, A.CapitalGeo) AS Distance
FROM      Customer C, City Y, State A
WHERE     C.CityKey = Y.CityKey AND Y.StateKey = A.StateKey
ORDER BY  C.CompanyName
```

The above query computes, using the function **ST_Distance**, the distance between the geometry of the customer and the capital of its state.

Query 12.5. *Total sales amount of each customer to its closest supplier.*

```
SELECT    C.CompanyName AS CustomerName, SUM(S.SalesAmount) AS SalesAmount
FROM      Sales S, Customer C, Supplier U
WHERE     S.CustomerKey = C.CustomerKey AND S.SupplierKey = U.SupplierKey AND
          ST_Distance(C.CustomerGeo, U.SupplierGeo) <= (
          SELECT MIN(ST_Distance(C.CustomerGeo, U1.SupplierGeo))
          FROM   Supplier U1 )
GROUP BY  C.CompanyName
```

In the above query, we use the inner query to compute the minimum distance of a given customer to all its suppliers.

Query 12.6. *Total sales amount for customers that have orders delivered by suppliers such that their locations are less than 200 km from each other.*

```
SELECT     C.CompanyName AS CustomerName, SUM(S.SalesAmount) AS SalesAmount
FROM       Sales S, Customer C, Supplier U
WHERE      S.CustomerKey = C.CustomerKey AND S.SupplierKey = U.SupplierKey AND
           ST_Distance(C.CustomerGeo, U.SupplierGeo) < 200000
GROUP BY C.CompanyName
```

This query selects, for each customer, the suppliers related to the customer through at least one order and located less than 200 km from the customer.

Query 12.7. *Distance between the customer and supplier for customers that have orders delivered by suppliers of the same country.*

```
SELECT DISTINCT C.CompanyName AS CustomerName,
       U.CompanyName AS SupplierName,
       ST_Distance(C.CustomerGeo, U.SupplierGeo) AS Distance
FROM   Sales S, Customer C, City CC, State CS, Supplier U, City SC, State SS
WHERE  S.CustomerKey = C.CustomerKey AND
       C.CityKey = CC.CityKey AND CC.StateKey = CS.StateKey AND
       S.SupplierKey = U.SupplierKey AND U.CityKey = SC.CityKey AND
       SC.StateKey = SS.StateKey AND SS.CountryKey = CS.CountryKey
ORDER BY C.CompanyName, U.CompanyName
```

In the above query we obtain for each customer the suppliers located in the same country, provided that they are both involved in at least one order.

Query 12.8. *Number of customers from European countries with an area larger than 50,000 km².*

```
SELECT     C.CountryName, COUNT(U.CustomerKey) AS NbCustomers
FROM       Customer U, City Y, State T, Country C, Continent O
WHERE      U.CityKey = Y.CityKey AND Y.StateKey = T.StateKey AND
           T.CountryKey = C.CountryKey AND O.ContinentName = 'Europe' AND
           C.ContinentKey = O.ContinentKey AND
           ST_Area(C.CountryGeo)/1000000 > 50000
GROUP BY C.CountryName
```

In this query, the function **ST_Area** computes the area of a country, which is then expressed in square kilometers. Then, we count the number of customers located in each of the European countries whose area is greater than 50,000.

Query 12.9. *For each supplier, number of customers located at more than 100 km from the supplier.*

```
SELECT     U.CompanyName, COUNT(DISTINCT C.CustomerKey) AS NbCustomers
FROM       Sales S, Supplier U, Customer C
WHERE      S.SupplierKey = U.SupplierKey AND S.CustomerKey = C.CustomerKey AND
           ST_Distance(U.SupplierGeo, C.CustomerGeo) > 100000
GROUP BY U.CompanyName
```

The function **ST_Distance** is used to select the customers located at more than 100 km from the current supplier. Then, the aggretate function **COUNT** is used to obtain the number of selected customers.

Query 12.10. *For each supplier, distance between the location of the supplier and the centroid of the locations of all its customers.*

```
SELECT     U.CompanyName, ST_Distance(U.SupplierGeo, ST_Centroid(
           ST_Union(DISTINCT C.CustomerGeo::Geometry))::Geography) AS Distance
FROM       Sales S, Supplier U, Customer C
WHERE      S.SupplierKey = U.SupplierKey AND S.CustomerKey = C.CustomerKey
GROUP BY U.CompanyName, U.SupplierGeo
```

The **ST_Union** function is used for aggregating into a single geometry the locations of all customers of the current supplier. Then, the function **ST_Centroid** function is used to compute the centroid of these locations. Finally, the function **ST_Distance** function is used to compute the distance between the location of the supplier and the centroid of all its customers.

Next, we give examples of queries that involve raster data.

Query 12.11. *Total sales by customers located at more than 1000 m of altitude.*

```
SELECT     C.CompanyName AS CustomerName, SUM(F.SalesAmount) AS SalesAmount
FROM       Sales F, Customer C, City Y, State A, Country O, CountryElevation E
WHERE      F.CustomerKey = C.CustomerKey AND C.CityKey = Y.CityKey AND
           Y.StateKey = A.StateKey AND A.CountryKey = O.CountryKey AND
           ST_Value(E.Elevation, CustomerGeo::Geometry) > 1000
GROUP BY C.CompanyName
```

This query uses the **ST_Value** function to obtain the elevation value of customers.

Query 12.12. *Total sales by customers located in cities whose altitude is greater than 1500 m to suppliers located in cities whose altitude is less than 1000 m.*

```
SELECT     C.CompanyName AS CustomerName, SUM(F.SalesAmount) AS SalesAmount
FROM       Sales F, Customer C, City CC, State CS, Country CO, CountryElevation E,
           Supplier S, City SC, State SS, Country SO
WHERE      F.CustomerKey = C.CustomerKey AND C.CityKey = CC.CityKey AND
           CC.StateKey = CS.StateKey AND CS.CountryKey = CO.CountryKey AND
           ST_Value(E.Elevation, CC.CityGeo::Geometry) > 1500 AND
           F.SupplierKey = S.SupplierKey AND S.CityKey = SC.CityKey AND
           SC.StateKey = SS.StateKey AND SS.CountryKey = SO.CountryKey AND
           ST_Value(E.Elevation, SC.CityGeo::Geometry) < 1000
GROUP BY C.CompanyName
```

Query 12.13. *Total sales of customers located in states of Belgium that have at least 70% of their extent at an altitude smaller than 100 m.*

```
SELECT    C.CompanyName AS CustomerName, SUM(F.SalesAmount) AS SalesAmount
FROM      Sales F, Customer C, City Y, State S, Country O
WHERE     F.CustomerKey = C.CustomerKey AND C.CityKey = Y.CityKey AND
          Y.StateKey = S.StateKey AND S.CountryKey = O.CountryKey AND
          O.CountryName = 'Belgium' AND ST_Area(S.StateGeo) * 0.7 < (
          SELECT ST_Area(ST_Union(SE.Geom))
          FROM   ( SELECT (ST_Intersection(Elevation, S.StateGeo::Geometry)).*
                   FROM   CountryElevation E
                   WHERE  O.CountryKey = E.CountryKey ) AS SE
          WHERE SE.Val < 100 )
GROUP BY C.CompanyName
```

This query uses the **ST_Area** function to compare the area of a state, with the area of the state at an altitude less than 100 m. For obtaining the latter, in the innermost query the **ST_Intersection** function is used to intersect the geometry of the state with the raster containing the elevation of Belgium. This results in a set of **(Geom, Val)** pairs. Then, the pairs with value less than 100 are selected in the outer query and the **ST_Union**, and **ST_Area** functions are applied to the corresponding geometries.

12.6 Mobility Data Analysis

The previous sections of this chapter focused on the analysis of the spatial features of **static objects**, that is, objects whose spatial features do not change (or change exceptionally) over time. For example, the location of a store can change at a certain instant. Similarly, the borders of a state or a country can change over time. In the remainder of this chapter we focus on **moving objects**, that is, objects whose spatial extent change over time. We only consider moving points, which are typically used to represent the location of cars and persons. However, many applications must also deal with moving geometries of arbitrary type such as lines or regions. These moving geometries can be rigid, as in the case of autonomous vehicles, or deforming, as in the case of polluting clouds or spills in bodies of water. The analysis of data generated by moving objects is called **mobility data analysis**.

The interest in mobility data analysis has expanded dramatically with the availability of embedded positioning devices such as GPS. With these devices, traffic data, for example, can be captured as a collection of sequences of positioning signals transmitted by the vehicles' GPS along their itineraries. Since such sequences can be very long, they are often processed by dividing them into segments. For instance, the movement of a car can be segmented with respect to the duration of the time intervals in which it stops at a certain location. These segments of movement are called **trajectories**, and they are the unit of interest in the analysis of movement data. Mobility analysis can be applied, for example, in traffic management, which requires traffic flows to be monitored and analyzed to capture their characteristics. Other applications aim at tracking the position of persons recorded by the electronic devices they carry, such as smartphones, in order to analyze their behavior.

Trajectories can be represented in two possible ways. A **continuous trajectory** represents the movement of an object by a sequence of spatiotemporal points, together with interpolation functions that allows the computation, with a reasonable degree of confidence, of the position of the object at any instant in the period of observation. On the other hand, a **discrete trajectory** contains only a sequence of spatiotemporal points but there is no plausible interpolation function. As a typical example, consider the case of check-in services in social networks. A user checks-in at a place at 2 p.m. and the next day she checks-in at another place at 4 p.m. Interpolation between these spatiotemporal points will most likely be useless for any application that wants to analyze the movement of this user. However, an application aimed at analyzing the presence of people in a given area may find this information useful. Note that the difference between discrete and continuous trajectories has to do with the application semantics rather than with the time between two consecutive trajectory points.

Spatiotemporal or **moving-object databases** are databases that manipulate data pertaining to moving objects. For example, a query to a moving-object database would be "When will the next train from Rome arrive?". However, these databases do not enable analytical queries such as "Number of deliveries that started in Brussels in the last quarter of 2012" or "Average duration of deliveries by city." **Spatiotemporal** or **mobility data warehouses** are data warehouses that contain data about the trajectories of moving objects. Such trajectories are typically analyzed in conjunction with other spatial data, for instance, a road network or continuous field data such as elevation.

To represent spatiotemporal data we use a collection of data types that capture the evolution over time of base types. These types are referred to as *temporal types*, and we study them in detail in the next section.

12.7 Temporal Types

Temporal types represent values that change over time, for instance, to keep track of the evolution of the salaries of employees. Conceptually, temporal types are functions that assign to each instant a value of a particular domain. They are obtained by applying a constructor $t(\cdot)$, where t stands for temporal. Hence, a value of type t(integer), e.g., representing the evolution of the salary of an employee, is a partial function $f : \text{instant} \to \text{integer}$. Temporal types are partial functions since they may be undefined for certain periods of time.

In what follows, we only consider **valid time**. As we have seen in Sect. 11.1, valid time represents the time in the application domain, independently of when this information is stored in the database.

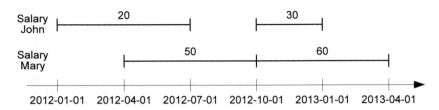

Fig. 12.10 Graphical representation of the evolution of salaries of two employees.

For example, Fig. 12.10 shows two values of type t(integer), which represent the evolution of the salary of two employees. For instance, John has a salary of 20 in the period [2012-01-01, 2012-07-01) and a salary of 30 in the period [2012-10-01, 2013-01-01), while his salary remains undefined in between 2012-07-01 and 2012-09-30. We denote by '⊥' this undefined value. As a convention, we use closed-open periods for representing the evolution of values of a temporal type.

Table 12.1 Classes of operations on temporal types

Class	Operations
Projection to domain/range	getTime, getValues, trajectory
Interaction with domain/range	atInstant, atInstantSet, atPeriod, atPeriodSet,
	atValue, atRange, atGeometry, atMin, atMax
	startInstant, startValue, endInstant, endValue,
	minValue, maxValue
Rate of change	derivative, speed, direction, turn
Temporal aggregation	integral, duration, length, TMin, TMax, TSum, TAvg,
	TVariance, TStDev
Lifting	All new operations inferred

Temporal types have an associated set of operations, which can be grouped into several classes, as shown in Table 12.1. We discuss next some of these operations; others will be explained later in this chapter.

Some operations perform the *projection to the domain and range*. Operations getTime and getValues return, respectively, the domain and range of a temporal type. For example, getTime(SalaryMary) and getValues(SalaryMary) return, respectively, [2012-04-01, 2013-04-01) and {50, 60}.

Other operations allow the *interaction with the domain and range*. The operations atInstant, atInstantSet, atPeriod, and atPeriodSet restrict the function to a given instant (set) or period (set), while the operations atValue, and atRange restrict the temporal type to a value or to a range of values in the range of the function. The operations atMin and atMax restrict the function to the instants when its value is minimal or maximal, respectively. Operations startInstant and startValue return, respectively, the first instant at which the function is defined and the corresponding value. The operations endInstant and endValue are analogous.

For example, atInstant(SalaryJohn, 2012-03-15) and atInstant(SalaryJohn, 2012-07-15) return, respectively, the value 20 and '⊥', because John's salary is undefined at the latter date. Similarly, atPeriod(SalaryJohn, [2012-04-01, 2012-11-01)) results in a temporal real with value 20 at [2012-04-01, 2012-07-01) and 30 at [2012-10-01, 2012-11-01), where the periods have been projected to the period specified in the operation. Further, startInstant(SalaryJohn) and startValue(SalaryJohn) return 2012-01-01 and 20, which are, respectively, the start time and value of the temporal value. Moreover, atValue(SalaryJohn, 20) and atValue(SalaryJohn, 25) return, respectively, a temporal real with value 20 at [2012-01-01, 2012-07-01) and '⊥', because there is no temporal real with value 25 whatsoever. Finally, atMin(SalaryJohn) and atMax(SalaryJohn) return, respectively, a temporal real with value 20 at [2012-01-01, 2012-07-01) and a temporal real with value 30 at [2012-10-01, 2013-01-01).

There are three basic **temporal aggregation operations** that take as argument a temporal integer or real and return a real value. Operation integral returns the area under the curve defined by the function, duration returns the duration of the temporal extent on which the function is defined, and length returns the length of the curve defined by the function. From these operations, other derived operations such as TAvg, TVariance, or TStDev can be defined. These are prefixed with a 'T' (temporal) in order to distinguish them from the usual aggregation operations generalized to temporal types, which we discuss below. For example, the operation TAvg computes the weighted average of a temporal value, taking into account the duration in which the function takes a value. In our example, TAvg(SalaryJohn) yields 23.36, given that John had a salary of 20 during 182 days and a salary of 30 during 92 days. Further, TVariance and TStDev compute the variance and the standard deviation of a temporal type. Finally, TMin and TMax return, respectively, the minimum and maximum value taken by the function. These are obtained by min(getValues(·)) and max(getValues(·)), where min and max are the classic operations over numeric values.

The generalization of operations on nontemporal types to temporal types is called **lifting**. An operation for nontemporal types is lifted to allow any of the arguments to be replaced by a temporal type and returns a temporal type. As an example, the less than (<) operation has lifted versions where one or both of its arguments can be temporal types and the result is a temporal Boolean. Intuitively, the semantics of such lifted operations is that the result is computed at each instant using the nonlifted operation.

When two temporal values are defined on different temporal extents, the result of a lifted operation can be defined in two possible ways. On the one hand, the result is defined on the *intersection* of both extents and undefined elsewhere. On the other, the result is defined on the *union* of the two extents, and a default value (such as 0, for the addition) is used for extents that belong to only one temporal type. For lifted operations, we assume that the result is defined on the *intersection* of the two extents. For example, in Fig. 12.10, the comparison SalaryJohn < SalaryMary results in a temporal Boolean with value true during [2012-04-01, 2012-07-01) and [2012-10-01, 2013-01-01).

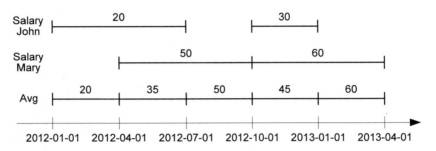

Fig. 12.11 Graphical representation of the temporal average

Aggregation operations can also be lifted. For example, a lifted Avg operation combines a set of temporal reals and results in a new temporal real where the average is computed *at each instant*. For example, Fig. 12.11 shows the average of the temporal values in Fig. 12.10. Notice that for temporal aggregation, we assume that the result is defined on the *union* of all the extents.

The definition of temporal types discussed so far is also valid for spatial types, leading to **spatiotemporal types**. For example, a value of type t(point), which can represent the trajectory of a vehicle, is a partial function f : instant → point. We present next some of the operations of Table 12.1 for the spatial case using the example in Fig. 12.12a, which depicts two temporal points RouteV1 and RouteV2 that represent the delivery routes followed by two vehicles V1 and V2 on a particular day. We can see, for instance, that vehicle V1 took 15 min to go from point (0,0) to point (3 3), and then it stopped for 10 min at that point. Thus, vehicle V1 traveled a distance of $\sqrt{18}$ = 4.24 in 15 min, while vehicle V2 traveled a distance of $\sqrt{5}$ = 2.23 in the first 10 min and a distance of 1 in the following 5 min. We assume a constant speed between consecutive pairs of points.

The operation trajectory (see Table 12.1) projects temporal geometries into the spatial plane. The projection of a temporal point into the plane may consist of points and lines, the projection of a temporal line into the plane may consist of lines and regions, and the projection of a temporal region into the plane consists of a region. In our example, trajectory(RouteV1) results in the leftmost line in Fig. 12.12a, without any temporal information.

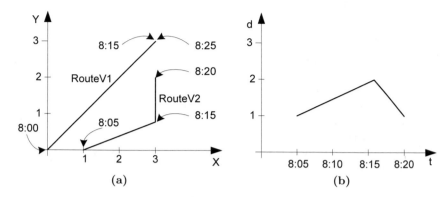

Fig. 12.12 Graphical representation of (**a**) the trajectories of two vehicles, and (**b**) their temporal distance.

All operations over nontemporal spatial types are **lifted** to allow any of the arguments to be a temporal type and return a temporal type. Intuitively, the semantics of such lifted operations is that the result is computed at each instant using the nonlifted operation. As an example, the distance function, which returns the minimum distance between two geometries, has lifted versions where one or both of its arguments can be temporal points and the result is a temporal real. In our example, distance(RouteV1, RouteV2) returns a temporal real shown in Fig. 12.12b, where, for instance, the function has a value 1.5 at 8:10 and 2 at 8:15.[1]

Topological operations can also be lifted. In this case, the semantics is that the operation returns a temporal Boolean that computes the topological relationship at each instant. For example, Intersects(RouteV1, RouteV2) returns a temporal Boolean with value **false** during [8:05, 8:20] since the two vehicles were never at the same point at any instant of their route.

Several operations compute the rate of change for points. Operation speed yields the speed of a temporal point at any instant as a temporal real. Operation direction returns the direction of the movement, that is, the angle between the x-axis and the tangent to the trajectory of the moving point. Operation turn yields the change of direction at any instant. Finally, derivative returns the derivative of the movement as a temporal real. For example, speed(RouteV1) yields a temporal real with values 16.9 at [8:00, 8:10] and 0 at [8:20, 8:25], direction(RouteV1) yields a temporal real with value 45 at [8:00, 8:10], turn(RouteV1) yields a temporal real with value 0 at [8:00, 8:10], and derivative(RouteV1) yields a temporal real with value 1 at [8:00, 8:10]. Notice that during the while the vehicle is stopped, the direction and turn are undefined.

---

[1] Notice that the distance is a quadratic function and we have approximated the distance with a linear function.

12.8 Temporal Types in MobilityDB

Current DBMSs do not provide support for temporal types. In this section, we show the temporal types we presented in Sect. 12.7 are implemented on MobilityDB [278], an open-source mobility database based on PostgreSQL and PostGIS. As explained in Chap. 11, temporal support has been introduced in the SQL standard and some of its features have been implemented in SQL Server, DB2, Oracle, and Teradata. Such functionality adds temporality to tables, thus associating a period to each row. However, to cope with the needs of mobility applications, we need an alternative approach that allows the representation of the temporal evolution of individual attribute values.

In order to manipulate temporal types we need a set of time data types corresponding to those presented in Sect. 11.2.1. MobilityDB uses the times-tamptz (short for timestamp with time zone) type provided by PostgreSQL and three new types, namely period, timestampset, and periodset.

The period type represents the instants between two bounds, the lower and the upper bounds, which are timestamptz values. The bounds can be inclusive (represented by "[" and "]") or exclusive (represented by "(" and ")"). A period value with equal and inclusive bounds corresponds to a timestamptz value. An example of a period value is as follows

```
SELECT period '[2012-01-01 08:00:00, 2012-01-03 09:30:00)';
```

The timestampset type represents a set of distinct timestamptz values. A timestampset value must contain at least one element, in which case it corresponds to a timestamptz value. The elements composing a timestampset value must be ordered. Examples of timestampset values are as follows

```
SELECT timestampset '{2012-01-01 08:00:00, 2012-01-03 09:30:00}';
```

Finally, the periodset type represents a set of disjoint period values. A periodset value must contain at least one element, in which case it corresponds to a period value. The elements composing a periodset value must be ordered. An example of a periodset value is as follows

```
SELECT periodset '{[2012-01-01 08:00:00, 2012-01-01 08:10:00],
    [2012-01-01 08:20:00, '2012-01-01 08:40:00]}';
```

We have seen in the previous section that, conceptually, a temporal type is a function from the time domain to a base or spatial type. Currently, MobilityDB provides six built-in temporal types, tbool, tint, tfloat, ttext, tgeompoint, and tgeogpoint, which are, respectively, based on the bool, int, float, and text types provided by PostgreSQL, as well as the geometry and geography types provided by PostGIS (the last two types restricted to 2D and 3D points). Depending on their base type, temporal types may be discrete or continuous. **Discrete** temporal types (which are based on the boolean, int, or text subtypes) evolve in a stepwise manner, while **continuous** temporal types (which are based on the float, geometry, or geography subtypes) may evolve in a continuous or stepwise manner.

The **subtype** of a temporal value states the temporal extent at which the evolution of values is recorded. Temporal values come in four subtypes, namely, instant, instant set, sequence, and sequence set.

A temporal **instant** value represents the value at a time instant, such as

```
SELECT tfloat '17@2018-01-01 08:00:00';
```

A temporal **instant set** value represents the evolution of the value at a set of time instants, where the values between these instants are unknown. An example is as follows:

```
SELECT tfloat '{17@2018-01-01 08:00:00, 17.5@2018-01-01 08:05:00,
    18@2018-01-01 08:10:00}';
```

A temporal **sequence** value represents the evolution of the value during a period, where the values between these instants are interpolated using either a stepwise or a linear function. An example is as follows:

```
SELECT tint '(10@2018-01-01 08:00:00, 20@2018-01-01 08:05:00,
    15@2018-01-01 08:10:00]';
```

As can be seen, a value of a sequence type has a lower and an upper bound that can be inclusive (represented by '[' and ']') or exclusive (represented by '(' and ')'). The value of a temporal sequence is interpreted by assuming that the period of time defined by every pair of consecutive values v1@t1 and v2@t2 is lower inclusive and upper exclusive, unless they are the first or the last instants of the sequence and in that case the bounds of the whole sequence apply. Furthermore, the value taken by the temporal sequence between two consecutive instants depends on whether the subtype is discrete or continuous. For example, the temporal sequence above represents that the value is 10 during (2018-01-01 08:00:00, 2018-01-01 08:05:00), 20 during [2018-01-01 08:05:00, 2018-01-01 08:10:00), and 15 at the end instant 2018-01-01 08:10:00. On the other hand, the following temporal sequence

```
SELECT tfloat '(10@2018-01-01 08:00:00, 20@2018-01-01 08:05:00,
    15@2018-01-01 08:10:00]';
```

represents that the value evolves linearly from 10 to 20 during (2018-01-01 08:00:00, 2018-01-01 08:05:00) and from 20 to 15 during [2018-01-01 08:05:00, 2018-01-01 08:10:00].

Finally, a temporal **sequence set** value represents the evolution of the value over a set of sequences, where the values between these sequences are unknown. An example is as follows:

```
SELECT tfloat '{[17@2018-01-01 08:00:00, 17.5@2018-01-01 08:05:00],
    [18@2018-01-01 08:10:00, 18@2018-01-01 08:15:00]}';
```

Consider, for example, the following table definition:

```
CREATE TABLE Employee (
        SSN CHAR(9) PRIMARY KEY,
        FirstName VARCHAR(30),
        LastName VARCHAR(30),
        BirthDate DATE,
        Salary TINT );
```

Tuples can be inserted into this table as follows:

```
INSERT INTO Employee VALUES
( '123456789', 'John', 'Smith', '1980-01-01',
        TINT '{[20@2012-01-01, 20@2012-07-01), [30@2012-10-01, 30@2013-01-01)}'),
( '345345345', 'Mary', 'Brown', '1985-07-25',
        TINT '{[50@2012-04-01, 60@2012-10-01, 60@2013-04-01)}');
```

The values for the Salary attribute above correspond to those in Fig. 12.10.

We show next how some of the operations for temporal types defined in Table 12.1 can be expressed in MobilityDB. For example, given the above table with the two tuples inserted, the query

```
SELECT getTime(E.Salary), getValues(E.Salary)
FROM   Employee E
```

returns the following values

```
{[2012-01-01, 2012-07-01), [2012-10-01, 2013-01-01)} {20,30}
{[2012-04-01, 2013-04-01)}                            {50,60}
```

The first column of the result above is of type periodset, while the second column is of type integer[] (array of integers) provided by PostgreSQL. Similarly, the query

```
SELECT valueAtTimestamp(E.Salary, '2012-04-15'),
       valueAtTimestamp(E.Salary, '2012-07-15')
FROM   Employee E
```

returns the following values

```
20 NULL
50 50
```

where the NULL value above represents the fact that the salary of John is undefined on 2012-07-15. The following query

```
SELECT atPeriod(E.Salary, '[2012-04-01,2012-11-01)')
FROM   Employee E
```

returns

```
{[20@2012-04-01, 20@2012-07-01), [30@2012-10-01, 30@2012-11-01)}
{[50@2012-04-01, 60@2012-10-01, 60@2012-11-01)}
```

where the temporal attribute has been restricted to the period given in the query. Furthermore, the query

```
SELECT atMin(E.Salary), atMax(E.Salary)
FROM   Employee E
```

gives as result the minimum and maximum values and the periods when they occurred, as follows.

{[20@2012-01-01, 20@2012-07-01)} {[30@2012-10-01, 30@2013-01-01]}
{[50@2012-04-01, 50@2012-10-01)} {[60@2012-10-01, 60@2013-04-01]}

We show next the usage of lifted operations. Recall that the semantics of such operations is such that the nonlifted operation is applied at each instant. Then, the query

```
SELECT E1.Salary #< E2.Salary
FROM   Employee E1, Employee E2
WHERE  E1.FirstName = 'John' and E2.FirstName = 'Mary'
```

results in the temporal Boolean value

{[t@2012-04-01, t@2012-07-01), [t@2012-10-01, t@2013-01-01)}

Notice that the comparison is performed only on the time instants that are shared by the two temporal values. Similarly, the query

```
SELECT AVG(E.Salary)
FROM   Employee E
```

results in the value

{[20@2012-01-01, 20@2012-04-01), [35@2012-04-01, 35@2012-07-01),
    [50@2012-07-01, 50@2012-10-01), [45@2012-10-01, 45@2013-01-01),
    [60@2013-01-01, 60@2013-04-01)}

A graphical representation of this result was shown in Fig. 12.11.

In order to show the operations for temporal spatial types, we use the following table, which keeps track of the delivery routes followed by vehicles:

```
CREATE TABLE Delivery (
        VehicleId CHAR(6) PRIMARY KEY,
        DeliveryDate DATE,
        Route TGEOMPOINT )
```

We insert now two tuples into this table, containing information about two deliveries performed by two vehicles V1 and V2 shown in Fig. 12.12a:

```
INSERT INTO Delivery VALUES
( 'V1', '2012-01-10', TGEOMPOINT '[Point(0 0)@2012-01-10 08:00,
        Point(3 3)@2012-01-10 08:15, Point(3 3)@2012-01-10 08:25]' ),
( 'V2', '2012-01-10', TGEOMPOINT '[Point(1 0)@2012-01-10 08:05,
        Point(3 1)@2012-01-10 08:15, Point(3 2)@2012-01-10 08:20]' );
```

Recall that these are *continuous trajectories* and thus, we assume a constant speed between any two consecutive points and use linear interpolation to determine the position of the vehicles at any instant.

We show next examples of lifted spatial operations. The following query computes the distance between the two vehicles whose graphical representation was given in Fig. 12.12b:

```
SELECT distance(D1.Route, D2.Route)
FROM   Delivery D1, Delivery D2
WHERE  D1.VehicleId = 'V1' AND D2.VehicleId = 'V2'
```

This query returns

```
[1@2012-01-10 08:05:00, 2@2012-01-10 08:15:00, 1@2012-01-10 08:20:00]
```

Finally, the following query uses the lifted **ST_Intersects** topological operation to test whether the routes of the two vehicles intersect, as follows:

```
SELECT tintersects(D1.Route, D2.Route)
FROM   Delivery D1, Delivery D2
WHERE  D1.VehicleId = 'V1' AND D2.VehicleId = 'V2'
```

12.9 Mobility Data Warehouses

We study next how data warehouses can be extended with temporal types in order to support the analysis of mobility data. We use the Northwind case study in order to introduce the main concepts.

The Northwind company wants to build a mobility data warehouse that keeps track of the deliveries of goods to their customers in order to optimize the shipping costs. Nonspatial data include the characteristics of the vehicles performing the deliveries. Spatial data include the road network, the warehouses that store the goods to be delivered, the customers, and the geographical information related to these locations (city, state, and country). Spatiotemporal data include the trajectories followed by the vehicles. In our scenario, vehicles load the goods in a warehouse, perform a delivery serving several customers, and then return to the warehouse. We will analyze the deliveries by vehicles, days, warehouses, and delivery locations.

Figure 12.13 shows the conceptual schema depicting the above scenario using the MultiDim model extended to support spatial data and temporal types. As shown in the figure, the fact **DeliverySegment** is related to five dimensions: **Vehicle**, **Delivery**, **Date**, **From**, and **To**, where the latter two link to either a **Customer** or a **Warehouse**. Consider for example a delivery that serves two clients. This delivery will have three segments: the first one going from the warehouse to the first client, the second one going from the first to the second client, and the third one going from the second client back

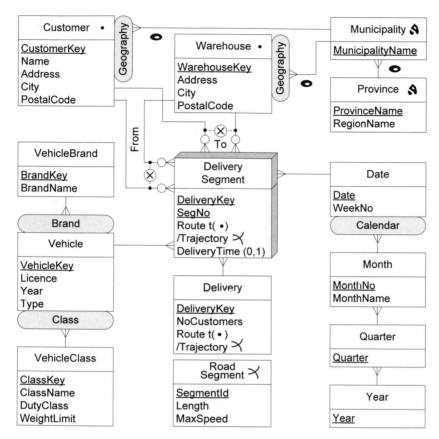

Fig. 12.13 Conceptual schema of the Northwind mobility data warehouse

to the warehouse. Dimensions are composed of levels and hierarchies. For example, the Customer dimension is composed of three levels, with a one-to-many parent-child relationship defined between each couple of levels. Levels have attributes that describe their members. For example, level Vehicle has attributes VehicleKey, Licence, Year, and Type. Spatial levels or attributes have an associated geometry (e.g., point, line, or region), which is indicated by a pictogram. In our example, dimensions Customer and Warehouse are spatial and share a Geography hierarchy where a geometry is associated with each level in both dimensions.

Topological constraints are represented using pictograms in parent-child relationships. For example, the topological constraints in dimension Geography indicate that a customer is contained in its parent municipality and a municipality is contained in its parent province.

The fact DeliverySegment has an identifier composed of DeliveryKey and SegNo, the latter being the segment number within the delivery. There are three measures. Route is a **spatiotemporal measure** of type temporal point, as indicated by the symbol 't($\bullet$)', which keeps the position of the vehicle at any point in time. Trajectory is derived from Route and stores the route traversed by the vehicle, which is a line, without any temporal information. Finally, DeliveryTime keeps the time needed to deliver to the client in the segment. This measure will be empty for the last segment of a delivery.

The translation of the conceptual schema in Fig. 12.13 into a logical schema, obtained as explained in Sect. 12.3, is shown in Fig. 12.14.

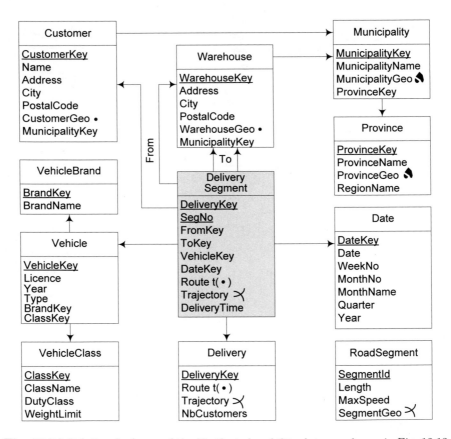

Fig. 12.14 Relational schema of the Northwind mobility data warehouse in Fig. 12.13

We used the BerlinMOD implementation in MobilityDB[2] to generate synthetic data for the Northwind mobility data warehouse based on OpenStreetMap data about Brussels, Belgium.[3] Figure 12.15 shows a visualization of the generated data using QGIS, a free and open-source geographic

---

[2] https://github.com/MobilityDB/MobilityDB-BerlinMOD

[3] Notice that you can generate synthetic data for any place in the world by changing the underlying OpenStreet data that is used by the BerlinMOD generator.

information system application for viewing, editing, and analyzing geospatial data[4]. Figure 12.16 shows a single delivery trip, which starts and ends at a warehouse and make deliveries to four customers.

Fig. 12.15 Data generated for the Northwind mobility data warehouse. The road network is shown with blue lines, the warehouses are shown with a red star, the routes taken by the deliveries are shown with black lines, and the location of the customers with black points.

Fig. 12.16 A trajectory of a single vehicle during one day serving four clients.

[4] http://www.qgis.org

12.10 Querying the Northwind Mobility Data Warehouse in SQL

We use MobilityDB[5] to address queries to the Northwind mobility data warehouse. In what follows, the functions that are prefixed by ST_ (e.g., ST_Length) are PostGIS functions, while the functions not prefixed (e.g., length) are the temporal extensions of these functions in MobilityDB.

Query 12.14. *Number of deliveries and number of customers served by warehouse.*

```
SELECT     WarehouseKey AS Warehouse, COUNT(*) AS NoDeliveries,
           SUM(NoCustomers) AS NoCustomers
FROM       Delivery D, Warehouse W
WHERE      startValue(D.Route) = W.WarehouseGeo
GROUP BY ROLLUP(WarehouseKey);
```

This query does not use the fact table. Since a delivery starts and ends at a warehouse, we use the function startValue to get the starting point of the deliveries, which is the location of a warehouse.

Query 12.15. *Deliveries that traversed at least two municipalities.*

```
SELECT     DeliveryKey
FROM       Delivery D, Municipality M1, Municipality M2
WHERE      M1.MunicipalityKey < M2.MunicipalityKey AND
           ST_Intersects(D.Trajectory, M1.Geom) AND
           ST_Intersects(D.Trajectory, M2.Geom)
```

This query uses the Trajectory attribute, which is a geometry obtained by projecting the route of the delivery into the spatial dimension. The query tests that the trajectory intersects two different municipalities using the function ST_Intersects.

Query 12.16. *Number of customers served by municipality.*

```
SELECT     M.MunicipalityName AS Municipality, COUNT(*) AS NoDeliveries,
           COUNT(DISTINCT C.CustomerKey) AS NoCustomers
FROM       DeliverySegment S, Customer C, Municipality M
WHERE      S.SegNo <> 1 AND S.FromKey = CustomerKey AND
           ST_Covers(M.MunicipalityGeo, C.CustomerGeo)
GROUP BY ROLLUP(M.MunicipalityName);
```

This query leverages the fact that a delivery segment which is not the first one starts from a customer. This query uses the function ST_Covers to obtain the municipality of the client. Notice that we could alternatively obtain the municipality of a client from the foreign key in table Customer.

---

[5] https://github.com/MobilityDB/MobilityDB

Query 12.17. *Number of customers served outside the province of Brussels.*

```
SELECT    COUNT(*) AS NoCustomers
FROM      DeliverySegment S, Customer C, Municipality M, Province P
WHERE     S.SegNo <> 1 AND S.FromKey = C.CustomerKey AND
          ST_Covers(M.MunicipalityGeo, C.CustomerGeo) AND
          M.ProvinceKey = P.ProvinceKey AND
          P.ProvinceName NOT LIKE '%Bruxelles%';
```

This query uses uses the same approach as the previous one, but we need to roll-up to the province level to know the province of a municipality.

Query 12.18. *Average duration per day of deliveries starting with a customer located in the municipality of Uccle.*

```
WITH UccleDeliveries AS (
          SELECT DISTINCT DeliveryKey
          FROM   DeliverySegment S, Customer C, Municipality M
          WHERE S.SegNo = 1 AND S.ToKey = C.CustomerKey AND
                ST_Covers(M.MunicipalityGeo, C.CustomerGeo) AND
                M.MunicipalityName LIKE 'Uccle%' )
SELECT    D.Day, SUM(timespan(D.Route)) / COUNT(*) AS AvgDuration
FROM      Delivery D
WHERE     D.DeliveryKey IN (SELECT DeliveryKey FROM UccleDeliveries)
GROUP BY D.Day
ORDER BY D.Day;
```

This query selects in table UccleDeliveries the deliveries whose first customer is located in the requested municipality. Then, in the main query, it uses function **timespan** to compute the duration of the delivery taking into account the time gaps, and computes the average of all the durations per day.

Query 12.19. *Average number of municipalities traversed by deliveries per warehouse.*

```
WITH DelivMunic AS (
          SELECT DeliveryKey, M.MunicipalityKey
          FROM Delivery D, Municipality M
          WHERE ST_Intersects(D.Trajectory, M.MunicipalityGeo) ),
    DelivNoMunic AS (
          SELECT DeliveryKey, COUNT(*) AS NoMunic
          FROM DelivMunic
          GROUP BY DeliveryKey ),
    DelivWareh AS (
          SELECT DeliveryKey, W.WarehouseKey
          FROM Delivery D, Warehouse W
          WHERE startValue(D.Route) = W.WarehouseGeo )
SELECT    W.WarehouseKey AS Warehouse, AVG(NoMunic) AS AvgNoMunicipalities
FROM      DelivMunic M, DelivWareh W
WHERE     M.DeliveryKey = W.DeliveryKey
GROUP BY W.WarehouseKey;
```

This query computes in table DelivMunic the pairs of delivery and municipality such that the delivery traversed the municipality. For this, the function ST_Intersects is used. Table DelivNoMunic computes from the previous table the number of municipalities traversed by a delivery. Table DelivWareh associates to each delivery its warehouse. Finally, the main query joins the last two tables to compute the requested answer.

Query 12.20. *Total distance traveled by vehicles per brand.*

```
SELECT    B.BrandName, SUM(length(S.Route) / 1000)
FROM      DeliverySegment S, Vehicle V, VehicleBrand B
WHERE     S.VehicleKey = V.VehicleKey AND V.BrandKey = B.BrandKey
GROUP BY B.BrandName
ORDER BY B.BrandName;
```

This query uses the function length to obtain the distance traveled in a delivery segment, which is divided by 1,000 to express it in kilometers, and then aggregates the distances per brand.

Query 12.21. *Number of deliveries per day such that their route intersects the municipality of Ixelles for more than 20 minutes.*

```
SELECT    Day, COUNT(DISTINCT DeliveryKey) AS NoDeliveries
FROM      Delivery D, Municipality M
WHERE     M.MunicipalityName LIKE 'Ixelles%' AND
          D.Route && M.MunicipalityGeo AND
          duration(atGeometry(D.Route, M.MunicipalityGeo)) >= interval '20 min'
GROUP BY Day
ORDER BY Day;
```

This query uses the function atGeometry to restrict the route of the delivery to the geometry of the requested municipality. Then, function duration computes the time spent within the province and verifies that this duration is at least of 20 minutes. Remark that this duration of 20 minutes may not be continuous. Finally, the count of the selected deliveries is performed as usual.

The term D.Route && M.MunicipalityGeo is optional and it is included to enhance query performance. It verifies, using an index, that the spatio-temporal bounding box of the delivery projected into the spatial dimension intersects with the bounding box of the municipality. In this way, the atGeometry function is only applied to deliveries satisfying the bounding box condition.

Query 12.22. *Same as the previous query but with the condition that the route intersects the municipality of Ixelles for more than consecutive 20 minutes.*

```
SELECT    Day, COUNT(DISTINCT DeliveryKey) AS NoDeliveries
FROM      Delivery D, Municipality M,
          unnest(periods(getTime(atGeometry(D.Route, M.MunicipalityGeo)))) P
WHERE     M.MunicipalityName LIKE 'Ixelles%' AND
          D.Route && M.MunicipalityGeo AND duration(P) >= interval '20 min'
GROUP BY Day
ORDER BY Day;
```

As in the previous query, the function atGeometry restricts the route of the delivery to the requested municipality. This results in a route that may be discontinuous in time, because the route may enter and leave the municipality. The query uses the function getTime to obtain the set of periods of the restricted delivery, represented as a periodSet value. The function periods converts the latter value into an array of periods, and the PostgreSQL function unnest expands this array to a set of rows, each row containing a single period. Then, it is possible to verify that the duration of one of the periods is at least 20 minutes.

Query 12.23. *Average speed of deliveries per hour and day.*

```
WITH Days AS (
            SELECT MIN(startTimestamp(Day)::date) AS StartDay,
                   MAX(endTimestamp(Day)::date) + interval '1 day' AS EndDay
            FROM Delivery ),
        TimeSplit AS (
            SELECT period(H, H + interval '1 hour') AS Period
            FROM Days D, generate_series(StartDay, EndDay, interval '1 hour') AS H )
SELECT    T.Period, AVG(twAvg(speed(atPeriod(D.Route, T.Period)))) AS AvgSpeed
FROM      Delivery D, TimeSplit T
WHERE     atPeriod(D.Route, T.Period) IS NOT NULL
GROUP BY T.Period
ORDER BY T.Period;
```

This query computes in table Days the minimal and maximal day of the deliveries. For this, we compute the start and end timestamp of each delivery with functions startTimestamp and endTimestamp, cast these values to dates using the PostgreSQL operator ::, and apply the MIN and MAX traditional aggregate functions. Table TimeSplit splits the range of days found in the previous table into one-hour periods. Notice that in table Days we added one day to the maximal date to also split the maximal date in table TimeSplit. In the main query, with function atPeriod we restrict each delivery to a given one-hour period, compute the speed of the restricted trip as a temporal float, and apply the function twAvg to compute the time-weighted average of the speed as a single float value. Finally, the traditional AVG aggregate function is used to obtain the average of these values per period.

Query 12.24. *For each speed range of 20 km/h, give the total distance traveled by all deliveries within that range.*

```
WITH Ranges AS (
            SELECT I AS RangeKey, floatrange(((I - 1) * 20), I * 20) AS Range
            FROM generate_series(1, 10) I )
SELECT    R.Range, SUM(length(atPeriodSet(D.Route,
          getTime(atRange(speed(D.Route) * 3.6, R.Range)))) / 1000)
FROM      Delivery D, Ranges R
WHERE     atRange(speed(D.Route) * 3.6, R.Range) IS NOT NULL
GROUP BY R.RangeKey, R.Range
ORDER BY R.RangeKey;
```

The idea of this query is to have an overall view of the speed behavior of the entire fleet of delivery vehicles. Table Ranges computes the speed ranges $[0, 20)$, $[20, 40)$, ... $[180, 200)$. In the main query, the speed of the trips, obtained in meters per second, is multiplied by 3.6 to convert it to km/h. Then, function atRange restricts the speed to the portions having a given range and function getTime obtains the time when the speed was within the range. The overall route is then restricted to the obtained time periods with the function atPeriodSet. Function length computes the distance traveled by the vehicle within this speed range and this value is divided by 1,000 to express the distance in kilometers. Finally, all the distances for all vehicles at the given speed range are obtained with the SUM aggregate function.

Query 12.25. *Number of deliveries per month that traveled at least 20 km at a speed higher than 100 km/h.*

```
SELECT     DT.Year, DT.MonthNumber, COUNT(DISTINCT DeliveryKey)
FROM       Delivery D, Date T
WHERE      D.DateKey = T.DateKey AND length(atPeriodSet(D.Route,
             getTime(atRange(speed(Route) * 3.6, floatrange(100,200))))) / 1000 >= 20
GROUP BY DT.Year, DT.MonthNumber
ORDER BY DT.Year, DT.MonthNumber
```

The query uses the function speed to obtain the speed of the vehicle at each instant. The function atRange restricts the speed, expressed in kilometers per hour, to the range [100,200). The getTime function computes the set of periods during which the delivery travels within that range. The function atPeriodSet restricts the overall delivery to these periods and the length function computes the distance traveled by the restricted deliveries. Finally, we verify that this distance, converted to kilometers, is at least 20 km.

Query 12.26. *Pairs of deliveries that traveled at less than one kilometer from each other during more than 20 minutes.*

```
SELECT     D1.DeliveryKey, D2.DeliveryKey
FROM       Delivery D1, Delivery D2
WHERE      D1.DeliveryKey < D2.DeliveryKey AND duration(getTime(
             atValue(tdwithin(D1.Route, D2.Route, 1000), true))) > '20 min'
```

The function tdwithin is the temporal version of the PostGIS function ST_DWithin. It returns a temporal Boolean which is true during the periods when the two routes are within the specified distance from each other. The function atValue restricts the temporal Boolean to the periods when its value is true, and the function getTime obtains these periods. Finally, the query uses the duration function to obtain the corresponding interval and verifies that it is greater than 20 minutes.

To conclude, we show in the visualization of Fig. 12.17 how often a road segment is traversed by the deliveries. We use color gradients, where the darker the color, the higher the number of times the road segment is traversed. We determine how many deliveries traversed each road segment as follows.

```
CREATE TABLE HeatMap AS
SELECT     E.Id, E.geom, COUNT(*) AS noDels
FROM       Edges E, Delivery S
WHERE      ST_Intersects(E.geom, S.trajectory)
GROUP BY E.Id, E.geom;
INSERT INTO HeatMap
SELECT E.Id, E.geom, 0 FROM Edges E WHERE E.Id NOT IN (
           SELECT Id FROM HeatMap );
```

The CREATE TABLE above uses the ST_Intersects function to compute the number of deliveries that used each road segment. Then, the INSERT statement adds to the table those segments that were not used by any delivery. We need some statistics about the attribute noDels to define the gradient.

```
SELECT MIN(noDels), MAX(noDels), round(AVG(noDels),3), round(STDDEV(noDels),3)
FROM HeatMap;
-- 0 299 11.194 26.803
```

As can be seen, on average, a road segment is traversed by 11 deliveries. We use the following expression to display the road segments in QGIS with a gradient according to the attribute noDels.

```
ramp_color('Blues', scale_linear(noDels, 0, 20, 0, 1))
```

The scale_linear function above transforms the value of the attribute noDels from a value in [0, 20] into a value in [0,1]. Therefore, we decided to assign a full blue color to a road segment as soon as there are at least 20 deliveries that traverse it. The ramp_color function states the gradient to be used for the display, in our case shades of blue.

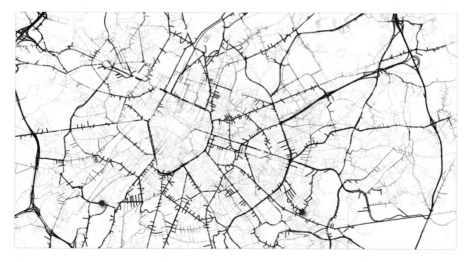

Fig. 12.17 Visualizing how often the road segments are taken by the deliveries.

12.11 Summary

In this chapter, we first studied how data warehouses can be extended with spatial data. For this, we presented a spatial extension of the MultiDim conceptual model with spatial types, field types, and topological relationships. We used as example the GeoNorthwind data warehouse, which extends the Northwind data warehouse with spatial data. We also generalized the rules for translating conceptual to logical models to account for spatial data. Then, we addressed the vector and raster models to explain how spatial data types at the conceptual level can be represented at the logical level. We implemented the above concepts using the PostgreSQL database with its spatial extension PostGIS. We also showed how the GeoNorthwind data warehouse can be queried with SQL extended with spatial functions.

We then discussed how data warehousing techniques can be applied to mobility data. For this, we first defined temporal types, which capture the variation of a value across time. Applying temporal types to spatial data leads to spatiotemporal types, which provide a conceptual view of trajectories. We then presented how temporal types are implemented in MobilityDB, an open-source moving-object database based on PostgreSQL and PostGIS. We illustrated these concepts by extending the Northwind data warehouse with mobility data and showed how to query this data warehouse in MobilityDB.

12.12 Bibliographic Notes

A recent introduction to the technologies underlying spatial computing is given in [217]. Popular books on spatial databases and geographic information systems (GIS) are [195, 263]. SQL/MM, the spatial extension of SQL, is an ISO standard described in [151]. A book introducing the main features of PostGIS is [169]. The book [165] describes GRASS, an open-source GIS that includes advanced capabilities for manipulating raster data. Recent spatial data management systems based on Hadoop or Spark include SpatialHadoop [69] and Sedona [270].

The extension of the MultiDim model presented in this chapter is based on the conceptual model MADS [182] and on the work on field types by the present authors [90, 249]. The notion of SOLAP was introduced in [196, 24]. Other relevant work on SOLAP can be found in [27, 38]. The work done on the topic of OLAP analysis of continuous fields (e.g., [29, 43]) is typically based on an algebra for fields, or map algebra. This work started in the classic book of Tomlin [235] and continued by the work of several authors [42, 156, 180]. Rasdaman [23] is an open-source database management sytems for multidimensional arrays, such as raster data satellite images. Spatial data warehouses on the cloud are discussed in [149].

An overall perspective of the state of the art in mobility data management can be found in the books [155, 194, 275]. The mobility data warehouses presented in chapter are based on previous work performed by the authors [249, 250, 251]. A general framework for the analysis of trajectories of moving objects designed around a trajectory data warehouse is given in [160] The data type system for temporal types presented in this chapter follows the approach of [99]. An SQL extension for spatiotemporal data is proposed in [255]. The view of continuous fields as cubes was introduced in [90]. The GeoPKDD trajectory data warehouse, its associated ETL process, and the double-counting problem during aggregation are studied in [175]. A discussion on mobility data warehouses is presented in [7, 187]. The books [8, 257] are devoted to visual analytics for mobility data.

There are a few moving-object database management systems. The first one was SECONDO [267], which is based on the model proposed by Güting *et al.* [99]. MobilityDB, developed by one of the authors of this book, is described in [20, 213, 278]. Hermes is described in [188]. Recent systems based on Hadoop or Spark include TrajMesa [139], Summit [6], and DITA [215].

12.13 Review Questions

12.1 What are spatial databases? Describe two complementary ways of modeling spatial data in database applications.

12.2 Describe the various spatial data types at a conceptual level, giving for each one of them an example of its use.

12.3 Define the various topological relationships in terms of the boundary, interior, and exterior of spatial values.

12.4 What are continuous fields? How are them implemented at a conceptual level?

12.5 Discuss the following concepts: spatial dimension, spatial level, spatial attribute, spatial fact, spatial measure, spatial hierarchy, and topological relationship.

12.6 What are the differences between a spatial level, a spatial level with spatial attributes, and a nonspatial level with spatial attributes?

12.7 How does a spatial measure differ from a numerical measure computed with spatial operators? Does a spatial measure require to be related to spatial dimensions?

12.8 Give an example of a multidimensional schema containing a spatial measure. Transform the spatial measure into a spatial dimension. Compare the two schemas with respect to the various queries that can be addressed to them.

12.9 Define the geoid and the ellipsoid. What are they used for? What are the difference between them? What is a datum?

12.10 What are spatial reference systems?

12.11 What is the difference between the vector and the raster data models for representing spatial data?

12.12 Describe the spatial data types implemented in SQL/MM.

12.13 Discuss the mapping rules for translating a spatial MultiDim schema into an relational schema.

12.14 How are topological relationships represented in a logical schema? How can these relationships be checked in a logical schema ?

12.15 What are moving objects? How are they different from spatial objects?

12.16 Give examples of different types of moving objects and illustrate with scenarios the importance of their analysis.

12.17 Discuss various criteria that can be used to segment movement data taking into different analysis requirements.

12.18 What is a trajectory? What is the difference between continuous and discrete trajectories?

12.19 Define the terms mobility databases and mobility data warehouses. Mention the main differences between the two concepts.

12.20 What are temporal types? How are they constructed?

12.21 Give examples of a temporal base type and a spatiotemporal type. Give examples of operations associated to each of these types.

12.22 Explain why traditional operations must be lifted for temporal types. Illustrate this with examples.

12.23 Give a hint about how temporal types can be implemented in a platform such as PostGIS. How does this implementation differ from the abstract definition of temporal types?

12.24 Discuss how temporal types can be added to a multidimensional schema.

12.25 Discuss the implications of including trajectories as dimensions or measures in a data warehouse.

12.14 Exercises

Exercise 12.1. Consider the conceptual schema of the GeoFoodmart data warehouse given in Fig. 12.18. Translate the schema into a relational one.

Exercise 12.2. Given the relational schema obtained in the previous exercise, write in SQL the following queries.

a. Display all measures summarized for the stores located in California or Washington, considering only stores in California that are less than 200 km from Los Angeles, and stores in Washington that are less than 200 km from Seattle.

b. For each store, give the total sales to customers from the same city than the store.

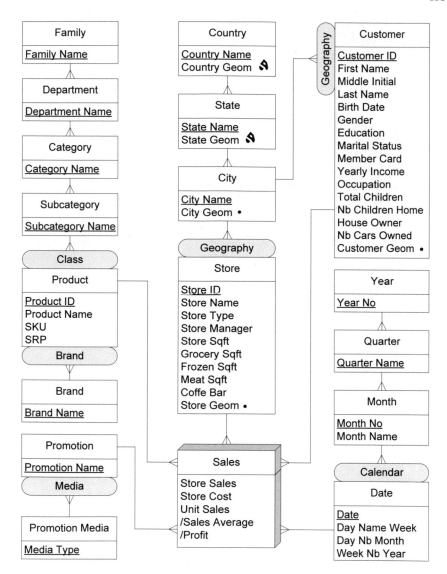

Fig. 12.18 Conceptual schema of the GeoFoodmart cube

c. For each store, obtain the ratio between the sales to customers from the same state against its total sales, in 2013.

d. Total sales of stores located at less than 5 km from the city center against total sales for all stores in their state.

e. Display the unit sales by product brand, only considering sales to customers from a country different than the country of the store.

f. For each store list total sales to customers living closer than 10 km to the store, against total sales for the store.

g. For each city give the store closest to the city center and its the best sold brand name.

h. Give the spatial union of all the cities that have more than one store with a surface of more than 10,000 square feet.

i. Give the spatial union of the states such that the average of the total sales by customer in 2017 is greater than $60 per month.

j. Give the spatial union of all the cities where all customers have purchased for more than $100.

k. Display the spatial union of the cities whose sales count accounts for more than 5% of all the sales.

Exercise 12.3. Add spatial data to the data warehouse schema you created as a solution of Ex. 5.11 for the AirCarrier application. You must analyze the dimensions, facts, and measures and define which of them can be extended with spatial features. You should also consider adding continuous field data representing altitude so you can enhance the analysis trying to find a correlation between the results and the elevation of the geographic sites.

Exercise 12.4. Use a reverse engineering technique to produce a multidimensional schema from the logical schema obtained as a solution of Ex. 12.3.

Exercise 12.5. Given the logical schema obtained in Ex. 12.3, write in SQL the following queries.

a. For each carrier and year, give the number of scheduled and performed flights.

b. For each airport, give the number of scheduled and performed flights in the last two years.

c. For each carrier and distance group, give the total number of seats sold in 2012.

d. Display for each city the three closest airports and their distance to the city independently of the country in which the city and the airport are located.

e. Give the total number of persons arriving to or departing from airports closer than 15 km from the city center in 2012.

f. Give for 2012 the ratio between the number of persons arriving to or departing from aiports closer than 15 km from the city center and the number of persons arriving to or departing from airports located between 15 and 40 km from the city center.

g. Display the spatial union of all airports with more than 5,000 departures in 2012.

h. Display the spatial union of all airports where more than 100 carriers operate.

i. For cities operated by more than one airport, give the total number of arriving and departing passengers.

j. For cities operated by more than one airport, give the total number of arriving and departing passengers at the airport closest to the city center, and the ratio between this value and the city total.

k. Display the spatial union of all airports located at more than 1,000 m above sea level.

l. Compare the number of departed and scheduled flights for airports located above and below 1,000 m above sea level in 2012.

Exercise 12.6. Consider the train company application described in Ex. 3.2 and whose conceptual multidimensional schema was obtained in Ex. 4.3. Add spatiotemporal data to this schema to transform it into a mobility data warehouse. You must analyze the dimensions, facts, and measures, and define which of them can be extended with spatiotemporal features.

Exercise 12.7. Transform the conceptual schema obtained as solution for Ex. 12.6 into a relational one. This schema should correspond to the relational schema without spatiotemporal features obtained in Ex. 5.3.

Exercise 12.8. Write in SQL the following queries on the relational schema obtained in Ex. 12.7:

a. Give the trip number, origin, and destination of trips that contain segments with a duration of more than 3 h and whose length is shorter than 200 km.

b. Give the trip number, origin, and destination of trips that contain at least two segments served by trains from different constructors.

c. Give the trip number of trips that cross at least three cities in less than 2 h.

d. Give the total number of trips that cross at least two country borders in less than 4 h.

e. Give the average speed by train constructor. This should be computed taking the sum of the durations and lengths of all segments with the same constructor and obtaining the average. The result must be ordered by average speed.

f. For each possible number of total segments, give the number of trips in each group and the average length, ordered by number of segments. Each answer should look like (5, 50, 85), meaning that there are 50 trips that have 5 segments with an average length of 85 km, and so on.

g. Give the trip number, origin, and destination stations for trips with at least one segment of the trip runs for at least 100 km within Germany.

Exercise 12.9. Consider an application that monitors air quality measuring the values of a set of pollutants (such as particulate matter or sulfur dioxide) at a fixed number of stations. Measures are collected hourly or daily and are expressed both in traditional units (like micrograms per cubic meter, or parts per million) or using an air quality index, which in Europe has five levels using a scale from 0 (very low) to greater than 100 (very high). Stations are located

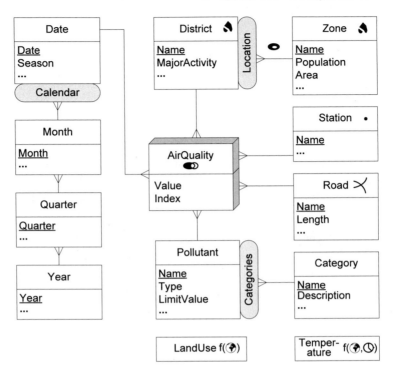

Fig. 12.19 A multidimensional schema for analyzing air quality

in districts alongside roads. Finally, there is also field data corresponding to land use and temperature.

The conceptual multidimensional schema of this application is given in Fig. 12.19. Translate the schema into a logical schema.

Exercise 12.10. Write in SQL the following queries on the relational schema obtained in Ex. 12.9.

a. For pollutants belonging to the organic category, give the maximum value by station and month.
b. For stations located on the Autostrada del Sole, give the average values of lead registered in the last quarter of 2010.
c. For stations located at a distance of at most 1 km of the Autostrada del Sole, give the average values of lead registered in the last quarter of 2010.
d. For zones with at least 20% of industrial land use, give the average value for carbon monoxide on February 1, 2012.
e. Roads located in industrial zones, such that the average temperature in 2012 along the road was higher than 20°C.
f. Maximum temperature by land use type in 2012.
g. Maximum temperature in 2012 in stations where organic pollutants were over the limit more than five times.

Chapter 13
Graph Data Warehouses

The explosion of the web and, in particular, of social networks, produced a renewed interest in graph databases, since graphs are the natural choice for modeling highly connected data, not only in social networks, but also for transport networks, biological data, and so on. A **graph database system** is a database management system that allows storage and manipulation of graph data. In domains where users are interested in specifying graph patterns that involve paths of arbitrary lengths between nodes, graph databases may be more appropriate than relational databases. This is especially true when systems use native graph storage, which means they are designed and optimized for storing and managing graph data structures. There are, however, graph database systems that serialize graph data into, for example, a relational database. The drawback of graph databases is their relatively limited scalability. When the volume of graph data becomes large, parallel processing is required. **Graph processing frameworks** are used to handle these large volumes, most often in distributed environments.

In this context, *graph analytics* has been steadily gaining momentum in the data management community. Further, there are situations where traditional data warehousing and OLAP operations on cubes are not enough to cope with data analysis requirements. On the other hand, from a graph analytics point of view, OLAP operations and models like the ones studied in this book can expand the possibilities of analysis beyond the traditional graph-based computation, with tools allowing shortest-path computation, centrality analysis, and so on. This chapter studies methods and techniques proposed to extend OLAP concepts to the graph data model. This chapter starts with a description of basic concepts about graph data models and graph databases. After this, Neo4j, one of the most popular graph databases, is described in detail. Then, a comprehensive study of how OLAP and data warehousing concepts can be applied to graph data making use of the notion of hypergraph. Finally, graph processing frameworks are briefly presented.

13.1 Graph Data Models

Formally, a **graph** is a mathematical structure that consists in a collection
of vertices and edges. Intuitively, a graph represents entities as nodes and the
relationships between those entities and edges. This simple structure allows
the representation of a wide variety of real-world scenarios, mainly situations
where the entities involved are highly connected, as in the case of social
networks, and, in general, in any problem that can be naturally represented
as a network. Figure 13.1 shows an example of a simple graph representing
a relationship between persons in a social network.

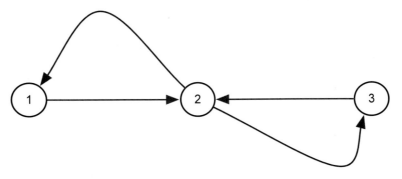

Fig. 13.1 A simple graph

Graphs like the one in Fig. 13.1 do not suffice when more expressiveness
is required. For example, the lack of edge labels prevents indication of the
kind of relationship that each edge represents. Adding labels to the edges
in the graph leads to the notion of edge-labeled graphs. In general, more
sophisticated graph data models are needed to address the problems that
appear in real-world situations. **Graph data models** have been extensively
studied in the literature. In practice, the three models mainly used are based
on either the Resource Description Framework (RDF), property graphs, and
hypergraphs.

Models based on **RDF** represent data as sets of triples where, as we will
study in Chap. 14, each triple consists of three elements that are referred to
as the subject, the predicate, and the object of the triple. These triples allow the description of arbitrary objects in terms of their attributes and their
relationships with other objects. Intuitively, a collection of RDF triples is an
RDF graph. An important feature of RDF-based graph models is that they
follow a standard, which is not yet the case of the other graph databases,
although at the time of writing this book, efforts are being carried out for
standardization. Therefore, RDF graphs are mainly used to represent metadata. However, since RDF graphs are typically stored using so-called triple
stores, which normally rely on underlying relational databases with special-

ized index structures, they are not the best choice when complex path computations are required. The standard query language associated with RDF graphs is **SPARQL**. RDF and the Semantic Web are extensively studied in Chap. 14 of this book, and are thus not covered in this chapter. An example of a commercial graph database built upon this model is AllegroGraph.[1]

In models based on **property graphs**, both nodes and edges can be labeled and can be associated with a collection of (attribute, value) pairs. Property graphs are the usual choice in practical implementations of modern graph databases. Unlike the case of RDF, there is no standard language for property graphs, although there is an emerging standard called GQL[2] (Graph Query Language). Examples of graph databases based on the property graph data model are Neo4j[3] and Sparksee.[4] Neo4j will be described in detail in Section 13.2, since it is one of the most-used graph database systems.

Figure 13.2 shows a property graph version of the graph in Fig. 13.1. In this graph, nodes are labeled Person, with attributes Name and Gender, and edges are labeled Follows, with no attribute associated. In this example, the Neo4j notation has been used.

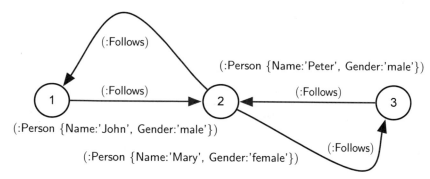

Fig. 13.2 A property graph extending the graph in Fig. 13.1

It has been proved that there is a formal way of reconciling the property graph and RDF models through a collection of well-defined transformations between the two models.

In models based on **hypergraphs**, any number of nodes can be connected through a relationship, which is represented as a hyperedge. On the contrary, the property graph model allows only binary relationships. Hypergraphs can model many-to-many relationships in a natural way. As an example, Fig. 13.3 represents group calls where many users are involved. In this figure, for example, there is a hyperedge involving nodes 1, 2, and 3, indicating that Mario

---

[1] http://franz.com/agraph/allegrograph/

[2] http://www.gqlstandards.org/

[3] https://neo4j.com/

[4] http://www.sparsity-technologies.com/

(represented by node 3) initiated a group call with Mary and Julia (nodes 1 and 2, respectively). Here, again, Neo4j notation has been used. There are nodes of type Phone, with attributes Nbr and Name, representing the phone numbers and the person's name, respectively. There are also nodes of type Call, representing a phone call, with attributes Date and Duration, representing the date and duration of the call, respectively. We will come back to the phone call example in more detail in Sect. 13.3.

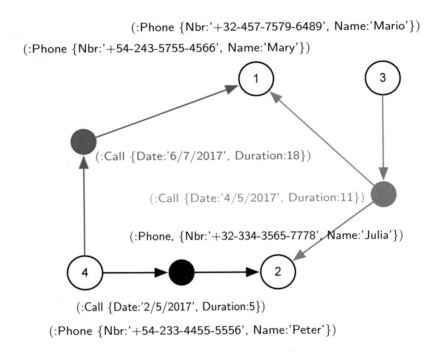

Fig. 13.3 A hypergraph example representing group calls

Having presented the main graph data models, we are now ready to discuss graph database systems based on the property graph model.

13.2 Property Graph Database Systems

A **graph database management system** allows manipulation of graphs using a graph data model. From a data storage point of view, graph database systems can be of two kinds. Those that use a *native storage* use graph data structures that are designed and optimized for storing and managing actual graphs. Graph database systems that use a *non-native storage* serialize graph data into, for example, a relational database, or some other kind of data store. In what follows we will focus on native graph database systems based on the property graph data model. We call them **property graph database systems**.

We explained above that a property graph is composed of nodes, relationships, and properties. Nodes have a label (i.e., the name of the node), and are annotated with properties (attributes). These annotations are represented as (property, value) pairs, where property represents the name of the property (i.e., a string) and value its actual value. Relationships connect and structure nodes, and have a label, a direction, a start node, and an end node. Like the nodes, relationships may also have properties. Figure 13.4 shows a simplified portion of the Northwind operational database represented as a property graph. Here, a node with name Employee has properties EmployeeID, First-Name, and LastName. There is also a node with name Order, and properties OrderID and OrderDate, and a node with name Product, and with properties ProductID and ProductName. A relationship Contains is defined from the Order node to the Product node, with properties Quantity and UnitPrice, indicating that the product is contained in the order.

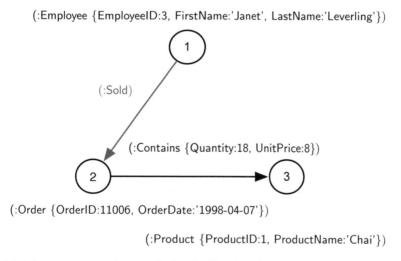

Fig. 13.4 A property graph example for the Northwind database

Currently, there is a wide range of graph database systems in the marketplace based on the property graph data model. Since Neo4j is one of the most popular ones, in the next sections we will be using it to explain how data warehouses can be deployed over a graph database management system.

13.2.1 Neo4j

Neo4j is an open-source graph database system written in Java. It follows the
property graph model and uses a native graph storage. Each node in Neo4j
has a pointer to all its outgoing relationships. Analogously, each relationship
knows its associated nodes. In other words, internally, data are stored as
double-chained lists. To find the neighbors of a node, Neo4j just needs to
look at its relationships, a feature known as index-free adjacency.

The query language for Neo4j is called **Cypher**. It is a declarative query
language based on pattern matching designed to operate over property
graphs. A Cypher query defines a graph pattern with a MATCH clause and returns the subgraph (i.e., all nodes and/or paths) that matches that pattern.
Cypher also supports Create, Read, Update, and Delete operations (called
CRUD operations). Neo4j comes with a web interface from which queries can
be run and results can be visualized as graphs or tables. Queries can also be
run from a command-line console.

A node in Neo4j has the form:

(n:label1: ... :labeln {prop1:val1, ..., propk:valk})

where n is a variable representing the node. Labels (or types) are optional and
a node can have more than one of them. There are also optional (property,
value) pairs. In the example of Fig. 13.4, the statement in Cypher for creating
a Product node is:

CREATE(:Product {ProductID:'1', Name:'Chai'});

Analogously, an edge in Neo4j has the form:

(n1)-[e:label {prop1:val1, ..., propk:valk}]->(n2)

Each edge has exactly one label (or type). As for nodes, properties are optional and there can be many of them. The Cypher statement for creating
the edge of type Contains between the order and the product of Fig. 13.4,
indicating that the product is contained in the order, is written as follows:

MATCH (p:Product {ProductID:1}), (o:Order {OrderID:'11006'})
CREATE (o)-[:Contains {Quantity:18, UnitPrice:8}]->(p)

First, MATCH is used to find the product and the order. The results are stored
in the variables p and o, and an edge labeled Contains is created between the
order and the product. In this case, the edge also includes two attributes,
namely Quantity and UnitPrice. Note that, unlike the case of relational databases, there is no formal database schema in Neo4j, and this is, in general,
the case in most graph database systems. This means that instances do not
have to comply with a predefined structure and thus nodes and edges of the
same type may have different components at the instance level. Therefore, in
the example above, we may create another Contains edge with no attributes,

or another **Product** node without a value for **ProductName**. All of these nodes and edges will coexist in the database.

In the following sections we will show how data warehouses can be represented at the logical and physical levels using Neo4j. As an example, we will use the Northwind data cube.

13.2.2 Introduction to Cypher

We start this section by showing how Cypher can be used for creating graphs. Then, we show the basics of Cypher as a query language, and finally we briefly discuss Cypher's semantics.

Representing the Northwind Cube in Neo4j

Graph databases (and, in general NoSQL databases, which will be studied in Chap. 15) are schemaless. This means that their instances must not comply with a predefined schema, like in the case of relational DBMSs. Nevertheless, given a certain database instance we can induce a corresponding schema. This schema is useful to provide a view of the structure of the data. Actually in Cypher (explained below), the statement **Call db.schema.visualization()** produces such schema based of the current graph instance. In this chapter we introduce an intuitive notation to represent a graph schema. In this notation, an ellipse represents a node type and an edge ending with a single arrow says that a node of a certain type may be linked with at most one node of another type. For example, any **Sales** node is linked with at most one node of type a **Product**. This is analogous to the **One2many** multiplicity property that will be explained in Sect. 13.4.2 (note that the same product may be contained in many different sales). A self-referencing arrow indicates a recursive relationship between nodes of the same type.

Figure 13.5 shows the schema of the Northwind data warehouse represented as a graph using the notation introduced above. For clarity, the attributes are not shown since they can easily be inferred from the corresponding logical relational schema depicted in Fig. 5.4. Sales facts are represented by a **Sales** node. Edges outgoing from the **Sales** node link the fact with the nodes representing the dimensions, namely, **Customer, Employee, Supplier, Product, Shipper**, and the three role-playing dimensions **Date**. Note that although in this example a sales fact is related to exactly one product, we will see in Sect. 13.3 that a fact node may be linked to many nodes of the same type (and viceversa), in which case a double arrow will point to such node type in the schema. The **Employee** node has a self-referencing edge labeled **ReportsTo** which represents the recursive relationship between an employee and her supervisor. There is also the **Product** hierarchy with level **Category**.

The Geography hierarchy is represented by the nodes City, State, Country, and Continent, and the edges between them.

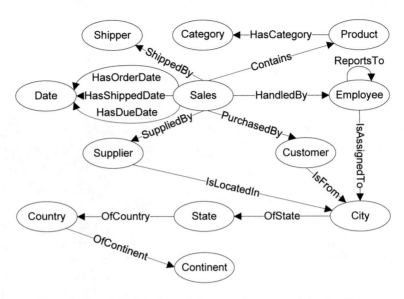

Fig. 13.5 The schema of the Northwind data warehouse graph in Neo4j

Figure 13.6 shows a portion of an instance of the Northwind data warehouse graph corresponding to the schema of Fig. 13.5. Each Sales node represents a fact instance associated with the Sales schema node. The outgoing edges are the links between the dimension members represented as nodes in the instance graph. As in the graphic interface that comes with Neo4j, only one attribute (chosen by the user) is displayed in the figure.

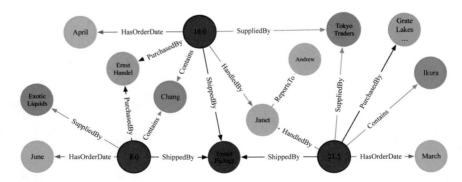

Fig. 13.6 An instance of the schema of Fig. 13.5

In the Northwind example we adopted a convention where a Sales fact node has outgoing edges to its related dimensions and the relationships representing a hierarchy follow its natural semantics, meaning that the edges go from the finer to the coarser node type. However, given the double-linked list structure implemented in Neo4j, any direction can be adopted. Thus, the Cypher queries must take into account the directions chosen in the design, as we will show later.

There are many other design decisions that must be taken when planning a graph database. Since graph databases are mainly used for real-world problems that can be naturally represented as networks, we cannot limit to translate a relational design into a graph. Instead, we must rethink the problem in terms of nodes and relationships. Further, the "One size fits all" approach, typical in relational databases, does not apply to graph databases. Therefore, we must consider the queries that will be submitted to the database in order to define whether a data object will be represented as a node, an attribute, or a relationship in the graph.

Consider the case of the Northwind data warehouse introduced above. As in classic relational data warehouse design, we can choose between a "Star", a "Snowflake" and a "Starflake" representation for the dimensions. In Fig. 13.5 we can see that for the geographic dimension we defined each level as a node type, yielding the node hierarchy City $\rightarrow$ State $\rightarrow$ Country $\rightarrow$ Continent. On the other hand, for the Date dimension we have chosen a flat (i.e., Star) representation, where there is one attribute (or property) for each dimension level (e.g., Month, Year). A Snowflake design allows reusing nodes. For example, we only use one city node (and its corresponding hierarchy) for all employees and suppliers of the same city. Otherwise, information about the city would be heavily replicated. On the other hand, since redundancy is low for the Date dimension in the Northwind case study, we chose a Star design. However, in a real-world situation we may have many sales on the same date which may worsen the redundancy problem.

As mentioned, the queries that the database will support must be accounted for in the design, since this will have an impact in the way in which graph data will be accessed. The database to be used plays an important role here. For example Neo4j allows indexing nodes *and* relationship properties, which was not the case in previous versions. This impacts on the design because without this feature we may be forced to define some data objects as nodes or node properties to be able to index them.

Discussing the issues above in depth is beyond the scope of this book. Thus, the graph database designs shown in this chapter are aimed at exposing the reader to different alternatives rather than providing the "best" solution to a particular problem.

Importing Graph Data

There are many ways to import the graph from the relational database storing the Northwind data warehouse. For example, to perform a bulk import of the Customer dimension table we may proceed as follows. First, we create a CSV file containing the tuples in the Customer table. Then, we write:

```
LOAD CSV WITH HEADERS FROM "file:/NWdata/customer.csv" AS row
CREATE (:Customer {CustomerID:row.CustomerID, CompanyName:row.CompanyName,
        Address:row.Address});
```

The LOAD statement above retrieves each row in the CSV file, and instantiates the variable row, one row at a time. Then, the CREATE statement creates the customer node using the values in the row variable. Creating a relationship is analogous. For example, assuming that the Employee and City nodes have been created, the IsAssignedTo relationship, indicating that an employee is assigned to a city, can be created as follows:

```
LOAD CSV WITH HEADERS FROM "file:/NWdata/territories.csv" AS row
MATCH (employee:Employee {EmployeeKey:row.EmployeeKey})
MATCH (city:City {CityKey:row.CityKey})
MERGE (employee)-[:IsAssignedTo]->(city);
```

Here, the file territories.csv contains the relationship between the cities and the employees. The row variable contains the values in each row of the CSV file. We need two matches then, one for the city nodes (i.e., matching the CityKey property in the City nodes in the graph with the CityKey value in the CSV file), and another one for the employee nodes. Finally, the MERGE clause creates the edge. This clause eliminates the duplicates, in case a link with the same name between the same nodes already exists. Otherwise, duplicates will be kept using CREATE.

Another way to import data from the relational database makes use of one of the popular libraries developed for Neo4j, namely the APOC library.[5] This library contains many useful functions, among them, functions allowing connection to a database and retrieval of tuples that are used for populating a graph. For example, to load the Product nodes we may write:

```
WITH "jdbc:postgresql://localhost:5433/NorthwindDW?
        user=postgres&password=postgres" AS url
CALL apoc.load.jdbc(url, 'SELECT * FROM Product') YIELD row
CREATE (:Product {ProductKey:row.ProductKey, ProductName:row.ProductName,
        UnitPrice:row.UnitPrice, Discontinued:row.Discontinued});
```

The connection string in the WITH clause has the credentials of the database (in this case, NorthwindDW in a PostgreSQL DBMS), and it is passed on using the variable url. Then, the apoc.load.jdbc function is called. The YIELD clause retrieves the data in a variable, in this case, named row, which is used as above to populate the Product nodes.

We could also update node attributes similarly. The following statement:

---

[5] https://neo4j.com/developer/neo4j-apoc/

```
WITH "jdbc:postgresql://localhost:5433/NorthwindDW?
          user=postgres&password=postgres" AS url
CALL apoc.load.jdbc(url, 'SELECT * FROM Sales') YIELD row
MATCH (s:Sales) WHERE s.OrderNo = row.OrderNo AND
          s.OrderLineNo = row.OrderLineNo
SET s += {Discount:row.Discount, Freight:row.Freight}
```

will add the Discount and Freight attributes to the existing Sales nodes. All
other attributes are kept unchanged. If we remove the + in the above statement, the node will end up with only these two attributes.

Querying with Cypher

Queries in Cypher are based on pattern matching. As mentioned, a typical
query starts with a MATCH clause, which defines a query pattern. The result
returns all nodes and/or paths that match the pattern. For example, a query
over the Northwind graph asking for all product names and unit prices, sorted
by unit price, will read:

```
MATCH (p:Product)
RETURN p.ProductName, p.UnitPrice
ORDER BY p.UnitPrice DESC
```

The MATCH clause retrieves all product nodes in the variable p. The type
of this variable is node, which means that all attributes of the nodes will be
retrieved. Since we are only interested in two of them, the RETURN clause
returns only the product names and unit prices, and finally, the ORDER BY
clause sorts the result in descending order according to the unit price. If we
only want the products with name Chocolade, the first line above should be
replaced with

```
MATCH (p:Product) WHERE p.ProductName = "Chocolade"
```

To ask for the name of the products belonging to the Beverages category,
we write:

```
MATCH (p:Product)-[:HasCategory]->(c:Category {CategoryName:'Beverages'})
RETURN p.ProductName
```

The MATCH clause matches the paths in the Product hierarchy such that a
Beverages node is at the top and the product node is at the bottom of the
hierarchy. Finally, the name is returned. Note that if instead of the graph
nodes we want the whole paths that match the pattern, we should write

```
MATCH path = (p:Product)-[:HasCategory]->(c:Category {CategoryName:'Beverages'})
RETURN path
```

Writing aggregate queries in Cypher is straightforward. For example, the
following query in SQL:

```
SELECT      ProductName, CompanyName, SUM(SalesAmount)
FROM        Sales
GROUP BY ProductName, CompanyName
```

is written in Cypher as:

```
MATCH (p:Product)<-[:Contains]-(s:Sales)-[:PurchasedBy]->(c:Customer)
RETURN p.ProductName, c.CompanyName, sum(s.SalesAmount)
```

As can be seen, the **GROUP BY** clause in SQL is implicit in Cypher.

Lists and collections are also supported. For example, the next query retrieves, for each employee, the list of cities she is assigned to.

```
MATCH (c:City)<-[:IsAssignedTo]-(e:Employee)
RETURN e, COLLECT(c.CityName) AS collection
```

The **COLLECT** clause produces, for each employee in the result of the **MATCH** clause, a list of the associated city names. To flatten this collection, and obtain a table as a result, the **UNWIND** clause is used.

```
MATCH (c:City)<-[:IsAssignedTo]-(e:Employee)
WITH e, COLLECT(c.CityName) AS collection
UNWIND collection AS col
RETURN e, col
```

The **WITH** clause in Cypher acts like a "pipe", passing variables on to the following step. In this case, the pairs (e, collection) are passed on to the **UNWIND** clause and a table is then returned.

We explain now how the window functions introduced in Sect. 5.8 can be expressed in Cypher. Consider the following query over the Northwind data warehouse: "*For each sale of a product to a customer, compare the sales amount against the overall sales of the product.*" This query is written in SQL using window functions as follows:

```
SELECT ProductName, CompanyName, SalesAmount,
        SUM(SalesAmount) OVER (PARTITION BY ProductName) AS TotAmount
FROM    Sales
```

The same query in Cypher reads:

```
MATCH (p:Product)<-[:Contains]-(s:Sales)-[:PurchasedBy]->(c:Customer)
WITH p, c, sum(s.SalesAmount) AS salesPC
WITH p, sum(salesPC) AS salesP, COLLECT(Customer:c, salesPC:salesPC) AS custSales
UNWIND custSales AS cs
RETURN p.ProductName AS ProductName, cs.Customer.CompanyName
        AS CompanyName, cs.salesPC AS SalesCustomer, salesP As SalesProduct
ORDER BY ProductName, CompanyName DESC
```

In the query above, the **MATCH** clause computes all the sales of products to customers. With such data, two computations are performed in the **WITH** clauses. First, the total sales by customer and product are computed in the variable **salesPC**. In the second **WITH** clause, the total sales for each product is computed in the variable salesP, which is returned together with a list, denoted custSales, containing the pairs (Customer, salesPC) representing the total sales of that product to a customer. Then, custSales is flattened using the UNWIND clause. The query returns a table containing for each product and each customer the total sales amount of the product to the customer and the total product sales. Note that cs.Customer.CompanyName obtains an attribute from a node in the table built with the UNWIND statement.

Cypher Semantics

We have explained that query evaluation in Cypher is based on pattern matching. The underlying semantics of Cypher is based on the notions of graph isomorphism and homomorphism, which we explain next. Let $V(G)$ and $E(G)$ denote, respectively, the vertices and the edges of a graph G. An **isomorphism** from a graph G to a graph H is a bijective mapping $\alpha : V(G) \rightarrow V(G)$ such that

$$xy \in E(G) \Leftrightarrow \alpha(x)\alpha(y) \in E(H).$$

The above definition implies that α maps edges to edges and vertices to vertices. On the other hand, a **homomorphism** from a graph G to a graph H is a mapping (not necessarily bijective) $\alpha : V(G) \rightarrow V(G)$ such that

$$xy \in E(G) \Rightarrow \alpha(x)\alpha(y) \in E(H).$$

Notice that the difference between the two definitions is that the if and only if condition in the first one is replaced with an implication in the second one. As a consequence, a homomorphism α maps edges to edges but may map a vertex to either a vertex or an edge. Note that an isomorphism is a special type of homomorphism.

Cypher semantics is formalized through the graph isomorphism problem, defined as follows: Given a property graph G and a pattern graph P, a matching P to G results in all subgraphs of G that are isomorphic to P. It is well known that this is a hard problem, in general NP-complete. For property graphs, the problem is based on **basic graph patterns** (BGPs), which is equivalent to the problem of conjunctive queries, well studied by the database community. A BGP for querying property graphs is a property graph where variables can appear in place of any constant (either labels or properties). A match for a BGP is a mapping from variables to constants such that when the mapping is applied to the BGP, the result is contained in the original graph. The results for a BGP are then all the mappings from variables in the query to constants that comprise a match.

Given the definitions above, evaluating a BGP Q against a graph database G corresponds to listing all possible matches of Q with respect to G. There are several semantics to produce this matching:

- *Homomorphism-based semantics*, where multiple variables in Q can map to the same term in G. This corresponds to the SQL and SPARQL semantics.
- *Isomorphism-based semantics*, where the match function must be injective. In this case, three variants are possible:
  - *No-repeated-anything semantics*, which corresponds to strict isomorphism.
  - *No-repeated-node semantics*, where the match function is only injective for nodes.
  - *No-repeated-edge semantics*, where the match function is only injective for edges. This is the semantics adopted by Cypher, sometimes called Cyphermorphism.

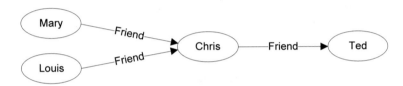

Fig. 13.7 An example of Cypher semantics

Consider Fig. 13.7 to explain the practical consequences of the no-repeated-edge semantics. Here, we have two persons who are friends of a third one, who is in turn a friend of a fourth one. Cypher semantics imply that all relationships matched by the same clause must be different, although this is not the case for nodes. That means that two query edges cannot map to the same data edge. Therefore, the following query returns the empty set, since the edge between Chris and Ted can only be used once in the MATCH clause.

```
MATCH (p1:Person)-[:Friend]->(:Person)-[:Friend]->(c),
      (p2:Person)-[:Friend]->(:Person)-[:Friend]->(c)
WHERE p1 <> p2
RETURN p1.Name, p2.Name
```

However, writing two MATCH clauses, as in the following query,

```
MATCH (p1:Person)-[:Friend]->(:Person)-[:Friend]->(c),
MATCH (p2:Person)-[:Friend]->(:Person)-[:Friend]->(c)
WHERE p1 <> p2
RETURN p1.Name, p2.Name
```

will enable the edge between Chris and Ted to be used in the two clauses. In fact, the query returns duplicated results, since p1 and p2 are matched indistinctly to Louis and Mary.

We next show how to query the Northwind data warehouse using Cypher.

13.2.3 Querying the Northwind Cube with Cypher

Given the schema of the Northwind cube represented as a Neo4j graph in
Fig. 13.5, we now revisit the queries of Sect. 4.4 and write them in Cypher.

Query 13.1. *Total sales amount per customer, year, and product category.*

```
MATCH   (c:Category)<-[:HasCategory]-(:Product)<-[:Contains]-(s:Sales)-
        [:PurchasedBy]->(u:Customer)
MATCH   (s)-[:HasOrderDate]->(d:Date)
RETURN u.CompanyName AS Customer, d.Year AS Year, c.CategoryName AS Category,
       sum(s.SalesAmount) AS SalesAmount
ORDER BY Customer, Year, Category
```

In this query, the roll-up to the Category level along the product dimension is
performed through the first MATCH clause. The second MATCH clause performs the roll-up to the Year level, although this is straightforward, since all
the date information is stored as properties of the Date nodes. The aggregation is performed in the RETURN clause, and finally the results are ordered
by the company name of the customer, the year, and the category.

Query 13.2. *Yearly sales amount for each pair of customer and supplier
countries.*

```
MATCH   (cc:Country)<-[:OfCountry]-(:State)<-[:OfState]-(:City)<-[:IsLocatedIn]-
        (:Customer)<-[:PurchasedBy]-(s:Sales)
MATCH   (sc:Country)<-[:OfCountry]-(:State)<-[:OfState]-(:City)<-[:IsFrom]-
        (:Supplier)<-[:SuppliedBy]-(s:Sales)-[:HasOrderDate]->(d:Date)
RETURN cc.CountryName AS CustomerCountry, sc.CountryName AS SupplierCountry,
       d.Year AS Year, sum(s.SalesAmount) AS SalesAmount
ORDER BY CustomerCountry, SupplierCountry, Year
```

The first MATCH performs a roll-up to the customer country level, while
the second MATCH performs a roll-up to the supplier contry and the Year
levels. The aggregated result is computed in the RETURN clause. Here we
can see the impact of the Cypher semantics that we studied in Sect. 13.2.2.
If, instead of writing the two roll-ups to the Country level using two different
statements we had used only one statement, some tuples would have been
missed because of the no-repeated-edge semantics.

Query 13.3. *Monthly sales by customer state compared to those of the previous year.*

```
// All months and customer states
MATCH   (d:Date)
MATCH   (:Customer)-[:IsLocatedIn]->(:City)-[:OfState]->(t:State)
WITH DISTINCT t.StateName AS State, d.Year AS Year, d.MonthNumber AS Month
// Sales amount by month and state including months without sales
OPTIONAL MATCH (d:Date)<-[:HasOrderDate]-(s:Sales)-[:PurchasedBy]->
        (:Customer)-[:IsLocatedIn]->(:City)-[:OfState]->(t:State)
WHERE   t.StateName = State AND d.Year = Year AND d.MonthNumber = Month
```

```
WITH     State, Year, Month, sum(s.SalesAmount) AS SalesAmount
ORDER BY State, Year, Month
WITH     State, COLLECT({y:Year, m:Month, s:SalesAmount}) AS rows
UNWIND range(0, size(rows) - 1) AS i
// Same month previous year using row number
WITH     State, rows[i].y AS Year, rows[i].m AS Month, rows[i].s AS SalesAmount,
         CASE WHEN i-12 < 0 THEN 0 ELSE rows[i-12].s END AS SalesAmountPY
WHERE  SalesAmount <> 0 OR SalesAmountPY <> 0
RETURN State, Year, Month, SalesAmount, SalesAmountPY
ORDER BY State, Year, Month
```

This query is more involved. One of the issues to solve here is that we need to produce the aggregation of all possible combinations of customer state and month, including those combinations for which there have been no sales. This is done through the Cartesian product in the first two **MATCH** clauses and the **WITH** clause, which passes all possible combinations of state, year, and month in the database. The **OPTIONAL MATCH** clause, which behaves like an outer join, returns a null value for **salesAmount** when there are no sales for a combination. Over the result, the total sales per state, year, and month are computed in the **WITH** clause. If there were no sales for a combination, zero is returned (i.e., the operation **sum(s.SalesAmount) AS SalesAmount** returns 0 if there was no match in the outer join). The result is sorted by state, year, and month. Then, for each state, a list is produced by the **COLLECT** function, composed of triples containing the sales for each month and year. This list is stored in the variable **rows**. For each state, the list has the same length. The **UNWIND** clause produces an index, which is used to iterate over the elements in the list. This index is used to compute the sales amount value of the same month of the previous year in the last **WITH** clause. For example, for each state, **rows[i].y** returns the year in position [i] in the list. Since the list is sorted by year and month, the operation **rows[i-12]** returns the sales of the same month in the previous year, and the value is stored in variable **SalesAmountPY**.

Query 13.4. *Monthly sales growth per product, that is, total sales per product compared to those of the previous month.*

```
// All months and products
MATCH   (d:Date)
MATCH   (p:Product)
WITH DISTINCT p.ProductName AS Product, d.Year AS Year, d.MonthNumber AS Month
// Sales amount by month and product including months without sales
OPTIONAL MATCH (p:Product)<-[:Contains]-(s:Sales)-[:HasOrderDate]->(d:Date)
WHERE  p.ProductName = Product AND d.Year = Year AND d.MonthNumber = Month
WITH     Product, Year, Month, sum(s.SalesAmount) AS SalesAmount
ORDER BY Product, Year, Month
// Add row number
WITH     Product, collect({y:Year, m:Month, s:SalesAmount}) AS rows
UNWIND range(0, size(rows) - 1) AS i
// Previous month using row number
WITH     Product, rows[i].y AS Year, rows[i].m AS Month, rows[i].s AS SalesAmount,
```

```
          CASE WHEN i-1 < 0 THEN 0 ELSE rows[i-1].s END AS SalesAmountPM
RETURN Product, Year, Month, SalesAmount, SalesAmountPM,
          SalesAmount - SalesAmountPM AS SalesGrowth
ORDER BY Product, Year, Month
```

This query uses a similar strategy to the previous one to compute aggregate values for all combinations of products and months. The OPTIONAL MATCH and the WITH clauses perform the aggregation, also producing a zero as aggregated value for missing combinations. The call to the COLLECT function and the subsequent UNWIND generates a row number per product in the variable i. This row number is used to access the sales amount value of the previous month in the last WITH clause to compute the growth in the RETURN clause.

Query 13.5. *Three best-selling employees.*

```
MATCH   (e:Employee)<-[:HandledBy]-(s:Sales)
RETURN e.FirstName + ' ' + e.LastName, SUM(s.SalesAmount) AS SalesAmount
ORDER BY SalesAmount DESC LIMIT 3
```

This query is simple to express in Cypher. Once the matching of the employees and their sales is performed, we have all we need for the aggregation. In the RETURN clause, the first and last name of each employee are concatenated, separated by a blank space. Finally, the LIMIT clause retains the first three employees and their total sales.

Query 13.6. *Best-selling employee per product and year.*

```
MATCH   (e:Employee)<-[:HandledBy]-(s:Sales)-[:Contains]->(p:Product)
MATCH   (d:Date)<-[:HasOrderDate]-(s)
WITH    p.ProductName AS Product, d.Year AS Year, e.FirstName + ' ' + e.LastName
          AS Employee, SUM(s.SalesAmount) AS SalesAmount
ORDER BY Product, Year, SalesAmount DESC
WITH    Product, Year, COLLECT({e:Employee, s:SalesAmount}) AS rows
WITH    Product, Year, head(rows) AS top
RETURN Product, Year, top.e AS Employee, top.s AS SalesAmount
ORDER BY Product, Year
```

Here, the first two MATCH clauses perform the roll-up along the employee, product, and date dimensions, to collect the data needed later. The first WITH clause aggregates sales by product and year. The second WITH clause uses COLLECT to build, for each (product, year) pair, a list with each employee and her sales of that product that year, and passes these sets in the variable rows. Finally, the first element of each list is extracted using head(rows).

Query 13.7. *Countries that account for top 50% of the sales amount.*

```
MATCH   (c:Country)<-[:OfCountry]-(:State)<-[:OfState]-(:City)<-[:IsLocatedIn]-
          (:Customer)<-[:PurchasedBy]-(s:Sales)
WITH    c.CountryName AS CountryName, sum(s.SalesAmount) AS SalesAmount
ORDER BY SalesAmount DESC
```

```
WITH    COLLECT({CountryName:CountryName, SalesAmount:SalesAmount})
        AS Countries, sum(SalesAmount) * 0.5 AS Sales50Perc
UNWIND Countries AS c
WITH    c.CountryName AS CountryName, c.SalesAmount AS SalesAmount,
        apoc.coll.sum([c1 IN Countries where c1.SalesAmount >= c.SalesAmount |
        c1.SalesAmount]) AS CumulSales, Sales50Perc
WITH    COLLECT({CountryName:CountryName, SalesAmount:SalesAmount,
        CumulSales:CumulSales}) AS CumulCountries, Sales50Perc
UNWIND [c1 IN CumulCountries where c1.CumulSales <= Sales50Perc] +
        [c1 IN CumulCountries where c1.CumulSales > Sales50Perc][0] AS r
RETURN r.CountryName AS CountryName, r.SalesAmount AS SalesAmount,
        r.CumulSales As CumulativeSales
ORDER BY r.SalesAmount DESC
```

This query requires the computation of a cumulative sum of the sales. The
solution requires the use of some advanced Cypher features. First, the sales
per country are computed and passed, sorted in descending order of the sales
amount, to the first COLLECT function. This builds the collection Countries,
as a list of (Country, Sales) pairs. The value accounting for the top 50% of
the overall sales amount is attached to the Countries list. Then, the UNWIND
clause transforms the collection back to a table c, where each row consists of a
(Country, Sales) pair. For each tuple in c, the expression with the apoc.coll.sum
function of the APOC library computes the cumulative sum in the collection
Countries. As a result, we get a table with the country name, the cumulative
sum for the country, the total sales for it, and the 50 percent value of the
total sales (this is repeated for every tuple). At this point we have everything
we need to produce a result. For this, a collection is built again, containing
triples of the form (CountryName, SalesAmount, CumulSales). The trick to
compute what we need is performed by the next UNWIND clause. The first
line of this clause produces a table with the countries whose cumulative sales
are *less than* 50% of the total sales. Since we need to add a last country
to exceed the 50%, we must add the first element of the remainder of the
collection. This is done in the second line of the UNWIND clause. The +
operation performs the union of the two tables.

Query 13.8. *Total sales and average monthly sales by employee and year.*

```
MATCH   (e:Employee)<-[:HandledBy]-(s:Sales)-[:HasOrderDate]->(d:Date)
WITH    e.FirstName + ' ' + e.LastName AS Employee, d.Year AS Year,
        d.MonthNumber AS Month, sum(s.SalesAmount) AS MonthSales
WITH    Employee, Year, sum(MonthSales) AS YearSales, COUNT(*) AS count
RETURN Employee, Year, YearSales, YearSales / count AS avgMonthlySales
ORDER BY Employee, Year
```

In this query, the MATCH clause performs the roll-up along the employee
and date dimensions. The first WITH clause computes the sales amount per
year and month, while the second one computes the sales amount per year
together with the number of tuples composing each year's sales in the variable
count. Finally, in the RETURN clause, the average is computed.

Query 13.9. *Total sales amount and total discount amount per product and month.*

```
MATCH   (d:Date)<-[:HasOrderDate]-(s:Sales)-[:Contains]->(p:Product)
WITH    p.ProductName AS Product, d.Year AS Year, d.MonthNumber AS Month,
        sum(s.SalesAmount) AS SalesAmount,
        sum(s.UnitPrice * s.Quantity * s.Discount) AS TotalDiscount
RETURN Product, Year, Month, SalesAmount, TotalDiscount
ORDER BY Product, Year, Month
```

Here, to compute the total discount, we need to use the quantity sold of each product, along with its unit price, instead of using the **SalesAmount** attribute. The rest of the query is straightforward.

Query 13.10. *Monthly year-to-date sales for each product category.*

```
MATCH   (c:Category)<-[:HasCategory]-(:Product)<-[:Contains]-
        (s:Sales)-[:HasOrderDate]->(d:Date)
WITH    c.CategoryName AS Category, d.Year AS Year, d.MonthNumber AS Month,
        sum(s.SalesAmount) AS SalesAmount
MATCH   (c1:Category)<-[:HasCategory]-(:Product)<-[:Contains]-
        (s1:Sales)-[:HasOrderDate]->(d1:Date)
WHERE   c1.CategoryName = Category AND d1.MonthNumber <= Month AND
        d1.Year = Year
RETURN Category, Year, Month, SalesAmount, SUM(s1.SalesAmount) AS YTDSalesAmount
ORDER BY Category, Year, Month
```

Recall that this query is written in SQL using window functions. Here, the MATCH clause collects all sales with their associated category and date. The WITH clause aggregates the sales by category, month, and year. Then, a new MATCH allows these results to be compared with the sales of the same year and previous months, performing the running sum.

Query 13.11. *Moving average over the last 3 months of the sales amount by product category.*

```
// Sales amount by month and category including months without sales
MATCH   (d:Date)
MATCH   (c:Category)
WITH DISTINCT c.CategoryName AS Category, d.Year AS Year, d.MonthNumber AS Month
OPTIONAL MATCH (d:Date)<-[:HasOrderDate]-(s:Sales)-[:Contains]->(p:Product)-
        [:HasCategory]->(c:Category)
WHERE   c.CategoryName = Category AND d.Year = Year AND d.MonthNumber = Month
WITH    Category, Year, Month, sum(s.SalesAmount) AS SalesAmount
ORDER BY Category, Year, Month
// Add row number
WITH    Category, COLLECT({y:Year, m:Month, s:SalesAmount}) AS rows
UNWIND range(0, size(rows) - 1) AS i
// Moving average using row number
WITH    Category, rows[i].y AS Year, rows[i].m AS Month, rows[i].s AS SalesAmount,
        rows[CASE WHEN i-2 < 0 THEN 0 ELSE i-2 END..i+1] AS Values
UNWIND Values AS Value
RETURN Category, Year, Month, SalesAmount, collect(Value.s) AS Values,
        avg(Value.s) AS MovAvg3M
ORDER BY Category, Year, Month
```

In this query, we proceed as in Query 13.3 to compute the aggregated sales by category, year, and month including also the months when no product in some category was sold. These values are passed, sorted, to the COLLECT function to generate, per category, a list of triples (Year, Month, SalesAmount). We proceed as in Query 13.3 using the index produced by the UNWIND clause, to select the sales values of the current month and the two preceding ones, where the CASE expression takes care of the case when there are fewer than two previous values for the current category. The average of these values is then computed in the RETURN clause. Notice that the values over which the average is computed are given in the output for illustration purposes.

Query 13.12. *Personal sales amount made by an employee compared with the total sales amount made by herself and her subordinates during 2017.*

```
MATCH    (e:Employee)<-[:HandledBy]-(s:Sales)-[:HasOrderDate]->(d:Date)
WHERE    d.Year = 2017
WITH     e, e.FirstName + ' ' + e.LastName AS Employee,
         sum(s.SalesAmount) AS PersSales
OPTIONAL MATCH (e2:Employee)-[:ReportsTo*]->(e:Employee)
OPTIONAL MATCH (e2:Employee)<-[:HandledBy]-(s:Sales)-[:HasOrderDate]->(d:Date)
WHERE    d.Year = 2017
RETURN Employee, PersSales, sum(s.SalesAmount) AS SubordSales
         (PersSales + sum(s.SalesAmount)) AS PersonalAndSubordSales
ORDER BY Employee
```

This is a recursive query, which makes use of one of the main features of graph databases in general, and Neo4j in particular, which is the easy and efficient computation of the transitive closure of a graph. At the start of the query, the sales by employee in 2017 are computed and passed forward. For each employee in this result, the first OPTIONAL MATCH is used to compute recursively all her subordinates with the construct [:ReportsTo*]. The second OPTIONAL MATCH computes the sales of these subordinates, which are aggregated in the RETURN clause.

Query 13.13. *Total sales amount, number of products, and sum of the quantities sold for each order.*

```
MATCH    (p:Product)<-[:Contains]-(s:Sales)-[:HasOrderDate]->(d:Date)
WITH     s.OrderNo AS Order, sum(s.UnitPrice * s.Quantity) AS OrderAmount,
         sum(s.Quantity) AS TotalQty, count(*) AS NbrOfProducts
RETURN Order, OrderAmount, TotalQty, NbrOfProducts
ORDER BY Order
```

Here, the product sales and their dates are computed first. The WITH clause computes, for each order, the total amount by multiplying the unit price and the quantity sold, and also computes the number of products for each order.

Query 13.14. *For each month, total number of orders, total sales amount, and average sales amount by order.*

```
MATCH   (s:Sales)-[:HasOrderDate]->(d:Date)
WITH    d.Year AS Year, d.MonthNumber AS Month, s.OrderNo AS Order,
        sum(s.SalesAmount) AS OrderAmount
RETURN Year, Month, count(*) AS NoOrders, sum(OrderAmount) AS SalesAmount,
        avg(OrderAmount) AS AvgOrderAmount
ORDER BY Year, Month
```

The first **MATCH** associates to each order its date to find all dates at which an order was placed. The **WITH** clause computes the total amount of each order and associates to it its year and month. In the **RETURN** clause, the required aggregations are computed.

Query 13.15. *For each employee, total sales amount, and number of cities to which she is assigned.*

```
MATCH   (e:Employee)<-[:HandledBy]-(s:Sales)
MATCH   (e:Employee)-[:IsAssignedTo]->(c:City)-[:OfState]->(t:State)
RETURN e.FirstName + ' ' + e.LastName AS Employee,
        sum(s.SalesAmount) AS SalesAmount, count(DISTINCT c) AS NoCities,
        count(DISTINCT t) AS NoStates
ORDER BY Employee
```

The first **MATCH** retrieves the sales of each employee, while the second one retrieves the employee's cities and states. The **RETURN** clause computes the aggregated sales as well as the number of distinct cities and states.

13.3 OLAP on Hypergraphs

Traditional data warehousing and OLAP operations on cubes are not sufficient to address the data analysis requirements in modern big data systems, where data are highly connected. Given the extensive use of graphs to represent practical problems, multidimensional analysis of graph data and **graph data warehouses** is increasingly being studied. There is a need to perform graph analysis from different perspectives and at multiple granularities. Although OLAP operations and models can expand the possibilities of graph analysis beyond the traditional graph-based computation, this poses new challenges to traditional OLAP technology.

Consider a social network represented as a graph where nodes are used to represent persons. We can enrich this graph with additional nodes, edges, and properties describing multidimensional information associated to the nodes. For persons, such information may include Gender, Profession, City, State, etc. Therefore, while in traditional OLAP as studied in this book queries are of the kind "Average income by location and profession?", in our multidimensional network the natural queries would be of the kind "What is the network structure between the various professions?" To answer such a query we need to aggregate all user nodes of a given profession into a single node and aggregate all edges between persons into edges between professions.

Most proposals to perform OLAP over graphs only address graphs whose nodes are of the same kind, which are referred to as **homogeneous**. Contrary to this, **heterogeneous** graphs can have nodes of different kinds. Work on OLAP over heterogeneous graphs is still at a preliminary stage. This section presents **Hypergraph GOLAP (HGOLAP)**, an extension of OLAP concepts to hypergraphs, which are heterogeneous graphs that allow many-to-many relationships between nodes.

The hypergraph model is appropriate for representing facts having a variable number of dimensions, which can even be of different types. A typical example is the analysis of phone calls that we will use in this section. Here, we represent *point-to-point calls* between two participants, but also *group calls* between any number of participants, initiated by one of them. As discussed in Sect. 5.6.2, a relational representation of this scenario typically requires a bridge table to represent the many-to-many relationship between the fact representing the calls (with measures such as call duration) and the dimension representing the participants. The hypergraph model described next allows a more natural representation of this scenario.

A **hypergraph** is composed of *nodes* and *hyperedges*. Nodes have a *type* and are described by *attributes*. Attributes, which correspond to dimension levels, have an associated *domain*. For formal reasons (not covered in this chapter) the first attribute in a node type corresponds to a distinguished *identifier attribute*. *Hyperedges* are defined analogously to nodes but without an identifier attribute. Figure 13.8 illustrates this model, based on the example of the group calls mentioned above. The figure depicts a node of type **Person**, having an identifier attribute and three dimensions representing the name, the city, and the phone number. There is also a hyperedge of type **Call** with dimension **Date** and a measure denoted **Duration** (recall that OLAP measures can be considered as dimensions). This hyperedge says that the person represented by node 1 initiates a call where persons represented by nodes 2 and 3 participate. We keep the Neo4j notation for nodes and edges. As mentioned in Sect. 13.2.2, although conceptually the direction of the arrows indicates the role of each node in the hyperedge, this is not an issue in a Neo4j implementation. Therefore, in Fig. 13.8 we follow the semantics of the problem and define an edge going from a **Person** node to the **Call** node to indicate the initiator of the call. Analogously, an edge going from a **Call** node to a **Person** node indicates the receiver of the call.

We can now define the model as follows. Given n dimensions $D_1, ..., D_n$ defined at granularity levels $l_1, ..., l_n$, a *hypergraph by* $(D_1.l_1, ..., D_n.l_n)$ is a multi-hypergraph (i.e., there can be several hyperedges between the same pair of nodes) where all attributes in nodes and edges are defined at the granularity $D_i.l_i$. The **base hypergraph** is the graph where all information in the data cube is at the finest granularity level (i.e., the bottom level).

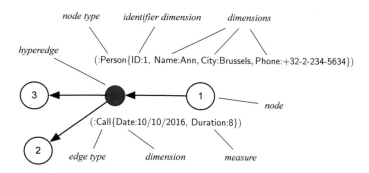

Fig. 13.8 A hyperedge in the HGOLAP model

In what follows we explain the HGOLAP model and operations in detail, using the phone call example. To describe the schema of the phone call graph we use the notation introduced in Sect. 13.2.2. We extend such notation in two ways: (a) We introduce a double-lined ellipse to indicate a hyperdegde; (b) We use double arrows to indicate "multivalued" nodes, meaning that a node may have many nodes associated with it and each of them can be associated at most with one node. This is analogous to the multiplicity Multi that will be explained in Sect. 13.4.2 (for example, a phone number can be involved in many calls and a call may be associated with many phone numbers). Using this notation, Fig. 13.9 depicts the schema of the phone call graph. This schema allows representing group calls between a variable number of participants. There are nodes, such as Person, Phone, and Operator, and edges connecting the nodes, such as Has and Connected. The cardinalities of the edges are also shown, indicating that a person may have several phones and each phone is connected to a single operator. Attributes are attached to the nodes and edges, such as Name, BirthDate, Gender, and Profession for persons. For readability, the identifier attribute for nodes is not shown. There is also a hyperedge of type Call (as indicated by the double line in the ellipse) with attributes StartTime and Duration. This hyperedge has a single incoming edge Initiates and one or multiple outgoing edges Participates.

We illustrate the hypergraph model with the graph excerpt given in Fig. 13.10, which represents calls between a variable number of participants. For readability, we omit the property names and only show the property values, and we show only the date part of the StartTime property of calls. For the same reason we also omit the relationship names of the hyperedges (i.e., Receives and Creates). As shown in the figure, there is a group call started by phone 3, which called phones 2 and 5 on October 10, 2017, with a duration of 6 minutes. There are also point-to-point calls, for instance, two calls from phone 1 to 2. We do not show the dimensional information in the figures. For example, each call will is related to a date, each phone to an operator, and each person a geographic hierarchy composed of city, state, and coun-

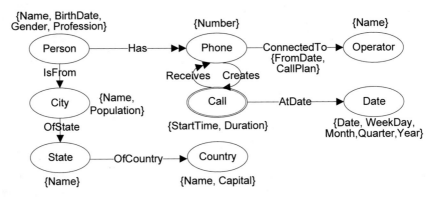

Fig. 13.9 Schema of the phone calls hypergraph

try. These are denoted *contextual dimensions* in the HGOLAP model. We use these dimensions to define hypergraphs at several aggregation levels, as explained next.

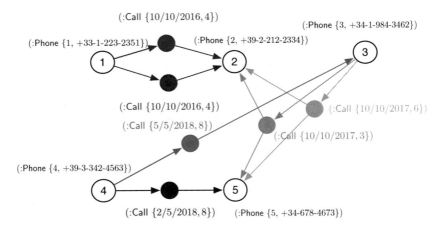

Fig. 13.10 Base hypergraph representing phone calls

The graph depicted in Fig. 13.10 is actually the base graph. Note that several hypergraphs at the same granularity can exist for a given base graph. Suppose that the phone 1 corresponds to the operator Orange, phones 2 and 4 to Vodafone, and phones 3 and 5 to Movistar. A hypergraph by (Date.Day, Phone.Operator), shown in Fig. 13.11, is obtained from the base graph in Fig. 13.10 by replacing all phone numbers in the graph with their corresponding operators, keeping the rest of the graph unchanged. As can be seen in the figure, the hypergraph has the same number of nodes, but at a coarser granularity level.

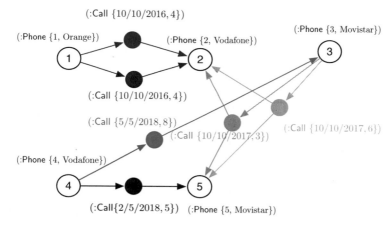

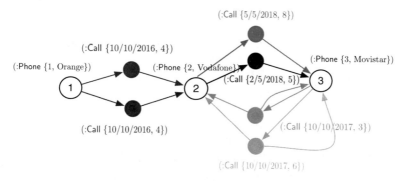

Fig. 13.11 Hypergraph by (Date.Day, Phone.Operator) for the hypergraph of Fig. 13.10

Fig. 13.12 A minimal hypergraph by (Date.Day, Phone.Operator) for the graph in Fig. 13.10

However, a more concise version of the hypergraph in Fig. 13.11 can be obtained by merging all nodes which are identical except for the node identifier. This is shown in Fig. 13.12. In this case, all the nodes corresponding to the same operator are merged. As a convention, the node with the smallest identifier is kept (call it n) and the other nodes are deleted. This merging is obtained by deleting all edges leaving from the deleted nodes and redirecting these edges to n. A hypergraph built in this way is called a *minimal hypergraph*, and it can be proved that there is exactly one minimal hypergraph for a given graph at a specified granularity. This is relevant for the model, since the result of OLAP operations over a hypergraph gives as result a minimal hypergraph, which is unique. Thus, Fig. 13.12 depicts the minimal hypergraph by (Date.Day, Phone.Operator) for the base graph in Fig. 13.10. Here, the pairs of nodes (2,4) and (3,5) have been merged together and the edges have been accommodated accordingly.

13.3.1 Operations on Hypergraphs

This section explains intuitively the OLAP operations on hypergraphs. These correspond to the typical OLAP operations on cubes.

Climb Consider a hypergraph G with a dimension D and a level L in that dimension. The **climb** operation over D up to L produces a hypergraph G' at a coarser granularity for D, leaving the granularity of all the other dimensions unchanged. In practice, the operation simply replaces a value v at the current level in dimension D, with the value v' to which v rolls up in level L. The hypergraph shown in Fig. 13.11 was produced by applying to the hypergraph in Fig. 13.10 the climb operation over the **Phone** dimension up to the **Operator** level. As mentioned before, the resulting hypergraph is not necessarily minimal.

Aggregation Consider a hypergraph G with a measure M and an aggregate function F. The **aggregation** over M using F returns a hypergraph G' built by replacing by a single hyperedge all hyperedges of the same type that coincide in all attributes except the identifier attribute and the measure M. The value of M in the new hyperedge is the result of applying function F to the values of M in the original edges. Figure 13.13 illustrates this. We start from the minimal hypergraph in Fig. 13.12, where we can see two hyperedges between nodes 1 and 2. Both hyperedges coincide in their type **Call** and their attribute **Date**. Thus, we can replace them by one edge that contains the aggregated value of the measure using the function **SUM**. We proceed analogously with the two hyperedges between nodes 2, 3, and 5. However, the two calls between nodes 2 and 3 cannot be aggregated, because they do not coincide on the date.

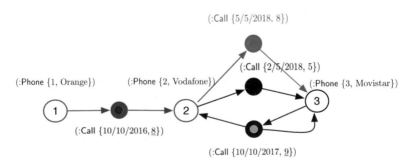

Fig. 13.13 Aggregation operation over the minimal hypergraph of Fig. 13.12

Roll-up and drill-down The **roll-up** operation can be defined from the climb and aggregation operations given above. Given a hypergraph G, a dimension D with a level L, a measure M, and an aggregate function F, the roll-up over M using F along the dimension D up to level L is defined as the result of three operations: (1) Compute the climb operation along D up to L, yielding a hypergraph G'; (2) Compute the minimal hypergraph of G'; (3) Perform an aggregation of G' over the measure M using the function F. The **drill-down** operation does the opposite of roll-up, taking a hypergraph to a finer granularity level, along the dimension D.

To illustrate this concept, consider the hypergraph in Fig. 13.10. A roll-up operation over this hypergraph along the Phone dimension up to level Operator, and along the Date dimension up to level Year, using the function Sum, produces the hypergraph of Fig. 13.16. First, a climb up to the Year and Operator levels is produced. The result is depicted in Fig. 13.14. Then, a minimal hypergraph of this last result is built, as shown in Fig. 13.15. Finally, an aggregation over this hypergraph applying the Sum function to the measures is performed as follows. The two Call hyperedges corresponding to calls from an Orange to a Vodafone line in 2016 are aggregated using the Sum function over the measure Duration. The same occurs with the calls between the nodes 2 and 3.

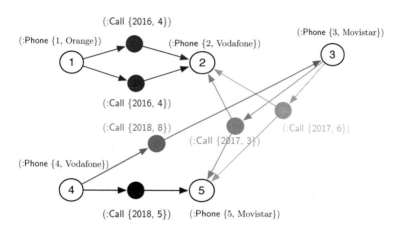

Fig. 13.14 Hypergraph produced by climbing up to Year and Operator levels

Dice Given a hypergraph G and a Boolean formula φ over the dimension levels and the measures, the **dice** operation produces a hypergraph G' whose nodes are the nodes of G and whose edges satisfy the conditions expressed by φ. When an edge does not satisfy φ, the whole hyperedge is deleted. All other edges of G are kept. For example, applying Dice(G, Operator.OperatorName $\neq$ "Orange") to the hypergraph depicted in Fig. 13.11 produces the hypergraph of Fig. 13.17.

Slice The slice operation on cubes drops a dimension D and aggregates all measures over D. Before a slicing operation, the dropped dimension must have a unique element. Thus, before slicing a roll-up to the All level along

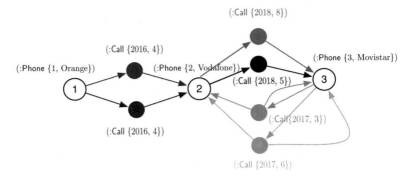

Fig. 13.15 Minimal hypergraph produced by climbing up to Year and Operator levels

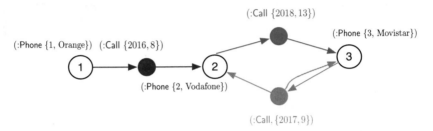

Fig. 13.16 Roll-up to levels Year and Operator for the base hypergraph in Fig. 13.10

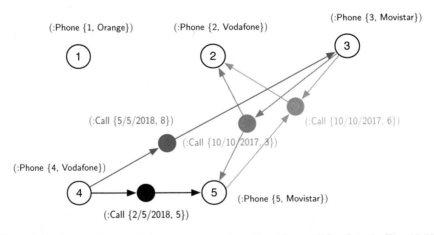

Fig. 13.17 Dicing the graph for operators other than "Orange" for data in Fig. 13.10

the dimension to be deleted is required. Thus, the **slice** operation on hypergraphs is just defined as a roll-up to $D.\text{All}$. Fig. 13.18 depicts a slice over the dimension Date for the graph in Fig. 13.10.

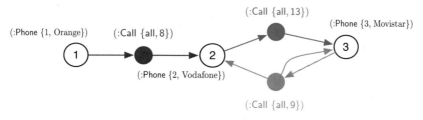

Fig. 13.18 Slicing the Date dimension for the graph in Fig. 13.10

Hypergraph Implementation in Neo4j

We can represent in Neo4j the hypergraph whose schema was shown in
Fig. 13.9. For this, we create node types for each level of a contextual dimension and for each hyperedge. For example, node Phone represents the phone
dimension and node Call represents the call fact. These are linked through
edges labeled Creates and Receives, the former going from the phone that
initiated the call to the node representing the call, and the latter from the
call node to the phones receiving the call. Background dimensions are represented in the same graph, using the entity nodes Operator, User, City, and
Country for the dimension levels. Finally, dimension levels are linked, respectively, using the edges of types ConnectedTo, Has, and IsFrom. Figure 13.19
shows a portion of the running example implemented in Neo4j.

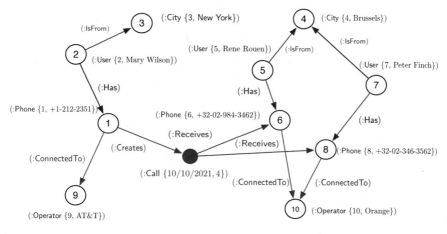

Fig. 13.19 Portion of the call graph in Neo4j

We now show how different kinds of analytical queries can be expressed
on the Neo4j graph representing the hypergraph model. We show three kinds
of OLAP queries: (a) queries where aggregations are performed in groups

of n objects, where $n > 2$; (b) roll-up queries up to dimension levels; (c) aggregations performed over graph measures.

Query 13.16. *Average duration of the calls between groups of n phones.*
This query computes all the hyperedges involving n phones participating in some call. The Cypher query for $n = 3$ is shown below.

```
MATCH   (t1:Phone)<-[:Creates]-(c:Call),
        (t2:Phone)<-[:Receives]-(c:Call)-[:Receives]->(t3:Phone)
WHERE   t1.Number < t2.Number AND t2.Number < t3.Number
RETURN  t1.Number, t2.Number, t3.Number, avg(c.Duration)
```

Query 13.17. *Average duration of the calls between groups of n different users.*

```
MATCH   (u1:User)<-[:Has]-(t1:Phone)<-[:Creates]-
        (c:Call)-[:Receives]->(t2:Phone)<-[:Has]-(u2:User),
        (c:Call)-[:Receives]->(t3:Phone)<-[:Has]-(u3:User)
WHERE   u1.Id < u2.id AND u2.Id < u3.Id
RETURN  u1.Name, u2.Name, u3.Name, avg(c.Duration)
```

This query shows a roll-up along the Phone dimension up to the level User. The climb is done by the MATCH clause (the climbing path is explicit in this clause), while the aggregation is performed in the RETURN clause. Note that a single user can have several phones. The condition in the WHERE clause above only considers calls between phones belonging to different users.

Query 13.18. *Compute the shortest path between each pair of phones.*
This query aims at analyzing the connections between phone users, and has many real-world applications (for example, to investigate calls made between two persons who use a third one as an intermediary). From a technical point of view, this is an aggregation over the whole graph, using as a metric the shortest path between every pair of nodes. We next show the Cypher query.

```
MATCH   (m:Phone), (n:Phone)
WITH    m, n WHERE m < n
MATCH   p = shortestPath((m)-[:Receives|:Creates*]-(n))
RETURN  p, length(p)
```

In the query above, shortestPath is a built-in function in Cypher. This path is assigned to variable p using the = operator.

13.3.2 OLAP on Trajectory Graphs

Chapter 12 introduced the notion of **moving objects**, which produce trajectory data that can be analyzed to obtain interesting mobility patterns. Trajectory analysis can be performed over the original trajectories, but also over other geospatial objects that are semantically related to the trajectories. These objects are typically referred to as *places of interest* (PoIs), and they depend on the application domain. For example, in a tourist application, usual examples of PoIs are hotels, restaurants, and historical buildings, while for traffic analysis, examples of PoIs could be road junctions or parking lots. A PoI is considered a *stop* in a trajectory when the moving object remains in it for a duration longer than some threshold. Thus, each trajectory, being a sequence of points, can be transformed into a sequence of stops and moves, and trajectory analysis can be applied to these transformed trajectories, which are called **semantic trajectories**. An example is given next.

Assume we have a tourist application for New York where the PoIs include hotels, restaurants, and buildings. There is also information about moving objects telling how tourists move in the city. For example, a moving object can go from Hotel 1 to St. Patrick's Cathedral, then to the Empire State Building, and finally return to the hotel. In this setting, a data scientist may pose queries like "How many persons went from a hotel to St. Patrick's Cathedral and then to the Empire State Building (stopping to visit both places) in the same day." An analyst may also want to identify interesting patterns in the trajectory data with queries like "Give the percentage of trajectories visiting two restaurants in the same day."

As shown in this section, graph databases can be used to manipulate semantic trajectory data. We focus on analytical queries that typically require the trajectory graph to be aggregated at various granularities, as shown in Sect. 13.3. For this, we use a real-world dataset containing about ten months of check-in data in New York City, collected by the Foursquare social network.[6] The dataset has been enriched with geographic data about New York City.[7] In addition, we define Time and Stop dimensions used as contextual information to perform OLAP on this trajectory graph.

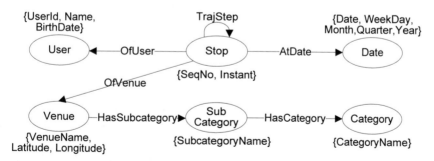

Fig. 13.20 Graph schema of the trajectory database

---

[6] https://www.kaggle.com/chetanism/foursquare-nyc-and-tokyo-checkin-dataset
[7] Maps were downloaded from http://www.mapcruzin.com

Figure 13.20 depicts the schema of the semantic trajectory graph using the hypergraph OLAP model described in Sect. 13.3. The base hypergraph is composed of the trajectories themselves. Each step in a trajectory is represented by the fact **Stop**, which has a self-referencing edge labeled **TrajStep**. **Stop** has properties **UserId** (the user identifier), **Position** (the relative position of the stop in the trajectory), and **Instant** (the time instant when reaching the stop). **Stop** is associated with the contextual dimensions **Venue** and **Date**. The **Date** dimension aggregates data from the instants represented in the stops up to the **Year** level. The **Venue** dimension is associated with level **Subcategory**, which is further associated with level **Category**. For example, a node **Afghan Restaurant** at the **Subcategory** level is associated with the node **Restaurant** at the **Category** level. **Venue** has properties **VenueId**, **Latitude**, and **Longitude**. Thus, through the **Venue** dimension, a trajectory consisting of sequences of stops becomes a sequence of the form ⟨Home, Station, Restaurant, . . .⟩. Examples of OLAP queries defined over this dataset are:

- Users that travel to an airport by taxi during the night.
- Trajectories in which users go from their homes to an airport after 5 p.m.
- Trajectories where users go from a restaurant to a sports event and then to a coffee shop.
- Number of users moving between two or more boroughs in the same day.
- Average distance traveled per user and per day.

We show next some analytical queries over the trajectory graph, expressed in Cypher using the Graph OLAP operations explained in Sect. 13.3.

Query 13.19. *Find the trajectories that go from a private home to a station and then to an airport, without intermediate stops.*

```
MATCH   (c1:Category {CategoryType:'Home'})<-[*3..3]-(s1:Stop)-[:TrajStep]->
        (s2:Stop)-[:TrajStep]->(s3:Stop)-[*3..3]-(c3:Category {CategoryType:'Airport'})
WHERE   s2.Position = s1.Position + 1 AND s3.Position = s2.Position + 1
MATCH   (s2)-[*3..3]->(c2:Category {CategoryType:'Station'})
WITH    s1 ORDER BY s1.Position
RETURN  s1.userid, COLLECT(distinct s1.Position) ORDER BY s1.UserId
```

The first **MATCH** clause describes a pattern as a sequence of three consecutive stops; the first and last ones include climb operations along the **Stop** dimension up to the **Category** dimension level. The second **MATCH** describes the same climbing pattern for the intermediate stop. At the **Category** level, a dice operation is performed, keeping the desired category, such that only the required three-stop patterns are kept. The **WITH** clause before the last line acts like a pipe, which passes a variable **s1** from one portion of the code to the next one (in this case, it passes **s1**). The result is given as pairs of the form (**UserId**, **Positions**), where **UserId** identifies the trajectory, and **Positions** is a list of the initial position of each pattern within the trajectory. Note that in the climbs a shorthand is used, since there is only one possible path up to the **Category** level, and no variables are needed over any intermediate level.

Query 13.20. *For each trajectory, compute the distance traveled between each pair of consecutive stops.*

```
MATCH   (s1:Stop)-[:TrajStep]->(s2:Stop)
WITH    point({Longitude: s1.Longitude, Latitude:s1.Latitude}) AS p1,
        point({Longitude:s2.Longitude, Latitude:s2.Latitude}) AS p2,
        s1, s2, s1.UserId AS User
RETURN User, s1.Position, s2.Position, round(distance(p1, p2)) AS TravelDistance
ORDER BY s1.UserId ASC, TravelDistance DESC
```

In this query, all consecutive pairs of stops are computed first (by pattern matching, rather than joins, which would be the case in the relational model). Then, the (Latitude, Longitude) pairs of each stop are obtained. Finally, for each trajectory, the distance between two consecutive stops is computed.

As a last example, we show a query requiring the computation of the transitive closure of the trajectory graph.

Query 13.21. *For each trajectory, find the paths that go from a private home to an airport on the same day.*

```
MATCH   (cat1:Category {CategoryType:'Home'})<-[*3..3]-(s1:Stop)
MATCH   (cat2:Category {CategoryType:'Airport'})<-[*3..3]-(s2:Stop)
WHERE   s1.UserId = s2.userid AND s1.Position < s2.Position AND
        apoc.date.fields(s1.Instant, 'yyyy-MM-dd HH:mm:ss').years =
        apoc.date.fields(s2.Instant, 'yyyy-MM-dd HH:mm:ss').years AND
        apoc.date.fields(s1.Instant, 'yyyy-MM-dd HH:mm:ss').months =
        apoc.date.fields(s2.Instant, 'yyyy-MM-dd HH:mm:ss').months AND
        apoc.date.fields(s2.Instant, 'yyyy-MM-dd HH:mm:ss').days =
        apoc.date.fields(s1.Instant, 'yyyy-MM-dd HH:mm:ss').days
WITH    s1, apoc.coll.sort(collect(s2.Position)) AS FirstAirports
WITH    s1, head(FirstAirports) AS s2pos
MATCH   path = (s1)-[:TrajStep*]->(s2:Stop {Position:s2pos})
RETURN s1, path
```

This query requires some explanation. Several climb operations are required along both background dimensions: (1) along the Stop dimension up to the Category level, to find the stops corresponding to homes and airports; (2) along the Time dimension up to the Day level. Further, dice operations are used to filter out the subtrajectories not occurring during the same day, and to keep only the trajectories going from a home to an airport. The climbs and dices are computed in the first two MATCH clauses. The transitive closure of the resulting subgraph is finally computed.

The climb along the Time dimension is performed through a conjunction of Boolean conditions over the Instant property of the Stop nodes. Note that to operate with dates, we could have written:

```
MATCH (s1)-[:IsInstantOf]->()-[:IsMinuteOf]->()-[:IsHourOf]->(d:Day),
      (s2)-[:IsInstantOf]->()-[:IsMinuteOf]->()-[:IsHourOf]->(d:Day)
```

Instead, we used the APOC library, which is more efficient than performing the two matchings along the Time hierarchy.

13.4 Graph Processing Frameworks

Graph database systems like Neo4j are in general adequate for medium-sized graphs, since, in general, they do not partition the graph for parallel processing. The so-called **graph processing frameworks** are used when there is a need to handle very large graphs. These frameworks provide specific APIs for parallel execution of complex graph algorithms over very large data volumes. Most of these frameworks use a graph traversal query language called Gremlin. In the first part of this section we introduce this language, and then briefly comment on JanusGraph, a graph processing framework that uses Gremlin as query language. In this section, we use the term *vertex* instead of *node*, to follow the terminology used in Gremlin and JanusGraph.

13.4.1 Gremlin

Unlike Cypher, which is based on *pattern matching*, Gremlin is a functional language based on *path traversal*. A *traversal* is composed of a sequence of *steps* from a *starting point*. Every step returns objects to which the next step operation is applied. This is explained next.

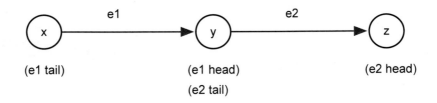

Fig. 13.21 Traversing paths in Gremlin

For moving *from vertices to edges*, the basic operations are given next. The operations outE() and inE() navigate from a vertex to the outgoing and incoming edges, respectively. For example, in Fig. 13.21, if while navigating the graph we are at vertex y, outE() moves us to the edge e2, while inE() takes us to e1. The operation bothE() combines the two operations. For example, standing at y, the operation bothE() moves us to e1 and e2.

For moving *from edges to vertices*, the basic operations are as follows. The operations outV() and inV() navigate from edges to their tail and head vertices, respectively. For example, standing at e1, outV() takes us to x, while inV() takes us to y. The operator otherV() navigates from an edge and arrives at the vertex from which it did not come. In Fig. 13.21, standing at e1, if we arrived at that edge from x, otherV() takes us to y.

To indicate paths between vertices when we do not need to indicate the edges that are traversed, we can use the operators out(), in(), or both(). In Fig. 13.21, standing at y, out() takes us to z, while in() takes us to x. These operations can be composed in a functional style. Thus, starting at x, the operations out().out() would take us to z.

The operations that obtain properties of vertices and edges, called FlatMap steps, are as follows:

- id(): returns the identifiers of an element;
- label(): returns the labels of an element;
- properties() : returns the (key, value) pairs of an element;
- properties(list of keys): returns the (key, value) pairs of an element matching the keys;
- values(): returns the values of an element;
- values(list of keys): returns the values of an element matching the keys;

The operations that obtain vertices and edges according to their identifiers, labels, or property values, called filter steps, are as follows:

- hasLabel(list of labels): returns the elements containing the labels in the list;
- has(key, value): returns the elements containing the (key, value) pair;
- has(key, predicate): returns the elements containing a (key, value) pair that satisfies the predicate;
- hasKey(key): returns the properties of an element containing the key;
- hasNot(key): the opposite to hasKey(key);
- where(predicate): returns the elements satisfying the predicate.

Iterators define a starting point for the navigation. These are:

- V(): given a graph, returns an iterator over vertices;
- V(ids) given a graph, returns an iterator over vertices containing the identifiers indicated as argument;
- E() given a graph, returns an iterator over edges;
- E(ids) given a graph, returns an iterator over edges containing the identifiers indicated as argument.

Graph navigation in Gremlin is typically performed using path traversal operations. This is referred to as *imperative traversal*, since the traversers are told how to proceed in each step. Examples of traversals are:

```
1. graph.traversal().V().outE();
2. graph.traversal().V().outE().otherV();
3. graph.traversal().E().properties('Score', 'Time');
4. graph.traversal().V().out().out();
5. graph.traversal().V().has('Country', 'CA').out().out();
6. graph.traversal().V().has('Country', 'CA').repeat(out()).times(2).count();
7. graph.traversal().V().has('Country', 'CA').out().out().path()
8. graph.traversal().E().has('Score', lt(3))
```

The first expression above returns all the outgoing edges in the graph. The second expression returns the vertices at the other end of the outgoing edges of the graph. Expression 3 returns a list of properties of the edges containing properties Score and Time. Expression 4 returns the two-hop vertices from the starting ones. Expression 5 returns the two-hop vertices from the vertices with value 'CA' in the Country key. Expression 6 shows an equivalent way of writing Expression 5 with a repeat operator. This allows more concise expressions, to avoid long sequences of out operations. Expression 7 does the same as the previous two, but returning the paths. Finally, Expression 8 returns the edges with a property Score with value less than 3.

Gremlin can also define traversals using pattern matching, where the properties of the vertices and edges are declared, leaving to Gremlin the decision of computing the most appropriate traversals to match the pattern. This is called *declarative traversal*, since the order of the traversals is not defined a priori. Each traverser will select a pattern to execute from a collection of patterns, which may yield several different query plans. A pattern-matching traversal uses the match() step to evaluate a graph pattern. Each graph pattern in a match() is interpreted individually, allowing construction of composite graph patterns by joining each of the traversals. These graph patterns are represented using the as() step (called step modulators), which mark the start and end of particular graph patterns or path traversals (note that all patterns must start with _.as()).

For example, the query over the Northwind graph "List the products supplied by suppliers located in London" can be expressed as follows:

```
g.V().match(
        _.as('s'). hasLabel('Sales').outE('SuppliedBy').outE('isFrom').inV().hasLabel('City').
            has('CityName', 'London'),
        _.as('s'). hasLabel('Sales').outE('Contains').inV().hasLabel('Product').as('p1').
            select('p1').values('ProductName').dedup() )
```

The query starts by defining a variable g for the graph traversal. Then, two traversals are defined (separated by a comma), one for the supplier and another one for the products. Variable 's' binds the patterns, and variable 'p1' is used to find the product names. The result is listed with the select() step, and duplicates are removed with the dedup() step.

We now compare Cypher and Gremlin using the Northwind data warehouse graph. In Cypher, the query "Find the customers who purchased a product with name Pavlova and another product" reads :

```
MATCH   (c:Customer)<-[:PurchasedBy]-(s1:Sales)-[:Contains]->(p1:Product)
WHERE   p1.ProductName = 'Pavlova'
MATCH   (c:Customer)<-[:PurchasedBy]-(s2:Sales)-[:Contains]->(p2:Product)
WHERE   p1 <> p2
RETURN DISTINCT c.CustomerKey
```

The same query in Gremlin can be written as:

```
g.V().hasLabel("Customer").as('c').match(
```

```
_as('a').inE('PurchasedBy').outV().hasLabel('Sales').outE('Contains').inV().
    hasLabel('Product').has('ProductName', 'Pavlova').as('p1'),
_.as('a').inE('PurchasedBy').outV().hasLabel('Sales').outE('Contains').inV().
    hasLabel('Product').as('p2').where('p1', neq('p2')) ).
select('c').values('CustomerKey').dedup()
```

The Cypher query performs two matches to find the customers buying at least two products, one of them being Pavlova and the other being different from the first one. On the other hand, the Gremlin query starts by defining a variable g for the graph traversal. Then two graph patterns are defined, with traversals that define variables p1 and p2 using an alias (the as() step). The final dedup() step after the select step is analogous to the DISTINCT clause in Cypher.

13.4.2 JanusGraph

JanusGraph is a graph database system based on the property graph data model. JanusGraph integrates with Hadoop for distributed processing and can process very large graphs in a clustered environment. For storing graphs JanusGraph supports Cassandra, HBase, and BerkeleyDB. Therefore, the behavior with respect to consistency and availability depends on the database choice. On Cassandra we will get availability and partitioning, on HBase we will get consistency and partitioning, and with BerkeleyDB we will get consistency and availability. These issues will be studied in Chap. 15. External indices based on Apache Lucene, Elastic Search, and Apache Solr are supported. JanusGraph uses Gremlin as high-level query language.

JanusGraph follows the property graph data model but, contrary to Neo4j, a schema can be explicitly or implicitly defined. However, it is recommended to define a schema explicitly. A schema is composed of vertex and edge labels, as well as property keys. These must be unique in the graph.

We create an edge label with the expression makeEdgeLabel(String). After that, we can define its properties and multiplicities. The multiplicity of an edge with a given label is one of the following:

- **Multi**: For every pair of vertices, there is no limit on the number of edges with the label.
- **Simple**: For every pair of vertices, there is at most one edge with the label.
- **Many2one**: For each vertex, there is no limit for incoming edges and at most one outgoing edge with the label.
- **One2many**: For each vertex, there is at most one incoming edge and no limit for outgoing edges with the label.
- **One2one**: For each vertex, there is at most one incoming and one outgoing edge with the label.

As an example, Fig. 13.22a shows that two **Speaks** edges are allowed between the same pair of vertices, meaning that a multiplicity **Multi** has been defined. On the contrary, a multiplicity of One2one would not allow us to represent the situation where a vertex has more than one incoming edge with the same label, as shown on Fig. 13.22b.

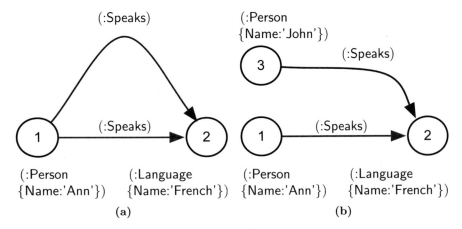

Fig. 13.22 Multiplicity in JanusGraph. (a) Multiplicity Multi; (b) Multiplicity One2one.

To create a vertex label we write makeVertexLabel(String). Unlike edges, vertices may have no label. JanusGraph assigns by default to all vertices an internal default label. Vertices created by the addVertex methods use this default label.

To define a property key we write makePropertyKey(String). In Janus-Graph, the property key values can be of the classic types string, character, Boolean, Geoshape (a point, a circle, or a box), or UUID (Universally Unique Identifier). Their cardinality can be Single (at most one value per element per key, which is the default), List (an arbitrary number of values per element per key), or Set (multiple values per element per key but with no duplicates).

To conclude, we illustrate how a graph is created and populated in Janus-Graph. For this, we show how an excerpt of the Northwind data warehouse graph would be created. We focus on the statements that create the graph and omit coding details. We start by creating the schema.

```
graph = ConfiguredGraphFactory.open("NorthwindDW");
m = graph.openManagement()
// Vertices
Category = m.makeVertexLabel('Category').make();
Customer = m.makeVertexLabel('Customer').make();
...
// Edges
HasCategory = m.makeEdgeLabel('HasCategory').multiplicity(Multi).make();
Contains = m.makeEdgeLabel('Contains').multiplicity(Multi).make();
...
```

```
// Properties
CategoryKey = m.makePropertyKey('CategoryKey').dataType(Integer.class).make();
CategoryName = m.makePropertyKey('CategoryName').dataType(String.class).make();
...
m.commit()
```

The ConfiguredGraphFactory is an access point to the graph. This factory provides methods for dynamically managing the graphs hosted on the server. The openManagement() method opens a transaction. The make() method returns the defined element, and commit() finishes the transaction.

We next populate the graph by importing data from CSV files. This is an iterative program; we just show the main parts and omit the details. We first load the vertices data.

```
// Define the path
Category = ".../Category.csv"
// Start traversal of the graph
g = graph.traversal();
// Load categories iterating over the lines of the CSV file.
new File(Category).eachLine {
    ...
    v = graph.addVertex("Category");
    v.property('id', field[0]);
    v.property('CategoryKey', field[2]);
    v.property('CategoryName', field[3]);
    v.property('Description', field[4]);
    ... }
```

Category defines the path to the CSV file that contains the records for the categories. The code iterates over every line in the file. A vertex is created with the addVertex method. Then, the values for the properties of the vertex are set with the property method using the various columns in the file.

Finally, we show next how the edges are loaded.

```
// Load category edges iterating over the lines of the CSV file.
new File(HasCategory).eachLine {
    ...
    src = g.V().has('id', field[2]).next(); // source
    dst = g.V().has('id', field[3]).next(); // destination
    e = src.addEdge('HasCategory', dst); // add the edge
    ... }
```

As in the case of vertices, first the path to the CSV file should be defined in HasCategory, and then the code iterates over the lines of this file. Here, the source and the destination of an edge are taken, respectively, from the second and third fields of the file. Then, the edge can be created.

13.5 Bibliographic Notes

An introduction to graph databases can be found in [199]. Fundamental aspects of graph data management are presented in the book [77]. Graph data models are comprehensively studied in [12, 13]. Angles [10] compares the graph data models underlying the most-used NoSQL graph databases, leaving out physical implementation issues. Foundations of graph query languages are studied in [11]. A comprehensive coverage of property graphs can be found in the book by Bonifati et al. [36]. The work in [269] proposes a framework for multidimensional analysis of heterogeneous graphs. Neo4j is covered in the book [258]. Practical issues about graph algorithms in Neo4j and in Spark are studied in [105]. The Gremlin language is described in [200, 233]

Graph summarization (also called graph coarsening) allows performing multilevel analysis of graph data, also producing a smaller representation of the input graph which can reveal patterns in the original data, preserving specific structural properties. A well-known solution to the problem of graph summarization is the SNAP (Summarization by grouping Nodes on Attributes and Pairwise relationships) operation, which produces a summary graph by grouping nodes based on node attributes and relationships selected by the user. Further, the k-SNAP operation makes it possible to drill-down and roll-up at different aggregation levels. This topic is studied in [234]. The main difference between OLAP-style aggregation and SNAP is that the latter does not take into account roll-up functions, but aggregates nodes based on the strength of the relationships between them.

A first proposal for performing OLAP on graphs is called Graph OLAP, which presents a multidimensional and multilevel view of graphs. This is described in [47]. Its sequel, called Graph Cube, introduces a model for graph data warehouses that supports OLAP queries on large multidimensional networks accounting for attribute aggregation and structure summarization of the networks. Graph Cube is discussed in [274].

The example used to explain Cypher's semantics is taken from a presentation by Oskar van Rest[8], who also coined the term Cyphermorphism.

The hypergraph model for OLAP is studied in [92]. Trajectory graph OLAP data warehouses are studied in [91].

13.6 Review Questions

13.1 What are the main characteristics of graph databases? How do they differ from relational databases?

13.2 What are graph data warehouses?

---

[8]   https://s3.amazonaws.com/artifacts.opencypher.org/website/ocim1/slides/cypher_implementers_day_2017_pattern_matching_semantics.pdf

13.3 Discuss at least three scenarios where graph data warehouses can be more convenient than relational-based data warehousing. Elaborate on the reasons for your choices.

13.4 Give five typical queries that can exploit a graph data warehouse for the scenarios discussed in your previous answer.

13.5 What is a property graph? How do property graphs differ from traditional graphs?

13.6 Discuss the main data models underlying graph databases.

13.7 Explain the main characteristics of Neo4j.

13.8 Discuss different ways of populating a Neo4j database.

13.9 How does Neo4j qualify with respect to the CAP theorem?

13.10 Explain the differences between graph databases and graph processing frameworks. In which scenarios you would use each one.

13.11 Compare Cypher and Gremlin as query languages for graphs. When would you use each one of them?

13.12 Discuss different relational data warehouse representations for the phone calls example given in this chapter. Compare them against the HGOLAP solution.

13.13 Give real-world examples where the hypergraph data model can be naturally used.

13.7 Exercises

Exercise 13.1. Given the Northwind operational database in Fig. 2.4, propose a graph representation using property graphs. Export the data into a Neo4j database, and express the following queries in Cypher. The schema of the Northwind operational database in Neo4j in given in Fig. **??**.

a. List products and their unit price.

b. List information about products 'Chocolade' and 'Pavlova'.

c. List information about products with names starting with a 'C', whose unit price is greater than 50.

d. Same as the previous query, but considering the sales price, not the product's price.

e. Total amount purchased by customer and product.

f. Top 10 employees, considering the number of orders sold.

g. For each territory, list the assigned employees.

h. For each city, list the number of customers and number of suppliers located in that city.

i. For employees who have subordinates, list the number of direct or indirect subordinates.

j. Direct or indirect supervisors of employees whose first name is "Robert".

k. List the employees who do not have supervisors.

l. List the suppliers, number of categories they supply, and a list of such categories.
m. List the suppliers who supply beverages.
n. List the customer who purchased the largest amount of beverages.
o. List the five most popular products considering number of orders.
p. Products ordered by customers from the same country as their suppliers.

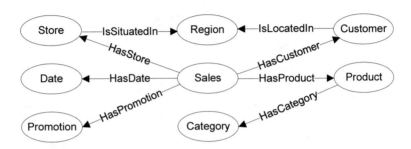

Fig. 13.23 Schema of the Foodmart data warehouse in Neo4j

Exercise 13.2. Consider the relational schema of the Foodmart data warehouse given in Fig. 5.41 and its implementation in Neo4j given in Fig. 13.23. Write in Cypher the queries given in Ex. 7.3.

Exercise 13.3. Consider the schema of the graph trajectory database given in Fig. 13.20, obtained from the Foursquare check-ins database from Kaggle.com. Write the following queries in Cypher.

a. List the trajectories that go from a bar (or similar) to a restaurant, again to a bar (or similar) and finish at a restaurant, without intermediate stops.
b. For all trajectories that go directly from a private home to an airport, list the user identifier, together with the distance traveled between these two places each time that this pattern occurs.
c. Compute the number of different categories of venues visited by month.
d. Compute the number of stops per day per user, along with the starting position of each subtrajectory for each day.
e. For each trajectory, compute its total length, as the sum of the distances between each pair of stops.
f. For each day, and for each trajectory, find the longest subtrajectory.
g. Write the previous query in SQL, and compare against the Cypher equivalent. For this, use the PostgreSQL database dump provided.

Exercise 13.4. We will query a river system represented as a graph. Each segment of the river is represented as a node with label :Segment, and its

FlowsTo

Segment

{SegmentId, SegmentName, SegmentLength, SegmentCategory,
StartLongitude, StartLatitude, EndLongitude,EndLatitude}

Fig. 13.24 Graph schema of the rivers database

corresponding properties. There is a FlowsTo relationship defined as follows: there exists a relation FlowsTo from node A to node B if the water flows from segment A to segment B. The schema and properties are shown in Fig. 13.24. Note that, given what was explained in the chapter, there is no need to have a relationship ComesFrom. Also, the double arrow in the schema indicates that a segment can split and provide water to several ones. Express in Cypher the following queries.

a. Compute the average segment length.
b. Compute the average segment length by segment category.
c. Find all segments that have a length within a 10% margin of the length of segment with ID 6020612.
d. For each segment find the number of incoming and outgoing segments.
e. Find the segments with the maximum number of incoming segments.
f. Find the number of splits in the downstream path of segment 6020612.
g. Find the branches of downstream flow starting at a given position (identified by a segment's identifier), together with the length and number of segments of each branch.
h. Find all segments reachable from the segment closest to the central square of Antwerp.

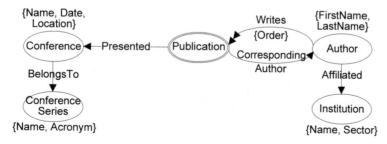

Fig. 13.25 An instance of the conference database using the HGOLAP model

Exercise 13.5. Figure 13.25 depicts the schema of a conference database modeled using HGOLAP as explained in this chapter. Fig. 13.26 depicts a

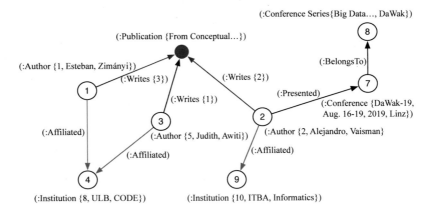

Fig. 13.26 An instance of the conference database using the HGOLAP model

portion of an instance corresponding to this schema. An arrow from an author node to the node representing the Publication hyperedge indicates that she is a co-author of the paper. An arrow labeled :Writes going from the Author node to the Publication node indicates that she is a co-author. An arrow labeled :Corresponding Author from the Publication node to the Author node indicates that she is the corresponding author of the paper. Contextual dimension levels shown are Institution (to which authors are affiliated), Conference (where papers are published), and Conference Series (to which conferences belong). There can be other hierarchies which you must define as part of the design (e.g., Date).

Define the contextual dimensions that you consider necessary to complete the schema of Fig. 13.25. Then, express the following queries using the Cypher query language.

a. For each pair of authors, compute the number of papers they published together per year.
b. Compute the average number of papers per author per year.
c. Rank the authors according to the number of papers in which they are first authors.
d. Compute number of publications by university and year.
e. Compute the graph containing only the nodes corresponding to publications in the last five years where there is at least one author affiliated to ULB.
f. Compute the total number of papers by author and by tear, such that the author is the corresponding author of the paper.

Chapter 14
Semantic Web Data Warehouses

The availability of enormous amounts of data from many different domains is continuously challenging data analysts to find out ways to deliver knowledge from these data. One of such domains in the World Wide Web. In particular, the so-called semantic web, that aims at representing web content in a way such that the human participation can be dramatically reduced, taking advantage of semantic information that is added the web documents. Large repositories of semantically annotated data are becoming available, providing new opportunities for enhancing decision-support systems. In this scenario, two approaches are clearly identified. One focuses on automating multidimensional design, using semantic web artifacts, for example, existing ontologies. In this approach, data warehouses are (semi)automatically designed using available metadata, and then populated with semantic web data. The other approach aims at analyzing large amounts of semantic web data using OLAP tools. In this chapter, we tackle the latter approach, which requires the definition of a precise vocabulary allowing to represent OLAP data on the semantic web. Over this vocabulary, multidimensional models and OLAP operations on the semantic web can be defined. For this, we use the QB4OLAP vocabulary, which follows closely the classic multidimensional models studied in this book. The QB4OLAP vocabulary extends the data cube vocabulary (called QB), which is used for representing statistical data.

In this chapter, we first introduce in Sect. 14.1 the basic semantic web concepts, including the RDF and RDFS data models, together with a study of RDF representation of relational data, and a review of R2RML, the standard language to define mappings from relational to RDF data. In Sect. 14.2, we give an introduction to SPARQL, the standard query language for RDF data. In Sect. 14.3, we discuss the representation of multidimensional data in RDF using the QB4OLAP vocabulary. We continue in Sect. 14.4 showing how the Northwind data cube can be represented using this vocabulary. We conclude in Sect. 14.5 by showing how to query the QB4OLAP representation of the Northwind data warehouse in SPARQL.

© Springer-Verlag GmbH Germany, part of Springer Nature 2022
A. Vaisman, E. Zimányi, *Data Warehouse Systems*, Data-Centric Systems
and Applications, https://doi.org/10.1007/978-3-662-65167-4_14

14.1 Semantic Web

The **semantic web** is a proposal oriented to represent web content in a machine-processable way. The basic layer for data representation on the semantic web recommended by the World Wide Web Consortium (W3C) is the resource description framework (RDF). In a semantic web scenario, domain ontologies are used to define a common terminology for the concepts involved in a particular domain. These ontologies are expressed in RDF or in languages defined on top of RDF like the Web Ontology Language (OWL)[1] and are especially useful for describing unstructured, semistructured, and text data. Many applications attach metadata and semantic annotations to the information they produce (e.g., in medical applications, medical images and laboratory tests). The availability of large repositories of semantically annotated data will open new opportunities for enhancing current decision-support systems.

14.1.1 Introduction to RDF and RDFS

The **resource description framework** (RDF)[2] is a formal language for describing structured information. One of the main goals of RDF is to enable the composition of distributed data to allow data exchange over the web. To uniquely identify resources, RDF uses *internationalized resource identifiers* (IRIs). IRIs generalize the concept of *universal resource locators* (URLs) since they do not necessarily refer to resources located on the web. Further, IRIs generalize the concept of the *uniform resource identifiers* (URIs): while URIs are limited to a subset of the ASCII character set, IRIs may contain Unicode characters.

RDF can be used to express assertions over resources. These assertions are expressed in the form of *subject-predicate-object* triples, where *subject* are resources or *blank nodes*, *predicate* are resources, and *object* are resources or *literals* (i.e., data values). Blank nodes are used to represent resources without an IRI, typically with a structural function, for example, to group a set of statements. A set of RDF triples or *RDF data set* can be seen as a directed graph where subjects and objects are nodes, and predicates are arcs. RDF, together with the property graphs model, are the two mainly used data models for graphs used in practice.

RDF provides a way to express statements about resources using named properties and values. However, sometimes we also need to define kinds or classes of resources and the specific properties describing those resources.

---

[1] http://www.w3.org/2004/OWL/

[2] http://www.w3.org/TR/rdf11-concepts/

A set of reserved words, called **RDF Schema** (RDFS),[3] is used to define
properties and represent relationships between resources, adding semantics
to the terms in a vocabulary. Intuitively, RDF allows us to describe instances
while RDFS adds schema information to those instances. A comprehensive
study of the formal semantics of RDFS is beyond the scope of the book, but
we provide below the basic concepts we will use in the next sections.

Among the many terms in the RDFS vocabulary, the fragment which represents the essential features of RDF is composed of the following ones: rdf:type,
rdf:Class, rdfs:Resource, rdfs:Property, rdfs:range, rdfs:domain, rdfs:subClassOf,
and rdfs:subPropertyOf. For example, a triple Employee rdf:type Class tells that
Employee is a class that aggregates objects of the same kind, in this case employees. The triple Davolio rdf:type Employee tells that Davolio is an instance
of the class Employee. The term rdfs:Resource denotes the class of all resources,
and rdf:Property the class of all properties. Importantly, class membership is
not exclusive, since a resource may belong to several different classes. Elements belonging to the class rdf:Property represent relationships between
resources, and are used in the predicate part of RDF triples. For example,
hasSalary is a property defined as hasSalary rdf:type rdf:Property. The predicate rdfs:subClassOf allows us to define generalization relationships between
classes. For example, the triple TemporaryEmployee rdfs:subClassOf Employee
tells that every temporary employee is also an employee. Analogously, the
predicate rdfs:subPropertyOf allows us to define generalization relationships
between properties. For example, hasLowSalary rdfs:subPropertyof hasSalary
indicates a subproperty to describe employees with low salaries. A rule system can be defined using these and other predicates, thus allowing to infer
knowledge from an RDF graph. The RDF Semantics[4] specification defines a
precise semantics and corresponding complete systems of inference rules for
RDF and RDFS. Finally, let us remark that, in general, triples representing
schema and instance data coexist in RDF data sets.

14.1.2 RDF Serializations

An RDF graph is a collection of triples given in any order, which can be
serialized in many ways. Two widely used notations are **RDF/XML**,[5] which
defines an XML syntax for RDF, and **Turtle**,[6] which provides a simple way
of representing RDF triples.

---

[3] http://www.w3.org/TR/rdf-schema/

[4] http://www.w3.org/TR/rdf11-mt/

[5] http://www.w3.org/TR/rdf-syntax-grammar/

[6] http://www.w3.org/TR/turtle/

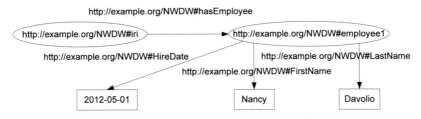

Fig. 14.1 An example of an RDF graph

Figure 14.1 depicts an RDF graph representing an employee of the North-wind company, her first name, last name, and hire date. The following piece of RDF/XML code describes this graph.

```
<xml version "1.0" encoding= "utf8"?>
<rdf:RDF
    xmlns:rdf="http://www.w3.org/1999/02/22-rdf-syntax-ns#"
    xmlns:ex="http://example.org/NWDW#">
    <rdf:Description rdf:about="http://example.org/NWDW#iri">
        <ex:hasEmployee>
            <rdf:Description rdf:about="http://example.org/NWDW#employee1">
                <ex:FirstName>Nancy</ex:FirstName>
                <ex:LastName>Davolio</ex:LastName>
                <ex:HireDate>2012-05-01</ex:HireDate>
            </rdf:Description>
        </ex:hasEmployee>
    </rdf:Description>
</rdf:RDF>
```

The first line is the typical XML heading line, and the document starts with the RDF element. The xmlns attribute is used to define XML namespaces composed of a prefix and an IRI, making the text less verbose. The subject and object of the triple representing the company and its employee are within Description elements, where the attribute rdf:about indicates the IRIs of the resources. The ex prefix refers to the Northwind data warehouse.

The same triple will be written as follows using Turtle.

```
@prefix rdf: <http://www.w3.org/1999/02/22-rdf-syntax-ns#> .
@prefix ex: <http://example.org/NWDW#> .

ex:iri ex:hasEmployee ex:employee1 .
ex:employee1 rdf:type ex:Employee ; ex:FirstName "Nancy" ;
    ex:LastName "Davolio" ; ex:HireDate "2012-05-01" .
```

Note that Turtle provides a much simpler, less verbose syntax, compared to RDF/XML, so we use Turtle in the remainder of the chapter.

Data types are supported in RDF through the XML data type system. For example, by default ex:HireDate would be interpreted as a string value rather than a date value. To explicitly define the data types for the example above, we would write in Turtle:

@prefix rdf: <http://www.w3.org/1999/02/22-rdf-syntax-ns#> .
@prefix ex: <http://example.org/NWDW#> .
@prefix xsd: <http://www.w3.org/2001/XMLSchema#> .

ex:iri ex:hasEmployee ex:employee1 .
ex:employee1 rdf:type ex:Employee ; ex:FirstName "Nancy"^^xsd:string ;
   ex:LastName "Davolio"^^xsd:string ; ex:HireDate "2012-05-01"^^xsd:date .

To further simplify the notation, Turtle allows to replace rdf:type with 'a'. Thus, instead of

ex:employee1 rdf:type ex:Employee ;

we could write

ex:employee1 a ex:Employee ;

Also, the xml:lang attribute allows us to indicate the language of the text in the triple. For example, to indicate that the name of the employee is an English name, we may write in Turtle:

ex:employee1 ex:FirstName "Nancy"@en ; ex:LastName "Davolio"@en .

Finally, blank nodes are represented either explicitly with a blank node identifier of the form _:name, or with no name using square brackets. The latter is used if the identifier is not needed elsewhere in the document. For example, the following triples state that the employee identified by ex:employee1, who corresponds to Nancy Davolio in the triples above, has a supervisor who is an employee called Andrew Fuller:

ex:employee1 a ex:Employee ;
   ex:Supervisor [a ex:Employee ; ex:FirstName "Andrew" ; ex:LastName "Fuller"] .

In this case, the blank node is used as object, and this object is an anonymous resource; we are not interested in who this person is.

A blank node can be used as subject in triples. If we need to use the blank node in other part of the document, we may use the following Turtle notation:

ex:employee1 a ex:Employee ; ex:Supervisor _:employee2 .
_:employee2 a ex:Employee ; ex:FirstName "Andrew"; ex:LastName "Fuller" .

The expression above thells that there is an employee who has a supervisor who is also an employee and whose first name in Andrew and whose last name is Fuller.

14.1.3 RDF Representation of Relational Data

In this section, we describe how relational data can be represented in RDF in order to be used and shared on the semantic web. The World Wide Web Consortium (W3C) has proposed two ways of mapping relational data to RDF:

the direct mapping and the R2RML mapping. We next explain both of them using as an example a portion of the Northwind data warehouse, which is stored in a relational database. Suppose that the Northwind company wants to share their warehouse data on the web, for example, to be accessible to all their branches. We want to publish the Sales fact table and the Product dimension table of Fig. 14.2, which are simplified versions of the corresponding data warehouse tables. Note that we added an identifier SalesKey for each tuple in the Sales fact table.

SalesKey	ProductKey	CustomerKey	DateKey	Quantity
s1	p1	c1	d1	100
s2	p1	c2	d2	100
...	...	...	...	...

(a)

ProductKey	ProductName	QuantityPerUnit	UnitPrice	Discontinued	CategoryName
p1	prod1	25	60	No	c1
p2	prod2	45	60	No	c1
...	...	...	...	...	...

(b)

Fig. 14.2 An excerpt of a simplified version of the Northwind data warehouse. (a) Sales fact table; (b) Product dimension table

Direct Mapping

The **direct mapping**[7] defines an RDF graph representation of the data in a relational database. This mapping takes as input the schema and instance of a relational database, and produces an RDF graph called the *direct graph*, whose triples are formed concatenating column names and values with a **base IRI**. In the examples below, the base IRI is <http://example.org/>. The mapping also accounts for the foreign keys in the databases being mapped. The direct mapping for the Sales fact table and the Product dimension table in Fig. 14.2 results in an RDF graph, from which we show below some triples.

```
@base <http://example.org/>
@prefix rdf:<http://www.w3.org/1999/02/22-rdf-syntax-ns#>

<Sales/SalesKey="s1"> rdf:type <Sales> .
<Sales/SalesKey="s1"> <Sales#SalesKey> "s1" .
<Sales/SalesKey="s1"> <Sales#ProductKey> "p1" .
<Sales/SalesKey="s1"> <Sales#ref-ProductKey> <Product/ProductKey="p1"> .
<Sales/SalesKey="s1"> <Sales#CustomerKey> "c1" .
```

---

[7] http://www.w3.org/TR/rdb-direct-mapping/

```
<Sales/SalesKey="s1"> <Sales#ref-CustomerKey> <Customer/CustomerKey="c1"> .
<Sales/SalesKey="s1"> <Sales#DateKey> "d1" .
<Sales/SalesKey="s1"> <Sales#ref-DateKey> <Date/DateKey="d1"> .
<Sales/SalesKey="s1"> <Sales#Quantity> "100" .
...
<Product/ProductKey="p1"> rdf:type <Product> .
<Product/ProductKey="p1"> <Product#ProductKey> "p1" .
<Product/ProductKey="p1"> <Sales#ProductName> "prod1" .
<Product/ProductKey="p1"> <Sales#QuantityPerUnit> "25" .
<Product/ProductKey="p1"> <Sales#UnitPrice> "60" .
<Product/ProductKey="p1"> <Sales#Discontinued> "No" .
<Product/ProductKey="p1"> <Sales#CategoryKey> "c1" .
<Product/ProductKey="p1"> <Sales#ref-CategoryKey> <Category/CategoryKey="c1"> .
...
```

Each row in Sales produces a set of triples with a common subject. The subject is an IRI formed from the concatenation of the base IRI, the table name, the primary key column name (SalesKey), and the primary key value (s1 for the first tuple). The predicate for each column is an IRI formed as the concatenation of the base IRI, the table name, and the column name. The values are RDF literals taken from the column values. Each foreign key produces a triple with a predicate composed of the foreign key column names, the referenced table, and the referenced column names. The object of these triples is the row identifier for the referenced triple. The reference row identifiers must coincide with the subject used for the triples generated from the referenced row. For example, the triple

```
<Sales/SalesKey="s1"> <Sales#ref-ProductKey> <Product/ProductKey="p1">
```

tells that the subject (the first row in Sales) contains a foreign key in the column ProductKey (the predicate in the triple) which refers to the triple identified in the object (the triple whose subject is <Product/ProductKey="p1">).

As it can be seen above, the direct mapping is straightforward but it does not allow any kind of customization. Indeed, the structure of the resulting RDF graph directly reflects the structure of the database, the target RDF vocabulary directly reflects the names of database schema elements, and neither the structure nor the vocabulary can be changed.

R2RML Mapping

RDB to RDF Mapping Language (R2RML)[8] is a language for expressing mappings from relational databases to RDF data sets. Such mappings provide the ability to view relational data in RDF using a customized structure and vocabulary. As with the direct mapping, an R2RML mapping results in an RDF graph.

An R2RML mapping is an RDF graph written in Turtle syntax, called the *mapping document*. The main object of an R2RML mapping is the so-called

---

[8] http://www.w3.org/TR/r2rml

triples map. Each triples map is a collection of triples, composed of a *logical table*, a *subject map*, and zero or more *predicate object maps*. A logical table is either a base table, a view (using the predicate rr:tableName), or an SQL query (using the predicate rr:sqlQuery). A predicate object map is composed of a predicate map and an object map. Subject maps, predicate maps, and object maps are either constants (rr:constant), column-based maps (rr:column), or template-based maps (rr:template). Templates use brace-enclosed column names as placeholders. As an example, Fig. 14.3 shows how a portion of the dimension table Product is mapped to RDF using R2RML. This mapping can be then applied to any instance of the table, to produce the triples. We next show the mapping document, which, together with the instance of the table, will produce the RDF graph.

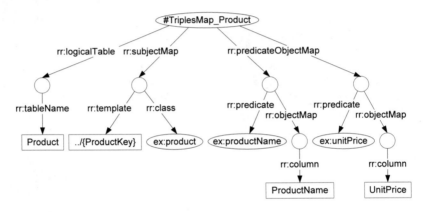

Fig. 14.3 R2RML mapping of the Product dimension

```
@prefix rr: <http://www.w3.org/ns/r2rml#> .
@prefix rdf: <http://www.w3.org/1999/02/22-rdf-syntax-ns#> .
@prefix rdfs: <http://www.w3.org/2000/01/rdf-schema#> .
@prefix ex: <http://example.org/> .

<#TriplesMap_Product>
    a rr:TriplesMap ;
    rr:logicalTable [ rr:tableName "Product" ] ;
    rr:subjectMap [
        rr:template "http://example.org/product/{ProductKey}" ;
        rr:class ex:product ] ;
    rr:predicateObjectMap [
        rr:predicate ex:productName ;
        rr:objectMap [ rr:column "ProductName" ; rr:language "en" ] ; ] ;
    rr:predicateObjectMap [
        rr:predicate ex:unitPrice ;
        rr:objectMap [ rr:column "UnitPrice" ; rr:datatype rdfs:integer ] ; ] .
```

The triples map above (corresponding to the table Product) is called <#TriplesMap_Product>. The logical table is the table Product, and the subject is the template for the key, ProductKey. Applied to the input table, this will produce the subject of the triples. For each such subject, the predicate-object mapping will produce the mapping of the columns we wish to map. For example, rr:predicate ex:productName will map the column ProductName. Note that this procedure allows us to customize the name of the column, for example, according to a given vocabulary. Below, we show some of the triples produced by this mapping when applied to the table Product in Fig. 14.2b:

```
<http://example.org/product/p1>
   a <http://example.org/product> ;
   <http://example.org/productName> "prod1"@en ;
   <http://example.org/unitPrice> "60"^^
       <http://www.w3.org/2000/01/rdf-schema#integer>
   .... ;
```

Foreign keys are handled through *referencing object maps*, which use the subjects of another triples map as the objects generated by a predicate-object map.

```
<#TriplesMap_Sales>
   rr:predicateObjectMap [
       rr:predicate ex:product ;
       rr:objectMap [
           rr:parentTriplesMap <#TriplesMap_Product> ;
           rr:joinCondition [
               rr:child "ProductKey" ;
               rr:parent "ProductKey" ] ; ] ; ] .
```

The rr:parentTriplesMap predicate references an existing triples map in the same mapping file that generates the desired resource. In the example above, in the mapping file for the Sales fact table, when mapping the foreign key for the table Product we reference the mapping for the latter (which we have called <#TriplesMap_Product>). The join condition (rr:joinCondition) contains two elements, namely, rr:child and rr:parent. The former is associated with a column name of the logical table of the triples map containing the referencing object map. The latter is associated with a logical column name of the referenced triples map.

14.2 Introduction to SPARQL

In this section, we introduce **SPARQL**[9], the standard query language for RDF graphs. We start introducing the basic constructs of the language and then we explain its semantics.

---

[9] http://www.w3.org/TR/sparql11-query/

14.2.1 SPARQL Basics

SPARQL queries are built using variables, which are denoted by using either '?' or '$' as a prefix, although the former is normally used. The query evaluation mechanism of SPARQL is based on subgraph matching, where the selection criteria is expressed as a graph pattern. This pattern is matched against an RDF graph instantiating the variables in the query.

In what follows, we will work with the Northwind data warehouse represented as an RDF graph, as studied in Sect. 14.1.3. To get started, consider the following SPARQL query, which asks for names and hire date of employees.

```
PREFIX ex:<http://example.org/NWDW#>
PREFIX rdf:<http://www.w3.org/1999/02/22-rdf-syntax-ns#>

SELECT ?firstName ?lastName ?hireDate
WHERE { ?emp a ex:Employee .
          ?emp ex:Employee#FirstName ?firstName .
          ?emp ex:Employee#LastName ?lastName .
          ?emp ex:Employee#HireDate ?hireDate . }
```

There are three parts in the query. A sequence of **PREFIX** clauses declares the namespaces. The **SELECT** clause indicates the format of the result. The **WHERE** clause contains a graph pattern composed of four triples in Turtle notation. The triples in the query are matched against the triples in an RDF graph that instantiates the variables in the pattern. In our case, this is the default RDF graph that represents the Northwind data warehouse. If we want to include other graphs, a **FROM** clause must be added, followed by a list of named graphs. The query can be more succinctly written as follows (we omit the prefix part) :

```
SELECT ?firstName ?lastName ?hireDate
WHERE { ?emp a ex:Employee ; ex:Employee#FirstName ?firstName ;
          ex:Employee#LastName ?lastName ; ex:Employee#HireDate ?hireDate . }
```

To evaluate this query, we instantiate the variable ?emp with an IRI whose type is http://example.org/NWDW#Employee. Then, we look if there is a triple with the same subject and property ex:Employee#FirstName, and, if so, we instantiate the variable ?firstName. We proceed similarly to instantiate the other variables in the query and return the result. Note that in this case the result of the query is not an RDF graph, but a set of literals. Alternatively, the **CONSTRUCT** clause can be used to return an RDF graph built by substituting variables in a set of triple templates.

From now on, we omit the prefix clauses in queries for brevity. The keyword **DISTINCT** is used to remove duplicates in the result. For example, the following query returns the cities of the Northwind customers, without duplicates.

```
SELECT DISTINCT ?city
WHERE { ?customer a ex:Customer ; ex:Customer#City ?city . }
```

The **FILTER** keyword selects patterns that meet a certain condition. For example, the query "First name and last name of the employees hired between 2012 and 2014" reads in SPARQL as follows:

```
SELECT ?firstName ?lastName
WHERE { ?emp a ex:Employee ; ex:Employee#FirstName ?firstName ;
         ex:Employee#LastName ?lastName ; ex:Employee#HireDate ?hireDate .
         FILTER( ?hireDate >= "2012-01-01"^^xsd:date &&
         ?hireDate <= "2014-12-31"^^xsd:date) }
```

Filter conditions are Boolean expressions constructed using the logical connectives **&&** (and), **||** (or), and **!** (not).

The **FILTER** keyword can be combined with the **NOT EXISTS** keyword to test the absence of a pattern. For example, the query "First name and last name of employees without supervisor" reads in SPARQL as follows:

```
SELECT ?firstName ?lastName
WHERE { ?emp a ex:Employee ; ex:Employee#FirstName ?firstName ;
         ex:Employee#LastName ?lastName .
         FILTER NOT EXISTS { ?emp ex:Employee#Supervisor ?sup . } }
```

The **OPTIONAL** keyword is used to specify a graph pattern for which the values will be shown if they are found. It behaves in a way similar to an outer join in SQL. For example, the query "First and last name of employees, along with the first and last name of her supervisor, if she has one" can be written in SPARQL as follows:

```
SELECT ?empFirstName ?empLastName ?supFirstName ?supLastName
WHERE { ?emp a ex:Employee ; ex:Employee#FirstName ?empFirstName ;
         ex:Employee#LastName ?empLastName .
         OPTIONAL { ?emp ex:Employee#Supervisor ?sup .
             ?sup a ex:Employee ; ex:Employee#FirstName ?supFirstName ;
             ex:Employee#LastName ?supLastName . } }
```

Aggregate functions summarize information from multiple triple patterns into a single one. SPARQL provides the usual aggregate functions **COUNT**, **SUM**, **MAX**, **MIN**, and **AVG**. In addition, along the lines of SQL, before summarization, triples may be grouped using the **GROUP BY** keyword, and then the aggregate function is applied to every group. Furthermore, filtering of groups may also be performed with the **HAVING** keyword, like it is done with the **FILTER** clause for ungrouped sets. Finally, the result can be sorted with the **ORDER BY** clause, where every attribute in the list can be ordered either in ascending or descending order by specifying **ASC** or **DESC**, respectively.

Consider the query "Total number of orders handled by each employee, in descending order of number of orders. Only list employees that handled more than 100 orders." This query is expressed in SPARQL as follows:

```
SELECT      ?emp (COUNT(DISTINCT ?orderNo) AS ?ordersByEmployee)
WHERE       { ?sales a ex:Sales ; ex:Sales#Employee ?emp ;
            ex:Sales#OrderNo ?orderNo .
            ?emp a ex:Employee . }
GROUP BY ?emp
HAVING      COUNT(DISTINCT ?orderNo) > 100
ORDER BY DESC(COUNT(DISTINCT ?orderNo))
```

The **GROUP BY** clause collects the orders associated to each employee, the **HAVING** clause keeps only the employees who have more than 100 distinct orders, and the **ORDER BY** clause orders the result in descending order according to the number of orders.

Consider now the query "For customers from San Francisco, list the total quantity of each product ordered. Order the result by customer key, in ascending order, and by quantity of products ordered, in descending order."

```
SELECT      ?cust ?prod (SUM(?qty) AS ?totalQty)
WHERE       { ?sales a ex:Sales ; ex:Sales#Customer ?cust ;
            ex:Sales#Product ?prod ; ex:Sales#Quantity ?qty .
            ?cust a ex:Customer ; ex:Customer#City ?city .
            ?city a ex:City ; ex:City#Name ?cityName .
            FILTER(?cityName = "San Francisco") }
GROUP BY ?cust ?prod
ORDER BY ASC(?cust) DESC(?totalQty)
```

This query defines a graph pattern linking sales to customers and cities. Prior to grouping, we need to find the triples satisfying the graph pattern, and select the customers from San Francisco. We then group by pairs of **?cust** and **?prod** and, for each group, take the sum of the attribute **?qty**. Finally, the resulting triples are ordered.

In SPARQL, a **subquery** is used to look for a certain value in a database, and then use this value in a comparison condition. A subquery is a query enclosed into curly braces used within a **WHERE** clause. As an example, the query "For each customer compute the maximum sales amount among all her orders" is written as follows:

```
SELECT      ?cust (MAX(?totalSales) AS ?maxSales)
WHERE       { {
            SELECT      ?cust ?orderNo (SUM(?sales) AS ?totalSales)
            WHERE       { ?sales a ex:Sales ; ex:Sales#Customer ?cust ;
                        ex:Sales#OrderNo ?orderNo ; ex:Sales#SalesAmount ?sales .
                        ?cust a ex:Customer . }
            GROUP BY ?cust ?orderNo } }
GROUP BY ?cust
```

The inner query computes the total sales amount for each customer and order. Then, in the outer query, for each customer we select the maximum sales amount among all its orders.

Subqueries are commonly used with the **UNION** and **MINUS** keywords. The **UNION** combines graph patterns so that one of several alternative graph patterns may match. For example, the query "Products that have been ordered by customers from San Francisco or supplied by suppliers from San Jose" can be written as follows:

```
SELECT DISTINCT ?prodName
WHERE { {
        SELECT ?prod
        WHERE { ?sales a ex:Sales ; ex:Sales#Product ?prod ;
                ex:Sales#Customer ?cust .
                ?cust a ex:Customer ; ex:Customer#City ?custCity .
                ?custCity a ex:City ; ex:City#Name ?custCityName .
                FILTER(?custCityName = "San Francisco") } }
        UNION {
        SELECT ?prod
        WHERE { ?sales a ex:Sales ; ex:Sales#Product ?prod ;
                ex:Sales#Supplier ?sup .
                ?sup a ex:Supplier ; ex:Supplier#City ?supCity .
                ?supCity a ex:City ; ex:City#Name ?supCityName .
                FILTER(?supCityName = "San Jose") } } }
```

Analogously, the MINUS operation computes the difference between the results of two subqueries. For example, the query "Products that have not been ordered by customers from San Francisco" can be written as follows:

```
SELECT DISTINCT ?prod
WHERE { ?sales a ex:Sales ; ex:Sales#Product ?prod .
        MINUS { {
        SELECT ?prod
        WHERE { ?sales a ex:Sales ; ex:Sales#Product ?prod ;
                ex:Sales#Customer ?cust .
                ?cust a ex:Customer ; ex:Customer#City ?city .
                ?city a ex:City ; ex:City#Name ?cityName .
                FILTER(?cityName = "San Francisco") } } } }
```

The inner query computes the products ordered by customers from San Francisco. The outer query obtains all products that have been ordered and subtracts from them the products obtained in the inner query.

14.2.2 SPARQL Semantics

We explained in Sect. 13.2.2 the importance of knowing the semantics that graph query languages use to evaluate basic graph patterns. We also mentioned that Cypher follows the variant of isomorphism-based semantics known as no-repeated-edge semantics. On the contrary, SPARQL follows the homomorphism-based semantics, which implies that multiple variables in a query Q can map to the same term in a graph G. In other words, we can say that SPARQL semantics corresponds to the *repeated nodes-repeated relationships semantics*. As a consequence, we will not miss any result, but we may obtain matches that are worthless or redundant in practice.

Consider the example depicted in Fig. 13.7. In the case of Cypher, the query returned the empty set, because of its no-repeated-edge semantics. In SPARQL's semantics, the result is the correct one (except for duplicated results).

```
SELECT ?x4
FROM <SocialNetwork>
WHERE {
        ?x1 a <http://xmlns.com/foaf/0.1/Person> .
        ?x2 a <http://xmlns.com/foaf/0.1/Person> .
        ?x3 a <http://xmlns.com/foaf/0.1/Person> .
        ?x4 a <http://xmlns.com/foaf/0.1/Person> .
        ?x1 <http://www.lib.org/schema#friendOf> ?x3 .
        ?x2 <http://www.lib.org/schema#friendOf> ?x3 .
        ?x3 <http://www.lib.org/schema#friendOf> ?x4 .
}
```

The answer to this query will be obtained by performing all the possible assignments according to SPARQL's homomorphism-based semantics. For example, the basic graph pattern in the WHERE clause will be true if we instantiate variable x1 to the constant John, x2 to Ann, x3 to Klara and x4 to Amber. Then, x4 will be projected as the result in the SELECT clause. The following table indicates all the matchings that satisfy the homomorphic conditions in this query.

x1	x2	x3	x4
John	Ann	Klara	Amber
John	John	Klara	Amber
Ann	John	Klara	Amber
Ann	Ann	Klara	Amber

Thus, the query returns four tuples corresponding to the four isomorphic matches of Amber. Adding the condition FILTER(?x1 < ?x2) we would obtain just the answer we need.

14.3 RDF Representation of Multidimensional Data

We are now ready to study how to represent multidimensional data in RDF. Suppose that the Northwind company wants to analyze sales data against economic and demographic data, published as open data on the web. Instead of loading and maintaining those data permanently in the local data warehouse, it could be more efficient to either temporarily load them into the warehouse for analysis, or to operate over a cube directly in RDF format, as we will study in the next sections. Being able to publish data cubes in RDF will also allow the company to publish data over the web to be shared by all the company branches.

We will use the GeoNames ontology containing geographical data in the world.[10] In this ontology, the toponymes (e.g., cities, states, countries) are defined as classes (called **Features**) and the geographic relationships between them are defined through properties (e.g., **children** for the administrative subdivisions of a country). For instance, a portion of the ontology corresponding to Paris is shown below.

```
<gn:Feature rdf:about="http://sws.geonames.org/2968815/">
    gn:name "Paris" ; gn:alternateName "Departement de Paris" ;
    gn:countryCode "FR" ; gn:population 2257981 ;
    wgs84_pos:lat 48.8534 ; wgs84_pos:long 2.3486 ;
    gn:parentFeature <http://sws.geonames.org/3012874/> ;
    gn:parentCountry <http://sws.geonames.org/3017382/> ;
    gn:wikipediaArticle <http://en.wikipedia.org/wiki/Paris> .
```

The IRI in the first line represents the resource (Paris), and it is the subject of the triples formed with the predicate-object pairs below it (telling, e.g., that the country code of Paris is FR).

For representing multidimensional data in RDF we use the **QB4OLAP vocabulary**.[11] QB4OLAP is an extension of the **RDF data cube vocabulary**[12] or **QB**. The QB vocabulary is compatible with the cube model underlying the Statistical Data and Metadata eXchange (SDMX)[13] standard, an ISO standard for exchanging and sharing statistical data and metadata among organizations. QB is also compatible with the Simple Knowledge Organization System (SKOS)[14] vocabulary.

Figure 14.4 depicts the QB4OLAP vocabulary. Capitalized terms represent RDF classes and noncapitalized terms represent RDF properties. Classes and properties in QB have a prefix qb. Classes and properties added to QB (with prefix qb4o) are depicted with light gray background and black font. Classes in external vocabularies are depicted in light gray font.

A data structure definition or DSD, defined as an instance of the class qb:DataStructureDefinition, specifies the schema of a data set (i.e., a cube), the latter defined as an instance of the class qb:DataSet. This structure can be shared among different data sets. The DSD of a data set is defined by means of the qb:structure property. The DSD has **component** properties for representing dimensions, dimension levels, measures, and attributes, called qb:dimension, qb4o:level, qb:measure, and qb:attribute, respectively. Component specifications are linked to DSDs via the property qb:component.

Observations (i.e., facts), which are instances of qb:Observation, represent points in a multidimensional data space. They are grouped into data sets by means of the qb:dataSet property. An observation is linked to a value in each

---

[10] http://www.geonames.org/ontology/

[11] http://purl.org/qb4olap/cubes

[12] http://www.w3.org/TR/vocab-data-cube/

[13] http://sdmx.org/

[14] http://www.w3.org/2009/08/skos-reference/skos.html

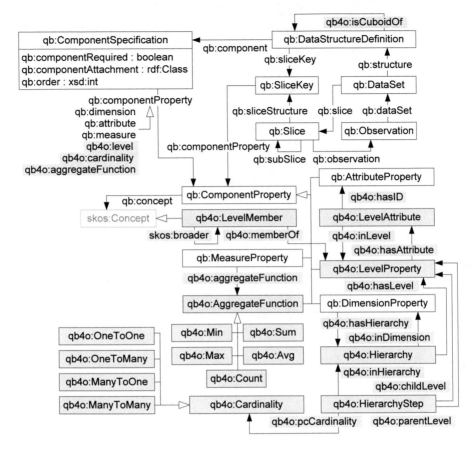

Fig. 14.4 The QB4OLAP vocabulary

dimension level of the DSD using instances of qb4o:LevelProperty. This class models dimension levels. Level attributes are defined via the qb4o:hasAttribute property. Instances of the class qb4o:LevelMember represent level members, and the relations between them are expressed using the skos:broader property.

Dimension hierarchies are defined via the class qb4o:HierarchyProperty. The relationships between dimensions and hierarchies are represented via the property qb4o:hasHierarchy and its inverse qb4o:inDimension. A level may belong to different hierarchies, and in each hierarchy it may have a different parent level. Also, the relationships between level members may have different cardinalities (e.g., one-to-many, many-to-many, etc.). The qb4o:HierarchyStep class represents parent-child relationships in a hierarchy, and properties are provided to describe these relationships: qb4o:inHierarchy, qb4o:childLevel, and qb4o:parentLevel. The cardinality of this relationship is represented via the qb4o:cardinality property and members of the qb4o:Cardinality class. This property can also be used to represent the cardinality of the relationship between a fact and a level.

A set of measure values is associated with an observation using the property qb:MeasureProperty in the DSD. Aggregate functions are defined via the qb4o:AggregateFunction class. The association between measures and aggregate functions is represented using the property qb4o:aggregateFunction. This property, together with the concept of component sets, allows a given measure to be associated with different aggregate functions in different cubes.

14.4 Representation of the Northwind Cube in QB4OLAP

In this section, we show how the Northwind data cube in Fig. 4.1 can be represented in RDF using the QB4OLAP vocabulary.

We start by defining the namespace prefixes as follows:

```
@prefix qb: <http://purl.org/linked-data/cube#> .
@prefix qb4o: <http://purl.org/qb4olap/cubes#> .
@prefix nw: <http://dwbook.org/cubes/schemas/northwind#> .
@prefix nwi: <http://dwbook.org/cubes/instances/northwind#> .
@prefix rdf: <http://www.w3.org/1999/02/22-rdf-syntax-ns#> .
@prefix rdfs: <http://www.w3.org/2000/01/rdf-schema#> .
@prefix sdmx-concept: <http://purl.org/linked-data/sdmx/2009/concept#> .
@prefix sdmx-dimension: <http://purl.org/linked-data/sdmx/2009/dimension#> .
@prefix skos: <http://www.w3.org/2004/02/skos/core#> .
@prefix db: <http://dbpedia.org/resource/> .
```

Dimensions are defined using the property qb:DimensionProperty as follows:

```
nw:employeeDim a rdf:Property, qb:DimensionProperty ;
    rdfs:label "Employee Dimension"@en .
nw:orderDateDim a rdf:Property, qb:DimensionProperty ;
    rdfs:label "Order Date Dimension"@en ;
    rdfs:subPropertyOf sdmx-dimension:refPeriod ; qb:concept sdmx-concept:refPeriod .
nw:dueDateDim a rdf:Property, qb:DimensionProperty ;
    rdfs:label "Due Date Dimension"@en ;
    rdfs:subPropertyOf sdmx-dimension:refPeriod ; qb:concept sdmx-concept:refPeriod .
nw:shippedDateDim a rdf:Property, qb:DimensionProperty ;
    rdfs:label "Shipped Date Dimension"@en ;
    rdfs:subPropertyOf sdmx-dimension:refPeriod ; qb:concept sdmx-concept:refPeriod .
nw:productDim a rdf:Property, qb:DimensionProperty ;
    rdfs:label "Product Dimension"@en .
    ...
```

Dimension levels are defined with the property qb4o:LevelProperty. Attributes of levels are defined with the property qb4o:LevelAttribute. The property qb4o:hasAttribute is used to associate attributes with a dimension level.

For example, the definition of the Product level and its attributes is shown next.

```
nw:product a qb4o:LevelProperty ; rdfs:label "Product Level"@en ;
    qb4o:hasAttribute nw:productKey ; qb4o:hasAttribute nw:productName ;
    qb4o:hasAttribute nw:quantityPerUnit ; qb4o:hasAttribute nw:unitPrice ;
    qb4o:hasAttribute nw:discontinued .
nw:productKey a qb4o:LevelAttribute ; rdfs:label "Product Key"@en .
nw:productName a qb4o:LevelAttribute ; rdfs:label "Product Name"@en .
nw:quantityPerUnit a qb4o:LevelAttribute ; rdfs:label "Quantity per Unit"@en .
nw:unitPrice a qb4o:LevelAttribute ; rdfs:label "Unit Price"@en .
nw:discontinued a qb4o:LevelAttribute ; rdfs:label "Discontinued"@en .
```

Hierarchies are defined as instances of the class qb:HierarchyProperty. The relationships between dimensions and hierarchies are defined with the properties qb4o:inDimension and qb4o:hasHierarchy. The levels in a hierarchy are defined with the property qb4o:hasLevel. For example, the hierarchies for the Employee dimension are defined as follows:

```
nw:supervision a qb4o:HierarchyProperty ; qb4o:inDimension nw:employeeDim ;
    qb4o:hasLevel nw:employee ; rdfs:label "Supervision Hierarchy"@en .
nw:territories a qb4o:HierarchyProperty ; qb4o:inDimension nw:employeeDim ;
    qb4o:hasLevel nw:employee , nw:city , nw:state , nw:region , nw:country ,
    nw:continent ; rdfs:label "Territories Hierarchy"@en .
nw:employeeDim qb4o:hasHierarchy nw:supervision , nw:territories .
```

Parent-child relationships in a hierarchy are defined as instances of the class qb4o:HierarchyStep. They have associated properties qb4o:inHierarchy, qb4o:childLevel, qb4o:parentLevel, and qb4o:cardinality as follows.

```
_:hs1 a qb4o:HierarchyStep ; qb4o:inHierarchy nw:territories ;
    qb4o:childLevel nw:employee ; qb4o:parentLevel nw:city ;
    qb4o:cardinality qb4o:ManyToMany .
_:hs2 a qb4o:HierarchyStep ; qb4o:inHierarchy nw:territories ;
    qb4o:childLevel nw:city ; qb4o:parentLevel nw:state ;
    qb4o:cardinality qb4o:OneToMany .
_:hs3 a qb4o:HierarchyStep ; qb4o:inHierarchy nw:territories ;
    qb4o:childLevel nw:city ; qb4o:parentLevel nw:country ;
    qb4o:cardinality qb4o:OneToMany .
    ...
_:hs7 a qb4o:HierarchyStep ; qb4o:inHierarchy nw:territories ;
    qb4o:childLevel nw:country ; qb4o:parentLevel nw:continent ;
    qb4o:cardinality qb4o:OneToMany .
```

Measures are defined as instances of qb:MeasureProperty, where the range of the measure can be defined with the using the property rdfs:range.

```
nw:quantity a qb:MeasureProperty ; rdfs:label "Quantity"@en ; rdfs:range xsd:integer .
nw:unitPrice a qb:MeasureProperty ; rdfs:label "Unit Price"@en ; rdfs:range xsd:decimal .
nw:discount a qb:MeasureProperty ; rdfs:label "Discount"@en ; rdfs:range xsd:decimal .
nw:salesAmount a qb:MeasureProperty ; rdfs:label "Sales Amount"@en ;
    rdfs:range xsd:decimal .
nw:freight a qb:MeasureProperty ; rdfs:label "Freight"@en ; rdfs:range xsd:decimal .
nw:netAmount a qb:MeasureProperty ; rdfs:label "Net Amount"@en ;
    rdfs:range xsd:decimal .
```

A cube is defined as an instance of the class qb:DataStructureDefinition, its dimensions are defined using the property qb4o:level, and its measures are defined using the property qb4o:measure as follows:

```
nw:Northwind a qb:DataStructureDefinition ;
    qb:component [qb4o:level nw:employee ; qb4o:cardinality qb4o:ManyToOne] ;
    qb:component [qb4o:level nw:orderDate ; qb4o:cardinality qb4o:ManyToOne] ;
    qb:component [qb4o:level nw:dueDate ; qb4o:cardinality qb4o:ManyToOne] ;
    qb:component [qb4o:level nw:shippedDate ; qb4o:cardinality qb4o:ManyToOne] ;
    ...
    qb:component [qb:measure nw:quantity ; qb4o:aggregateFunction qb4o:sum] ;
    qb:component [qb:measure nw:unitPrice ; qb4o:aggregateFunction qb4o:avg] ;
    qb:component [qb:measure nw:discount ; qb4o:aggregateFunction qb4o:avg] ;
    qb:component [qb:measure nw:salesAmount ; qb4o:aggregateFunction qb4o:avg] ;
    qb:component [qb:measure nw:freight ; qb4o:aggregateFunction qb4o:avg] ;
    qb:component [qb:measure nw:netAmount ; qb4o:aggregateFunction qb4o:sum] .
```

14.5 Querying the Northwind Cube in SPARQL

Given the schema of the Northwind cube in Fig. 4.1 expressed in QB4OLAP, we revisit the queries of Sect. 4.4 in SPARQL.

Query 14.1. *Total sales amount per customer, year, and product category.*

```
SELECT ?custName ?catName ?yearNo (SUM(?sales) AS ?totalSales)
WHERE { ?o qb:dataSet nwi:dataset1 ; nw:Customer ?cust ;
          nw:OrderDate ?odate ; nw:Product ?prod ; nw:SalesAmount ?sales .
          ?cust nw:companyName ?custName . ?odate skos:broader ?month .
          ?month skos:broader ?quarter . ?quarter skos:broader ?sem .
          ?sem skos:broader ?year . ?year nw:year ?yearNo .
          ?prod skos:broader ?cat . ?cat nw:categoryName ?catName . }
GROUP BY ?custName ?catName ?yearNo
ORDER BY ?custName ?catName ?yearNo
```

In this query, we select the customer, order date, product, and sales amount of all sales, roll-up the date to the year level, roll-up the product to the category level, and aggregate the sales amount measure.

Query 14.2. *Yearly sales amount for each pair of customer country and supplier countries.*

```
SELECT ?custCountryName ?supCountryName ?yearNo (SUM(?sales) AS ?totalSales)
WHERE { ?o qb:dataSet nwi:dataset1 ; nw:Customer ?cust ; nw:Supplier ?sup ;
          nw:OrderDate ?odate ; nw:SalesAmount ?sales .
          ?cust skos:broader ?custCity . ?custCity skos:broader ?custState .
          { ?custState skos:broader ?custRegion .
          ?custRegion skos:broader ?custCountry . }
          UNION { ?custState skos:broader ?custCountry . }
          ?custCountry nw:countryName ?custCountryName .
```

```
        ?sup skos:broader ?supCity . ?supCity skos:broader ?supState .
        { ?supState skos:broader ?supRegion .
        ?supRegion skos:broader ?supCountry . }
        UNION { ?supState skos:broader ?supCountry . }
        ?supCountry nw:countryName ?supCountryName .
        ?odate skos:broader ?month . ?month skos:broader ?quarter .
        ?quarter skos:broader ?sem . ?sem skos:broader ?year .
        ?year nw:year ?yearNo . }
GROUP BY ?custCountryName ?supCountryName ?yearNo
ORDER BY ?custCountryName ?supCountryName ?yearNo
```

The above query performs a roll-up of the customer and supplier dimensions to the country level, a roll-up of the order date to the year level, and then aggregates the measure sales amount. Since a state rolls up to either a region or a country, the patterns between curly brackets before and after the **UNION** operator to take into account both alternative aggregation paths.

Query 14.3. *Monthly sales by customer state compared to those of the previous year.*

```
SELECT ?stateName ?yearNo ?monthNo ?totalSales ?salesPrevYear
WHERE {
        # Monthly sales by state
        { SELECT ?stateName ?yearNo ?monthNo (SUM(?sales) AS ?totalSales)
        WHERE { ?o qb:dataSet nwi:dataset1 ; nw:Customer ?cust ;
                nw:OrderDate ?odate ; nw:SalesAmount ?sales .
                ?cust skos:broader ?city . ?city skos:broader ?state .
                ?state nw:stateName ?stateName . ?odate skos:broader ?month .
                ?month nw:monthNumber ?monthNo ; skos:broader ?quarter .
                ?quarter skos:broader ?sem . ?sem skos:broader ?year .
                ?year nw:year ?yearNo . }
        GROUP BY ?stateName ?yearNo ?monthNo }
        # Monthly sales by state for the previous year
        OPTIONAL {
        { SELECT ?stateName ?yearNo1 ?monthNo
                (SUM(?sales1) AS ?salesPrevYear)
        WHERE { ?o1 qb:dataSet nwi:dataset1 ; nw:Customer ?cust1 ;
                nw:OrderDate ?odate1 ; nw:SalesAmount ?sales1 .
                ?cust1 skos:broader ?city1 . ?city1 skos:broader ?state .
                ?state nw:stateName ?stateName . ?odate1 skos:broader ?month1 .
                ?month1 nw:monthNumber ?monthNo ; skos:broader ?quarter1 .
                ?quarter1 skos:broader ?sem1 . ?sem1 skos:broader ?year1 .
                ?year1 nw:year ?yearNo1 . }
        GROUP BY ?stateName ?yearNo1 ?monthNo }
        FILTER ( ?yearNo = ?yearNo1 + 1) } }
ORDER BY ?stateName ?yearNo ?monthNo
```

The first inner query computes the monthly sales by state by rolling-up the customer dimension to the state level and the order date dimension to the month level. Then, after the **OPTIONAL** keyword, the second inner query computes again the monthly sales by state. The **FILTER** condition makes the join of the two inner queries relating the sales amount of a month and that of the corresponding month of the previous year.

Query 14.4. *Monthly sales growth per product, that is, total sales per product compared to those of the previous month.*

```
SELECT ?prodName ?yearNo ?monthNo ?totalSales ?prevMonthSales
       (?totalSales - ?prevMonthSales AS ?salesGrowth)
WHERE {
      # Monthly sales by product
      { SELECT ?prodName ?yearNo ?monthNo (SUM(?sales) AS ?totalSales)
        WHERE { ?o qb:dataSet nwi:dataset1 ; nw:Product ?prod ;
                nw:OrderDate ?odate ; nw:SalesAmount ?sales .
                ?prod nw:productName ?prodName . ?odate skos:broader ?month .
                ?month nw:monthNumber ?monthNo ; skos:broader ?quarter .
                ?quarter skos:broader ?sem . ?sem skos:broader ?year .
                ?year nw:year ?yearNo . }
        GROUP BY ?prodName ?yearNo ?monthNo }
      # Monthly sales by product for the previous month
      OPTIONAL {
      { SELECT ?prodName ?yearNo1 ?monthNo1
              (SUM(?sales1) AS ?prevMonthSales)
        WHERE { ?o1 qb:dataSet nwi:dataset1 ; nw:Product ?prod ;
                nw:OrderDate ?odate1 ; nw:SalesAmount ?sales1 .
                ?prod nw:productName ?prodName . ?odate1 skos:broader ?month1 .
                ?month1 nw:monthNumber ?monthNo1 ; skos:broader ?quarter1 .
                ?quarter1 skos:broader ?sem1 . ?sem1 skos:broader ?year1 .
                ?year1 nw:year ?yearNo1 . }
        GROUP BY ?prodName ?yearNo1 ?monthNo1 }
      FILTER( ( (?monthNo = ?monthNo1 + 1) && (?yearNo = ?yearNo1) ) ||
      ( (?monthNo = 1) && (?monthNo1 = 12) &&
      (?yearNo = ?yearNo1+1) ) ) } }
ORDER BY ?prodName ?yearNo ?monthNo
```

The first inner query computes the monthly sales by product. Then, after the **OPTIONAL** keyword, the second inner query computes again the monthly sales by product. The **FILTER** condition makes the join of the two inner queries relating the sales amount of a month and that of the previous month. The condition must take into account whether the previous month is in the same year or in the previous year.

Query 14.5. *Three best-selling employees.*

```
SELECT ?fName ?lName (SUM(?sales) AS ?totalSales)
WHERE { ?o qb:dataSet nwi:dataset1 ; nw:Employee ?emp ; nw:SalesAmount ?sales .
        ?emp nw:firstName ?fName ; nw:lastName ?lName . }
GROUP BY ?fName ?lName
ORDER BY DESC (?totalSales)
LIMIT 3
```

This query computes the total sales by employee, sorts them in descending order of total sales, and keeps the first three results.

Query 14.6. *Best-selling employee per product and year.*

```
SELECT ?prodName ?yearNo ?maxSales ?fName ?lName
WHERE {
        # Maximum employee sales per product and year
        { SELECT ?prodName ?yearNo (MAX(?totalSales) AS ?maxSales)
        WHERE {
                { SELECT ?prodName ?yearNo ?emp (SUM(?sales) AS ?totalSales)
                WHERE { ?o qb:dataSet nwi:dataset1 ; nw:Product ?prod ;
                nw:OrderDate ?odate ; nw:Employee ?emp ;
                nw:SalesAmount ?sales . ?prod nw:productName ?prodName .
                ?odate skos:broader ?month . ?month skos:broader ?quarter .
                ?quarter skos:broader ?sem . ?sem skos:broader ?year .
                ?year nw:year ?yearNo . }
                GROUP BY ?prodName ?yearNo ?emp } }
        GROUP BY ?prodName ?yearNo }
        # Sales per product, year, and employee
        { SELECT ?prodName ?yearNo ?fName ?lName
                (SUM(?sales1) AS ?empSales)
        WHERE { ?o1 qb:dataSet nwi:dataset1 ; nw:Product ?prod ;
                nw:OrderDate ?odate1 ; nw:Employee ?emp1 ;
                nw:SalesAmount ?sales1 . ?prod nw:productName ?prodName .
                ?emp1 nw:firstName ?fName ; nw:lastName ?lName .
                ?odate1 skos:broader ?month1 . ?month1 skos:broader ?quarter1 .
                ?quarter1 skos:broader ?sem1 . ?sem1 skos:broader ?year .
                ?year nw:year ?yearNo . }
        GROUP BY ?prodName ?yearNo ?fName ?lName }
        FILTER ( ?maxSales = ?empSales ) }
ORDER BY ?prodName ?yearNo
```

The first inner query computes the maximum employee sales by product and year. Then, the second inner query computes the sales per product, year, and employee. The FILTER condition makes the join of the two inner queries relating the maximum sales with the employee that realized those sales.

Query 14.7. *Countries that account for top 50% of the sales amount.*
    For simplicity, in this query we compute the top 50% of the sales amount by state, instead of by country. In this case, we must not take care of the fact that states roll-up to either regions or countries. This can be taken care by using a UNION operator as was we did in Query 14.2.

```
SELECT ?stateName ?totalSales ?cumSales
WHERE { ?state nw:stateName ?stateName .
        # Total sales and cumulative sales by state
        { SELECT ?state ?totalSales (SUM(?totalSales1) AS ?cumSales)
        WHERE {
                # Total sales by state
                { SELECT ?state (SUM(?sales) AS ?totalSales)
                WHERE { ?o qb:dataSet nwi:dataset1 ; nw:Customer ?cust ;
                        nw:SalesAmount ?sales . ?cust skos:broader ?city .
                        ?city skos:broader ?state . }
                GROUP BY ?state }
                # Total sales by state
```

```
                  { SELECT ?state1 (SUM(?sales1) AS ?totalSales1)
                    WHERE { ?o qb:dataSet nwi:dataset1 ; nw:Customer ?cust1 ;
                            nw:SalesAmount ?sales1 . ?cust1 skos:broader ?city1 .
                            ?city1 skos:broader ?state1 . }
                    GROUP BY ?state1 }
                    FILTER ( ?totalSales <= ?totalSales1 ) } }
          # Minimum cumulative sales >= 50% of the overall sales
          { SELECT (MIN(?cumSales2) AS ?threshold)
          WHERE {
                    # 50% of the overall sales
                    { SELECT (0.5 * SUM(?sales) AS ?halfOverallSales)
                    WHERE { ?o qb:dataSet nwi:dataset1 ; nw:SalesAmount ?sales . } }
                    # Total sales and cumulative sales by state
                    { SELECT ?state2 ?totalSales2
                            (SUM(?totalSales3) AS ?cumSales2)
                    WHERE {
                            { SELECT ?state2 (SUM(?sales2) AS ?totalSales2)
                            WHERE { ?o2 qb:dataSet nwi:dataset1 ;
                            nw:Customer ?cust2 ; nw:SalesAmount ?sales2 .
                            ?cust2 skos:broader ?city2 . ?city2 skos:broader ?state2 . }
                            GROUP BY ?state2 }
                            { SELECT ?state3 (SUM(?sales3) AS ?totalSales3)
                            WHERE { ?o3 qb:dataSet nwi:dataset1 ;
                            nw:Customer ?cust3 ; nw:SalesAmount ?sales3 .
                            ?cust3 skos:broader ?city3 . ?city3 skos:broader ?state3 . }
                            GROUP BY ?state3 }
                            FILTER ( ?totalSales2 <= ?totalSales3 ) } }
                    FILTER(?cumSales2 >= ?halfOverallSales) } }
          FILTER(?cumSales <= ?threshold) }
ORDER BY DESC(?totalSales)
```

The first inner query computes for each country the total sales and the cumulative sales of all countries having total sales greater than or equal to the total sales of the country. The second inner query computes the threshold value, which represents the minimum cumulative sales greater than or equal to the 50% of the overall sales. Finally, the FILTER selects all countries whose cumulative sales are less than or equal to the threshold value.

Query 14.8. *Total sales and average monthly sales by employee and year.*

```
SELECT ?fName ?lName ?yearNo (SUM(?monthlySales) AS ?totalSales)
        (AVG(?monthlySales) AS ?avgMonthlySales)
WHERE {
        # Monthly sales by employee
        { SELECT ?fName ?lName ?month (SUM(?sales) AS ?monthlySales)
        WHERE { ?o qb:dataSet nwi:dataset1 ; nw:Employee ?emp ;
                nw:OrderDate ?odate ; nw:SalesAmount ?sales .
                ?emp nw:firstName ?fName ; nw:lastName ?lName .
                ?odate skos:broader ?month . }
        GROUP BY ?fName ?lName ?month }
        ?month skos:broader ?quarter . ?quarter skos:broader ?sem .
        ?sem skos:broader ?year . ?year nw:year ?yearNo . }
GROUP BY ?fName ?lName ?yearNo
ORDER BY ?fName ?lName ?yearNo
```

In the query above, the inner query computes the total sales amount by employee and month. The outer query rolls-up the previous result to the year level while computing the total yearly sales and the average monthly sales.

Query 14.9. *Total sales amount and total discount amount per product and month.*

```
SELECT ?prodName ?yearNo ?monthNo (SUM(?sales) AS ?totalSales)
       (SUM(?unitPrice * ?qty * ?disc) AS ?totalDiscAmount)
WHERE { ?o qb:dataSet nwi:dataset1 ; nw:Product ?prod ;
       nw:OrderDate ?odate ; nw:SalesAmount ?sales ;
       nw:Quantity ?qty ; nw:Discount ?disc ; nw:UnitPrice ?unitPrice .
       ?prod nw:productName ?prodName . ?odate skos:broader ?month .
       ?month nw:monthNumber ?monthNo ; skos:broader ?quarter .
       ?quarter skos:broader ?sem . ?sem skos:broader ?year . ?year nw:year ?yearNo . }
GROUP BY ?prodName ?yearNo ?monthNo
ORDER BY ?prodName ?yearNo ?monthNo
```

Here, we roll-up to the month level and compute the requested measures.

Query 14.10. *Monthly year-to-date sales for each product category.*

```
SELECT ?catName ?yearNo ?monthNo (SUM(?totalSales1) AS ?YTDSales)
WHERE { ?cat nw:categoryName ?catName .
       ?month nw:monthNumber ?monthNo ; skos:broader ?quarter .
       ?quarter skos:broader ?sem . ?sem skos:broader ?year . ?year nw:year ?yearNo.
       { SELECT ?catName ?yearNo ?monthNo1 (SUM(?sales1) AS ?totalSales1)
         WHERE { ?o1 qb:dataSet nwi:dataset1 ; nw:Product ?prod1 ;
                 nw:OrderDate ?odate1 ; nw:SalesAmount ?sales1 .
                 ?prod1 skos:broader ?cat1 . ?cat1 nw:categoryName ?catName .
                 ?odate1 skos:broader ?month1 .
                 ?month1 nw:monthNumber ?monthNo1 ; skos:broader ?quarter1 .
                 ?quarter1 skos:broader ?sem1 . ?sem1 skos:broader ?year1 .
                 ?year1 nw:year ?yearNo. }
         GROUP BY ?catName ?yearNo ?monthNo1 }
       FILTER( ?monthNo >= ?monthNo1 ) }
GROUP BY ?catName ?yearNo ?monthNo
ORDER BY ?catName ?yearNo ?monthNo
```

This query starts by selecting the category, month, and year levels. Then, for each category, month, and year, it selects all facts whose order date is in the same year but whose month is less than or equal to the current month.

Query 14.11. *Moving average over the last 3 months of the sales amount by product category.*

```
SELECT ?catName ?yearNo ?monthNo (AVG(?totalSales1) AS ?MovAvg3MSales)
WHERE { ?cat nw:categoryName ?catName .
       ?month nw:monthNumber ?monthNo ; skos:broader ?quarter .
       ?quarter skos:broader ?sem . ?sem skos:broader ?year . ?year nw:year ?yearNo.
       OPTIONAL {
       { SELECT ?catName ?yearNo1 ?monthNo1 (SUM(?sales1) AS ?totalSales1)
         WHERE { ?o1 qb:dataSet nwi:dataset1 ; nw:Product ?prod1 ;
```

```
                    nw:OrderDate ?odate1 ; nw:SalesAmount ?sales1 .
                    ?prod1 skos:broader ?cat1 . ?cat1 nw:categoryName ?catName .
                    ?odate1 skos:broader ?month1 .
                    ?month1 nw:monthNumber ?monthNo1 ; skos:broader ?quarter1 .
                    ?quarter1 skos:broader ?sem1 . ?sem1 skos:broader ?year1 .
                    ?year1 nw:year ?yearNo1. }
             GROUP BY ?catName ?yearNo1 ?monthNo1 }
             FILTER( (( ?monthNo >= 3 && ?yearNo = ?yearNo1 &&
             ?monthNo >= ?monthNo1 && ?monthNo-2 <= ?monthNo1 ) ||
             ( ?monthNo = 2 && (( ?yearNo = ?yearNo1 && ?monthNo1 <= 2 ) ||
             ( ?yearNo = ?yearNo1+1 && ?monthNo1 = 12 ))) ||
             ( ?monthNo = 1 && ((?yearNo = ?yearNo1 && ?monthNo1 = 1 ) ||
             (?yearNo = ?yearNo1+1 && ?monthNo1 >= 11 ))))) } }
GROUP BY ?catName ?yearNo ?monthNo
ORDER BY ?catName ?yearNo ?monthNo
```

This query starts by selecting the category, month, and year levels. Then, for each category, month, and year, the query selects all facts whose order date is within a three-month window from the current month. This selection involves an elaborated condition in the FILTER clause, which covers three cases, depending on whether the month is March or later, the month is February, or the month is January.

Query 14.12. *Personal sales amount made by an employee compared with the total sales amount made by herself and her subordinates during 2017.*

```
SELECT ?fName ?lName ?persSales ?subordSales
WHERE { ?emp nw:firstName ?fName ; nw:lastName ?lName .
        { SELECT ?emp (SUM(?sales) AS ?persSales)
        WHERE { ?o qb:dataSet nwi:dataset1 ; nw:Employee ?emp ;
                nw:OrderDate ?odate ; nw:SalesAmount ?sales .
                ?odate skos:broader ?month . ?month skos:broader ?quarter .
                ?quarter skos:broader ?sem . ?sem skos:broader ?year .
                ?year nw:year ?yearNo .
                FILTER(?yearNo = 2017) }
        GROUP BY ?emp }
        { SELECT ?emp (SUM(?sales1) AS ?subordSales)
        WHERE { ?subord nw:supervisor* ?emp .
                ?o1 qb:dataSet nwi:dataset1 ; nw:Employee ?subord ;
                nw:OrderDate ?odate1 ; nw:SalesAmount ?sales .
                ?odate1 skos:broader ?month1 . ?month1 skos:broader ?quarter1 .
                ?quarter1 skos:broader ?sem1 . ?sem1 skos:broader ?year1 .
                ?year1 nw:year ?yearNo1 .
                FILTER(?yearNo1 = 2017) }
        GROUP BY ?emp } }
ORDER BY ?emp
```

The first inner query computes by employee the personal sales in 2017. The second inner query exploits the recursive hierarchy Supervision with a property path expression in SPARQL. The '*' character states that the transitive closure of the supervision hierarchy must be taken into account for obtaining all subordinates of an employee. Then, the sales in 2017 of all these subordinates are aggregated.

Query 14.13. *Total sales amount, number of products, and sum of the quantities sold for each order.*

```
SELECT ?orderNo (SUM(?sales) AS ?totalSales)
           (COUNT(?prod) AS ?nbProducts) (SUM(?qty) AS ?nbUnits)
WHERE { ?o qb:dataSet nwi:dataset1 ; nw:Order ?order ;
          nw:Product ?prod ; nw:SalesAmount ?sales ; nw:Quantity ?qty .
          ?order nw:orderNo ?orderNo . }
GROUP BY ?orderNo
ORDER BY ?orderNo
```

Here, we group sales by order number and compute the requested measures.

Query 14.14. *For each month, total number of orders, total sales amount, and average sales amount by order.*

```
SELECT ?yearNo ?monthNo (COUNT(?orderNo) AS ?nbOrders)
           (SUM(?totalSales) AS ?totalSalesMonth)
           (AVG(?totalSales) AS ?avgSalesOrder)
WHERE {
          { SELECT ?orderNo ?odate (SUM(?sales) AS ?totalSales)
            WHERE { ?o qb:dataSet nwi:dataset1 ; nw:Order ?order ;
                    nw:OrderDate ?odate ; nw:SalesAmount ?sales .
                    ?order nw:orderNo ?orderNo . }
            GROUP BY ?orderNo ?odate }
          ?odate skos:broader ?month .
          ?month nw:monthNumber ?monthNo ; skos:broader ?quarter .
          ?quarter skos:broader ?sem . ?sem skos:broader ?year . ?year nw:year ?yearNo . }
GROUP BY ?yearNo ?monthNo
ORDER BY ?yearNo ?monthNo
```

Here, the inner query computes the total sales by order. The outer query then rolls-up the previous result to the month level and computes the requested measures.

Query 14.15. *For each employee, total sales amount, number of cities, and number of states to which she is assigned.*

```
SELECT ?fName ?lName (SUM(?sales)/COUNT(DISTINCT ?city) AS ?totalSales)
           (COUNT(DISTINCT ?city) AS ?noCities)
           (COUNT(DISTINCT ?state) AS ?noStates)
WHERE { ?o qb:dataSet nwi:dataset1 ; nw:Employee ?emp ; nw:SalesAmount ?sales .
          ?emp nw:firstName ?fName ; nw:lastName ?lName ; skos:broader ?city .
          ?city skos:broader ?state . }
GROUP BY ?fName ?lName
ORDER BY ?fName ?lName
```

Recall that there is a many-to-many relationship between employees and cities. Thus, the above query rolls-up to the city and state levels and then groups the result by employee. Then, in the SELECT clause, we sum the sales amount measure and divide it by the number of distinct cities assigned to an employee. This solves the double-counting problem to which we referred in Sect. 4.2.6.

14.6 Summary

In this chapter, we studied how OLAP techniques can be applied to analyzed data on the semantic web. The RDF graph data model is the way in
which data are represented on the semantic web. We first introduced the main
concepts of the RDF graph data model. Then, we studied how to represent relational data in RDF. We also introduced SPARQL, the standard language to
query RDF graphs, and compare its homomorphism-based semantics against
the isomorphism-based semantics of Cypher studied in Chap. 13. We then
showed how OLAP techniques can be directly applied to RDF data sets without the need of first transforming RDF data into OLAP data cubes. For this,
we need vocabularies that allow us to represent OLAP data and metadata.
We studied and compared two of these vocabularies: the Data Cube Vocabulary (QB) and the QB4OLAP vocabulary. We studied the limitations of the
former when trying to define the OLAP operations and showed, based on a
portion of a real-world case study, how these operations can be implemented
in SPARQL. Finally, we applied QB4OLAP to the Northwind data cube and
query the resulting RDF cube using SPARQL.

14.7 Bibliographic Notes

There are many books explaining the basics of the semantic web, for example, [102, 106]. The book [101] provides an introduction to Linked Data, a
paradigm in which data is seen as a first-class citizen of the Web, thereby
enabling the extension of the Web with a global data space – the Web of
Data. The book [207] provides a recent view of methods, technologies, and
systems related to Linked Data. A book entirely devoted to SPARQL is [63].
A recent survey on the topic is [104].

A review on the application of semantic web techologies for data warehousing is [78]. Sect. 14.3 of this chapter is based on research work by Etcheverry
and Vaisman on QB4OLAP [72, 73] and on [246]. Kämpgen and Harth [125]
propose to load statistical linked data into an RDF triple store and to answer OLAP queries using SPARQL. For this, they implement an OLAP
to SPARQL engine which translates OLAP queries into SPARQL. Further,
Breucker et al. [39] proposed SEO4OLAP, a tool for generating search engine
optimized web pages for every possible view of a statistical linked dataset
modeled in the RDF Data Cube Vocabulary. This approach to querying statistical linked open data is comprehensively studied in [124]. QB4OLAP has
also been used to enrich statistical data represented in the QB vocabulary
with dimensional data [252]. Matei et al. [148] propose a framework for integrating OLAP and semantic web data, also based in QB4OLAP. A proposal
to perform OLAP analysis over RDF graphs is presented in [19]. Knowledge
graphs are large networks of entities, their semantic types, properties, and

relationships. In [214] is presented an adaptation of the OLAP cube model for knowledge graphs that enables the representation of the knowledge at various abstraction levels.

We also mentioned that another research approach studies how to extract multidimensional data from the semantic web, and then analyze these data using traditional OLAP techniques. The methods to do this are based on ontologies, which allow us to extract data in a semiautomatic fashion. The idea is to use ontologies to identify facts and dimensions that can populate a data cube. We briefly mention next some of this work. Niinimäki and Niemi [167] use ontology mapping to convert data sources to RDF and then query this RDF data with SPARQL to populate the OLAP schema. The ETL process is guided by the ontology. In addition, the authors create an OLAP ontology, somehow similar to the vocabularies discussed in this chapter. Ontologies are expressed in RDF and OWL. Along the same lines, Romero and Abelló [201] address the design of the data warehouse starting from an OWL ontology that describes the data sources. They identify the dimensions that characterize a central concept under analysis (the fact concept) by looking for concepts connected to it through one-to-many relationships. The same idea is used for discovering the different levels of the dimension hierarchies, starting from the concept that represents the base level. The output of the method is a star or snowflake schema that guarantees the summarizability of the data, suitable to be instantiated in a traditional multidimensional database. Finally, Nebot and Berlanga [164] proposed a semiautomatic method for extracting semantic data on-demand into a multidimensional database. In this way, data could be analyzed using traditional OLAP techniques. Here, the authors assume that data are represented as an OWL ontology. A portion of this ontology contains the application and domain ontology axioms, while the other part contains the actual instance store. A multidimensional schema must first be created from the requirements and the knowledge that can be inferred from the ontologies. This schema is then semiautomatically populated from the ontology.

The semantic web has been extended to cover spatial [107, 122, 174] and spatiotemporal [168, 247, 256] aspects, which we have covered in Chap. 12. A recent survey on RDF for spatial and spatiotemporal data management is given [273]. Spatial data warehouses and the semantic web have been studied in [98, 97, 162, 163].

14.8 Review Questions

14.1 What are the two main approaches to perform OLAP analysis with semantic web data?

14.2 Briefly describe RDF and RDFS and their main constructs.

14.3 Give an example of the RDF/XML and Turtle serializations of RDF data.

14.4 What is SPARQL? How does its semantics differ from the one of SQL?

14.5 Give an example of a SPARQL query, describe its elements, and discuss how it will be evaluated.

14.6 Explain the two standard approaches to represent relational data in RDF. How do they differ from each other?

14.7 How can we represent multidimensional data in RDF?

14.8 Briefly explain the QB4OLAP vocabulary. How is QB4OLAP related to the Data Cube vocabulary QB?

14.9 How facts, dimensions, and hierarchies are represented in QB4OLAP?

14.10 Analyze and discuss the implementation of roll-up in QB4OLAP.

14.11 Explain how to perform OLAP queries in SPARQL.

14.9 Exercises

Exercise 14.1. Given the Northwind data cube shown in Fig. 4.2, give the QB4OLAP representation of the Sales fact. Provide at least two observations.

Exercise 14.2. Given the Northwind data cube shown in Fig. 4.2, give the QB4OLAP representation of the Customer dimension.

Exercise 14.3. Do the same as Ex. 14.2 for the Employee dimension.

Exercise 14.4. Write the R2RML mapping that represents the Northwind data warehouse using the QB4OLAP vocabulary.

Exercise 14.5. Show the SPARQL query implementing the operation

ROLLUP(Northwind, Product → Category, SUM(SalesAmount)).

Exercise 14.6. Show the SPARQL query implementing the operation

SLICE(Northwind, Customer, City='Paris')

Exercise 14.7. Represent the Foodmart cube given in Fig. 4.24 using the QB4OLAP vocabulary.

Exercise 14.8. Consider the Foodmart table instances given in Fig. 14.5. Represent sales facts as observations, adhering to the Data Structure Definition specified in the previous exercise.

Exercise 14.9. Write in SPARQL the queries over the Foodmart cube given in Ex. 4.9.

Sales

StoreID	DateID	ProductID	PromotionID	CustomerID	StoreSales	StoreCost	UnitSales
1	738	219	0	567	7.16	2.4344	3
1	738	684	0	567	12.88	5.0232	2
2	739	551	7	639	5.20	2.236	4

Product

ProductID	ProductName	BrandName	ProductClassID
219	Best Choice Corn Chips	Best Choice	12
551	Fast Low Fat Chips	Fast	12
684	Gorilla Blueberry Yogurt	Gorilla	6

ProductClass

ProductClassID	ProductSubcategory	ProductCategory	ProductDepartment	ProductFamily
6	Yogurt	Dairy	Dairy	Food
12	Chips	Snack Foods	Snack Foods	Food

Date

DateID	Date	WeekdayName	Month	Year	Day	Week	Month	Quarter
738	2018-01-07	Wednesday	January	2018	7	4	1	Q1
739	2018-01-08	Thursday	January	2018	8	4	1	Q1

Customer

CustID	FName	MI	LName	City	State	Country	Marital Status	YearlyIncome	Gender	Education
567	Charles	L.	Mank	Santa Fe	DF	Mexico	S	$50K-$70K	F	Bachelors
639	Michael	J.	Troyer	Kirkland	WA	USA	M	$30K-$50K	M	High School

Promotion

PromID	PromName	MediaType
0	No Promotion	No Media
7	Fantastic Discounts	Sunday paper, Radio, TV

Store

StoreID	StoreType	StoreName	StoreCity	StoreState	StoreCountry	StoreSqft
1	Supermarket	Store 1	Acapulco	Guerrero	Mexico	23593
2	Small Grocery	Store 2	Bellingham	WA	USA	28206

Fig. 14.5 An instance of the Foodmart data warehouse

Chapter 15
Recent Developments in Big Data Warehouses

Big data is usually defined as data that is so big, that may arrive at a pace or with such a variety that makes it difficult to manage them with methods and tools. Social networks, the Internet of Things (IoT), smart city devices, and mobility data, among others, produce enormous volumes of data that must be analyzed for decision making. Management and analysis of these massive amounts of data demand new solutions that go beyond the traditional processes or tools. All of these have great implications for data warehousing architectures and practices. For instance, big data analytics typically requires dramatically reduced data latency, which is the time elapsed between the moment some data are collected and the action based on such data is taken.

This chapter discusses the main technologies that address the challenges introduced by big data. We start by motivating the problem in Sect. 15.1. Distributed processing is studied in Sect. 15.2, where we address Hadoop, the Hadoop Distributed File System (HDFS), and Spark. The section concludes by discussing Apache Kylin, a big data warehouse system running on Hadoop or Spark, built using the concepts covered in this book. We then study modern database technologies designed for storing and querying large data volumes. We first introduce in Sect. 15.3 distributed database systems. We then study new approaches, as in-memory database systems (Sect. 15.4), and column-store database systems (Sect. 15.5), NoSQL database systems (Sect. 15.6), NewSQL database systems (Sect. 15.7), array database systems (Sect. 15.8), the new Hybrid Transactional and Analytical Processing (HTAP) paradigm (Sect. 15.9), which allows OLTP and OLAP processing on the same system, and polystores (Sect. 15.10), which provide integrated access to multiple cloud data stores. Cloud data warehouses are discussed in Sect. 15.11. We continue in Sect. 15.12 by discussing data lakes and Delta Lake. The former is an approach aimed at loading data right after the ingestion phase, while the latter consists of a layer on top of the data lake. We conclude the chapter in Sect. 15.13 by describing future perspectives on data warehousing in the context of big data.

© Springer-Verlag GmbH Germany, part of Springer Nature 2022
A. Vaisman, E. Zimányi, *Data Warehouse Systems*, Data-Centric Systems and Applications, https://doi.org/10.1007/978-3-662-65167-4_15

15.1 Data Warehousing in the Age of Big Data

The amount of data currently available from a wide variety of sources increasingly poses challenges to scientific and commercial applications. Datasets are continuously growing beyond the limits that traditional database and computing technologies can handle. Applications over such amounts of data are called *big data applications* or *data-centric applications*, and require appropriate solutions to be developed. These applications share some typical characteristics: the amount of data, the complexity of data, and the speed at which data arrive to the system.

Big data is normally defined using four dimensions (informally characterized by the well-known "four Vs"), namely:

- *Volume*: Big datasets are in the range of petabytes or zettabytes.
- *Variety*: Relational DBMSs are designed to work on structured data, compliant with a schema. In big data applications, data may come in any format, not necessarily structured, such as images, text, audio, video, etc.
- *Velocity*: Big data applications usually deal with real-time data processing, not only with batch processing, since data may come at a speed that systems cannot store before processing.
- *Veracity*: The reliability of big data sources usually varies. For example, data coming from social networks is not always reliable, while sensor data is usually more reliable.

From the above, it follows that a single tool or DBMS cannot meet all the data processing and storage requirements of big data applications. Big data systems are usually decomposed into tasks that can be performed efficiently by specific software tools. Those tasks are orchestrated and integrated by ad hoc applications. In this way, there are tools specific for capturing data in real time (e.g., Kafka), indexing data (e.g., ElasticSearch), storing data (e.g., Cassandra), and analyzing data (e.g., R, Python).

Furthermore, the continuously increasing data volumes to be processed require the computing infrastructure to scale. This can be done in two ways. **Vertical scaling** or *scaling up* consists in adding more resources to an existing system. This includes adding more hardware resources such as processing power, memory, storage, or network, but also adding more software resources such as more threads, more connections, or increasing cache sizes. On the other hand, **horizontal scaling** or *scaling out* consists in adding additional machines to a distributed computing infrastructure, such as a cluster or a cloud. This enables data partitioning across multiple nodes and the use of distributed processing algorithms where the core of the computation is performed locally at each node. In this way, applications can scale out by adding nodes as the dataset size grows. Horizontal scaling also enables **elasticity**, which is defined as the degree to which a system is able to *automatically* adapt to workload changes by provisioning and de-provisioning resources, such that at each point in time the available resources match the current demand as closely as possible.

For decades, organizations have invested in implementing enterprise data warehouses to support their BI systems. Modern data warehousing aims at delivering **self-service BI**, which empowers users at all organizational levels to produce their own analytical reports. However, big data greatly impacts on the design of data warehouses, which not only must ingest and store large data volumes coming at high speed, but also deliver query performance under these conditions and support new kinds of applications. For example, data warehouses provide consistent datasets for artificial intelligence and machine learning applications and, conversely, artificial intelligence and machine learning can enhance the capabilities of data warehouses. As an example, Google has incorporated machine learning into its BigQuery data warehouse. Also, new kinds of data warehouses are emerging, such as cloud data warehouses, which we discuss in Sect. 15.11. Indeed, organizations are increasingly moving their data warehouses to the cloud to take advantage of its flexibility, although many questions remain open in this respect.

In summary, to cope with the new requirements discussed above, new data warehousing approaches must be developed. Data warehouses must evolve to deliver the scalability, agility, and flexibility that data-driven applications need. Agility and flexibility are provided by new database technologies, supporting unstructured, schemaless data, and new ways of ingesting data, reducing the time required to make data available to users. Scalability is achieved through both distributed computing frameworks and distributed data storage. Scalability requirements are due to increasing data volumes. However, in cloud applications elastic scalability is needed, so the system is able to scale up and down dynamically as the computation requirements change. We study these new technologies in this chapter.

15.2 Distributed Processing Frameworks

To comply with the scalability requirements mentioned above, many applications can be easily partitioned into smaller portions that can be executed in parallel. The **MapReduce** programming model uses this approach to process large amounts of data on a very large number of commodity machines, hiding the complexity of knowing how to parallelize a job. The main idea is to divide a task into small parts and assign them to many computers, where the tasks are executed. The partial results are collected at one place and integrated to obtain the final result. The goal is to simplify parallel processing using a distributed computing platform that offers only two interfaces, namely, Map and Reduce. Splitting the computation into these two functions works well for coding simple problems in a variety of languages and over many data formats. Further, for simple tasks MapReduce allows distributed computa-

tion in applications that do not require the overhead of a DBMS, which are
typical in big data scenarios. Finally, MapReduce is a very efficient model
for applications that require processing the data only once. However, when
programs require processing the data iteratively, the MapReduce approach
becomes inefficient. This is true of machine learning code or complex SQL
queries. Spark, studied in Sect. 15.2.3 is typically used in those cases.

Figure 15.1 shows an example of how MapReduce works. Consider that
orders in the Northwind database come from many sources, each from one
country. We are interested in analyzing product sales. The files in this example
contain pairs of the form (ProductKey, Quantity). In the Map phase, the
input is divided into a list of key-value pairs with ProductKey as the key and
Quantity as the value. This list is sent to the so-called Shuffle phase in which
it is sorted such that values with the same ProductKey are put together.
The output of the Shuffle phase is a collection of tuples of the form (key,
list-of-values). This is forwarded to the Reduce phase where many different
operations such as average, sum, or count can be performed. Since the key-
list pairs are independent of each other, they can be forwarded to multiple
workers for parallel execution.

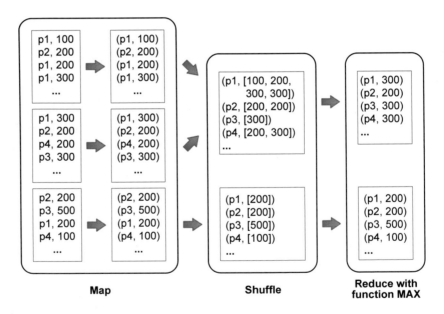

Fig. 15.1 A MapReduce process for products

The most popular MapReduce implementation is Hadoop, an open-source
framework written in Java. It has the capability to handle structured,
semistructured, or unstructured data, dividing a task into parallel chunks
of jobs and data. In the next section we describe Hadoop in detail.

15.2.1 Hadoop

Hadoop is a platform consisting of a collection of components working together for distributing data storage and processing. The core components of Hadoop are the Hadoop Distributed File System (HDFS) (although it can work with other storage systems), the MapReduce processsing model, and YARN (Yet Another Resource Negotiator), a software module for resource allocation and application scheduling.

The **Hadoop Distributed File System (HDFS)** is the component of Hadoop in charge of storing data in a distributed way. Nodes in HDFS have different roles. There are several **DataNodes** and one **NameNode**. The DataNodes are the servers that actually store the data, and are physically organized in racks. The NameNode contains metadata with information about the data stored in the different nodes. An application only interacts with the NameNode, which communicates with the DataNodes as required. HDFS uses blocks (of 64 MB by default) to store files on the file system. One block of Hadoop may consist of many blocks of the underlying operating system. Blocks can be replicated in several different nodes. For example, block1 can be stored in node1 and node3, block2 in node2 and node4, and so on. The NameNode and DataNodes communicate with each other using the TCP IP protocol. When the NameNode starts, a file (called FsImage) is loaded into main memory, containing the latest state of the file system. To avoid the single-point-of-failure problem, the content of the FsImage file is recorded at regular intervals in a secondary NameNode. The NameNode manages the file system's namespace, the client's access to files, and performs typical file system tasks such as naming, closing, and opening files and directories. The DataNodes store the file blocks, manage **replication**, and perform application data tasks. They also send messages to the NameNode at regular intervals (e.g., every three seconds), informing about the status of their own blocks. To improve network traffic management in large Hadoop clusters, the NameNode chooses the DataNode which is closest to the same rack, or the closest nearby rack, for reading and writing blocks. The NameNode maintains the rack ids of each DataNode. Taking decisions through this rack information is called **rack awareness**. Figure 15.2 depicts the schema of the HDFS components and how they interact with each other.

Hadoop MapReduce is the Hadoop framework for running MapReduce programs. This framework takes care of scheduling tasks, monitoring them and re-executing tasks that fail. The MapReduce framework and the HDFS run on the same set of nodes, allowing the framework to schedule tasks on the nodes where data is already present. The MapReduce framework consists of a single master called the ResourceManager, one worker NodeManager per cluster-node, and a MRAppMaster per application. Applications specify the input/output locations and supply map and reduce functions via implementations of appropriate interfaces and/or abstract-classes. These, and other job parameters, comprise the job configuration. The Hadoop job client then sub-

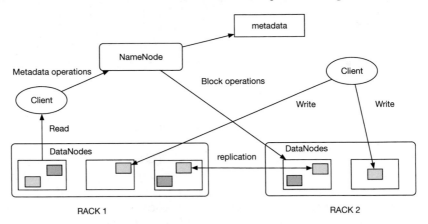

Fig. 15.2 Hadoop distributed file system (HDFS) architecture

mits the job (e.g., a .jar file) and the configuration to the ResourceManager, who distributes them to the workers, scheduling and monitoring the tasks, and returning status and diagnostic information to the job client. Note that although the Hadoop framework is implemented in Java, MapReduce applications can be written also in other programming languages.

The key idea of **YARN** is to split the functionality of resource management and job scheduling and monitoring into separate programs. To do this, there is a global ResourceManager and one ApplicationMaster per application. An application is either a single job or a Directed Acyclic Graph (DAG) of jobs. There is one NodeManager at each node in the cluster, which works together with the ResourceManager. The ResourceManager assigns resources to all the applications in the system. The NodeManager monitors the usage of computing resources such as CPU, network, etc., and reports to the ResourceManager. The ApplicationMaster negotiates resources from the ResourceManager, and works together with the NodeManager(s) to run and monitor tasks. Figure 15.3 shows the scheme explained above. Clients submit jobs to the ResourceManager, which has two components: the Scheduler and the ApplicationsManager. The former allocates resources to the (in general, many) running applications. The latter accepts job submissions and negotiates the first container (memory resource) for executing the ApplicationMaster, also taking care of the ApplicationMaster container in case of failure. The ApplicationMaster negotiates resource containers with the Scheduler, and tracks their status. Each NodeManager reports its status to the ResourceManager. An application, for example, MapReduce, is usually spanned into many containers (holding one MR task each), coordinated by (in this example) the MapReduce ApplicationMaster.

The interaction between YARN and Hadoop is as follows: The NameNode and the ResourceManager live on two different hosts, since they store key metadata. The DataNode and the NodeManager processes are placed on

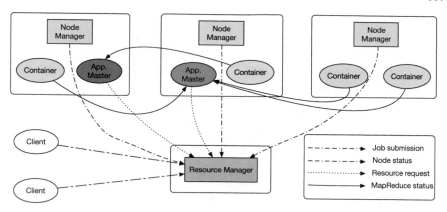

Fig. 15.3 The scheme of YARN

the same host (see Fig. 15.3). Since a file is split and saved to the HDFS DataNodes, to access it, a YARN application (such as MapReduce) is written using a YARN client, which reads data using an HDFS client. The application looks for the file location in the NameNode, and asks the ResourceManager to provide containers on the hosts that hold the file blocks. Since the distributed job gets a container on a host which keeps the DataNode, the read operation will be local and not over the network, which enhances reading performance.

In a big data environment like Hadoop, tasks are performed by specialized modules, which compose the **Hadoop ecosystem**. Key components of this ecosystem are Hive, a high-level query language for querying HDFS (studied in Sect. 15.2.2), and HBase, a column-oriented, non-relational database (studied in Sect. 15.6). Other key components are:

- Sqoop: Standing for "SQL to Hadoop", is a data ingestion tool like Flume, but, while Flume works on unstructured or semi-structured data, Sqoop is used to export and import data from and to relational databases.
- Zookeeper: A service that coordinates distributed applications. It has information about the cluster of the distributed servers it manages.
- Kafka: A distributed messaging system, used with Hadoop for fast data transfers in real time.

15.2.2 Hive

Using Hadoop is not easy for end users not familiar with MapReduce. They need to write MapReduce code even for simple tasks suh as counting or averaging. High-level query languages provide a solution to this problem; they enable a higher level of abstraction than Java or other lower-level languages supported by Hadoop. The most commonly used is **Hive**. Hive queries are translated into MapReduce jobs, resulting in programs that are much smaller than the equivalent Java ones. Besides, Hive can be extended, for example, by writing user-defined functions in Java. This can work the other way round: Programs written in Hive can be embedded in other languages as well.

Hive brings the concepts of tables, columns, partitions, and SQL into the Hadoop architecture. Hive organizes data in tables and partitions, which are then stored into directories in the HDFS. A popular format for storing data in Hive is **ORC** (standing for Optimized Row Columnar) format, which is a columnar format for storing data. Another widely used format is **Parquet**, which is also columnar and includes metadata information. Parquet is supported by many data processing systems.

In addition, Hive provides an SQL dialect called **Hive Query Language** (HiveQL) for querying data stored in a Hadoop cluster. Hive works as follows. Clients communicate with a Hive server. The request is handled by a driver, which calls the compiler and the execution engine, which sends the job to the MapReduce layer and receives the results, which are finally sent back to the driver. The job is executed at the processing layer, where it is handled by YARN, as explained above. A relational database, such as MySQL or PostgreSQL, holds Hive metadata, which is used to translate the queries written in HiveQL. The actual data are stored in HDFS, in the storage layer.

The Hive data model includes primitive data types such as Boolean and int, and collection data types such as Struct, Map, and Array. Collection data types allow many-to-many relationships to be represented, avoiding foreign key relationships between tables. On the other hand, they introduce data duplication and do not enforce referential integrity. We next show a simplified representation of the table Employees from the Northwind database, where the attributes composing a full address are stored as a Struct data type, and the Territories attribute is an Array that contains the set of territory names to which the employee is related. Hive has no control over how data are stored, and supports different file and record formats. The table schema is applied when the data are read from storage. The example below includes the file format definition (Textfile in this case) and the delimiter characters needed to parse each record:

```
CREATE TABLE Employees (
        EmployeeID int, Name String,
        Address Struct<Street:String, City:String,
                Region:String, PostalCode:String, Country:String>,
        Territories Array<String> )
ROW FORMAT
DELIMITED FIELDS TERMINATED BY ','
COLLECTION ITEMS TERMINATED BY '|'
LINES TERMINATED BY '\n'
STORED AS Textfile;
```

HiveQL supports the typical relational operations, such as INNER JOIN, OUTER JOIN, LEFT SEMI JOIN, GROUP BY, HAVING, and ORDER BY. They are analogous to the usual SQL expressions.

Hive also supports computations that go beyond SQL-like languages, for example, machine learning models. For this, Hive provides language constructs that allow users to plug their own transformation scripts into an SQL statement. This is done through the MAP, REDUCE, TRANSFORM, DISTRIBUTE BY, SORT BY, and CLUSTER BY keywords in the SQL extensions. As an example, the Hive program below counts the occurrences of products in an input file.

```
CREATE TABLE Products (Content STRING);
FROM            (MAP Products.Content
                USING 'tokenizerScript' AS ProductID, Count
                FROM Products
                CLUSTER BY ProductID) mapOut
                REDUCE mapOut.ProductID, mapOut.Count
                USING 'countScript' AS ProductID, Count;
```

The scripts tokenizerScript and countScript can be implemented in any language, such as Python or Java. The former produces a tuple for each new product in the input; the latter counts the number of occurrences of each product. The CLUSTER BY clause tells Hive to distribute the Map output (mapOut) to the reducers by hashing on ProductID.

15.2.3 Spark

The MapReduce programming model can be efficiently used for applications that can be expressed as acyclic data flows over large distributed datasets. However, MapReduce is not adequate for dealing with jobs that repeatedly apply a function to the same dataset, as in machine learning algorithms. In such cases, where the MapReduce task must reload the data, the costs become unacceptable. This is also the case in exploratory data analysis when it is done using high-level query languages that are translated into MapReduce (e.g., HiveQL). The Spark cluster computing framework solves this problem, while keeping the other properties of MapReduce, such as scalability and fault tolerance. Spark was initially developed at the University of Berkeley and later became one of the top Apache projects. Spark is written in Scala on top of the Mesos cluster operating system and allows development of libraries for complex algorithms such as machine learning and graph ones. It can run stand alone, or integrated with Hadoop running as an application for YARN.

Unlike Hadoop, Spark works in memory. While Hadoop reads and writes files from and to a storage system such as HDFS, Spark processes data in RAM, based on the notion of **resilient distributed datasets** (RDDs), which are read-only, immutable collections of objects partitioned across a cluster that can be reused in parallel operations. In case of a node failure, RDDs can be rebuilt. If a partition of an RDD is lost, the RDD has the information (typically, how it was derived from other RDDs) to rebuild it. We explain RDDs and provide an example later in this section.

Every Spark application needs an entry point for communicating with data sources and performing certain operations such as reading and writing data. In Spark version 1, three entry points existed: SparkContext, SQLContext, and HiveContext. In Spark version 2, a new entry point called SparkSession has been introduced, which essentially combines all functionalities available in the above. Spark uses a master-slave architecture. The SparkContext is used by the driver process of the Spark application running on a master node. It communicates with a coordinator, called the cluster manager, which manages workers running on worker nodes (the slave nodes), where executors run a set of tasks. Thus, the SparkContext splits a job into tasks performed by the workers. The application code, written by the user, interacts with the driver, creating RDDs and performing a series of transformations leading to the result. These RDD transformations are then translated into a DAG. This logical graph is converted into a physical execution plan containing many stages, each stage containing physical execution units, namely, the tasks. This is then submitted to the scheduler for execution on the worker nodes. The cluster manager then negotiates the resources. Figure 15.4 illustrates these processes.

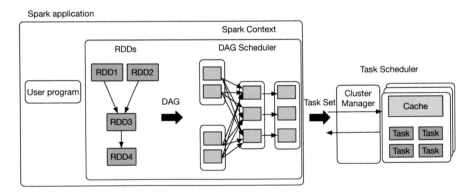

Fig. 15.4 Spark processing scheme

SparkContext also enables access to the other two contexts mentioned above, SQLContext and HiveContext. SQLContext is the entry point to SparkSQL, a Spark module for structured data processing over Datasets and DataFrames, which we explain later in this section. Similarly, HiveContext is used to communicate with Hive. For example, to create a session with Hive support, we would write in Scala:

```
import org.apache.spark.sql.SparkSession;
val spark = SparkSession
        .builder()
```

```
.appName("a name for the application")
.enableHiveSupport()
.getOrCreate();
```

Analogous to Hadoop, the **Spark ecosystem** allows many different applications to be run in a distributed way. This ecosystem is composed of:

- Spark Core: The base engine for large-scale parallel and distributed data processing. It is responsible for memory management and fault recovery, scheduling, distributing and monitoring jobs on a cluster, and interacting with storage systems.
- Spark Streaming: The component of Spark used to process real-time streaming data.
- Spark SQL: Integrates relational processing with Spark's functional programming API. It supports querying data either via SQL or via HiveQL. We give details in Sect. 15.2.3.
- GraphX: The Spark API for graphs and graph-parallel computation. It extends the Spark RDD with a Resilient Distributed Property Graph.
- MLlib: the Machine Learning Library used to perform machine learning in Apache Spark.
- SparkR: An R package that provides a distributed DataFrame implementation. It also supports operations such as selection, filtering, and aggregation on large datasets.

Running Spark Applications

A Spark application (i.e., the Driver program) can run in a cluster coordinated by a SparkContext object, which connects to the cluster. Once the resources for the application are allocated, the worker nodes receive the .jar file (if we are running a Java program) and the SparkContext sends to the nodes the tasks to execute. Finally, the Driver program collects the results. Spark applications can be executed on several different kinds of clusters:

- Local Cluster: There is no distribution of tasks. This is only useful for development environments.
- Standalone Spark Cluster: A Hadoop distribution comes equipped with this cluster. It is composed of a master JobTracker and TaskTrackers running on the workers.
- YARN Cluster, explained before.

The last two cluster types can run in different modes, depending on where the driver runs, namely outside or inside the cluster.

- Client mode: The client launches the driver. Thus, the client process cannot exit until the driver finishes the execution. The driver connects to the cluster via the master node. The master node is in charge of distributing the processing among the workers, since it manages the resources. The task is executed by the workers.

- Cluster mode: the client submits the driver and finishes immediately. The master node chooses one worker node and this node launches the driver. Thus, all the processes run inside the cluster.

In practice, a Spark application in client mode is submitted as follows, assuming that node1 is the coordinator:

```
node1:$ spark-submit --master yarn --deploy-mode client
    --class example.SparkAppMain $HOME/myCode.jar
```

Here, SparkAppMain is the name of the main program, myCode.jar is the file to execute, and example is the name of the software package.

As mentioned above, Spark applications are built upon the notion of RDDs. Spark provides an API for caching, partitioning, transforming, and materializing data. An RDD can be created either from an external storage or from another RDD. The RDD stores information about its parents to optimize execution (via pipelining of operations), and to recompute the partition in case of failure. RDDs provide an interface based on coarse-grained transformations that apply the same operation to many data items. The **operations on RDDs** can be:

- Transformations: Apply a user function to every element in a partition or to the whole partition, apply an aggregate function to the whole dataset (through **GROUP BY** and **SORT BY** operations), and introduce dependencies between RDDs to form the DAG. All transformations receive an RDD and produce another RDD. Some operations are only available on RDDs of key-value pairs. This is true of the join operation. Other operations include map, a one-to-one mapping; flatMap, which maps each input value to one or more outputs (similarly to the map in MapReduce); filter, which keeps the elements in an RDD satisfying a condition; and union.
- Actions: Launch a computation to return a value to the program or write data to external storage. Actions receive an RDD and return values. For example, count() receives an RDD and returns the count of its elements, collect() returns a sequence. Other operations are reduce, lookup, and save. The latter receives an RDD and stores it in HDFS or another storage system.
- Other operations: Provide RDD persistence, by storing RDDs on disk.

A Spark application transforms data into RDDs. To obtain RDDs, two strategies can be followed: parallelizing an existing Java collection in the driver, or reading a file via a SparkContext. That means that we can read data from different sources, but in order to process data in a distributed fashion, we always need to transform data into RDDs, and here is where Spark offers specific methods. We next give an example of a Java program running a Spark application, called SparkAppMain. The application reads a CSV file containing tweets, such that each line contains the tweet identifier, the sentiment, the author, and the content. We want to count the number of tweets that have been categorized as expressing "happiness" or "enthusiasm" by a sentiment analysis process.

```
package example;
import java.util.ArrayList;
import org.apache.spark.SparkConf;
import org.apache.spark.api.java.JavaRDD;
import org.apache.spark.api.java.JavaSparkContext;
import org.apache.spark.api.java.function.Function;
public class SparkAppMain {
    public static void main(String[] args) {
    SparkConf spark = new SparkConf().setAppName("Example");
    JavaSparkContext sparkContext = new JavaSparkContext(spark);
    JavaRDD<String> originalRDD = sparkContext.textFile(args[0]);
    JavaRDD<String> matchingRDD = originalRDD.filter(
        new Function<String, Boolean>() {
        public Boolean call(String v1) throws Exception {
            if (v1.contains("happiness") OR v1.contains("enthusiasm")) {
                System.out.println(v1); return true;
            }
            return false;
        }
    } );
    System.out.println("# of elements = " + originalRDD.count());
    System.out.println("# of happiness or enthusiasm = " + matchingRDD.count());
    sparkContext.close();
    }
}
```

First, the Spark application creates a **SparkContext** handle, and from there on, the methods can be invoked. This handle is used to load the text file into RDDs, using the method textFile(args[0]). The RDD variable is called original-RDD. Then, another transformation operation takes place: filter, creating a new RDD (recall that RDDs are immutable structures) called matchingRDD. Then, an action is invoked to compute the lines satisfying the condition (using an anonymous function). Finally, the number of elements of the RDDs is displayed. Note that each RDD computes its result, and the Driver aggregates the partial results. To execute the application in YARN mode, we would write

```
node1:$ spark-submit --master yarn --deploy-mode cluster
    --class example.SparkAppMain $HOME/myCode.jar file:///$HOME/text_emotion.csv
```

Spark SQL

Spark SQL is a Spark module for structured data processing. For this, Spark SQL uses the concepts of DataFrame and Dataset. Like an RDD, a **DataFrame** is an immutable distributed collection of data. However, unlike an RDD, a DataFrame is organized into named columns, like a table in a relational database. DataFrames allow developers to impose a structure on a distributed collection of data, allowing higher-level abstraction, where syntax errors (such as invoking a function that is not part of the API) are detected at compile time. Finally, **Datasets** are an extension of DataFrames which provide an object-oriented programming interface that enables static-typing and runtime type-safety, where both syntax and analysis errors (such as mismatch of typed-parameters) can be detected at compile time.

Spark SQL provides Spark with more information about the structure of both the data and the computation being performed. This information is used internally to optimize the processing. There are several ways to interact with Spark SQL including SQL and the Dataset API. When computing a result, the same execution engine is used, independent of which API/language is used to express the computation. This enables developers to choose among the different APIs the one that provides the most natural way to express a given transformation.

The DataFrame API can perform relational operations on both external data sources and RDDs. This API is similar to the widely used data frame concept in R. The main, but key difference is that it can perform lazy evaluation of the operations, allowing relational optimization. In addition, Spark SQL introduces an extensible optimizer denoted *Catalyst*, which facilitates adding data sources, optimization rules, and data types for different domains. DataFrames can be created directly from RDDs, enabling relational processing in existing Spark programs. DataFrames make it easy to compute multiple aggregates in one pass using an SQL statement, which is not straightforward in traditional functional APIs. They also automatically store data in a columnar format that is significantly more compact than Java or Python objects. The Catalyst optimizer mentioned above uses features of the Scala programming language such as pattern-matching and allows transforming trees used for query optimization and code generation.

RDDs, like DataFrames, are evaluated lazily, in such a way that we can consider an RDD as a logical plan to compute a dataset. This allows a simple form of query optimization, for example, pipelining, which avoids materializing intermediate results. However, this optimization is limited because the engine does not understand the structure of the data in the RDDs, which are either Java or Python objects, as seen in the example in Sect. 15.2.3. DataFrames are distributed collections of rows with the same schema, similar to a relational database table, and thus can keep track of their schema and support various relational operations that lead to more optimized execution. DataFrames can be constructed from a wide array of sources, such as structured data files, tables in Hive, external databases (e.g., in HDFS), or existing RDDs of native Java or Python objects. They can be manipulated with various relational operators, such as WHERE and GROUP BY. In a sense, a DataFrame can also be viewed as an RDD of row objects, which allows procedural Spark APIs such as map to be called.

For writing Spark SQL applications, the typical entry point into all SQL functionality in Spark is the SparkSession class. For example, a SparkSession handle can be obtained in a Java program as follows:

```
import org.apache.spark.sql.SparkSession;
val spark = SparkSession
        .builder()
        .appName("a name for the application")
        .config("spark.some.config.option", "some-value")
        .getOrCreate();
```

After a SparkSession has been created, applications can create DataFrames. The DataFrame API is available in Scala, Java, Python, and R. For example, a DataFrame obtained from a JSON document is created using the Java API as follows:

```
import org.apache.spark.sql.Dataset;
import org.apache.spark.sql.Row;
Dataset<Row> df = spark.read().json("local/src/main/resources/employee.json");
```

Associated with the DataFrame object df, there are a series of methods that allow it to be manipulated, for example select, filter, groupBy, and many more. In other words, a Spark SQL program can be written over this DataFrame.

Spark SQL can also be run programatically, that is, SQL statements can be passed as arguments to the API. For this, views must be defined. *Temporary views* in Spark SQL are views that are valid within a session. If a view must be shared across several sessions, a *global* temporary view must be created, associated with a system database global_temp. A view can be used as follows.

```
import org.apache.spark.sql.Dataset;
import org.apache.spark.sql.Row;
// Registers the Dataset as an SQL temporary view
df.createOrReplaceTempView("Employee");
Dataset<Row> sqlDF = spark.sql("SELECT * FROM Employee");
sqlDF.show();
```

Two or more DataFrames can be joined. For this, different views must be defined, e.g., with a statement like

```
df.createOrReplaceTempView("Department");
```

Datasets can be created in Java and Scala. They use a specialized encoder to serialize the objects for processing or transmitting over the network. RDDs can be converted into Datasets using two methods. One of them infers the schema, and the other one uses a programmatic interface that allows construction of a schema and its application to an existing RDD.

Parquet files are another popular data source allowed by Spark. Spark SQL provides support for both reading and writing Parquet files that automatically capture the schema of the original data. Columnar storage is efficient for summarizing data, and follows type-specific encoding. RDD data can be easily converted into a Parquet file with a simple statement like DataFrame.write.parquet("myPath"). Analogously, Parquet files are read into Spark SQL using spark.read.parquet("myPath").

Spark SQL allows several optimizations such as caching, join hints, configuration of partition sizes, configuration of partitions when shuffling, among others. Diving into this is outside the scope of this book.

15.2.4 Comparison of Hadoop and Spark

The discussion about Hadoop versus Spark has been going on since Spark first appeared. The two systems are appropriate for different scenarios, and can even work together, as we explain next.

In Sect. 15.2.1, we have seen that Hadoop is written in Java, and Map-Reduce programs can be written on Hadoop using many different programming languages. There is a software ecosystem for performing specialized tasks on Hadoop, including data capturing, transforming, analyzing, and querying. Further, Hadoop is also used for cloud storage, as in the case of Amazon S3 buckets or Azure blobs. Unlike Hadoop, which relies on permanent disk storage, Spark processes data in RAM in a distributed way, using RDDs, DataFrames, or Datasets, and can obtain data from HDFS, S3, or any RDBMs. Further, Spark comes equipped with APIs for executing SQL queries and running machine learning or graph data algorithms, using different programming languages.

Given the characteristics above, reports indicating that Spark runs up to two orders of magnitude faster in memory, and one order of magnitude on disk are not surprising. Obviously, Spark is faster on machine learning applications since MapReduce is not efficient in these cases. Anyway, there are situations where Hadoop may be more efficient than Spark, for example when Spark runs on YARN with other shared services, because of the RAM overhead. For this reason, Hadoop has been found to be more efficient than Spark for batch processing. Also, Hadoop is highly fault-tolerant because of the data replication across many nodes. In Spark, since RDDs reside in memory, data may become corrupted if there is a node or network failure, although in general they can be rebuilt.

Regarding query languages, Hive QL is used to query data stored on HDFS, to avoid writing MapReduce code. Spark SQL, on the other hand, can be used to query data within Spark, although these data could be obtained from different sources, and it is mainly used to query real-time data. Hive QL is typically used with Java programs, while Spark SQL supports APIs for Scala, Java, Python, and R. Since the original goal of Hive has been to provide data warehouse functionality for big data, its main use is to run aggregate queries. However, as we mentioned above, Spark SQL can be used also for querying Hive tables.

Nevertheless, there are many cases where the two systems work together and complement each other. When both batch and stream analysis are needed, Hadoop may be more convenient (because of lower hardware costs), and Spark can be used for real-time processing. Anyway, this is an ongoing debate at the present time.

15.2.5 Kylin

Kylin is an open-source distributed analytics engine initially developed at eBay that later became an Apache project. It provides an SQL interface and OLAP capabilities on Hadoop and Spark over very large datasets. It allows a star or snowflake schema to be defined, materialized cubes stored in HBase (a NoSQL database we study in Sect. 15.6) to be built, and data cubes to be queried with HiveQL or third-party tools, via ODBC, JDBC or a RESTful API. Kylin implements well-known logical and physical design concepts studied in this book, as well as many of the technologies studied in this chapter, as we explain next.

The classic OLAP tools studied so far in this book do not suffice to cope with situations where the size of the data grows exponentially, like in typical big data scenarios. In such situations, distributed and scalable storage and processing technologies must be considered, since otherwise, the latency of interactive OLAP queries would become unacceptable. However, at the time of writing this book, a mature SQL interface for Hadoop is still needed, and OLAP capabilities on the Hadoop ecosystem are limited. Performing OLAP in big data scenarios requires extremely low query latency on large data warehouses, standard SQL, integration with BI Tools, support for high cardinality and dimensionality, high concurrency capability, and a distributed architecture for large data volumes. Thus, providing OLAP on Hadoop is not a trivial task since Hadoop lacks many of those characteristics.

In Kylin, the user must first define a logical relational schema, either star or snowflake, as studied in Chap. 5. This schema is stored in Hive tables, typically in **ORC** format, which is an efficient columnar format for storing Hive data. The base data cube is built from these Hive tables. As studied in Chap. 8, materialized views are crucial to deliver efficient OLAP. Kylin applies this concept for materializing the cubes in the data cube lattice (as explained in Sect. 8.4), storing them in HFiles, the underlying file structure in HBase (see Sect. 15.6). Kylin provides ways to avoid materializing all the cubes in the lattice, through a mechanism called **aggregation groups**. Initially, cubes were computed from Hive using MapReduce. This was later replaced by Spark. For clarity, we first explain the concept using MapReduce and then using Spark. As an example, consider a **Sales** cube with three dimensions, namely **Product**, **Customer**, and **Supplier**, and one measure. Figure 15.5 shows two records in this cube, along with two tables containing all possi-

ble aggregations for these two records. For example, (p1,c1,*) contributes to
the aggregation by **Product** and **Customer**. The second table from the left
shows the shuffling that MapReduce computes for the same keys. Finally, the
aggregation is computed. The key-value pairs are then stored in HBase in
columnar format.

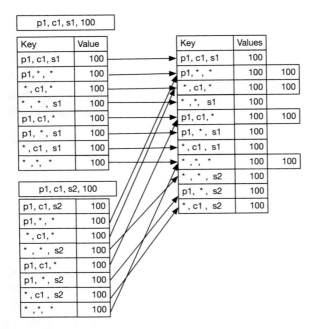

Fig. 15.5 Data cube computation with MapReduce

Kylin also supports Apache Spark for building the data cube. Here, RDDs
are at the cornerstone of data cube computation. These RDDs have a parent-
child relationship between them, as the parent RDD can be used to generate
the children RDDs. With the parent RDD cached in memory, the child RDD's
generation can be more efficient than reading from disk. Figure 15.6 describes
this process.

In summary, Kylin allows three abstraction levels of the OLAP model to
be defined. The end user works at the logical level with the star/snowflake
schema. The cube modeler is aware of the data cubes built from the logical
model and knows the cubes that are materialized. Finally, at the physical
level, the administrator takes care of the (distributed) storage in HBase.

From the technological side, the Kylin stack is composed as follows. The
logical model is stored in Hive files over Hadoop. The cubes are computed
with MapReduce or Spark and stored in HBase. Therefore, a Kylin installation requires, at least, Hadoop, YARN, Zookeeper, and HBase. In addition,
since typically a data warehouse is obtained from a relational database, Sqoop

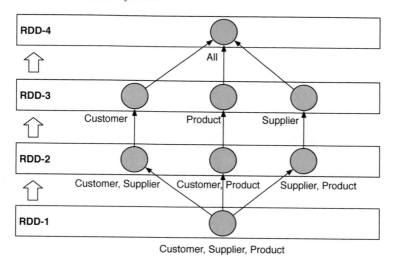

Fig. 15.6 Data cube computation with Spark

is normally used to import data from an RDBMS into Hive. Figure 15.7 depicts the Kylin architecture. Queries are submitted via third-party applications, the Kylin web interface, or via JDBC/ODBC from BI tools, such as Tableau or Saiku. Therefore, queries can be written in SQL or MDX, though they are finally submitted via SQL. SQL is handled by **Apache Calcite**, an open-source framework for building databases and DBMSs, which includes an SQL parser, an API for building expressions in relational algebra, and a query planning engine. An SQL query is handled as follows: If the query matches one of the materialized cubes, it is sent by the routing tool to the HBase repository where the cubes are stored as HFiles, thus achieving low latency. Otherwise, they are evaluated by the Hive server, which will obviously take much longer to execute.

15.3 Distributed Database Systems

A *distributed computing system* is a system made of a number of autonomous nodes (composed of processors, memory, and disks) connected by a network. These systems can be of two kinds. In *tightly coupled* systems the nodes have shared memory, as in the case of multicore processors, while in *loosely coupled* systems each node has its own memory, as in computer clusters. The distinction between distributed and *parallel* computing systems is rather vague. The main difference is that parallel computing allows multiple processors to execute tasks simultaneously while distributed computing divides a single task

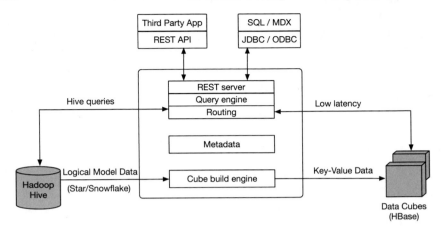

Fig. 15.7 Kylin architecture

between multiple computers. In the following, we refer to both systems as distributed, referring to parallel computing when needed.

Distributed database systems have been studied for decades by the database community and are currently used to process large data volumes in mixed OLTP and OLAP workloads. Most of the research on distributed database systems has been done in the context of the relational model because it provides a good basis for distributed data processing. Data distribution enhances performance by means of parallelism and availability through data replication. There are three kinds of architectures for distributed database systems: *shared memory*, *shared disk*, and *shared nothing*. In the remainder we focus on the last architecture, since it is the one adopted by most of the database systems studied in this chapter. In a **shared-nothing architecture**, each processor in a cluster of commodity servers has exclusive access to its main memory and disk and operates its own database and software.

As we have seen in Chap. 8, **partitioning** is the technique of distributing data across multiple tables, disks, or sites in order to improve query processing performance or increase database manageability. Once partitioning is performed, partitions must be allocated to nodes in a cluster. Due to the large volumes involved, query execution must be performed locally when possible. Therefore, data allocation must aim at distributing data uniformly since this is critical for performance. The degree of partitioning, i.e., the number of nodes over which a relation is partitioned, should be a function of the size of the relation and the access frequency. Thus, increasing the degree of partitioning may result in data reorganization. For example, if a relation initially allocated across eight nodes doubles its size, ideally it should be allocated across sixteen nodes. However, the complexity of this depends on the partitioning technique used. This can be easy with range partitioning, but becomes harder with hash partitioning, since it may require use of a different hash function on an attribute different from the initial one.

Parallel algorithms for efficient query processing are designed to take advantage of data partitioning. This requires a trade-off between parallelism and communication costs. Since not all operations in a program can be parallelized, algorithms for relational algebra operators aim at maximizing the degree of parallelism. For example, highly sequential algorithms, such as Quicksort, are not good for parallelization. On the other hand, the sort-merge algorithm is appropriate for parallel execution, and thus it is normally used in shared-nothing architectures.

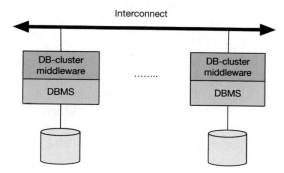

Fig. 15.8 Cluster database architecture

A **database cluster** is a cluster of autonomous databases in a shared-nothing architecture, each managed by an off-the-shelf DBMS. Parallel data management is implemented via middleware, as depicted in Fig. 15.8. This middleware takes care of transaction processing, load balancing, replication, query processing, and fault tolerance. In a database cluster, parallel query processing can be used to achieve high performance.

Sharding consists in distributing data across multiple machines, where each partition is referred to as a *shard*. We discuss later how sharding is accomplished in different database systems.

Distribution and data partitioning are used to achieve scalability in NoSQL database systems (studied in Sect. 15.6). However, database systems usually have other requirements, such as consistency and availability. Consider a database that stores a data item replicated in several nodes, and at some point there is an error in the network. When an update is submitted to one of the nodes where the data item is stored, it may not be possible to update all the replicas immediately, leaving the database in an inconsistent state. In this case, we must choose between availability and consistency.

The above situation is captured by the **CAP theorem**, which states that any distributed data store can only provide two of the following three guarantees: Consistency, Availability, and Partition tolerance. Consistency refers to strong consistency of updates, meaning that simultaneous reads of the same data item from different nodes must return the same result. Availability guarantees that every request receives a response whether it succeeded or failed when retrieving data. Finally, partition tolerance implies that the system continues to operate despite arbitrary message loss or failure of a part of it. Therefore, distributed systems are classified as CA, ensuring consistency and availability (which is the case of classic relational database systems), CP, where consistency is guaranteed under partitioning, and PA, which does not guarantee consistency, but availability instead.

We describe next two representative distributed database systems, MySQL Cluster and Citus.

15.3.1 MySQL Cluster

MySQL Cluster is a distributed database that aims at providing linear scalability and high availability. Being an in-memory database (explained in Sect. 15.4 below), it allows efficient real-time access. MySQL Cluster is designed to run on a shared-nothing architecture on commodity hardware and also in the cloud (see Sect. 15.11). MySQL provides a wide array of APIs that allow concurrent access to different data models. These include APIs for relational SQL, key-value NoSQL databases, HTTP/REST, Java, and C++, among others.

MySQL Cluster integrates the standard MySQL server with a clustered storage engine called **NDB** (standing for Network Database). The difference between MySQL and MySQL Cluster is as follows: The standard MySQL database engine is called InnoDB. When the standard MySQL updates one or more replicas, transactions are committed sequentially, which means a transaction is replicated after it has been committed. This can be a slow process; therefore, in case of a failure the replica may abort transactions already committed in other nodes (because InnoDB is ACID compliant). As a consequence, the node where the transaction was executed and committed and the node storing a replica will not contain the same data. In other words, standard MySQL replication is *asynchronous*, and therefore consistency is not guaranteed. In MySQL Cluster running the NDB engine, all nodes are *synchronously* updated, because a transaction committed in one node of the cluster (the source node), is committed in all other nodes. If there is a node failure, all nodes remain in a consistent state, since NDB takes care of this. Note that *asynchronous replication* may occur if we have two MySQL Clusters connected by a network. In this case, consistency between nodes in both clusters is not guaranteed.

In MySQL Cluster architectures, tables are automatically sharded across the nodes, which allows horizontal scaling. Also, nodes can be added online as needed for scalability. This **automatic sharding** is transparent to the application, which can connect to any node in the cluster and then queries will automatically access the right shard(s). While queries are processed in parallel, join and filter operations are executed locally on the partitions and data nodes. A mechanism called *Adaptive Query Localization* (AQL) allows joins to be distributed across the data nodes, enhancing local computation and reducing the number of messages being passed around the system. In other words, joins are pushed down to the data nodes.

A typical MySQL Cluster architecture has three layers: the client, the application, and the data layer. The core of the architecture is the data layer, which is composed of two kinds of nodes: data nodes and management nodes. The application layer is composed of application nodes, which receive the clients' requests and pass them on to the data nodes.

Data nodes are organized in groups. There can be more than one data node per physical server, and a set of physical servers compose a cluster. The data nodes receive read and write requests from the clients and also take care of several tasks in the cluster as follows:

- Storage and management of both in-memory and disk-based data. MySQL can store all data in memory or some of these data can be stored on disk. However, *only non-indexed data can be stored on disk*, indexed columns must always be in memory.
- Automatic and user-defined sharding of tables.
- Synchronous replication of data between data nodes.
- Transactions, data retrieval, recovery, and rollback to a consistent state.

Management nodes provide services for the cluster as a whole. They are responsible for publishing the cluster configuration to all nodes in the cluster and also for startup, shutdown, and backups. They are also used when a node wants to join the cluster and when there is a system reconfiguration. Management nodes can be stopped and restarted without affecting the ongoing execution of the other kinds of nodes. Note that there can be more than one management node per cluster, and they are defined in a configuration file.

Application nodes, also called *SQL nodes*, compose the application layer and are instances of MySQL Server that connect to all of the data nodes for data storage and retrieval and support the NDB Cluster storage engine. Thus, MySQL Server is used to provide an SQL interface to the cluster. Data nodes can also be queried using any of the APIs mentioned at the beginning of this section. All application nodes can access all data nodes. Therefore if a data node fails applications can simply use the remaining nodes.

In-memory data are regularly saved to disk for recovery, performing checkpoints (this is coordinated for all the data nodes). Data can be stored on disk when the data set is bigger than the available RAM and has less-strict performance requirements. Again, this is similar to other in-memory systems that are studied in Sect. 15.4. These in-memory optimized tables provide the ability to serve *real-time workloads with low latency*, one of the main features of MySQL Cluster. However, note that for large databases the hardware and memory requirements can become important. It is recommended to keep for each data node a disk space that should be about five times the amount of data memory. This space is needed for storing local checkpoints, the redo log and three backups. A rough estimation of the required RAM memory suggested by the vendor is given by the expression (Size of database × Number of replicas × 1.1)/Number of data nodes.

Replication aims at providing availability under a network failure between database nodes or a failure of the database nodes themselves. Under a failure event, a network may become partitioned. In this case, the nodes in a partition may remain isolated from the network, unable to know the status of a node in another network partition. That is, a node may not know whether the other nodes are dead, alive and isolated from clients, or reachable by clients. Note that in the last case, a node could be updated without other nodes knowing this, and consistency would be lost. MySQL supports fully replicated tables, normally of small size, that can be used for static lookup tables, for instance tables containing provinces, categories, and so on. This means that the entire table is replicated in every data node. This is similar to what in Citus (see below) are called reference tables.

In light of the above, we now analyze MySQL Cluster with respect to the CAP theorem. For this, we need to consider that there are different possible cluster configurations. In the case of a *single* MySQL Cluster data are, as mentioned above, synchronously replicated between data nodes using the two-phase commit protocol. In this case, MySQL Cluster prioritizes data consistency over availability under network partitions since, when a network partition occurs, the nodes that are still alive in each partition regroup and decide either to *shutdown* or continue serving data. Therefore, with respect to the CAP theorem stated above, a single MySQL Cluster is a *CP database system*. When the configuration has two clusters connected through a network and replicated asynchronously, and a partition of the network between the two clusters occurs, reads and writes can still be performed locally at both clusters, and data consistency within each cluster is guaranteed, but *data consistency across the two clusters is not*. However, *availability* is preserved, since each cluster can still accept requests to all of the data from any connected client. In this case, MySQL Cluster prioritizes service availability over data consistency, and the pair of MySQL clusters is an *AP database system* with respect to the CAP theorem.

In spite of the features of MySQL Cluster and the NDB engine, it still has certain drawbacks and limitations. First, it does not support the full SQL standard. For example, temporary tables are not allowed and indexes on BLOBS and text data are not supported either, nor are fulltext and geospatial indexes. However, geospatial data are supported. Second, memory consumed when data is inserted into a table is not automatically recovered when these data are deleted. There is also a limit in the number of data nodes. Third, regarding ACID transactions, only the transaction isolation level **read committed** is supported, while the standard MySQL InnoDB engine supports up to the serializable level. Further, no partial rollbacks of transactions are supported.

We now briefly comment on two alternatives to MySQL Cluster, based on the MySQL database system, namely Vitess and XtraDB Cluster.

Vitess is a popular implementation of a distributed database based on MySQL, with the same idea as the NDB-based MySQL Cluster engine, that is, to build a middleware to allow automatic sharding of data across nodes. Basically, Vitess is composed of a collection of proxy servers (that can dynamically grow according with the requirements) called *vtgates*, to which the users' applications connect. When a query is submitted to the database, the vtgate is responsible for deciding where to route it. Also, if a vtgate fails, the applications connected to it connects through the load balancer to another vtgate. The information of the system is kept in a *lock server*, which is a third-party tool, typically Zookeeper (mentioned in Sect 15.2.1). The other components of Vitess' architecture are the *vttablets*, which lie between the vtgates and the MySQL instances. Queries are sent from the vtgates to the vttablets, which analyze them, and, if necessary, kill a query. Finally, the *vtctld* is a dashboard where the network topology can be monitored.

Compared with MySQL Cluster studied above, Vitess is particularly appropriate for larger loads of data writes while the former (being an in-memory database) provides good real-time read performance. However, many basic database functionalities are lacking in Vitess, such as user-friendly interfaces to monitor the database load and, importantly, better support for automated failover management. To override the above, Vitess can be integrated with third-party tools. Also, since Vitess is not focused on ACID transactions but on scalability, compared to MySQL Cluster, the latter offers better support for high availability.

XtraDB Cluster is another distributed database option. It is based on the XtraDB database system, which is san extension of the InnoDB engine. Over this database a middleware is built. Also the standard MySQL is supported by XtraDB Cluster. In XtraDB Cluster all nodes have the same consistent data, which is achieved by a synchronous replication software. Given that in this architecture all nodes must have the same data, XtraDB Cluster is more appropriate to read workloads but not for scaling heavy write loads.

15.3.2 Citus

Citus is an extension to PostgreSQL that distributes data and queries across nodes in a cluster of commodity machines. Citus horizontally scales PostgreSQL using **sharding** and **replication**. Its query engine parallelizes incoming SQL queries across these servers to enable real-time responses on large datasets. However, this also allows OLAP queries to be run in parallel.

In a Citus cluster, the nodes are database servers organized in a shared-nothing architecture. This architecture allows the database to scale horizontally by just adding nodes to the cluster. Every cluster has one distinguished node called the **coordinator**, while the others are called **workers**, as usual. The coordinator is equipped with a distributed PostgreSQL engine that rewrites SQL queries and routes these queries to the shards on the worker nodes. Applications send their queries to the coordinator. For each query, the coordinator either sends it to a single worker node, or parallelizes it across several ones depending on where the required data are stored. For this, the coordinator queries the Citus metadata tables.

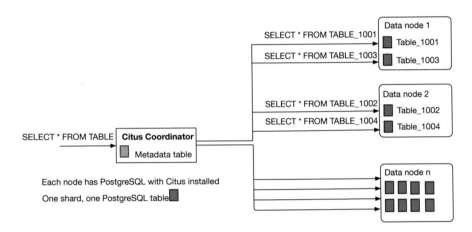

Fig. 15.9 Citus architecture

There are three types of tables in a cluster, each used for different purposes.

- **Distributed tables**, which are horizontally partitioned across worker nodes. Citus uses algorithmic sharding to assign rows to shards. This assignment is made based on the value of a particular table column called the **distribution column**. The cluster administrator must designate this column when distributing a table. Figure 15.9 shows an example of this partitioning.
- **Reference tables**, which are replicated on every worker. Thus, queries on any worker can access the reference information locally, without the network overhead of requesting rows from another node. Reference tables are typically small, and are used to store data that is relevant to queries running on any worker node. Examples are enumerated values such as product categories or customer types.
- **Local tables**, which are traditional tables that are not distributed. This is useful for small tables that do not participate in join queries.

Since Citus uses the distribution column to assign table rows to shards, choosing the best distribution column for each table is crucial to put related data together on the same physical nodes, even across different tables. This is called *data co-location*. As long as the distribution column provides a meaningful grouping of data, relational operations can be performed within the groups. In Citus, a row is stored in a shard if the hash of the value in the distribution column falls within the shard's hash range. To ensure co-location, shards with the same hash range are always placed on the same node. As an example, consider the Northwind data warehouse, shown in Fig. 5.4. The Employee table can be defined as a reference table, as follows:

```
SELECT create_reference_table('Employee');
```

The fact table Sales can be defined as a distributed table with distribution column CustomerKey.

```
SELECT create_distributed_table('Sales', 'CustomerKey');
```

That means that, for example, if the Customer table is also partitioned using the CustomerKey attribute, it will be co-located, and thus efficiently joined, with the Sales table.

The pg_dist_shard metadata table on the coordinator node contains a row for each shard of each distributed table in the system. This row matches a shardid with a range of integers in a hash space (shardminvalue, shardmaxvalue). If the coordinator node wants to determine which shard holds a row of a given table, it hashes the value of the distribution column in the row, and checks which shard's range contains the hashed value.

Citus uses a two-stage optimizer when planning SQL queries. The first phase involves transforming the queries so that query fragments can be pushed down and run on the workers in parallel. The distributed query planner applies several optimizations to the queries depending on the distribution column and distribution method. The query fragments are then sent to the workers to start the second phase of query optimization. The workers simply apply PostgreSQL's standard planning and execution algorithms to run the SQL query fragment. Explaining query processing in Citus in more detail is outside the scope of this chapter.

15.4 In-Memory Database Systems

An **in-memory database system** (IMDBS) is a DBMS that stores data in main memory, as opposed to traditional database systems, which store data on persistent media such as hard disks. Because working with data in memory is much faster than writing to and reading from a file system, IMDBSs can run applications orders of magnitude faster. IMDBSs come in many flavors: They can be DBMSs that only use main memory to load and execute real-time analytics, they can be used as a cache for disk-based DBMSs, or they can be commercialized as software-hardware licensed packages, called *appliances*, particularly for BI applications. In most cases, they are combined with column-store technology (discussed in Sect. 15.5), given the compression rate that the latter achieves.

The typical way in which traditional DBMSs operate is based on reading data from disk to buffer pages located in main memory. When a query is submitted, data are first fetched into these buffers, and, if not found, new data are loaded from disk into main memory. If there is an update, the modified page is marked and written back to disk. The process where disk-based databases keep frequently accessed records in memory for faster access is called *caching*. Note, however, that caching only speeds up database reads, while updates or writes must still be written from the cache to disk. Therefore, the performance benefit only applies to a subset of database tasks. In addition, managing the cache is itself a process that requires substantial memory and CPU resources. An IMDBS reduces to a minimum these data transfers, since data are mainly in memory. It follows that the optimization objectives of disk-based database systems are opposed to those of an IMDBS. Traditional DBMSs try to minimize input/output using the cache, consuming CPU cycles to maintain this cache. In addition, they keep redundant data, for example in index structures, to enable direct access to records without the need to go down to the actual data. On the contrary, an IMDBS is designed with the optimization goal of reducing both memory consumption and CPU cycles.

Traditional relational DBMSs enable the safe sharing of data through transactions, which ensure the **ACID properties**, standing for Atomicity, Consistency, Isolation, and Durability. IMDBSs support the first three as in traditional DBMSs. Since the main memory is volatile, durability is supported by transaction logging, in which snapshots of the database are stored periodically at certain time instants (referred to as **savepoints** or **checkpoints**) and are written to nonvolatile media. If the system fails and must be restarted, the database either rolls back to the last completed transaction or rolls forward to complete any transaction that was in progress when the system failed. IMDBSs also support durability by **replication**, maintaining one or more copies of the database. Nonvolatile RAM provides another means of in-memory database persistence.

Finally, disk-based storage can be applied selectively in an IMDBS. For example, certain record types can be written to disk, while others are managed entirely in memory. Functions specific for disk-based databases, such as cache management, are applied only to records stored on disk, minimizing the impact of these activities over performance and CPU demands.

Figure 15.10 depicts the typical data storage architecture of an IMDBS.[1] The database is stored in main memory, and it is composed of three main parts. The main store contains data stored in a column-oriented fashion. For query optimization reasons, some systems also store together groups of columns that are usually accessed together. These are called combined

---

[1] This figure is inspired by the SAP HANA architecture (Sect. 15.7.2), although most IMDBSs follow a similar architecture.

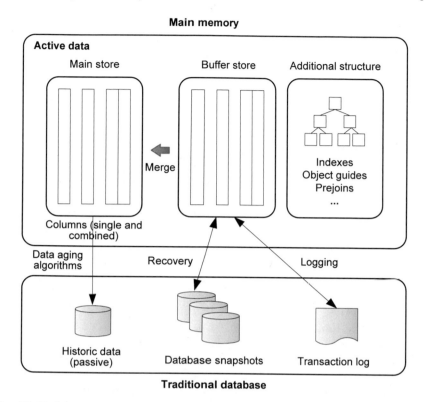

Fig. 15.10 A typical in-memory database system architecture

columns. The buffer store is a write-optimized data structure that holds data that have not yet been moved to the main store. This means that a query can need data from both the main store and the buffer. The special data structure of the buffer normally requires more space per record than the main store. Thus, data are periodically moved from the buffer to the main store, a process that requires a merge operation. There are also data structures used to support special features. An example is inverted indexes for fast retrieval of low-cardinality data.

Finally, although data in the database are stored in main memory, to save memory space, IMDBSs also store data persistently. This is done as follows. The most recent data are kept in main memory, since these are the data most likely to be accessed and/or updated. These data are called **active**. By contrast, passive data are data not currently used by a business process, used mostly for analytical purposes. Passive data are stored on nonvolatile memory, even using traditional DBMSs. This supports so-called time-travel queries, which allow the status of the database as of a certain point in time to be known. Data partition between active and passive data is performed by **data aging** algorithms. Nonvolatile memory is also used to guarantee consistency and recovery under failure: Data updates are written in a log file, and database snapshots are kept in nonvolatile memory, to be read in case of failure. This combination of main and nonvolatile memory allows IMDBSs to support OLTP transactions and OLAP analysis at the same time, which is the basis of HTAP systems (see Sect. 15.9).

15.4.1 Oracle TimesTen

Oracle TimesTen is an in-memory RDBMS that also supports transaction processing. TimesTen stores all its data in optimized data structures in memory, and includes query algorithms designed for in-memory processing. TimesTen is mainly used for OLTP transactions that require very low latency. It can be used as a stand-alone RDBMS or as an application-tier cache that works together with traditional disk-based RDBMSs, for example, the Oracle database itself: Existing applications over an Oracle database can use TimesTen to cache a subset of the data to improve response time. Thus, read and write operations can be performed on the cache tables using SQL and PL/SQL with automatic persistence, transactional consistency, and synchronization with the Oracle database.

Unlike in traditional DBMSs, where query optimizers are based on disk input/output costs, namely, the number of disk accesses, the cost function of the TimesTen optimizer is based on the cost of evaluating predicates. TimesTen's cache provides range, hash, and bitmap indexes, and supports typical join algorithms such as nested-loop join and merge-join. Also, the optimizer can create temporary indexes as needed, and accepts hints from the user, as in traditional databases.

Two key features of the TimesTen **data storage architecture** are the in-memory database cache and the data aging algorithms. The *in-memory database cache* (IMDB cache) creates a real-time updatable cache where a subset of the tables are loaded. For instance, in the Northwind database, the cache can be used to store recent orders, while data about customers can be stored in a traditional Oracle database. Thus, information that requires real-time access is stored in the IMDB cache while information needed for longer-term analysis, auditing, and archiving is stored in the Oracle database. This is analogous to the general architecture depicted in Fig. 15.10. Moreover, the scenario above can be distributed. For example, a company may have a centralized Oracle database and many applications running at several application server nodes in various countries. To perform analysis of orders and sales in near real time, we may install an IMDB cache database at each node. On the other hand, the customer profiles do not need to be stored at every node. When a node addresses a sales order, the customer's profile is uploaded from the most up-to-date location, which could be either a node, or the central database. When the transaction is finished, the customer's profile is updated and stored back into the central database. The IMDB cache can also be used as a read-only cache, for example, to provide fast access to auxiliary data structures, such as look-up tables. **Data aging** is an operation that removes data that are no longer needed. There are two kinds of data aging algorithms: ones that remove old data based on a timestamp value, and ones that remove the least recently used data.

Like the other systems described in this chapter, TimesTen uses **compression** of tables at the column level. This mechanism provides space reduction for tables by eliminating duplicate values within columns, improving the performance of SQL queries that must perform full table scans.

Finally, TimesTen achieves **durability** through transaction logging over a disk-based version of the database. TimesTen maintains the disk-based version using a **checkpoint** operation that occurs in the background, with low impact on database applications. TimesTen also has a blocking checkpoint that does not require transaction log files for recovery and must be initiated by the application. TimesTen uses the transaction log to recover transactions under failure, undo transactions that are rolled back, replicate changes to other TimesTen databases and/or to Oracle tables, and enable applications to detect changes to tables.

Oracle commercializes an appliance called **Oracle Exalytics In-Memory Machine**, which is similar to the SAP HANA appliance (Sect. 15.7.2). Exalytics is composed of hardware, BI software, and an Oracle TimesTen IMDBS. The hardware consists of a single server configured for in-memory analytics of business intelligence workloads. Exalytics comes with the Oracle BI Foundation Suite and Essbase, a multidimensional OLAP server enhanced with a more powerful MDX syntax and a high-performance MDX query engine. Oracle Exalytics complements the Oracle Exadata Database Machine, which supports high performance for both OLAP and OLTP applications.

15.4.2 Redis

Redis is a key-value (see Sect. 15.6 for details) in-memory storage system. It enables data to be stored across nodes over a network and also supports **replication**. Multiple machines provide data storage services together. These are called *master nodes*. Each master node is responsible for storing parts of the data. Different clients can visit these nodes independently, and read and write data. To ensure data safety, there is at least one *slave node* for each master node to replicate data, so when the master is down, the slave node can replace it to restore the service.

Since Redis is a key-value storage system, the main problem is the assignment of keys to nodes. Redis uses a key-slot-node mapping strategy to maintain the data distribution status. To map keys to nodes, there is first a hash stage, where, for a given key, Redis calculates its hash value. All hash

values are evenly assigned to slots and there are 16,382 slots in total. In a
second stage, called the slot mapping stage, the corresponding slot is assigned
to a key based on its hash value. All slots can be dynamically assigned to
different nodes. In this case, if any node is under heavy workload, some parts
can be moved from their slots to other nodes or new nodes can even be created. Thus, in a third stage, the corresponding node of the given key is found
based on the slot-node mapping status. In summary, given a key, it is hashed,
a slot is found, and, finally, the key is assigned to a node.

   We have seen that in clustered systems such as Hadoop, important information (e.g., number of nodes, their IP addresses and port numbers, current
status) is stored on a central node of the cluster, to simplify the design of the
distributed system, at the cost of creating a single point of failure. To avoid
this, Redis uses a fully decentralized design, which uses the *Gossip protocol*
to maintain this information on all nodes. All nodes in the system are fully
connected and know the current state of the system. Every time the system's
status changes, this new info is propagated to every node. Nodes will also
randomly send PING messages to other nodes and expect to receive PONG
messages to prove that the cluster is working correctly. If any node is found
to be not working properly, all other nodes will participate in a vote to use
a slave node to replace the crashed master node. With this design, clients
can connect to any master node which, upon reception of a key-value request
from a client, checks whether this key belongs to this node using the key-
slot-node mapping. If so, it processes the request and returns the results to
the client. Otherwise, it returns an error containing the right node for this
request, so the client knows which node it should send the request to.

   Redis uses two mechanisms for data protection: **persistence** and **replication**. The so-called RDB (Redis DB) persistence periodically performs
snapshots of the data in memory and writes the compressed file on disk. Alternatively, the AOF (Append Only File) persistence mechanism logs every
write operation received by the server. To restore the service, these operations are processed again. Data replication is more efficient than persistence,
since, when data is replicated on different nodes, upon a crash, the service
can be restored very fast, replacing the master node with the slave node. On
the other hand, for data persistence it takes longer to read data from disk.

15.5 Column-Store Database Systems

Typically, in relational DBMS architectures data are stored in a record-
oriented fashion, where attributes of a record are placed contiguously in disk
pages. Thus, a disk page contains a certain number of database tuples, which
at the moment of being queried are accessed either sequentially or through
some of the indexes studiesd in Chap. 8. These architectures are appropriate
for OLTP systems. For systems oriented to ad hoc querying large amounts of

data (as in OLAP), other structures can do better. This is true of **column-store database systems**, where the values for each column (or attribute) are stored contiguously on disk pages, such that a disk page contains a number of database columns, and thus, a database record is scattered across many different disk pages. We study this architecture next.

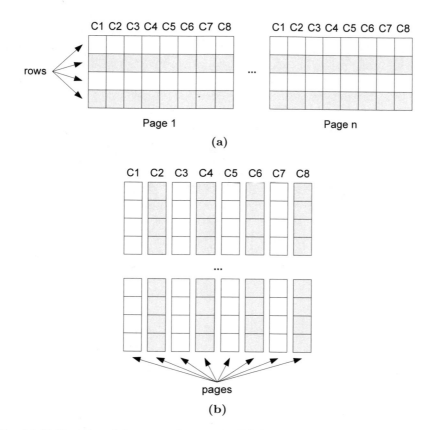

Fig. 15.11 Row-store (a) versus column-store (b) database systems

Figure 15.11a shows the row-store organization, where records are stored in disk pages, while Fig. 15.11b shows the column-store alternative. In most systems, a page contains a single column. However, if a column does not fit in a page, it is stored in as many pages as needed. When evaluating a query over a column-store architecture, a DBMS just needs to read the values of the columns involved in the query, thus avoiding loading into memory irrelevant attributes. For example, consider a typical query over the Northwind data warehouse:

```
SELECT    CustomerName, SUM(SalesAmount)
FROM      Sales S, Customer C, Product P, Date D, Employee E
```

WHERE   S.CustomerKey = C.CustomerKey AND
            S.ProductKey = P.ProductKey AND S.DateKey = D.DateKey AND
            S.EmployeeKey = E.EmployeeKey AND
            P.Discontinued = 'Yes' AND D.Year = '2012' AND E.City = 'Berlin'
GROUP BY C.CustomerName

Depending on the query evaluation strategy, the query above may require all columns of all the tables in the FROM clause to be accessed, totaling 51 columns. The number of columns can increase considerably in a real-world enterprise data warehouse. However, only 12 of them are actually needed to evaluate this query. Therefore, a row-oriented DBMS will read into main memory a large number of columns that do not contribute to the result and which will probably be pruned by a query optimizer. As opposed to this, a column-store database system will just look for the pages containing the columns actually used in the query. Further, it is likely that the values for E.City, T.Year, and P.Discontinued will fit in main memory.

RowId	EmployeeKey	CustomerKey	ProductKey	⋯
1	e1	c1	p1	⋯
2	e1	c1	p4	⋯
3	e1	c2	p4	⋯
4	e1	c2	p4	⋯
5	e1	c2	p4	⋯
6	e2	c2	p5	⋯
7	e2	c2	p5	⋯
8	e2	c2	p1	⋯
9	e3	c3	p2	⋯
10	e3	c3	p2	⋯
⋯	⋯	⋯	⋯	⋯

(a)

f	v	l
1	e1	5
6	e2	3
9	e3	2
...	...	...
...	...	...
...	...	...

(b)

f	v	l
1	c1	2
3	c2	6
9	c3	2
...	...	...
...	...	...
...	...	...

(c)

f	v	l
1	p1	1
2	p4	4
6	p5	2
8	p1	1
9	p2	2
...	...	...

(d)

Fig. 15.12 Storing columns of the Sales fact table: one table per column. (a) Fact table Sales; (b) Column EmployeeKey; (c) Column CustomerKey; (d) Column ProductKey

To save space, column-store database systems normally store columns in pages in a compressed form. For example, consider the portion of the Sales fact table shown in Fig. 15.12a. Figures 15.12b–d show a possible encoding scheme for the columns EmployeeKey, CustomerKey, and ProductKey, respectively. **Compression** is based on run-length encoding, already discussed in Chap. 8. For example, Fig. 15.12b shows a three-column table, with attributes f, v, and l, where f indicates the first of l consecutive records with value v. For instance, the first row in Fig. 15.12b says that in column EmployeeKey there is a run of length five that starts in the first position and whose value is e1. Analogously, the next record says that there are three e2 in positions 6–8. Over this scheme, we want to evaluate the following query.

SELECT ProductKey, CustomerKey
FROM   Sales

We can perform a variation of a sort-merge join which just accesses the pages containing the required columns. Thus, we set two cursors at the beginning of the partitions for ProductKey and CustomerKey. The first runs of values of these attributes have lengths one and two, respectively. Thus, the first pair (p1, c1) is produced. We advance the cursors. Now the cursor for ProductKey is at the first position of the second run, and the cursor CustomerKey is at the second position of the first run; thus, we build the second tuple, (p4, c1). The run for CustomerKey = c1, is finished so when we advance this cursor it positions at the beginning of a run of length six with the value c2; the cursor over ProductKey is at the second position of a run of length four with the value p4. Therefore, we will now retrieve three tuples of the form (p4, c2). We continue in this fashion. Note that once the column stores are sorted, this join between columns can be done in linear time.

15.5.1 Vertica

Vertica is a distributed massively parallel relational DBMS, based on the C-Store research project. Although Vertica supports the SQL operations IN-SERT, UPDATE, and DELETE , it is mainly designed to support analytical workloads. Vertica has a hybrid in-memory/on-disk architecture. This is the main difference from our general architecture in Fig. 15.10, where the main and buffer stores reside in memory and only passive data are stored on disk. Vertica groups data on disk by column rather than by row, with the advantages already mentioned for analytical queries. Further, data are compressed using different techniques, not only run-length encoding.

From a logical view, a schema in Vertica consists of objects such as tables, constraints, and views. This is why Vertica qualifies as a relational columnar DBMS rather than a NoSQL database, like HBase or Cassandra (which we will see in Sect. 15.6). Physically, Vertica organizes data into sorted subsets of the attributes of a table. These are called **projections**. Normally, there is one large projection called a super projection (which contains every column in the table) and many small projections. Note that this can be considered analogous to the combined columns in Fig. 15.10. In a distributed architecture, projections are distributed and replicated across the nodes in a cluster. Data are replicated using the notion of K-safety, where K is the number of times the data in the database cluster is replicated. Values for K range between zero and two. For example, if K=1, if Vertica loses a node, it will still run. Vertica also supports prejoin projections, although it has been reported that actually they are not frequently used. Figure 15.13 shows a schema of the above. There is the relational view of a portion of the Northwind Sales fact table, at the logical level. This is physically stored in columnar format, so it can be then split into several partitions which duplicate data to be able to give fast answers to different queries. For example, a SalesCustomer projection might be stored sorted on CustomerId to efficiently answer the query "Total product sales by customer", while the SalesPrice projection could be sorted on OrderDate and ProductId to answer the query "Total daily sales by product." To save space, data are encoded and compressed. In addition, data can be distributed (i.e., partitioned) across a cluster.

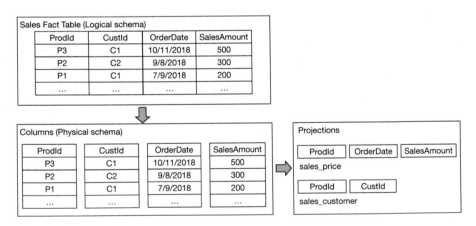

Fig. 15.13 Vertica projections

Vertica's architecture is based on two read- and write-optimized stores, which are variants of the main and buffer stores of Fig. 15.10. The **write-optimized store** (WOS) is an in-memory structure which is optimized for data inserts, deletes, and updates. Data in the WOS are uncompressed, unindexed, unsorted, and segmented and could be stored in a row- or column-oriented manner. This allows low latency for fast real-time data analysis. The **read-optimized store** (ROS) is a disk-based store where most of the data reside. Data in the ROS are stored as sets of index-value pairs, called ROS containers. Each ROS container is composed of two files per database column: one contains the column itself and the other contains the position index. At the ROS, **partitioning** and **segmentation** are applied to facilitate parallelism. The former, also called intra-node partitioning, splits data horizontally, based on data values, for example, by date intervals. Segmentation (also called inter-node partitioning) splits data across nodes according to a hash key. When the WOS is full, data are moved to the ROS by a moveout function. To save space in the ROS, a mergeout function is applied (this is analogous to the merge operation in Fig. 15.10).

Finally, although inserts, deletes, and updates are supported, Vertica may not be appropriate for update-intensive applications, such as heavy OLTP workloads that, roughly speaking, exceed 10% of the total load.

15.5.2 MonetDB

MonetDB is a column-store database system developed at the Centrum Wiskunde & Informatica (CWI) in the Netherlands. The main characteristics of MonetDB are a columnar storage, a bulk query algebra, which allows fast implementation on modern hardware, cache-conscious algorithms, and cost models that account for the cost of memory access.

Usually, in RDBMS query processing, when executing a query plan we typically need to scan a relation R and filter it using a condition ϕ. The format of R is only known at query time, and thus an expression interpreter is needed. The idea of MonetDB is based on the fact that the CPU is basically used to analyze the query expression, thus processing costs can be reduced by optimizing CPU usage. To simplify query interpretation, the relational algebra was replaced by a simpler algebra.

MonetDB also uses vertical **partitioning**, where each database column is stored in a so-called *binary association table* (BAT). A BAT is a two-column table where the left column is called the head (actually an object identifier) and the right column, the tail (the column value). The query language of MonetDB is a column algebra called MIL (Monet Interpreter Language). The parameters of the operators have a fixed format: They are two-column tables or constants. The expression calculated by an operator is also fixed, as well as the format of the result. However, performance is not optimal since each operation consumes materialized BATs and produces a materialized BAT. Therefore, since MIL uses a column-at-a-time evaluation technique, it does not have the problem of spending 90% of its query execution time in a tuple-at-a-time interpretation overhead, like in traditional RDBMSs. Furthermore, queries that contain complex calculations over many tuples materialize an entire result column for each function in the expression, even when they are not required in the query result, but just as input to other functions in the expression. If the intermediate results are small, materialization is not actually necessary and produces a large overhead.

To solve the drawbacks of MonetDB, a new query processor, called X100, was devised, where columns are fragmented vertically and compressed. These fragments are efficiently processed using a technique called vectorized processing, which operates over small vertical chunks of data items in the cache rather than single records. X100 uses a variant of the relational algebra as query language. The relational operations can process multiple columns at the same time. The primitives of MonetDB/X100 algebra resemble those in an extended relational algebra: Scan, Select, Project, Join, Aggr (for aggregation), TopN, and Order. All operators, except for Order, TopN, and Select, return a data flow with the same format as the input. A typical query scans one column at a time, and then the column is passed to the query tree, where the operators above are applied to the data flow.

15.5.3 Citus Columnar

Citus (described in Sect. 15.3.2) recently added columnar storage for read-only operations. This enhances its capability for handling OLAP queries. As a consequence, Citus now has three features that are relevant for data warehouses: distribution, columnar storage, and data compression (which comes together with columnar storage). To illustrate the relevance of columnar storage for OLAP queries, we use the example below.[2]

```
CREATE EXTENSION Citus;
CREATE TABLE perf_row_30(c00 int8, c01 int8, c02 int8, c03 int8, c04 int8, ..
... c28 int8, c29 int8);
CREATE TABLE perf_columnar_30 (LIKE perf_row_30) USING COLUMNAR;
```

We first add the Citus extension to PostgreSQL. Then, we create a 30-column table using traditional row storage in Citus. Finally, we create the same table, but using columnar storage. When populating both tables with 30 million records, it can be seen that the compression rate achieved by the columnar alternative is about twenty-three times; it also reduced by a factor of seven the time needed to populate the table with the same number of records.

We now create two tables with 100 columns and 30 million records using both row and columnar storage. Here the compression rate is around seven.

```
CREATE TABLE perf_row_100 (c00 int8, c01 int8, c02 int8, c03 int8, c04 int8, ..
... c28 int8, c99 int8);
CREATE TABLE perf_columnar_100(LIKE perf_row_100) USING COLUMNAR;
```

Now, consider the following query over the row-storage version:

```
SELECT c00, SUM(c28), SUM(c29)
FROM perf_row_30
GROUP BY c00
```

---

[2] This example is based on `https://www.citusdata.com/blog/2021/03/06/citus-10-columnar-compression-for-postgres/`

On a four-machine cluster, the query took amost two minutes to run. The same query using columnar storage took less than seven seconds, because it only makes use of the columns mentioned in the query, instead of the 30 columns, which is the case of the row-storage alternative. Running the same query over the perf_row_100 table takes almost 5 minutes since, of course, the table occupies more pages, although the number of records is the same, therefore there are more pages to read. However, the columnar alternative still takes seven seconds, since only the required columns are used. This shows that columnar storage is crucial for a large variety of OLAP queries, particularly over wide tables. Of course, using the distribution capabilities of Citus would further enhance query performance.

15.6 NoSQL Database Systems

Relational databases are designed for storing and querying structured data under strong consistency requirements. However, traditional database solutions do not suffice for managing massive amounts of data. To cope with such big data scenarios, a new generation of databases have been developed, known as **NoSQL database systems**. This term accounts for databases that do not use relations to store data, do not use SQL for querying data, and are typically schemaless. Therefore, they go beyond the "one size fits all" paradigm of classic relational databases, which refers to the fact that the traditional DBMS architecture has been used to support many data-centric applications with widely varying characteristics and requirements. NoSQL data stores are categorized in four classes, as follows:

- *Key-value stores*, which consist of a set of key-value pairs with unique keys. A value represents data of arbitrary type, structure, and size, uniquely identified by a key. This very simple structure allows these systems to store large amounts of data, although they only support very simple update operations.
- *Wide-column stores*, in which data are represented in a tabular format of rows and a fixed number of column families, each family containing an arbitrary number of columns that are logically related to each other and usually accessed together. Data here are physically stored per column-family instead of per row. The schema of a column-family is flexible as its columns can be added or removed at runtime.
- *Document stores*, where values in the key-value pairs are represented as a document encoded in standard semistructured formats such as XML, JSON, or BSON (Binary JSON). This brings great flexibility for accessing the data, compared with simple key-value stores. A document has a flexible schema, and attributes can be added or deleted at runtime.
- *Graph stores*, typically used to store highly connected data, where queries require intensive computation of paths and path traversals. Although

some authors do not classify these data stores as being NoSQL, it is generally accepted that graph stores fit into this class, particularly since they are schemaless databases.

In this section, we focus on wide-column stores and discuss two relevant examples of NoSQL data stores: HBase and Cassandra. Graph data stores are covered in depth in Chap. 13.

15.6.1 HBase

HBase is a column-oriented and horizontally scalable database system that runs on top of HDFS. The HBase data model is based on Google's big table, and it is designed to provide quick random access to huge amounts of structured data, taking advantage of the fault tolerance of the HDFS. HBase does not have an associated query language like SQL. Rather than this, HBase applications (including MapReduce applications) are written in Java. A table in HBase is a collection of rows, such that each row is a collection of column families, which in turn are a collection of columns, such that a column is a collection of key-value pairs. Therefore, data in HBase are denormalized. In addition, a primary key must be defined for the table.

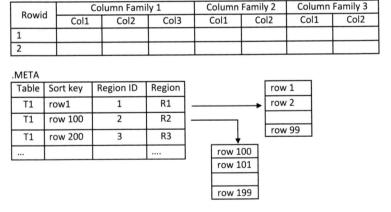

Fig. 15.14 HBase data model

Figure 15.14 depicts a scheme of the HBase data model. We can see that there is a row identifier which acts as the primary key for the table. Columns can be added on the fly to any column family at any time, and, of course, null values are allowed for any column. Therefore, HBase is schemaless, since there is not a fixed schema, and only the column families are defined in advance. Further, when inserting data into HBase, there is an associated timestamp, which is generated automatically by a so-called RegionServer or supplied by the user, and defines the version of a value. Note that, physically, data are stored in column-family basis rather than in column basis. That is, groups of rows of the form (row key, timestamp, column family) are stored together. With respect to the CAP theorem, being based on Hadoop, there is a single point of failure; thus HBase supports *partitioning* and *consistency*, at the expense of availability. HBase provides auto-sharding, which means that it dynamically distributes tables when they become large.

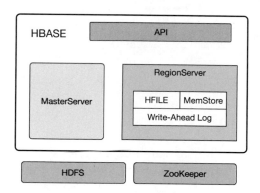

Fig. 15.15 HBase architecture

Figure 15.15 shows the HBase architecture, built on top of HDFS. The main components are the MasterServer and the RegionServer. The Master-Server assigns regions to a RegionServer using ZooKeeper, the task coordinator introduced in Sect. 15.2.1. The clients communicate with a RegionServer via ZooKeeper. The MasterServer also carries out load balancing of the regions in the RegionServers. The RegionServers host and manage regions, split them automatically, handle read/write requests, and communicate with the clients directly. Each RegionServer contains a write-ahead log (called HLog) and serves multiple regions. Each region is composed of a MemStore and multiple store files, each called an **HFile**, where data live as column families. The MemStore holds in-memory modifications to the data, and an HFile is generated when the MemStore is full and flushed to disk. The process is further explained in Fig. 15.16. The mapping from the regions to a RegionServer is kept in a system table called .META, where each RegionServer maps to a collection of regions within a range of row identifiers. Each region (i.e., a machine, called m*.host in the figure) holds a collection of indexed rows, stored in column family basis. When trying to read or write data, the HBase clients read the required region information from the .META table and communicate with the appropriate RegionServer. When a client asks for rows in HBase, the process is similar to what happens in a typical DBMS: It first reads the MemStore. If the record is not there, it reads the RegionServer's block cache (which is an MRU cache of rows), and, if it fails, it loads the HFiles in memory.

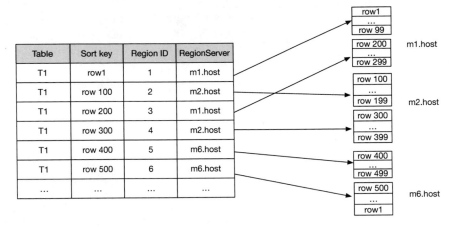

Fig. 15.16 HBase data storage distribution

HBase provides a shell to launch commands, for example, to create, modify, list, and drop tables in the database. There are also data manipulation commands for example, to put, get, and delete values from a cell. Since it is written in Java, it also provides a Java API for the above tasks. For example, to create a table **Orders** with two column families **OrNbr** and **OrDetails**, the put command is used (actually, one should use some bulk import procedure):

```
create 'Orders', 'OrNbr', 'OrDetails'
```

To insert an order with two items using HBase shell we write:

```
put 'Orders', '1', 'OrNbr:nbr', '123'
put 'Orders', '1', 'OrDetails:item1', '12'
put 'Orders', '1', 'OrDetails:item2', '25'
```

Here, the value 1 indicates the row number and the key-value pairs are (nbr,123), (item1,12), and (item2, 25).

Listing the table with the command scan 'Orders' results in:

```
1 column = OrNbr:nbr, timestamp = 3545355, value = 123
1 column = OrDetails: item1, timestamp = 3545445, value = 12
1 column = OrDetails: item2, timestamp = 3545567, value = 25
...
```

Note that the timestamps are inserted automatically.

15.6.2 Cassandra

Cassandra is an open source non-relational database originally developed at Facebook, becoming later an Apache project. Cassandra uses a ring-based architecture, instead of a master-slave one, where all nodes have the same role. In this architecture, one or more nodes in a cluster act as replicas for given data. Therefore, with respect to the CAP theorem, Cassandra supports partitioning and availability at the expense of consistency. Cassandra uses the Gossip protocol to allow the nodes to communicate with each other to detect any failing nodes in the cluster. Figure 15.17 shows the replication scheme.

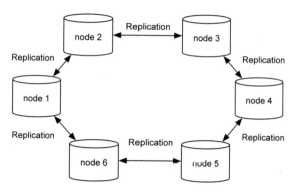

Fig. 15.17 Cassandra's ring architecture

When storing data, Cassandra first writes in a disk-based commit log. Then, data are written in a memory-based structure called a memtable, and finally, when this table is full, data are flushed to an immutable file (on disk) called an SSTable. This results in a very efficient write performance, which is one of the key features of Cassandra. Note that many SSTables can correspond to a single Cassandra logical table. Periodically, these tables are coalesced into one, to enhance performance. To read data, Cassandra queries a data structure called a Bloom filter, stored in memory, which checks the probability that a piece of data is in an SSTable. If the data are likely to be there, Cassandra queries another layer of in-memory caches, and fetches the compressed data on disk. Otherwise, Cassandra moves on to the next SStable.

Figure 15.18 shows the data model underlying Cassandra. The outermost container of data is called a Keyspace, which is a data container similar to a database in relational RDBMSs. The main attributes of a Keyspace are:

- The *replication factor*: the number of machines in the cluster that will receive copies of the same data.
- The *replica placement strategy*: the strategy to place replicas in the ring architecture mentioned above. These strategies can be SimpleStrategy or NetworkTopologyStrategy, where the latter is aware of the network topology, that is, location of nodes in racks, data centers, etc.
- The *column families*: a Keyspace is a container for at least one or several column families. A column family, in turn, is a container for a collection

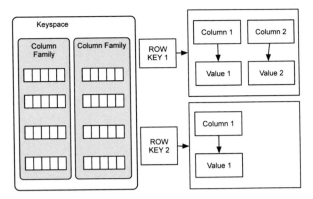

Fig. 15.18 Cassandra data model

of rows. From a user's point of view, a column family is analogous to a table in the relational model. However, in Cassandra it is not mandatory that individual rows have all the columns. Also, any column can be added to a column family at all times. A column has three values: column name (key), value, and a timestamp (like in HBase).

Consistency in Cassandra refers to the synchronization of all replicas of a data row at any given moment. The repair operations in Cassandra guarantee that all replicas of a row will eventually become consistent, which is called **eventual consistency**. This means that when an update occurs, it is guaranteed that eventually all accesses will return the last updated value, provided that no new updates are made to the object. It follows from the above that it is not possible to ensure consistency at all times, since network traffic may cause inconsistency. This suggests that consistency is associated with **replication**: As the number of replicas grows, the probability of inconsistency in some of the nodes increases. Cassandra defines the *consistency level* as the minimum number of nodes that must acknowledge a read or write operation before the operation can be considered successful. Different Keyspaces may have different consistency levels. Cassandra uses the LOCAL_QUORUM value to specify the consistency level for a keyspace, calculated for a data center as: LOCAL_QUORUM = (replication_factor/2) + 1. This number is rounded down to an integer. Thus, for a replication factor of three, LOCAL_QUORUM = 2, meaning that at least two nodes in the data center must respond to a read/write operation to consider the operation successful.

We explained that the typical one-size-fits-all design used for relational databases is not appropriate in a big data scenario. Also, disk space is generally cheap, compared to other resources, and writing in Cassandra is very efficiently done. Further, to efficiently read data, duplication is often needed, leading to a query-based database design. Therefore, Cassandra and also HBase databases are typically designed in denormalized fashion. Before explaining design basics, we need to elaborate roughly on how data are stored in the cluster. When a table (column family) is created in a Keyspace, a Primary Key (PK) is defined, as it is done in relational databases. This PK can have more than one column (in this case it is called a compound PK). Rows are distributed in the cluster based on a hash of the data **partition key**, which is the first element mentioned in the PK. In other words, partitions are groups of rows that share the same partition key. There are some well-known best-practice rules for designing a Cassandra database, namely:

- Every node in the cluster must have about the same amount of data.
- The number of partitions read must be kept to the minimum possible.
- If possible, a query must be answered by reading a single partition.

To satisfy the first rule, the designer must choose an appropriate PK, since the partition key determines which data will be stored together in a partition. Satisfying the second rule depends on the query. Since different queries will have different access patterns, and therefore require reading a different number of partitions, it is usual to define more than one table for the same problem, such that one table targets a given query. In the requirements elicitation stage, the most relevant queries for the design are defined. For each of these relevant queries, a table should be defined in order to satisfy the second rule. Regarding query efficiency, we also remark that Cassandra allows the definition of materialized views referring to a base table. When changes are made to the base table, the materialized view will be automatically updated.

Cassandra provides a query language shell (cqlsh). Using this shell, queries written in the **Cassandra Query Language** (CQL) can be executed for defining and modifying a schema, inserting and querying data, etc. We conclude this section by presenting the main CQL statements and discussing keys and partitions. For example, to create a Keyspace we must write:

```
CREATE KEYSPACE "Northwind"
WITH replication = 'class': 'simpleStrategy', 'replication_factor': 3;
```

The CREATE TABLE statement is used to create a table (that is, a column family) as follows:

```
CREATE TABLE Customer (
    CompanyName text,
    CustEmail text,
    City text,
    State text,
    Country text,
    PRIMARY KEY (CompanyName)
);
```

Here, Cassandra will store, for each customer, the data specified in the columns together with a system-generated timestamp. Columns can be added and dropped with the ALTER TABLE commands.

We can insert data into the previous table as follows:

```
INSERT INTO Customer(CompanyName, CustEmail, City, State, Country) VALUES
    ('Europe Travel', 'etravel@gmail.com', 'Antwerp', 'Antwerp', 'Belgium')
```

Such data will be stored as:

```
Partition Key: 'Europe Travel'
(column = CustEmail, value= 'etravel@gmail.com', timestamp = 456397177000)
(column = City, value= 'Antwerp', timestamp = 456397177000)
(column = State, value= 'Antwerp', timestamp = 456397177000)
(column = Country, value= 'Belgium', timestamp = 4563971770000)
```

If we would also like the partition key to be the customer's email, for example, because our queries will perform a lookup based on the email, we would need to define another table where the email is defined as the primary key. Note that if we want to get all customers from the same country stored together, the partition key must be defined to be the country; therefore the primary key must be (Country, CompanyName), because the partition key is the first element in the primary key. If we define the partition key as a multicolumn key, we have a composite key. For instance, defining ((Country, State), CompanyName) as primary key, data would be partitioned by country and state, because now the pair (Country, State) is the first element of the composite primary key.

15.7 NewSQL Database Systems

NoSQL database systems achieve scalability typically by means of partitioning data among several nodes. However, enterprise information systems require the consistency and availability properties offered by traditional relational DBMSs. **NewSQL database systems** aim at providing at the same time the scalable performance of NoSQL and compliance with **ACID properties** for transactions as in relational DBMSs. NewSQL database systems are the first step that allows the so-called Hybrid Transaction and Analytics Processing (HTAP), which is aimed at performing OLAP, OLTP, and real-time analysis over the same database. We will discusse this topic in Sect. 15.9.

NewSQL systems, although very different from each other, basically present the following common features:

- Main-memory storage of OLTP databases.
- Scaling out by splitting a database into disjoint subsets (shards).
- ACID properties and concurrency control.
- Secondary indexing supporting fast query processing times.
- High availability and strong data durability made possible with the use of replication mechanisms.
- Fault tolerance through a crash recovery mechanism.

We describe next three representative NewSQL systems, namely, Cloud Spanner, SAP HANA, and VoltDB.

15.7.1 Cloud Spanner

Cloud Spanner is a distributed data management system developed and used at Google. Like typical NewSQL systems, Spanner provides scalability, automatic sharding, fault tolerance, consistent replication, wide-area distribution, distributed query execution, and blockwise columnar storage. This started from the first "key-value" stores such as Google's Bigtable. For the SQL interface, Spanner borrows ideas originally used to manage Google's AdWords data, which included a federated query processor. Spanner is used as an OLTP database management system for structured data at Google, used in production systems like Google Play. The system provides transactional consistency, strong consistent replication, and therefore high availability. The Spanner query processor implements a dialect of SQL, called Standard SQL, shared by several query subsystems within Google. Standard SQL is based on standard ANSI SQL, fully using standard features such as array and row types (called Struct) to support nested data. Spanner's query processor can serve a mix of transactional and analytical workloads, supporting low-latency and long-running queries. Given the distributed nature of data storage in Spanner, the query processor is itself distributed and uses standard optimization techniques such as shipping code close to data, parallel processing of parts of a single request on multiple machines, and partition pruning. However, the SQL dialect used in Spanner is not strictly Standard SQL, since Google manages proprietary data types and other protocols.

15.7.2 SAP HANA

The SAP approach to business intelligence, known as **HANA** is based on two main components.

1. The SAP HANA database system (also called SAP IMDBS), a hybrid IMDBS that combines row-based, column-based, and object-based technologies, optimized to take advantage of parallel processing.
2. The SAP HANA appliance (SAP HANA), used for analyzing large volumes of data in real time without the need to materialize aggregations. It is a combination of hardware and software delivered by SAP in cooperation with hardware partners, such as IBM.

We next focus on the SAP HANA database system.

The core of the SAP HANA database is composed of two relational database engines. The first one is a column-based engine, holding tables with large amounts of data that can be aggregated in real time and used in analytical operations. The second one is a row-based engine, optimized for row operations, such as frequent inserts and updates. The latter has a lower compression rate and lower query performance compared to the column-based engine.

This architecture allows mixed workloads to be supported in the same server, performing complex analytical computations without the need to materialize tables. The two relational engines support SQL and MDX. Row or column storage can be selected at the time a table is created, but can be changed afterwards. Both engines share a common persistence layer (the nonvolatile data store in Fig. 15.10), where page management and logging are supported as in traditional databases.

The **data storage architecture** is similar to the generic one depicted in Fig. 15.10, with an optimized column-store area and a non-optimized buffer area to allow insertions and updates. Insertions, deletions, and updates are handled following the notion of lifetime management of a data record. Data storage in SAP HANA is organized in three levels, called *main storage, L1 delta storage*, and *L2 delta storage*. The main storage stores records in columnar format, has a sorted data dictionary, and achieves the highest compression rate. The L2 Delta also stores records in a column format although with a lower compression rate; there is an unsorted data dictionary (data dictionaries are explained below), and this storage works well for storing up to ten million records. Finally, the L1 delta storage stores records in a row format, thus it is optimized for write operations, achieving fast data inserts and deletions, although the data compression is low. The main storage is optimized for read operations, the L1 delta for write operations, and the L2 delta lies between the other two. Therefore, this storage structure supports different kinds of workloads. Typically, during their life cycle, records are moved from level L1, to level L2, and to the main store. This is because L1 is faster for writing. Then, data are moved to the colunm storage for querying.

Regarding **partitioning**, data are divided into subsets and stored in a cluster of servers, forming a distributed database. An individual database table can be placed on different servers within a cluster, or can be split into several partitions, either horizontally (a group of rows per partition) or vertically (a group of columns per partition), with each partition residing in a separate server within the cluster.

Atomicity, consistency, and isolation are **ACID properties** that are not affected by in-memory storage. However, as explained above, durability cannot be met by just storing data in main memory since this is volatile storage. To make data persistent, it must reside on nonvolatile storage such as hard drives or flash devices. HANA divides the main memory into pages. When a transaction changes data, the affected pages are marked and written to nonvolatile storage at regular intervals. In addition, a database log captures all changes made by transactions. Each committed transaction generates a log entry that is written to nonvolatile storage, ensuring that all transactions are permanent. SAP HANA stores changed pages at **savepoints**, which are asynchronously written to persistent storage at regular intervals (by default, every 5 min). A transaction does not commit before the corresponding log entry is written to persistent storage, to meet the durability requirement (in traditional database management this is called *write-ahead logging*). After a power failure, the database can be restarted from the savepoints like a disk-based database: The database logs are applied to restore the changes that were not captured in the savepoints, ensuring that the database can be restored in memory to the same state as before the failure.

Finally, **compression** is performed using data dictionaries. For this, each attribute value in a table is replaced by an integer code, and the correspondence of codes and values is stored in a dictionary. For example, in the City column of the Customer table, the value Berlin can be encoded as 1, and the tuple (Berlin, 1) will be stored in the dictionary. Thus, if needed, the corresponding value (Berlin, in this case) will be accessed just once. Therefore, data movement is reduced without imposing additional CPU load for decompression, for example, in run-length encoding. The compression factor achieved is highly dependent on the data being compressed. Attributes with few distinct values compress well (e.g., if we have many customers from the same city), while attributes with many distinct values do not benefit as much.

15.7.3 VoltDB

VoltDB is an in-memory relational DBMS designed for high-throughput, operational applications, which uses SQL as its native data language, supports ACID transactions to ensure data consistency, and provides high availability and fault tolerance. Replication across data centers allows high availability. Finally, VoltDB also provides geospatial query support. VoltDB runs entirely in memory with optional periodic disk snapshots. It runs on Linux on premises, and on a variety of cloud services like Amazon Web Services (AWS), Google, and Azure. VoltDB implements a horizontally scalable architecture.

The above is achieved by **partitioning** both data and processes and distributing them across CPU cores in a shared-nothing hardware cluster. Data are kept in memory, eliminating the need for buffer management (which is a bottleneck of traditional relational DBMSs). Each partition operates autonomously, which avoids the need for locking. Data are automatically replicated for intra- and inter-cluster high availability. Updates are applied in parallel to multiple machines in memory. The **replication** strategy in VoltDB is called "K-safety". When a database is configured for K-safety, VoltDB automatically and transparently replicates the database partitions so that the database can support the loss of K nodes without stopping the database. For example, a K-Safety of 2 guarantees no data loss even if two machines fail, since data is committed to at least three in-memory nodes. Transactions are submitted as Java stored procedures which can be executed asynchronously in the database, and data are automatically partitioned across nodes in the system. Reference data can be cloned to maximize join performance. At predefined intervals, VoltDB writes database snapshots to disk. Snapshot files can be used to restore the database to a previous, known state after a failure or scheduled service event. Snapshots are guaranteed to be transactionally consistent at the point in time at which the snapshot was completed. This provides durability.

A key feature when querying in VoltDB is that database calls are reduced to just one client-server trip per transaction, through a stored procedure interface. Each stored procedure is defined as a transaction that either succeeds or rolls back as a whole, ensuring database consistency. For developing applications, API libraries are provided for multiple programming languages. JSON data structures are supported as well. Materialized views are also supported in VoltDB. A JDBC API is also provided to process ad hoc SQL.

Given that VoltDB is designed to handle large volumes of OLTP transactions, it is not so appropriate for OLAP querying over large data warehouses. In these cases, VoltDB has an export integration subsystem that spools VoltDB data to analytic DBMS products (such as columnar data stores and Hadoop), providing a sort of HTAP capability (see Sect. 15.9).

15.8 Array Database Systems

We have seen when studying MOLAP and MDX that multidimensional arrays are the natural representation for data cubes. Similarly, in most science and engineering domains, arrays represent spatiotemporal sensor, image, and simulation output, among other kinds of data. For example, temperature data can be seen as a data cube with four dimensions (latitude, longitude, altitude, and time), and one or more measures representing temperatures (e.g., minimum, maximum, average). Classic database technology does not support arrays adequately. Therefore, most solutions are proprietary, which produces information silos and requires data to be moved between relational and multidimensional databases. Array database systems attempt to close this gap by providing declarative query support for flexible ad-hoc analytics on large multidimensional arrays. Potentially, array databases can offer significant advantages in terms of flexibility, functionality, extensibility, performance, and scalability. The possibility of having data cubes in array databases may also close the gap between ROLAP and MOLAP approaches. There are systems in the database market that may be be considered a serious option for data cube storage and querying.

Arrays are partitioned in subarrays, called *tiles* or *chunks*, which are the unit of access to disk storage. This partition strategy impacts on query performance. Thus, it is desirable to allow dynamic partitioning, or to statically define a partition strategy appropriate to the expected query workload. Array database systems such as rasdaman and SciDB, which we introduce in this section, use different strategies. Based on the degree of grid alignment, tiling schemes can be classified into *aligned* and *non-aligned*. The former can be regular (a grid of fixed-domain tiles) or irregular. Figure 15.19 depicts the tiling schemes.

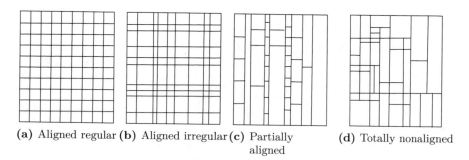

(a) Aligned regular (b) Aligned irregular (c) Partially   (d) Totally nonaligned
                                            aligned

Fig. 15.19 Tiling schemes in rasdaman

Array database systems require a high-level, SQL-like declarative language where the iteration over the partitions is implicit, based on a formal algebra. This algebra (and its derived query language) must provide three core operators: an array constructor, an aggregator, and an array sort operation. Operations to build subarrays from a given one must be provided as well, for example, to produce subcubes from a data cube.

Some systems operate on arrays standalone, and others embed them into a host data model, typically the relational model. In the latter case, arrays are introduced as a new column type. This is used in most array database systems, such as rasdaman, PostgreSQL, Oracle, and Teradata, since it makes query optimization easier. For example, in these systems, a table can be created as follows.

```
CREATE TABLE ImageSat(
        id: integer not null,
        readDate: date,
        content: cell(band1:int,...,band7) mdarray[0:4999,0:4999])
```

In the above statement, **ImageSat** is a table containing an object identifier, the date when a satellite image was acquired, and a content, which is an array with an extent of 5,000 × 5,000 pixels, each containing seven color bands. This table can then be queried in any SQL-like language extended with array algebra operations. For example:

```
SELECT id, encode(content.band1, "image/tiff")
FROM    ImageSat
WHERE mdavg(content.band2 - content.band3) > 0
```

In the query above, **mdavg** performs an iterative average over the array extent, and an image is produced as a result. We do not give details on array algebras, and refer to the bibliography for details. Languages are further commented below, for the rasdaman and SciDB systems.

Regarding query processing, unlike relational DBMSs, array operations are strongly CPU bound. Some array operations can be easily parallelized, such as simple aggregations, and distributed on either local or remote processing nodes. In other cases, queries must be rewritten as parallelizable operations. In the first case, parallelization across several cores in one node allows vertical scalability to be exploited; in the second case, distributed processing requires strategies based on data location, intermediate results transfer costs, and resource availability, among others. Two main techniques are used: query rewriting and cost-based optimization. Query rewriting takes a query and rewrites it into an equivalent one. The array algebra facilitates this task, since it allows equivalence rules to be defined. Different systems use different sets of rules. For example, rasdaman (Sect. 15.8.1) has about 150 such rules. Cost-based optimization aims at finding an efficient query execution plan from a space of possible plans. This involves knowing the approximate costs of processing different operations.

Array DBMSs can be classified in three groups, described next.

First, *generic array DBMSs* provide characteristic features such as a query language, multi-user concurrent operation, dedicated storage management, and so on. Examples of these kinds of system are discussed next.

Second, *object-relational extensions* are based on object-relational DBMSs, which allow users to define new data types and operators. However, in these systems, an array is a type constructor, not a data type; thus it cannot provide abstraction, only instantiated data types. Examples of this kinds of systems are PostGIS raster, Oracle GeoRaster, and Teradata arrays.

Finally, *array tools* are specific-purpose tools for operating with arrays. Examples are TensorFlow, a machine learning library, Xarray, a Python package for working with arrays, and Xtensor, a C++ library for numerical analysis. Finally, attempts have been made to implement partitioned array management and processing on top of MapReduce. Examples are SciHadoop, an experimental Hadoop plugin allowing scientists to specify logical queries over array-based data models, which are executed as MapReduce programs. Since MapReduce presents the problems already mentioned when iterations are needed, SciSpark (a NASA project) aims at augmenting Spark with the ability to load, process, and deliver scientific data and results. SciSpark produces methods to create RDDs that preserve the logical representation of structured and dimensional data.

15.8.1 Rasdaman

Rasdaman (standing for "raster data manager") was the first array database system. It was developed initially as an academic project, and then became a commercial spin-off. Currently, rasdaman has a vast contributing community around the world, supporting a complete array DBMS as an open-source project. Rasdaman allows efficient storage and querying of massive multidimensional arrays, such as sensor, image, simulation, and statistics data over domains such as Earth, space, and life sciences, complying with OGC standards. It allows parallel access to huge files and objects, as well as being scalable and providing high availability. Array data can reside in a conventional database, in files optimized by rasdaman, or in some pre-existing archive.

In rasdaman's data model, arrays are determined by their extent or domain and their cells (called pixels and voxels). Extents are given by lower and upper bound integer values. Cells have a type, which is defined by composing typical C/C++ base data types in nested structs. For example, a type to represent red, blue, and green channels of a color image would be a composite of three char channels. Over such typed arrays, collections are built; these have two attributes, an object identifier maintained by the system, and the array itself, which allows arrays to be embedded into the relational model. This follows an "array-as-attribute" approach, as opposed to the "array-as-table" approach followed by SciDB (see Sect. 15.8).

In more detail, a multidimensional array is a set of elements ordered in a discretized space where only integer coordinates are allowed. The number of integers needed to refer to a particular position in this space is called the *dimensionality* or dimension. An array element or cell is located in space through its *coordinates*. A base type (whether built in or user-defined composite) along with a dimension and an optional maximum spatial domain are the components of an *array type*. Finally, an array type combined with optional null values define a *collection type*. Arrays in rasdaman are stored inside a standard database, partitioned into subarrays called tiles, where each tile is stored as a BLOB (binary large object) in a relational table. This allows conventional relational database systems to maintain arrays of unlimited size. A spatial index allows the tiles required by a query to be quickly located. The partitioning scheme is open, and any kind of tiling shown in Fig. 15.19 can be specified during array instantiation.

Rasdaman's high-level query language, called rasql, allows raster processing through expressions over SQL-like raster operations. The language supports the typical data manipulation expressions such as SELECT, INSERT, UPDATE, and DELETE. In rasql, the type and format of the query result are specified in the SELECT clause, and the result type can be a multidimensional array or an atomic value. The SELECT clause can reference the collection. In the FROM clause, a list of collections is specified, optionally aliased to variable names, like in SQL. These collection names and aliases serve as an iterator variable over the collection which can be used in the SELECT or WHERE clauses. Conditions are specified in the WHERE clause. Predicates are built as Boolean expressions using comparison, logical operations, parenthesis, functions, etc. Unlike SQL, however, rasql offers mechanisms to express selection criteria on multidimensional items, for example, to restrict the input of the query to those images where at least one difference pixel value is greater than a certain value. An example query is shown below.

```
SELECT arr1 - arr2
FROM    arr1, arr2
WHERE  cells(arr1 - arr2 > 50)
```

For development, rasdaman provides a C++ API, raslib, and a Java API, rasj, both adhering to the ODMG standard.

The core part of rasdaman responsible for query evaluation is called rasserver. Rasdaman runs several rasserver processes, each responsible for the evaluation of a single query. Therefore, multiple queries are dispatched to multiple rasservers. The rasserver processes are supervised by a process called rasmgr. Client queries are sent to rasmgr, which allocates a rasserver for the client. Rasserver connects to a backend database RASBASE, to store details of persistent data, such as collection names, types, dimensions, indices, etc. Arrays also need to be persisted. This is performed on the file system as ordinary files, or as blobs within RASBASE. On top of the core rasdaman there is a geo-services layer called *petascope*, where the data model is composed of coverages associated with geo-referencing information, supporting regular and irregular grids, and implementing several OGC standards.

15.8.2 SciDB

SciDB is an open-source analytical database oriented toward the data management needs of scientific workflows. It is based on a nested multidimensional array data model and provides statistical and linear algebra operations over these arrays. SciDB has a shared-nothing system architecture, shown in Figure 15.20, which supports the scalability of the system. SciDB is deployed on a cluster of servers, each with processing, memory, and local storage, interconnected using a standard Ethernet and TCP/IP network. Each physical server hosts a SciDB instance that is responsible for local storage and processing. Query processing occurs at each node on its local data. When creating an array, a user may specify the distribution of the array data: whether chunks will be stored primarily on one node or replicated on all nodes.

Upon creating an array, the user specifies its dimensions and attributes. Each unique set of dimensions maps to a single cell in the array. Each cell is defined by a collection of attributes, where an attribute represents a single data value. Both dimensions and attribute data types can be user defined. If dimensions are not specified, SciDB creates a data frame, which is an unordered group of cells. Users can also create temporary arrays, which are stored in memory and do not keep deltas of changes like non-temporary arrays do. In addition to the dimension size attributes, the user must define two parameters for each dimension: the chunk size and chunk overlap. These parameters affect the distribution of the array data among the worker nodes.

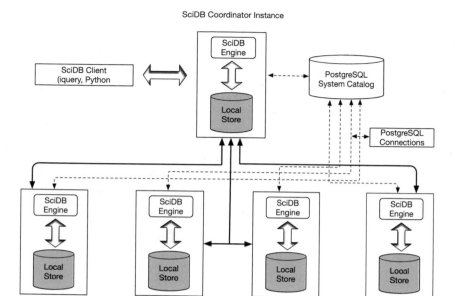

Fig. 15.20 SciDB architecture

Unlike in rasdaman, foreign keys are not part of the array data model used by SciDB. SciDB does not use an index, but maps chunks of an array to specific nodes by hashing the chunk's coordinates. It also has a map that allows dimensions specified with user-defined data types to be represented internally as integers, which is called an index in the SciDB documentation.

In SciDB, users define how each attribute of an array is compressed when the array is created. The default is no compression. Other options are zlib, bzlib, or null filter compression. Since data are stored by attribute, where logical chunks of an array are vertically partitioned into single-attribute physical chunks, the specified compression is used on a chunk-by-chunk basis. If certain parts of a chunk are accessed more often than others, SciDB can partition a chunk into tiles and compress on a tile-by-tile basis. Run-length encoding (see bitmap compression in Chap. 8) is used to compress recurring sequences of data. In addition, SciDB's storage manager compression engine can split or group logical chunks in order to optimize memory usage while remaining within the limit of the buffer pool's fixed-size slots. During the creation of an array in SciDB the user must specify an array name, the dimensions of the array, and at least one attribute for the array. Attributes can be added to an array as the result of an operation in SciDB. For example:

```
CREATE ARRAY myArray <val:double>[I=0:9,10,0, J=0:*,10,0];
```

The array myArray has two dimensions, I and J. I is a bounded dimension with values ranging from 0 to 9, with chunk size 10 and chunk overlap 0. The other dimension Y is analogous to I, but its size is unbounded.

SciDB supports two query languages: the Array Query Language (AQL) and the Array Functional Language (AFL). AQL is very similar to SQL, where operations are described as SELECT, INSERT, and UPDATE, and several kinds of JOINS. On the other hand, AFL allows for a more functional description of array operations, using a function syntax which allows for nesting of operations.

The following kinds of array aggregation are supported: (a) Grand aggregates, which compute aggregates over entire arrays; (b) Group-by aggregates, which compute summaries by grouping array data by dimension values; (c) Grid aggregates, which compute summaries for non-overlapping subarrays; and (d) Window aggregates, which compute summaries over a moving window in an array, like SQL window functions. The five SQL aggregate functions are supported. For example, the type (b) query

SELECT MAX(Altitude) FROM AltMap GROUP BY y;

computes the maximum values for attribute Altitude of array AltMap, grouped by dimension y, where the latter refers to the traditional coordinate axis.

15.9 Hybrid Transactional and Analytical Processing

Many current big data applications require both to acquire huge amounts of data in very short times, such as data coming from Internet of Thing (IoT) or real-time data from social networks, and to perform analytics over such data. The typical division between concurrent transaction processing (i.e., OLTP) and analytical queries (i.e., OLAP) is not appropriate for these applications, since they require the best from both worlds. For these data processing requirements Gartner coined the term **hybrid transactional and analytical processing (HTAP)**, which combines OLTP and OLAP. The database technologies studied in this chapter allow these kinds of systems to be built. As we have seen, since OLTP and OLAP systems have different requirements, they are tuned very differently. Further, the idea of general-purpose systems has been losing strength, and specialized database systems have appeared. Essentially, in HTAP systems, an OLTP engine continuously updates the data, which serves OLAP queries. Thus, data freshness depends on transactional throughput. Ideally, an HTAP system provides OLAP over up-to-date data without affecting the performance of the OLTP system, and also OLAP query response should remain unaffected by OLTP traffic. However, these assumptions are not accomplished in actual systems. It is the case that performance of either the OLTP or the OLAP part of an HTAP system is affected by the other one.

Three main HTAP architectures have been proposed. In all them, the data is logically shared among the OLTP and OLAP components. However, the various architectures differ in how they implement the sharing of data.

The two-copy, mixed-format (TCMF) architecture keeps two copies of the data, one for OLTP in row format and one for OLAP in columnar format. This requires the data to be converted between the two formats. To keep the data consistent across the OLTP and OLAP components, an intermediate data structure, referred to as delta, is used, which keeps track of the recently modified, fresh tuples. Periodically, TCMF propagates the fresh tuples from the OLTP side to the OLAP side by scanning the delta. Therefore, the latest committed data might not be available to the analytical queries right away.

The single-copy, mixed-format (SCMF) architecture keeps a single copy of the data and uses the intermediate delta data structure as the OLTP store. The delta is in row format, whereas the main copy of the data is in columnar format. OLTP transactions only modify the delta, whereas the OLAP queries read both the delta and the main copy of the data.

Lastly, the single-copy, single-format (SCSF) architecture keeps a single copy of the data and uses a single format, that is, either row or columnar, for both for OLTP and OLAP workloads. This requires mechanisms such as multi-version concurrency control to keep multiple versions of the data, through which analytical queries can access the most recent transactional data.

We briefly describe examples of HTAP systems next.

15.9.1 SingleStore

SingleStore (formerly called memSQL) is a distributed relational database that handles both transactions and real-time analytics. It is able to scale for large data volumes and is accessible through standard SQL drivers and supports standard SQL. SingleStore can ingest data continuously, support ACID transactions, and perform operational analytics. It can read streaming data from Kafka and Spark, relational data from multiple database systems, and data from HDFS and Amazon S3, and supports data in relational SQL, JSON, geospatial, and full-text search formats.

SingleStore can store data in either row- or column-oriented tables. The format is defined by the user when creating the table. Row stores are optimized for small insert, update, or delete queries and are associated with OLTP use cases. Data for row-oriented tables are stored in memory, making random reads fast, with snapshots and transaction logs persisted to disk. Column-oriented tables are optimized for OLAP queries and data warehousing use cases. Data for column-store tables are stored on disk, supporting fast sequential reads and compression up to ten times. SingleStore is a distributed system, so data are **sharded** automatically among nodes in a cluster of commodity machines, optimizing query performance for both distributed aggregate queries and filtered queries with equality predicates. Nodes can be added at will, and shards can be moved as needed. Data are stored in partitions on leaf nodes, and users connect to aggregator nodes. An aggregator node is responsible for receiving SQL queries, breaking them up across leaf nodes, and aggregating results back to the client. A leaf node stores Single-Store data and processes queries from the aggregators. All communication between aggregators and leaf nodes is done over the network using SQL. SingleStore uses hash **partitioning** to distribute data uniformly across the leaf nodes. In addition, to support high concurrency, a distributed query optimizer evenly divides the processing workload for efficient CPU usage. SingleStore uses multi-version concurrency control (MVCC) and lock-free data structures, to keep data accessible under a high volume of concurrent reads and writes.

Durability for the in-memory row store is implemented with a write-ahead log and snapshots (checkpoints). With default settings, as soon as a transaction is acknowledged in memory, the database asynchronously writes the transaction to disk. A SingleStore cluster can be configured in high-availability mode, where every data partition is automatically created with master and slave versions on two separate leaf nodes. In high-availability mode, aggregators send transactions to the master partitions, which then send logs to the slave partitions. Under an unexpected master failure, the slave partitions take over as master partitions, in a fully online operation with no downtime.

Efficient OLAP querying is achieved by means of shared-nothing horizontal scaling and distributed parallel query execution, column-store query processing (for aggregation), and optimized disk consumption, query compilation, and query vectorization.

15.9.2 LeanXcale

LeanXcale is a scalable SQL OLTP database supporting ACID transactions. It natively supports SQL and key-value pairs, as well as data streaming. It uses a proprietary parallel-distributed transactional manager called Iguazu, which enables analytical queries over the operational data, without the need for ETL processes.

LeanXcale's architecture has three distributed layers:

- A distributed SQL query engine that provides full SQL and a JDBC driver to access the database. It supports both scaling out OLTP workloads (distributing transactions across nodes) and OLAP workloads (using multiple nodes for a single large analytical query).
- A distributed transaction manager that uses the Iguazu technology.

- A distributed relational key-value data store engine called KiVi. Users can access the relational tables through both the SQL and the key-value interfaces. The key-value interface has all the power of SQL (selections, aggregations, grouping, and sorting) except joins.

LeanXcale is a polyglot database (Sect. 15.10), allowing queries to performed across multiple data stores. In this way, organizations can break their data silos and query across all their databases. LeanXcale supports querying MongoDB, HBase, Neo4j, and any SQL relational DBMS, thus combining SQL with the native APIs and query languages of the mentioned data stores. Further, by means of metadata and parsing of HDFS files, these files become read-only SQL, where SQL queries can be run.

15.10 Polystores

As discussed in previous sections, a large number of new database technologies have appeared to cope with the problems raised by big data applications. This results in a rich offering of services that can be used to build data-intensive applications that can scale and exhibit high performance. However, this has also led to a wide diversification of DBMS interfaces and the loss of a common paradigm, which makes it very hard to integrate and analyze data in the different data stores. Several efforts have been made to build **polystores**, which provide integrated access to multiple, heterogeneous storage engines, such as relational DBMS, NoSQL DBMS, and HDFS repositories. They typically support just read-only queries, since supporting distributed transactions across heterogeneous data stores is a hard problem.

Polystores can be classified based on the level of coupling with the underlying data stores, as described next.

Loosely coupled polystores keep the autonomy of the data stores, which are accessed through a common interface, and also separately through their own local API. Integration is achieved through wrappers, one for each data store. A query processor contains a catalog of the associated data stores, and each wrapper has a local catalog of its data store. The problem of this approach is that when accessing multiple data stores, loosely coupled polystores typically perform centralized access, and thus cannot exploit parallelism to enhance query performance.

Tightly coupled polystores typically work over a shared-nothing cluster architecture, so that data stores can only be accessed through the polystore. Like loosely coupled systems, they provide a single language for querying structured and unstructured data, and the query processor directly uses the data store local interfaces. In the case of HDFS, they can interface with a data processing framework such as MapReduce or Spark. Thus, during query execution, the query processor directly accesses the data stores. This approach takes advantage of massive parallelism by bringing in parallel shards from HDFS tables to the SQL database nodes and doing parallel joins. On the other hand, they can access only specific data stores, usually through SQL mappings, which is costly compared to accessing directly the data store.

Hybrid polystores combine the advantages of loosely coupled and tightly coupled systems, that is, they combine the high expressiveness of native queries with massive parallelism. Therefore, the architecture follows the mediator-wrapper architecture, and the query processor can also directly access some data stores, e.g., HDFS through MapReduce or Spark. One example of a hybrid polystore is Spark SQL (see Sect. 15.2.3). We next describe two other representative polystore efforts.

15.10.1 CloudMdsQL

CloudMdsQL (Cloud Multidatastore Query Language) is an SQL-like database capable of querying multiple heterogeneous data stores (e.g. relational, NoSQL, and HDFS). It is based on five main ideas: (a) Evaluate queries against different NoSQL and SQL databases using their native query mechanism; (b) Allow nested queries, where the result of a query may be used as input of another one; (c) Allows databases with or without schemas to be easily integrated; (d) Support data-metadata transformations, that is, attributes or relations into data and the other way round; (e) Reuse the classic database machinery for query optimization.

CloudMdsQL's common data model is table-based and has rich datatypes that capture a wide range of datatypes from the underlying data stores, such as arrays and JSON objects, in order to handle non-flat and nested data. CloudMdsQL integrates datasets by means of relational operations, although to be able integrate NoSQL systems it adopts a hybrid approach keeping the common data model schemaless.

In CloudMdsQL, a single query can embed native queries and constructs of different data stores. A *table expression* is an expression that returns a table and has a name and signature, which defines the names and types of the columns of the returned relation. A table expression can be an SQL statement (that can be optimized) or a native expression (that is delegated to the data store). Each query, although agnostic to the schemas of the underlying data stores, is executed in the context of an ad hoc schema, formed by all table expressions within the query. For example, the following query contains two subqueries addressed, respectively, to an SQL database rdb and a MongoDB database mongo:

```
T1(CustKey int, CustName string, City string)@rdb =
        ( SELECT CustKey, CustName, City FROM Customer )
T2(CustKey int, LastTweet timestamp)@mongo = {* ...MongoDB query... *}
SELECT T1.CustKey, T1.CustName, T2.LastTweet
FROM   T1, T2
WHERE  T1.CustKey = T2.CustKey AND T1.City = 'Brussels'
```

In the above query, the table expression T1 is defined by an SQL subquery, while T2 is a native expression (identified by the special symbols {* *}) defining a native MongoDB call. The two subqueries are sent independently to the data stores and the retrieved relations are joined in the main SELECT statement. The expression T1 can be rewritten by pushing into it the filter condition on city specified in the WHERE clause, thus reducing the amount of data retrieved.

CloudMdsQL has been extended to address distributed processing frameworks such as Apache Spark by enabling the ad hoc usage of user-defined map-filter-reduce operators as subqueries allowing for pushing down predicates and join conditions.

15.10.2 BigDAWG

BigDAWG (Big Data Analytics Working Group) is a polystore supporting multiple database systems. Its design is motivated by three goals. The first one is to support **location transparency**, which enables users to write queries without being concerned about the present location of the data or how to assign work to each storage engine. The second goal is *semantic completeness*, by which users exploit all capabilities provided by the underlying storage engines. Finally, the third goal is to enable objects stored in a given database system to be accessed from other systems in their own languages.

In BigDAWG, an *island of information* is a collection of storage engines sharing the same data model. For example, a polystore may have relational, array, and key-value islands. Each island has a set of database systems connected to it and each of them provides a *shim*, which is an adapter mapping the island language to its native language. *Cast* operations allow for the migration of data from one island to another. Finally, *scopes* allow an island to correctly interpret the syntax of a query and to select the correct shim. Cross-island queries may involve multiple scope operations.

The BigDAWG middleware has four components. The *query planner* parses an incoming query and creates a set of possible query plans that highlight the possible engines for each collection of objects. The *performance monitor* uses information about the performance of previous queries to determine a plan with the best engine for each collection of objects. The plan is then passed to the *query executor*, which determines the best method to combine the collections of objects and executes the query. The executor can use the *data migrator* to move objects between engines and islands, if required by the query plan. For example, suppose that Customer and Tweet are located, respectively, in a relational and a key-value store and consider the following cross-island operation:

```
RELATIONAL(SELECT T1.CustKey, T1.CustName, T2.LastTweet
FROM    Customer T1, CAST(Tweet, relation) T2
```

WHERE T1.CustKey = T2.CustKey AND T1.City = 'Brussels')

This query performs a join between the relational and key-value stores that is executed in a RELATIONAL scope. The CAST operation translates Tweet into a table when it is initially accessed. The user does not care whether the query is executed in the relational store or the key-value one provided his prescribed island semantics are obeyed.

The middleware relies on a *catalog* that stores metadata about the system components. This is maintained in a database that includes information about (a) engine names and connection information, (b) databases, their engine membership, and connection authentication information, (c) data objects (e.g., tables and column names) stored on each engine, (d) the shims that integrate the engines within each island, and (e) the available casts between engines.

15.11 Cloud Data Warehouses

Cloud computing is defined as the on-demand availability of computing resources, such as server time and network storage, without direct management by the user. The cloud computing model has five essential characteristics:

- On-demand self-service: A customer can unilaterally provision the resources. This can be done automatically and without requiring human interaction with a service provider.
- Broad network access: The resources are available over the network and are accessed through standard mechanisms and protocols using standard clients, such as a Web browser.
- Resource pooling: The resources are pooled to serve multiple users through a multi-tenant model.
- Rapid elasticity: The resources can be increased and decreased, in some cases automatically, to meet fluctuating and unpredictable demand.
- Measured service: Providers can measure storage, processing, bandwidth, and number of user accounts. The resources can be monitored and controlled by both customers and the provider.

The way in which cloud services are made available to users is called the *deployment model*. There are four of them, described next.

- *Private* or *on-premises* clouds are used by a single organization to support various user groups. Private clouds may be managed by the organization itself or by a service provider either on-site or off-site. They better address security and privacy concerns than the other alternatives.
- *Public clouds* support all users who access the resources on a subscription basis. Public clouds typically allow fast application deployment and elasticity. However, data safety and privacy can be at risk.

- *Community clouds* support multiple organizations that are part of a community, for instance, universities cooperating in certain areas or public administrations within a province. Access is normally restricted to the members of the community.
- *Hybrid clouds* are a composition of two or more of the above models that remain unique entities but are bound together by standardized or proprietary technology that enables data and application portability.

In an orthogonal classification, there are three classic *service models* in cloud computing:

- **Software as a service** (SaaS): In this model, also known as *cloud application services*, software is hosted online and made available to customers, typically on a subscription basis. The provider is responsible for developing, maintaining, and updating the software. This enables users to easily start using it, without installing or hosting it locally, at the expense of losing control over the software.
- **Infrastructure as a service** (IaaS): This model provides the technology and capabilities of high-standard data centers to customers without a significant investment on infrastructure. Customers access their infrastructure via a dashboard or API, without physically managing it.
- **Platform as a service** (PaaS): This model provides a ready-to-use environment for developing, testing, managing, and distributing software applications. This model prevents developers from being aware of the operating system, storage or updates, and makes the process of developing and deploying applications simpler and cost-effective.

The popularity of the SaaS model expanded to scenarios related to the database industry. In **database as a service** (DBaaS), users access and use a cloud database system without purchasing and setting up their own hardware, installing their own database software, or managing the database themselves. Once a database is set up, the platform is responsible for all the back end operations to maintain it, including configuration management, automating backups, patches and upgrades, service monitoring, etc. From the operational side, scaling is easy with this cloud computing model.

Similarly, data warehouses began to be delivered on the cloud, leading to **cloud data warehouses**. There are different models for this, described next.

- Data warehouse software deployed in the cloud. This is similar to conventional data warehouses, where the customer builds and manages the data warehouse, including tuning, configuration, and backups.
- Data warehouse hosted and managed in the cloud by a provider. Here, the provider manages the hardware deployment, as well as the software installation and configuration, while the customer manages, tunes, and optimizes the software. Amazon Redshift and Azure Synapse Analytics are examples of this category.

- **Data warehouse as a service** (DWaaS), also called *serverless cloud data warehouses*. Here, the provider manages the hardware and the software, and is responsible of managing performance, governance, and security, as well as scaling up and down on demand. Google BigQuery and Snowflake are examples of this category. In this case, customers pay for the storage and computing resources they use, when they use them. However, costs are difficult to predict. For example, Google BigQuery and Snowflake offer on-demand pricing options based on the amount of data scanned or compute time used.

Cloud data warehouses still faces many challenges. Ingesting data into a cloud data warehouse is not a trivial task, since it normally requires writing ETL code, which consumes time and expensive resources. Besides, moving between cloud providers can be problematic, since an organization may become tied to a provider or pay huge costs for moving from one cloud provider to another. Data latency, the time it takes to store or retrieve data, may be a challenge, depending on performance requirements, for example in the case of real-time data. Latency depends on the location of data sources, the amount of data, and the type of data. In the end, the choice between on-premises and cloud data warehouses will be based on the requirements of the application and the available resources. Among these factors, we can mention:

- The users and applications that will access the data warehouse and the analytic services to be offered using it.
- The types of data in the data warehouse, the speed at which these data come, how data can be accessed, the costs of moving data into the data warehouse, where data are located.
- The types of queries that will be run, how much data users will access, the frequency of the queries, the workload variation (whether constant or periodic, whether it has peaks and valleys), the required performance, the number of users. All of these have an impact on the costs, both for the on-premises solution and the cloud alternative.
- The security policies, which account for how data is shared across the organization with customers and partners.
- Legal requirements, which vary with the kind of business, the company's national law, and so on.
- Human resources available to manage the data warehouse.

15.12 Data Lakes and Data Lakehouses

A **data lake** is a central storage repository that holds vast amounts of raw data coming from multiple sources. The term **raw data** refers to data that is kept in its original format and that has not yet been processed for a purpose. Intuitively, the term data lake refers to the ad hoc nature of the data contained in it, as opposed to the curated data stored in traditional data warehouse systems. A data lake can store structured, semi-structured, or unstructured data, typically in a Hadoop environment. Data lakes are usually implemented on a cluster of commodity hardware, either locally or in the cloud, although the latter alternative is steadily growing.

The data lake concept is based on the **extraction, loading, and transformation** (ELT) paradigm, which opposes the traditional ETL approach used in classic data warehousing. The ELT paradigm aims to address situations where the ETL approach cannot cope with the analytical requirements, since the time needed to refresh the data warehouse using the traditional ETL process cannot be afforded. Other differences between a data lake and a data warehouse are given next.

- A data lake works on a **schema-on-read** principle, as opposed to data warehouses, which are based on a **schema-on-write** principle. In the former, data is stored in any format since a predefined schema into which data needs to be fitted does not exist. In other words, data preparation takes place when the data are actually being used. In the latter, as studied in previous chapters, data preparation takes place before processing.

- A data lake makes data acquisition easier and allows low-latency and near real-time data to be accessed, deferring the schema definition to the moment when requirements become clear. While a data warehouse only contains data that are needed for a well-defined purpose, a data lake typically ingests all types of data and keeps them in case they will eventually be needed. The data lake approach encourages what is called *early data exploration*, to satisfy the need for fast answers, which the data warehouse approach cannot address.

- The purpose of data acquisition is not predetermined in a data lake. Since raw data are captured without any preconceived purpose, data lakes sometimes lack organization and data filtering. By contrast, a data warehouse only stores processed data acquired for a specific task and for a specific purpose.

- In a data lake, early exploration is performed over the raw data, and only after this exploration, a schema may be defined over a portion of the data using typical cleansing and transformation tasks. As a consequence, data lakes usually demand larger storage capacity than data warehouses. Further, raw data can be quickly analyzed, which is typical in machine learning applications, obviously at the risk of lower data quality.

- Data lake users are typically data scientists, since non-technical users may not be able to interact with unstructured data, although many tools exist to alleviate this using self-service BI. In contrast, data warehouses use highly processed data exploited through easy-to-use OLAP clients or dashboards, making a data warehouse appropriate for users.

- Data lakes are more flexible than data warehouses. Changes in the former are relatively simple, while data warehouses are more structured and rigid, making changes to them more complicated.

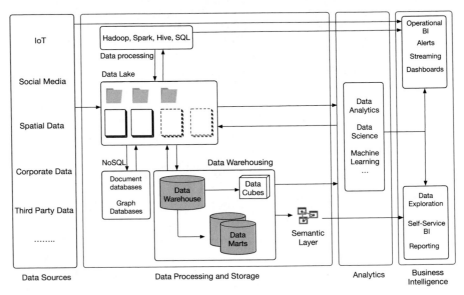

Fig. 15.21 A typical data lake architecture

Data lakes do not replace data warehouses; modern data architectures combine the two technologies, where the data warehouse and the data lake coexist and complement each other. Figure 15.21 summarizes this idea. The figure depicts the diversity of data sources and technological tools at the service of complex requirements for performing analytics. This confluence of different storage technologies is usually called **polyglot persistence**. It is worth noting that Hadoop is not the only choice to implement data lakes (although it is the most usual one); relational technologies are also used, typically in an ELT mode. However, the advantage of Hadoop is that data can also be exploited in a relational way, using tools like Hive, retaining Hadoop's very high data ingestion speed.

A data lake may be implemented either on premises or in the cloud, a topic addressed in Sect. 15.11. The former allows better control of data privacy and security, with higher physical space requirement and set up costs. The latter is easily scalable, with a pay-as-you-use cost model, also avoiding the maintenance of a usually large and expensive infrastructure, likely to become obsolete over time. Further, since a data warehouse already exists in many organizations, this favors the on-premises solution or a hybrid one, where only unstructured data are ingested from the cloud.

A main drawback of data lakes is their lack of data reliability. This requires building long data processing pipelines that ingest raw data, clean, structure and enrich them, until these data become useful for machine learning and business analytics. Lack of reliability is in particular a consequence of lack of consistency because data lake storage is not ACID compliant. We explain this next, to introduce the notion of Delta Lake, which attempts to solve this problem.

Data in data lakes are typically stored using file formats such as **ORC** or **Parquet** (Sect. 15.2.2), possibly partitioned. Achieving ACID properties using these file formats is very difficult since, when multiple objects need to be updated, users will see partial updates on individual objects. A similar situation occurs with rollbacks. **Delta Lake** is an open-source storage layer that brings transactions with **ACID properties** to Apache Spark and big data workloads. The goal of Delta Lake is to unify stream and batch data processing to solve the inconsistency problems explained above.

The main abstraction in the Delta Lake solution is the Delta table, a Spark table that stores data as Parquet files in the file system, and maintains a transaction log that efficiently tracks changes to the table. Data can be read, written, and stored in the Delta format using Spark SQL. The transaction log allows ACID transactions, so users can concurrently modify a dataset and get consistent views.

The general problem consists in capturing changes in data sources and merging these changes into target tables. This is called **change data capturing** (CDC). The basic idea is to maintain a staging table that accumulates all updates, and then produce a final table that contains the current up-to-date snapshot that users can query. This is done in a two-step process. Data are read and inserted into a Parquet table acting as a staging table. This table is read by a job running at regular intervals and the new data are loaded into the final Delta table, which complies with the ACID properties.

The snapshots of data mentioned above can be accessed and reverted to earlier versions of data for audits or rollbacks. Delta Lake also allows a table schema to be changed and this change is applied automatically. For this, Delta Lake uses schema validation on write, where all new writes to a table are checked for compatibility with the table schema at write time. If the schema is not compatible, the transaction is cancelled. This is called *schema enforcement*. If the user wants to add the rejected data into the schema, she can enable *schema evolution*. When this occurs, any column in the Apache Spark DataFrame (where processing is occurring) but not in the target table is automatically added at the end of the schema.

The combined data lake and data warehouse architecture presented above, which is increasingly being used in industry, suffers from the following problems. (a) Reliability: Keeping the data lake and data warehouse consistent is difficult and costly. (b) Data staleness: The data in the warehouse is stale compared to that of the data lake, with new data frequently taking days to load. (c) Limited support for advanced analytics: None of the leading machine learning systems work well on top of data warehouses. (d) Total cost of ownership: In addition to the ETL costs, users double the storage cost for data extracted from the data lake into the data warehouse.

A **data lakehouse** is a recent architecture that aims to enable both artificial intelligence and business intelligence tasks directly on data lakes. This is made possible due to recent technical advances, detailed next. (a) Multiple solutions, such as Delta Lake mentioned above, add to traditional data lakes reliable data management features such as ACID, schema evolution, time travel, incremental consumption, etc. (b) Many data science systems have adopted DataFrames as the abstraction for manipulating data, and recent declarative DataFrame APIs enable machine learning workloads to directly benefit from many optimizations in lakehouses. (c) Lakehouses provide SQL performance on top of the massive Parquet/ORC datasets that have been collected over the last decade. Recent results have shown that an SQL engine over Parquet outperforms leading cloud data warehouses on the well-known TPC-DS analytical benchmark. Nevertheless, it still remains to be proven that a unified data platform architecture that implements data warehousing functionality over open data lake file formats can provide performance competitive with today's data warehouse systems and considerably simplify enterprise data architectures.

15.13 Future Perspectives

Big data has become the standard setting in todays' applications, and this state of affairs will remain in the years to come. In the last decades, the data management domain has explored various approaches to solve the multiple challenges posed by big data. Since traditional relational databases have limitations for coping with these challenges, the initial approaches abandoned many of their foundational aspects. The advent of the first generation of NoSQL systems represents this situation. Although NoSQL systems provided relevant solutions for scalability and elasticity, over the years it became clear that many characteristics of traditional databases, in particular the ACID properties for transaction processing, were still relevant. The advent of the first NewSQL systems represent this situation. Around the same time, the HTAP (Hybrid transaction and analytical processing) paradigm was proposed as a solution to the limitations of the ETL (extraction, transformation, and loading) approach for coping with big data, in particular for reducing the latency for processing real-time data, as well as for reducing the high overhead, complexity, and costs of maintaining two parallel systems, one for coping with OLTP (online transaction processing) workloads and another for OLAP (online analytical processing) workloads.

Each one of the solutions proposed during the last decades tackle some, but not all, of the multiple challenges posed by big data. The CAP theorem was fundamental in this respect, showing that a compromise between the various challenges must be made depending on the application requirements. Over the years, initial solutions were replaced by newer, more efficient ones. The long-standing debate between MapReduce and Spark represents this situation. Gradually, the proposed approaches blended several of the previous ones into a single framework. For example, several of the new database systems provide both in-memory and columnar storage. However, the most recent solutions lack the maturity of those proposed many years ago. Examples are polyglot database systems or delta lakes. In conclusion, what is still missing are robust approaches that encompass many of the ones proposed in the last decades within a single framework.

In this chapter, we surveyed the approaches proposed so far to address the big data challenges. The choice of the technologies and systems covered reflects the current understanding of the authors, at the time of writing this book, about which of them will still be relevant in the years to come. Although only time will tell whether our choice was correct, what we are completely sure of is that big data management and analytics represents nowadays one of the foundational disciplines of computer science.

15.14 Summary

We have studied the challenges that big data analytics brought to data warehousing, and the approaches that have been proposed for addressing these challenges. We presented a comprehensive state of the art in the field. We addressed the problem along two dimensions: distributed processing frameworks and distributed data storage and querying. For the first dimension, we studied the two main frameworks, namely, Hadoop and Spark, as well as high-level query languages for them, namely, HiveQL and Spark SQL. For the second dimension, we presented various database technologies enabling big data processing. These are distributed database systems, in-memory database systems, columnar database systems, NoSQL database systems, NewSQL database systems, and array database systems. For each of these technologies we also presented two representative systems. We covered the HTAP paradigm, which proposes performing OLAP and OLTP workloads on the same system. An analogous approach is behind polystores, which aim at querying heterogeneous database systems through a single query language. Crossing all of the above, we discussed cloud data warehousing, and the classic dilemma of on-premises against in-cloud processing was also addressed. We concluded by presenting the data lake approach, used for making the data available right after the ingestion phase, including the notion of Delta Lake, an open-source layer on top of a data lake, allowing ACID transactions on the data lake.

15.15 Bibliographic Notes

There is a wide corpus of academic literature and industrial white papers on the topics covered in this chapter. A survey of more than 20 years of research on data warehouse systems, from their early relational implementations up to the challenges posed by the integration with big data settings is given in [88]. The "one size fits all" approach followed by traditional DBMSs is discussed in [225]. Gilbert and Lynch formalized the CAP theorem in [81]. Distributed and parallel databases are covered in [177], which also discusses big data processing. A general description of Hadoop can be found in [261]. Hive is described in the book [62]. The seminal Spark paper was published by Zaharia et al. [271], while a recent book on Spark is [46]. Davoudian et al. [57] present a comprehensive survey on NoSQL databases. HBase is covered in [80] and Cassandra in [44]. Regarding column stores, MonetDB is reviewed in [115] and Vertica is studied in [134]. IMDBSs are studied in [190], where SAP HANA is also studied. Redis is discussed in [48]. Pavlo and Aslett [184] discuss NewSQL, relate it to HTAP, and also comment on the commercial and open-source systems supporting this approach. A survey on HTAP is presented in [176], while a performance characterization of HTAP workloads is given in [219]. VoltDB is studied in [226]. Array databases are covered in [22], rasdaman is described in [23], and SciDB is described in [224]. An Ontology Based Data Access (OBDA) to polystores is described in [126]. The Cloud-MdsQL engine is described in [131], while the BigDAWG polystore system is studied in [64]. Cloud data warehouses are discussed in [132], while Snowflake is covered in [54]. Self-service BI is studied in [243]. Finally, data lakes are described in [93, 216], Delta Lake is introduced in [14], and Lakehouse is introduced in [15].

15.16 Review Questions

15.1 What is big data? How can we characterize this notion?

15.2 What are the challenges that big data poses to data warehousing?

15.3 What are the requirements for efficient OLAP querying in big data? Can they be achieved with standard data warehousing technology?

15.4 Describe the main characteristics of the MapReduce paradigm.

15.5 Describe the main features of Hadoop.

15.6 What is Hive? Explain its main characteristics.

15.7 Describe the main features of Spark and compare it with Hadoop.

15.8 Describe Kylin's implementations on Hadoop and Spark. Explain how materialized cubes are built and stored.

15.9 Explain the main characteristics of distributed database systems.

15.10 Explain and compare the data distribution architectures in MySQL Cluster and Citus.

15.11 Describe in-memory database systems and their general architecture.

15.12 How do in-memory database systems guarantee the ACID properties?

15.13 What is data aging? How is this concept used in in-memory database systems?

15.14 Compare Times Ten and Redis against the characteristics of in-memory database systems. Which mechanisms do they use to comply with the ACID properties?

15.15 Explain the main characteristics of column-store database systems.

15.16 Why do column-store database systems achieve better efficiency than row-store database systems for data warehouses?

15.17 How do column-store database systems compress the data? Why is compression important?

15.18 Explain the architectures of Vertica and MonetDB, and compare them against a general column-store database architecture.

15.19 What do columnar capabilities add to Citus?

15.20 Define NoSQL database systems. Classify them and give examples.

15.21 Explain the CAP theorem and its relevance for NoSQL database systems.

15.22 Compare the architectures of HBase and Cassandra and classify them with respect to the CAP theorem.

15.23 What are NewSQL database systems? What do they try to achieve?

15.24 Describe the main features of Cloud Spanner.

15.25 Compare SAP HANA and VoltDB against the NewSQL goals. Do they achieve such goals? Elaborate on this topic.

15.26 Explain the general architecture of array database systems.

15.27 Explain the main features of rasdaman and SciDB and compare them against each other.

15.28 What is Hybrid Transactional and Analytical Processing (HTAP)?

15.29 Explain the three typical HTAP architectures.

15.30 Discuss why SingleStore and LeanXcale are examples of HTAP architectures.

15.31 Define polystores and explain the three different kinds of polystores.

15.32 Compare CloudMdsQL and BigDAWG and explain their query processing mechanisms.

15.33 Explain the deployment and service models in cloud computing.

15.34 What are cloud data warehouses? Explain the three possible ways of deploying a cloud data warehouse.

15.35 Discuss pros and cons of on-premises and cloud data warehouses.

15.36 How does extraction, loading, and transformation (ELT) differ from extraction, transformation, and loading (ETL)? Choose an application scenario you are familiar with to motivate the use of ELT.

15.37 What are data lakes? Do they replace data warehouses?

15.38 Describe the main components of a data lake architecture.

15.39 How does a data lakehouse differ from a data lake? What would you use a data lakehouse for?

15.40 Elaborate on a vision of future scenarios for data warehousing.

Appendix A
Graphical Notation

In the following, we summarize the graphical notation used in this book.

A.1 Entity-Relationship Model

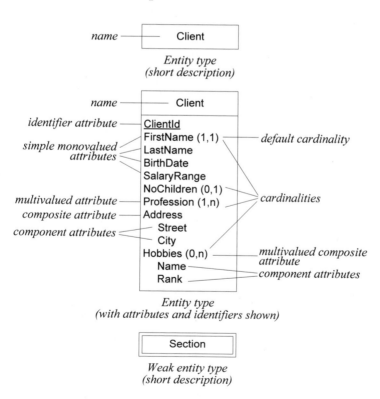

Entity type
(short description)

Entity type
(with attributes and identifiers shown)

Weak entity type
(short description)

Section

Semester
Year
Homepage (0,1)

Weak entity type
(with attributes and partial identifiers shown)

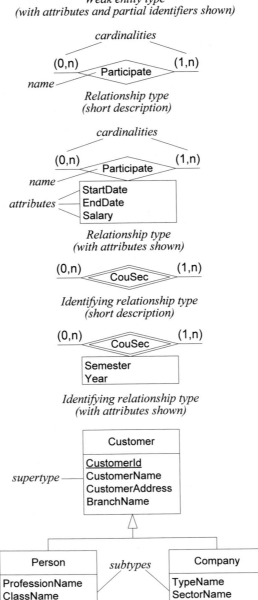

cardinalities

(0,n)   (1,n)
Participate

name

Relationship type
(short description)

cardinalities

(0,n)   (1,n)
Participate

name

attributes   StartDate
EndDate
Salary

Relationship type
(with attributes shown)

(0,n)   (1,n)
CouSec

Identifying relationship type
(short description)

(0,n)   (1,n)
CouSec

Semester
Year

Identifying relationship type
(with attributes shown)

Customer

CustomerId
CustomerName
CustomerAddress
BranchName

supertype

Person

ProfessionName
ClassName

subtypes

Company

TypeName
SectorName

Generalization/specialization
relationship type

A.2 Relational Model

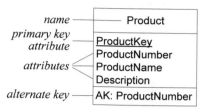

name — Product
primary key attribute — ProductKey
ProductNumber
attributes — ProductName
Description
alternate key — AK: ProductNumber

Relational table
(with attributes and keys shown)

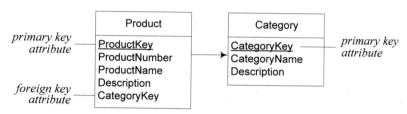

primary key attribute — Product / ProductKey
foreign key attribute — CategoryKey
primary key attribute — Category / CategoryKey

Referential integrity

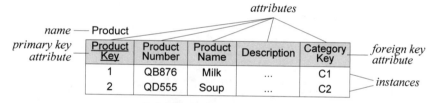

Relational table with instances

A.3 MultiDim Model for Data Warehouses

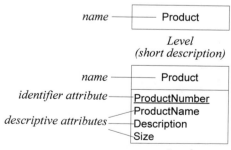

name — Product

Level
(short description)

name — Product
identifier attribute — ProductNumber
descriptive attributes — ProductName
Description
Size

Level
(with attributes and identifiers shown)

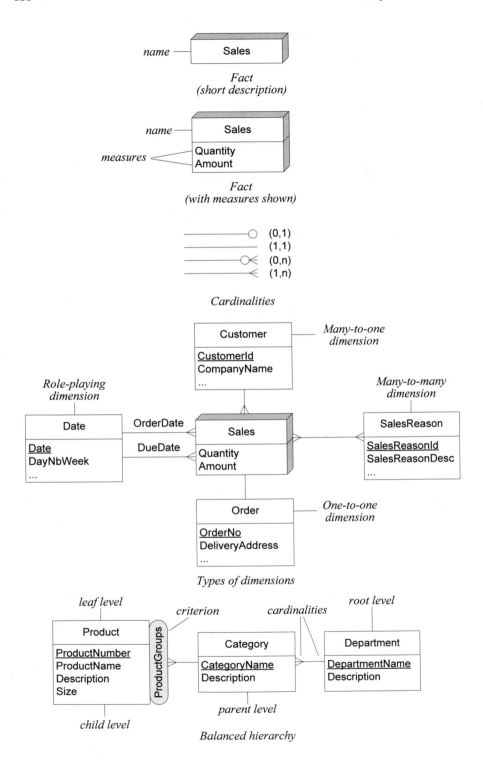

name — Sales

*Fact
(short description)*

name — Sales
measures — Quantity
Amount

*Fact
(with measures shown)*

(0,1)
(1,1)
(0,n)
(1,n)

Cardinalities

*Many-to-one
dimension*

Customer

CustomerId
CompanyName
...

*Role-playing
dimension*

*Many-to-many
dimension*

Date   OrderDate   Sales   SalesReason

Date   DueDate   Quantity   SalesReasonId
DayNbWeek   Amount   SalesReasonDesc
...   ...

*One-to-one
dimension*

Order

OrderNo
DeliveryAddress
...

Types of dimensions

leaf level   *criterion*   *cardinalities*   *root level*

Product   ProductGroups   Category   Department

ProductNumber   CategoryName   DepartmentName
ProductName   Description   Description
Description
Size

child level   *parent level*

Balanced hierarchy

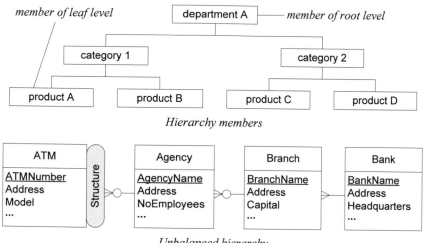

member of leaf level department A — *member of root level*

Hierarchy members

ATM

ATMNumber
Address
Model
...

Structure

Agency

AgencyName
Address
NoEmployees
...

Branch

BranchName
Address
Capital
...

Bank

BankName
Address
Headquarters
...

Unbalanced hierarchy

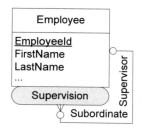

Employee

EmployeeId
FirstName
LastName
...

Supervision

Supervisor

Subordinate

Parent-child hierarchy

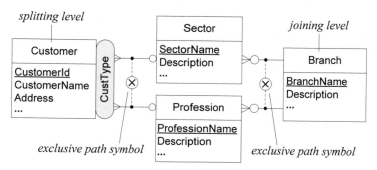

splitting level

Customer

CustomerId
CustomerName
Address
...

CustType

Sector

SectorName
Description
...

joining level

Branch

BranchName
Description
...

Profession

ProfessionName
Description
...

exclusive path symbol   *exclusive path symbol*

Generalized hierarchy

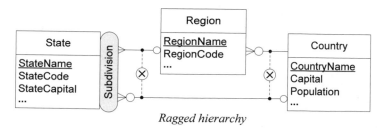

State

StateName
StateCode
StateCapital
...

Subdivision

Region

RegionName
RegionCode
...

Country

CountryName
Capital
Population
...

Ragged hierarchy

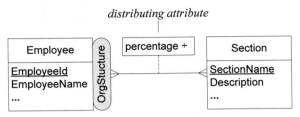

Nonstrict hierarchy

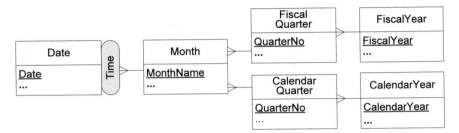

Alternative hierarchy

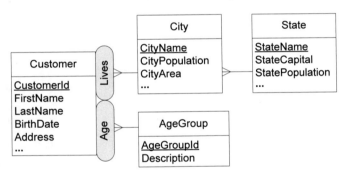

Parallel independant hierarchies

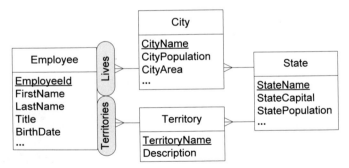

Parallel dependant hierarchies

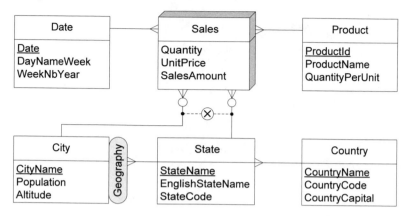

Fact with multiple granularities

A.4 MultiDim Model for Spatial Data Warehouses

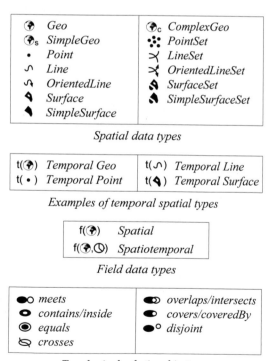

Spatial data types

Examples of temporal spatial types

Field data types

Topological relationship types

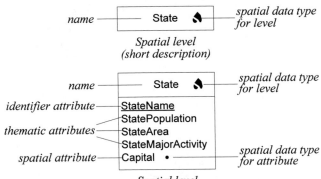

*Spatial level
(short description)*

*Spatial level
(with attributes and identifiers shown)*

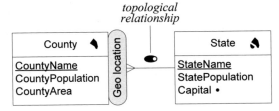

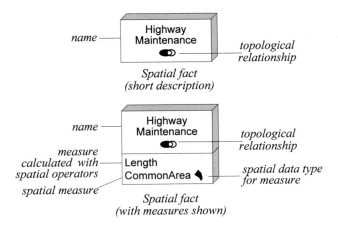

Spatial hierarchy

*Spatial fact
(short description)*

*Spatial fact
(with measures shown)*

A.5 MultiDim Model for Temporal Data Warehouses

◐ Time	◐c ComplexTime
◐s SimpleTime	◑ InstantSet
◐ Instant	❂ IntervalSet
◑ Interval	

Time data types

⊢⊣ meets	⊢⊣ overlaps/intersects
⊟ contains/inside	⊡ covers/coveredBy
⊨ equals	⊣⊢ disjoint
⊢ starts	⊣ finishes
⇠ precedes	⇢ succeeds

Synchronization predicates

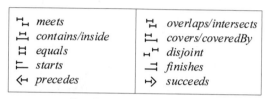

temporality type of level — ❂ Product — *name*

*Temporal level
(short description)*

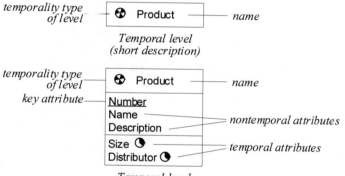

temporality type of level — ❂ Product — *name*
key attribute — Number
Name — *nontemporal attributes*
Description
Size ◑ — *temporal attributes*
Distributor ◑

*Temporal level
(with attributes and key shown)*

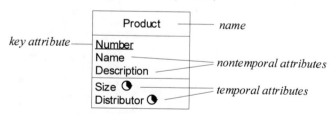

Product — *name*
key attribute — Number
Name — *nontemporal attributes*
Description
Size ◑ — *temporal attributes*
Distributor ◑

*Nontemporal level
with temporal attributes*

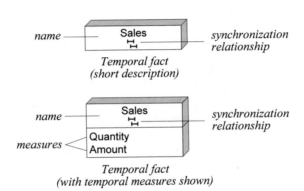

synchronization
relationship

snapshot
cardinality

temporal parent-child
relationship

Temporal hierarchy

name ———

synchronization
relationship

Temporal fact
(short description)

name ———

synchronization
relationship

measures ———

Temporal fact
(with temporal measures shown)

A.6 BPMN Notation for ETL

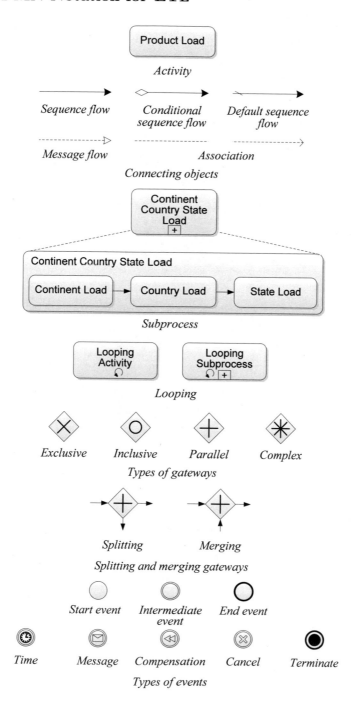

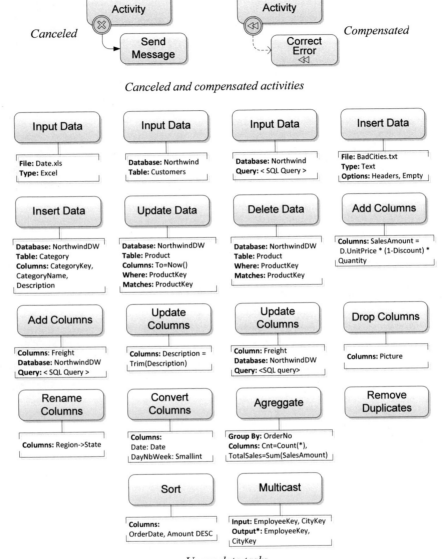

Canceled and compensated activities

Unary data tasks

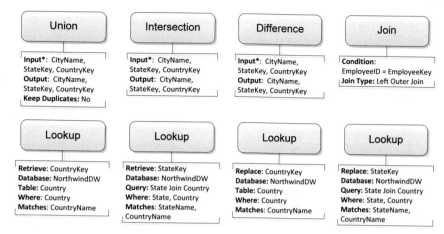

Union

Input*: CityName,
StateKey, CountryKey
Output: CityName,
StateKey, CountryKey
Keep Duplicates: No

Intersection

Input*: CityName,
StateKey, CountryKey
Output: CityName,
StateKey, CountryKey

Difference

Input*: CityName,
StateKey, CountryKey
Output: CityName,
StateKey, CountryKey

Join

Condition:
EmployeeID = EmployeeKey
Join Type: Left Outer Join

Lookup

Retrieve: CountryKey
Database: NorthwindDW
Table: Country
Where: Country
Matches: CountryName

Lookup

Retrieve: StateKey
Database: NorthwindDW
Query: State Join Country
Where: State, Country
Matches: StateName,
CountryName

Lookup

Replace: CountryKey
Database: NorthwindDW
Table: Country
Where: Country
Matches: CountryName

Lookup

Replace: StateKey
Database: NorthwindDW
Query: State Join Country
Where: State, Country
Matches: StateName,
CountryName

N-ary data tasks

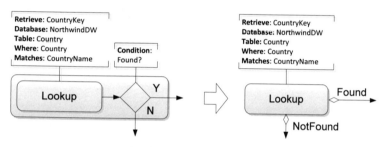

Retrieve: CountryKey
Database: NorthwindDW
Table: Country
Where: Country
Matches: CountryName

Condition:
Found?

Lookup Y N

Retrieve: CountryKey
Database: NorthwindDW
Table: Country
Where: Country
Matches: CountryName

Lookup Found

NotFound

Shorthand notation for lookup

References

[1] A. Abelló and C. Martín. A bitemporal storage structure for a corporate data warehouse. In *Proc. of the 5th International Conference on Enterprise Information Systems, ICEIS'03*, pages 177–183, 2003.

[2] A. Abelló, J. Samos, and F. Saltor. YAM^2 (Yet Another Multidimensional Model): An extension of UML. *Information Systems*, 32(6):541–567, 2006.

[3] S. Agarwal, R. Agrawal, P. Deshpande, A. Gupta, J.F. Naughton, R. Ramakrishnan, and S. Sarawagi. On the computation of multidimensional aggregates. In *Proc. of the 22nd International Conference on Very Large Data Bases, VLDB'96*, pages 506–521. Morgan Kaufmann, 1996.

[4] W. Ahmed, E. Zimányi, A.A. Vaisman, and R. Wrembel. A temporal multidimensional model and OLAP operators. *International Journal of Data Warehousing and Mining*, 16(4):112–143, 2020.

[5] W. Ahmed, E. Zimányi, A.A. Vaisman, and R. Wrembel. A multiversion data warehouse model and its implementation. *International Journal of Data Warehousing and Mining*, 17(4):1–28, 2021.

[6] L. Alarabi. Summit: a scalable system for massive trajectory data management. *ACM SIGSPATIAL Special*, 10(3):2–3, 2018.

[7] O. Andersen, B.B. Krogh, C. Thomsen, and K. Torp. An advanced data warehouse for integrating large sets of GPS data. In *Proc. of the 17th ACM International Workshop on Data Warehousing and OLAP, DOLAP 2014*, pages 13–22. ACM Press, 2014.

[8] G. Andrienko, N. Andrienko, P. Bak, D. Keim, and S. Wrobel. *Visual Analytics of Movement*. Springer, 2014.

[9] N. Andrienko, G. Andrienko, G. Fuchs, A. Slingsby, C. Turkay, and S. Wrobel. *Visual Analytics for Data Scientists*. Springer, 2020.

[10] R. Angles. A comparison of current graph database models. In *Workshop Proc. of the IEEE 28th International Conference on Data Engineering, ICDE 2012*, pages 171–177. IEEE Computer Society, 2012.

© Springer-Verlag GmbH Germany, part of Springer Nature 2022
A. Vaisman, E. Zimányi, *Data Warehouse Systems*, Data-Centric Systems and Applications, https://doi.org/10.1007/978-3-662-65167-4

[11] R. Angles, M. Arenas, P. Barceló, A. Hogan, J.L. Reutter, and D. Vrgoc. Foundations of modern query languages for graph databases. *ACM Computing Surveys*, 50(5):68:1–68:40, 2017.

[12] R. Angles and C. Gutiérrez. Survey of graph database models. *ACM Computing Surveys*, 40(1):1:1–1:39, 2008.

[13] R. Angles and C. Gutiérrez. An introduction to graph data management. *CoRR*, abs/1801.00036, 2018.

[14] M. Armbrust, T. Das, L. Sun, et al. Delta Lake: High-performance ACID table storage over cloud object stores. *Proc. of VLDB Endowment*, 13(12):3411–3424, 2020.

[15] M. Armbrust, A. Ghodsi, R. Xin, and M. Zaharia. Lakehouse: A new generation of open platforms that unify data warehousing and advanced analytics. In *Proc. of the 11th Conference on Innovative Data Systems Research, CIDR 2021*, 2021.

[16] M.-A. Aufaure and E. Zimányi, editors. *Tutorial Lectures of the 2nd European Business Intelligence Summer School, eBISS 2012*, number 138 in Lecture Notes in Business Information Processing. Springer, 2012.

[17] J. Awiti, A.A. Vaisman, and E. Zimányi. Design and implementation of ETL processes using BPMN and relational algebra. *Data Knowledge Engineering*, 129:101837, 2020.

[18] J. Awiti and E. Zimányi. An XML interchange format for ETL models. In *Proc. of ADBIS 2019 Short Papers, Workshops and Doctoral Consortium*, number 1064 in Communications in Computer and Information Science, pages 427–439. Springer, 2019.

[19] E.A. Azirani, F. Goasdoué, I. Manolescu, and A. Roatis. Efficient OLAP operations for RDF analytics. In *Workshop Proc. of the 31st International Conference on Data Engineering, ICDE 2015*, pages 71–76. IEEE Computer Society Press, 2015.

[20] M.S. Bakli, M.A. Sakr, and E. Zimányi. Distributed spatiotemporal trajectory query processing in SQL. In *Proc. of the 28th International Conference on Advances in Geographic Information Systems, SIGSPATIAL'20*. ACM, 2020.

[21] D. Barone, L. Jiang, D. Amyot, and J. Mylopoulos. Composite indicators for business intelligence. In *Proc. of the 30th International Conference on Conceptual Modeling, ER 2011*, number 6998 in Lecture Notes in Computer Science, pages 448–458. Springer, 2011.

[22] P. Baumann, D. Misev, V. Merticariu, and B.P. Huu. Array databases: concepts, standards, implementations. *Journal of Big Data*, 8(28), 2021.

[23] P. Baumann, D. Misev, V. Merticariu, B.P. Huu, and B. Bell. rasdaman: Spatio-temporal datacubes on steroids. In *Proc. of the 26th ACM SIGSPATIAL International Conference on Advances in Geographic Information Systems, SIGSPATIAL 2018*, pages 604–607. ACM, 2018.

[24] Y. Bédard, S. Rivest, and M. Proulx. Spatial online analytical processing (SOLAP): Concepts, architectures, and solutions from a geomatics engineering perspective. In [265], chapter 13, pages 298–319.

[25] L. Bellatreche, M. Schneider, H. Lorinquer, and M.K. Mohania. Bringing together partitioning, materialized views and indexes to optimize performance of relational data warehouses. In *Proc. of the 6th International Conference on Data Warehousing and Knowledge Discovery, DaWaK'04*, number 3181 in Lecture Notes in Computer Science, pages 15–25. Springer, 2004.

[26] S. Bimonte, L. Antonelli, and S. Rizzi. Requirements-driven data warehouse design based on enhanced pivot tables. *Requirements Engineering*, 26(1):43–65, 2021.

[27] S. Bimonte, M. Bertolotto, J. Gensel, and O. Boussaid. Spatial OLAP and map generalization: Model and algebra. *International Journal of Data Warehouse and Mining*, 8(1):24–51, 2012.

[28] S. Bimonte, M. Schneider, and O. Boussaid. Business intelligence indicators: Types, models and implementation. *International Journal of Data Warehousing and Mining*, 12:75–98, 2016.

[29] S. Bimonte, M. Zaamoune, and P. Beaune. Conceptual design and implementation of spatial data warehouses integrating regular grids of points. *International Journal of Digital Earth*, 10(9):901–922, 2017.

[30] M. Blaschka, C. Sapia, and G. Höfling. On schema evolution in multidimensional databases. In *Proc. of the 1st International Conference on Data Warehousing and Knowledge Discovery, DaWaK'99*, number 1676 in Lecture Notes in Computer Science, pages 153–164. Springer, 1999.

[31] R. Bliujute, S. Saltenis, G. Slivinskas, and C.S. Jensen. Systematic change management in dimensional data warehousing. Technical Report TR-23, Time Center, 1998.

[32] M. Body, M. Miquel, Y. Bédard, and A. Tchounikine. Handling evolution in multidimensional structures. In *Proc. of the 19th International Conference on Data Engineering, ICDE'03*, pages 581–592. IEEE Computer Society Press, 2003.

[33] M. Böhlen, J. Gamper, and C.S. Jensen. Towards general temporal aggregation. In *Proc. of the 25th British National Conference on Databases, BNCOD 2008*, number 5071 in Lecture Notes in Computer Science, pages 257–269. Springer, 2008.

[34] M. Böhnlein and A. Ulbrich-vom Ende. Deriving initial data warehouses structures from the conceptual data models of the underlying operational information systems. In [222], pages 15–21.

[35] A. Bonifati, F. Cattaneo, S. Ceri, A. Fuggetta, and S. Paraboschi. Designing data marts for data warehouses. *ACM Transactions on Software Engineering and Methodology*, 10(4):452–483, 2001.

[36] A. Bonifati, G. Fletcher, H. Voigt, and N. Yakovets. *Querying Graphs*. Synthesis Lectures on Data Management. Morgan & Claypool, 2018.

[37] G. Booch, I. Jacobson, and J. Rumbaugh. *The Unified Modeling Language: User Guide*. Addison-Wesley, second edition, 2005.

[38] K. Boulil, S. Bimonte, and F. Pinet. Conceptual model for spatial data cubes: A UML profile and its automatic implementation. *Computer Standards & Interfaces*, 38:113–132, 2015.

[39] D. Breucker, B. Kämpgen, and A. Harth. SEO4OLAP - search engine optimized presentation of statistical linked data. In *46. Jahrestagung der Gesellschaft für Informatik, Informatik 2016*, volume P-259 of *LNI*, pages 395–407. GI, 2016.

[40] L. Cabibbo and R. Torlone. A logical approach to multidimensional databases. In [212], pages 183–197.

[41] J. Cabot, A. Olivé, and E. Teniente. Representing temporal information in UML. In *Proc. of the 6th International Conference on the Unified Modeling Language, UML'2003*, number 2863 in Lecture Notes in Computer Science, pages 44–59. Springer, 2003.

[42] G. Câmara, D. Palomo, R.C.M. de Souza, F. de Oliveira, and O. Regina. Towards a generalized map algebra: Principles and data types. In *Proc. of the VII Brazilian Symposium on Geoinformatics, GeoInfo 2005*, pages 66–81, 2005.

[43] J. Carabaño, J. Westerholm, and T. Sarjakoski. A compiler approach to map algebra: automatic parallelization, locality optimization, and GPU acceleration of raster spatial analysis. *GeoInformatica*, 22(2):211–235, 2018.

[44] J. Carpenter and E. Hewitt. *Cassandra: The Definitive Guide. Distributed Data at Web Scale*. O'Reilly Media, 2016.

[45] J. Celko. *Joe Celko's SQL for Smarties: Advanced SQL Programming*. Morgan Kaufmann, fifth edition, 2014.

[46] B. Chambers and M. Zaharia. *Spark: The Definitive Guide. Big Data Processing Made Simple*. O'Reilly Media, 2018.

[47] C. Chen, X. Yan, F. Zhu, J. Han, and P.S. Yu. Graph OLAP: A multidimensional framework for graph data analysis. *Knowledge Information Systems*, 21(1):41–63, 2009.

[48] S. Chen, X. Tang, H. Wang, H. Zhao, and M. Guo. Towards scalable and reliable in-memory storage system: A case study with redis. In *Proc. of the 2016 IEEE Trustcom/BigDataSE/ISPA Conferences*, pages 1660–1667. IEEE, 2016.

[49] J. Chmiel, T. Morzy, and R. Wrembel. Multiversion join index for multiversion data warehouse. *Information and Software Technology*, 51(1):98–108, 2009.

[50] C. Ciferri, R. Ciferri, L.I. Gómez, M. Schneider, A.A. Vaisman, and E. Zimányi. Cube algebra: A generic user-centric model and query language for OLAP cubes. *International Journal of Data Warehousing and Mining*, 9(2):39–65, 2013.

[51] C. Combi, B. Oliboni, G. Pozzi, A. Sabaini, and E. Zimányi. Enabling instant- and interval-based semantics in multidimensional data models: the T+MultiDim model. *Information Sciences*, 518:413–435, 2020.

[52] C. Cote, M. Lah, and D. Sarka. *SQL Server 2017 Integration Services Cookbook: Powerful ETL techniques to load and transform data from almost any source*. Packt Publishing, 2017.

[53] C. Curino, H.-J. Moon, A. Deutsch, and C. Zaniolo. Automating the database schema evolution process. *The VLDB Journal*, 22(1):73–98, 2013.

[54] B. Dageville, T. Cruanes, M. Zukowski, et al. The Snowflake elastic data warehouse. In *Proc. of the ACM SIGMOD International Conference on Management of Data, SIGMOD 2016*, pages 215–226. ACM Press, 2016.

[55] C.J. Date, H. Darwen, and N.A. Lorentzos. *Time and Relational Theory: Temporal Databases in the Relational Model and SQL*. Morgan Kaufmann, second edition, 2014.

[56] L. Davidson. *Pro SQL Server Relational Database Design and Implementation: Best Practices for Scalability and Performance*. APress, sixth edition, 2020.

[57] A. Davoudian, L. Chen, and M. Liu. A survey on NoSQL stores. *ACM Comput. Surv.*, 51(2):40:1–40:43, 2018.

[58] C. Diamantini, D. Potena, and E. Storti. Extended drill-down operator: Digging into the structure of performance indicators. *Concurrency and Computation: Practice and Experience*, 28(15):3948–3968, 2016.

[59] J. Dick, E. Hull, and K. Jackson. *Requirements Engineering*. Springer, fourth edition, 2017.

[60] Anton Dignös, Michael H. Böhlen, Johann Gamper, and Christian S. Jensen. Extending the kernel of a relational DBMS with comprehensive support for sequenced temporal queries. *ACM Transactions of Database Systems*, 41(4):26:1–26:46, 2016.

[61] E. Domínguez, B. Pérez, A.L. Rubio, and M.A. Zapata. A taxonomy for key performance indicators management. *Computer Standards & Interfaces*, 64:24–40, 2019.

[62] D. Du. *Apache Hive Essentials*. Packt Publishing, second edition, 2018.

[63] B. DuCharme. *Learning SPARQL: Querying and Updating with SPARQL 1.1*. O'Reilly Media, second edition, 2013.

[64] J. Duggan, A.J. Elmore, M. Stonebraker, M. Balazinska, B. Howe, J. Kepner, S. Madden, D. Maier, T. Mattson, and S.B. Zdonik. The BigDAWG polystore system. *SIGMOD Record*, 44(2):11–16, 2015.

[65] J. Eder, C. Koncilia, and T. Morzy. The COMET metamodel for temporal data warehouses. In *Proc. of the 14th International Conference on Advanced Information Systems Engineering, CAiSE'02*, number 2348 in Lecture Notes in Computer Science, pages 83–99. Springer, 2002.

[66] Z. El Akkaoui and E. Zimányi. Defining ETL workflows using BPMN and BPEL. In *Proc. of the 12th ACM International Workshop on Data Warehousing and OLAP, DOLAP 2009*, pages 41–48. ACM Press, 2009.

[67] Z. El Akkaoui, E. Zimányi, J.-N. Mazón, and J. Trujillo. A BPMN-based design and maintenance framework for ETL processes. *International Journal of Data Warehousing and Mining*, 9(3):46–72, 2013.

[68] E. Elamin, S. Alshomrani, and J. Feki. Ssreq: A method for designing star schemas from decisional requirements. *2017 International Conference on Communication, Control, Computing and Electronics Engineering (ICCCEE)*, pages 1–7, 2017.

[69] A. Eldawy and M.F. Mokbel. SpatialHadoop: A MapReduce framework for spatial data. In *Proc. of the 31st International Conference on Data Engineering, ICDE 2015*, pages 1352–1363. IEEE Computer Society Press, 2015.

[70] R. Elmasri and S. Navathe. *Fundamentals of Database Systems*. Pearson, seventh edition, 2016.

[71] R. Elmasri and G. Wuu. A temporal model and query language for ER databases. In *Proc. of the 6th International Conference on Data Engineering, ICDE'90*, pages 76–83. IEEE Computer Society Press, 1990.

[72] L. Etcheverry and A.A. Vaisman. QB4OLAP: A vocabulary for OLAP cubes on the semantic web. In *Proc. of the Third International Workshop on Consuming Linked Data, COLD 2012*, number 905 in CEUR Workshop Proceedings, 2012.

[73] L. Etcheverry and A.A. Vaisman. Efficient analytical queries on semantic web data cubes. *Journal on Data Semantics*, 6(4):199–219, 2017.

[74] A. Ferrari and M. Russo. *Analyzing Data with Power BI and Power Pivot for Excel*. Microsoft Press, 2017.

[75] S. Few. *Information Dashboard Design: Displaying Data for At-a-Glance Monitoring*. Analytics Press, second edition, 2013.

[76] S. Flesca, S. Greco, E. Masciari, and D. Saccà, editors. *A Comprehensive Guide Through the Italian Database Research Over the Last 25 Years*, volume 31 of *Studies in Big Data*. Springer, 2018.

[77] G. Fletcher, J. Hidders, and J.L. Larriba-Pey, editors. *Graph Data Management: Fundamental Issues and Recent Developments*. Springer, 2018.

[78] R. Gacitua, J.-N. Mazón, and Ania Cravero. Using semantic web technologies in the development of data warehouses: A systematic mapping. *Wiley Interdisciplinary Reviews Data Mining and Knowledge Discovery*, 9(3), 2019.

[79] H. Garcia-Molina, J.D. Ullman, and J. Widom. *Database systems: The complete book*. Prentice Hall, second edition, 2008.

[80] L. George. *HBase: The Definitive Guide*. O'Reilly Media, 2011.

[81] S. Gilbert and N. A. Lynch. Perspectives on the CAP theorem. *IEEE Computer*, 45(2):30–36, 2012.

[82] M. Golfarelli, J. Lechtenbörger, S. Rizzi, and G. Vossen. Schema versioning in data warehouses: Enabling cross-version querying via schema augmentation. *Data & Knowledge Engineering*, 59:435–459, 2006.

[83] M. Golfarelli, D. Maio, and S. Rizzi. Conceptual design of data warehouses from E/R schemes. In *Proc. of the 31st Hawaii International Conference on System Sciences, HICSS-31*, volume 7, pages 334–343. IEEE Computer Society Press, 1998.

[84] M. Golfarelli and S. Rizzi. A methodological framework for data warehouse design. In *Proc. of the 1st ACM International Workshop on Data Warehousing and OLAP, DOLAP'98*, pages 3–9. ACM Press, 1998.

[85] M. Golfarelli and S. Rizzi. Index selection for data warehousing. In *Proc. of the 4th International Workshop on Design and Management of Data Warehouses, DMDW'02*, number 58 in CEUR Workshop Proceedings, pages 33–42, 2002.

[86] M. Golfarelli and S. Rizzi. *Data Warehouse Design: Modern Principles and Methodologies*. McGraw-Hill, 2009.

[87] M. Golfarelli and S. Rizzi. Temporal data warehousing: Approaches and techniques. In [228], pages 1–18.

[88] M. Golfarelli and S. Rizzi. From star schemas to big data: 20+ years of data warehouse research. In [76], pages 93–107.

[89] M. Goller and S. Berger. Handling measurement function changes with slowly changing measures. *Information Systems*, 53:107–123, 2015.

[90] L.I. Gómez, S. Gómez, and A.A. Vaisman. A generic data model and query language for spatiotemporal OLAP cube analysis. In *Proc. of the 15th International Conference on Extending Database Technology, EDBT 2012*, pages 300–311. ACM Press, 2012.

[91] L.I. Gómez, B. Kuijpers, and A.A. Vaisman. Analytical queries on semantic trajectories using graph databases. *Transactions in GIS*, 23(5):1078–1101, 2019.

[92] L.I. Gómez, B. Kuijpers, and A.A. Vaisman. Online analytical processsing on graph data. *Intelligent Data Analysis*, 24(3):515–541, 2020.

[93] A. Gorelik. *The Enterprise Big Data Lake: Delivering the Promise of Big Data and Data Science*. O'Reilly Media, 2019.

[94] J. Gray, S. Chaudhuri, A. Basworth, A. Layman, D. Reichart, M. Venkatrao, F. Pellow, and H. Pirahesh. Data cube: A relational aggregation operator generalizing group-by, cross-tab, and sub-totals. *Data Mining and Knowledge Discovery*, 1(1):29–53, 1997.

[95] A. Gupta and I.S. Mumick. Maintenance of materialized views: Problems, techniques, and applications. *IEEE Data Engineering Bulletin*, 18(2):3–18, 1995.

[96] A. Gupta, I.S. Mumick, and V.S. Subrahmanian. Maintaining views incrementally. In *Proc. of the ACM SIGMOD International Conference on Management of Data, SIGMOD'93*, pages 157–166. ACM Press, 1993.

[97] N. Gür, T.B. Pedersen, K. Hose, and M. Midtgaard. Multidimensional enrichment of spatial RDF data for SOLAP – full version. *CoRR*, abs/2002.06608, 2020.

[98] N. Gür, T.B. Pedersen, E. Zimányi, and K. Hose. A foundation for spatial data warehouses on the semantic web. *Semantic Web*, 9(5):557–587, 2018.

[99] R.H. Güting and M. Schneider. *Moving Objects Databases*. Morgan Kaufmann, 2005.

[100] V. Harinarayan, A. Rajaraman, and J.D. Ullman. Implementing data cubes efficiently. In *Proc. of the 1996 ACM SIGMOD International Conference on Management of Data*, pages 205–216. ACM Press, 1996.

[101] T. Heath and C. Bizer. *Linked Data: Evolving the Web into a Global Data Space*. Synthesis Lectures on the Semantic Web: Theory and Technology. Morgan & Claypool, 2011.

[102] J.A. Hendler, F. Gandon, and D. Allemang. *Semantic Web for the Working Ontologist: Effective Modeling for Linked Data, RDFS, and OWL*. ACM Books, third edition, 2020.

[103] K. Herrmann, H. Voigt, A. Behrend, and W. Lehner. CoDEL: A relationally complete language for database evolution. In *Proc. of the 19th East European Conference on Advances in Databases and Information Systems, ADBIS'15*, number 9282 in Lecture Notes in Computer Science, pages 63–76. Springer, 2015.

[104] P. Hitzler. A review of the semantic web field. *Communications of the ACM*, 64(2):76–83, 2021.

[105] A. Hodler and M. Needham. *Graph Algorithms: Practical Examples in Apache Spark and Neo4j*. O'Reilly Media, 2019.

[106] A. Hogan. *The Web of Data*. Springer, 2020.

[107] T. Homburg, S. Staab, and D. Janke. GeoSPARQL+: Syntax, semantics and system for integrated querying of graph, raster and vector data. In *Proc. of the 19th International Semantic Web Conference, ISWC 2020, Part I*, volume 12506 of *Lecture Notes in Computer Science*, pages 258–275. Springer, 2020.

[108] S. Hughes. *Hands-On SQL Server 2019 Analysis Services: Design and query tabular and multi-dimensional models using Microsoft's SQL Server Analysis Services*. Packt Publishing, 2020.

[109] C.A. Hurtado and C. Gutierrez. Handling structural heterogeneity in OLAP. In [265], chapter 2, pages 27–57.

[110] C.A. Hurtado, C. Gutierrez, and A. Mendelzon. Capturing summarizability with integrity constraints in OLAP. *ACM Transactions on Database Systems*, 30(3):854–886, 2005.

[111] C.A. Hurtado and A. Mendelzon. Reasoning about summarizability in heterogeneous multidimensional schemas. In *Proc. of the 8th International Conference on Database Theory, ICDT'01*, number 1973 in Lecture Notes in Computer Science, pages 375–389. Springer, 2001.

[112] C.A. Hurtado and A. Mendelzon. OLAP dimension constraints. In *Proc. of the 3rd ACM SIGACT-SIGMOD Symposium on Principles of Database Systems, PODS'02*, pages 375–389. ACM Press, 2002.

[113] C.A. Hurtado, A. Mendelzon, and A.A. Vaisman. Updating OLAP dimensions. In [222], pages 60–66.

[114] B. Hüsemann, J. Lechtenbörger, and G. Vossen. Conceptual data warehouse design. In *Proc. of the 2nd International Workshop on Design and Management of Data Warehouses, DMDW'00*, number 28 in CEUR Workshop Proceedings, page 6, 2000.

[115] S. Idreos, F. Groffen, N. Nes, S. Manegold, K.S. Mullender, and M.L. Kersten. MonetDB: Two decades of research in column-oriented database architectures. *IEEE Data Engineering Bulletin*, 35(1):40–45, 2012.

[116] N. Iftikhar and T.B. Pedersen. Using a time granularity table for gradual granular data aggregation. *Fundamenta Informaticae*, 132(2):153–176, 2014.

[117] W.H. Inmon. *Building the Data Warehouse*. Wiley, fourth edition, 2005.

[118] W.H. Inmon and F. Puppini. *The Unified Star Schema: An Agile and Resilient Approach to Data Warehouse and Analytics Design*. Technics Publications, 2020.

[119] H. Jagadish, L. Lakshmanan, and D. Srivastava. What can hierarchies do for data warehouses. In *Proc. of the 25th International Conference on Very Large Data Bases, VLDB'99*, pages 530–541. Morgan Kaufmann, 1999.

[120] M. Jarke, M. Lanzerini, C. Quix, T. Sellis, and P. Vassiliadis. Quality-driven data warehouse design. In *Fundamentals of Data Warehouses*, pages 165–179. Springer, second edition, 2003.

[121] T. Johnston. *Bitemporal Data: Theory and Practice*. Morgan Kaufmann, 2014.

[122] M. Jovanovik, T. Homburg, and M. Spasic. A GeoSPARQL compliance benchmark. *ISPRS International Journal Geo-Information*, 10(7):487, 2021.

[123] M. Jürgens. *Index Structures for Data Warehouses*. Number 1859 in Lecture Notes in Computer Science. Springer, 2002.

[124] B. Kämpgen. *Flexible Integration and Efficient Analysis of Multidimensional Datasets from the Web*. PhD thesis, Karlsruhe Institute of Technology, 2015.

[125] B. Kämpgen and A. Harth. No size fits all: Running the star schema benchmark with SPARQL and RDF aggregate views. In *Proc. of the 10th International Conference on the Semantic Web, ESWC 2013*, number 7882 in Lecture Notes in Computer Science, pages 290–304. Springer, 2013.

[126] E. Kharlamov, T.P. Mailis, K. Bereta, et al. A semantic approach to polystores. In *Proc. of the 2016 IEEE International Conference on Big*

Data, BigData 2016, , December 5-8, 2016, pages 2565–2573. IEEE Computer Society, 2016.

[127] V. Khatri, S. Ram, and R.T. Snodgrass. Augmenting a conceptual model with geospatiotemporal annotations. *IEEE Transactions on Knowledge and Data Engineering*, 16(11):1324–1338, 2004.

[128] R. Kimball and J. Caserta. *The Data Warehouse ETL Toolkit: Practical Techniques for Extracting, Cleaning, Conforming, and Delivering Data*. Wiley, 2004.

[129] R. Kimball and M. Ross. *The Data Warehouse Toolkit: The Complete Guide to Dimensional Modeling*. Wiley, third edition, 2013.

[130] R. Kimball, M. Ross, W. Thornthwaite, J. Mundy, and B. Becker. *The Data Warehouse Lifecycle Toolkit*. Wiley, second edition, 2007.

[131] B. Kolev, P. Valduriez, C. Bondiombouy, R. Jiménez-Peris, R. Pau, and J. Pereira. CloudMdsQL: querying heterogeneous cloud data stores with a common language. *Distributed Parallel Databases*, 34(4):463–503, 2016.

[132] J. Kraynak and D. Baum. *Cloud Data Warehousing For Dummies*. Wiley, second edition, 2020.

[133] K. Kulkarni and J.-E. Michels. Temporal features in SQL:2011. *SIGMOD Record*, 41(3):34–43, 2012.

[134] A. Lamb, M. Fuller, R. Varadarajan, N. Tran, B. Vandier, L. Doshi, and C. Bear. The Vertica analytic database: C-Store 7 years later. *Proc. of the VLDB*, 5(12):1790–1801, 2012.

[135] B. Larson. *Microsoft SQL Server 2016 Reporting Services*. McGraw-Hill Education, fifth edition, 2016.

[136] J. Lechtenbörger and G. Vossen. Multidimensional normal forms for data warehouse design. *Information Systems*, 28(5):415–434, 2003.

[137] W. Lehner, J. Albrecht, and H. Wedekind. Normal forms for multidimensional databases. In *Proc. of the 10th International Conference on Scientific and Statistical Database Management, SSDBM'98*, pages 63–72. IEEE Computer Society Press, 1998.

[138] H. Lenz and A. Shoshani. Summarizability in OLAP and statistical databases. In *Proc. of the 9th International Conference on Scientific and Statistical Database Management, SSDBM'97*, pages 132–143. IEEE Computer Society Press, 1997.

[139] R. Li, H. He, R. Wang, S. Ruan, Y. Sui, J. Bao, and Y. Zheng. TrajMesa: A distributed NoSQL storage engine for big trajectory data. In *Proc. of the 36th IEEE International Conference on Data Engineering, ICDE 2020*, pages 2002–2005. IEEE, 2020.

[140] S.S. Lightstone, T.J. Teorey, and T. Nadeau. *Physical Database Design: The database professional's guide to exploiting indexes, views, storage, and more*. Morgan Kaufmann, fourth edition, 2007.

[141] D. Linstedt and M. Olschimke. *Building a Scalable Data Warehouse with Data Vault 2.0*. Morgan Kaufmann, 2015.

[142] S. Luján-Mora and J. Trujillo. A comprehensive method for data warehouse design. In *Proc. of the 5th International Workshop on Design and Management of Data Warehouses, DMDW'03*, number 77 in CEUR Workshop Proceedings, 2003.

[143] S. Luján-Mora, J. Trujillo, and I.-Y. Song. A UML profile for multidimensional modeling in data warehouses. *Data & Knowledge Engineering*, 59(3):725–769, 2006.

[144] E. Malinowski and E. Zimányi. Hierarchies in a multidimensional model: From conceptual modeling to logical representation. *Data & Knowledge Engineering*, 59(2):348–377, 2006.

[145] E. Malinowski and E. Zimányi. *Advanced Data Warehouse Design: From Conventional to Spatial and Temporal Applications*. Springer, 2008.

[146] I. Mami and Z. Bellahsene. A survey of view selection methods. *SIGMOD Record*, 41(1):20–29, 2012.

[147] P. Manousis, P. Vassiliadis, A.V. Zarras, and G. Papastefanatos. Schema evolution for databases and data warehouses. In *Tutorial Lectures of the 5th European Business Intelligence Summer School, eBISS 2015*, number 253 in Lecture Notes in Business Information Processing, pages 1–31. Springer, 2015.

[148] A. Matei, K.-M. Chao, and N. Godwin. OLAP for multidimensional semantic web databases. In *Enabling Real-Time Business Intelligence: Proc. of the BIRTE 2013 and BIRTE 2014 International Workshops*, number 206 in Lecture Notes in Business Information Processing, pages 81–96. Springer, 2015.

[149] R. Mateus, T. Siqueira, V. Times, R. Ciferri, and C. Ciferri. Spatial data warehouses and spatial OLAP come towards the cloud: Design and performance. *Distributed Parallel Databases*, 34(3):425–461, 2016.

[150] J.-N. Mazón, J. Trujillo, M. Serrano, and M. Piattini. Designing data warehouses: From business requirement analysis to multidimensional modeling. In *Proc. of the 1st International Workshop on Requirements Engineering for Business Need and IT Alignment, REBN'05*, pages 44–53, 2005.

[151] J. Melton. *Advanced SQL:1999. Understanding Object-Relational and Other Advanced Features*. Morgan Kaufmann, 2003.

[152] J. Melton. SQL:2003 has been published. *SIGMOD Record*, 33(1):119–125, 2003.

[153] J. Melton and A. Simon. *SQL:1999. Understanding Relational Language Components*. Morgan Kaufmann, 2002.

[154] A. Mendelzon and A.A. Vaisman. Time in multidimensional databases. In [193], pages 166–199.

[155] X. Meng, Z. Ding, and J. Xu. *Moving Objects Management: Models, Techniques and Applications*. Springer, second edition, 2014.

[156] J. Mennis. Multidimensional map algebra: Design and implementation of a spatio-temporal GIS processing language. *Transactions in GIS*, 14(1):1–21, 2010.

[157] J.-E. Michels, K. Hare, K.G. Kulkarni, C. Zuzarte, Z.H. Liu, B.C. Hammerschmidt, and F. Zemke. The new and improved SQL:2016 standard. *SIGMOD Record*, 47(2):51–60, 2018.

[158] T. Morzy and R. Wrembel. On querying versions of multiversion data warehouse. In *Proc. of the 7th ACM International Workshop on Data Warehousing and OLAP, DOLAP'04*, pages 92–101. ACM Press, 2004.

[159] I.S. Mumick, D. Quass, and B.S. Mumick. Maintenance of data cubes and summary tables in a warehouse. In *Proc. of the ACM SIGMOD International Conference on Management of Data, SIGMOD'97*, pages 100–111. ACM Press, 1997.

[160] F.M. Nardini, S. Orlando, R. Perego, A. Raffaetà, C. Renso, and C. Silvestri. Analysing trajectories of mobile users: From data warehouses to recommender systems. In [76], pages 407–421.

[161] A. Nasiri, E. Zimányi, and R. Wrembel. Requirements engineering for data warehouse systems. In [277].

[162] R. Nath, K. Hose, T.B. Pedersen, and O. Romero. SETL: A programmable semantic extract-transform-load framework for semantic data warehouses. *Information Systems*, 68:17–43, 2017.

[163] R. Nath, O. Romero, T.B. Pedersen, and K. Hose. High-level ETL for semantic data warehouses – full version. *CoRR*, abs/2006.07180, 2020.

[164] V. Nebot and R. Berlanga Llavori. Building data warehouses with semantic web data. *Decision Support Systems*, 52(4):853–868, 2011.

[165] M. Neteler and H. Mitasova. *Open Source GIS: A GRASS GIS Approach*. Springer, third edition, 2008.

[166] T. Niemi, M. Niinimäkia, P. Thanisch, and J. Nummenmaa. Detecting summarizability in OLAP. *Data & Knowledge Engineering*, 89(1):1–20, 2014.

[167] M. Niinimäki and T. Niemi. An ETL process for OLAP using RDF/OWL ontologies. In *Journal on Data Semantics XIII*, number 1396 in Lecture Notes in Computer Science, pages 97–119. Springer, 2009.

[168] P. Nikitopoulos, A. Vlachou, C. Doulkeridis, and G.A. Vouros. DiStRDF: Distributed spatio-temporal RDF queries on Spark. In *Proc. of the Workshops of the EDBT/ICDT 2018 Joint Conference, (EDBT/ICDT 2018)*, volume 2083 of *CEUR Workshop Proceedings*, pages 125–132. CEUR-WS.org, 2018.

[169] R.O. Obe and L.S. Hsu. *PostGIS in Action*. Manning Publications Co., third edition, 2021.

[170] E. O'Connor. *Microsoft Power BI Dashboards Step by Step*. Microsoft Press, second edition, 2018.

[171] A. Olivé. *Conceptual Modeling of Information Systems*. Springer, 2007.

[172] E. O'Neil and G. Graefe. Multi-table joins through bitmapped join indices. *SIGMOD Record*, 24(3):8–11, 1995.

[173] P.E. O'Neil. Model 204 architecture and performance. In *Proc. of the 2nd International Workshop on High Performance Transaction Systems*, number 359 in Lecture Notes in Computer Science, pages 40–59. Springer, 1989.

[174] Open Geospatial Consortium Inc. GeoSPARQL – A Geographic Query Language for RDF Data. OGC 11-052r4, 2012.

[175] S. Orlando, R. Orsini, A. Raffaetà, A. Roncato, and C. Silvestri. Spatio-temporal aggregations in trajectory data warehouses. *Journal of Computing Science and Engineering*, 1(2):211–232, 2007.

[176] F. Özcan, Y. Tian, and P. Tözün. Hybrid transactional/analytical processing: A survey. In *Proc. of the 2017 ACM International Conference on Management of Data, SIGMOD 2017*, pages 1771–1775. ACM, 2017.

[177] M.T. Özsu and P. Valduriez. *Principles of Distributed Database Systems*. Springer, fourth edition, 2020.

[178] F. Paim, A. Carvalho, and J. Castro. Towards a methodology for requirements analysis of data warehouse systems. In *Proc. of the 16th Brazilian Symposium on Software Engineering, SBES'02*, pages 1–16, 2002.

[179] F. Paim and J. Castro. DWARF: An approach for requirements definition and management of data warehouse systems. In *Proc. of the 11th IEEE International Requirements Engineering Conference, RE'03*, pages 75–84. IEEE Computer Society Press, 2003.

[180] L. Paolino, G. Tortora, M. Sebillo, G. Vitiello, and R. Laurini. Phenomena: A visual query language for continuous fields. In *Proc. of the 11th ACM Symposium on Advances in Geographic Information Systems, ACM-GIS'03*, pages 147–153. ACM Press, 2003.

[181] G. Papastefanatos, P. Vassiliadis, A. Simitsis, and Y. Vassiliou. Metrics for the prediction of evolution impact in ETL ecosystems: A case study. *Journal on Data Semantics*, 1(3):75–97, 2012.

[182] C. Parent, S. Spaccapietra, and E. Zimányi. *Conceptual Modeling for Traditional and Spatio-Temporal Applications: The MADS Approach*. Springer, 2006.

[183] D. Parmenter. *Key Performance Indicators (KPI): Developing, Implementing, and Using Winning KPIs*. Wiley, fourth edition, 2019.

[184] A. Pavlo and M. Aslett. What's really new with NewSQL? *SIGMOD Record*, 45(2):45–55, 2016.

[185] T.B. Pedersen. Managing complex multidimensional data. In [16], pages 1–28.

[186] T.B. Pedersen, C.S. Jensen, and C. Dyreson. A foundation for capturing and querying complex multidimensional data. *Information Systems*, 26(5):383–423, 2001.

[187] N. Pelekis, A. Raffaetà, M.L. Damiani, C. Vangenot, G. Marketos, E. Frentzos, I. Ntoutsi, and Y. Theodoridis. Towards trajectory data

warehouses. In F. Giannotti and D. Pedreschi, editors, *Mobility, Data Mining and Privacy: Geographic Knowledge Discovery*, chapter 9, pages 189–211. Springer, 2008.

[188] N. Pelekis and Y. Theodoridis. *Mobility Data Management and Exploration*. Springer, 2014.

[189] T. Piasevoli and S. Li. *MDX with Microsoft SQL Server 2016 Analysis Services Cookbook*. Packt Publishing, third edition, 2016.

[190] H. Plattner and A. Zeier. *In-Memory Data Management: Technology and Applications*. Springer, second edition, 2012.

[191] E. Pourabbas and M. Rafanelli. Hierarchies. In [193], pages 91–115.

[192] N. Prakash and D. Prakash. *Data Warehouse Requirements Engineering: A Decision Based Approach*. Springer, 2018.

[193] M. Rafanelli, editor. *Multidimensional Databases: Problems and Solutions*. Idea Group, 2003.

[194] C. Renso, S. Spaccapietra, and E. Zimányi, editors. *Mobility Data: Modeling, Management, and Understanding*. Cambridge Press, 2013.

[195] P. Rigaux, M. Scholl, and A. Voisard. *Spatial Databases with Application to GIS*. Morgan Kaufmann, 2002.

[196] S. Rivest, Y. Bédard, and P. Marchand. Toward better suppport for spatial decision making: Defining the characteristics of spatial on-line analytical processing (SOLAP). *Geomatica*, 55(4):539–555, 2001.

[197] S. Rizzi and M. Golfarelli. X-Time: Schema versioning and cross-version querying in data warehouses. In *Proc. of the 23rd International Conference on Data Engineering, ICDE'07*, pages 1471–1472. IEEE Computer Society Press, 2007.

[198] S. Rizzi and E. Saltarelli. View materialization vs. indexing: Balancing space constraints in data warehouse design. In *Proc. of the 15th International Conference on Advanced Information Systems Engineering, CAiSE'03*, number 2681 in Lecture Notes in Computer Science, pages 502–519. Springer, 2003.

[199] I. Robinson, J. Webber, and E. Eifrem. *Graph Databases*. O'Reilly Media, 2013.

[200] M.A. Rodriguez. The Gremlin graph traversal machine and language. *CoRR*, abs/1508.03843, 2015.

[201] O. Romero and A. Abelló. Automating multidimensional design from ontologies. In *Proc. of the 10th ACM International Workshop on Data Warehousing and OLAP, DOLAP'07*, pages 1–8. ACM Press, 2007.

[202] O. Romero and A. Abelló. On the need of a reference algebra for OLAP. In *Proc. of the 9th International Conference on Data Warehousing and Knowledge Discovery, DaWaK'07*, number 4654 in Lecture Notes in Computer Science, pages 99–110. Springer, 2007.

[203] O. Romero and A. Abelló. Multidimensional design methods for data warehousing. In [228], pages 78–105.

[204] M. Russo and A. Ferrari. *Tabular Modeling in Microsoft SQL Server Analysis Services*. Microsoft Press, second edition, 2017.

[205] M. Russo and A. Ferrari. *The Definitive Guide to DAX: Business intelligence for Microsoft Power BI, SQL Server Analysis Services, and Excel.* Microsoft Press, second edition, 2019.

[206] A. Sabaini, E. Zimányi, and C. Combi. Extending the multidimensional model for linking cubes. In [277], pages 17–32.

[207] S. Sakr, M. Wylot, R. Mutharaju, D. Le Phuoc, and I. Fundulaki. *Linked Data: Storing, Querying, and Reasoning.* Springer, 2018.

[208] V. Santos and O. Belo. Slowly changing dimensions specification a relational algebra approach. *International Journal on Information Technology*, 1(3):63–68, 2011.

[209] V. Santos and O. Belo. Using relational algebra on the specification of real world ETL processes. In *Proc. of CIT 2015, IUCC 2015, DASC 2015, PICom 2015*, pages 861–866. IEEE, 2015.

[210] C. Sapia, M. Blaschka, G. Höfling, and B. Dinter. Extending the E/R model for multidimensional paradigm. In *Proc. of the 17th International Conference on Conceptual Modeling, ER'98*, number 1507 in Lecture Notes in Computer Science, pages 105–116. Springer, 1998.

[211] L. Sautot, S. Bimonte, and L. Journaux. A semi-automatic design methodology for (big) data warehouse transforming facts into dimensions. *IEEE Transactions on Knowledge and Data Engineering*, 33(1):28–42, 2021.

[212] H. Schek, F. Saltor, I. Ramos, and G. Alonso, editors. *Proc. of the 6th International Conference on Extending Database Technology, EDBT'98*, number 1377 in Lecture Notes in Computer Science. Springer, 1998.

[213] M. Schoemans, M.A. Sakr, and E. Zimányi. Implementing rigid temporal geometries in moving object databases. In *Proc. of 37th IEEE International Conference on Data Engineering, ICDE 2021*, pages 2547–2558. IEEE, 2021.

[214] C.G. Schuetz, L. Bozzato, B. Neumayr, M. Schrefl, and L. Serafini. Knowledge graph OLAP. *Semantic Web*, 12(4):649–683, 2021.

[215] Z. Shang, G. Li, and Z. Bao. DITA: Distributed in-memory trajectory analytics. In *Proc. of the 2018 International Conference on Management of Data, SIGMOD 2018*, pages 725–740. ACM, 2018.

[216] B. Sharma. *Architecting Data Lakes.* O'Reilly Media, 2018.

[217] S. Shekhar and P. Vold. *Spatial Computing.* The MIT Press, 2020.

[218] A. Simitsis. Mapping conceptual to logical models for ETL processes. In *Proc. of the 8th ACM International Workshop on Data Warehousing and OLAP, DOLAP'05*, pages 67–76. ACM Press, 2005.

[219] U. Sirin, S. Dwarkadas, and A. Ailamaki. Performance characterization of HTAP workloads. In *Proc. of the 37th IEEE International Conference on Data Engineering, ICDE 2021*, pages 1829–1834. IEEE, 2021.

[220] R.T. Snodgrass, editor. *The TSQL2 Temporal Query Language.* Kluwer Academic, 1995.

[221] R.T. Snodgrass. *Developing Time-Oriented Database Applications in SQL.* Morgan Kaufmann, 2000.

[222] I.-Y. Song and T.J. Teorey, editors. *Proc. of the 2nd ACM International Workshop on Data Warehousing and OLAP, DOLAP'99.* ACM Press, 1999.

[223] K. Stockinger and K. Wu. Bitmap indices for data warehouses. In [265], chapter 7, pages 157–178.

[224] M. Stonebraker, P. Brown, A. Poliakov, and S. Raman. The architecture of SciDB. In *Proc. of the 23rd International Conference on Scientific and Statistical Database Management, SSDBM 2011,* volume 6809 of *Lecture Notes in Computer Science,* pages 1–16. Springer, 2011.

[225] M. Stonebraker and U. Çetintemel. "One size fits all": an idea whose time has come and gone. In M.L. Brodie, editor, *Making Databases Work: the Pragmatic Wisdom of Michael Stonebraker,* pages 441–462. ACM / Morgan & Claypool, 2019.

[226] M. Stonebraker and A. Weisberg. The VoltDB main memory DBMS. *IEEE Data Engineering Bulletin,* 36(2):21–27, 2013.

[227] J. Strate. *Expert Performance Indexing in SQL Server 2019: Toward Faster Results and Lower Maintenance.* APress, third edition, 2019.

[228] D. Taniar and L. Chen, editors. *Integrations of Data Warehousing, Data Mining and Database Technologies: Innovative Approaches.* IGI Global, 2011.

[229] A.U. Tansel, J. Clifford, S. Gadia, S. Jajodia, A. Segev, and R.T. Snodgrass. *Temporal Databases: Theory, Design, and Implementation.* Benjamin Cummings, 1993.

[230] T.J. Teorey, S.S. Lightstone, T. Nadeau, and H.V. Jagadish. *Database Modeling and Design: Logical Design.* Morgan Kaufmann, fifth edition, 2011.

[231] P. Terenziani. Temporal aggregation on user-defined granularities. *Journal of Intelligent Information Systems,* 38(3):785–813, 2012.

[232] P. Terenziani and R.T. Snodgrass. Reconciling point-based and interval-based semantics in temporal relational databases: A treatment of the telic/atelic distinction. *IEEE Transactions on Knowledge and Data Engineering,* 16(5):540–551, 2004.

[233] H. Thakkar, S. Auer, and M.-E. Vidal. Formalizing Gremlin pattern matching traversals in an integrated graph algebra. In *Proc. of the BlockSW and CKG Workshops of the 18th International Semantic Web Conference,* volume 2599 of *CEUR Workshop Proceedings.* CEUR-WS.org, 2019.

[234] Y. Tian, R. Hankins, and J.M. Patel. Efficient aggregation for graph summarization. In *Proc. of the ACM SIGMOD International Conference on Management of Data, SIGMOD 2008,* pages 567–580. ACM, 2008.

[235] D. Tomlin. *Geographic Information Systems and Cartographic Modeling.* Prentice Hall, 1990.

[236] R. Torlone. Conceptual multidimensional models. In [193], pages 69–90.

[237] FF.Di Tria, E. Lefons, and F. Tangorra. Cost-benefit analysis of data warehouse design methodologies. *Information Systems*, 63:47–62, 2017.

[238] F.Di Tria, E. Lefons, and F. Tangorra. A framework for evaluating design methodologies for big data warehouses: Measurement of the design process. *International Journal of Data Warehousing and Mining*, 14(1):15–39, 2018.

[239] J. Trujillo, M. Palomar, J. Gomez, and I.-Y. Song. Designing data warehouses with OO conceptual models. *IEEE Computer*, 34(12):66–75, 2001.

[240] N. Tryfona, F. Busborg, and J. Borch. StarER: A conceptual model for data warehouse design. In [222], pages 3–8.

[241] A. Tsois, N. Karayannidis, and T. Sellis. MAC: Conceptual data modelling for OLAP. In *Proc. of the 3rd International Workshop on Design and Management of Data Warehouses, DMDW'01*, number 39 in CEUR Workshop Proceedings, page 5, 2001.

[242] P. Turley. *Professional Microsoft SQL Server 2016 Reporting Services and Mobile Reports*. Wrox, 2016.

[243] S. Uttamchandani. *The Self-Service Data Roadmap: Democratize Data and Reduce Time to Insight*. O'Reilly Media, 2020.

[244] A.A. Vaisman. Data quality-based requirements elicitation for decision support systems. In [265], chapter 16, pages 58–86.

[245] A.A. Vaisman. An introduction to business process modeling. In [16], pages 29–61.

[246] A.A. Vaisman. Publishing OLAP cubes on the semantic web. In *Tutorial Lectures of the 5th European Business Intelligence Summer School, eBISS 2015*, volume 253 of *Lecture Notes in Business Information Processing*, pages 32–61. Springer, 2016.

[247] A.A. Vaisman and K. Chentout. Mapping spatiotemporal data to RDF: A SPARQL endpoint for Brussels. *ISPRS International Journal Geo-Information*, 8(8):353, 2019.

[248] A.A. Vaisman, A. Izquierdo, and M. Ktenas. A web-based architecture for temporal OLAP. *International Journal of Web Engineering and Technology*, 4(4):465–494, 2008.

[249] A.A. Vaisman and E. Zimányi. A multidimensional model representing continuous fields in spatial data warehouses. In *Proc. of the 17th ACM SIGSPATIAL Symposium on Advances in Geographic Information Systems, ACM-GIS'09*, pages 168–177. ACM Press, 2009.

[250] A.A. Vaisman and E. Zimányi. What is spatio-temporal data warehousing? In *Proc. of the 11th International Conference on Data Warehousing and Knowledge Discovery, DaWaK'09*, number 5691 in Lecture Notes in Computer Science, pages 9–23. Springer, 2009.

[251] A.A. Vaisman and E. Zimányi. Mobility data warehouses. *ISPRS International Journal of Geo-Information*, 8(4):170, 2019.

[252] J. Varga, O. Romero, A.A. Vaisman, L. Etcheverry, T.B. Pedersen, and C. Thomsen. Dimensional enrichment of statistical linked open data. *Journal of Web Semantics*, 40:22–51, 2016.

[253] P. Vassiliadis. A survey of extract-transform-load technology. In [228], chapter 8, pages 171–199.

[254] P. Vassiliadis, A. Simitsis, and S. Skiadopoulos. Conceptual modeling for ETL processes. In *Proc. of the 5th ACM International Workshop on Data Warehousing and OLAP, DOLAP'02*, pages 14–21. ACM Press, 2002.

[255] J. Viqueira and N. Lorentzos. SQL extension for spatio-temporal data. *The VLDB Journal*, 16(2):179–200, 2007.

[256] A. Vlachou, C. Doulkeridis, A. Glenis, G.M. Santipantakis, and G.A. Vouros. Efficient spatio-temporal RDF query processing in large dynamic knowledge bases. In *Proc. of the 34th ACM/SIGAPP Symposium on Applied Computing, SAC 2019*, pages 439–447. ACM, 2019.

[257] G.A. Vouros, G.L. Andrienko, C. Doulkeridis, N. Pelekis, A. Artikis, A.-L. Jousselme, C. Ray, J.M. Cordero Garcia, and D. Scarlatti, editors. *Big Data Analytics for Time-Critical Mobility Forecasting, From Raw Data to Trajectory-Oriented Mobility Analytics in the Aviation and Maritime Domains*. Springer, 2020.

[258] A. Vukotic, N. Watt, T Abedrabbo, D. Fox, and J. Partner. *Neo4j in Action*. Manning Publications Co., 2021.

[259] H.-C. Wei and R. Elmasri. Schema versioning and database conversion techniques for bi-temporal databases. *Annals of Mathematics and Artificial Intelligence*, 30(1–4):23–52, 2000.

[260] S. Wexler, J. Shaffer, and A. Cotgreave. *The Big Book of Dashboards: Visualizing Your Data Using Real-World Business Scenarios*. Wiley, 2017.

[261] T. White. *Hadoop: The Definitive Guide, Storage and Analysis at Internet Scale*. O'Reilly Media, fourth edition, 2015.

[262] A. Wojciechowski and R. Wrembel. On case-based reasoning for ETL process repairs: Making cases fine-grained. In *Proc. of the 14th International Baltic Conference on Databases and Information Systems, DB&IS 2020*, volume 1243 of *Communications in Computer and Information Science*, pages 235–249. Springer, 2020.

[263] M. Worboys and M. Duckham. *GIS: A Computing Perspective*. CRC Press, second edition, 2004.

[264] R. Wrembel and B. Bebel. Metadata management in a multiversion data warehouse. In S. Spaccapietra et al., editors, *Journal on Data Semantics VIII*, number 4380 in Lecture Notes in Computer Science, pages 118–157. Springer, 2007.

[265] R. Wrembel and C. Koncilia, editors. *Data Warehouses and OLAP: Concepts, Architectures and Solutions*. IRM Press, 2007.

[266] K. Wu, E. J. Otoo, and A. Shoshani. Optimizing bitmap indices with efficient compression. *ACM Transactions on Database Systems*, 31(1):1–38, 2006.

[267] J. Xu and R.H. Güting. A generic data model for moving objects. *GeoInformatica*, 17(1):125–172, 2013.

[268] J. Yang and J. Widom. Maintaining temporal views over non-temporal information sources for data warehousing. In [212], pages 389–403.

[269] M. Yin, B. Wu, and Z. Zeng. HMGraph OLAP: A novel framework for multi-dimensional heterogeneous network analysis. In *Proc. of the 15th ACM International Workshop on Data Warehousing and OLAP, DOLAP 2012*, pages 137–144. ACM Press, 2012.

[270] J. Yu, Z. Zhang, and M. Sarwat. Spatial data management in Apache Spark: the GeoSpark perspective and beyond. *GeoInformatica*, 23(1):37–78, 2019.

[271] M. Zaharia, M. Chowdhury, M. J. Franklin, S. Shenker, and I. Stoica. Spark: Cluster computing with working sets. In *Proc. of the 2nd USENIX Workshop on Hot Topics in Cloud Computing, HotCloud'10*. USENIX Association, 2010.

[272] F. Zemke. What's new in SQL:2011. *SIGMOD Record*, 41(1):67–73, 2012.

[273] F. Zhang, Q. Lu, Z. Du, X. Chen, and C. Cao. A comprehensive overview of RDF for spatial and spatiotemporal data management. *The Knowledge Engineering Review*, 36(e10), 2021.

[274] P. Zhao, X. Li, D. Xin, and J. Han. Graph Cube: On warehousing and OLAP multidimensional networks. In *Proc. of the ACM SIGMOD International Conference on Management of Data, SIGMOD 2011*, pages 853–864. ACM Press, 2011.

[275] Y. Zheng and X. Zhou, editors. *Computing with Spatial Trajectories*. Springer, 2011.

[276] E. Zimányi. Temporal aggregates and temporal universal quantifiers in standard SQL. *SIGMOD Record*, 32(2):16–21, 2006.

[277] E. Zimányi, T. Calders, and S. Vansummeren, editors. *Proc. of the Journées francophones sur les Entrepôts de Données et l'Analyse en ligne, EDA 2015*. Editions Hermann, 2015.

[278] E. Zimányi, M.A. Sakr, and A. Lesuisse. MobilityDB: A mobility database based on PostgreSQL and PostGIS. *ACM Transactions on Database Systems*, 45(4):19:1–19:42, 2020.

Glossary

ACID properties: A set of properties, namely atomicity, consistency, isolation, and durability, that transactions must satisfy to guarantee data validity despite any error or failure thay may occur.

ad hoc query: A request for information in a database that is created as the need arises and about which the system has no prior knowledge. This is to be contrasted with a predefined query.

additive measure: A measure that can be meaningfully aggregated by addition along all of its dimensions. It is the most common type of measure. This is to be contrasted with a semiadditive and a nonadditive measure.

aggregation function: A function that computes an aggregated value from a set of values. Examples include count, sum, and average. In a data warehouse, it is used for aggregating measures across dimensions and hierarchies.

algebraic measure: A measure that can be computed by a scalar function of distributive ones. Examples include count and average. This is to be contrasted with a distributive and a holistic measure.

alternate key: A key of a relation that is not the primary key.

analytical application: An application that produces information for decision support.

array DBMS: A database management system that manipulates multidimensional arrays, such as sensor data or satellite images, typically in a distributed way.

atelic measure: A measure that satisfies the downward inheritance property, which means that if the measure has a given value during a time period p, it has the same value in any subperiod of p. This is to be contrasted with a telic measure.

attribute: In a conceptual model, a structural property of an entity or relationship types.

B-tree index: A kind of index that uses B-tree. Such an index is the most commun index in relational databases.

© Springer-Verlag GmbH Germany, part of Springer Nature 2022
A. Vaisman, E. Zimányi, *Data Warehouse Systems*, Data-Centric Systems
and Applications, https://doi.org/10.1007/978-3-662-65167-4

back-end process: A process that populates a data warehouse with data from operational and external data sources. This is to be contrasted with a front-end process.

base hypergraph: A hypergraph where all information is represented at the finest granularity level.

basic graph pattern: A property graph where variables can appear in place of any constant (either labels or properties), used to define a query in a graph database.

big data: Data that are so big, that arrives at a pace, or with such a variety that makes it difficult to process with traditional methods and tools. Big data are usually defined in terms of volume, variety, velocity, and veracity.

binary relationship type: A relationship type between two entity types or between two levels.

bitemporal time: A temporal specification that associates both valid time and transaction time with a schema element.

bitmap index: A kind of index that uses bitmaps. Such an index is typically used for a column in a relation with a low number of distinct values.

bridge table: A relation that represents a many-to-many relationship either between a fact table and a dimension table or between two dimension tables in a hierarchy.

business process: A collection of related activities or tasks in an organization whose goal is to produce a specific service or product.

Business Process Model and Notation (BPMN): A graphical representation for specifying business processes. It is a standard proposed by OMG.

business-driven design: An approach to design a data warehouse based on the business requirements. It is also called *requirements-* or *analysis-driven design*. This is to be contrasted with data-driven design.

business/data-driven design: An approach to design a data warehouse that is a combination of the business-driven and the data-driven design approaches.

business intelligence (BI): The process of collecting and analyzing information to derive strategic knowledge from business data. It is also called *data analytics*.

CAP theorem: A theorem that states that any distributed data store can only provide two of the following three guarantees: consistency, availability, and partition tolerance.

cardinality: The number of elements in a collection. In a conceptual model, it is an integrity constraint that restricts either the number of values that an attribute may take, or the number of instances of a relationship type in which an entity type or a level may participate.

cell: A single element in a cube defined by a set of coordinates, one for each of the cube's dimensions.

check constraint: An integrity constraint that specifies a Boolean predicate that must be satisfied by each row in a relation.

child level: Given two related levels in a hierarchy, the lower level, containing more detailed data. This is to be contrasted with a parent level.

cloud computing: The on-demand delivery of computing services, such as servers, storage, databases, or software, over the Internet without direct active management by the user.

cluster: A set of computers connected by a network that work together so that they can be viewed as a single system. Each node in a cluster performs the same task, controlled and scheduled by software.

coalescing: In a temporal database, the process of combining several value-equivalent rows into one provided that their time periods overlap.

column-oriented DBMS: A database management system that uses column-oriented storage. Examples include PostgreSQL and MySQL. This is to be contrasted with a row-oriented DBMS.

column-oriented storage: A storage method that organizes data by column, keeping all of the data associated with a column next to each other in memory. This is to be contrasted with a row-oriented storage.

complex attribute: An attribute that is composed of several other attributes. This is to be contrasted with a simple attribute.

composite key: A key of a relation that is composed of two or more attributes.

conceptual design: The process of building a user-oriented representation of a database or a data warehouse that does not contain any implementation considerations, which results in a conceptual model.

conceptual model: A set of modeling concepts and rules for describing conceptual schemas.

conceptual schema: A schema that is as close as possible to the users' perception of the data, without any implementation consideration. This is to be contrasted with a logical schema and a physical schema.

constellation schema: A relational schema for representing multidimensional data composed of multiple fact tables that share dimension tables.

continuous field: A technique to represent phenomena that change continuously in space and/or time, such as altitude and temperature.

continuous trajectory: A trajectory for which an interpolation function is used to determine the position of its object at any instant in the period of observation. This is to be contrasted with a discrete trajectory.

conventional attribute: An attribute that has a conventional data type as its domain. This is to be contrasted with a temporal and a spatial attribute.

conventional data type: A data type that represents conventional alphanumeric information. Examples include Boolean, integer, float, and string. This is to be contrasted with a temporal and a spatial data type.

conventional database: A database that only manipulates conventional data. This is to be contrasted with temporal, a spatial, and a moving-object database.

conventional data warehouse: A data warehouse that only manipulates conventional data. This is to be contrasted with a temporal, a multiversion, a spatial, and a mobility data warehouse.

conventional dimension: A dimension composed of only conventional hierarchies. This is to be contrasted with a temporal and a spatial dimension.

conventional fact relationship: A fact relationship that requires a classical join between its dimensions. This is to be contrasted with a temporal and a spatial fact relationship.

conventional hierarchy: A hierarchy composed of only conventional levels. This is to be contrasted with a temporal and a spatial hierarchy.

conventional level: A level that includes only conventional attributes. This is to be contrasted with a temporal and a spatial level.

conventional measure: A measure that has a conventional data type as its domain. This is to be contrasted with a temporal and a spatial measure.

cube: A multidimensional structure that contains a set of measures in each cell. Cubes are used to implement OLAP. It is also called a *hypercube* or *multidimensional cube*.

current data: Data from the current time period used for the daily operations of an organization. This is to be contrasted with historical data.

Common Warehouse Metamodel (CWM): A metamodel to enable interchange metadata of data warehouses between tools, platforms, and metadata repositories. It is a standard proposed by OMG.

Cypher: The most used high-level query language for Neo4j.

dashboard: An interactive report that presents summarized key information in visual, easy-to-read form, providing an overview of the performance of an organization for decision support.

data aggregation: The process of combining a set of values into a single value. It is typically done during OLAP operations but also as part of the ETL process. It is also called *summarization*.

data cleaning: The process of transforming source data by removing errors and inconsistencies or by converting it into a standardized format. This is typically done as part of the ETL process.

data cube lattice: A lattice that represents how to compute all possible aggregations of a fact table with respect to a combination of its dimensions and hierarchies from other combinations.

data-driven design: An approach to design a data warehouse based on the data available in the data sources. It is also called *source-driven design*. This is to be contrasted with business-driven design.

data extraction: The process of obtaining data from operational and external data sources to prepare these data for a data warehouse. This is typically done as part of the ETL process.

data integration: The process of reconciling data coming from various data sources both at the schema and the data level. This is typically done as part of the ETL process.

data lake: A repository that stores structured and unstructured data in its original format to be used for data analytics. This is to be contrasted with delta lake.

data loading: The process of populating a data warehouse, typically done as part of the ETL process.

data mart: A data warehouse targeted at a particular functional area or user group in an organization. Its data can be derived from an organization-wide data warehouse or be extracted from data sources.

data mining: The process of analyzing large amounts of data to identify unsuspected or unknown relationships, trends, patterns, and associations that might be of value to an organization.

data model: A set of modeling concepts and rules for describing the schema of a database or a data warehouse.

data quality: The degree of excellence of data. Various factors contribute to data quality, such as whether the data are consistent, nonredundant, complete, timely, well understood, and follows business rules.

data refreshing: The process of propagating updates from data sources to a data warehouse in order to keep it up to date. This is typically done as part of the ETL process.

data source: A system from which data are collected in order to be integrated into a data warehouse. Such a system may be a database, an application, a repository, or a file.

data staging area: A storage area where the ETL process is executed and where the source data are prepared in order to be introduced into a data warehouse or a data mart.

data transformation: The process of cleaning, aggregating, and integrating data to make it conform with business rules, domain rules, integrity rules, and other data. This is typically done as part of the ETL process.

data type: A domain of values with associated operators. The data types in this book include conventional, spatial, temporal, and spatiotemporal data types.

data warehouse: A database that is targeted at analytical applications. It contains historical data about an organization obtained from operational and external data sources.

database: A shared collection of logically related data, and a description of these data, designed to meet the information needs of an organization and to support its activities.

database management system (DBMS): A software system that allows users to define, create, manipulate, and manage a database.

database reverse engineering: The process through which the logical and conceptual schemas of a database or of a set of files are reconstructed from various information sources.

DataFrame: In Spark, an immutable distributed collection of data organized into named columns, which is conceptually equal to a relation. This is to be contrasted with an RDD and a DataSet.

DataSet: In Spark, an extension of a DataFrame that provides static-typing and runtime type-safety. This is to be contrasted with an RDD and a DataFrame.

delta lake: A repository that extends a data lake with transactions and ACID properties for both stream and batch processing.

denormalization: The modification of the schema of a relation so that it does not satisfy a normal form. This is done to improve performance but results in data redundancy. This is to be contrasted with normalization.

derived attribute: An attribute whose value for each instance of a type is derived, by means of an expression, from other values in a database.

derived measure: A measure whose value for each instance of a fact is derived, by means of an expression, from other measures in a data warehouse.

dice: An OLAP operation that keeps the cells in a cube that satisfy a Boolean condition.

dimension: One or several related levels that provide a viewpoint for analyzing facts. Dimensions may be composed of hierarchies.

dimension table: A relation that contains dimension data.

discrete trajectory: A trajectory that has no associated interpolation function so that the position of its object is only known at the reported observations. This is to be contrasted with a continuous trajectory.

distributed DBMS: A database management system that enables the perception of physically separate databases as a single logical system.

distributed processing framework: A platform for developing applications that run on distributed computer systems. Examples are MapReduce and Spark.

distributing attribute: An attribute that determines how measures are split between parent members in a many-to-many parent-child relationship.

distributive measure: A measure that can be computed in a distributed way. Examples include sum, minimum, and maximum. This is to be contrasted with an algebraic and a holistic measure.

double counting: The problem of counting the same thing twice, or more than twice. In data warehouses this problem appears in the presence of many-to-many relationships in hierarchies.

drill-across: An OLAP operation that queries related data, moving from one fact to another through common dimensions.

drill-down: An OLAP operation that queries detailed data, moving down one or several levels in a hierarchy. This is to be contrasted with roll-up.

drill-through: An OLAP operation that queries detailed data, moving from data in a data warehouse to the source data in an operational database.

elasticity: In computing, the degree to which a system is able to automatically adapt to workload changes by provisioning and de-provisioning resources, such that at each point in time the available resources match the current demand as closely as possible.

enterprise data warehouse: A centralized data warehouse that encompasses an entire enterprise.

entity: In the entity-relationship model, an instance of an entity type.

entity-relationship (ER) model: A popular conceptual model defined by Peter Chen in a seminal paper of 1976.

entity type: In the entity-relationship model, a description of a set of entities that share the same attributes, relationships, and semantics.

external data source: A system from an organization external to the one under consideration that is used for providing data to a data warehouse. This is to be contrasted with an operational data source.

extraction-loading-transformation (ELT): A process that extracts data from data sources and stores them in their original format, so it may be transformed and loaded into a data warehouse when it is needed. This is to be contrasted with ETL.

extraction-transformation-loading (ETL): A process that extracts data from data sources, transform it, and load it into a data warehouse. It also includes refreshing the data warehouse at a specified frequency to keep it up to date. This is to be contrasted with ELT.

fact: A central component of a data warehouse that contains the measures to be analyzed. Facts are related to dimensions.

fact dimension: A dimension that does not have an associated dimension table because all its attributes are stored in a fact table or in other dimensions. It is also called a *degenerate dimension*.

fact relationship: In the MultiDim model, a relationship that contains fact data.

fact table: A relation that contains fact data.

foreign key: One or several columns in a relation that are related through referential integrity to other columns of the same or other relation.

front-end process: A process that exploits the contents of a data warehouse. This can be done in many ways, including OLAP analysis, reporting, and data mining. This is to be contrasted with a back-end process.

functional dependency: An integrity constraint defined between two sets of columns X and Y in a relation to state that the rows that have the same values for X must have the same values for Y. Functional dependencies are used to define various normal forms.

generalization hierarchy: A set of generalization relationships between entity types that have the same supertype. It is also called an *is-a hierarchy*.

generalization relationship: A directed relationship between a supertype and a subtype that states that instances of the subtype also belong to the supertype. It is also called an *is-a relationship*.

geographic information system (GIS): A software system that allows users to manipulate a database that contains geographic information.

granularity: A partition of a domain into groups of elements, where each element is perceived as an indivisible unit (a granule) at a particular abstraction level. In a multidimensional model, it is the level of detail at which data are captured in dimensions and facts.

graph: A mathematical structure that consists of a collection of vertices and a collection of edges, where each edge connects exactly two vertices.

graph data model: A data model in which information is represented as a graph. Examples include the property graph and the RDF graph models.

graph database: A database that manipulates graph data.

graph DBMS: A database management system that manipulates graphs structured according to a graph data model.

graph data warehouse: A data warehouse that uses a graph as its logical model.

graph processing framework: A distributed processing framework that allows manipulation of graphs.

Hadoop: A distributed processing framework for big data based on the Map-Reduce programming model. It is an alternative to Spark.

Hadoop Distributed File System (HDFS): A distributed file system that stores data on commodity machines, providing high aggregate bandwidth across a cluster. It is the primary data storage system used in Hadoop.

HGOLAP: An extension of OLAP concepts to hypergraphs.

hierarchy: Several related levels of a dimension that define aggregation paths for roll-up and drill-down operations.

historical data: Data from previous time periods which is used for trend analysis and for comparison with previous periods. This is to be contrasted with current data.

holistic measure: A measure that cannot be computed in a distributed way. Examples include median and rank. This is to be contrasted with a distributive and an algebraic measure.

horizontal partitioning: A partitioning of a relation that distributes the rows into relations that have the same structure as the original one. It is also called *sharding*. This is to be contrasted with vertical partitioning.

horizontal scaling: The process of adding additional machines to a computing infrastructure to cope with increasing demands. It is also called *scaling out*. This is to be contrasted with vertical scaling.

hybrid OLAP (HOLAP): A storage method for multidimensional data that stores detailed data in a relational database and aggregated data in a multidimensional database. This is to be contrasted with ROLAP and MOLAP.

hybrid transactional and analytical processing (HTAP): A workload of a database that is a combination of the OLTP and OLAP approaches.

hypergraph: A generalization of a graph in which an edge can link any number of vertices.

identifier: In a conceptual model, a set of attributes whose values uniquely identify an instance of an entity type or a level.

in-memory DBMS: A database management system that stores data in main memory, as opposed to traditional DBMSs, which store data on persistent media such as hard disks.

index: A mechanism to locate and access data in a relation. It involves one or more columns and may be used to enforce uniqueness of their values.

inheritance: The mechanism by which a subtype in a generalization hierarchy incorporates the properties of its supertypes.

instance: An element of an entity or a relationship type. In a multidimensional model, instances of a level are called members.

instant cardinality: A cardinality specification that is valid at each instant of the temporal extent of a database. It is also called the *snapshot cardinality*. This is to be contrasted with of a lifespan cardinality.

integrity constraint: A condition that restricts the possible states of a database in order to enforce their consistency with the rules of the applications using the database.

Java Database Connectivity (JDBC): An application programming interface (API) that enables Java programs to access data in a database management system. This is to be contrasted with ODBC.

join index: A kind of index that materializes a join between two relations by keeping pairs of row identifiers that participate in the join. In a data warehouse, it relates the values of dimensions to rows in a fact table.

joining level: In the MultiDim model, a level in which two alternative aggregation paths are merged.

key: In the relational model, a set of one or more columns in a relation whose values uniquely identify a row in the relation.

key performance indicator (KPI): A measurable organizational objective that is used for characterizing how an organization is performing.

leaf level: A level in a hierarchy that is not related to a child level, so it contains the most detailed data. This is to be contrasted with a root level.

legacy system: An existing system that has been in place for several years and uses languages, platforms, and techniques prior to current technology. Legacy systems are difficult to modify and maintain.

level: In a multidimensional model, a type that belongs to a dimension. A level defines a set of attributes and is typically related to other levels to define hierarchies.

lifespan (LS): The time extent that represents the membership of an instance to its type.

lifespan cardinality: A cardinality specification that is valid over the whole temporal extent of a database. This is to be contrasted with an instant cardinality.

lifting: A technique to derive operations for temporal data types from the corresponding operations on the underlying data types, where each argument (and thus the result) may be time dependent.

location transparency: A characteristic of distributed DBMSs that allows the manipulation of data without being aware of its actual location.

logical design: The process of translating a conceptual design of a database or a data warehouse into a logical model targeted to a class of database management systems.

logical model: A set of modeling concepts and rules for describing a logical schema. Examples are the relational and the object-oriented model.

logical schema: A schema that is targeted to a family of database management systems. This is to be contrasted with a conceptual schema and a physical schema.

MapReduce: A programming model and an associated implementation for processing big data on a cluster with a distributed algorithm.

materialized view: A view that is stored in a database. It is used to improve query performance by precalculating costly operations.

materialized view selection: The process of selecting a set of materialized views in a database to improve overall query performance given a limited amount of ressources such as storage space or materialization time.

mandatory attribute: An attribute that has at least one value in the instances of a type. This is to be contrasted with an optional attribute.

mandatory role: A role in which the instances of an entity type must participate. This is to be contrasted with an optional role.

measure: A particular piece of information that has to be analyzed in a data warehouse. Measures are associated with cells in a cube.

member: In a multidimensional model, an instance of a level.

metadata: Literally, data about data. It is information about the contents and uses of a database or a data warehouse.

metamodel: A modeling framework that represents the properties of a modeling language.

mobility data warehouse: A data warehouse that manipulates moving-object data. It is also called a *spatiotemporal data warehouse*. This is to be contrasted with a conventional, a temporal, a multiversion, and a spatial data warehouse.

model: A representation of the essential characteristics of a system, process, or phenomenon intended to enhance our ability to understand, predict, or control its behavior.

modeling: The process of constructing or modifying a model.

monovalued attribute: An attribute that may have at most one value in the instances of a type. This is to be contrasted with a multivalued attribute.

moving object: An object whose spatial extent change over time.

moving-object database: A database that manipulates moving object data. It is also called a *spatiotemporal database*. This is to be contrasted with a spatial and a temporal database.

MultiDim model: A conceptual model for data warehouse and OLAP applications.

multidimensional database: A database that represents data according to the multidimensional model.

multidimensional model: A model in which information is represented as facts, measures, dimensions, and hierarchies. It is used to represent the information requirements of analytical applications.

multidimensional OLAP (MOLAP): A storage method for multidimensional data in which both detailed and aggregated data are stored in a multidimensional database. This is to be contrasted with ROLAP and HOLAP.

multiple inheritance: The possibility for an entity type to have more than one direct supertype.

multivalued attribute: An attribute that may have several values in the instances of a type. This is to be contrasted with a monovalued attribute.

multivalued dependency: A constraint between two sets of columns X and Y in a relation stating that the rows that have the same values for X have a set of possible values for Y independently of any other column. Multivalued dependencies are used to define various normal forms.

multiversion data warehouse: A data warehouse that records the evolution over time of its schema. This is to be contrasted with a conventional, a temporal, a spatial, and a mobility data warehouse.

n-ary relationship type: A relationship type among three or more entity types.

NewSQL DBMS: A class of relational database management systems that provide scalability for OLTP workloads while maintaining the consistency guarantees required by ACID properties. This is to be contrasted with a NoSQL DBMS.

Neo4j: An open-source graph DBMS written in Java.

nonadditive measure: A measure that cannot be meaningfully aggregated by addition across any dimension. This is to be contrasted with an additive and a semiadditive measure.

normal form: A set of conditions that a relation must satisfy to guarantee some desirable properties, typically to eliminate data redundancy.

normalization: The modification of the schema of a relation so that it satisfies some normal form. This is to be contrasted with denormalization.

NoSQL DBMS: A class of database management systems that supports flexible schemas and provide scalability through weaker consistency models than the ACID properties. This is to be contrasted with a NewSQL DBMS.

null value: A particular marker that indicates that the value of a column in a relation is missing, unknown, or inapplicable.

object: A phenomenon in the real world that is perceived as having existence independently of other phenomena.

Open Geospatial Consortium (OGC): An international standards organization that define open standards for geospatial content and services, sensor web and Internet of Things, GIS data processing, and data sharing.

Object Management Group (OMG): An international computer industry consortium that develops standards for a wide range of technologies and industries.

object-oriented model: A logical model in which an application is modeled as a set of cooperating objects that exchange messages between them. It includes features such as inheritance, encapsulation, polymorphism, complex types, and methods.

online analytical processing (OLAP): Typical workload of a data warehouse that supports interactive analysis of data for decision support. This is to be contrasted with OLTP and HTAP.

online transaction processing (OLTP): Typical workload of an operational database that supports daily operations of an organization. This is to be contrasted with OLAP and HTAP.

Open Database Connectivity (ODBC): An application programming interface (API) for accessing data in a database management system in a language-independent manner. This is to be contrasted with JDBC.

operational data source: An operational system in an organization that provides data for a data warehouse. This is to be contrasted with an external data source.

operational database: A database that supports the daily operations of an organization in real time. This is to be contrasted with a data warehouse.

Optimized Row Columnar (ORC): A column-oriented storage format of the Hadoop ecosystem. It is an alternative to Parquet.

optional attribute: An attribute that may have no value in the instances of a type. This is to be contrasted with a mandatory attribute.

optional role: A role in which the instances of an entity type may not participate. This is to be contrasted with a mandatory role.

parent-child relationship: In a multidimensional model, a binary relationship type that links a parent and a child levels in a hierarchy.

parent level: Given two related levels in a hierarchy, the upper level, containing more general data. This is to be contrasted with a child level.

Parquet: A column-oriented storage format of the Hadoop ecosystem. It is an alternative to ORC.

partitioning: The process to split data in a relation into multiple relations to improve performance or security. It is also called *fragmentation*. A relation can be partitioned using horizontal and/or vertical partitioning.

physical design: The process of translating a logical design of a database or a data warehouse into a physical model targeted to a specific database management system.

physical model: A set of modeling concepts and rules for describing the physical schema of a database.

physical schema: A schema customized to maximize efficiency and performance on a particular database management system. This is to be contrasted with a conceptual schema and a logical schema.

polystore: A database management system that provides integrated access to multiple, heterogeneous storage engines, such as relational DBMSs, NoSQL DBMSs, and HDFS repositories. This is to be contrasted with a distributed DBMS.

population: The set of instances of an entity or a relationship type.

predefined query: A request for information in a database that is performed on a regular basis. This is to be contrasted with an ad hoc query.

primary key: A privileged key among all keys in a relation that is used to represent the links of the relation to other relations.

property graph: A type of graph in which both vertices and edges may be annotated with properties represented as key-value pairs.

QB4OLAP: An extension of the QB vocabulary that enables the manipulation of multidimensional datasets using OLAP operations.

query rewriting: The process of modifying a query to exploit available materialized views or indexes to improve query performance.

RDB to RDF Mapping Language (R2RML): A language for expressing mappings from relational databases to RDF data sets.

RDF Data Cube Vocabulary (QB): An RDF vocabulary that allows the publication of multidimensional data on the web.

RDF graph: A type of graph that structures information according to the RDF data model.

RDF Schema (RDFS): A set of classes with properties expressed in RDF that provides basic elements for the description of RDF vocabularies.

recursive relationship type: A relationship type in which the same entity type is linked by two or more roles.

referential integrity: An integrity constraint specifying that the values of one or more columns of a relation (the foreign key) must appear in other columns (typically the primary key) of the same or another relation.

relation: A two-dimensional structure for storing information in a relational database. A relation has a specified number of columns but can have any number of rows. Relations are also called *tables*.

relational database: A database that represents data according to the relational model.

relational DBMS (RDBMS): A database management system that manipulates data structured according to the relational model.

relational model: A logical model in which information is represented using relations.

relational OLAP (ROLAP): A storage method for multidimensional data in which both detailed and aggregated data are stored in a relational database. This is to be contrasted with MOLAP and HOLAP.

relational schema: A schema targeted at a relational database management system.

relationship: In the entity-relationship model, an instance of a relationship type. Its existence is subject to the existence of the linked entities.

relationship type: A description of a set of relationships that share the same attributes, roles, and semantics. In the MultiDim model, a relationship type can be either a fact or a parent-child relationship.

reporting: The process of extracting data from a database or a data warehouse and presenting them in reports containing graphs, charts, etc.

requirements specification: The process of collecting information about the users' needs pertaining to a database or a data warehouse application.

Resilient Distributed Dataset (RDD): In Spark, an immutable distributed collection of data elements that can be operated on in parallel. This is to be contrasted with a DataFrame and a DataSet.

resource description framework (RDF): A formal language for describing structured information that uses triples composed of a subject, a predicate, and an object. It is a basic component of the semantic web.

role: The participation of an entity type in a relationship type.

roll-up: An OLAP operation that queries summarized data, moving up one or several levels in a hierarchy. This is to be contrasted with drill-down.

root level: A level in a hierarchy that does not have a parent level, so it contains the most general data. This is to be contrasted with a leaf level.

row-oriented DBMS: A database management system that uses row-oriented storage. Examples include PostgreSQL and MySQL. This is to be contrasted with a column-oriented DBMS.

row-oriented storage: A storage method that organizes data by record, keeping all of the data associated with a record next to each other in memory. This is to be contrasted with a column-oriented storage.

schema: A specification in a data model that defines how the data are structured, the type of values that each data element can contain, and the rules that govern how these values may be input and may evolve.

schema diagram: A diagram that illustrates a schema according to a diagrammatic notation that corresponds to a data model.

self-service BI: An approach to business intelligence that enables business users to access and explore data even if they do not have a background in BI or related domains like data mining and statistical analysis.

semantic trajectory: A trajectory where the original spatiotemporal information has been replaced with a temporal sequence of geolocalized objects or of other annotations.

semantic web: A development of the World Wide Web to represent web content in a machine-processable way.

semiadditive measure: A measure that can be meaningfully aggregated by addition along some, but not all, of its dimensions. This is to be contrasted with an additive and a nonadditive measure.

simple attribute: An attribute that is not composed of other attributes. It is also called an *atomic attribute*. This is to be contrasted with a complex attribute.

slice: An OLAP operation that removes one dimension in a cube by selecting one instance in a level.

slowly changing dimension: A dimension whose data changes over time. The term *slowly* emphasizes the fact that the data in the dimension changes less frequently than the data in related facts.

snowflake schema: A relational schema for representing multidimensional data composed of a single fact table related to normalized dimensions. This is to be contrasted with a star and a starflake schema.

Spark: A distributed processing framework for big data analytics. It is an alternative to Hadoop.

SPARQL: The standard query language for RDF graphs.

spatial attribute: An attribute that has a spatial data type as its domain. This is to be contrasted with a conventional and a temporal attribute.

spatial constraint: An integrity constraint that imposes a restriction on spatial extents. This is to be contrasted with a temporal constraint.

spatial data type: A data type that represents the spatial extent of phenomena. Examples are point, line, and surface. This is to be contrasted with a conventional, a time, and a temporal data type.

spatial database: A database that manipulates spatial data. This is to be contrasted with a conventional, a temporal, and a moving-object database.

spatial data warehouse: A data warehouse that manipulates spatial data. This is to be contrasted with a conventional, a temporal, a multiversion, and a mobility data warehouse.

spatial dimension: A dimension that includes a spatial hierarchy. This is to be contrasted with a conventional and a temporal dimension.

spatial fact relationship: A fact relationship that requires a spatial join between two or more spatial dimensions. This is to be contrasted with a conventional and a temporal fact relationship.

spatial hierarchy: A hierarchy that includes a spatial level. This is to be contrasted with a conventional and a temporal hierarchy.

spatial level: A level that stores the spatial extent of its members. This is to be contrasted with a conventional and a temporal level.

spatial measure: A measure that has a spatial data type as its domain. This is to be contrasted with a conventional and a temporal measure.

spatial reference system (SRS): A framework used to precisely measure locations on the surface of the Earth as coordinates.

spatiotemporal data type: A temporal data type that is based on a spatial data type and thus represents the evolution over time of the spatial extent of phenomena.

splitting level: In the MultiDim model, a level in which two alternative aggregation paths start.

star schema: A relational schema for representing multidimensional data composed of a single fact table related to denormalized dimensions. This is to be contrasted with a snowflake and a starflake schema.

starflake schema: A relational schema for representing multidimensional data that is a combination of the star and the snowflake schemas, i.e., it is composed of both normalized and denormalized dimensions.

strong entity type: An entity type that has at least one identifier of its own. This is to be contrasted with a weak entity type.

subtype: In a generalization relationship, the most specific type. This is to be contrasted with the supertype of the relationship.

summarizability: A characteristic referring to the possibility of correctly aggregating measures in a higher level of a hierarchy by taking into account existing aggregations in a lower level.

supertype: In a generalization relationship, the most generic type. This is to be contrasted with the subtype of the relationship.

surrogate key: A system-generated artificial primary key of a relation that is not derived from any data in the database.

synchronization relationship: A relationship that states a temporal constraint on the lifespan of the linked entities. Examples include starts, finishes, precedes, or succeeds. It is similar to a topological relationship for spatial values.

telic measure: A measure that does not satisfy the downward inheritance property, which means that if the measure has a given value during a time period p, its value must be subdivided for any subperiod of p.

temporal attribute: An attribute that has a temporal data type as its domain. This is to be contrasted with a conventional and a spatial attribute.

temporal constraint: An integrity constraint that imposes a restriction on temporal extents. This is to be contrasted with a spatial constraint.

temporal data type: A data type that represents the evolution over time of the value of a conventional or spatial data type. Examples include temporal integer, temporal float, and temporal geometry.

temporal database: A database that manages information that varies over time. It allows previous or future data to be stored, as well as the time when the changes in these data occurred or will occur. This is to be contrasted with a conventional database.

temporal data warehouse: A data warehouse that records the evolution over time of its members. This is to be contrasted with a conventional, a multiversion, a spatial, and a mobility data warehouse.

temporal dimension: A dimension that includes a temporal hierarchy. This is to be contrasted with a conventional and a spatial dimension.

temporal fact relationship: A fact relationship that requires a temporal join between two or more temporal dimensions. This is to be contrasted with a conventional and a spatial fact relationship.

temporal hierarchy: A hierarchy that includes a temporal level or a temporal relationship. This is to be contrasted with a conventional and a spatial hierarchy.

temporal level: A level that stores the lifespan of its members. This is to be contrasted with a conventional and a spatial level.

temporal measure: A measure that records the evolution of its values. It is also called a *slowly changing measure*. This is to be contrasted with a conventional measure and a spatial measure.

temporal relationship: A relationship that records the evolution of the links between its instances.

temporally consistent query: An interpretation of a query addressed to a temporal database or a temporal data warehouse that considers the state of the data at the time when it ocurred. This is to be contrasted with a time-slice query.

time data type: A data type that represents the time extent associated with phenomena. Examples include instant, period, instant set, and period set. This is to be contrasted with a conventional and a spatial data type.

time-slice query: A query addressed to a temporal database or a temporal data warehouse that extracts the state of the data at a particular point in time. This is to be contrasted with a temporally consistent query.

topological relationship: A relationship that states a spatial constraint on the spatial extent of the linked entities. Examples include overlaps, contains, disjoint, or crosses. It is similar to a synchronization relationship for temporal values.

trajectory: The path followed by a moving object as it moves. A trajectory may be continuous or discrete.

transaction: An operation in a database or a data storage system that is treated as a single unit of work, which either completes fully or does not complete at all, and leaves the system in a consistent state.

transaction time (TT): A specification that records when a data element is stored in and deleted from a temporal database or a temporal data warehouse. This is to be contrasted with valid time.

trigger: A piece of code automatically executed by a database management system in response to certain events happening in a database.

valid time (VT): A specification that records when a data element stored in a temporal database or a temporal data warehouse is valid from the application perspective. This is to be contrasted with transaction time.

value-equivalent rows: In a temporal database, a set of rows that have the same value for all columns in a relation excepted those that define their time extent.

vertical partitioning: A partitioning of a relation in which the columns are distributed into several relations, each one containing a subset of the original columns. This is to be contrasted with horizontal partitioning.

vertical scaling: The process of adding more processing power to a computer to cope with increasing demands. It is also called *scaling up*. This is to be contrasted with horizontal scaling.

view: A relation whose content is derived from one or several relations or other views. It may be computed during query processing or may pre-computed and stored, in which case it is a materialized view.

view maintenance: The process of updating a materialized view in response to changes in the relations on which the view is defined.

weak entity type: An entity type that does not have an identifier of its own. This is to be contrasted with a strong entity type.

Yet Another Resource Negotiator (YARN): A Hadoop component responsible for allocating system resources to applications running in a cluster and scheduling tasks to be executed on cluster nodes.

Index

Printed in the United States
by Baker & Taylor Publisher Services